Dedication

ENTRY

To my friend:

From:

Date:

Message:

`D1404770`

...so that, together, we can grow in our friendships...with God, with those in our lives, and with each other.

FIELD MANUAL No. 06-OAE-29

FRIENDSHIP

★ No.1 **FIRST**™ | DOCUMENT: *New testament*

LIFETIME QUALITY GUARANTEE

LIVING IN FRIENDSHIP WITH GOD AND OTHERS

NEW LIVING TRANSLATION

Group
Loveland, Colorado

New Living Translation®
SECOND EDITION

Tyndale House Publishers, Inc.
Carol Stream, Illinois

Tyndale House Publishers and Wycliffe Bible Translators share the vision for an understandable, accurate translation of the Bible for every person in the world. Each sale of the *Holy Bible,* New Living Translation, benefits Wycliffe Bible Translators. Wycliffe is working with partners around the world to accomplish Vision 2025—an initiative to start a Bible translation program in every language group that needs it by the year 2025.

Acknowledgments

Celebrate the friends who cast the vision and made this Friendship First™ New Testament a reality

Group Publishing, Inc.

Chief Creative Officer: Joani Schultz
Vice President of Product Division: Sue Geiman
Creative Development Editor: Matt Lockhart
Editor: Roxanne Wieman
Copy Editors: Lyndsay E. Gerwing and Amber Van Schooneveld
Senior Designer: Josh Emrich
Designer: Susan Tripp

Tyndale House Publishers, Inc.

Publisher: Douglas R. Knox
Director of Bibles: Kevin O'Brien
Director of Product Development, Bibles and Bible Reference: Mark Norton
Acquisitions Editor: Kim Johnson
Consulting Editor: Pat LaCosse
Editorial Assistant: Anisa Baker
Proofreading Coordinator: Keith Williams

Writers:

Linda Crawford
Cheri R. Gillard
Kate S. Holburn
Keith D. Johnson
Mikal Keefer
Joy-Elizabeth F. Lawrence
Karl Leuthauser
Jeanette Gardner Littleton

Mark Littleton
Keith Madsen
James W. Miller
A. Koshy Muthalaly
Lori Niles
Dean Ridings
Beth Robinson
Jeff White

BIBLE TRANSLATION TEAM
HOLY BIBLE, NEW LIVING TRANSLATION

Give thanks to the friends who worked hard to translate the Bible into the New Living Translation

GOSPEL AND ACTS
Grant R. Osborne, *Senior Translator, Trinity Evangelical Divinity School*

MATTHEW
Craig Blomberg, *Denver Seminary*
Donald A. Hagner, *Fuller Theological Seminary*
David Turner, *Grand Rapids Baptist Seminary*

MARK
Robert Guelich (deceased), *Fuller Theological Seminary*
George Guthrie, *Union University*
Grant R. Osborne, *Trinity Evangelical Divinity School*

LUKE
Darrell Bock, *Dallas Theological Seminary*
Scot McKnight, *North Park University*
Robert Stein, *The Southern Baptist Theological Seminary*

JOHN
Gary M. Burge, *Wheaton College*
Philip W. Comfort, *Coastal Carolina University*
Marianne Meye Thompson, *Fuller Theological Seminary*

ACTS
D. A. Carson, *Trinity Evangelical Divinity School*
William J. Larkin, *Columbia International University*
Roger Mohrlang, *Whitworth College*

LETTERS AND REVELATION
Norman R. Ericson, *Senior Translator, Wheaton College*

ROMANS, GALATIANS
Gerald Borchert, *Northern Baptist Theological Seminary*
Douglas J. Moo, *Wheaton College*
Thomas R. Schreiner, *The Southern Baptist Theological Seminary*

1 & 2 CORINTHIANS
Joseph Alexanian, *Trinity International University*
Linda Belleville, *North Park Theological Seminary*

Douglas A. Oss, *Central Bible College*
Robert Sloan, *Baylor University*

EPHESIANS–PHILEMON
Harold W. Hoehner, *Dallas Theological Seminary*
Moises Silva, *Gordon-Conwell Theological Seminary*
Klyne Snodgrass, *North Park Theological Seminary*

HEBREWS, JAMES, 1 & 2 PETER, JUDE
Peter Davids, *Schloss Mittersill Study Centre*
Norman R. Ericson, *Wheaton College*
William Lane (deceased), *Seattle Pacific University*
J. Ramsey Michaels, *S.W. Missouri State University*

1–3 JOHN, REVELATION
Greg Beale, *Wheaton College*
Robert Mounce, *Whitworth College*
M. Robert Mulholland Jr., *Asbury Theological Seminary*

SPECIAL REVIEWERS
F. F. Bruce (deceased), *University of Manchester*
Kenneth N. Taylor (deceased), *Translator, The Living Bible*

BIBLE TRANSLATION COMMITTEE
Mark D. Taylor, *Director and Chief Stylist*
Ronald A. Beers, *Executive Director and Stylist*
Mark R. Norton, *Managing Editor*
Philip W. Comfort, *N.T. Coordinating Editor*
Daniel W. Taylor, *Senior Stylist, Bethel University*
Daniel I. Block, *Wheaton College*
Barry J. Beitzel, *Trinity Evangelical Divinity School*
Tremper Longman III, *Westmont College*
John N. Oswalt, *Wesley Biblical Seminary*
Grant R. Osborne, *Trinity Evangelical Divinity School*
Norman R. Ericson, *Wheaton College*

To our Friends:

The *Holy Bible*, New Living Translation, was first published in 1996. It quickly became one of the most popular Bible translations in the English-speaking world. While the NLT's influence was rapidly growing, the Bible Translation Committee determined that an additional investment in scholarly review and text refinement could make it even better. So shortly after its initial publication, the committee began an eight-year process with the purpose of increasing the level of the NLT's precision without sacrificing its easy-to-understand quality. This second-generation text was completed in 2004 and is reflected in this edition of the New Living Translation.

The goal of any Bible translation is to convey the meaning and content of the ancient Hebrew, Aramaic, and Greek texts as accurately as possible to contemporary readers. The challenge for our translators was to create a text that would communicate as clearly and powerfully to today's readers as the original texts did to readers and listeners in the ancient biblical world. The resulting translation is easy-to-read and understand, while also accurately communicating the meaning and content of the original biblical texts. The NLT is a general-purpose text especially good for study and devotional reading and to be read aloud in public worship.

We believe that the New Living Translation—which combines the latest biblical scholarship with a clear, dynamic writing style—will communicate God's Word powerfully to all who read it. We publish it with the prayer that God will use it to speak his timeless truth to the church and the world in a fresh, new way.

~ Tyndale House Publishers
July 2004

Friendship First™ NEW TESTAMENT

You're about to embark on a journey of the heart. We designed this *Friendship First*™ *New Testament* to give you a glimpse on Earth of what a friendship with God is all about.

God made us.

And he made us to be in relationship with him and others.

We all long to experience the richness of relationships. We wonder: What is it like to really know God? How can we understand what a true connection with the Creator of the universe must be like? What must we do to really "get it"?

Someone once asked Jesus a question. It was meant to be a stumper. Yet Jesus' reply put our lives and relationships in perspective. In Matthew 22:36 someone asks, "Teacher, which is the most important commandment in the law of Moses?" (In other words, boil everything down to something simple so I can understand what I'm supposed to do.)

In a stunning display of simplicity, Jesus replied, "'You must love the Lord your God with all your heart, all your soul, and all your mind.' This is the first and greatest commandment. A second is equally important: 'Love your neighbor as yourself.'"

Simply love God and love others.

Jesus lets us in on the secret of a fulfilling life. We need to be in relationship.

God gave us a picture of what it means to be in relationship with him. In experiencing healthy friendships with other people, we get a glimpse of a real friendship with God. For example, when a new friend accepts us—warts and all—we get a small indication of God's unconditional acceptance and grace.

God gave us permission to look at our relationship with him as a friendship. In John 15:15, he says, "I no longer call you slaves...Now you are my friends." The relationship moves from a boss/subordinate relationship to a unique friendship.

We've had God's Word for thousands of years. "In the beginning the Word already existed," we read in John 1:1. But God chose to make his Word more personal, more relational. "So the Word became human and made his home among us" (John 1:14).

Some view the Bible as a textbook. They pursue faith in God as a subject to be mastered—such as geology, physics, or history. But when "the Word became human," we see that God isn't looking for mere readers of text. He's looking for friends.

The Bible you're holding in your hand is unlike any other Bible. It's designed to show you the ultimate joy and fulfillment in connecting with

God. It's not a heady, academic, informational exercise but a journey of the heart—a transformational experience. The New Living Translation communicates more like an intimate letter between friends than a dry textbook. And the additional material throughout this book helps you make the connection between befriending others and befriending God.

Jump in. Accept the invitation and become a friend of God.

Thom Schultz

Joani Schultz

Mark D. Taylor

> *" 'You must love the LORD your God with all your heart, all your soul, and all your mind.' This is the first and greatest commandment. A second is equally important: 'Love your neighbor as yourself.' "*
>
> *~ Jesus (Matthew 22:37-39)*

Table of Contents

THE BOOKS OF THE NEW TESTAMENT

EXTRAS

Friendship First NEW TESTAMENT

WHAT'S IN STORE WITH THE
Friendship First NEW TESTAMENT?

> "Friendship is unnecessary, like philosophy, like art, like the universe itself (for God did not need to create). It has no survival value; rather it is one of those things that give value to survival."
>
> ~ C.S. Lewis

It's about friendship. Friendship with God. Friendship with others.

It's about authentic community. Where people can be themselves and share life, laughter, tears—companionship.

It's about life…and how much better it is with friendships.

Everyone hungers for friendship—in fact, God designed us that way!

God wants you to have friendships with others and with him.

And the truth is, friendships with God and others look a lot alike. A friendship with God may seem like some sort of impossible, intangible, impractical idea…but it's not. Friendship with God is within reach; it's as real and enjoyable as friendship with another person. God made us to be friends with him, just as God made us to have meaningful friendships with other people. In fact, our friendships with people are the greatest metaphor for our friendship with God. Just as you spend time with friends talking and hanging out, God desires to spend time with us and be in conversation with us. Just as it's important to trust a friend—to be open and honest—it's important to trust God and be vulnerable with him. God is still *God*—mysterious, powerful, infinite—but that doesn't mean you can't engage in a friendship with God. It won't be *exactly* the same as your friendships with people—especially considering that God is the *perfect* friend—but there will be similarities, and those similarities can help you grow deeper friendships with God and with others.

But how do you have authentic, intimate, *lasting* friendships with people and with God? You know, the kinds of friendships that "give value to survival"?

Well, you've picked up the right book! Consider it your field guide to friendship—what you need to start, build, and keep valuable friendships. With scriptural insights, practical advice, and real ways to *experience* friendship, this *Friendship First New Testament* will help you reach new levels in your friendships with others and with God.

The Friendship Guide

Five Types of Friendship

	NEIGHBORS	HARD-TO-LOVE PEOPLE	FAMILY	FRIENDS	JESUS
GETTING ACQUAINTED (greeting and engaging in small talk)	Luke 10:25-37 (The Good Samaritan)	Acts 9:10-19a (Saul and Ananias)	2 Timothy 1:5-7 (Generational Faith)	John 1:35-50 (Calling of the First Disciples)	John 4:1-30 (The Woman at the Well)
ACCEPTANCE (reaching out and listening)	James 2:1-13 (A Warning Against Prejudice)	Acts 9:19b-28 (Barnabas Accepts Saul)	Luke 15:11-31 (The Parable of the Prodigal Son)	Mark 2:13-17 (The Calling of Levi)	John 1:10-14 (Yet to All Who Receive Him…)
TRUST (opening up, being transparent, sharing confidences)	Acts 27:13-44 (Paul Encourages the Sailors)	Ephesians 2:11-22 (Gentiles and Jews Are One in Christ)	Luke 1:39-45 (Mary Visits Elizabeth)	Mark 2:1-12 (Four Friends Help a Paralytic)	Matthew 14:22-36 (Peter Walks on Water)
DEEPENING (showing affection, revealing emotions, working through conflict, forgiving)	Ephesians 4:25-32 (Living as Children of Light)	Matthew 5:38-48 (Love Your Enemies)	Matthew 18:21-35 (The Parable of the Unmerciful Servant)	Acts 15:36-41 (Paul and Barnabas' Disagreement)	Mark 14:66-72 (Peter Disowns Jesus)
COMPANIONSHIP (cooperating and spending quality time together)	Romans 12:9-18 (Rejoice With Those Who Rejoice)	2 Corinthians 2:5-11 (Forgiveness for the Sinner)	Ephesians 5:31–6:4 (Spirit-Guided Family Relationships)	John 13:1-17 (The Last Supper)	Luke 10:38-42 (Martha and Mary)
COMMITMENT (serving, sacrificing, and sharing)	1 Corinthians 13:1-7 (The Love Chapter)	Luke 19:1-10 (Jesus and Zacchaeus)	1 Timothy 5:3-8 (Take Care of Your Family)	John 15:12-17 (Love Each Other as I've Loved You)	Matthew 28:16-20 (The Great Commission)

Six Layers of Friendship

Useful Directions

He did it again! You slam your door shut as you walk into the house. You're so sick of dealing with him. He doesn't care about your projects. He doesn't seem to notice that it bothers you when he makes those snide comments. You're thinking about calling in sick just so you don't have to be *near* him.

We all have them—those hard-to-love people who can make our lives miserable. But the truth is, God loves those people…and he has called you to love them, too.

So when you need help ***accepting*** those ***hard-to-love people***, here's what you do: Run your finger down the "Hard-to-Love People" column (under *Friendship Types*) and across the "Acceptance" column (under *Friendship Layers*)…and when your fingers meet…well, that's the box you're looking for. Inside the box you'll find a reference to an Anchor Passage.

That passage and its accompanying feature are going to get you started on some powerful experiences and insights that will help you accept hard-to-love people.

Five Types of Friendship

Six Layers of Friendship		NEIGHBORS	HARD-TO-LOVE PEOPLE	FAMILY	FRIENDS	JESUS
	GETTING ACQUAINTED (greeting and engaging in small talk)	Luke 10:25-37 (The Good Samaritan)	Acts 9:1-19a (Saul and Ananias)	2 Timothy 1:5-7 (Generational Faith)	John 1:35-50 (Calling of the First Disciples)	John 4:1-30 (The Woman at the Well)
	ACCEPTANCE (reaching out and listening)	James 2:1-13 (A Warning Against Prejudice)	Acts 9:19b-28 (Barnabas Accepts Saul)	Luke 15:11-31 (The Parable of the Prodigal Son)	Mark 2:13-17 (The Calling of Levi)	John 1:10-14 (Yet to All Who Receive Him…)
	TRUST (opening up, being transparent, sharing confidences)	Acts 27:13-44 (Paul Encourages the Sailors)	Ephesians 2:11-22 (Gentiles and Jews Are One in Christ)	Luke 1:39-45 (Mary Visits Elizabeth)	Mark 2:1-12 (Four Friends Help a Paralytic)	Matthew 14:22-36 (Peter Walks on Water)
	DEEPENING (showing affection, revealing emotions, working through conflict, forgiving)	Ephesians 4:25-32 (Living as Children of Light)	Matthew 5:38-48 (Love Your Enemies)	Matthew 18:21-35 (The Parable of the Unmerciful Servant)	Acts 15:36-41 (Paul and Barnabas' Disagreement)	Mark 14:66-72 (Peter Disowns Jesus)
	COMPANIONSHIP (cooperating and spending quality time together)	Romans 12:9-18 (Rejoice With Those Who Rejoice)	2 Corinthians 2:5-11 (Forgiveness for the Sinner)	Ephesians 5:31–6:4 (Spirit-Guided Family Relationships)	John 13:1-17 (The Last Supper)	Luke 10:38-42 (Martha and Mary)
	COMMITMENT (serving, sacrificing, and sharing)	1 Corinthians 13:1-7 (The Love Chapter)	Luke 19:1-10 (Jesus and Zacchaeus)	1 Timothy 5:3-8 (Take Care of Your Family)	John 15:12-17 (Love Each Other as I've Loved You)	Matthew 28:16-20 (The Great Commission)

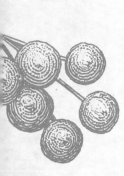

SCENARIO #2

Your small group is on a mission. You want to learn to fully accept people. You want to be a reflection of God's love and acceptance to your co-workers, family, and friends.

What's the first step? Where do you begin?

How about with your neighbors?

As a small group, go through the experiences connected with the "Acceptance" and "Neighbors" box. You'll get practical ideas for accepting the people with whom you live and work…and learning to become better friends with them.

And once your small group has gone through that box, move on to the "Acceptance" and "Hard-to-Love" box, and then the "Acceptance" and "Family" box…You get the idea!

Five Types of Friendship

Six Layers of Friendship		NEIGHBORS	HARD-TO-LOVE PEOPLE	FAMILY	FRIENDS	JESUS
	GETTING ACQUAINTED (greeting and engaging in small talk)	Luke 10:25-37 (The Good Samaritan)	Acts 9:10-19a (Saul and Ananias)	2 Timothy 1:5-7 (Generational Faith)	John 1:35-50 (Calling of the First Disciples)	John 4:1-30 (The Woman at the Well)
	ACCEPTANCE (reaching out and listening)	James 2:1-13 (A Warning Against Prejudice)	Acts 9:19b-28 (Barnabas Accepts Saul)	Luke 15:11-31 (The Parable of the Prodigal Son)	Mark 2:13-17 (The Calling of Levi)	John 1:10-14 (Yet to All Who Receive Him…)
	TRUST (opening up, being transparent, sharing confidences)	Acts 27:13-44 (Paul Encourages the Sailors)	Ephesians 2:11-22 (Gentiles and Jews Are One in Christ)	Luke 1:39-45 (Mary Visits Elizabeth)	Mark 2:1-12 (Four Friends Help a Paralytic)	Matthew 14:22-36 (Peter Walks on Water)
	DEEPENING (showing affection, revealing emotions, working through conflict, forgiving)	Ephesians 4:25-32 (Living as Children of Light)	Matthew 5:38-48 (Love Your Enemies)	Matthew 18:21-35 (The Parable of the Unmerciful Servant)	Acts 15:36-41 (Paul and Barnabas' Disagreement)	Mark 14:66-72 (Peter Disowns Jesus)
	COMPANIONSHIP (cooperating and spending quality time together)	Romans 12:9-18 (Rejoice With Those Who Rejoice)	2 Corinthians 2:5-11 (Forgiveness for the Sinner)	Ephesians 5:31–6:4 (Spirit-Guided Family Relationships)	John 13:1-17 (The Last Supper)	Luke 10:38-42 (Martha and Mary)
	COMMITMENT (serving, sacrificing, and sharing)	1 Corinthians 13:1-7 (The Love Chapter)	Luke 19:1-10 (Jesus and Zacchaeus)	1 Timothy 5:3-8 (Take Care of Your Family)	John 15:12-17 (Love Each Other as I've Loved You)	Matthew 28:16-20 (The Great Commission)

SCENARIO #3

Your friend doesn't know much about the Bible or about Jesus, but she has come to you with questions. You're not sure where to begin, but you desperately want your friend to know Jesus...to become *friends* with him. You ask her if she's willing to meet with you once a week to talk. She says she is...so you give her a *Friendship First New Testament* and tell her to read through the experiences for the "Jesus" and "Getting Acquainted" box. You set up a time next week to talk about it.

After a few weeks of working through the experiences in the "Jesus" column, your friend is beginning to understand. She tells you that she never realized having a friendship with Jesus could be so *easy*, so *natural*. "I never thought it would be like a real friendship, but it is. It's kind of like being friends with you," she says.

Five Types of Friendship

Six Layers of Friendship	NEIGHBORS	HARD-TO-LOVE PEOPLE	FAMILY	FRIENDS	JESUS
GETTING ACQUAINTED (greeting and engaging in small talk)	Luke 10:25-37 (The Good Samaritan)	Acts 9:10-19a (Saul and Ananias)	2 Timothy 1:5-7 (Generational Faith)	John 1:35-50 (Calling of the First Disciples)	John 4:1-30 (The Woman at the Well)
ACCEPTANCE (reaching out and listening)	James 2:1-13 (A Warning Against Prejudice)	Acts 9:19b-28 (Barnabas Accepts Saul)	Luke 15:11-31 (The Parable of the Prodigal Son)	Mark 2:13-17 (The Calling of Levi)	John 1:10-14 (Yet to All Who Receive Him...)
TRUST (opening up, being transparent, sharing confidences)	Acts 27:13-44 (Paul Encourages the Sailors)	Ephesians 2:11-22 (Gentiles and Jews Are One in Christ)	Luke 1:39-45 (Mary Visits Elizabeth)	Mark 2:1-12 (Four Friends Help a Paralytic)	Matthew 14:22-36 (Peter Walks on Water)
DEEPENING (showing affection, revealing emotions, working through conflict, forgiving)	Ephesians 4:25-32 (Living as Children of Light)	Matthew 5:38-48 (Love Your Enemies)	Matthew 18:21-35 (The Parable of the Unmerciful Servant)	Acts 15:36-41 (Paul and Barnabas' Disagreement)	Mark 14:66-72 (Peter Disowns Jesus)
COMPANIONSHIP (cooperating and spending quality time together)	Romans 12:9-18 (Rejoice With Those Who Rejoice)	2 Corinthians 2:5-11 (Forgiveness for the Sinner)	Ephesians 5:31–6:4 (Spirit-Guided Family Relationships)	John 13:1-17 (The Last Supper)	Luke 10:38-42 (Martha and Mary)
COMMITMENT (serving, sacrificing, and sharing)	1 Corinthians 13:1-7 (The Love Chapter)	Luke 19:1-10 (Jesus and Zacchaeus)	1 Timothy 5:3-8 (Take Care of Your Family)	John 15:12-17 (Love Each Other as I've Loved You)	Matthew 28:16-20 (The Great Commission)

"Christ did not
lay down his life
for us as enemies
so that we should
remain enemies,
but so that he could
make us friends."

~ Thomas Aquinas

Friendship First NEW TESTAMENT

WHAT YOU'LL FIND IN THE
Friendship First NEW TESTAMENT

LOOK INSIDE each box of the Friendship Guide to see a Scripture reference. That Scripture reference is the Anchor Passage for that topic. It's the launching point for your study into that topic. When you flip to the page with the Anchor Passage, you'll find a highlighted section of Scripture as well as a reading and experience in the margin of that page.

READ IT. Soak up every word. Delight in fresh glimpses of God and people as you read the Scripture passage and the accompanying text. You'll see how the passage relates to the Friendship Type and Friendship Layer you're exploring. You'll also find great—and *practical*—ideas for living out that friendship in your life.

EPHESIANS 4   PAGE 374

⚓ *Anchor Passage*

PASSAGE: **Ephesians 4:25-32**

FRIENDSHIP TYPE: *Neighbors*   FRIENDSHIP LAYER: *Deepening*

Getting Messy

Write on a piece of paper five things that could break a relationship apart.

Remember the old parental adage "if you can't say something nice, don't say anything at all"? Good advice, but not God's advice. **Ephesians 4:25-32** is God's advice—go ahead, read it right now.

At first glance this passage may sound like a parent's laundry list of the "don'ts" for proper behavior. Don't lie, don't be angry, and stop saying bad things! Your heavenly Father *is* trying to teach you the don'ts, but his real desire is to teach you the do's: *Do* be useful to others, *do* be kind and compassionate, and *do* forgive others as Christ has forgiven you!

Great advice…but hard to do in the heat of an argument, when your emotions are on high and your judgment is, well…at a low. It's during those times, though, that you have your greatest opportunity for *building* that friendship…or destroying it.

In order to build it, you have to really dig in and learn to love as God loves—even when it's tough. You have to forgive as he forgives. You have to build others up instead of tearing them down. You have to bless them instead of cursing them. You have to be tenderhearted instead of hardhearted. And here's the good news: God's power can help you do these tough things.

When it comes to deepening in friendship with your neighbors, you can't always avoid the messes. But there's a reward for getting your hands dirty and learning to work through the conflicts: a deeper friendship that lasts!

Anchor Passage continues on page 375…

Friendship First NEW TESTAMENT

---

and build up the church, the body of Christ. [13] This will continue until we all come to such unity in our faith and knowledge of God's Son that we will be mature in the Lord, measuring up to the full and complete standard of Christ.

[14] Then we will no longer be immature like children. We won't be tossed and blown about by every wind of new teaching. We will not be influenced when people try to trick us with lies so clever they sound like the truth. [15] Instead, we will speak the truth in love, growing in every way more and more like Christ, who is the head of his body, the church. [16] He makes the whole body fit together perfectly. As each part does its own special work, it helps the other parts grow, so that the whole body is healthy and growing and full of love.

Living as Children of Light

[17] With the Lord's authority I say this: Live no longer as the Gentiles do, for they are hopelessly confused. [18] Their minds are full of darkness; they wander far from the life God gives because they have closed their minds and hardened their hearts against him. [19] They have no sense of shame. They live for lustful pleasure and eagerly practice every kind of impurity.

[20] But that isn't what you learned about Christ. [21] Since you have heard about Jesus and have learned the truth that comes from him, [22] throw off your old sinful nature and your former way of life, which is corrupted by lust and deception. [23] Instead, let the Spirit renew your thoughts and attitudes. [24] Put on your new nature, created to be like God—truly righteous and holy.

[25] So stop telling lies. Let us tell our neighbors the truth, for we are all parts of the same body. [26] And "don't sin by letting anger control you."* Don't let the sun go down while you are still angry, [27] for anger gives a foothold to the devil.

[28] If you are a thief, quit stealing. Instead, use your hands for good hard work, and then give generously to others in need. [29] Don't use foul or abusive language. Let everything you say be good and helpful, so that your words will be an encouragement to those who hear them.

[30] And do not bring sorrow to God's Holy Spirit

4:26 Ps 4:4.

★ Anchor Passages ★

PAGE 375

EPHESIANS 5

by the way you live. Remember, he has identified you as his own,* guaranteeing that you will be saved on the day of redemption. ³¹Get rid of all bitterness, rage, anger, harsh words, and slander, as well as all types of evil behavior. ³²Instead, be kind to each other, tenderhearted, forgiving one another, just as God through Christ has forgiven you. ⚓

CHAPTER 5

Living in the Light

Imitate God, therefore, in everything you do, because you are his dear children. ²Live a life filled with love, following the example of Christ. He loved us* and offered himself as a sacrifice for us, a pleasing aroma to God.

³Let there be no sexual immorality, impurity, or greed among you. Such sins have no place among God's people. ⁴Obscene stories, foolish talk, and coarse jokes—these are not for you. Instead, let there be thankfulness to God. ⁵You can be sure that no immoral, impure, or greedy person will inherit the Kingdom of Christ and of God. For a greedy person is an idolater, worshiping the things of this world.

⁶Don't be fooled by those who try to excuse these sins, for the anger of God will fall on all who disobey him. ⁷Don't participate in the things these people do. ⁸For once you were full of darkness, but now you have light from the Lord. So live as people of light! ⁹For this light within you produces only what is good and right and true.

¹⁰Carefully determine what pleases the Lord. ¹¹Take no part in the worthless deeds of evil and darkness; instead, expose them. ¹²It is shameful even to talk about the things that ungodly people do in secret. ¹³But their evil intentions will be exposed when the light shines on them, ¹⁴for the light makes everything visible. This is why it is said,

"Awake, O sleeper,
     rise up from the dead,
     and Christ will give you light."

Living by the Spirit's Power

¹⁵So be careful how you live. Don't live like fools, but like those who are wise. ¹⁶Make the most of every opportunity in these

4:30 Or *has put his seal on you.*   5:2 Some manuscripts read *loved you.*

Anchor Passage continued from page 374...

Experience

Take your list of things that could break apart a relationship, and tear it into pieces. Use tape to reassemble the pieces in the shape of a building. As you build, identify each piece of tape as something that could repair a friendship.

Choose a neighbor in your life whom you've had trouble getting along with but would like to deepen your relationship with. Pick one of the do's from **Ephesians 4:25-32** that would help you build that deeper friendship...and do it! (And don't be afraid of making a mess!)

Reflect

★ What friendship troubles are you having right now?
★ Underline the specific things from the Scripture passage that can help you deal with the relationship messes in your life. How can those words help you deepen your friendships?

DIGGING DEEPER

FRIENDSHIP TYPE:	FRIENDSHIP LAYER:
Neighbors	*Deepening*

For deepening in friendship with your neighbors, check out...

➻ The Friendship Experience .... on page 387
➻ The Friendship Story .... on page 502
➻ What to Say and What Not to Say .... on page 391

Friendship First NEW TESTAMENT

DO IT. Don't just read it and move on. Accept the challenge. Then go out and *experience* friendship in everyday, down-to-earth ways. *Live out* the lessons of Scripture.

REFLECT ON YOUR EXPERIENCES. Use the questions at the end of the Anchor Passage and the journal space around it to jot down your thoughts regarding the Scripture, the insights you've gained, and the experiences you've had.

MOVE ON. At the end of each Anchor Passage is a "Digging Deeper" box that will direct you to more experiences, stories, and laughs! The "Digging Deeper" section will help you find the *Friendship Experience*, *Friendship Story*, and *What to Say and What Not to Say* related to the topic you're studying within the Friendship Guide.

★ *Friendship Experiences* ★

Experience friendship—with people and with God. The *Friendship Experiences* offer you the opportunity to dig deeper into the type of friendship and layer of friendship you're exploring.

Relevant, practical challenges for experiencing friendship will help you see the connection between friendship with others and friendship with God.

A photo scavenger hunt. A prayer walk. A Saturday at the homeless shelter. A long hike with an old friend. Sometimes the experiences are quick and easy. Sometimes they're intense and challenging. But they're always inspiring… and they'll always help you grow your friendships!

These fellowship activities will help you create meaningful experiences—shared memories— of each type of friendship and at every layer of friendship…both with your friends and with God.

Experience the connection between friendship with others and friendship with God.

FRIENDSHIP EXPERIENCE

FRIENDSHIP TYPE: *Neighbors*   FRIENDSHIP LAYER: *Acceptance*

Smash Through

We often blame prejudice on ignorance. And that's certainly part of the problem but not all of it—there are plenty of educated people who are also highly prejudiced. And nearly *everyone* has some level of prejudice.

Many who are free from racial prejudice harbor religious prejudice. Others make judgments about people based on what they've heard from family, from the media, or even (sadly) at church.

Prejudice is usually the result of an indulgence in stereotypes and a refusal to get to know a person or group of people.

Sure, education is great, and it may help a little, but the best cure for judgment and prejudice is exposure. It's tough to hate someone you truly know and understand.

Getting to know someone is the first step toward acceptance. If there's a person or a group you struggle with, try getting to know them. Your efforts might turn people you dislike or fear into friends. And remember, God loves those people…deeply.

FRIENDSHIP EXPERIENCE *continues on page 451…*

Friendship First NEW TESTAMENT

---

7 So humble yourselves before God. Resist the devil, and he will flee from you. 8 Come close to God, and God will come close to you. Wash your hands, you sinners; purify your hearts, for your loyalty is divided between God and the world. 9 Let there be tears for what you have done. Let there be sorrow and deep grief. Let there be sadness instead of laughter, and gloom instead of joy. 10 Humble yourselves before the Lord, and he will lift you up in honor.

Warning against Judging Others

11 Don't speak evil against each other, dear brothers and sisters.* If you criticize and judge each other, then you are criticizing and judging God's law. But your job is to obey the law, not to judge whether it applies to you. 12 God alone, who gave the law, is the Judge. He alone has the power to save or to destroy. So what right do you have to judge your neighbor?

Warning about Self-Confidence

13 Look here, you who say, "Today or tomorrow we are going to a certain town and will stay there a year. We will do business there and make a profit." 14 How do you know what your life will be like tomorrow? Your life is like the morning fog—it's here a little while, then it's gone. 15 What you ought to say is, "If the Lord wants us to, we will live and do this or that." 16 Otherwise you are boasting about your own plans, and all such boasting is evil. 17 Remember, it is sin to know what you ought to do and then not do it.

CHAPTER 5
Warning to the Rich

Look here, you rich people: Weep and groan with anguish because of all the terrible troubles ahead of you. 2 Your wealth is rotting away, and your fine clothes are moth-eaten rags. 3 Your gold and silver have become worthless. The very wealth you were counting on will eat away your flesh like fire. This treasure you have accumulated will stand as evidence against you on the day of judgment. 4 For listen! Hear the cries of the field workers whom you have cheated of their pay. The wages you held back cry out against you. The cries of those who harvest your fields have reached the ears of the LORD of Heaven's Armies. 5 You have spent your years on earth in luxury, satisfying your every desire. You have fattened yourselves for the day of slaugh-

4:11 Greek *brothers*.

---

ter. 6 You have condemned and killed innocent people,* who do not resist you.*

Patience and Endurance

7 Dear brothers and sisters,* be patient as you wait for the Lord's return. Consider the farmers who patiently wait for the rains in the fall and in the spring. They eagerly look for the valuable harvest to ripen. 8 You, too, must be patient. Take courage, for the coming of the Lord is near.

9 Don't grumble about each other, brothers and sisters, or you will be judged. For look—the Judge is standing at the door!

10 For examples of patience in suffering, dear brothers and sisters, look at the prophets who spoke in the name of the Lord. 11 We give great honor to those who endure under suffering. For instance, you know about Job, a man of great endurance. You can see how the Lord was kind to him at the end, for the Lord is full of tenderness and mercy.

12 But most of all, my brothers and sisters, never take an oath, by heaven or earth or anything else. Just say a simple yes or no, so that you will not sin and be condemned.

The Power of Prayer

13 Are any of you suffering hardships? You should pray. Are any of you happy? You should sing praises. 14 Are any of you sick? You should call for the elders of the church to come and pray over you, anointing you with oil in the name of the Lord. 15 Such a prayer offered in faith will heal the sick, and the Lord will make you well. And if you have committed any sins, you will be forgiven.

16 Confess your sins to each other and pray for each other so that you may be healed. The earnest prayer of a righteous person has great power and produces wonderful results. 17 Elijah was as human as we are, and yet when he prayed earnestly that no rain would fall, none fell for three and a half years! 18 Then, when he prayed again, the sky sent down rain and the earth began to yield its crops.

Restore Wandering Believers

19 My dear brothers and sisters, if someone among you wanders away from the truth and is brought back, 20 you can be sure that whoever brings the sinner back will save that person from death and bring about the forgiveness of many sins.

5:6a Or *killed the Righteous One.* 5:6b Or *Don't they resist you?* or *Doesn't God oppose you?* or *Aren't they now accusing you before God?* 5:7 Greek *brothers;* also in 5:9, 10, 12, 19.

FRIENDSHIP EXPERIENCE *continued from page 450…*

THE ONE THING 1 YOU CAN DO TODAY

Experience

Begin by being really honest with yourself. There is likely a certain type of person you avoid, are afraid of, don't like, or feel uncomfortable around. Do you hold hidden prejudice against a race? a social or economic group? people without education? people with certain interests or behaviors?

Make an effort to get to know that race, group, or type of person. Perhaps you can start up a conversation with someone during lunch or a break at work. If you don't have direct contact with that type of person, gain exposure by learning about them. Read about their history. Search for stories about respected men and women who share the same race, economic background, or level of education.

Virtually every people group and demographic has been reached by the message of Jesus at some level. Check with a mission agency or missions program to find out what God is doing with different groups of people around the world. For the ultimate exposure, go on a mission trip and learn more (remember, a mission trip doesn't have to be to a foreign country; it could be to the inner city, a rural area, or another state).

Reflect

★ What prejudices do you struggle with? Why do you feel that way?

★ In what ways are your prejudices or judgments off-base?

★ Read James 2:1-13. How can you move from judgment toward acceptance?

Friendship First NEW TESTAMENT

★ *Friendship Stories* ★

The world is full of real-life friendship stories. Some of them are heroic, some of them everyday, some of them funny…all of them inspiring.

Here you'll get a glimpse at what real friendship looks like—how it's lived out in daily life. Each story is a real-life illustration of the type of friendship and layer of friendship on which you're reflecting.

• **Based on True Events***—These everyday, contemporary stories reveal the value of authentic friendships—with people and with God—in our fast-paced, grab-and-go society.

• **From the Archives**—Abraham Lincoln, Mother Teresa, John Wesley…What do they have in common? Well, they all had friends! In these historic stories, you'll read about friendships that changed history.

• **Found in Scripture**—These Old Testament accounts of friendship show how God has been shaping friendships since the beginning of time.

From David and Jonathan to C.S. Lewis and J.R.R. Tolkien to the neighbors down the street, these true stories of friendship will move you to grow your own relationships with people and with God.

*In most of these stories, names have been changed.

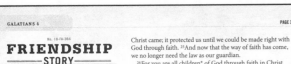

GALATIANS 4   PAGE 364

FRIENDSHIP
— STORY —

No. 18-FA-364

FRIENDSHIP TYPE:	FRIENDSHIP LAYER:
Jesus	*Companionship*
	FROM THE ARCHIVES

When Jesus Rubs Off on You

To say Ben was on a fast track is an understatement.

The son of minor nobility, Ben grew up with every advantage he could desire. He was well-connected, his future was wide open with possibilities, and he was receiving a first-rate classical education in the capital of the empire. Ben was going places.

So why did he drop out of school? Why would a young man accustomed to comfort and companionship choose solitary confinement in a remote cave at the far end of a rocky Italian ravine?

What was *wrong* with this guy?

Nothing, actually.

Ben walked away from his easy life to seek companionship with Jesus, far away from the temptations and distractions of fifth-century Rome. And the several years he spent in prayer and companionship with Jesus changed Ben.

He moved into the cave a confused young man, escaping an overwhelming world.

He emerged sure of who he was in Christ and secure in his friendship with Jesus.

Ben—we now know him as St. Benedict—spent enough time with Jesus that he started viewing life as Jesus viewed it. The scrambling for wealth and influence in Rome? Meaningless. His education? Ben saw that knowledge without wisdom wasn't worth much.

Ben summed up his learning in the *Benedictine Rule*, which inspires and informs millions to this day.

What changed Ben into St. Benedict? Companionship—with Jesus.

FRIENDSHIP STORY *continues on page 365...*

Friendship First NEW TESTAMENT

Christ came; it protected us until we could be made right with God through faith. [25]And now that the way of faith has come, we no longer need the law as our guardian.

[26]For you are all children* of God through faith in Christ Jesus. [27]And all who have been united with Christ in baptism have put on Christ, like putting on new clothes.* [28]There is no longer Jew or Gentile,* slave or free, male and female. For you are all one in Christ Jesus. [29]And now that you belong to Christ, you are the true children* of Abraham. You are his heirs, and God's promise to Abraham belongs to you.

CHAPTER 4

Think of it this way. If a father dies and leaves an inheritance for his young children, those children are not much better off than slaves until they grow up, even though they actually own everything their father had. [2]They have to obey their guardians until they reach whatever age their father set. [3]And that's the way it was with us before Christ came. We were like children; we were slaves to the basic spiritual principles* of this world.

[4]But when the right time came, God sent his Son, born of a woman, subject to the law. [5]God sent him to buy freedom for us who were slaves to the law, so that he could adopt us as his very own children.* [6]And because we* are his children, God has sent the Spirit of his Son into our hearts, prompting us to call out, "Abba, Father."* [7]Now you are no longer a slave but God's own child.* And since you are his child, God has made you his heir.

Paul's Concern for the Galatians

[8]Before you Gentiles knew God, you were slaves to so-called gods that do not even exist. [9]So now that you know God (or should I say, now that God knows you), why do you want to go back again and become slaves once more to the weak and useless spiritual principles of this world? [10]You are trying to earn favor with God by observing certain days or months or seasons or years. [11]I fear for you. Perhaps all my hard work with you was for nothing. [12]Dear brothers and sisters,* I plead with you to live as I do in freedom from these things, for I have become like you Gentiles—free from those laws.

You did not mistreat me when I first preached to you. [13]Surely you remember that I was sick when I first brought you the Good News. [14]But even though my condition tempted

3:26 Greek *sons.*   3:27 Greek *have put on Christ.*   3:28 Greek *Jew or Greek.*   3:29 Greek *seed.* 4:3 Or *powers;* also in 4:9.   4:5 Greek *sons;* also in 4:6.   4:6a Greek *you.*   4:6b *Abba* is an Aramaic term for "father."   4:7 Greek *son;* also in 4:7b.   4:12 Greek *brothers;* also in 4:28, 31.

PAGE 365   GALATIANS 4

you to reject me, you did not despise me or turn me away. No, you took me in and cared for me as though I were an angel from God or even Christ Jesus himself. [15]Where is that joyful and grateful spirit you felt then? I am sure you would have taken out your own eyes and given them to me if it had been possible. [16]Have I now become your enemy because I am telling you the truth?

[17]Those false teachers are so eager to win your favor, but their intentions are not good. They are trying to shut you off from me so that you will pay attention only to them. [18]If someone is eager to do good things for you, that's all right; but let them do it all the time, not just when I'm with you.

[19]Oh, my dear children! I feel as if I'm going through labor pains for you again, and they will continue until Christ is fully developed in your lives. [20]I wish I were with you right now so I could change my tone. But at this distance I don't know how else to help you.

Abraham's Two Children

[21]Tell me, you who want to live under the law, do you know what the law actually says? [22]The Scriptures say that Abraham had two sons, one from his slave wife and one from his freeborn wife.* [23]The son of the slave wife was born in a human attempt to bring about the fulfillment of God's promise. But the son of the freeborn wife was born as God's own fulfillment of his promise.

[24]These two women serve as an illustration of God's two covenants. The first woman, Hagar, represents Mount Sinai where people received the law that enslaved them. [25]And now Jerusalem is just like Mount Sinai in Arabia,* because she and her children live in slavery to the law. [26]But the other woman, Sarah, represents the heavenly Jerusalem. She is the free woman, and she is our mother. [27]As Isaiah said,

"Rejoice, O childless woman,
   you who have never given birth!
Break into a joyful shout,
   you who have never been in labor!
For the desolate woman now has more children
   than the woman who lives with her husband!"*

[28]And you, dear brothers and sisters, are children of the promise, just like Isaac. [29]But you are now being persecuted

4:22 See Gen 16:15; 21:2-3.   4:25 Greek *And Hagar, which is Mount Sinai in Arabia, is now like Jerusalem;* other manuscripts read *And Mount Sinai in Arabia is now like Jerusalem.*   4:27 Isa 54:1.

FRIENDSHIP STORY *continued from page 364...*

Experience

THE ONE THING YOU CAN DO THIS WEEK **1**

Companions check in with each other often. This week do the same with Jesus by using these reminders: When you stop at a red light, ask Jesus what you should be praying about, and use that time to pray. When you hang up a phone, ask Jesus to help you see people the way he sees them, and treat them accordingly. When you touch a doorknob, quickly ask Jesus how he wants to use you in the next five minutes, and look for his leading.

Let Jesus rub off on you; it'll make for an interesting week.

Reflect

★ What actions or attitudes in your life show a new acquaintance that you've been spending time with Jesus?

★ In what ways do you regularly spend time with Jesus? What's hard about making that happen?

★ What's the best thing that could happen if you were a companion of Jesus? What's the worst? What do you expect to happen between you and Jesus?

★ *What to Say and What Not to Say* ★

They're funny. They're witty. They're entertaining.

They're nuggets of truth that you can't ignore.

Each *What to Say and What Not to Say* is jam-packed with fun, practical, often hilarious tips on what to say and do—and what *not* to say or do—in everyday situations.

Ever been annoyed by a friend who talks with his mouth full? Or what about a family member who always asks for money? Have you ever been invited to a party you *didn't* want to attend?

We all face awkward situations like that. And a lot of the time, we don't know what to say or do. We stumble through and hope we come out looking OK…and that we don't offend anyone.

The *What to Say and What Not to Say* readings will make you laugh, but they'll also give you practical insights into social appropriateness and loving responses.

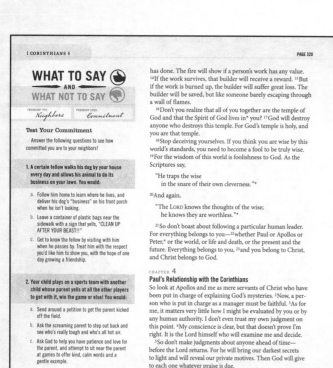

★ Extra! Extra! ★

Insightful thoughts and quotes on friendship.

"There is always an intangible something which makes a friend, it is not what he does, but what he is."

~ Oswald Chambers

"Pass the cheesecake, please..." Of those surveyed, 71% said they have **developed friendships** with others in church over a shared meal or meals.

—from "Friendship and Faith," a Gallup Research Study Commissioned by Group Publishing, Inc.

Statistics revealing the connection between faith and friendship.

JOURNAL

Journal space to record your reflections, insights, and discoveries as you study and experience your *Friendship First New Testament.*

Old Testament wisdom on friendships with others and with God.

"Love prospers when a fault is forgiven, but dwelling on it separates close friends."

~ Proverbs 17:9

More Scripture passages on friendship in the **Friendship Reading Plan** on page 512. Check it out, and follow the plan with a friend this year!

HOW TO BE A FRIEND TO NEIGHBORS
- **MARK 10:35-45** (Jesus teaches us to serve others.)

How to Use This New Testament

It's for small-group Bible study.

It's for weekly get-togethers with a friend.

It's for personal devotions.

It's all three—and more!

This Friendship Guide is endlessly versatile and creative. It can be used with your small group, with a friend, and in your own reflection times. Study down a column, study across a row, or study a box as it's needed in your life. Go through a box a week or a feature a day, or just grab it when you need it!

It doesn't matter how you use this New Testament; what matters is how you *live* it.

We're called to true friendship with God and with the people around us. The two greatest commandments God has given us (Matthew 22:37-39)?

Love God.

Love people.

So what are you waiting for? The promises of authentic friendship are just pages away…

The New Testament

Matthew

AUTHOR:	DATE WRITTEN:
Matthew (Levi)	Approximately A.D. 60–65

JOURNAL

CHAPTER 1

The Ancestors of the Messiah

This is a record of the ancestors of Jesus the Messiah, a descendant of David* and of Abraham:

² Abraham was the father of Isaac.
Isaac was the father of Jacob.
Jacob was the father of Judah and his brothers.
³ Judah was the father of Perez and Zerah (whose mother was Tamar).
Perez was the father of Hezron.
Hezron was the father of Ram.*
⁴ Ram was the father of Amminadab.
Amminadab was the father of Nahshon.
Nahshon was the father of Salmon.
⁵ Salmon was the father of Boaz (whose mother was Rahab).
Boaz was the father of Obed (whose mother was Ruth).
Obed was the father of Jesse.
⁶ Jesse was the father of King David.
David was the father of Solomon (whose mother was Bathsheba, the widow of Uriah).
⁷ Solomon was the father of Rehoboam.
Rehoboam was the father of Abijah.
Abijah was the father of Asa.*
⁸ Asa was the father of Jehoshaphat.
Jehoshaphat was the father of Jehoram.*
Jehoram was the father* of Uzziah.
⁹ Uzziah was the father of Jotham.
Jotham was the father of Ahaz.
Ahaz was the father of Hezekiah.

1:1 Greek *Jesus the Messiah, son of David.* 1:3 Greek *Aram,* a variant spelling of Ram; also in 1:4. See 1 Chr 2:9-10. 1:7 Greek *Asaph,* a variant spelling of Asa; also in 1:8. See 1 Chr 3:10. 1:8a Greek *Joram,* a variant spelling of Jehoram; also in 1:8b. See 1 Kgs 22:50 and note at 1 Chr 3:11. 1:8b Or *ancestor;* also in 1:11.

¹⁰ Hezekiah was the father of Manasseh.
   Manasseh was the father of Amon.*
   Amon was the father of Josiah.
¹¹ Josiah was the father of Jehoiachin* and his brothers
      (born at the time of the exile to Babylon).
¹² After the Babylonian exile:
   Jehoiachin was the father of Shealtiel.
   Shealtiel was the father of Zerubbabel.
¹³ Zerubbabel was the father of Abiud.
   Abiud was the father of Eliakim.
   Eliakim was the father of Azor.
¹⁴ Azor was the father of Zadok.
   Zadok was the father of Akim.
   Akim was the father of Eliud.
¹⁵ Eliud was the father of Eleazar.
   Eleazar was the father of Matthan.
   Matthan was the father of Jacob.
¹⁶ Jacob was the father of Joseph, the husband of Mary.
   Mary gave birth to Jesus, who is called the Messiah.

¹⁷All those listed above include fourteen generations from Abraham to David, fourteen from David to the Babylonian exile, and fourteen from the Babylonian exile to the Messiah.

The Birth of Jesus the Messiah

¹⁸This is how Jesus the Messiah was born. His mother, Mary, was engaged to be married to Joseph. But before the marriage took place, while she was still a virgin, she became pregnant through the power of the Holy Spirit. ¹⁹Joseph, her fiancé, was a good man and did not want to disgrace her publicly, so he decided to break the engagement* quietly.

²⁰As he considered this, an angel of the Lord appeared to him in a dream. "Joseph, son of David," the angel said, "do not be afraid to take Mary as your wife. For the child within her was conceived by the Holy Spirit. ²¹And she will have a son, and you are to name him Jesus,* for he will save his people from their sins."

²²All of this occurred to fulfill the Lord's message through his prophet:

²³ "Look! The virgin will conceive a child!
   She will give birth to a son,

1:10 Greek *Amos,* a variant spelling of Amon; also in 1:10b. See 1 Chr 3:14. 1:11 Greek *Jeconiah,* a variant spelling of Jehoiachin; also in 1:12. See 2 Kgs 24:6 and note at 1 Chr 3:16. 1:19 Greek *to divorce her.* 1:21 *Jesus* means "The LORD saves."

FRIENDSHIP EXPERIENCE

| FRIENDSHIP TYPE: *Family* | FRIENDSHIP LAYER: *Deepening* |

Patterned Forgiveness

Ever been forgiven for something really big? How did you feel after being forgiven? Grateful? Undeserving? Resentful? Guilty?

Consider this: The feelings you have when you are forgiven can affect your own ability and willingness to forgive others.

If you're grateful for forgiveness, you're quick to give it away. If you feel undeserving of forgiveness, you might try to pay it off and then expect the same from others. If you're resentful of forgiveness, you might withhold it from people you love. If you still feel guilty, even after being forgiven, then you may be unable to completely forgive someone else.

Read **Matthew 18:21-35**, and consider how the servant might have felt when his huge debt was forgiven. Why do you think he, after receiving such lavish forgiveness, turned around and refused to forgive his fellow servant?

Was he simply ungrateful and incredibly stingy? Or did he feel guilty and want to push his guilt onto someone else? Or maybe he still felt he should pay off his debt to the king and wanted to begin collecting the money.

How do you receive forgiveness?

It has a lot to do with how you forgive others.

FRIENDSHIP EXPERIENCE *continues on page 4...*

Friendship First NEW TESTAMENT

FRIENDSHIP EXPERIENCE *continued from page 3...*

Experience

Get together with one or more family members. Ask everyone to make two lists: one list of times you forgave someone in your family (remember when he wrecked your car?) and one list of times you received forgiveness from someone in your family (how about when you forgot that birthday?).

Finish the list, and then write down one feeling you associate with each event. *Gratitude? Anger? Sadness? Guilt? Relief?*

Talk about your lists. Are they filled with positive or negative words? Is anyone still hurting? Is anyone holding a grudge? Or have you mostly moved on?

Discuss this: How do you think these feelings reflect your ability to give and receive forgiveness—from God and others? How can you, as a family, grow in giving and receiving forgiveness?

Maybe you can remind each other that forgiveness comes with no strings attached. Or perhaps you can pray together each day and thank God for his perfect forgiveness.

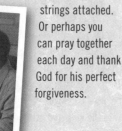

Reflect

★ How do you think God wants you to feel toward the forgiveness he offers? How can that attitude enable you to give and receive forgiveness from others?

★ Why is forgiveness an important part of deepening the friendships in your family?

and they will call him Immanuel,*
which means 'God is with us.'"

24 When Joseph woke up, he did as the angel of the Lord commanded and took Mary as his wife. 25 But he did not have sexual relations with her until her son was born. And Joseph named him Jesus.

CHAPTER **2**

Visitors from the East

Jesus was born in Bethlehem in Judea, during the reign of King Herod. About that time some wise men* from eastern lands arrived in Jerusalem, asking, 2 "Where is the newborn king of the Jews? We saw his star as it rose,* and we have come to worship him."

3 King Herod was deeply disturbed when he heard this, as was everyone in Jerusalem. 4 He called a meeting of the leading priests and teachers of religious law and asked, "Where is the Messiah supposed to be born?"

5 "In Bethlehem in Judea," they said, "for this is what the prophet wrote:

6 'And you, O Bethlehem in the land of Judah,
    are not least among the ruling cities* of Judah,
for a ruler will come from you
    who will be the shepherd for my people Israel.'*"

7 Then Herod called for a private meeting with the wise men, and he learned from them the time when the star first appeared. 8 Then he told them, "Go to Bethlehem and search carefully for the child. And when you find him, come back and tell me so that I can go and worship him, too!"

9 After this interview the wise men went their way. And the star they had seen in the east guided them to Bethlehem. It went ahead of them and stopped over the place where the child was. 10 When they saw the star, they were filled with joy! 11 They entered the house and saw the child with his mother, Mary, and they bowed down and worshiped him. Then they opened their treasure chests and gave him gifts of gold, frankincense, and myrrh.

12 When it was time to leave, they returned to their own country by another route, for God had warned them in a dream not to return to Herod.

1:23 Isa 7:14; 8:8, 10 (Greek version).   2:1 Or *royal astrologers;* Greek reads *magi;* also in 2:7, 16.
2:2 Or *star in the east.*   2:6a Greek *the rulers.*   2:6b Mic 5:2; 2 Sam 5:2.

The Escape to Egypt

¹³After the wise men were gone, an angel of the Lord appeared to Joseph in a dream. "Get up! Flee to Egypt with the child and his mother," the angel said. "Stay there until I tell you to return, because Herod is going to search for the child to kill him."

¹⁴That night Joseph left for Egypt with the child and Mary, his mother, ¹⁵and they stayed there until Herod's death. This fulfilled what the Lord had spoken through the prophet: "I called my Son out of Egypt."*

¹⁶Herod was furious when he realized that the wise men had outwitted him. He sent soldiers to kill all the boys in and around Bethlehem who were two years old and under, based on the wise men's report of the star's first appearance. ¹⁷Herod's brutal action fulfilled what God had spoken through the prophet Jeremiah:

¹⁸ "A cry was heard in Ramah—
    weeping and great mourning.
Rachel weeps for her children,
    refusing to be comforted,
    for they are dead."*

The Return to Nazareth

¹⁹When Herod died, an angel of the Lord appeared in a dream to Joseph in Egypt. ²⁰"Get up!" the angel said. "Take the child and his mother back to the land of Israel, because those who were trying to kill the child are dead."

²¹So Joseph got up and returned to the land of Israel with Jesus and his mother. ²²But when he learned that the new ruler of Judea was Herod's son Archelaus, he was afraid to go there. Then, after being warned in a dream, he left for the region of Galilee. ²³So the family went and lived in a town called Nazareth. This fulfilled what the prophets had said: "He will be called a Nazarene."

CHAPTER **3**

John the Baptist Prepares the Way

In those days John the Baptist came to the Judean wilderness and began preaching. His message was, ²"Repent of your sins and turn to God, for the Kingdom of Heaven is near.*" ³The prophet Isaiah was speaking about John when he said,

"He is a voice shouting in the wilderness,
'Prepare the way for the LORD's coming!
    Clear the road for him!'"*

2:15 Hos 11:1.   **2:18** Jer 31:15.   **3:2** Or *has come,* or *is coming soon.*   **3:3** Isa 40:3 (Greek version).

"To err is human, to forgive divine."
~ Alexander Pope

JOURNAL

⁴John's clothes were woven from coarse camel hair, and he wore a leather belt around his waist. For food he ate locusts and wild honey. ⁵People from Jerusalem and from all of Judea and all over the Jordan Valley went out to see and hear John. ⁶And when they confessed their sins, he baptized them in the Jordan River.

⁷But when he saw many Pharisees and Sadducees coming to watch him baptize,* he denounced them. "You brood of snakes!" he exclaimed. "Who warned you to flee God's coming wrath? ⁸Prove by the way you live that you have repented of your sins and turned to God. ⁹Don't just say to each other, 'We're safe, for we are descendants of Abraham.' That means nothing, for I tell you, God can create children of Abraham from these very stones. ¹⁰Even now the ax of God's judgment is poised, ready to sever the roots of the trees. Yes, every tree that does not produce good fruit will be chopped down and thrown into the fire.

¹¹"I baptize with* water those who repent of their sins and turn to God. But someone is coming soon who is greater than I am—so much greater that I'm not worthy even to be his slave and carry his sandals. He will baptize you with the Holy Spirit and with fire.* ¹²He is ready to separate the chaff from the wheat with his winnowing fork. Then he will clean up the threshing area, gathering the wheat into his barn but burning the chaff with never-ending fire."

The Baptism of Jesus

¹³Then Jesus went from Galilee to the Jordan River to be baptized by John. ¹⁴But John tried to talk him out of it. "I am the one who needs to be baptized by you," he said, "so why are you coming to me?"

¹⁵But Jesus said, "It should be done, for we must carry out all that God requires.*" So John agreed to baptize him.

¹⁶After his baptism, as Jesus came up out of the water, the heavens were opened* and he saw the Spirit of God descending like a dove and settling on him. ¹⁷And a voice from heaven said, "This is my dearly loved Son, who brings me great joy."

CHAPTER 4
The Temptation of Jesus

Then Jesus was led by the Spirit into the wilderness to be tempted there by the devil. ²For forty days and forty nights he fasted and became very hungry.

3:7 Or *coming to be baptized.*   3:11a Or *in.*   3:11b Or *in the Holy Spirit and in fire.*   3:15 Or *for we must fulfill all righteousness.*   3:16 Some manuscripts read *opened to him.*

3During that time the devil* came and said to him, "If you are the Son of God, tell these stones to become loaves of bread."
4But Jesus told him, "No! The Scriptures say,

'People do not live by bread alone,
    but by every word that comes from the mouth of God.'*"

5Then the devil took him to the holy city, Jerusalem, to the highest point of the Temple, 6and said, "If you are the Son of God, jump off! For the Scriptures say,

'He will order his angels to protect you.
And they will hold you up with their hands
    so you won't even hurt your foot on a stone.'*"

7Jesus responded, "The Scriptures also say, 'You must not test the LORD your God.'*"
8Next the devil took him to the peak of a very high mountain and showed him all the kingdoms of the world and their glory. 9"I will give it all to you," he said, "if you will kneel down and worship me."
10"Get out of here, Satan," Jesus told him. "For the Scriptures say,

'You must worship the LORD your God
    and serve only him.'*"

11Then the devil went away, and angels came and took care of Jesus.

The Ministry of Jesus Begins

12When Jesus heard that John had been arrested, he left Judea and returned to Galilee. 13He went first to Nazareth, then left there and moved to Capernaum, beside the Sea of Galilee, in the region of Zebulun and Naphtali. 14This fulfilled what God said through the prophet Isaiah:

15 "In the land of Zebulun and of Naphtali,
        beside the sea, beyond the Jordan River,
        in Galilee where so many Gentiles live,
16   the people who sat in darkness
        have seen a great light.
    And for those who lived in the land where death casts
        its shadow,
        a light has shined."*

4:3 Greek *the tempter.*   4:4 Deut 8:3.   4:6 Ps 91:11-12.   4:7 Deut 6:16.   4:10 Deut 6:13.
4:15-16 Isa 9:1-2 (Greek version).

WHAT TO SAY
AND
WHAT NOT TO SAY

FRIENDSHIP TYPE: *Jesus*   FRIENDSHIP LAYER: *Commitment*

Do I Have To?

The Scene: You're driving to a friend's house with the dinner you just picked up for everyone to share. You won't be late if you hit all green lights…though it's not like that ever happens. And sure enough, the car in front of you is the last one to get through on yellow. You sigh and mutter, drum your fingers on the wheel, and think about what movie you and your friends will go to tonight. Suddenly, it occurs to you that nobody checked theater times yet. Instantly irritated, you reach for your cell phone…and lock eyes with a man standing on the corner next to your car. He's holding a cardboard sign with a plea for food, for any kind of help. The man's legs are bent at an unnatural angle, and he looks like he's in pain. A woman and three small children sit nearby. It looks as if they have only one duffel bag between them and that they've been on that corner for a while. Hungry. Hurting. Suddenly, you have the very distinct feeling that God's saying something to you…

 ## WHAT NOT TO SAY:

★ "Who, me? No way; what would we do about dinner? Besides, I have to get reimbursed for this stuff."

★ "But I'm not really sure what I could even do to help…OK, what about if I pass some change through the window? Looks like I have quite a few pennies here…"

★ "You're right, Lord—I can help. If I say a quick prayer while I'm driving, I'm sure that would do a lot of good. Right? I'm sure somebody else will come by soon and help out anyway."

WHAT TO SAY AND WHAT NOT TO SAY *continues on page 8…*

WHAT TO SAY AND WHAT NOT TO SAY *continued from page 7...*

WHAT TO SAY:

★ "Thank you, Jesus, for the ways you love all of us. I pray you would help me share your love with this family as an overflow of my friendship with you."

★ "Jesus, I have to admit that I'm angry. And sad. And confused. It's hard to understand why these people would be in such a painful situation. Please relieve their suffering. Please also be with me as I go talk to them. Show me what to say and do."

★ "Jesus, thank you for blessing this food. It's a small gift, but please use it in the way you want."

"For I was hungry, and you fed me. I was thirsty, and you gave me a drink. I was a stranger, and you invited me into your home. I was naked, and you gave me clothing. I was sick, and you cared for me. I was in prison, and you visited me...I tell you the truth, when you did it to one of the least of these my brothers and sisters, you were doing it to me!"

— Jesus (Matthew 25:35-36, 40)

[17] From then on Jesus began to preach, "Repent of your sins and turn to God, for the Kingdom of Heaven is near.*"

The First Disciples

[18] One day as Jesus was walking along the shore of the Sea of Galilee, he saw two brothers—Simon, also called Peter, and Andrew—throwing a net into the water, for they fished for a living. [19] Jesus called out to them, "Come, follow me, and I will show you how to fish for people!" [20] And they left their nets at once and followed him.

[21] A little farther up the shore he saw two other brothers, James and John, sitting in a boat with their father, Zebedee, repairing their nets. And he called them to come, too. [22] They immediately followed him, leaving the boat and their father behind.

Crowds Follow Jesus

[23] Jesus traveled throughout the region of Galilee, teaching in the synagogues and announcing the Good News about the Kingdom. And he healed every kind of disease and illness. [24] News about him spread as far as Syria, and people soon began bringing to him all who were sick. And whatever their sickness or disease, or if they were demon possessed or epileptic or paralyzed—he healed them all. [25] Large crowds followed him wherever he went—people from Galilee, the Ten Towns,* Jerusalem, from all over Judea, and from east of the Jordan River.

CHAPTER **5**

The Sermon on the Mount

One day as he saw the crowds gathering, Jesus went up on the mountainside and sat down. His disciples gathered around him, [2] and he began to teach them.

The Beatitudes

[3] "God blesses those who are poor and realize their need
    for him,*
    for the Kingdom of Heaven is theirs.
[4] God blesses those who mourn,
    for they will be comforted.
[5] God blesses those who are humble,
    for they will inherit the whole earth.
[6] God blesses those who hunger and thirst for justice,*
    for they will be satisfied.

4:17 Or *has come,* or *is coming soon.*   **4:25** Greek *Decapolis.*   **5:3** Greek *poor in spirit.*   **5:6** Or *for righteousness.*

7 God blesses those who are merciful,
     for they will be shown mercy.
8 God blesses those whose hearts are pure,
     for they will see God.
9 God blesses those who work for peace,
     for they will be called the children of God.
10 God blesses those who are persecuted for doing right,
     for the Kingdom of Heaven is theirs.

11 "God blesses you when people mock you and persecute you and lie about you* and say all sorts of evil things against you because you are my followers. 12 Be happy about it! Be very glad! For a great reward awaits you in heaven. And remember, the ancient prophets were persecuted in the same way.

Teaching about Salt and Light

13 "You are the salt of the earth. But what good is salt if it has lost its flavor? Can you make it salty again? It will be thrown out and trampled underfoot as worthless.

14 "You are the light of the world—like a city on a hilltop that cannot be hidden. 15 No one lights a lamp and then puts it under a basket. Instead, a lamp is placed on a stand, where it gives light to everyone in the house. 16 In the same way, let your good deeds shine out for all to see, so that everyone will praise your heavenly Father.

Teaching about the Law

17 "Don't misunderstand why I have come. I did not come to abolish the law of Moses or the writings of the prophets. No, I came to accomplish their purpose. 18 I tell you the truth, until heaven and earth disappear, not even the smallest detail of God's law will disappear until its purpose is achieved. 19 So if you ignore the least commandment and teach others to do the same, you will be called the least in the Kingdom of Heaven. But anyone who obeys God's laws and teaches them will be called great in the Kingdom of Heaven.

20 "But I warn you—unless your righteousness is better than the righteousness of the teachers of religious law and the Pharisees, you will never enter the Kingdom of Heaven!

Teaching about Anger

21 "You have heard that our ancestors were told, 'You must not murder. If you commit murder, you are subject to judgment.'*

5:11 Some manuscripts omit *and lie about you.*   5:21 Exod 20:13; Deut 5:17.

JOURNAL

22But I say, if you are even angry with someone,* you are subject to judgment! If you call someone an idiot,* you are in danger of being brought before the court. And if you curse someone,* you are in danger of the fires of hell.*

23"So if you are presenting a sacrifice* at the altar in the Temple and you suddenly remember that someone has something against you, 24leave your sacrifice there at the altar. Go and be reconciled to that person. Then come and offer your sacrifice to God.

25"When you are on the way to court with your adversary, settle your differences quickly. Otherwise, your accuser may hand you over to the judge, who will hand you over to an officer, and you will be thrown into prison. 26And if that happens, you surely won't be free again until you have paid the last penny.*

Teaching about Adultery

27"You have heard the commandment that says, 'You must not commit adultery.'* 28But I say, anyone who even looks at a woman with lust has already committed adultery with her in his heart. 29So if your eye—even your good eye*—causes you to lust, gouge it out and throw it away. It is better for you to lose one part of your body than for your whole body to be thrown into hell. 30And if your hand—even your stronger hand*—causes you to sin, cut it off and throw it away. It is better for you to lose one part of your body than for your whole body to be thrown into hell.

Teaching about Divorce

31"You have heard the law that says, 'A man can divorce his wife by merely giving her a written notice of divorce.'* 32But I say that a man who divorces his wife, unless she has been unfaithful, causes her to commit adultery. And anyone who marries a divorced woman also commits adultery.

Teaching about Vows

33"You have also heard that our ancestors were told, 'You must not break your vows; you must carry out the vows you make to the LORD.'* 34But I say, do not make any vows! Do not say, 'By heaven!' because heaven is God's throne. 35And do not say, 'By the earth!' because the earth is his footstool. And do not say, 'By Jerusalem!' for Jerusalem is the city of the great King. 36Do not even say, 'By my head!' for you can't turn one hair

5:22a Some manuscripts add *without cause.*   5:22b Greek uses an Aramaic term of contempt: *If you say to your brother, 'Raca.'*   5:22c Greek *if you say, 'You fool.'*   5:22d Greek *Gehenna;* also in 5:29, 30.   5:23 Greek *gift;* also in 5:24.   5:26 Greek *the last kodrantes* [i.e., quadrans].   5:27 Exod 20:14; Deut 5:18.   5:29 Greek *your right eye.*   5:30 Greek *your right hand.*   5:31 Deut 24:1.   5:33 Num 30:2.

white or black. 37 Just say a simple, 'Yes, I will,' or 'No, I won't.' Anything beyond this is from the evil one.

Teaching about Revenge

38 "You have heard the law that says the punishment must match the injury: 'An eye for an eye, and a tooth for a tooth.'* 39 But I say, do not resist an evil person! If someone slaps you on the right cheek, offer the other cheek also. 40 If you are sued in court and your shirt is taken from you, give your coat, too. 41 If a soldier demands that you carry his gear for a mile,* carry it two miles. 42 Give to those who ask, and don't turn away from those who want to borrow.

Teaching about Love for Enemies

43 "You have heard the law that says, 'Love your neighbor'* and hate your enemy. 44 But I say, love your enemies!* Pray for those who persecute you! 45 In that way, you will be acting as true children of your Father in heaven. For he gives his sunlight to both the evil and the good, and he sends rain on the just and the unjust alike. 46 If you love only those who love you, what reward is there for that? Even corrupt tax collectors do that much. 47 If you are kind only to your friends,* how are you different from anyone else? Even pagans do that. 48 But you are to be perfect, even as your Father in heaven is perfect.   ⚓

CHAPTER **6**

Teaching about Giving to the Needy

"Watch out! Don't do your good deeds publicly, to be admired by others, for you will lose the reward from your Father in heaven. 2 When you give to someone in need, don't do as the hypocrites do—blowing trumpets in the synagogues and streets to call attention to their acts of charity! I tell you the truth, they have received all the reward they will ever get. 3 But when you give to someone in need, don't let your left hand know what your right hand is doing. 4 Give your gifts in private, and your Father, who sees everything, will reward you.

5:38 Greek *the law that says: 'An eye for an eye and a tooth for a tooth.'* Exod 21:24; Lev 24:20; Deut 19:21.   5:41 Greek *milion* [4,854 feet or 1,478 meters].   5:43 Lev 19:18.   5:44 Some manuscripts add *Bless those who curse you. Do good to those who hate you.* Compare Luke 6:27-28.   5:47 Greek *your brothers.*

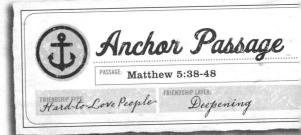

Anchor Passage

PASSAGE: Matthew 5:38-48

FRIENDSHIP TYPE: *Hard-to-Love People*   FRIENDSHIP LAYER: *Deepening*

Sure...Be Glad To

Think about the last time you hiked a mile. Read **Matthew 5:38-48**.

Hey, you think you have annoying people in *your* life?

Consider this: In Jesus' day, Roman soldiers could legally demand that civilians carry their packs for one Roman mile—approximately 4,854 feet.

Picture dragging yourself home after a long day at the carpentry shop when—*wham*—a soldier grabs you by the shoulder and you're hiking a mile out of your way hauling a fully loaded pack. And do you get a tip or a thank you?

All you get is the opportunity to hike back to where you started.

Annoying? You bet. The Romans not only conquer your country and tax you for the privilege but also make you haul their stuff all over the countryside.

Note what Jesus recommends in this situation: Go a second mile. *Voluntarily.*

Jesus isn't encouraging his people to become doormats for Roman abuse. Rather, he's encouraging his followers to adopt God's outlook when it comes to loving others.

God is absolutely *surrounded* by annoying people. People who call only when they want something. Who whine. Who are disobedient. Who sin.

You know—people like *us.*

Yet God continues to give...to answer...to love.

What to do with annoying people? We could do nothing and hope they'll go away. Eventually they will, but that's not what Jesus calls us to do.

Anchor Passage continues on page 12...

Anchor Passage continued from page 11...

We could do only what's absolutely required, teeth clenched and game face on, and then feel noble about an hour spent listening or 10 bucks passed to someone in need.

Or we could open up our hearts and lives, treating others the way God treats us. To not only endure annoying people but seek to deepen our relationship with them.

"Be perfect, even as your Father in heaven is perfect."

Experience

You could use some exercise, right? Ask that co-worker or neighbor who's annoying you to join you for a brief, refreshing hike during a break in your day. Ask open-ended questions to get to know the person better. And if God uses the time to open doors or to remove some barriers, go the second mile—twice around the block!

THE ONE THING
1
YOU CAN DO THIS WEEK

Anchor Passage continues on page 13...

Teaching about Prayer and Fasting

⁵"When you pray, don't be like the hypocrites who love to pray publicly on street corners and in the synagogues where everyone can see them. I tell you the truth, that is all the reward they will ever get. ⁶But when you pray, go away by yourself, shut the door behind you, and pray to your Father in private. Then your Father, who sees everything, will reward you.

⁷"When you pray, don't babble on and on as people of other religions do. They think their prayers are answered merely by repeating their words again and again. ⁸Don't be like them, for your Father knows exactly what you need even before you ask him! ⁹Pray like this:

Our Father in heaven,
    may your name be kept holy.
¹⁰ May your Kingdom come soon.
May your will be done on earth,
    as it is in heaven.
¹¹ Give us today the food we need,*
¹² and forgive us our sins,
    as we have forgiven those who sin against us.
¹³ And don't let us yield to temptation,*
    but rescue us from the evil one.*

¹⁴"If you forgive those who sin against you, your heavenly Father will forgive you. ¹⁵But if you refuse to forgive others, your Father will not forgive your sins.

¹⁶"And when you fast, don't make it obvious, as the hypocrites do, for they try to look miserable and disheveled so people will admire them for their fasting. I tell you the truth, that is the only reward they will ever get. ¹⁷But when you fast, comb your hair and wash your face. ¹⁸Then no one will notice that you are fasting, except your Father, who knows what you do in private. And your Father, who sees everything, will reward you.

Teaching about Money and Possessions

¹⁹"Don't store up treasures here on earth, where moths eat them and rust destroys them, and where thieves break in and steal. ²⁰Store your treasures in heaven, where moths and rust cannot destroy, and thieves do not break in and steal. ²¹Wherever your treasure is, there the desires of your heart will also be.

6:11 Or *Give us today our food for the day;* or *Give us today our food for tomorrow.* **6:13a** Or *And keep us from being tested.* **6:13b** Or *from evil.* Some manuscripts add *For yours is the kingdom and the power and the glory forever. Amen.*

²²"Your eye is a lamp that provides light for your body. When your eye is good, your whole body is filled with light. ²³But when your eye is bad, your whole body is filled with darkness. And if the light you think you have is actually darkness, how deep that darkness is!

²⁴"No one can serve two masters. For you will hate one and love the other; you will be devoted to one and despise the other. You cannot serve both God and money.

²⁵"That is why I tell you not to worry about everyday life—whether you have enough food and drink, or enough clothes to wear. Isn't life more than food, and your body more than clothing? ²⁶Look at the birds. They don't plant or harvest or store food in barns, for your heavenly Father feeds them. And aren't you far more valuable to him than they are? ²⁷Can all your worries add a single moment to your life?

²⁸"And why worry about your clothing? Look at the lilies of the field and how they grow. They don't work or make their clothing, ²⁹yet Solomon in all his glory was not dressed as beautifully as they are. ³⁰And if God cares so wonderfully for wildflowers that are here today and thrown into the fire tomorrow, he will certainly care for you. Why do you have so little faith?

³¹"So don't worry about these things, saying, 'What will we eat? What will we drink? What will we wear?' ³²These things dominate the thoughts of unbelievers, but your heavenly Father already knows all your needs. ³³Seek the Kingdom of God* above all else, and live righteously, and he will give you everything you need.

³⁴"So don't worry about tomorrow, for tomorrow will bring its own worries. Today's trouble is enough for today.

CHAPTER 7

Do Not Judge Others

"Do not judge others, and you will not be judged. ²For you will be treated as you treat others.* The standard you use in judging is the standard by which you will be judged.*

³"And why worry about a speck in your friend's eye* when you have a log in your own? ⁴How can you think of saying to your friend,* 'Let me help you get rid of that speck in your eye,' when you can't see past the log in your own eye? ⁵Hypocrite! First get rid of the log in your own eye; then you will see well enough to deal with the speck in your friend's eye.

6:33 Some manuscripts do not include *of God.*   **7:2a** Or *For God will judge you as you judge others.*
7:2b Or *The measure you give will be the measure you get back.*   **7:3** Greek *your brother's eye;* also
in 7:5.   **7:4** Greek *your brother.*

Anchor Passage continued from page 12...

Reflect

★ What's your default attitude toward adding a voluntary second mile to an obligatory first mile? Why?

★ Who's gone a "second mile" for you? How did it impact you?

★ In what ways did God use the voluntary second mile to improve your relationship with that "hard-to-love" person?

DIGGING DEEPER

FRIENDSHIP TYPE:
Hard-to-Love People

FRIENDSHIP LAYER:
Deepening

For deepening your friendship with hard-to-love people, check out...

➻ The Friendship Experience .... on page 43

➻ The Friendship Story .... on page 49

➻ What to Say and What Not to Say .... on page 25

JOURNAL

6 "Don't waste what is holy on people who are unholy.* Don't throw your pearls to pigs! They will trample the pearls, then turn and attack you.

Effective Prayer

7 "Keep on asking, and you will receive what you ask for. Keep on seeking, and you will find. Keep on knocking, and the door will be opened to you. 8 For everyone who asks, receives. Everyone who seeks, finds. And to everyone who knocks, the door will be opened.

9 "You parents—if your children ask for a loaf of bread, do you give them a stone instead? 10 Or if they ask for a fish, do you give them a snake? Of course not! 11 So if you sinful people know how to give good gifts to your children, how much more will your heavenly Father give good gifts to those who ask him.

The Golden Rule

12 "Do to others whatever you would like them to do to you. This is the essence of all that is taught in the law and the prophets.

The Narrow Gate

13 "You can enter God's Kingdom only through the narrow gate. The highway to hell* is broad, and its gate is wide for the many who choose that way. 14 But the gateway to life is very narrow and the road is difficult, and only a few ever find it.

The Tree and Its Fruit

15 "Beware of false prophets who come disguised as harmless sheep but are really vicious wolves. 16 You can identify them by their fruit, that is, by the way they act. Can you pick grapes from thornbushes, or figs from thistles? 17 A good tree produces good fruit, and a bad tree produces bad fruit. 18 A good tree can't produce bad fruit, and a bad tree can't produce good fruit. 19 So every tree that does not produce good fruit is chopped down and thrown into the fire. 20 Yes, just as you can identify a tree by its fruit, so you can identify people by their actions.

True Disciples

21 "Not everyone who calls out to me, 'Lord! Lord!' will enter the Kingdom of Heaven. Only those who actually do the will of my Father in heaven will enter. 22 On judgment day many will say to me, 'Lord! Lord! We prophesied in your name and cast out

7:6 Greek *Don't give the sacred to dogs.*   7:13 Greek *The road that leads to destruction.*

demons in your name and performed many miracles in your name.' [23]But I will reply, 'I never knew you. Get away from me, you who break God's laws.'

Building on a Solid Foundation

[24]"Anyone who listens to my teaching and follows it is wise, like a person who builds a house on solid rock. [25]Though the rain comes in torrents and the floodwaters rise and the winds beat against that house, it won't collapse because it is built on bedrock. [26]But anyone who hears my teaching and doesn't obey it is foolish, like a person who builds a house on sand. [27]When the rains and floods come and the winds beat against that house, it will collapse with a mighty crash."

[28]When Jesus had finished saying these things, the crowds were amazed at his teaching, [29]for he taught with real authority—quite unlike their teachers of religious law.

CHAPTER **8**

Jesus Heals a Man with Leprosy

Large crowds followed Jesus as he came down the mountainside. [2]Suddenly, a man with leprosy approached him and knelt before him. "Lord," the man said, "if you are willing, you can heal me and make me clean."

[3]Jesus reached out and touched him. "I am willing," he said. "Be healed!" And instantly the leprosy disappeared. [4]Then Jesus said to him, "Don't tell anyone about this. Instead, go to the priest and let him examine you. Take along the offering required in the law of Moses for those who have been healed of leprosy.* This will be a public testimony that you have been cleansed."

The Faith of a Roman Officer

[5]When Jesus returned to Capernaum, a Roman officer* came and pleaded with him, [6]"Lord, my young servant* lies in bed, paralyzed and in terrible pain."

[7]Jesus said, "I will come and heal him."

[8]But the officer said, "Lord, I am not worthy to have you come into my home. Just say the word from where you are, and my servant will be healed. [9]I know this because I am under the authority of my superior officers, and I have authority over my soldiers. I only need to say, 'Go,' and they go, or 'Come,' and they come. And if I say to my slaves, 'Do this,' they do it."

8:4 See Lev 14:2-32.   **8:5** Greek *a centurion;* similarly in 8:8, 13.   **8:6** Or *child;* also in 8:13.

No. 01-TE-015

FRIENDSHIP STORY

FRIENDSHIP TYPE:	FRIENDSHIP LAYER:
Jesus	*Trust*

BASED ON TRUE EVENTS

Coming Home

No introduction necessary. George had grown up in this town. Nearly everyone in the congregation knew him or his family. But not from church.

His family hadn't really been the churchgoing type. George had attended Sunday school as a child, but he'd drifted away at an early age. George had a rough childhood in a big family with little money, but he grew up to be a successful businessman. He was happy...for the most part. Inside, he had a nagging feeling that, well, maybe there was something he was missing out on...but mostly he just ignored that feeling.

George lived far away from his hometown, but he kept in touch with his high school buddy, Dick. Dick had ALS, and the outlook wasn't promising. But through the long sickness, Dick didn't doubt God's love. Ever. And George couldn't quite figure it out...this unshakeable faith. So when Dick died, George e-mailed Guy, another old football teammate: "Dick had something that I want."

That brief e-mail started a long conversation—months long—about life, faith, and God.

Yup, there should've been trumpets, spotlights, and a really loud choir because one day—through those e-mails—George realized what he'd been missing: *Jesus.*

FRIENDSHIP STORY *continues on page 16...*

Friendship First NEW TESTAMENT

FRIENDSHIP STORY *continued from page 15…*

Guy helped George understand that Jesus wanted to be a part of George's everyday life… and, if that wasn't amazing enough, actually wanted to be his trusted *friend*. Over time George came to realize what Dick had—that carried him through even a terminal sickness—was a friendship with Jesus. And George knew he wanted and *needed* this friendship.

So George, successful businessman and long-time skeptic, took a daring, extraordinary leap into a friendship with Jesus. And Sunday morning, a few weeks later, George stood next to his old friend, Pastor Guy, and proudly announced his new friendship with Jesus to a congregation of people who had always known him…and yet were seeing him for the first time.

Experience

George decided to trust Jesus because he was inspired by someone else's example of trust. Has someone inspired you with his or her deep trust in Jesus? Has your friendship with Jesus grown as a result of learning from someone else? Friendship with Jesus doesn't come about in a vacuum; the people we interact with have a major impact on our faith…for good or ill.

Write an e-mail (or letter) to someone who positively impacted and inspired your friendship with Jesus. Thank the person for helping you trust Jesus…and grow in your friendship with him.

Reflect

★ Read **Romans 15:5-7, 13**. How were harmony, unity, acceptance, and trust evident in this story?

★ How has friendship made a difference in your life? in your faith?

★ How does trusting Jesus affect your daily life?

[10] When Jesus heard this, he was amazed. Turning to those who were following him, he said, "I tell you the truth, I haven't seen faith like this in all Israel! [11] And I tell you this, that many Gentiles will come from all over the world—from east and west—and sit down with Abraham, Isaac, and Jacob at the feast in the Kingdom of Heaven. [12] But many Israelites—those for whom the Kingdom was prepared—will be thrown into outer darkness, where there will be weeping and gnashing of teeth."

[13] Then Jesus said to the Roman officer, "Go back home. Because you believed, it has happened." And the young servant was healed that same hour.

Jesus Heals Many People

[14] When Jesus arrived at Peter's house, Peter's mother-in-law was sick in bed with a high fever. [15] But when Jesus touched her hand, the fever left her. Then she got up and prepared a meal for him.

[16] That evening many demon-possessed people were brought to Jesus. He cast out the evil spirits with a simple command, and he healed all the sick. [17] This fulfilled the word of the Lord through the prophet Isaiah, who said,

"He took our sicknesses
     and removed our diseases."*

The Cost of Following Jesus

[18] When Jesus saw the crowd around him, he instructed his disciples to cross to the other side of the lake.

[19] Then one of the teachers of religious law said to him, "Teacher, I will follow you wherever you go."

[20] But Jesus replied, "Foxes have dens to live in, and birds have nests, but the Son of Man* has no place even to lay his head."

[21] Another of his disciples said, "Lord, first let me return home and bury my father."

[22] But Jesus told him, "Follow me now. Let the spiritually dead bury their own dead.*"

Jesus Calms the Storm

[23] Then Jesus got into the boat and started across the lake with his disciples. [24] Suddenly, a fierce storm struck the lake, with waves breaking into the boat. But Jesus was sleeping. [25] The disciples went and woke him up, shouting, "Lord, save us! We're going to drown!"

8:17 Isa 53:4.   **8:20** "Son of Man" is a title Jesus used for himself.   **8:22** Greek *Let the dead bury their own dead.*

[26] Jesus responded, "Why are you afraid? You have so little faith!" Then he got up and rebuked the wind and waves, and suddenly there was a great calm.

[27] The disciples were amazed. "Who is this man?" they asked. "Even the winds and waves obey him!"

Jesus Heals Two Demon-Possessed Men

[28] When Jesus arrived on the other side of the lake, in the region of the Gadarenes,* two men who were possessed by demons met him. They lived in a cemetery and were so violent that no one could go through that area.

[29] They began screaming at him, "Why are you interfering with us, Son of God? Have you come here to torture us before God's appointed time?"

[30] There happened to be a large herd of pigs feeding in the distance. [31] So the demons begged, "If you cast us out, send us into that herd of pigs."

[32] "All right, go!" Jesus commanded them. So the demons came out of the men and entered the pigs, and the whole herd plunged down the steep hillside into the lake and drowned in the water.

[33] The herdsmen fled to the nearby town, telling everyone what happened to the demon-possessed men. [34] Then the entire town came out to meet Jesus, but they begged him to go away and leave them alone.

CHAPTER 9

Jesus Heals a Paralyzed Man

Jesus climbed into a boat and went back across the lake to his own town. [2] Some people brought to him a paralyzed man on a mat. Seeing their faith, Jesus said to the paralyzed man, "Be encouraged, my child! Your sins are forgiven."

[3] But some of the teachers of religious law said to themselves, "That's blasphemy! Does he think he's God?"

[4] Jesus knew* what they were thinking, so he asked them, "Why do you have such evil thoughts in your hearts? [5] Is it easier to say 'Your sins are forgiven,' or 'Stand up and walk'? [6] So I will prove to you that the Son of Man* has the authority on earth to forgive sins." Then Jesus turned to the paralyzed man and said, "Stand up, pick up your mat, and go home!"

[7] And the man jumped up and went home! [8] Fear swept

8:28 Other manuscripts read *Gerasenes;* still others read *Gergesenes.* Compare Mark 5:1; Luke 8:26. **9:4** Some manuscripts read *saw.* **9:6** "Son of Man" is a title Jesus used for himself.

Almost 9 in 10 church members who feel loved and accepted by their church also say they are very satisfied with their church.

—from "Friendship and Faith," a Gallup Research Study Commissioned by Group Publishing, Inc.

JOURNAL

through the crowd as they saw this happen. And they praised God for sending a man with such great authority.*

Jesus Calls Matthew

9 As Jesus was walking along, he saw a man named Matthew sitting at his tax collector's booth. "Follow me and be my disciple," Jesus said to him. So Matthew got up and followed him.

10 Later, Matthew invited Jesus and his disciples to his home as dinner guests, along with many tax collectors and other disreputable sinners. 11 But when the Pharisees saw this, they asked his disciples, "Why does your teacher eat with such scum?*"

12 When Jesus heard this, he said, "Healthy people don't need a doctor—sick people do." 13 Then he added, "Now go and learn the meaning of this Scripture: 'I want you to show mercy, not offer sacrifices.'* For I have come to call not those who think they are righteous, but those who know they are sinners."

A Discussion about Fasting

14 One day the disciples of John the Baptist came to Jesus and asked him, "Why don't your disciples fast* like we do and the Pharisees do?"

15 Jesus replied, "Do wedding guests mourn while celebrating with the groom? Of course not. But someday the groom will be taken away from them, and then they will fast.

16 "Besides, who would patch old clothing with new cloth? For the new patch would shrink and rip away from the old cloth, leaving an even bigger tear than before.

17 "And no one puts new wine into old wineskins. For the old skins would burst from the pressure, spilling the wine and ruining the skins. New wine is stored in new wineskins so that both are preserved."

Jesus Heals in Response to Faith

18 As Jesus was saying this, the leader of a synagogue came and knelt before him. "My daughter has just died," he said, "but you can bring her back to life again if you just come and lay your hand on her."

19 So Jesus and his disciples got up and went with him. 20 Just then a woman who had suffered for twelve years with constant

9:8 Greek *for giving such authority to human beings.* 　9:11 Greek *with tax collectors and sinners?* 9:13 Hos 6:6 (Greek version). 　9:14 Some manuscripts read *fast often.*

bleeding came up behind him. She touched the fringe of his robe, 21 for she thought, "If I can just touch his robe, I will be healed."

22 Jesus turned around, and when he saw her he said, "Daughter, be encouraged! Your faith has made you well." And the woman was healed at that moment.

23 When Jesus arrived at the official's home, he saw the noisy crowd and heard the funeral music. 24 "Get out!" he told them. "The girl isn't dead; she's only asleep." But the crowd laughed at him. 25 After the crowd was put outside, however, Jesus went in and took the girl by the hand, and she stood up! 26 The report of this miracle swept through the entire countryside.

Jesus Heals the Blind

27 After Jesus left the girl's home, two blind men followed along behind him, shouting, "Son of David, have mercy on us!"

28 They went right into the house where he was staying, and Jesus asked them, "Do you believe I can make you see?"

"Yes, Lord," they told him, "we do."

29 Then he touched their eyes and said, "Because of your faith, it will happen." 30 Then their eyes were opened, and they could see! Jesus sternly warned them, "Don't tell anyone about this." 31 But instead, they went out and spread his fame all over the region.

32 When they left, a demon-possessed man who couldn't speak was brought to Jesus. 33 So Jesus cast out the demon, and then the man began to speak. The crowds were amazed. "Nothing like this has ever happened in Israel!" they exclaimed.

34 But the Pharisees said, "He can cast out demons because he is empowered by the prince of demons."

The Need for Workers

35 Jesus traveled through all the towns and villages of that area, teaching in the synagogues and announcing the Good News about the Kingdom. And he healed every kind of disease and illness. 36 When he saw the crowds, he had compassion on them because they were confused and helpless, like sheep without a shepherd. 37 He said to his disciples, "The harvest is great, but the workers are few. 38 So pray to the Lord who is in charge of the harvest; ask him to send more workers into his fields."

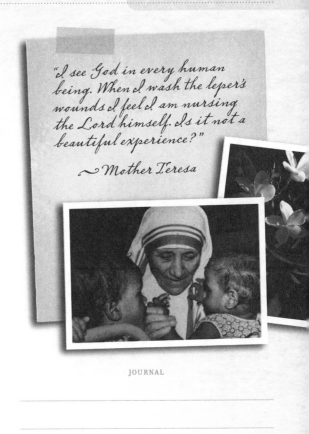

"I see God in every human being. When I wash the leper's wounds I feel I am nursing the Lord himself. Is it not a beautiful experience?"

~ *Mother Teresa*

JOURNAL

_____
_____
_____
_____
_____
_____
_____
_____
_____
_____
_____
_____
_____
_____
_____
_____
_____
_____
_____
_____
_____
_____
_____
_____
_____
_____
_____
_____
_____
_____
_____
_____

CHAPTER **10**

Jesus Sends Out the Twelve Apostles

Jesus called his twelve disciples together and gave them authority to cast out evil* spirits and to heal every kind of disease and illness. ²Here are the names of the twelve apostles:

first, Simon (also called Peter),
then Andrew (Peter's brother),
James (son of Zebedee),
John (James's brother),
³ Philip,
Bartholomew,
Thomas,
Matthew (the tax collector),
James (son of Alphaeus),
Thaddaeus,*
⁴ Simon (the zealot*),
Judas Iscariot (who later betrayed him).

⁵Jesus sent out the twelve apostles with these instructions: "Don't go to the Gentiles or the Samaritans, ⁶but only to the people of Israel—God's lost sheep. ⁷Go and announce to them that the Kingdom of Heaven is near.* ⁸Heal the sick, raise the dead, cure those with leprosy, and cast out demons. Give as freely as you have received!

⁹"Don't take any money in your money belts—no gold, silver, or even copper coins. ¹⁰Don't carry a traveler's bag with a change of clothes and sandals or even a walking stick. Don't hesitate to accept hospitality, because those who work deserve to be fed.

¹¹"Whenever you enter a city or village, search for a worthy person and stay in his home until you leave town. ¹²When you enter the home, give it your blessing. ¹³If it turns out to be a worthy home, let your blessing stand; if it is not, take back the blessing. ¹⁴If any household or town refuses to welcome you or listen to your message, shake its dust from your feet as you leave. ¹⁵I tell you the truth, the wicked cities of Sodom and Gomorrah will be better off than such a town on the judgment day.

¹⁶"Look, I am sending you out as sheep among wolves. So be as shrewd as snakes and harmless as doves. ¹⁷But beware! For you will be handed over to the courts and will be flogged with whips in the synagogues. ¹⁸You will stand trial before governors

10:1 Greek *unclean.*   10:3 Other manuscripts read *Lebbaeus;* still others read *Lebbaeus who is called Thaddaeus.*   10:4 Greek *the Cananean,* an Aramaic term for Jewish nationalists.   10:7 Or *has come,* or *is coming soon.*

and kings because you are my followers. But this will be your opportunity to tell the rulers and other unbelievers about me.* ¹⁹When you are arrested, don't worry about how to respond or what to say. God will give you the right words at the right time. ²⁰For it is not you who will be speaking—it will be the Spirit of your Father speaking through you.

²¹"A brother will betray his brother to death, a father will betray his own child, and children will rebel against their parents and cause them to be killed. ²²And all nations will hate you because you are my followers.* But everyone who endures to the end will be saved. ²³When you are persecuted in one town, flee to the next. I tell you the truth, the Son of Man* will return before you have reached all the towns of Israel.

²⁴"Students* are not greater than their teacher, and slaves are not greater than their master. ²⁵Students are to be like their teacher, and slaves are to be like their master. And since I, the master of the household, have been called the prince of demons,* the members of my household will be called by even worse names!

²⁶"But don't be afraid of those who threaten you. For the time is coming when everything that is covered will be revealed, and all that is secret will be made known to all. ²⁷What I tell you now in the darkness, shout abroad when daybreak comes. What I whisper in your ear, shout from the housetops for all to hear!

²⁸"Don't be afraid of those who want to kill your body; they cannot touch your soul. Fear only God, who can destroy both soul and body in hell.* ²⁹What is the price of two sparrows— one copper coin*? But not a single sparrow can fall to the ground without your Father knowing it. ³⁰And the very hairs on your head are all numbered. ³¹So don't be afraid; you are more valuable to God than a whole flock of sparrows.

³²"Everyone who acknowledges me publicly here on earth, I will also acknowledge before my Father in heaven. ³³But everyone who denies me here on earth, I will also deny before my Father in heaven.

³⁴"Don't imagine that I came to bring peace to the earth! I came not to bring peace, but a sword.

³⁵ 'I have come to set a man against his father,
    a daughter against her mother,

10:18 Or *But this will be your testimony against the rulers and other unbelievers.* 10:22 Greek *on account of my name.* 10:23 "Son of Man" is a title Jesus used for himself. 10:24 Or *Disciples.* 10:25 Greek *Beelzeboul;* other manuscripts read *Beezeboul;* Latin version reads *Beelzebub.* 10:28 Greek *Gehenna.* 10:29 Greek *one assarion* [i.e., one "as," a Roman coin equal to 1/16 of a denarius].

FRIENDSHIP EXPERIENCE

FRIENDSHIP TYPE: *Jesus*   FRIENDSHIP LAYER: *Trust*

Take a Risk

The world can be a scary place. You've heard it. You've witnessed it. You've even experienced it. Life's not as simple as it looks on TV.

It seems easier to play it safe…really safe. Go to work or school, come home, spend the evening doing chores, watch a little television, and go to bed. Safe…predictable…*boring!*

God doesn't mean for you to lead a safe, predictable, boring life. God wants to give you a satisfying, abundant life—but grabbing hold of that life is going to involve risk, unpredictability, and discomfort. (Think of Peter stepping out of that boat.)

But guess what!

You'll also get excitement, adventure, and fulfillment. That's because God created you, and he knows your passions, desires, and needs. When you truly trust Jesus, he'll enable you to step out of the boat and discover the life you were created to live!

Read about the satisfying life in **John 10:1-10** and **Ephesians 3:14-21**.

FRIENDSHIP EXPERIENCE *continues on page 22…*

FRIENDSHIP EXPERIENCE *continued from page 21…*

Experience

Invite a good friend to do something that you'd both consider a little bit risky. You might…

★ take a ride in a glider,

★ hike up a mountain or high hill,

★ audition for community theater,

★ host a dinner party, or

★ tell a stranger why you decided to trust Jesus.

While you're engaged in this risky adventure, trust your friend and trust Jesus to help you survive…and have fun!

Reflect

★ How did it feel to step out of your comfort zone? How did your thoughts and feelings differ before and after your adventure?

★ In what ways did you have to trust your friend? How was trusting your friend like trusting Jesus?

★ How can you trust Jesus to help you live a satisfying, abundant day-to-day life?

and a daughter-in-law against her mother-in-law.

36   Your enemies will be right in your own household!'*

37 "If you love your father or mother more than you love me, you are not worthy of being mine; or if you love your son or daughter more than me, you are not worthy of being mine. 38 If you refuse to take up your cross and follow me, you are not worthy of being mine. 39 If you cling to your life, you will lose it; but if you give up your life for me, you will find it.

40 "Anyone who receives you receives me, and anyone who receives me receives the Father who sent me. 41 If you receive a prophet as one who speaks for God,* you will be given the same reward as a prophet. And if you receive righteous people because of their righteousness, you will be given a reward like theirs. 42 And if you give even a cup of cold water to one of the least of my followers, you will surely be rewarded."

CHAPTER **11**

Jesus and John the Baptist

When Jesus had finished giving these instructions to his twelve disciples, he went out to teach and preach in towns throughout the region.

2 John the Baptist, who was in prison, heard about all the things the Messiah was doing. So he sent his disciples to ask Jesus, 3 "Are you the Messiah we've been expecting,* or should we keep looking for someone else?"

4 Jesus told them, "Go back to John and tell him what you have heard and seen—5 the blind see, the lame walk, the lepers are cured, the deaf hear, the dead are raised to life, and the Good News is being preached to the poor. 6 And tell him, 'God blesses those who do not turn away because of me.*'"

7 As John's disciples were leaving, Jesus began talking about him to the crowds. "What kind of man did you go into the wilderness to see? Was he a weak reed, swayed by every breath of wind? 8 Or were you expecting to see a man dressed in expensive clothes? No, people with expensive clothes live in palaces. 9 Were you looking for a prophet? Yes, and he is more than a prophet. 10 John is the man to whom the Scriptures refer when they say,

'Look, I am sending my messenger ahead of you,
    and he will prepare your way before you.'*

10:35-36 Mic 7:6.   **10:41** Greek *receive a prophet in the name of a prophet.*   **11:3** Greek *Are you the one who is coming?*   **11:6** Or *who are not offended by me.*   **11:10** Mal 3:1.

11 "I tell you the truth, of all who have ever lived, none is greater than John the Baptist. Yet even the least person in the Kingdom of Heaven is greater than he is! 12And from the time John the Baptist began preaching until now, the Kingdom of Heaven has been forcefully advancing,* and violent people are attacking it. 13For before John came, all the prophets and the law of Moses looked forward to this present time. 14And if you are willing to accept what I say, he is Elijah, the one the prophets said would come.* 15Anyone with ears to hear should listen and understand!

16 "To what can I compare this generation? It is like children playing a game in the public square. They complain to their friends,

17 'We played wedding songs,
     and you didn't dance,
   so we played funeral songs,
     and you didn't mourn.'

18For John didn't spend his time eating and drinking, and you say, 'He's possessed by a demon.' 19The Son of Man,* on the other hand, feasts and drinks, and you say, 'He's a glutton and a drunkard, and a friend of tax collectors and other sinners!' But wisdom is shown to be right by its results."

Judgment for the Unbelievers

20Then Jesus began to denounce the towns where he had done so many of his miracles, because they hadn't repented of their sins and turned to God. 21 "What sorrow awaits you, Korazin and Bethsaida! For if the miracles I did in you had been done in wicked Tyre and Sidon, their people would have repented of their sins long ago, clothing themselves in burlap and throwing ashes on their heads to show their remorse. 22I tell you, Tyre and Sidon will be better off on judgment day than you.

23 "And you people of Capernaum, will you be honored in heaven? No, you will go down to the place of the dead.* For if the miracles I did for you had been done in wicked Sodom, it would still be here today. 24I tell you, even Sodom will be better off on judgment day than you."

Jesus' Prayer of Thanksgiving

25At that time Jesus prayed this prayer: "O Father, Lord of heaven and earth, thank you for hiding these things from those

11:12 Or *the Kingdom of Heaven has suffered violence.*   11:14 See Mal 4:5.   11:19 "Son of Man" is a title Jesus used for himself.   11:23 Greek *to Hades.*

who think themselves wise and clever, and for revealing them to the childlike. 26 Yes, Father, it pleased you to do it this way!

27 "My Father has entrusted everything to me. No one truly knows the Son except the Father, and no one truly knows the Father except the Son and those to whom the Son chooses to reveal him."

28 Then Jesus said, "Come to me, all of you who are weary and carry heavy burdens, and I will give you rest. 29 Take my yoke upon you. Let me teach you, because I am humble and gentle at heart, and you will find rest for your souls. 30 For my yoke is easy to bear, and the burden I give you is light."

CHAPTER 12

A Discussion about the Sabbath

At about that time Jesus was walking through some grainfields on the Sabbath. His disciples were hungry, so they began breaking off some heads of grain and eating them. 2 But some Pharisees saw them do it and protested, "Look, your disciples are breaking the law by harvesting grain on the Sabbath."

3 Jesus said to them, "Haven't you read in the Scriptures what David did when he and his companions were hungry? 4 He went into the house of God, and he and his companions broke the law by eating the sacred loaves of bread that only the priests are allowed to eat. 5 And haven't you read in the law of Moses that the priests on duty in the Temple may work on the Sabbath? 6 I tell you, there is one here who is even greater than the Temple! 7 But you would not have condemned my innocent disciples if you knew the meaning of this Scripture: 'I want you to show mercy, not offer sacrifices.'* 8 For the Son of Man* is Lord, even over the Sabbath!"

Jesus Heals on the Sabbath

9 Then Jesus went over to their synagogue, 10 where he noticed a man with a deformed hand. The Pharisees asked Jesus, "Does the law permit a person to work by healing on the Sabbath?" (They were hoping he would say yes, so they could bring charges against him.)

11 And he answered, "If you had a sheep that fell into a well on the Sabbath, wouldn't you work to pull it out? Of course you would. 12 And how much more valuable is a person than a sheep! Yes, the law permits a person to do good on the Sabbath."

13 Then he said to the man, "Hold out your hand." So the man

12:7 Hos 6:6 (Greek version).   12:8 "Son of Man" is a title Jesus used for himself.

held out his hand, and it was restored, just like the other one! ¹⁴Then the Pharisees called a meeting to plot how to kill Jesus.

Jesus, God's Chosen Servant

¹⁵But Jesus knew what they were planning. So he left that area, and many people followed him. He healed all the sick among them, ¹⁶but he warned them not to reveal who he was. ¹⁷This fulfilled the prophecy of Isaiah concerning him:

¹⁸ "Look at my Servant, whom I have chosen.
     He is my Beloved, who pleases me.
   I will put my Spirit upon him,
     and he will proclaim justice to the nations.
¹⁹ He will not fight or shout
     or raise his voice in public.
²⁰ He will not crush the weakest reed
     or put out a flickering candle.
     Finally he will cause justice to be victorious.
²¹ And his name will be the hope
     of all the world."*

Jesus and the Prince of Demons

²²Then a demon-possessed man, who was blind and couldn't speak, was brought to Jesus. He healed the man so that he could both speak and see. ²³The crowd was amazed and asked, "Could it be that Jesus is the Son of David, the Messiah?"

²⁴But when the Pharisees heard about the miracle, they said, "No wonder he can cast out demons. He gets his power from Satan,* the prince of demons."

²⁵Jesus knew their thoughts and replied, "Any kingdom divided by civil war is doomed. A town or family splintered by feuding will fall apart. ²⁶And if Satan is casting out Satan, he is divided and fighting against himself. His own kingdom will not survive. ²⁷And if I am empowered by Satan, what about your own exorcists? They cast out demons, too, so they will condemn you for what you have said. ²⁸But if I am casting out demons by the Spirit of God, then the Kingdom of God has arrived among you. ²⁹For who is powerful enough to enter the house of a strong man like Satan and plunder his goods? Only someone even stronger—someone who could tie him up and then plunder his house.

³⁰ "Anyone who isn't with me opposes me, and anyone who isn't working with me is actually working against me.

12:18-21 Isa 42:1-4 (Greek version for 42:4). 12:24 Greek *Beelzeboul;* also in 12:27. Other manuscripts read *Beezeboul;* Latin version reads *Beelzebub.*

WHAT TO SAY AND **WHAT NOT TO SAY**

FRIENDSHIP TYPE: *Hard-to-Love People*   FRIENDSHIP LAYER: *Deepening*

When Annoying People Win... and Lose

Nothing makes an annoying person even *more* annoying than when he or she becomes successful. *You* know she has a laugh like a buzz saw. *You* noticed he steals paper clips from the supply drawer. *You* see how she never mows her grass, yet she was elected Chairperson of the Garden Committee.

So why is *she* being interviewed in the paper? Why is *he* getting promoted? Is there no *justice* in life?

Not so much, actually, at least in the short run. In **Matthew 5:45,** Jesus points out that God's rain nourishes the crops of both the righteous and unrighteous.

So what about when that annoying person loses? You want to rub it in, right? Let 'em know they deserved it. Secretly you're laughing—rejoicing even. But that's not what God wants you to do. Nope. God wants you to pray for them. Even weep for them.

Assuming you want to deepen your relationship with annoying people, here's a quick tutorial about what to say and not say when they're successful and when they're not.

1. Your annoying acquaintance, Frank, bought a house at a truly great price.

 WHAT NOT TO SAY: "Wow! Think how easy it'll be to drive to work with that new interstate cutting through your backyard. Oh, you didn't hear about that? Well, maybe it's just a rumor."

 WHAT TO SAY: "Hey, good news! I hope you'll be happy there." (See **Romans 12:15-16.**)

WHAT TO SAY AND WHAT NOT TO SAY *continues on page 26...*

WHAT TO SAY AND WHAT NOT TO SAY *continued from page 25...*

2. Your annoying acquaintance, Frank, just lost his new house in a fire.

 WHAT NOT TO SAY: "Well, I told you those new builders didn't install enough fire alarms. Guess you'll be more careful in the future."

 WHAT TO SAY: "I'm so sorry. Is there anything I can do to help? Do you need a place to stay for a while?"(See **Romans 12:15-16**.)

3. Sheila has just been promoted... and you weren't.

 WHAT NOT TO SAY: *(Speaking to other disgruntled, passed-over employees)* "Guess they don't always ask the right questions at job interviews…"

 WHAT TO SAY: *(Speaking to Sheila)* "Congratulations on the new job duties. Let me know if I can be of help as you settle in." (See **Romans 12:15-16**.)

4. Sheila has just been fired from her new job.

 WHAT NOT TO SAY: *(Speaking to other elated employees)* "Well, we all knew what she was really like. I guess they finally saw through her."

 WHAT TO SAY: *(Speaking to Sheila)* "I'm really sorry to hear about your job. Can I pray for you or help you in any way?" (See **Romans 12:15-16**. Noticing a trend here?)

Friendship First NEW TESTAMENT

31 "So I tell you, every sin and blasphemy can be forgiven—except blasphemy against the Holy Spirit, which will never be forgiven. 32 Anyone who speaks against the Son of Man can be forgiven, but anyone who speaks against the Holy Spirit will never be forgiven, either in this world or in the world to come.

33 "A tree is identified by its fruit. If a tree is good, its fruit will be good. If a tree is bad, its fruit will be bad. 34 You brood of snakes! How could evil men like you speak what is good and right? For whatever is in your heart determines what you say. 35 A good person produces good things from the treasury of a good heart, and an evil person produces evil things from the treasury of an evil heart. 36 And I tell you this, you must give an account on judgment day for every idle word you speak. 37 The words you say will either acquit you or condemn you."

The Sign of Jonah

38 One day some teachers of religious law and Pharisees came to Jesus and said, "Teacher, we want you to show us a miraculous sign to prove your authority."

39 But Jesus replied, "Only an evil, adulterous generation would demand a miraculous sign; but the only sign I will give them is the sign of the prophet Jonah. 40 For as Jonah was in the belly of the great fish for three days and three nights, so will the Son of Man be in the heart of the earth for three days and three nights.

41 "The people of Nineveh will stand up against this generation on judgment day and condemn it, for they repented of their sins at the preaching of Jonah. Now someone greater than Jonah is here—but you refuse to repent. 42 The queen of Sheba* will also stand up against this generation on judgment day and condemn it, for she came from a distant land to hear the wisdom of Solomon. Now someone greater than Solomon is here—but you refuse to listen.

43 "When an evil* spirit leaves a person, it goes into the desert, seeking rest but finding none. 44 Then it says, 'I will return to the person I came from.' So it returns and finds its former home empty, swept, and in order. 45 Then the spirit finds seven other spirits more evil than itself, and they all enter the person and live there. And so that person is worse off than before. That will be the experience of this evil generation."

12:42 Greek *The queen of the south.* **12:43** Greek *unclean.*

The True Family of Jesus

46As Jesus was speaking to the crowd, his mother and brothers stood outside, asking to speak to him. 47Someone told Jesus, "Your mother and your brothers are outside, and they want to speak to you."*

48Jesus asked, "Who is my mother? Who are my brothers?" 49Then he pointed to his disciples and said, "Look, these are my mother and brothers. 50Anyone who does the will of my Father in heaven is my brother and sister and mother!"

CHAPTER 13

Parable of the Farmer Scattering Seed

Later that same day Jesus left the house and sat beside the lake. 2A large crowd soon gathered around him, so he got into a boat. Then he sat there and taught as the people stood on the shore. 3He told many stories in the form of parables, such as this one:

"Listen! A farmer went out to plant some seeds. 4As he scattered them across his field, some seeds fell on a footpath, and the birds came and ate them. 5Other seeds fell on shallow soil with underlying rock. The seeds sprouted quickly because the soil was shallow. 6But the plants soon wilted under the hot sun, and since they didn't have deep roots, they died. 7Other seeds fell among thorns that grew up and choked out the tender plants. 8Still other seeds fell on fertile soil, and they produced a crop that was thirty, sixty, and even a hundred times as much as had been planted! 9Anyone with ears to hear should listen and understand."

10His disciples came and asked him, "Why do you use parables when you talk to the people?"

11He replied, "You are permitted to understand the secrets* of the Kingdom of Heaven, but others are not. 12To those who listen to my teaching, more understanding will be given, and they will have an abundance of knowledge. But for those who are not listening, even what little understanding they have will be taken away from them. 13That is why I use these parables,

For they look, but they don't really see.
They hear, but they don't really listen or understand.

14This fulfills the prophecy of Isaiah that says,

'When you hear what I say,
you will not understand.

12:47 Some manuscripts do not include verse 47. Compare Mark 3:32 and Luke 8:20. 13:11 Greek *the mysteries.*

"Friendship should be surrounded with ceremonies and respects, and not crushed into corners. Friendship requires more time than poor busy men can usually command."

~ Ralph Waldo Emerson

JOURNAL

When you see what I do,
    you will not comprehend.
15 For the hearts of these people are hardened,
    and their ears cannot hear,
and they have closed their eyes—
    so their eyes cannot see,
and their ears cannot hear,
    and their hearts cannot understand,
and they cannot turn to me
    and let me heal them.'*

16 "But blessed are your eyes, because they see; and your ears, because they hear. 17 I tell you the truth, many prophets and righteous people longed to see what you see, but they didn't see it. And they longed to hear what you hear, but they didn't hear it.

18 "Now listen to the explanation of the parable about the farmer planting seeds: 19 The seed that fell on the footpath represents those who hear the message about the Kingdom and don't understand it. Then the evil one comes and snatches away the seed that was planted in their hearts. 20 The seed on the rocky soil represents those who hear the message and immediately receive it with joy. 21 But since they don't have deep roots, they don't last long. They fall away as soon as they have problems or are persecuted for believing God's word. 22 The seed that fell among the thorns represents those who hear God's word, but all too quickly the message is crowded out by the worries of this life and the lure of wealth, so no fruit is produced. 23 The seed that fell on good soil represents those who truly hear and understand God's word and produce a harvest of thirty, sixty, or even a hundred times as much as had been planted!"

Parable of the Wheat and Weeds

24 Here is another story Jesus told: "The Kingdom of Heaven is like a farmer who planted good seed in his field. 25 But that night as the workers slept, his enemy came and planted weeds among the wheat, then slipped away. 26 When the crop began to grow and produce grain, the weeds also grew.

27 "The farmer's workers went to him and said, 'Sir, the field where you planted that good seed is full of weeds! Where did they come from?'

28 "'An enemy has done this!' the farmer exclaimed.

13:14-15 Isa 6:9-10 (Greek version).

"'Should we pull out the weeds?' they asked.

²⁹"'No,' he replied, 'you'll uproot the wheat if you do. ³⁰Let both grow together until the harvest. Then I will tell the harvesters to sort out the weeds, tie them into bundles, and burn them, and to put the wheat in the barn.'"

Parable of the Mustard Seed

³¹Here is another illustration Jesus used: "The Kingdom of Heaven is like a mustard seed planted in a field. ³²It is the smallest of all seeds, but it becomes the largest of garden plants; it grows into a tree, and birds come and make nests in its branches."

Parable of the Yeast

³³Jesus also used this illustration: "The Kingdom of Heaven is like the yeast a woman used in making bread. Even though she put only a little yeast in three measures of flour, it permeated every part of the dough."

³⁴Jesus always used stories and illustrations like these when speaking to the crowds. In fact, he never spoke to them without using such parables. ³⁵This fulfilled what God had spoken through the prophet:

"I will speak to you in parables.
    I will explain things hidden since the creation of the
        world.*"

Parable of the Wheat and Weeds Explained

³⁶Then, leaving the crowds outside, Jesus went into the house. His disciples said, "Please explain to us the story of the weeds in the field."

³⁷Jesus replied, "The Son of Man* is the farmer who plants the good seed. ³⁸The field is the world, and the good seed represents the people of the Kingdom. The weeds are the people who belong to the evil one. ³⁹The enemy who planted the weeds among the wheat is the devil. The harvest is the end of the world,* and the harvesters are the angels.

⁴⁰"Just as the weeds are sorted out and burned in the fire, so it will be at the end of the world. ⁴¹The Son of Man will send his angels, and they will remove from his Kingdom everything that causes sin and all who do evil. ⁴²And the angels will throw them into the fiery furnace, where there will be weeping and gnashing of teeth. ⁴³Then the righteous will shine like the sun in their

13:35 Some manuscripts do not include *of the world.* Ps 78:2.   **13:37** "Son of Man" is a title Jesus used for himself.   **13:39** Or *the age;* also in 13:40, 49.

No. 02-FA-029

FRIENDSHIP STORY

FRIENDSHIP TYPE:	FRIENDSHIP LAYER:
Jesus	*Commitment*

FROM THE ARCHIVES

How Sweet It Is

People around the world marvel at what a good, kind person Mother Teresa was, and who can deny it? She entered a convent at 18 and taught at the Sisters of Loreto's school in India but left the school to "follow Christ into the slums" of Calcutta. She began the Missionaries of Charity, an organization of orphanages, shelters, hospitals, and food centers. She took care of lepers nobody else would touch, comforted the dying, championed the poor and oppressed, and welcomed the outcast. She won the Nobel Peace Prize in 1979. And at 87 she died in Calcutta, among the poor and hurting people she'd served for so long.

No wonder the world looks with astonishment at this humble nun. She was so…*good.* In a larger-than-life sort of way. But what most of the world may be more astonished to know is that Mother Teresa wasn't very interested in being a good person. And she was even less interested in getting any credit. In fact, when Pope Paul VI recognized her efforts with the gift of an expensive car, she immediately auctioned off the car and put the money toward a center for lepers.

So what was Mother Teresa most interested in? A glance at her prayers gives us the answer: "Dearest Lord, may I see you today and every day in the person of your sick, and, whilst nursing them, minister unto you. Though you hide yourself behind the unattractive disguise of the irritable, the exacting, the unreasonable, may I still recognize you, and say: 'Jesus, my patient, how sweet it is to serve you.' "

FRIENDSHIP STORY *continues on page 30…*

FRIENDSHIP STORY *continued from page 29...*

Mother Teresa's desire was for an intimate, genuine friendship with Jesus—which led her to nurse the sick, feed the hungry, and comfort the hurting. What Mother Teresa knew...what she *lived out*...was this: To serve Jesus means serving others. To love Jesus means loving others. This is what Jesus asks of us—that we are fully committed to others because we are fully committed to him.

Following Mother Teresa's example of commitment may seem unrealistic at best and impossible at worst. But believe it or not, you can also love and serve Jesus in larger-than-life ways...as only *you* can, with your unique life, in your special corner of the world. So how will *your* commitment to Jesus result in service, love, and compassion for others?

Experience

THE ONE THING / 1 / YOU CAN DO THIS WEEK

You might not be able to sell your car and give all the money away. However, you can make another kind of sacrifice...if you're willing to take the risk. Choose something you own that'd be pretty hard to give up. It may be an expensive TV, a nice computer, high-quality sports equipment, or something else of value to you. Then D.W.M.T.W.D. (that's "Do What Mother Teresa Would Do"): Take your offering to people in need. You may go to a homeless shelter, orphanage, recovery center, or soup kitchen. If you think the particular item wouldn't be put to good use, then sell it and purchase something that would be appreciated.

But don't just drop the item off; give of yourself as well. Offer your time, your help, your compassion, your listening ear, your unconditional love...and your prayers. Read **Matthew 28:16-20**, and ask God to help you be a committed friend to Jesus—and others— through your love, service, and sacrifice.

FRIENDSHIP STORY *continues on page 31...*

Father's Kingdom. Anyone with ears to hear should listen and understand!

Parables of the Hidden Treasure and the Pearl

[44]"The Kingdom of Heaven is like a treasure that a man discovered hidden in a field. In his excitement, he hid it again and sold everything he owned to get enough money to buy the field.

[45]"Again, the Kingdom of Heaven is like a merchant on the lookout for choice pearls. [46]When he discovered a pearl of great value, he sold everything he owned and bought it!

Parable of the Fishing Net

[47]"Again, the Kingdom of Heaven is like a fishing net that was thrown into the water and caught fish of every kind. [48]When the net was full, they dragged it up onto the shore, sat down, and sorted the good fish into crates, but threw the bad ones away. [49]That is the way it will be at the end of the world. The angels will come and separate the wicked people from the righteous, [50]throwing the wicked into the fiery furnace, where there will be weeping and gnashing of teeth. [51]Do you understand all these things?"

"Yes," they said, "we do."

[52]Then he added, "Every teacher of religious law who becomes a disciple in the Kingdom of Heaven is like a homeowner who brings from his storeroom new gems of truth as well as old."

Jesus Rejected at Nazareth

[53]When Jesus had finished telling these stories and illustrations, he left that part of the country. [54]He returned to Nazareth, his hometown. When he taught there in the synagogue, everyone was amazed and said, "Where does he get this wisdom and the power to do miracles?" [55]Then they scoffed, "He's just the carpenter's son, and we know Mary, his mother, and his brothers—James, Joseph,* Simon, and Judas. [56]All his sisters live right here among us. Where did he learn all these things?" [57]And they were deeply offended and refused to believe in him.

Then Jesus told them, "A prophet is honored everywhere except in his own hometown and among his own family." [58]And so he did only a few miracles there because of their unbelief.

13:55 Other manuscripts read *Joses;* still others read *John.*

CHAPTER **14**

The Death of John the Baptist

When Herod Antipas, the ruler of Galilee,* heard about Jesus, [2]he said to his advisers, "This must be John the Baptist raised from the dead! That is why he can do such miracles."

[3]For Herod had arrested and imprisoned John as a favor to his wife Herodias (the former wife of Herod's brother Philip). [4]John had been telling Herod, "It is against God's law for you to marry her." [5]Herod wanted to kill John, but he was afraid of a riot, because all the people believed John was a prophet.

[6]But at a birthday party for Herod, Herodias's daughter performed a dance that greatly pleased him, [7]so he promised with a vow to give her anything she wanted. [8]At her mother's urging, the girl said, "I want the head of John the Baptist on a tray!" [9]Then the king regretted what he had said; but because of the vow he had made in front of his guests, he issued the necessary orders. [10]So John was beheaded in the prison, [11]and his head was brought on a tray and given to the girl, who took it to her mother. [12]Later, John's disciples came for his body and buried it. Then they went and told Jesus what had happened.

Jesus Feeds Five Thousand

[13]As soon as Jesus heard the news, he left in a boat to a remote area to be alone. But the crowds heard where he was headed and followed on foot from many towns. [14]Jesus saw the huge crowd as he stepped from the boat, and he had compassion on them and healed their sick.

[15]That evening the disciples came to him and said, "This is a remote place, and it's already getting late. Send the crowds away so they can go to the villages and buy food for themselves."

[16]But Jesus said, "That isn't necessary—you feed them."

[17]"But we have only five loaves of bread and two fish!" they answered.

[18]"Bring them here," he said. [19]Then he told the people to sit down on the grass. Jesus took the five loaves and two fish, looked up toward heaven, and blessed them. Then, breaking the loaves into pieces, he gave the bread to the disciples, who distributed it to the people. [20]They all ate as much as they wanted, and afterward, the disciples picked up twelve baskets of leftovers. [21]About 5,000 men were fed that day, in addition to all the women and children!

14:1 Greek *Herod the tetrarch.* Herod Antipas was a son of King Herod and was ruler over Galilee.

FRIENDSHIP STORY *continued from page 30…*

Reflect

★ What about Mother Teresa's life inspires you?
★ Why do you think Jesus wants us to serve him by serving others? love him by loving others?
★ How did you feel giving away something of value?
★ How could you make this more than just a one-time thing but instead a lifestyle of generosity and service?

JOURNAL

JOURNAL

_____

_____

_____

_____

_____

_____

_____

_____

_____

_____

_____

_____

_____

_____

_____

_____

_____

_____

_____

_____

_____

_____

_____

_____

_____

_____

Jesus Walks on Water

22 Immediately after this, Jesus insisted that his disciples get back into the boat and cross to the other side of the lake, while he sent the people home. 23 After sending them home, he went up into the hills by himself to pray. Night fell while he was there alone.

24 Meanwhile, the disciples were in trouble far away from land, for a strong wind had risen, and they were fighting heavy waves. 25 About three o'clock in the morning* Jesus came toward them, walking on the water. 26 When the disciples saw him walking on the water, they were terrified. In their fear, they cried out, "It's a ghost!"

27 But Jesus spoke to them at once. "Don't be afraid," he said. "Take courage. I am here!*"

28 Then Peter called to him, "Lord, if it's really you, tell me to come to you, walking on the water."

29 "Yes, come," Jesus said.

So Peter went over the side of the boat and walked on the water toward Jesus. 30 But when he saw the strong* wind and the waves, he was terrified and began to sink. "Save me, Lord!" he shouted.

31 Jesus immediately reached out and grabbed him. "You have so little faith," Jesus said. "Why did you doubt me?"

32 When they climbed back into the boat, the wind stopped. 33 Then the disciples worshiped him. "You really are the Son of God!" they exclaimed.

34 After they had crossed the lake, they landed at Gennesaret. 35 When the people recognized Jesus, the news of his arrival spread quickly throughout the whole area, and soon people were bringing all their sick to be healed. 36 They begged him to let the sick touch at least the fringe of his robe, and all who touched him were healed.   ☩

CHAPTER **15**

Jesus Teaches about Inner Purity

Some Pharisees and teachers of religious law now arrived from Jerusalem to see Jesus. They asked him, 2 "Why do your disciples

14:25 Greek *In the fourth watch of the night.*   **14:27** Or *The 'I Am' is here;* Greek reads *I am.* See Exod 3:14.   **14:30** Some manuscripts do not include *strong.*

disobey our age-old tradition? For they ignore our tradition of ceremonial hand washing before they eat."

3Jesus replied, "And why do you, by your traditions, violate the direct commandments of God? 4For instance, God says, 'Honor your father and mother,'* and 'Anyone who speaks disrespectfully of father or mother must be put to death.'* 5But you say it is all right for people to say to their parents, 'Sorry, I can't help you. For I have vowed to give to God what I would have given to you.' 6In this way, you say they don't need to honor their parents.* And so you cancel the word of God for the sake of your own tradition. 7You hypocrites! Isaiah was right when he prophesied about you, for he wrote,

8 'These people honor me with their lips,
   but their hearts are far from me.
9 Their worship is a farce,
   for they teach man-made ideas as commands from God.'*"

10Then Jesus called to the crowd to come and hear. "Listen," he said, "and try to understand. 11It's not what goes into your mouth that defiles you; you are defiled by the words that come out of your mouth."

12Then the disciples came to him and asked, "Do you realize you offended the Pharisees by what you just said?"

13Jesus replied, "Every plant not planted by my heavenly Father will be uprooted, 14so ignore them. They are blind guides leading the blind, and if one blind person guides another, they will both fall into a ditch."

15Then Peter said to Jesus, "Explain to us the parable that says people aren't defiled by what they eat."

16"Don't you understand yet?" Jesus asked. 17"Anything you eat passes through the stomach and then goes into the sewer. 18But the words you speak come from the heart—that's what defiles you. 19For from the heart come evil thoughts, murder, adultery, all sexual immorality, theft, lying, and slander. 20These are what defile you. Eating with unwashed hands will never defile you."

The Faith of a Gentile Woman

21Then Jesus left Galilee and went north to the region of Tyre and Sidon. 22A Gentile* woman who lived there came to him, pleading, "Have mercy on me, O Lord, Son of David! For my daughter is possessed by a demon that torments her severely."

15:4a Exod 20:12; Deut 5:16.   15:4b Exod 21:17 (Greek version); Lev 20:9 (Greek version).
15:6 Greek *their father;* other manuscripts read *their father or their mother.*   15:8-9 Isa 29:13
(Greek version).   15:22 Greek *Canaanite.*

Anchor Passage

PASSAGE: **Matthew 14:22-36**

FRIENDSHIP TYPE: *Jesus*

FRIENDSHIP LAYER: *Trust*

Go Overboard!

Think about times you've been on a boat.

Read **Matthew 14:22-36**, and imagine this experience. It's late at night, the waves are crashing against your boat, and you look out into the night and see something—no, someone—*walking on top of the water!* It's easy to understand why the disciples decided they were seeing a ghost.

But it was Jesus! And Peter trusted Jesus enough to join him on the waves.

It can be easy to trust Jesus in a kind of big-picture way. He's God! The disciples trusted Jesus but not quite enough to leave the boat. Peter was different. His was the take-action, step-out-in-faith kind of trust. Sure, Peter ran into a little trouble when his fear overcame his faith. But Jesus, trustworthy to the end, rescued him.

So you want to put your trust in Jesus? Then go ahead—climb out of the boat and onto the water.

Trust him enough to seek his opinion the next time you have a decision to make.

Trust him enough to take a risk for him.

Trust him enough to become his friend.

Trust him with your life.

So how 'bout it? Are you in, or are you out?

Anchor Passage continues on page 34...

Friendship First NEW TESTAMENT

Anchor Passage continued from page 33...

Experience

THE ONE THING
1
YOU CAN DO THIS WEEK

Stand by a body of water. An ocean, a stream, or even a bathtub will do. Go ahead—take your shoes off, and wade on in. Imagine what Peter felt as he watched Jesus on the water and as he climbed out of the boat himself. What prompted Peter to take that step of faith?

Consider your life. Is Jesus asking you to deepen your trust in him? Is it time to take action? What's holding you back? What's compelling you forward? Ask Jesus what he wants from you...and trust his answer.

Reflect

★ When have you trusted Jesus and then "sunk in the waves" as Peter did? Why?

★ What's risky about stepping out in faith and trusting Jesus?

★ How can you trust Jesus right now?

DIGGING DEEPER

FRIENDSHIP TYPE:	FRIENDSHIP LAYER:
Jesus	*Trust*

For building trust with Jesus, check out...

➡ The Friendship Experience .... on page 21
➡ The Friendship Story .... on page 15
➡ What to Say and What Not to Say .... on page 464

23 But Jesus gave her no reply, not even a word. Then his disciples urged him to send her away. "Tell her to go away," they said. "She is bothering us with all her begging."

24 Then Jesus said to the woman, "I was sent only to help God's lost sheep—the people of Israel."

25 But she came and worshiped him, pleading again, "Lord, help me!"

26 Jesus responded, "It isn't right to take food from the children and throw it to the dogs."

27 She replied, "That's true, Lord, but even dogs are allowed to eat the scraps that fall beneath their masters' table."

28 "Dear woman," Jesus said to her, "your faith is great. Your request is granted." And her daughter was instantly healed.

Jesus Heals Many People

29 Jesus returned to the Sea of Galilee and climbed a hill and sat down. 30 A vast crowd brought to him people who were lame, blind, crippled, those who couldn't speak, and many others. They laid them before Jesus, and he healed them all. 31 The crowd was amazed! Those who hadn't been able to speak were talking, the crippled were made well, the lame were walking, and the blind could see again! And they praised the God of Israel.

Jesus Feeds Four Thousand

32 Then Jesus called his disciples and told them, "I feel sorry for these people. They have been here with me for three days, and they have nothing left to eat. I don't want to send them away hungry, or they will faint along the way."

33 The disciples replied, "Where would we get enough food here in the wilderness for such a huge crowd?"

34 Jesus asked, "How much bread do you have?"

They replied, "Seven loaves, and a few small fish."

35 So Jesus told all the people to sit down on the ground. 36 Then he took the seven loaves and the fish, thanked God for them, and broke them into pieces. He gave them to the disciples, who distributed the food to the crowd.

37 They all ate as much as they wanted. Afterward, the disciples picked up seven large baskets of leftover food. 38 There were 4,000 men who were fed that day, in addition to all the women and children. 39 Then Jesus sent the people home, and he got into a boat and crossed over to the region of Magadan.

CHAPTER 16

Leaders Demand a Miraculous Sign

One day the Pharisees and Sadducees came to test Jesus, demanding that he show them a miraculous sign from heaven to prove his authority.

²He replied, "You know the saying, 'Red sky at night means fair weather tomorrow; ³red sky in the morning means foul weather all day.' You know how to interpret the weather signs in the sky, but you don't know how to interpret the signs of the times!* ⁴Only an evil, adulterous generation would demand a miraculous sign, but the only sign I will give them is the sign of the prophet Jonah.*" Then Jesus left them and went away.

Yeast of the Pharisees and Sadducees

⁵Later, after they crossed to the other side of the lake, the disciples discovered they had forgotten to bring any bread. ⁶"Watch out!" Jesus warned them. "Beware of the yeast of the Pharisees and Sadducees."

⁷At this they began to argue with each other because they hadn't brought any bread. ⁸Jesus knew what they were saying, so he said, "You have so little faith! Why are you arguing with each other about having no bread? ⁹Don't you understand even yet? Don't you remember the 5,000 I fed with five loaves, and the baskets of leftovers you picked up? ¹⁰Or the 4,000 I fed with seven loaves, and the large baskets of leftovers you picked up? ¹¹Why can't you understand that I'm not talking about bread? So again I say, 'Beware of the yeast of the Pharisees and Sadducees.'"

¹²Then at last they understood that he wasn't speaking about the yeast in bread, but about the deceptive teaching of the Pharisees and Sadducees.

Peter's Declaration about Jesus

¹³When Jesus came to the region of Caesarea Philippi, he asked his disciples, "Who do people say that the Son of Man is?"*

¹⁴"Well," they replied, "some say John the Baptist, some say Elijah, and others say Jeremiah or one of the other prophets."

¹⁵Then he asked them, "But who do you say I am?"

¹⁶Simon Peter answered, "You are the Messiah,* the Son of the living God."

¹⁷Jesus replied, "You are blessed, Simon son of John,* because

16:2-3 Several manuscripts do not include any of the words in 16:2-3 after *He replied.*   16:4 Greek *the sign of Jonah.*   16:13 "Son of Man" is a title Jesus used for himself.   16:16 Or *the Christ. Messiah* (a Hebrew term) and *Christ* (a Greek term) both mean "the anointed one."   16:17 Greek *Simon bar-Jonah;* see John 1:42; 21:15-17.

_____

_____

_____

_____

_____

_____

_____

_____

_____

_____

_____

_____

_____

_____

_____

_____

_____

"For us to be involved, we must be willing to reach out and risk relating. This won't 'just happen'...May I urge you? Risk reaching. Take the initiative. Walk a few feet to your neighbor's yard...Open up. Be warm and transparent. You may be pleasantly surprised by the results."

~ Charles Swindoll

my Father in heaven has revealed this to you. You did not learn this from any human being. ¹⁸Now I say to you that you are Peter (which means 'rock'),* and upon this rock I will build my church, and all the powers of hell* will not conquer it. ¹⁹And I will give you the keys of the Kingdom of Heaven. Whatever you forbid* on earth will be forbidden in heaven, and whatever you permit* on earth will be permitted in heaven."

²⁰Then he sternly warned the disciples not to tell anyone that he was the Messiah.

Jesus Predicts His Death

²¹From then on Jesus* began to tell his disciples plainly that it was necessary for him to go to Jerusalem, and that he would suffer many terrible things at the hands of the elders, the leading priests, and the teachers of religious law. He would be killed, but on the third day he would be raised from the dead.

²²But Peter took him aside and began to reprimand him* for saying such things. "Heaven forbid, Lord," he said. "This will never happen to you!"

²³Jesus turned to Peter and said, "Get away from me, Satan! You are a dangerous trap to me. You are seeing things merely from a human point of view, not from God's."

²⁴Then Jesus said to his disciples, "If any of you wants to be my follower, you must turn from your selfish ways, take up your cross, and follow me. ²⁵If you try to hang on to your life, you will lose it. But if you give up your life for my sake, you will save it. ²⁶And what do you benefit if you gain the whole world but lose your own soul?* Is anything worth more than your soul? ²⁷For the Son of Man will come with his angels in the glory of his Father and will judge all people according to their deeds. ²⁸And I tell you the truth, some standing here right now will not die before they see the Son of Man coming in his Kingdom."

CHAPTER **17**
The Transfiguration

Six days later Jesus took Peter and the two brothers, James and John, and led them up a high mountain to be alone. ²As the men watched, Jesus' appearance was transformed so that his face shone like the sun, and his clothes became as white as light. ³Suddenly, Moses and Elijah appeared and began talking with Jesus.

⁴Peter exclaimed, "Lord, it's wonderful for us to be here! If

16:18a Greek *that you are Peter.*   16:18b Greek *and the gates of Hades.*   16:19a Or *bind,* or *lock.* 16:19b Or *loose,* or *open.*   16:21 Some manuscripts read *Jesus the Messiah.*   16:22 Or *began to correct him.*   16:26 Or *your self?* also in 16:26b.

you want, I'll make three shelters as memorials*—one for you, one for Moses, and one for Elijah."

⁵But even as he spoke, a bright cloud overshadowed them, and a voice from the cloud said, "This is my dearly loved Son, who brings me great joy. Listen to him." ⁶The disciples were terrified and fell face down on the ground.

⁷Then Jesus came over and touched them. "Get up," he said. "Don't be afraid." ⁸And when they looked up, Moses and Elijah were gone, and they saw only Jesus.

⁹As they went back down the mountain, Jesus commanded them, "Don't tell anyone what you have seen until the Son of Man* has been raised from the dead."

¹⁰Then his disciples asked him, "Why do the teachers of religious law insist that Elijah must return before the Messiah comes?*"

¹¹Jesus replied, "Elijah is indeed coming first to get everything ready. ¹²But I tell you, Elijah has already come, but he wasn't recognized, and they chose to abuse him. And in the same way they will also make the Son of Man suffer." ¹³Then the disciples realized he was talking about John the Baptist.

Jesus Heals a Demon-Possessed Boy

¹⁴At the foot of the mountain, a large crowd was waiting for them. A man came and knelt before Jesus and said, ¹⁵"Lord, have mercy on my son. He has seizures and suffers terribly. He often falls into the fire or into the water. ¹⁶So I brought him to your disciples, but they couldn't heal him."

¹⁷Jesus said, "You faithless and corrupt people! How long must I be with you? How long must I put up with you? Bring the boy here to me." ¹⁸Then Jesus rebuked the demon in the boy, and it left him. From that moment the boy was well.

¹⁹Afterward the disciples asked Jesus privately, "Why couldn't we cast out that demon?"

²⁰"You don't have enough faith," Jesus told them. "I tell you the truth, if you had faith even as small as a mustard seed, you could say to this mountain, 'Move from here to there,' and it would move. Nothing would be impossible.*"

Jesus Again Predicts His Death

²²After they gathered again in Galilee, Jesus told them, "The Son of Man is going to be betrayed into the hands of his enemies. ²³He will be killed, but on the third day he will be raised from the dead." And the disciples were filled with grief.

17:4 Greek *three tabernacles.* **17:9** "Son of Man" is a title Jesus used for himself. **17:10** Greek *that Elijah must come first?* **17:20** Some manuscripts add verse 21, *But this kind of demon won't leave except by prayer and fasting.* Compare Mark 9:29.

A full 83% of people who report their church is very friendly have friendships with other church members that extend outside the weekly worship service.

—from "Friendship and Faith," a Gallup Research Study Commissioned by Group Publishing, Inc.

JOURNAL

"*A gossip goes around telling secrets, but those who are trustworthy can keep a confidence.*"

~ Proverbs 12:13

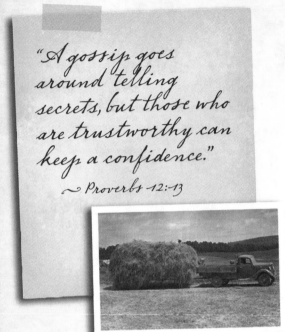

JOURNAL

Payment of the Temple Tax

24On their arrival in Capernaum, the collectors of the Temple tax* came to Peter and asked him, "Doesn't your teacher pay the Temple tax?"

25"Yes, he does," Peter replied. Then he went into the house.

But before he had a chance to speak, Jesus asked him, "What do you think, Peter?* Do kings tax their own people or the people they have conquered?*"

26"They tax the people they have conquered," Peter replied.

"Well, then," Jesus said, "the citizens are free! 27However, we don't want to offend them, so go down to the lake and throw in a line. Open the mouth of the first fish you catch, and you will find a large silver coin.* Take it and pay the tax for both of us."

CHAPTER **18**

The Greatest in the Kingdom

About that time the disciples came to Jesus and asked, "Who is greatest in the Kingdom of Heaven?"

2Jesus called a little child to him and put the child among them. 3Then he said, "I tell you the truth, unless you turn from your sins and become like little children, you will never get into the Kingdom of Heaven. 4So anyone who becomes as humble as this little child is the greatest in the Kingdom of Heaven.

5"And anyone who welcomes a little child like this on my behalf* is welcoming me. 6But if you cause one of these little ones who trusts in me to fall into sin, it would be better for you to have a large millstone tied around your neck and be drowned in the depths of the sea.

7"What sorrow awaits the world, because it tempts people to sin. Temptations are inevitable, but what sorrow awaits the person who does the tempting. 8So if your hand or foot causes you to sin, cut it off and throw it away. It's better to enter eternal life with only one hand or one foot than to be thrown into eternal fire with both of your hands and feet. 9And if your eye causes you to sin, gouge it out and throw it away. It's better to enter eternal life with only one eye than to have two eyes and be thrown into the fire of hell.*

10"Beware that you don't look down on any of these little ones. For I tell you that in heaven their angels are always in the presence of my heavenly Father.*

17:24 Greek *the two-drachma [tax];* also in 17:24b. See Exod 30:13-16; Neh 10:32-33.   **17:25a** Greek *Simon?*   **17:25b** Greek *their sons or others?*   **17:27** Greek *a stater* [a Greek coin equivalent to four drachmas].   **18:5** Greek *in my name.*   **18:9** Greek *the Gehenna of fire.*   **18:10** Some manuscripts add verse 11, *And the Son of Man came to save those who are lost.* Compare Luke 19:10.

Parable of the Lost Sheep

¹²"If a man has a hundred sheep and one of them wanders away, what will he do? Won't he leave the ninety-nine others on the hills and go out to search for the one that is lost? ¹³And if he finds it, I tell you the truth, he will rejoice over it more than over the ninety-nine that didn't wander away! ¹⁴In the same way, it is not my heavenly Father's will that even one of these little ones should perish.

Correcting Another Believer

¹⁵"If another believer* sins against you,* go privately and point out the offense. If the other person listens and confesses it, you have won that person back. ¹⁶But if you are unsuccessful, take one or two others with you and go back again, so that everything you say may be confirmed by two or three witnesses. ¹⁷If the person still refuses to listen, take your case to the church. Then if he or she won't accept the church's decision, treat that person as a pagan or a corrupt tax collector.

¹⁸"I tell you the truth, whatever you forbid* on earth will be forbidden in heaven, and whatever you permit* on earth will be permitted in heaven.

¹⁹"I also tell you this: If two of you agree here on earth concerning anything you ask, my Father in heaven will do it for you. ²⁰For where two or three gather together as my followers,* I am there among them."

Parable of the Unforgiving Debtor

²¹Then Peter came to him and asked, "Lord, how often should I forgive someone* who sins against me? Seven times?"

²²"No, not seven times," Jesus replied, "but seventy times seven!*

²³"Therefore, the Kingdom of Heaven can be compared to a king who decided to bring his accounts up to date with servants who had borrowed money from him. ²⁴In the process, one of his debtors was brought in who owed him millions of dollars.* ²⁵He couldn't pay, so his master ordered that he be sold—along with his wife, his children, and everything he owned—to pay the debt.

18:15a Greek *If your brother.*   18:15b Some manuscripts do not include *against you.*   18:18a Or *bind,* or *lock.*   18:18b Or *loose,* or *open.*   18:20 Greek *gather together in my name.*   18:21 Greek *my brother.*
18:22 Or *seventy-seven times.*   18:24 Greek *10,000 talents* [375 tons or 340 metric tons of silver].

Anchor Passage

PASSAGE: Matthew 18:21-35

FRIENDSHIP TYPE: Family

FRIENDSHIP LAYER: Deepening

From Your Heart

Read **Matthew 18:21-35.**

"Lord, how often should I forgive someone who sins against me? Seven times?"

Seven times? For the same thing? Seems like five or six times too many, doesn't it?

Nope. According to Jesus, seventy times seven is more like it.

What? You gotta be kidding, right?

Uh-uh…Jesus wanted his followers to understand that forgiveness isn't simply a numbers game; forgiveness is sincere, complete, and lasting—it's "from the heart." And to illustrate his point further, Jesus launched into a story contrasting a king's vast and lavish forgiveness with his servant's ungrateful and miserly behavior.

After being forgiven millions of dollars by the king, the servant turns around and is unable to forgive a fellow servant of even a few thousand dollars. And the king's reaction?

"You evil servant! I forgave you that tremendous debt because you pleaded with me. Shouldn't you have mercy on your fellow servant, just as I had mercy on you?"

This is like the Kingdom of Heaven. Jesus wanted his disciples—and us—to understand that our willingness to forgive others should reflect how God has forgiven us. In others words, it should be endless!

Anchor Passage continues on page 40…

Anchor Passage continued from page 39...

Whom do you most often have to forgive? Who do you think has to most often forgive you? If your answer is a family member, you're certainly not alone. Our family members definitely offer us plenty of opportunities to practice forgiveness. When things are going well, it's great to be part of a family, but when things turn sour, those four walls start to close in around us. One of the keys to deepening our relationships with family members is this "from the heart" sort of forgiveness that Jesus was talking about.

"No, not seven times," Jesus replied, "but seventy times seven!"

Experience

Forgive someone in your family. Remember, it must be "from your heart."

Dirty feet on a newly cleaned kitchen floor, a fresh dent in the car, or toilet seats left up...If you've told them once, you've told them a thousand times, right? When things like this happen over and over, it can be easy to start holding a grudge. Don't let that happen. Be a forgiver, not a grudge-holder.

This week, practice forgiving from your heart—when you find dirty footprints on your clean floor, when you stay up late waiting for someone who missed curfew, when you have to clean all the dirty dishes (again!), when you hear about a speeding ticket, and when you find a new dent in your door...and, and, and! Remember, not seven times but "seventy times seven" times! Forgiveness from the heart doesn't keep track.

God offers us forgiveness from everything we have done in our past and will do in our future. God's extravagant grace toward us—like the king's lavish forgiveness of his servant—is our inspiration to forgive those who have hurt us.

Anchor Passage continues on page 41...

²⁶"But the man fell down before his master and begged him, 'Please, be patient with me, and I will pay it all.' ²⁷Then his master was filled with pity for him, and he released him and forgave his debt.

²⁸"But when the man left the king, he went to a fellow servant who owed him a few thousand dollars.* He grabbed him by the throat and demanded instant payment.

²⁹"His fellow servant fell down before him and begged for a little more time. 'Be patient with me, and I will pay it,' he pleaded. ³⁰But his creditor wouldn't wait. He had the man arrested and put in prison until the debt could be paid in full.

³¹"When some of the other servants saw this, they were very upset. They went to the king and told him everything that had happened. ³²Then the king called in the man he had forgiven and said, 'You evil servant! I forgave you that tremendous debt because you pleaded with me. ³³Shouldn't you have mercy on your fellow servant, just as I had mercy on you?' ³⁴Then the angry king sent the man to prison to be tortured until he had paid his entire debt.

³⁵"That's what my heavenly Father will do to you if you refuse to forgive your brothers and sisters* from your heart." ⚓

CHAPTER **19**

Discussion about Divorce and Marriage

When Jesus had finished saying these things, he left Galilee and went down to the region of Judea east of the Jordan River. ²Large crowds followed him there, and he healed their sick.

³Some Pharisees came and tried to trap him with this question: "Should a man be allowed to divorce his wife for just any reason?"

⁴"Haven't you read the Scriptures?" Jesus replied. "They record that from the beginning 'God made them male and female.'* ⁵And he said, "This explains why a man leaves his father and mother and is joined to his wife, and the two are united into one.'* ⁶Since they are no longer two but one, let no one split apart what God has joined together."

18:28 Greek *100 denarii.* A denarius was equivalent to a laborer's full day's wage.   **18:35** Greek *your brother.*   **19:4** Gen 1:27; 5:2.   **19:5** Gen 2:24.

7 "Then why did Moses say in the law that a man could give his wife a written notice of divorce and send her away?"* they asked.

8 Jesus replied, "Moses permitted divorce only as a concession to your hard hearts, but it was not what God had originally intended. 9 And I tell you this, whoever divorces his wife and marries someone else commits adultery—unless his wife has been unfaithful.*"

10 Jesus' disciples then said to him, "If this is the case, it is better not to marry!"

11 "Not everyone can accept this statement," Jesus said. "Only those whom God helps. 12 Some are born as eunuchs, some have been made eunuchs by others, and some choose not to marry* for the sake of the Kingdom of Heaven. Let anyone accept this who can."

Jesus Blesses the Children

13 One day some parents brought their children to Jesus so he could lay his hands on them and pray for them. But the disciples scolded the parents for bothering him.

14 But Jesus said, "Let the children come to me. Don't stop them! For the Kingdom of Heaven belongs to those who are like these children." 15 And he placed his hands on their heads and blessed them before he left.

The Rich Man

16 Someone came to Jesus with this question: "Teacher,* what good deed must I do to have eternal life?"

17 "Why ask me about what is good?" Jesus replied. "There is only One who is good. But to answer your question—if you want to receive eternal life, keep* the commandments."

18 "Which ones?" the man asked.

And Jesus replied: "'You must not murder. You must not commit adultery. You must not steal. You must not testify falsely. 19 Honor your father and mother. Love your neighbor as yourself.'*"

20 "I've obeyed all these commandments," the young man replied. "What else must I do?"

21 Jesus told him, "If you want to be perfect, go and sell all your possessions and give the money to the poor, and you will have treasure in heaven. Then come, follow me."

19:7 See Deut 24:1. **19:9** Some manuscripts add *And anyone who marries a divorced woman commits adultery.* Compare Matt 5:32. **19:12** Greek *and some make themselves eunuchs* **19:16** Some manuscripts read *Good Teacher.* **19:17** Some manuscripts read *continue to keep.* **19:18-19** Exod 20:12-16; Deut 5:16-20; Lev 19:18.

Anchor Passage continued from page 40...

Reflect

★ What's special about forgiveness that comes "from the heart"?

★ Specifically, how can you offer "from the heart" forgiveness to someone in your family?

DIGGING DEEPER

FRIENDSHIP TYPE:	FRIENDSHIP LAYER:
Family	*Deepening*

For deepening your friendship with family, check out...

➡ The Friendship Experience .... on page 3
➡ The Friendship Story .... on page 510
➡ What to Say and What Not to Say .... on page 55

JOURNAL

²²But when the young man heard this, he went away sad, for he had many possessions.

²³Then Jesus said to his disciples, "I tell you the truth, it is very hard for a rich person to enter the Kingdom of Heaven. ²⁴I'll say it again—it is easier for a camel to go through the eye of a needle than for a rich person to enter the Kingdom of God!"

²⁵The disciples were astounded. "Then who in the world can be saved?" they asked.

²⁶Jesus looked at them intently and said, "Humanly speaking, it is impossible. But with God everything is possible."

²⁷Then Peter said to him, "We've given up everything to follow you. What will we get?"

²⁸Jesus replied, "I assure you that when the world is made new* and the Son of Man* sits upon his glorious throne, you who have been my followers will also sit on twelve thrones, judging the twelve tribes of Israel. ²⁹And everyone who has given up houses or brothers or sisters or father or mother or children or property, for my sake, will receive a hundred times as much in return and will inherit eternal life. ³⁰But many who are the greatest now will be least important then, and those who seem least important now will be the greatest then.*

CHAPTER **20**

Parable of the Vineyard Workers

"For the Kingdom of Heaven is like the landowner who went out early one morning to hire workers for his vineyard. ²He agreed to pay the normal daily wage* and sent them out to work.

³"At nine o'clock in the morning he was passing through the marketplace and saw some people standing around doing nothing. ⁴So he hired them, telling them he would pay them whatever was right at the end of the day. ⁵So they went to work in the vineyard. At noon and again at three o'clock he did the same thing.

⁶"At five o'clock that afternoon he was in town again and saw some more people standing around. He asked them, 'Why haven't you been working today?'

⁷"They replied, 'Because no one hired us.'

"The landowner told them, 'Then go out and join the others in my vineyard.'

19:28a Or *in the regeneration.*   **19:28b** "Son of Man" is a title Jesus used for himself.   **19:30** Greek *But many who are first will be last; and the last, first.*   **20:2** Greek *a denarius,* the payment for a full day's labor; similarly in 20:9, 10, 13.

⁸"That evening he told the foreman to call the workers in and pay them, beginning with the last workers first. ⁹When those hired at five o'clock were paid, each received a full day's wage. ¹⁰When those hired first came to get their pay, they assumed they would receive more. But they, too, were paid a day's wage. ¹¹When they received their pay, they protested to the owner, ¹²'Those people worked only one hour, and yet you've paid them just as much as you paid us who worked all day in the scorching heat.'

¹³"He answered one of them, 'Friend, I haven't been unfair! Didn't you agree to work all day for the usual wage? ¹⁴Take your money and go. I wanted to pay this last worker the same as you. ¹⁵Is it against the law for me to do what I want with my money? Should you be jealous because I am kind to others?'

¹⁶"So those who are last now will be first then, and those who are first will be last."

Jesus Again Predicts His Death

¹⁷As Jesus was going up to Jerusalem, he took the twelve disciples aside privately and told them what was going to happen to him. ¹⁸"Listen," he said, "we're going up to Jerusalem, where the Son of Man* will be betrayed to the leading priests and the teachers of religious law. They will sentence him to die. ¹⁹Then they will hand him over to the Romans* to be mocked, flogged with a whip, and crucified. But on the third day he will be raised from the dead."

Jesus Teaches about Serving Others

²⁰Then the mother of James and John, the sons of Zebedee, came to Jesus with her sons. She knelt respectfully to ask a favor. ²¹"What is your request?" he asked.

She replied, "In your Kingdom, please let my two sons sit in places of honor next to you, one on your right and the other on your left."

²²But Jesus answered by saying to them, "You don't know what you are asking! Are you able to drink from the bitter cup of suffering I am about to drink?"

"Oh yes," they replied, "we are able!"

²³Jesus told them, "You will indeed drink from my bitter cup. But I have no right to say who will sit on my right or my left. My Father has prepared those places for the ones he has chosen."

²⁴When the ten other disciples heard what James and John had asked, they were indignant. ²⁵But Jesus called them together

20:18 "Son of Man" is a title Jesus used for himself.　20:19 Greek *the Gentiles*.

FRIENDSHIP EXPERIENCE

FRIENDSHIP TYPE: *Hard-to-Love People*　　FRIENDSHIP LAYER: *Deepening*

Stay Connected

You gave it the old college try. You chatted with that person nobody else likes, and you discovered *why* that person isn't popular: *He's annoying.*

Nobody would blame you for letting your fledgling relationship die of neglect. You're not a match. There's no chemistry. He picks his teeth in public.

But consider what Jesus said in **Matthew 5:38-48**. If you relate only to people who are convenient or who raise your "cool quotient," where are God's values reflected in that?

You need to pursue an authentic relationship. But how?

FRIENDSHIP EXPERIENCE *continues on page 44...*

FRIENDSHIP EXPERIENCE *continued from page 43...*

Experience

Decide to look for something positive in your annoying acquaintance.

Nobody's perfect. And you may be so focused on what annoys you that you're failing to see what's praiseworthy in that person.

Check out your acquaintance's desk, yard, house, car, or other personal space. Does a photo or piece of artwork hint at something you can appreciate in the person? Is the person a parent? a volunteer? an excellent gardener?

No matter how you know your acquaintance, look for ways to engage him or her in conversation—and look for the best. It will feel familiar because that's precisely how God looks at you: through the eyes of grace.

You and God don't have all that much in common, you know. God is holy and perfect. You're a bit *less* than holy, and in your wildest dreams, you probably can't imagine someone describing you as "perfect."

Yet God continues to pursue a relationship with you in spite of things you do that disappoint him. God reaches out in love. God sees more than your failures; he sees the amazing qualities he created in you!

This week, ask God to help you see those annoying people through his eyes.

Reflect

★ How was spending time looking for what's praiseworthy in your acquaintance similar to how God views you?

★ Assuming your acquaintance won't change the attributes that annoy you, what will it take to continue deepening your friendship with that person?

and said, "You know that the rulers in this world lord it over their people, and officials flaunt their authority over those under them. 26But among you it will be different. Whoever wants to be a leader among you must be your servant, 27and whoever wants to be first among you must become your slave. 28For even the Son of Man came not to be served but to serve others and to give his life as a ransom for many."

Jesus Heals Two Blind Men

29As Jesus and the disciples left the town of Jericho, a large crowd followed behind. 30Two blind men were sitting beside the road. When they heard that Jesus was coming that way, they began shouting, "Lord, Son of David, have mercy on us!"

31"Be quiet!" the crowd yelled at them.

But they only shouted louder, "Lord, Son of David, have mercy on us!"

32When Jesus heard them, he stopped and called, "What do you want me to do for you?"

33"Lord," they said, "we want to see!" 34Jesus felt sorry for them and touched their eyes. Instantly they could see! Then they followed him.

CHAPTER **21**

Jesus' Triumphant Entry

As Jesus and the disciples approached Jerusalem, they came to the town of Bethphage on the Mount of Olives. Jesus sent two of them on ahead. 2"Go into the village over there," he said. "As soon as you enter it, you will see a donkey tied there, with its colt beside it. Untie them and bring them to me. 3If anyone asks what you are doing, just say, 'The Lord needs them,' and he will immediately let you take them."

4This took place to fulfill the prophecy that said,

5 "Tell the people of Israel,*
　'Look, your King is coming to you.
He is humble, riding on a donkey—
　riding on a donkey's colt.'"*

6The two disciples did as Jesus commanded. 7They brought the donkey and the colt to him and threw their garments over the colt, and he sat on it.*

8Most of the crowd spread their garments on the road ahead of him, and others cut branches from the trees and spread them

21:5a Greek *Tell the daughter of Zion.* Isa 62:11.　**21:5b** Zech 9:9.　**21:7** Greek *over them, and he sat on them.*

on the road. [9]Jesus was in the center of the procession, and the people all around him were shouting,

"Praise God* for the Son of David!
Blessings on the one who comes in the name
of the LORD!
Praise God in highest heaven!"*

[10]The entire city of Jerusalem was in an uproar as he entered. "Who is this?" they asked.

[11]And the crowds replied, "It's Jesus, the prophet from Nazareth in Galilee."

Jesus Clears the Temple

[12]Jesus entered the Temple and began to drive out all the people buying and selling animals for sacrifice. He knocked over the tables of the money changers and the chairs of those selling doves. [13]He said to them, "The Scriptures declare, 'My Temple will be called a house of prayer,' but you have turned it into a den of thieves!"*

[14]The blind and the lame came to him in the Temple, and he healed them. [15]The leading priests and the teachers of religious law saw these wonderful miracles and heard even the children in the Temple shouting, "Praise God for the Son of David."

But the leaders were indignant. [16]They asked Jesus, "Do you hear what these children are saying?"

"Yes," Jesus replied. "Haven't you ever read the Scriptures? For they say, 'You have taught children and infants to give you praise.'*" [17]Then he returned to Bethany, where he stayed overnight.

Jesus Curses the Fig Tree

[18]In the morning, as Jesus was returning to Jerusalem, he was hungry, [19]and he noticed a fig tree beside the road. He went over to see if there were any figs, but there were only leaves. Then he said to it, "May you never bear fruit again!" And immediately the fig tree withered up.

[20]The disciples were amazed when they saw this and asked, "How did the fig tree wither so quickly?"

[21]Then Jesus told them, "I tell you the truth, if you have faith and don't doubt, you can do things like this and much more. You can even say to this mountain, 'May you be lifted up and

21:9a Greek *Hosanna,* an exclamation of praise that literally means "save now"; also in 21:9b, 15. **21:9b** Pss 118:25-26; 148:1. **21:13** Isa 56:7; Jer 7:11. **21:16** Ps 8:2.

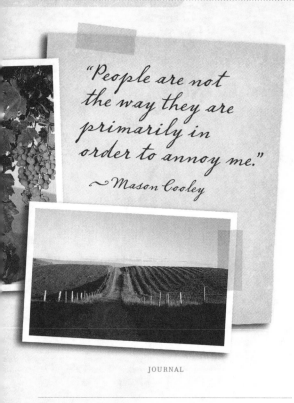

"People are not the way they are primarily in order to annoy me."

~ Mason Cooley

JOURNAL

thrown into the sea,' and it will happen. [22] You can pray for anything, and if you have faith, you will receive it."

The Authority of Jesus Challenged

[23] When Jesus returned to the Temple and began teaching, the leading priests and elders came up to him. They demanded, "By what authority are you doing all these things? Who gave you the right?"

[24] "I'll tell you by what authority I do these things if you answer one question," Jesus replied. [25] "Did John's authority to baptize come from heaven, or was it merely human?"

They talked it over among themselves. "If we say it was from heaven, he will ask us why we didn't believe John. [26] But if we say it was merely human, we'll be mobbed because the people believe John was a prophet." [27] So they finally replied, "We don't know."

And Jesus responded, "Then I won't tell you by what authority I do these things.

Parable of the Two Sons

[28] "But what do you think about this? A man with two sons told the older boy, 'Son, go out and work in the vineyard today.' [29] The son answered, 'No, I won't go,' but later he changed his mind and went anyway. [30] Then the father told the other son, 'You go,' and he said, 'Yes, sir, I will.' But he didn't go.

[31] "Which of the two obeyed his father?"

They replied, "The first."*

Then Jesus explained his meaning: "I tell you the truth, corrupt tax collectors and prostitutes will get into the Kingdom of God before you do. [32] For John the Baptist came and showed you the right way to live, but you didn't believe him, while tax collectors and prostitutes did. And even when you saw this happening, you refused to believe him and repent of your sins.

Parable of the Evil Farmers

[33] "Now listen to another story. A certain landowner planted a vineyard, built a wall around it, dug a pit for pressing out the grape juice, and built a lookout tower. Then he leased the vineyard to tenant farmers and moved to another country. [34] At the time of the grape harvest, he sent his servants to collect his share of the crop. [35] But the farmers grabbed his servants, beat one, killed one, and stoned another. [36] So the landowner sent a

21:29-31 Other manuscripts read *"The second."* In still other manuscripts the first son says "Yes" but does nothing, the second son says "No" but then repents and goes, and the answer to Jesus' question is that the second son obeyed his father.

larger group of his servants to collect for him, but the results were the same.

³⁷"Finally, the owner sent his son, thinking, 'Surely they will respect my son.'

³⁸"But when the tenant farmers saw his son coming, they said to one another, 'Here comes the heir to this estate. Come on, let's kill him and get the estate for ourselves!' ³⁹So they grabbed him, dragged him out of the vineyard, and murdered him.

⁴⁰"When the owner of the vineyard returns," Jesus asked, "what do you think he will do to those farmers?"

⁴¹The religious leaders replied, "He will put the wicked men to a horrible death and lease the vineyard to others who will give him his share of the crop after each harvest."

⁴²Then Jesus asked them, "Didn't you ever read this in the Scriptures?

'The stone that the builders rejected
   has now become the cornerstone.
This is the LORD's doing,
   and it is wonderful to see.'*

⁴³I tell you, the Kingdom of God will be taken away from you and given to a nation that will produce the proper fruit. ⁴⁴Anyone who stumbles over that stone will be broken to pieces, and it will crush anyone it falls on.*"

⁴⁵When the leading priests and Pharisees heard this parable, they realized he was telling the story against them—they were the wicked farmers. ⁴⁶They wanted to arrest him, but they were afraid of the crowds, who considered Jesus to be a prophet.

CHAPTER 22
Parable of the Great Feast

Jesus also told them other parables. He said, ²"The Kingdom of Heaven can be illustrated by the story of a king who prepared a great wedding feast for his son. ³When the banquet was ready, he sent his servants to notify those who were invited. But they all refused to come!

⁴"So he sent other servants to tell them, 'The feast has been prepared. The bulls and fattened cattle have been killed, and everything is ready. Come to the banquet!' ⁵But the guests he had invited ignored them and went their own way, one to his farm, another to his business. ⁶Others seized his messengers and insulted them and killed them.

21:42 Ps 118:22-23.   21:44 This verse is omitted in some early manuscripts. Compare Luke 20:18.

7 "The king was furious, and he sent out his army to destroy the murderers and burn their town. 8 And he said to his servants, 'The wedding feast is ready, and the guests I invited aren't worthy of the honor. 9 Now go out to the street corners and invite everyone you see.' 10 So the servants brought in everyone they could find, good and bad alike, and the banquet hall was filled with guests.

11 "But when the king came in to meet the guests, he noticed a man who wasn't wearing the proper clothes for a wedding. 12 'Friend,' he asked, 'how is it that you are here without wedding clothes?' But the man had no reply. 13 Then the king said to his aides, 'Bind his hands and feet and throw him into the outer darkness, where there will be weeping and gnashing of teeth.'

14 "For many are called, but few are chosen."

Taxes for Caesar

15 Then the Pharisees met together to plot how to trap Jesus into saying something for which he could be arrested. 16 They sent some of their disciples, along with the supporters of Herod, to meet with him. "Teacher," they said, "we know how honest you are. You teach the way of God truthfully. You are impartial and don't play favorites. 17 Now tell us what you think about this: Is it right to pay taxes to Caesar or not?"

18 But Jesus knew their evil motives. "You hypocrites!" he said. "Why are you trying to trap me? 19 Here, show me the coin used for the tax." When they handed him a Roman coin,* 20 he asked, "Whose picture and title are stamped on it?"

21 "Caesar's," they replied.

"Well, then," he said, "give to Caesar what belongs to Caesar, and give to God what belongs to God."

22 His reply amazed them, and they went away.

Discussion about Resurrection

23 That same day Jesus was approached by some Sadducees—religious leaders who say there is no resurrection from the dead. They posed this question: 24 "Teacher, Moses said, 'If a man dies without children, his brother should marry the widow and have a child who will carry on the brother's name.'* 25 Well, suppose there were seven brothers. The oldest one married and then died without children, so his brother married the widow. 26 But the second brother also died, and the third brother married her. This continued with all seven of them. 27 Last of all, the woman

22:19 Greek *a denarius*.   **22:24** Deut 25:5-6.

also died. ²⁸So tell us, whose wife will she be in the resurrection? For all seven were married to her."

²⁹Jesus replied, "Your mistake is that you don't know the Scriptures, and you don't know the power of God. ³⁰For when the dead rise, they will neither marry nor be given in marriage. In this respect they will be like the angels in heaven.

³¹"But now, as to whether there will be a resurrection of the dead—haven't you ever read about this in the Scriptures? Long after Abraham, Isaac, and Jacob had died, God said,* ³²'I am the God of Abraham, the God of Isaac, and the God of Jacob.'* So he is the God of the living, not the dead."

³³When the crowds heard him, they were astounded at his teaching.

The Most Important Commandment

³⁴But when the Pharisees heard that he had silenced the Sadducees with his reply, they met together to question him again. ³⁵One of them, an expert in religious law, tried to trap him with this question: ³⁶"Teacher, which is the most important commandment in the law of Moses?"

³⁷Jesus replied, "'You must love the LORD your God with all your heart, all your soul, and all your mind.'* ³⁸This is the first and greatest commandment. ³⁹A second is equally important: 'Love your neighbor as yourself.'* ⁴⁰The entire law and all the demands of the prophets are based on these two commandments."

Whose Son Is the Messiah?

⁴¹Then, surrounded by the Pharisees, Jesus asked them a question: ⁴²"What do you think about the Messiah? Whose son is he?"

They replied, "He is the son of David."

⁴³Jesus responded, "Then why does David, speaking under the inspiration of the Spirit, call the Messiah 'my Lord'? For David said,

⁴⁴ 'The LORD said to my Lord,
Sit in the place of honor at my right hand
until I humble your enemies beneath your feet.'*

⁴⁵Since David called the Messiah 'my Lord,' how can the Messiah be his son?"

⁴⁶No one could answer him. And after that, no one dared to ask him any more questions.

22:31 Greek *read about this? God said.*　22:32 Exod 3:6.　22:37 Deut 6:5.　22:39 Lev 19:18.
22:44 Ps 110:1.

No. 03-FA-049

FRIENDSHIP STORY

FRIENDSHIP TYPE: *Hard-to-Love People*

FRIENDSHIP LAYER: *Deepening*

FROM THE ARCHIVES

Unexpected Allies

When Abraham Lincoln ran for the 1860 Republican party presidential nomination, he was a major-league underdog.

The field was packed with more experienced, better-educated, more polished Republican hopefuls. Salmon Chase, Edward Bates, and William Seward campaigned hard against each other and Lincoln.

Lincoln's challengers did their level best to deprive Lincoln of the presidency. They questioned his character and attacked his credentials. But when the dust settled, Lincoln represented the Republicans in the national election...which he won.

So you might expect Lincoln to use his presidential influence to banish his rivals into the backwaters of the Republican Party, but you'd be wrong.

As critical as his political rivals had been during the election, Lincoln included all three in his new cabinet. Even Seward, whom Mrs. Lincoln disliked intensely.

Why would Lincoln surround himself with such hard-to-love people? There were political considerations, but there was also Lincoln's admiration for the good points he saw in each cabinet member.

FRIENDSHIP STORY *continues on page 50...*

FRIENDSHIP STORY *continued from page 49...*

Chase, Bates, and Seward had risen to their party's leadership because they each had abilities Lincoln—and the country—needed. Lincoln wasn't too proud to notice their skills or to request their service.

Not all of Lincoln's cabinet members came to appreciate him as a person. But history notes that two of his harshest critics—William Seward and Edwin Stanton, both of whom had publicly mocked Lincoln—became his close friends.

Seward was attacked by a would-be assassin the same night Lincoln was fatally shot at Ford's Theater.

And it was Stanton who, standing at Lincoln's bedside as the president died, eulogized, "Now he belongs to the ages."

Experience

THE ONE THING
1
YOU CAN DO THIS WEEK

Look at the portrait of Lincoln on a $5 bill as you think of a relative, co-worker, or someone else in your life who's hard to love. How can you use the bill to deepen your relationship with that person? Perhaps you could buy your co-worker a cup of coffee and, as you chat, look for something to respect. Or you could call your relative long-distance so you can catch up—and look for something to admire. Ask God: Whom should you contact? How should you use the $5?

Reflect

★ What was the genius in Lincoln's embracing hard-to-love people? What were the risks?

★ What were the benefits of investing your $5 in that difficult relationship?

★ In what ways have others invested in your life during those times you were less than easy to love?

CHAPTER 23

Jesus Criticizes the Religious Leaders

Then Jesus said to the crowds and to his disciples, ²"The teachers of religious law and the Pharisees are the official interpreters of the law of Moses.* ³So practice and obey whatever they tell you, but don't follow their example. For they don't practice what they teach. ⁴They crush people with unbearable religious demands and never lift a finger to ease the burden.

⁵"Everything they do is for show. On their arms they wear extra wide prayer boxes with Scripture verses inside, and they wear robes with extra long tassels.* ⁶And they love to sit at the head table at banquets and in the seats of honor in the synagogues. ⁷They love to receive respectful greetings as they walk in the marketplaces, and to be called 'Rabbi.'*

⁸"Don't let anyone call you 'Rabbi,' for you have only one teacher, and all of you are equal as brothers and sisters.* ⁹And don't address anyone here on earth as 'Father,' for only God in heaven is your spiritual Father. ¹⁰And don't let anyone call you 'Teacher,' for you have only one teacher, the Messiah. ¹¹The greatest among you must be a servant. ¹²But those who exalt themselves will be humbled, and those who humble themselves will be exalted.

¹³"What sorrow awaits you teachers of religious law and you Pharisees. Hypocrites! For you shut the door of the Kingdom of Heaven in people's faces. You won't go in yourselves, and you don't let others enter either.*

¹⁵"What sorrow awaits you teachers of religious law and you Pharisees. Hypocrites! For you cross land and sea to make one convert, and then you turn that person into twice the child of hell* you yourselves are!

¹⁶"Blind guides! What sorrow awaits you! For you say that it means nothing to swear 'by God's Temple,' but that it is binding to swear 'by the gold in the Temple.' ¹⁷Blind fools! Which is more important—the gold or the Temple that makes the gold sacred? ¹⁸And you say that to swear 'by the altar' is not binding, but to swear 'by the gifts on the altar' is binding. ¹⁹How blind! For which is more important—the gift on the altar or the altar that makes the gift sacred? ²⁰When you swear 'by the altar,' you are swearing by it and by everything on it. ²¹And when you

23:2 Greek *and the Pharisees sit in the seat of Moses.* 23:5 Greek *They enlarge their phylacteries and lengthen their tassels.* 23:7 *Rabbi,* from Aramaic, means "master" or "teacher." 23:8 Greek *brothers.* 23:13 Some manuscripts add verse 14, *What sorrow awaits you teachers of religious law and you Pharisees. Hypocrites! You shamelessly cheat widows out of their property and then pretend to be pious by making long prayers in public. Because of this, you will be severely punished.* Compare Mark 12:40 and Luke 20:47. 23:15 Greek *of Gehenna;* also in 23:33.

swear 'by the Temple,' you are swearing by it and by God, who lives in it. [22]And when you swear 'by heaven,' you are swearing by the throne of God and by God, who sits on the throne.

[23]"What sorrow awaits you teachers of religious law and you Pharisees. Hypocrites! For you are careful to tithe even the tiniest income from your herb gardens,* but you ignore the more important aspects of the law—justice, mercy, and faith. You should tithe, yes, but do not neglect the more important things. [24]Blind guides! You strain your water so you won't accidentally swallow a gnat, but you swallow a camel!*

[25]"What sorrow awaits you teachers of religious law and you Pharisees. Hypocrites! For you are so careful to clean the outside of the cup and the dish, but inside you are filthy—full of greed and self-indulgence! [26]You blind Pharisee! First wash the inside of the cup and the dish,* and then the outside will become clean, too.

[27]"What sorrow awaits you teachers of religious law and you Pharisees. Hypocrites! For you are like whitewashed tombs—beautiful on the outside but filled on the inside with dead people's bones and all sorts of impurity. [28]Outwardly you look like righteous people, but inwardly your hearts are filled with hypocrisy and lawlessness.

[29]"What sorrow awaits you teachers of religious law and you Pharisees. Hypocrites! For you build tombs for the prophets your ancestors killed, and you decorate the monuments of the godly people your ancestors destroyed. [30]Then you say, 'If we had lived in the days of our ancestors, we would never have joined them in killing the prophets.'

[31]"But in saying that, you testify against yourselves that you are indeed the descendants of those who murdered the prophets. [32]Go ahead and finish what your ancestors started. [33]Snakes! Sons of vipers! How will you escape the judgment of hell?

[34]"Therefore, I am sending you prophets and wise men and teachers of religious law. But you will kill some by crucifixion, and you will flog others with whips in your synagogues, chasing them from city to city. [35]As a result, you will be held responsible for the murder of all godly people of all time—from the murder of righteous Abel to the murder of Zechariah son of Barachiah, whom you killed in the Temple between the sanctuary and the altar. [36]I tell you the truth, this judgment will fall on this very generation.

★

A full 86% of those who describe their church as "very friendly" say they are "very satisfied" with their church, and an additional 12% report being "somewhat satisfied."

—from "Friendship and Faith," a Gallup Research Study Commissioned by Group Publishing, Inc.

★

JOURNAL

23:23 Greek *tithe the mint, the dill, and the cumin.* 23:24 See Lev 11:4, 23, where gnats and camels are both forbidden as food. 23:26 Some manuscripts do not include *and the dish.*

Jesus Grieves over Jerusalem

37"O Jerusalem, Jerusalem, the city that kills the prophets and stones God's messengers! How often I have wanted to gather your children together as a hen protects her chicks beneath her wings, but you wouldn't let me. 38And now, look, your house is abandoned and desolate.* 39For I tell you this, you will never see me again until you say, 'Blessings on the one who comes in the name of the LORD!'*"

CHAPTER 24

Jesus Foretells the Future

As Jesus was leaving the Temple grounds, his disciples pointed out to him the various Temple buildings. 2But he responded, "Do you see all these buildings? I tell you the truth, they will be completely demolished. Not one stone will be left on top of another!"

3Later, Jesus sat on the Mount of Olives. His disciples came to him privately and said, "Tell us, when will all this happen? What sign will signal your return and the end of the world?*"

4Jesus told them, "Don't let anyone mislead you, 5for many will come in my name, claiming, 'I am the Messiah.' They will deceive many. 6And you will hear of wars and threats of wars, but don't panic. Yes, these things must take place, but the end won't follow immediately. 7Nation will go to war against nation, and kingdom against kingdom. There will be famines and earthquakes in many parts of the world. 8But all this is only the first of the birth pains, with more to come.

9"Then you will be arrested, persecuted, and killed. You will be hated all over the world because you are my followers.* 10And many will turn away from me and betray and hate each other. 11And many false prophets will appear and will deceive many people. 12Sin will be rampant everywhere, and the love of many will grow cold. 13But the one who endures to the end will be saved. 14And the Good News about the Kingdom will be preached throughout the whole world, so that all nations* will hear it; and then the end will come.

15"The day is coming when you will see what Daniel the prophet spoke about—the sacrilegious object that causes desecration* standing in the Holy Place." (Reader, pay attention!) 16"Then those in Judea must flee to the hills. 17A person out on the deck of a roof must not go down into the house to pack.

23:38 Some manuscripts do not include *and desolate.*   23:39 Ps 118:26.   24:3 Or *the age?*   24:9 Greek *on account of my name.*   24:14 Or *all peoples.*   24:15 Greek *the abomination of desolation.* See Dan 9:27; 11:31; 12:11.

¹⁸A person out in the field must not return even to get a coat. ¹⁹How terrible it will be for pregnant women and for nursing mothers in those days. ²⁰And pray that your flight will not be in winter or on the Sabbath. ²¹For there will be greater anguish than at any time since the world began. And it will never be so great again. ²²In fact, unless that time of calamity is shortened, not a single person will survive. But it will be shortened for the sake of God's chosen ones.

²³"Then if anyone tells you, 'Look, here is the Messiah,' or 'There he is,' don't believe it. ²⁴For false messiahs and false prophets will rise up and perform great signs and wonders so as to deceive, if possible, even God's chosen ones. ²⁵See, I have warned you about this ahead of time.

²⁶"So if someone tells you, 'Look, the Messiah is out in the desert,' don't bother to go and look. Or, 'Look, he is hiding here,' don't believe it! ²⁷For as the lightning flashes in the east and shines to the west, so it will be when the Son of Man* comes. ²⁸Just as the gathering of vultures shows there is a carcass nearby, so these signs indicate that the end is near.*

²⁹"Immediately after the anguish of those days,

the sun will be darkened,
    the moon will give no light,
the stars will fall from the sky,
    and the powers in the heavens will be shaken.*

³⁰And then at last, the sign that the Son of Man is coming will appear in the heavens, and there will be deep mourning among all the peoples of the earth. And they will see the Son of Man coming on the clouds of heaven with power and great glory.* ³¹And he will send out his angels with the mighty blast of a trumpet, and they will gather his chosen ones from all over the world*—from the farthest ends of the earth and heaven.

³²"Now learn a lesson from the fig tree. When its branches bud and its leaves begin to sprout, you know that summer is near. ³³In the same way, when you see all these things, you can know his return is very near, right at the door. ³⁴I tell you the truth, this generation* will not pass from the scene until all these things take place. ³⁵Heaven and earth will disappear, but my words will never disappear.

³⁶"However, no one knows the day or hour when these things

"Security in a relationship lies neither in looking back to what it was in nostalgia, nor forward to what it might be in dread or anticipation, but living in the present relationship and accepting it as it is now."

~ Anne Morrow Lindbergh

JOURNAL

24:27 "Son of Man" is a title Jesus used for himself.   24:28 Greek *Wherever the carcass is, the vultures gather.*   24:29 See Isa 13:10; 34:4; Joel 2:10.   24:30 See Dan 7:13.   24:31 Greek *from the four winds.* 24:34 Or *this age,* or *this nation.*

will happen, not even the angels in heaven or the Son himself.* Only the Father knows.

37 "When the Son of Man returns, it will be like it was in Noah's day. 38 In those days before the flood, the people were enjoying banquets and parties and weddings right up to the time Noah entered his boat. 39 People didn't realize what was going to happen until the flood came and swept them all away. That is the way it will be when the Son of Man comes.

40 "Two men will be working together in the field; one will be taken, the other left. 41 Two women will be grinding flour at the mill; one will be taken, the other left.

42 "So you, too, must keep watch! For you don't know what day your Lord is coming. 43 Understand this: If a homeowner knew exactly when a burglar was coming, he would keep watch and not permit his house to be broken into. 44 You also must be ready all the time, for the Son of Man will come when least expected.

45 "A faithful, sensible servant is one to whom the master can give the responsibility of managing his other household servants and feeding them. 46 If the master returns and finds that the servant has done a good job, there will be a reward. 47 I tell you the truth, the master will put that servant in charge of all he owns. 48 But what if the servant is evil and thinks, 'My master won't be back for a while,' 49 and he begins beating the other servants, partying, and getting drunk? 50 The master will return unannounced and unexpected, 51 and he will cut the servant to pieces and assign him a place with the hypocrites. In that place there will be weeping and gnashing of teeth.

CHAPTER **25**

Parable of the Ten Bridesmaids

"Then the Kingdom of Heaven will be like ten bridesmaids* who took their lamps and went to meet the bridegroom. 2 Five of them were foolish, and five were wise. 3 The five who were foolish didn't take enough olive oil for their lamps, 4 but the other five were wise enough to take along extra oil. 5 When the bridegroom was delayed, they all became drowsy and fell asleep.

6 "At midnight they were roused by the shout, 'Look, the bridegroom is coming! Come out and meet him!'

7 "All the bridesmaids got up and prepared their lamps. 8 Then the five foolish ones asked the others, 'Please give us some of your oil because our lamps are going out.'

24:36 Some manuscripts do not include *or the Son himself.* 25:1 Or *virgins;* also in 25:7, 11.

9"But the others replied, "We don't have enough for all of us. Go to a shop and buy some for yourselves.'

10"But while they were gone to buy oil, the bridegroom came. Then those who were ready went in with him to the marriage feast, and the door was locked. 11Later, when the other five bridesmaids returned, they stood outside, calling, 'Lord! Lord! Open the door for us!'

12"But he called back, 'Believe me, I don't know you!'

13"So you, too, must keep watch! For you do not know the day or hour of my return.

Parable of the Three Servants

14"Again, the Kingdom of Heaven can be illustrated by the story of a man going on a long trip. He called together his servants and entrusted his money to them while he was gone. 15He gave five bags of silver* to one, two bags of silver to another, and one bag of silver to the last—dividing it in proportion to their abilities. He then left on his trip.

16"The servant who received the five bags of silver began to invest the money and earned five more. 17The servant with two bags of silver also went to work and earned two more. 18But the servant who received the one bag of silver dug a hole in the ground and hid the master's money.

19"After a long time their master returned from his trip and called them to give an account of how they had used his money. 20The servant to whom he had entrusted the five bags of silver came forward with five more and said, 'Master, you gave me five bags of silver to invest, and I have earned five more.'

21"The master was full of praise. "Well done, my good and faithful servant. You have been faithful in handling this small amount, so now I will give you many more responsibilities. Let's celebrate together!*'

22"The servant who had received the two bags of silver came forward and said, 'Master, you gave me two bags of silver to invest, and I have earned two more.'

23"The master said, "Well done, my good and faithful servant. You have been faithful in handling this small amount, so now I will give you many more responsibilities. Let's celebrate together!'

24"Then the servant with the one bag of silver came and said, 'Master, I knew you were a harsh man, harvesting crops you didn't plant and gathering crops you didn't cultivate. 25I was

25:15 Greek *talents*; also throughout the story. A talent is equal to 75 pounds or 34 kilograms.
25:21 Greek *Enter into the joy of your master* [or *your Lord*]; also in 25:23.

WHAT TO SAY
AND
WHAT NOT TO SAY

FRIENDSHIP TYPE: *Family* FRIENDSHIP LAYER: *Deepening*

When Forgiveness Really Isn't

In **Matthew 18:35**, Jesus tells us to forgive our brothers and sisters "from your heart." So what does that look like? Well, here's what it *doesn't* look like:

 WHAT NOT TO SAY:

★ *Passive-Aggressive:* "You know, I forgive you for hurting me so much by what you did."
★ *Conditional:* "I'm not going to forgive you until you really show you're sorry by not doing it anymore."
★ *Partial:* "I'll forgive you, but I won't forget!"
★ *Threatening:* "Yeah, I'll forgive you…but there have to be consequences!"

Forgiveness that comes from the heart is based in love. **First Corinthians 13:5-7** says love keeps no record of wrongs: "Love never gives up, never loses faith, is always hopeful, and endures through every circumstance."

Forgiveness from the heart looks like this:

 WHAT TO SAY:

★ *Perfect:* "I love you, and I forgive you."

No strings attached. No angry subtext. No subtle threats. No contingencies.

Friendship First NEW TESTAMENT

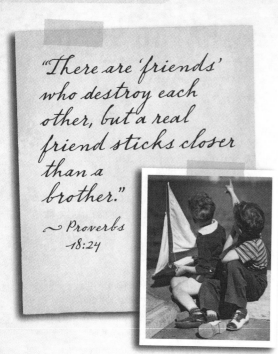

"There are 'friends' who destroy each other, but a real friend sticks closer than a brother."

~ Proverbs 18:24

JOURNAL

afraid I would lose your money, so I hid it in the earth. Look, here is your money back.'

26 "But the master replied, 'You wicked and lazy servant! If you knew I harvested crops I didn't plant and gathered crops I didn't cultivate, 27 why didn't you deposit my money in the bank? At least I could have gotten some interest on it.'

28 "Then he ordered, 'Take the money from this servant, and give it to the one with the ten bags of silver. 29 To those who use well what they are given, even more will be given, and they will have an abundance. But from those who do nothing, even what little they have will be taken away. 30 Now throw this useless servant into outer darkness, where there will be weeping and gnashing of teeth.'

The Final Judgment

31 "But when the Son of Man* comes in his glory, and all the angels with him, then he will sit upon his glorious throne. 32 All the nations* will be gathered in his presence, and he will separate the people as a shepherd separates the sheep from the goats. 33 He will place the sheep at his right hand and the goats at his left.

34 "Then the King will say to those on his right, 'Come, you who are blessed by my Father, inherit the Kingdom prepared for you from the creation of the world. 35 For I was hungry, and you fed me. I was thirsty, and you gave me a drink. I was a stranger, and you invited me into your home. 36 I was naked, and you gave me clothing. I was sick, and you cared for me. I was in prison, and you visited me.'

37 "Then these righteous ones will reply, 'Lord, when did we ever see you hungry and feed you? Or thirsty and give you something to drink? 38 Or a stranger and show you hospitality? Or naked and give you clothing? 39 When did we ever see you sick or in prison and visit you?'

40 "And the King will say, 'I tell you the truth, when you did it to one of the least of these my brothers and sisters,* you were doing it to me!'

41 "Then the King will turn to those on the left and say, 'Away with you, you cursed ones, into the eternal fire prepared for the devil and his demons.* 42 For I was hungry, and you didn't feed me. I was thirsty, and you didn't give me a drink. 43 I was a stranger, and you didn't invite me into your home. I was naked, and you didn't give me clothing. I was sick and in prison, and you didn't visit me.'

25:31 "Son of Man" is a title Jesus used for himself. 25:32 Or *peoples.* 25:40 Greek *my brothers.* 25:41 Greek *his angels.*

44 "Then they will reply, 'Lord, when did we ever see you hungry or thirsty or a stranger or naked or sick or in prison, and not help you?'

45 "And he will answer, 'I tell you the truth, when you refused to help the least of these my brothers and sisters, you were refusing to help me.'

46 "And they will go away into eternal punishment, but the righteous will go into eternal life."

CHAPTER 26

The Plot to Kill Jesus

When Jesus had finished saying all these things, he said to his disciples, 2 "As you know, Passover begins in two days, and the Son of Man* will be handed over to be crucified."

3 At that same time the leading priests and elders were meeting at the residence of Caiaphas, the high priest, 4 plotting how to capture Jesus secretly and kill him. 5 "But not during the Passover celebration," they agreed, "or the people may riot."

Jesus Anointed at Bethany

6 Meanwhile, Jesus was in Bethany at the home of Simon, a man who had previously had leprosy. 7 While he was eating,* a woman came in with a beautiful alabaster jar of expensive perfume and poured it over his head.

8 The disciples were indignant when they saw this. "What a waste!" they said. 9 "It could have been sold for a high price and the money given to the poor."

10 But Jesus, aware of this, replied, "Why criticize this woman for doing such a good thing to me? 11 You will always have the poor among you, but you will not always have me. 12 She has poured this perfume on me to prepare my body for burial. 13 I tell you the truth, wherever the Good News is preached throughout the world, this woman's deed will be remembered and discussed."

Judas Agrees to Betray Jesus

14 Then Judas Iscariot, one of the twelve disciples, went to the leading priests 15 and asked, "How much will you pay me to betray Jesus to you?" And they gave him thirty pieces of silver. 16 From that time on, Judas began looking for an opportunity to betray Jesus.

26:2 "Son of Man" is a title Jesus used for himself.   26:7 Or *reclining*.

About **77%** of highly satisfied church members have eaten a meal with people from their church in the last year. Only **23%** of those who haven't shared a meal with a friend from church say they are "very satisfied" with their church."

—from "Friendship and Faith," a Gallup Research Study
Commissioned by Group Publishing, Inc.

JOURNAL

The Last Supper

17 On the first day of the Festival of Unleavened Bread, the disciples came to Jesus and asked, "Where do you want us to prepare the Passover meal for you?"

18 "As you go into the city," he told them, "you will see a certain man. Tell him, 'The Teacher says: My time has come, and I will eat the Passover meal with my disciples at your house.'" 19 So the disciples did as Jesus told them and prepared the Passover meal there.

20 When it was evening, Jesus sat down at the table* with the twelve disciples.* 21 While they were eating, he said, "I tell you the truth, one of you will betray me."

22 Greatly distressed, each one asked in turn, "Am I the one, Lord?"

23 He replied, "One of you who has just eaten from this bowl with me will betray me. 24 For the Son of Man must die, as the Scriptures declared long ago. But how terrible it will be for the one who betrays him. It would be far better for that man if he had never been born!"

25 Judas, the one who would betray him, also asked, "Rabbi, am I the one?"

And Jesus told him, "You have said it."

26 As they were eating, Jesus took some bread and blessed it. Then he broke it in pieces and gave it to the disciples, saying, "Take this and eat it, for this is my body."

27 And he took a cup of wine and gave thanks to God for it. He gave it to them and said, "Each of you drink from it, 28 for this is my blood, which confirms the covenant* between God and his people. It is poured out as a sacrifice to forgive the sins of many. 29 Mark my words—I will not drink wine again until the day I drink it new with you in my Father's Kingdom."

30 Then they sang a hymn and went out to the Mount of Olives.

Jesus Predicts Peter's Denial

31 On the way, Jesus told them, "Tonight all of you will desert me. For the Scriptures say,

'God will strike* the Shepherd,
    and the sheep of the flock will be scattered.'

32 But after I have been raised from the dead, I will go ahead of you to Galilee and meet you there."

26:20a Or *Jesus reclined.*   26:20b Some manuscripts read *the Twelve.*   26:28 Some manuscripts read *the new covenant.*   26:31 Greek *I will strike.* Zech 13:7.

33 Peter declared, "Even if everyone else deserts you, I will never desert you."

34 Jesus replied, "I tell you the truth, Peter—this very night, before the rooster crows, you will deny three times that you even know me."

35 "No!" Peter insisted. "Even if I have to die with you, I will never deny you!" And all the other disciples vowed the same.

Jesus Prays in Gethsemane

36 Then Jesus went with them to the olive grove called Gethsemane, and he said, "Sit here while I go over there to pray." 37 He took Peter and Zebedee's two sons, James and John, and he became anguished and distressed. 38 He told them, "My soul is crushed with grief to the point of death. Stay here and keep watch with me."

39 He went on a little farther and bowed with his face to the ground, praying, "My Father! If it is possible, let this cup of suffering be taken away from me. Yet I want your will to be done, not mine."

40 Then he returned to the disciples and found them asleep. He said to Peter, "Couldn't you watch with me even one hour? 41 Keep watch and pray, so that you will not give in to temptation. For the spirit is willing, but the body is weak!"

42 Then Jesus left them a second time and prayed, "My Father! If this cup cannot be taken away* unless I drink it, your will be done." 43 When he returned to them again, he found them sleeping, for they couldn't keep their eyes open.

44 So he went to pray a third time, saying the same things again. 45 Then he came to the disciples and said, "Go ahead and sleep. Have your rest. But look—the time has come. The Son of Man is betrayed into the hands of sinners. 46 Up, let's be going. Look, my betrayer is here!"

Jesus Is Betrayed and Arrested

47 And even as Jesus said this, Judas, one of the twelve disciples, arrived with a crowd of men armed with swords and clubs. They had been sent by the leading priests and elders of the people. 48 The traitor, Judas, had given them a prearranged signal: "You will know which one to arrest when I greet him with a kiss." 49 So Judas came straight to Jesus. "Greetings, Rabbi!" he exclaimed and gave him the kiss.

50 Jesus said, "My friend, go ahead and do what you have come for."

26:42 Greek *If this cannot pass.*

FRIENDSHIP
EXPERIENCE

FRIENDSHIP TYPE: *Jesus*   FRIENDSHIP LAYER: *Commitment*

The Evidence...

Being totally committed to a friend is not always easy, painless, or risk-free. In fact, dedicating yourself to the friendship for the long haul—no matter what—means you'll experience some tough times. But it also means you'll experience what's *only* found in a committed friendship: unconditional love, intimate vulnerability, absolute acceptance, unmatched loyalty...and on and on.

It's the same when you commit to a no-matter-what friendship with Jesus; there will be tough times over the long haul, but what you'll experience is incomparably worthwhile. And Jesus, being, you know...the perfect friend, will never let you down. And how do you respond to the *perfect* friend? Well, 11 of Jesus' friends responded by dedicating their lives to his mission (check out **Matthew 28:16-20**)—they went out and shared his love, compassion, and joy with the world. This is evidence of a commitment to Jesus: compassionate, relentless, and selfless love for others.

FRIENDSHIP EXPERIENCE *continues on page 60...*

FRIENDSHIP EXPERIENCE *continued from page 59...*

Experience

THE ONE THING 1 YOU CAN DO THIS WEEK

Get an old piece of cloth or material you don't need anymore (any kind, but it should be something you can write on), and look closely at it. Closer. Study the intricacies of the material. What's it made of? How do the threads make it strong? As you look at the fabric, think about how it might symbolize your friendship with Jesus. Consider what your friendship is made of. What makes your friendship strong? When you take a close look at the "fabric" of your faith, where do you see commitment?

Using a marker or pen, write on the cloth one way you'll make commitment an essential thread of your friendship with Jesus. How might commitment make up the very fabric of your faith and keep it strong? You might pray daily or talk to a pastor about ways to serve God in your church. After writing, hold the cloth tightly in your hand, and ask God to help you grow in commitment to him so it's clear what your friendship with Jesus is made of...and what makes it strong.

Reflect

★ How did you feel as you took a closer look at the "fabric" of your friendship with Jesus?

★ Why is commitment such an important part of your friendship with Jesus?

★ How does active commitment strengthen a friendship with Jesus?

Then the others grabbed Jesus and arrested him. [51] But one of the men with Jesus pulled out his sword and struck the high priest's slave, slashing off his ear.

[52] "Put away your sword," Jesus told him. "Those who use the sword will die by the sword. [53] Don't you realize that I could ask my Father for thousands* of angels to protect us, and he would send them instantly? [54] But if I did, how would the Scriptures be fulfilled that describe what must happen now?"

[55] Then Jesus said to the crowd, "Am I some dangerous revolutionary, that you come with swords and clubs to arrest me? Why didn't you arrest me in the Temple? I was there teaching every day. [56] But this is all happening to fulfill the words of the prophets as recorded in the Scriptures." At that point, all the disciples deserted him and fled.

Jesus before the Council

[57] Then the people who had arrested Jesus led him to the home of Caiaphas, the high priest, where the teachers of religious law and the elders had gathered. [58] Meanwhile, Peter followed him at a distance and came to the high priest's courtyard. He went in and sat with the guards and waited to see how it would all end.

[59] Inside, the leading priests and the entire high council* were trying to find witnesses who would lie about Jesus, so they could put him to death. [60] But even though they found many who agreed to give false witness, they could not use anyone's testimony. Finally, two men came forward [61] who declared, "This man said, 'I am able to destroy the Temple of God and rebuild it in three days.'"

[62] Then the high priest stood up and said to Jesus, "Well, aren't you going to answer these charges? What do you have to say for yourself?" [63] But Jesus remained silent. Then the high priest said to him, "I demand in the name of the living God—tell us if you are the Messiah, the Son of God."

[64] Jesus replied, "You have said it. And in the future you will see the Son of Man seated in the place of power at God's right hand* and coming on the clouds of heaven."*

[65] Then the high priest tore his clothing to show his horror and said, "Blasphemy! Why do we need other witnesses? You have all heard his blasphemy. [66] What is your verdict?"

"Guilty!" they shouted. "He deserves to die!"

[67] Then they began to spit in Jesus' face and beat him with

26:53 Greek *twelve legions.*   26:59 Greek *the Sanhedrin.*   26:64a Greek *seated at the right hand of the power.* See Ps 110:1.   26:64b See Dan 7:13.

their fists. And some slapped him, [68]jeering, "Prophesy to us, you Messiah! Who hit you that time?"

Peter Denies Jesus

[69]Meanwhile, Peter was sitting outside in the courtyard. A servant girl came over and said to him, "You were one of those with Jesus the Galilean."

[70]But Peter denied it in front of everyone. "I don't know what you're talking about," he said.

[71]Later, out by the gate, another servant girl noticed him and said to those standing around, "This man was with Jesus of Nazareth.*"

[72]Again Peter denied it, this time with an oath. "I don't even know the man," he said.

[73]A little later some of the other bystanders came over to Peter and said, "You must be one of them; we can tell by your Galilean accent."

[74]Peter swore, "A curse on me if I'm lying—I don't know the man!" And immediately the rooster crowed.

[75]Suddenly, Jesus' words flashed through Peter's mind: "Before the rooster crows, you will deny three times that you even know me." And he went away, weeping bitterly.

CHAPTER **27**

Judas Hangs Himself

Very early in the morning the leading priests and the elders met again to lay plans for putting Jesus to death. [2]Then they bound him, led him away, and took him to Pilate, the Roman governor.

[3]When Judas, who had betrayed him, realized that Jesus had been condemned to die, he was filled with remorse. So he took the thirty pieces of silver back to the leading priests and the elders. [4]"I have sinned," he declared, "for I have betrayed an innocent man."

"What do we care?" they retorted. "That's your problem."

[5]Then Judas threw the silver coins down in the Temple and went out and hanged himself.

[6]The leading priests picked up the coins. "It wouldn't be right to put this money in the Temple treasury," they said, "since it was payment for murder."* [7]After some discussion they finally decided to buy the potter's field, and they made it into a cemetery for foreigners. [8]That is why the field is still called the Field of Blood. [9]This fulfilled the prophecy of Jeremiah that says,

26:71 Or *Jesus the Nazarene.*   **27:6** Greek *since it is the price for blood.*

"They took* the thirty pieces of silver—
the price at which he was valued by the people of Israel,
[10] and purchased the potter's field,
as the LORD directed.*"

Jesus' Trial before Pilate

[11] Now Jesus was standing before Pilate, the Roman governor. "Are you the king of the Jews?" the governor asked him.

Jesus replied, "You have said it."

[12] But when the leading priests and the elders made their accusations against him, Jesus remained silent. [13] "Don't you hear all these charges they are bringing against you?" Pilate demanded. [14] But Jesus made no response to any of the charges, much to the governor's surprise.

[15] Now it was the governor's custom each year during the Passover celebration to release one prisoner to the crowd—anyone they wanted. [16] This year there was a notorious prisoner, a man named Barabbas.* [17] As the crowds gathered before Pilate's house that morning, he asked them, "Which one do you want me to release to you—Barabbas, or Jesus who is called the Messiah?" [18] (He knew very well that the religious leaders had arrested Jesus out of envy.)

[19] Just then, as Pilate was sitting on the judgment seat, his wife sent him this message: "Leave that innocent man alone. I suffered through a terrible nightmare about him last night."

[20] Meanwhile, the leading priests and the elders persuaded the crowd to ask for Barabbas to be released and for Jesus to be put to death. [21] So the governor asked again, "Which of these two do you want me to release to you?"

The crowd shouted back, "Barabbas!"

[22] Pilate responded, "Then what should I do with Jesus who is called the Messiah?"

They shouted back, "Crucify him!"

[23] "Why?" Pilate demanded. "What crime has he committed?"

But the mob roared even louder, "Crucify him!"

[24] Pilate saw that he wasn't getting anywhere and that a riot was developing. So he sent for a bowl of water and washed his hands before the crowd, saying, "I am innocent of this man's blood. The responsibility is yours!"

[25] And all the people yelled back, "We will take responsibility for his death—we and our children!"*

[26] So Pilate released Barabbas to them. He ordered Jesus

27:9 Or *I took.* 27:9-10 Greek *as the LORD directed me.* Zech 11:12-13; Jer 32:6-9. 27:16 Some manuscripts read *Jesus Barabbas;* also in 27:17. 27:25 Greek *"His blood be on us and on our children."*

flogged with a lead-tipped whip, then turned him over to the Roman soldiers to be crucified.

The Soldiers Mock Jesus

27 Some of the governor's soldiers took Jesus into their headquarters* and called out the entire regiment. 28 They stripped him and put a scarlet robe on him. 29 They wove thorn branches into a crown and put it on his head, and they placed a reed stick in his right hand as a scepter. Then they knelt before him in mockery and taunted, "Hail! King of the Jews!" 30 And they spit on him and grabbed the stick and struck him on the head with it. 31 When they were finally tired of mocking him, they took off the robe and put his own clothes on him again. Then they led him away to be crucified.

The Crucifixion

32 Along the way, they came across a man named Simon, who was from Cyrene,* and the soldiers forced him to carry Jesus' cross. 33 And they went out to a place called Golgotha (which means "Place of the Skull"). 34 The soldiers gave him wine mixed with bitter gall, but when he had tasted it, he refused to drink it.

35 After they had nailed him to the cross, the soldiers gambled for his clothes by throwing dice.* 36 Then they sat around and kept guard as he hung there. 37 A sign was fastened to the cross above Jesus' head, announcing the charge against him. It read: "This is Jesus, the King of the Jews." 38 Two revolutionaries* were crucified with him, one on his right and one on his left.

39 The people passing by shouted abuse, shaking their heads in mockery. 40 "Look at you now!" they yelled at him. "You said you were going to destroy the Temple and rebuild it in three days. Well then, if you are the Son of God, save yourself and come down from the cross!"

41 The leading priests, the teachers of religious law, and the elders also mocked Jesus. 42 "He saved others," they scoffed, "but he can't save himself! So he is the King of Israel, is he? Let him come down from the cross right now, and we will believe in him! 43 He trusted God, so let God rescue him now if he wants him! For he said, 'I am the Son of God.'" 44 Even the revolutionaries who were crucified with him ridiculed him in the same way.

27:27 Or *into the Praetorium.* 27:32 *Cyrene* was a city in northern Africa. 27:35 Greek *by casting lots.* A few late manuscripts add *This fulfilled the word of the prophet: "They divided my garments among themselves and cast lots for my robe."* See Ps 22:18. 27:38 Or *criminals;* also in 27:44.

"See, from his head, his hands, his feet, sorrow and love flow mingled down. Did e'er such love and sorrow meet, or thorns compose so rich a crown?

Were the whole realm of nature mine, that were an offering far too small;

Love so amazing, so divine, demands my soul, my life, my all."

~ from "When I Survey the Wondrous Cross" by Isaac Watts

JOURNAL

The Death of Jesus

45 At noon, darkness fell across the whole land until three o'clock. 46 At about three o'clock, Jesus called out with a loud voice, *"Eli, Eli,* * *lema sabachthani?"* which means "My God, my God, why have you abandoned me?"*

47 Some of the bystanders misunderstood and thought he was calling for the prophet Elijah. 48 One of them ran and filled a sponge with sour wine, holding it up to him on a reed stick so he could drink. 49 But the rest said, "Wait! Let's see whether Elijah comes to save him."*

50 Then Jesus shouted out again, and he released his spirit. 51 At that moment the curtain in the sanctuary of the Temple was torn in two, from top to bottom. The earth shook, rocks split apart, 52 and tombs opened. The bodies of many godly men and women who had died were raised from the dead. 53 They left the cemetery after Jesus' resurrection, went into the holy city of Jerusalem, and appeared to many people.

54 The Roman officer* and the other soldiers at the crucifixion were terrified by the earthquake and all that had happened. They said, "This man truly was the Son of God!"

55 And many women who had come from Galilee with Jesus to care for him were watching from a distance. 56 Among them were Mary Magdalene, Mary (the mother of James and Joseph), and the mother of James and John, the sons of Zebedee.

The Burial of Jesus

57 As evening approached, Joseph, a rich man from Arimathea who had become a follower of Jesus, 58 went to Pilate and asked for Jesus' body. And Pilate issued an order to release it to him. 59 Joseph took the body and wrapped it in a long sheet of clean linen cloth. 60 He placed it in his own new tomb, which had been carved out of the rock. Then he rolled a great stone across the entrance and left. 61 Both Mary Magdalene and the other Mary were sitting across from the tomb and watching.

The Guard at the Tomb

62 The next day, on the Sabbath,* the leading priests and Pharisees went to see Pilate. 63 They told him, "Sir, we remember what that deceiver once said while he was still alive: 'After three days I will rise from the dead.' 64 So we request that you seal the tomb until the third day. This will prevent his disciples from

27:46a Some manuscripts read *Eloi, Eloi.*   27:46b Ps 22:1.   27:49 Some manuscripts add *And another took a spear and pierced his side, and out flowed water and blood.* Compare John 19:34.   27:54 Greek *The centurion.*   27:62 Or *On the next day, which is after the Preparation.*

coming and stealing his body and then telling everyone he was raised from the dead! If that happens, we'll be worse off than we were at first."

⁶⁵Pilate replied, "Take guards and secure it the best you can." ⁶⁶So they sealed the tomb and posted guards to protect it.

CHAPTER **28**

The Resurrection

Early on Sunday morning,* as the new day was dawning, Mary Magdalene and the other Mary went out to visit the tomb.

²Suddenly there was a great earthquake! For an angel of the Lord came down from heaven, rolled aside the stone, and sat on it. ³His face shone like lightning, and his clothing was as white as snow. ⁴The guards shook with fear when they saw him, and they fell into a dead faint.

⁵Then the angel spoke to the women. "Don't be afraid!" he said. "I know you are looking for Jesus, who was crucified. ⁶He isn't here! He is risen from the dead, just as he said would happen. Come, see where his body was lying. ⁷And now, go quickly and tell his disciples that he has risen from the dead, and he is going ahead of you to Galilee. You will see him there. Remember what I have told you."

⁸The women ran quickly from the tomb. They were very frightened but also filled with great joy, and they rushed to give the disciples the angel's message. ⁹And as they went, Jesus met them and greeted them. And they ran to him, grasped his feet, and worshiped him. ¹⁰Then Jesus said to them, "Don't be afraid! Go tell my brothers to leave for Galilee, and they will see me there."

The Report of the Guard

¹¹As the women were on their way, some of the guards went into the city and told the leading priests what had happened. ¹²A meeting with the elders was called, and they decided to give the soldiers a large bribe. ¹³They told the soldiers, "You must say, 'Jesus' disciples came during the night while we were sleeping, and they stole his body.' ¹⁴If the governor hears about it, we'll stand up for you so you won't get in trouble." ¹⁵So the guards accepted the bribe and said what they were told to say. Their story spread widely among the Jews, and they still tell it today.

28:1 Greek *After the Sabbath, on the first day of the week.*

Anchor Passage

PASSAGE: **Matthew 28:16-20**

FRIENDSHIP TYPE: *Jesus*

FRIENDSHIP LAYER: *Commitment*

Radical Commitment

Think of a time you did something truly radical because of a deep commitment. We're talking good kind of radical here—giving till people think you're crazy, going beyond the call of duty, sticking close by when nobody else does.

Now read **Matthew 28:16-20**. Jesus was asking the disciples—his closest friends—to do something pretty radical: Go out into the world, and spread the word that Jesus is the Son of God who died to free people from their sins. Yeah, that's definitely in the beyond-the-call-of-duty and people-might-think-you're-crazy categories.

But this was Jesus talking to them. Jesus, the friend who loved them. Jesus, the Savior who rescued them. Jesus, who said he'd be *with* them always! And these guys were deeply committed to Jesus. So committed that the only way they could respond was by doing exactly as Jesus said: leaving their comfortable lives, leaving the only country they'd ever known, leaving the relative safety of their homes…to go out and share Jesus' love with the world.

What made these guys so committed? They were responding to Jesus' own crazy, beyond-the-call-of-duty commitment to them.

In a friendship, radical commitment inspires radical commitment.

Now consider: How can you live out *radical* commitment in a friendship with Jesus, who loves you more than anyone else ever could? And how can you go out and share Jesus' love with the world?

Anchor Passage continues on page 66…

Anchor Passage continued from page 65...

After all, if you think of the radical commitment Jesus has for you (he *died* for you!), how can you respond with anything less than radical?

Experience

THE ONE THING
1
YOU CAN DO THIS WEEK

Carefully read the story of Jesus' death and resurrection (**Matthew 26–28**) and the Great Commission (**Matthew 28:16-20**). After reading both passages, write a letter to Jesus.

It doesn't have to be a specific kind of letter; just jot down your response to his sacrifice and his call for your commitment. Tell him what you think.

At the end of the letter, include a P.S. note. Write something tangible you'll do to radically live out your commitment to Jesus. You might read and discuss Matthew 26–28 with a friend. Or you might give up your own plans one night to encourage a lonely friend. Carry this letter with you as a symbol of your commitment to Jesus and a reminder to share his love with the world.

Reflect

★ How does true commitment impact a friendship? the people in the friendship?

★ In what specific ways can you radically commit to your friendship with Jesus?

★ How does sharing Jesus' love with others reflect your commitment to Jesus?

DIGGING DEEPER

FRIENDSHIP TYPE:	FRIENDSHIP LAYER:
Jesus	*Commitment*

For committing to your friendship with Jesus, check out...

➥ The Friendship Experience .... on page 59
➥ The Friendship Story .... on page 29
➥ What to Say and What Not to Say .... on page 7

The Great Commission

[16] Then the eleven disciples left for Galilee, going to the mountain where Jesus had told them to go. [17] When they saw him, they worshiped him—but some of them doubted!

[18] Jesus came and told his disciples, "I have been given all authority in heaven and on earth. [19] Therefore, go and make disciples of all the nations,* baptizing them in the name of the Father and the Son and the Holy Spirit. [20] Teach these new disciples to obey all the commands I have given you. And be sure of this: I am with you always, even to the end of the age." ⚓

28:19 Or *all peoples.*

Figure 1

Mark

AUTHOR:	DATE WRITTEN:
John Mark	Between A.D. 55–65

JOURNAL

CHAPTER 1

John the Baptist Prepares the Way

This is the Good News about Jesus the Messiah, the Son of God.* It began ²just as the prophet Isaiah had written:

"Look, I am sending my messenger ahead of you,
  and he will prepare your way.*
³ He is a voice shouting in the wilderness,
  'Prepare the way for the LORD's coming!
    Clear the road for him!'*"

⁴This messenger was John the Baptist. He was in the wilderness and preached that people should be baptized to show that they had repented of their sins and turned to God to be forgiven. ⁵All of Judea, including all the people of Jerusalem, went out to see and hear John. And when they confessed their sins, he baptized them in the Jordan River. ⁶His clothes were woven from coarse camel hair, and he wore a leather belt around his waist. For food he ate locusts and wild honey.

⁷John announced: "Someone is coming soon who is greater than I am—so much greater that I'm not even worthy to stoop down like a slave and untie the straps of his sandals. ⁸I baptize you with* water, but he will baptize you with the Holy Spirit!"

The Baptism and Temptation of Jesus

⁹One day Jesus came from Nazareth in Galilee, and John baptized him in the Jordan River. ¹⁰As Jesus came up out of the water, he saw the heavens splitting apart and the Holy Spirit descending on him* like a dove. ¹¹And a voice from heaven said, "You are my dearly loved Son, and you bring me great joy."

1:1 Some manuscripts do not include *the Son of God.*   1:2 Mal 3:1.   1:3 Isa 40:3 (Greek version).
1:8 Or *in;* also in 1:8b.   1:10 Or *toward him,* or *into him.*

Anchor Passage

PASSAGE: **Mark 2:1-12**

FRIENDSHIP TYPE: *Friends*   FRIENDSHIP LAYER: *Trust*

Through the Roof

Read **Mark 2:1-12**.

This story presents a powerful example of trust strengthening friendship…and transforming a life. The paralyzed man's friends weren't content to say nice things to him and wait passively in the hope that he got better. They took action—by putting their friend on a mat, digging a hole in the roof, and literally dropping their friend at Jesus' feet. No, really. Down *through the roof*.

And the paralyzed man trusted his friends enough to go along for the ride. He trusted them with his safety and his very life. How easy it would've been to say the practical thing, something along the lines of "No, that's OK, guys. Let's wait and maybe see Jesus on his way out." Instead, the paralyzed man risked embarrassment, let down his guard, and trusted his close friends to bring him before Jesus.

You see, his friends trusted Jesus. They believed Jesus could heal their friend, and they took action. Jesus saw their trust, and he told the paralyzed man to get up and walk home.

Their story shows us the power of trust—to heal, bring forgiveness, and deepen friendships. Trust isn't just an ideal; it's a *necessary* part of friendship. It causes friendship to grow and thrive. How can you put into action your trust for a friend? And how will your trust in *Jesus* transform a life— your own or a friend's?

Anchor Passage *continues on page 69…*

[12] The Spirit then compelled Jesus to go into the wilderness, [13] where he was tempted by Satan for forty days. He was out among the wild animals, and angels took care of him.

[14] Later on, after John was arrested, Jesus went into Galilee, where he preached God's Good News.* [15] "The time promised by God has come at last!" he announced. "The Kingdom of God is near! Repent of your sins and believe the Good News!"

The First Disciples

[16] One day as Jesus was walking along the shore of the Sea of Galilee, he saw Simon* and his brother Andrew throwing a net into the water, for they fished for a living. [17] Jesus called out to them, "Come, follow me, and I will show you how to fish for people!" [18] And they left their nets at once and followed him.

[19] A little farther up the shore Jesus saw Zebedee's sons, James and John, in a boat repairing their nets. [20] He called them at once, and they also followed him, leaving their father, Zebedee, in the boat with the hired men.

Jesus Casts Out an Evil Spirit

[21] Jesus and his companions went to the town of Capernaum. When the Sabbath day came, he went into the synagogue and began to teach. [22] The people were amazed at his teaching, for he taught with real authority—quite unlike the teachers of religious law.

[23] Suddenly, a man in the synagogue who was possessed by an evil* spirit began shouting, [24] "Why are you interfering with us, Jesus of Nazareth? Have you come to destroy us? I know who you are—the Holy One sent from God!"

[25] Jesus cut him short. "Be quiet! Come out of the man," he ordered. [26] At that, the evil spirit screamed, threw the man into a convulsion, and then came out of him.

[27] Amazement gripped the audience, and they began to discuss what had happened. "What sort of new teaching is this?" they asked excitedly. "It has such authority! Even evil spirits obey his orders!" [28] The news about Jesus spread quickly throughout the entire region of Galilee.

Jesus Heals Many People

[29] After Jesus left the synagogue with James and John, they went to Simon and Andrew's home. [30] Now Simon's mother-in-law was sick in bed with a high fever. They told Jesus about her right away. [31] So he went to her bedside, took her by the hand, and

1:14 Some manuscripts read *the Good News of the Kingdom of God.*   **1:16** *Simon* is called "Peter" in 3:16 and thereafter.   **1:23** Greek *unclean;* also in 1:26, 27.

helped her sit up. Then the fever left her, and she prepared a meal for them.

³²That evening after sunset, many sick and demon-possessed people were brought to Jesus. ³³The whole town gathered at the door to watch. ³⁴So Jesus healed many people who were sick with various diseases, and he cast out many demons. But because the demons knew who he was, he did not allow them to speak.

Jesus Preaches in Galilee

³⁵Before daybreak the next morning, Jesus got up and went out to an isolated place to pray. ³⁶Later Simon and the others went out to find him. ³⁷When they found him, they said, "Everyone is looking for you."

³⁸But Jesus replied, "We must go on to other towns as well, and I will preach to them, too. That is why I came." ³⁹So he traveled throughout the region of Galilee, preaching in the synagogues and casting out demons.

Jesus Heals a Man with Leprosy

⁴⁰A man with leprosy came and knelt in front of Jesus, begging to be healed. "If you are willing, you can heal me and make me clean," he said.

⁴¹Moved with compassion,* Jesus reached out and touched him. "I am willing," he said. "Be healed!" ⁴²Instantly the leprosy disappeared, and the man was healed. ⁴³Then Jesus sent him on his way with a stern warning: ⁴⁴"Don't tell anyone about this. Instead, go to the priest and let him examine you. Take along the offering required in the law of Moses for those who have been healed of leprosy.* This will be a public testimony that you have been cleansed."

⁴⁵But the man went and spread the word, proclaiming to everyone what had happened. As a result, large crowds soon surrounded Jesus, and he couldn't publicly enter a town anywhere. He had to stay out in the secluded places, but people from everywhere kept coming to him.

CHAPTER 2

Jesus Heals a Paralyzed Man

When Jesus returned to Capernaum several days later, the news spread quickly that he was back home. ²Soon the house where he was staying was so packed

1:41 Some manuscripts read *Moved with anger.*   1:44 See Lev 14:2-32.

Anchor Passage continued from page 68...

THE ONE THING 1 YOU CAN DO THIS WEEK

Experience

Grab a rubber band, and start stretching it as far as you can. Trusting a friend is a bit like stretching this rubber band. Trust will make your friendship grow and stretch. But trust is also a little risky. The rubber band could break. A friend could break your trust. There is risk in trust, but there is also great reward.

Think of something you'll do to build trust and stretch your friendship. Plan a weekend camping trip or other excursion together; ask the friend to teach you a sport or activity he or she is good at, something that intimidates you to learn; or take a friend to dinner and ask some important questions—digging-through-the-roof kinds of questions. Whatever you do, take the friendship to a new level of trust…and get ready to grow even closer!

Reflect

★ When have you been "paralyzed" due to a lack of trust?

★ Do you know someone who is "on the mat" and needs a trustworthy friend? How can you be that friend?

DIGGING DEEPER

FRIENDSHIP TYPE: *Friends*   FRIENDSHIP LAYER: *Trust*

For building trust with friends, check out…

➡ The Friendship Experience .... on page 83
➡ The Friendship Story .... on page 394
➡ What to Say and What Not to Say .... on page 397

JOURNAL

with visitors that there was no more room, even outside the door. While he was preaching God's word to them, ³four men arrived carrying a paralyzed man on a mat. ⁴They couldn't bring him to Jesus because of the crowd, so they dug a hole through the roof above his head. Then they lowered the man on his mat, right down in front of Jesus. ⁵Seeing their faith, Jesus said to the paralyzed man, "My child, your sins are forgiven."

⁶But some of the teachers of religious law who were sitting there thought to themselves, ⁷"What is he saying? This is blasphemy! Only God can forgive sins!"

⁸Jesus knew immediately what they were thinking, so he asked them, "Why do you question this in your hearts? ⁹Is it easier to say to the paralyzed man 'Your sins are forgiven,' or 'Stand up, pick up your mat, and walk'? ¹⁰So I will prove to you that the Son of Man* has the authority on earth to forgive sins." Then Jesus turned to the paralyzed man and said, ¹¹"Stand up, pick up your mat, and go home!"

¹²And the man jumped up, grabbed his mat, and walked out through the stunned onlookers. They were all amazed and praised God, exclaiming, "We've never seen anything like this before!" ⚓

Jesus Calls Levi (Matthew)

¹³Then Jesus went out to the lakeshore again and taught the crowds that were coming to him. ¹⁴As he walked along, he saw Levi son of Alphaeus sitting at his tax collector's booth. "Follow me and be my disciple," Jesus said to him. So Levi got up and followed him.

¹⁵Later, Levi invited Jesus and his disciples to his home as dinner guests, along with many tax collectors and other disreputable sinners. (There were many people of this kind among Jesus' followers.) ¹⁶But when the teachers of religious law who were Pharisees* saw him eating with tax collectors and other

2:10 "Son of Man" is a title Jesus used for himself.   **2:16a** Greek *the scribes of the Pharisees.*

sinners, they asked his disciples, "Why does he eat with such scum?*"

¹⁷When Jesus heard this, he told them, "Healthy people don't need a doctor—sick people do. I have come to call not those who think they are righteous, but those who know they are sinners." ⚓

A Discussion about Fasting

¹⁸Once when John's disciples and the Pharisees were fasting, some people came to Jesus and asked, "Why don't your disciples fast like John's disciples and the Pharisees do?"

¹⁹Jesus replied, "Do wedding guests fast while celebrating with the groom? Of course not. They can't fast while the groom is with them. ²⁰But someday the groom will be taken away from them, and then they will fast.

²¹"Besides, who would patch old clothing with new cloth? For the new patch would shrink and rip away from the old cloth, leaving an even bigger tear than before.

²²"And no one puts new wine into old wineskins. For the wine would burst the wineskins, and the wine and the skins would both be lost. New wine calls for new wineskins."

A Discussion about the Sabbath

²³One Sabbath day as Jesus was walking through some grainfields, his disciples began breaking off heads of grain to eat. ²⁴But the Pharisees said to Jesus, "Look, why are they breaking the law by harvesting grain on the Sabbath?"

²⁵Jesus said to them, "Haven't you ever read in the Scriptures what David did when he and his companions were hungry? ²⁶He went into the house of God (during the days when Abiathar was high priest) and broke the law by eating the sacred loaves of bread that only the priests are allowed to eat. He also gave some to his companions."

²⁷Then Jesus said to them, "The Sabbath was made to meet the needs of people, and not people to meet the requirements of the Sabbath. ²⁸So the Son of Man is Lord, even over the Sabbath!"

CHAPTER **3**

Jesus Heals on the Sabbath

Jesus went into the synagogue again and noticed a man with a deformed hand. ²Since it was the Sabbath, Jesus' enemies

2:16b Greek *with tax collectors and sinners?*

Anchor Passage

PASSAGE: Mark 2:13-17

FRIENDSHIP TYPE: *Friends*   FRIENDSHIP LAYER: *Acceptance*

Improved by Differences

He wants to go out for sushi; the rest of you were thinking hamburgers.

She's talking politics, and you're disagreeing with every word she says.

He wants you to go fishing; you want him to stay and watch the game.

Do you have any friends who are different from you? *really* different?

Read **Mark 2:13-17**.

Sure, we all have friends who are just like us. You know, the friend who always nods while you talk, the friend whose hobbies you enjoy, the friend who has all the same problems as you…the friend who it's so easy to be friends with.

But most of us also have that friend who's a little different. You know, the friend who challenges all your opinions, the friend whose hobbies don't appeal to you, the friend whose perspective and background are so different from yours.

Those friends can be frustrating—but also wonderful. They add a new perspective to your life. They change and grow you in ways other friends can't. They help you see things differently…and even *experience* things differently.

Anchor Passage continues on page 72…

Anchor Passage continued from page 71...

The thing is, though, you'll never have a friend like that until you learn to look past the differences and accept that friend just as he or she is.

When Jesus encountered Levi, he didn't make assumptions about Levi just because Levi was a tax collector. Jesus didn't just walk on by and never consider Levi as a potential friend. Jesus stopped. And Jesus accepted Levi as his friend—"issues" and all.

Experience

Write down ways your friends are different from you: political views, spiritual beliefs, hobbies, backgrounds.

Now write down ways your life is enhanced by knowing these friends.

In the next month, throw a party for your friends, just as Levi threw a party for Jesus. Start planning it this week, and invite *all* your friends so you can celebrate your friendships together!

Reflect

★ Thinking of the friend who is most different from you, what lessons have you learned from that friend?

★ What differences have you come to appreciate most in your friends?

★ What differences do you still need to accept? How can you do that?

Anchor Passage continues on page 73...

watched him closely. If he healed the man's hand, they planned to accuse him of working on the Sabbath.

³Jesus said to the man with the deformed hand, "Come and stand in front of everyone." ⁴Then he turned to his critics and asked, "Does the law permit good deeds on the Sabbath, or is it a day for doing evil? Is this a day to save life or to destroy it?" But they wouldn't answer him.

⁵He looked around at them angrily and was deeply saddened by their hard hearts. Then he said to the man, "Hold out your hand." So the man held out his hand, and it was restored! ⁶At once the Pharisees went away and met with the supporters of Herod to plot how to kill Jesus.

Crowds Follow Jesus

⁷Jesus went out to the lake with his disciples, and a large crowd followed him. They came from all over Galilee, Judea, ⁸Jerusalem, Idumea, from east of the Jordan River, and even from as far north as Tyre and Sidon. The news about his miracles had spread far and wide, and vast numbers of people came to see him.

⁹Jesus instructed his disciples to have a boat ready so the crowd would not crush him. ¹⁰He had healed many people that day, so all the sick people eagerly pushed forward to touch him. ¹¹And whenever those possessed by evil* spirits caught sight of him, the spirits would throw them to the ground in front of him shrieking, "You are the Son of God!" ¹²But Jesus sternly commanded the spirits not to reveal who he was.

Jesus Chooses the Twelve Apostles

¹³Afterward Jesus went up on a mountain and called out the ones he wanted to go with him. And they came to him. ¹⁴Then he appointed twelve of them and called them his apostles.* They were to accompany him, and he would send them out to preach, ¹⁵giving them authority to cast out demons. ¹⁶These are the twelve he chose:

Simon (whom he named Peter),
¹⁷ James and John (the sons of Zebedee, but Jesus nicknamed them "Sons of Thunder"*),
¹⁸ Andrew,
Philip,
Bartholomew,
Matthew,
Thomas,

3:11 Greek *unclean;* also in 3:30.   **3:14** Some manuscripts do not include *and called them his apostles.*
3:17 Greek *whom he named Boanerges, which means Sons of Thunder.*

James (son of Alphaeus),
Thaddaeus,
Simon (the zealot*),
19 Judas Iscariot (who later betrayed him).

Jesus and the Prince of Demons

20 One time Jesus entered a house, and the crowds began to gather again. Soon he and his disciples couldn't even find time to eat. 21 When his family heard what was happening, they tried to take him away. "He's out of his mind," they said.

22 But the teachers of religious law who had arrived from Jerusalem said, "He's possessed by Satan,* the prince of demons. That's where he gets the power to cast out demons."

23 Jesus called them over and responded with an illustration. "How can Satan cast out Satan?" he asked. 24 "A kingdom divided by civil war will collapse. 25 Similarly, a family splintered by feuding will fall apart. 26 And if Satan is divided and fights against himself, how can he stand? He would never survive. 27 Let me illustrate this further. Who is powerful enough to enter the house of a strong man like Satan and plunder his goods? Only someone even stronger—someone who could tie him up and then plunder his house.

28 "I tell you the truth, all sin and blasphemy can be forgiven, 29 but anyone who blasphemes the Holy Spirit will never be forgiven. This is a sin with eternal consequences." 30 He told them this because they were saying, "He's possessed by an evil spirit."

The True Family of Jesus

31 Then Jesus' mother and brothers came to see him. They stood outside and sent word for him to come out and talk with them. 32 There was a crowd sitting around Jesus, and someone said, "Your mother and your brothers* are outside asking for you."

33 Jesus replied, "Who is my mother? Who are my brothers?" 34 Then he looked at those around him and said, "Look, these are my mother and brothers. 35 Anyone who does God's will is my brother and sister and mother."

CHAPTER 4

Parable of the Farmer Scattering Seed

Once again Jesus began teaching by the lakeshore. A very large crowd soon gathered around him, so he got into a boat. Then he sat in the boat while all the people remained on the shore.

3:18 Greek *the Cananean,* an Aramaic term for Jewish nationalists.   3:22 Greek *Beelzeboul;* other manuscripts read *Beezeboul;* Latin version reads *Beelzebub.*   3:32 Some manuscripts add *and sisters.*

Anchor Passage continued from page 72...

DIGGING DEEPER

FRIENDSHIP TYPE:
Friends

FRIENDSHIP LAYER:
Acceptance

For accepting your friends, check out...

➡ The Friendship Experience .... on page 95
➡ The Friendship Story .... on page 79
➡ What to Say and What Not to Say .... on page 340

JOURNAL

JOURNAL

²He taught them by telling many stories in the form of parables, such as this one:

³"Listen! A farmer went out to plant some seed. ⁴As he scattered it across his field, some of the seed fell on a footpath, and the birds came and ate it. ⁵Other seed fell on shallow soil with underlying rock. The seed sprouted quickly because the soil was shallow. ⁶But the plant soon wilted under the hot sun, and since it didn't have deep roots, it died. ⁷Other seed fell among thorns that grew up and choked out the tender plants so they produced no grain. ⁸Still other seeds fell on fertile soil, and they sprouted, grew, and produced a crop that was thirty, sixty, and even a hundred times as much as had been planted!" ⁹Then he said, "Anyone with ears to hear should listen and understand."

¹⁰Later, when Jesus was alone with the twelve disciples and with the others who were gathered around, they asked him what the parables meant.

¹¹He replied, "You are permitted to understand the secret* of the Kingdom of God. But I use parables for everything I say to outsiders, ¹²so that the Scriptures might be fulfilled:

"When they see what I do,
    they will learn nothing.
When they hear what I say,
    they will not understand.
Otherwise, they will turn to me
    and be forgiven.'*"

¹³Then Jesus said to them, "If you can't understand the meaning of this parable, how will you understand all the other parables? ¹⁴The farmer plants seed by taking God's word to others. ¹⁵The seed that fell on the footpath represents those who hear the message, only to have Satan come at once and take it away. ¹⁶The seed on the rocky soil represents those who hear the message and immediately receive it with joy. ¹⁷But since they don't have deep roots, they don't last long. They fall away as soon as they have problems or are persecuted for believing God's word. ¹⁸The seed that fell among the thorns represents others who hear God's word, ¹⁹but all too quickly the message is crowded out by the worries of this life, the lure of wealth, and the desire for other things, so no fruit is produced. ²⁰And the seed that fell on good soil represents those who hear and accept God's word and produce a harvest of thirty, sixty, or even a hundred times as much as had been planted!"

4:11 Greek *mystery.*   4:12 Isa 6:9-10 (Greek version).

Parable of the Lamp

²¹Then Jesus asked them, "Would anyone light a lamp and then put it under a basket or under a bed? Of course not! A lamp is placed on a stand, where its light will shine. ²²For everything that is hidden will eventually be brought into the open, and every secret will be brought to light. ²³Anyone with ears to hear should listen and understand."

²⁴Then he added, "Pay close attention to what you hear. The closer you listen, the more understanding you will be given*— and you will receive even more. ²⁵To those who listen to my teaching, more understanding will be given. But for those who are not listening, even what little understanding they have will be taken away from them."

Parable of the Growing Seed

²⁶Jesus also said, "The Kingdom of God is like a farmer who scatters seed on the ground. ²⁷Night and day, while he's asleep or awake, the seed sprouts and grows, but he does not understand how it happens. ²⁸The earth produces the crops on its own. First a leaf blade pushes through, then the heads of wheat are formed, and finally the grain ripens. ²⁹And as soon as the grain is ready, the farmer comes and harvests it with a sickle, for the harvest time has come."

Parable of the Mustard Seed

³⁰Jesus said, "How can I describe the Kingdom of God? What story should I use to illustrate it? ³¹It is like a mustard seed planted in the ground. It is the smallest of all seeds, ³²but it becomes the largest of all garden plants; it grows long branches, and birds can make nests in its shade."

³³Jesus used many similar stories and illustrations to teach the people as much as they could understand. ³⁴In fact, in his public ministry he never taught without using parables; but afterward, when he was alone with his disciples, he explained everything to them.

Jesus Calms the Storm

³⁵As evening came, Jesus said to his disciples, "Let's cross to the other side of the lake." ³⁶So they took Jesus in the boat and started out, leaving the crowds behind (although other boats followed). ³⁷But soon a fierce storm came up. High waves were breaking into the boat, and it began to fill with water.

³⁸Jesus was sleeping at the back of the boat with his head

4:24 Or *The measure you give will be the measure you get back.*

FRIENDSHIP EXPERIENCE

FRIENDSHIP TYPE: *Jesus*　　　FRIENDSHIP LAYER: *Deepening*

Keeping It Real

It's easy to make friendship *sound* real. All you have to do is say the right things: "We should get together and do lunch sometime," "I'll be praying for you," "Anytime you need me, just call." You say things like this all the time, and perhaps you even mean them. But do you follow through? Do you make them real?

Peter knew what to say: "Even if everyone else deserts you, I never will" (**Mark 14:29**). But when it came down to it, Peter didn't follow through. Friendship based on nice words and no action is shallow and unsatisfying.

Moving beyond shallow friendship to deep friendship means consistently acting on the promises you make.

FRIENDSHIP EXPERIENCE *continues on page 76…*

FRIENDSHIP EXPERIENCE *continued from page 75...*

Experience

★ THE ONE THING ★
1
★ YOU CAN DO THIS WEEK ★

Keep a record of the promises you make to people. Make a chart in a notebook with these four headings: Friend, Promise Made, Date of Promise, My Follow-Through.

Each day write down the promises you made to others. To remember, you may want to carry this chart with you so you can write your promises down at the time. So if you say something about "doing lunch sometime," following through means setting up a specific time and being there!

Remember, making a promise and following through is a way to deepen your friendship with Jesus, too. Do you say to Jesus, "I'll spend more time with you next week" or "Sure, I'd really like to do something for the poor in my community...maybe next year"? If so, do you follow through with what you say? Include Jesus as one of the friends on your chart. Check out how you do with promises made to him.

Reflect

★ How did charting the promises you made affect your awareness of those promises? How do you think it affected your follow-through?

★ How has following through with promises deepened your friendships—with people and with Jesus?

on a cushion. The disciples woke him up, shouting, "Teacher, don't you care that we're going to drown?"

³⁹When Jesus woke up, he rebuked the wind and said to the waves, "Silence! Be still!" Suddenly the wind stopped, and there was a great calm. ⁴⁰Then he asked them, "Why are you afraid? Do you still have no faith?"

⁴¹The disciples were absolutely terrified. "Who is this man?" they asked each other. "Even the wind and waves obey him!"

CHAPTER **5**

Jesus Heals a Demon-Possessed Man

So they arrived at the other side of the lake, in the region of the Gerasenes.* ²When Jesus climbed out of the boat, a man possessed by an evil* spirit came out from a cemetery to meet him. ³This man lived among the burial caves and could no longer be restrained, even with a chain. ⁴Whenever he was put into chains and shackles—as he often was—he snapped the chains from his wrists and smashed the shackles. No one was strong enough to subdue him. ⁵Day and night he wandered among the burial caves and in the hills, howling and cutting himself with sharp stones.

⁶When Jesus was still some distance away, the man saw him, ran to meet him, and bowed low before him. ⁷With a shriek, he screamed, "Why are you interfering with me, Jesus, Son of the Most High God? In the name of God, I beg you, don't torture me!" ⁸For Jesus had already said to the spirit, "Come out of the man, you evil spirit."

⁹Then Jesus demanded, "What is your name?"

And he replied, "My name is Legion, because there are many of us inside this man." ¹⁰Then the evil spirits begged him again and again not to send them to some distant place.

¹¹There happened to be a large herd of pigs feeding on the hillside nearby. ¹²"Send us into those pigs," the spirits begged. "Let us enter them."

¹³So Jesus gave them permission. The evil spirits came out of the man and entered the pigs, and the entire herd of 2,000 pigs plunged down the steep hillside into the lake and drowned in the water.

¹⁴The herdsmen fled to the nearby town and the surrounding countryside, spreading the news as they ran. People rushed out to see what had happened. ¹⁵A crowd soon gathered around

5:1 Other manuscripts read *Gadarenes;* still others read *Gergesenes.* See Matt 8:28; Luke 8:26.
5:2 Greek *unclean;* also in 5:8, 13.

Jesus, and they saw the man who had been possessed by the legion of demons. He was sitting there fully clothed and perfectly sane, and they were all afraid. [16] Then those who had seen what happened told the others about the demon-possessed man and the pigs. [17] And the crowd began pleading with Jesus to go away and leave them alone.

[18] As Jesus was getting into the boat, the man who had been demon possessed begged to go with him. [19] But Jesus said, "No, go home to your family, and tell them everything the Lord has done for you and how merciful he has been." [20] So the man started off to visit the Ten Towns* of that region and began to proclaim the great things Jesus had done for him; and everyone was amazed at what he told them.

Jesus Heals in Response to Faith

[21] Jesus got into the boat again and went back to the other side of the lake, where a large crowd gathered around him on the shore. [22] Then a leader of the local synagogue, whose name was Jairus, arrived. When he saw Jesus, he fell at his feet, [23] pleading fervently with him. "My little daughter is dying," he said. "Please come and lay your hands on her; heal her so she can live."

[24] Jesus went with him, and all the people followed, crowding around him. [25] A woman in the crowd had suffered for twelve years with constant bleeding. [26] She had suffered a great deal from many doctors, and over the years she had spent everything she had to pay them, but she had gotten no better. In fact, she had gotten worse. [27] She had heard about Jesus, so she came up behind him through the crowd and touched his robe. [28] For she thought to herself, "If I can just touch his robe, I will be healed." [29] Immediately the bleeding stopped, and she could feel in her body that she had been healed of her terrible condition.

[30] Jesus realized at once that healing power had gone out from him, so he turned around in the crowd and asked, "Who touched my robe?"

[31] His disciples said to him, "Look at this crowd pressing around you. How can you ask, 'Who touched me?'"

[32] But he kept on looking around to see who had done it. [33] Then the frightened woman, trembling at the realization of what had happened to her, came and fell to her knees in front of him and told him what she had done. [34] And he said to her, "Daughter, your faith has made you well. Go in peace. Your suffering is over."

5:20 Greek *Decapolis*.

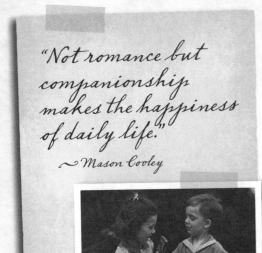

"Not romance but companionship makes the happiness of daily life."

~ Mason Cooley

JOURNAL

35 While he was still speaking to her, messengers arrived from the home of Jairus, the leader of the synagogue. They told him, "Your daughter is dead. There's no use troubling the Teacher now."

36 But Jesus overheard* them and said to Jairus, "Don't be afraid. Just have faith."

37 Then Jesus stopped the crowd and wouldn't let anyone go with him except Peter, James, and John (the brother of James). 38 When they came to the home of the synagogue leader, Jesus saw much commotion and weeping and wailing. 39 He went inside and asked, "Why all this commotion and weeping? The child isn't dead; she's only asleep."

40 The crowd laughed at him. But he made them all leave, and he took the girl's father and mother and his three disciples into the room where the girl was lying. 41 Holding her hand, he said to her, "*Talitha koum,*" which means "Little girl, get up!" 42 And the girl, who was twelve years old, immediately stood up and walked around! They were overwhelmed and totally amazed. 43 Jesus gave them strict orders not to tell anyone what had happened, and then he told them to give her something to eat.

CHAPTER **6**

Jesus Rejected at Nazareth

Jesus left that part of the country and returned with his disciples to Nazareth, his hometown. 2 The next Sabbath he began teaching in the synagogue, and many who heard him were amazed. They asked, "Where did he get all this wisdom and the power to perform such miracles?" 3 Then they scoffed, "He's just a carpenter, the son of Mary* and the brother of James, Joseph,* Judas, and Simon. And his sisters live right here among us." They were deeply offended and refused to believe in him.

4 Then Jesus told them, "A prophet is honored everywhere except in his own hometown and among his relatives and his own family." 5 And because of their unbelief, he couldn't do any miracles among them except to place his hands on a few sick people and heal them. 6 And he was amazed at their unbelief.

Jesus Sends Out the Twelve Disciples

Then Jesus went from village to village, teaching the people. 7 And he called his twelve disciples together and began sending them out two by two, giving them authority to cast out evil*

5:36 Or *ignored.*   6:3a Some manuscripts read *He's just the son of the carpenter and of Mary.*
6:3b Most manuscripts read *Joses;* see Matt 13:55.   6:7 Greek *unclean.*

spirits. [8]He told them to take nothing for their journey except a walking stick—no food, no traveler's bag, no money.* [9]He allowed them to wear sandals but not to take a change of clothes.

[10]"Wherever you go," he said, "stay in the same house until you leave town. [11]But if any place refuses to welcome you or listen to you, shake its dust from your feet as you leave to show that you have abandoned those people to their fate."

[12]So the disciples went out, telling everyone they met to repent of their sins and turn to God. [13]And they cast out many demons and healed many sick people, anointing them with olive oil.

The Death of John the Baptist

[14]Herod Antipas, the king, soon heard about Jesus, because everyone was talking about him. Some were saying,* "This must be John the Baptist raised from the dead. That is why he can do such miracles." [15]Others said, "He's the prophet Elijah." Still others said, "He's a prophet like the other great prophets of the past."

[16]When Herod heard about Jesus, he said, "John, the man I beheaded, has come back from the dead."

[17]For Herod had sent soldiers to arrest and imprison John as a favor to Herodias. She had been his brother Philip's wife, but Herod had married her. [18]John had been telling Herod, "It is against God's law for you to marry your brother's wife." [19]So Herodias bore a grudge against John and wanted to kill him. But without Herod's approval she was powerless, [20]for Herod respected John; and knowing that he was a good and holy man, he protected him. Herod was greatly disturbed whenever he talked with John, but even so, he liked to listen to him.

[21]Herodias's chance finally came on Herod's birthday. He gave a party for his high government officials, army officers, and the leading citizens of Galilee. [22]Then his daughter, also named Herodias,* came in and performed a dance that greatly pleased Herod and his guests. "Ask me for anything you like," the king said to the girl, "and I will give it to you." [23]He even vowed, "I will give you whatever you ask, up to half my kingdom!"

[24]She went out and asked her mother, "What should I ask for?"

Her mother told her, "Ask for the head of John the Baptist!"

[25]So the girl hurried back to the king and told him, "I want the head of John the Baptist, right now, on a tray!"

6:8 Greek *no copper coins in their money belts.* 6:14 Some manuscripts read *He was saying.*
6:22 Some manuscripts read *the daughter of Herodias herself.*

FRIENDSHIP STORY

No. 04-FS-079

FRIENDSHIP TYPE:	FRIENDSHIP LAYER:
Friends	*Acceptance*

FOUND IN SCRIPTURE

Forced Friendship

We've all heard them, those stories and jokes concerning the *awful, dreaded* mother-in-law.

Ruth had probably heard some of those stories, too. And, more than likely, she was a little worried when she first met her husband's mother. After all, this woman was from a different country, had a different background, worshipped a different God. Ruth probably figured that her mother-in-law would shun her—or worse.

But that wasn't the case. Against all expectations, Ruth's mother-in-law, Naomi, chose to accept her foreign daughter-in-law…and love her.

It likely wasn't easy for Naomi to accept Ruth. Probably, she had wished for her son to marry an Israelite woman who had the same background and beliefs as Naomi. But instead of obsessing about it or longing for what could have been, Naomi chose to accept the foreign woman as part of the family.

And she must have done a good job. Because 10 years later, when Naomi's son died, her daughter-in-law wanted nothing more than to follow Naomi back to her homeland of Judah.

Though they were very different, Ruth and Naomi accepted one another and had a friendship that lasted for years…and it's because of their friendship that Ruth came to know and love God.

FRIENDSHIP STORY *continues on page 80…*

Friendship First NEW TESTAMENT

FRIENDSHIP STORY *continued from page 79...*

It was an epic friendship—a friendship that changed the course of history. Because in the land of Judah, Ruth married a relative of Naomi's and began a family of her own. And from her family came the line of King David and Jesus.

Read the whole story of Ruth and Naomi in the Old Testament book of Ruth.

Experience

Get deeper with a friend who's different from you. Talk about your backgrounds. How are your backgrounds alike or different? Discuss how your backgrounds have shaped you into the people you are now. How do your different backgrounds make your experiences together more interesting?

THE ONE THING **1** YOU CAN DO THIS WEEK

Reflect

★ Is it hard for you to accept people from a different culture or background? Why or why not?

★ How have friendships with different people enriched your life?

★ **Romans 15:7** says, "Therefore, accept each other just as Christ has accepted you so that God will be given glory." Why is God glorified when we accept those who are very different from us?

²⁶Then the king deeply regretted what he had said; but because of the vows he had made in front of his guests, he couldn't refuse her. ²⁷So he immediately sent an executioner to the prison to cut off John's head and bring it to him. The soldier beheaded John in the prison, ²⁸brought his head on a tray, and gave it to the girl, who took it to her mother. ²⁹When John's disciples heard what had happened, they came to get his body and buried it in a tomb.

Jesus Feeds Five Thousand

³⁰The apostles returned to Jesus from their ministry tour and told him all they had done and taught. ³¹Then Jesus said, "Let's go off by ourselves to a quiet place and rest awhile." He said this because there were so many people coming and going that Jesus and his apostles didn't even have time to eat.

³²So they left by boat for a quiet place, where they could be alone. ³³But many people recognized them and saw them leaving, and people from many towns ran ahead along the shore and got there ahead of them. ³⁴Jesus saw the huge crowd as he stepped from the boat, and he had compassion on them because they were like sheep without a shepherd. So he began teaching them many things.

³⁵Late in the afternoon his disciples came to him and said, "This is a remote place, and it's already getting late. ³⁶Send the crowds away so they can go to the nearby farms and villages and buy something to eat."

³⁷But Jesus said, "You feed them."

"With what?" they asked. "We'd have to work for months to earn enough money* to buy food for all these people!"

³⁸"How much bread do you have?" he asked. "Go and find out."

They came back and reported, "We have five loaves of bread and two fish."

³⁹Then Jesus told the disciples to have the people sit down in groups on the green grass. ⁴⁰So they sat down in groups of fifty or a hundred.

⁴¹Jesus took the five loaves and two fish, looked up toward heaven, and blessed them. Then, breaking the loaves into pieces, he kept giving the bread to the disciples so they could distribute it to the people. He also divided the fish for everyone to share. ⁴²They all ate as much as they wanted, ⁴³and afterward, the disciples picked up twelve baskets of leftover bread and fish. ⁴⁴A total of 5,000 men and their families were fed from those loaves!

6:37 Greek *It would take 200 denarii.* A denarius was equivalent to a laborer's full day's wage.

Jesus Walks on Water

⁴⁵Immediately after this, Jesus insisted that his disciples get back into the boat and head across the lake to Bethsaida, while he sent the people home. ⁴⁶After telling everyone good-bye, he went up into the hills by himself to pray.

⁴⁷Late that night, the disciples were in their boat in the middle of the lake, and Jesus was alone on land. ⁴⁸He saw that they were in serious trouble, rowing hard and struggling against the wind and waves. About three o'clock in the morning* Jesus came toward them, walking on the water. He intended to go past them, ⁴⁹but when they saw him walking on the water, they cried out in terror, thinking he was a ghost. ⁵⁰They were all terrified when they saw him.

But Jesus spoke to them at once. "Don't be afraid," he said. "Take courage! I am here!*" ⁵¹Then he climbed into the boat, and the wind stopped. They were totally amazed, ⁵²for they still didn't understand the significance of the miracle of the loaves. Their hearts were too hard to take it in.

⁵³After they had crossed the lake, they landed at Gennesaret. They brought the boat to shore ⁵⁴and climbed out. The people recognized Jesus at once, ⁵⁵and they ran throughout the whole area, carrying sick people on mats to wherever they heard he was. ⁵⁶Wherever he went—in villages, cities, or the countryside—they brought the sick out to the marketplaces. They begged him to let the sick touch at least the fringe of his robe, and all who touched him were healed.

CHAPTER 7

Jesus Teaches about Inner Purity

One day some Pharisees and teachers of religious law arrived from Jerusalem to see Jesus. ²They noticed that some of his disciples failed to follow the Jewish ritual of hand washing before eating. ³(The Jews, especially the Pharisees, do not eat until they have poured water over their cupped hands,* as required by their ancient traditions. ⁴Similarly, they don't eat anything from the market until they immerse their hands* in water. This is but one of many traditions they have clung to—such as their ceremonial washing of cups, pitchers, and kettles.*)

⁵So the Pharisees and teachers of religious law asked him, "Why don't your disciples follow our age-old tradition? They eat without first performing the hand-washing ceremony."

6:48 Greek *About the fourth watch of the night.*   6:50 Or *The 'I Am' is here;* Greek reads *I am.* See Exod 3:14.   7:3 Greek *have washed with the fist.*   7:4a Some manuscripts read *sprinkle themselves.* 7:4b Some manuscripts add *and dining couches.*

JOURNAL

[6]Jesus replied, "You hypocrites! Isaiah was right when he prophesied about you, for he wrote,

'These people honor me with their lips,
    but their hearts are far from me.
[7] Their worship is a farce,
    for they teach man-made ideas as commands from God.'*

[8]For you ignore God's law and substitute your own tradition."

[9]Then he said, "You skillfully sidestep God's law in order to hold on to your own tradition. [10]For instance, Moses gave you this law from God: 'Honor your father and mother,'* and 'Anyone who speaks disrespectfully of father or mother must be put to death.'* [11]But you say it is all right for people to say to their parents, 'Sorry, I can't help you. For I have vowed to give to God what I would have given to you.'* [12]In this way, you let them disregard their needy parents. [13]And so you cancel the word of God in order to hand down your own tradition. And this is only one example among many others."

[14]Then Jesus called to the crowd to come and hear. "All of you listen," he said, "and try to understand. [15]It's not what goes into your body that defiles you; you are defiled by what comes from your heart.*"

[17]Then Jesus went into a house to get away from the crowd, and his disciples asked him what he meant by the parable he had just used. [18]"Don't you understand either?" he asked. "Can't you see that the food you put into your body cannot defile you? [19]Food doesn't go into your heart, but only passes through the stomach and then goes into the sewer." (By saying this, he declared that every kind of food is acceptable in God's eyes.)

[20]And then he added, "It is what comes from inside that defiles you. [21]For from within, out of a person's heart, come evil thoughts, sexual immorality, theft, murder, [22]adultery, greed, wickedness, deceit, lustful desires, envy, slander, pride, and foolishness. [23]All these vile things come from within; they are what defile you."

The Faith of a Gentile Woman

[24]Then Jesus left Galilee and went north to the region of Tyre.* He didn't want anyone to know which house he was staying in, but he couldn't keep it a secret. [25]Right away a woman who had heard about him came and fell at his feet. Her little girl was

7:7 Isa 29:13 (Greek version).   7:10a Exod 20:12; Deut 5:16.   7:10b Exod 21:17 (Greek version); Lev 20:9 (Greek version).   7:11 Greek "What I would have given to you is Corban' (that is, a gift). 7:15 Some manuscripts add verse 16, Anyone with ears to hear should listen and understand. Compare 4:9, 23.   7:24 Some manuscripts add and Sidon.

possessed by an evil* spirit, 26and she begged him to cast out the demon from her daughter.

Since she was a Gentile, born in Syrian Phoenicia, 27Jesus told her, "First I should feed the children—my own family, the Jews.* It isn't right to take food from the children and throw it to the dogs."

28She replied, "That's true, Lord, but even the dogs under the table are allowed to eat the scraps from the children's plates."

29"Good answer!" he said. "Now go home, for the demon has left your daughter." 30And when she arrived home, she found her little girl lying quietly in bed, and the demon was gone.

Jesus Heals a Deaf Man

31Jesus left Tyre and went up to Sidon before going back to the Sea of Galilee and the region of the Ten Towns.* 32A deaf man with a speech impediment was brought to him, and the people begged Jesus to lay his hands on the man to heal him.

33Jesus led him away from the crowd so they could be alone. He put his fingers into the man's ears. Then, spitting on his own fingers, he touched the man's tongue. 34Looking up to heaven, he sighed and said, *"Ephphatha,"* which means, "Be opened!" 35Instantly the man could hear perfectly, and his tongue was freed so he could speak plainly!

36Jesus told the crowd not to tell anyone, but the more he told them not to, the more they spread the news. 37They were completely amazed and said again and again, "Everything he does is wonderful. He even makes the deaf to hear and gives speech to those who cannot speak."

CHAPTER **8**

Jesus Feeds Four Thousand

About this time another large crowd had gathered, and the people ran out of food again. Jesus called his disciples and told them, 2"I feel sorry for these people. They have been here with me for three days, and they have nothing left to eat. 3If I send them home hungry, they will faint along the way. For some of them have come a long distance."

4His disciples replied, "How are we supposed to find enough food to feed them out here in the wilderness?"

5Jesus asked, "How much bread do you have?"

"Seven loaves," they replied.

6So Jesus told all the people to sit down on the ground. Then

7:25 Greek *unclean.*   7:27 Greek *Let the children eat first.*   7:31 Greek *Decapolis.*

FRIENDSHIP EXPERIENCE

FRIENDSHIP TYPE: *Friends*   FRIENDSHIP LAYER: *trust*

The Power of Trust

The friends in **Mark 2:1-12** weren't fair-weather friends, around only when things were going well. They weren't conditional friends, reliable only when they felt like it.

They were ever-faithful, always-committed friends who believed in Jesus' power to heal their paralyzed friend. And the paralyzed man knew he could trust them—all the time, even as they dropped him through a roof.

This is the kind of "always" trust Jesus wants us to have…in him and in our friends. When one of our close friends is hurting, we should trust Jesus and help that friend heal. When *we* are hurting, we must actively trust Jesus and our close friends to support and love us. Even if it means being carried…

FRIENDSHIP EXPERIENCE *continues on page 84…*

FRIENDSHIP EXPERIENCE *continued from page 83…*

Experience

Collect items that represent trust in your friendship—for example, a coffee mug that symbolizes your weekly time together at a coffee shop, a quarter because you once trusted your friend for money, or a fishing lure that represents your annual fishing trip. Show the items to your friend, and discuss how they represent trust in your friendship.

Now find images that symbolize trust in your friendship with Jesus, such as a cross, a Bible, a clock, a list of prayer requests, or your wedding ring. Sit down in a secluded spot, and look over the images, considering how each of the images represents trust in your friendship with Jesus.

THE ONE THING YOU CAN DO THIS WEEK **1**

Reflect

★ What words come to mind when you look at your images?

★ How is trusting a friend similar to trusting Jesus? How is it different?

★ How can you be a more trustworthy friend? In what ways will you trust Jesus more?

he took the seven loaves, thanked God for them, and broke them into pieces. He gave them to his disciples, who distributed the bread to the crowd. [7]A few small fish were found, too, so Jesus also blessed these and told the disciples to distribute them.

[8]They ate as much as they wanted. Afterward, the disciples picked up seven large baskets of leftover food. [9]There were about 4,000 people in the crowd that day, and Jesus sent them home after they had eaten. [10]Immediately after this, he got into a boat with his disciples and crossed over to the region of Dalmanutha.

Pharisees Demand a Miraculous Sign

[11]When the Pharisees heard that Jesus had arrived, they came and started to argue with him. Testing him, they demanded that he show them a miraculous sign from heaven to prove his authority.

[12]When he heard this, he sighed deeply in his spirit and said, "Why do these people keep demanding a miraculous sign? I tell you the truth, I will not give this generation any such sign." [13]So he got back into the boat and left them, and he crossed to the other side of the lake.

Yeast of the Pharisees and Herod

[14]But the disciples had forgotten to bring any food. They had only one loaf of bread with them in the boat. [15]As they were crossing the lake, Jesus warned them, "Watch out! Beware of the yeast of the Pharisees and of Herod."

[16]At this they began to argue with each other because they hadn't brought any bread. [17]Jesus knew what they were saying, so he said, "Why are you arguing about having no bread? Don't you know or understand even yet? Are your hearts too hard to take it in? [18]'You have eyes—can't you see? You have ears—can't you hear?'* Don't you remember anything at all? [19]When I fed the 5,000 with five loaves of bread, how many baskets of leftovers did you pick up afterward?"

"Twelve," they said.

[20]"And when I fed the 4,000 with seven loaves, how many large baskets of leftovers did you pick up?"

"Seven," they said.

[21]"Don't you understand yet?" he asked them.

Jesus Heals a Blind Man

[22]When they arrived at Bethsaida, some people brought a blind man to Jesus, and they begged him to touch the man and heal

8:18 Jer 5:21.

him. 23 Jesus took the blind man by the hand and led him out of the village. Then, spitting on the man's eyes, he laid his hands on him and asked, "Can you see anything now?"

24 The man looked around. "Yes," he said, "I see people, but I can't see them very clearly. They look like trees walking around."

25 Then Jesus placed his hands on the man's eyes again, and his eyes were opened. His sight was completely restored, and he could see everything clearly. 26 Jesus sent him away, saying, "Don't go back into the village on your way home."

Peter's Declaration about Jesus

27 Jesus and his disciples left Galilee and went up to the villages near Caesarea Philippi. As they were walking along, he asked them, "Who do people say I am?"

28 "Well," they replied, "some say John the Baptist, some say Elijah, and others say you are one of the other prophets."

29 Then he asked them, "But who do you say I am?"

Peter replied, "You are the Messiah.*"

30 But Jesus warned them not to tell anyone about him.

Jesus Predicts His Death

31 Then Jesus began to tell them that the Son of Man* must suffer many terrible things and be rejected by the elders, the leading priests, and the teachers of religious law. He would be killed, but three days later he would rise from the dead. 32 As he talked about this openly with his disciples, Peter took him aside and began to reprimand him for saying such things.*

33 Jesus turned around and looked at his disciples, then reprimanded Peter. "Get away from me, Satan!" he said. "You are seeing things merely from a human point of view, not from God's."

34 Then, calling the crowd to join his disciples, he said, "If any of you wants to be my follower, you must turn from your selfish ways, take up your cross, and follow me. 35 If you try to hang on to your life, you will lose it. But if you give up your life for my sake and for the sake of the Good News, you will save it. 36 And what do you benefit if you gain the whole world but lose your own soul?* 37 Is anything worth more than your soul? 38 If anyone is ashamed of me and my message in these adulterous and sinful days, the Son of Man will be ashamed of that person when he returns in the glory of his Father with the holy angels."

8:29 Or the Christ. Messiah (a Hebrew term) and Christ (a Greek term) both mean "the anointed one." 8:31 "Son of Man" is a title Jesus used for himself. 8:32 Or began to correct him. 8:36 Or your self? also in 8:37.

CHAPTER 9

Jesus went on to say, "I tell you the truth, some standing here right now will not die before they see the Kingdom of God arrive in great power!"

The Transfiguration

2 Six days later Jesus took Peter, James, and John, and led them up a high mountain to be alone. As the men watched, Jesus' appearance was transformed, 3 and his clothes became dazzling white, far whiter than any earthly bleach could ever make them. 4 Then Elijah and Moses appeared and began talking with Jesus.

5 Peter exclaimed, "Rabbi, it's wonderful for us to be here! Let's make three shelters as memorials*—one for you, one for Moses, and one for Elijah." 6 He said this because he didn't really know what else to say, for they were all terrified.

7 Then a cloud overshadowed them, and a voice from the cloud said, "This is my dearly loved Son. Listen to him." 8 Suddenly, when they looked around, Moses and Elijah were gone, and they saw only Jesus with them.

9 As they went back down the mountain, he told them not to tell anyone what they had seen until the Son of Man* had risen from the dead. 10 So they kept it to themselves, but they often asked each other what he meant by "rising from the dead."

11 Then they asked him, "Why do the teachers of religious law insist that Elijah must return before the Messiah comes?*"

12 Jesus responded, "Elijah is indeed coming first to get everything ready. Yet why do the Scriptures say that the Son of Man must suffer greatly and be treated with utter contempt? 13 But I tell you, Elijah has already come, and they chose to abuse him, just as the Scriptures predicted."

Jesus Heals a Demon-Possessed Boy

14 When they returned to the other disciples, they saw a large crowd surrounding them, and some teachers of religious law were arguing with them. 15 When the crowd saw Jesus, they were overwhelmed with awe, and they ran to greet him.

16 "What is all this arguing about?" Jesus asked.

17 One of the men in the crowd spoke up and said, "Teacher, I brought my son so you could heal him. He is possessed by an evil spirit that won't let him talk. 18 And whenever this spirit seizes him, it throws him violently to the ground. Then he foams at the mouth and grinds his teeth and becomes rigid.*

9:5 Greek three tabernacles.   9:9 "Son of Man" is a title Jesus used for himself.   9:11 Greek that Elijah must come first?   9:18 Or becomes weak.

So I asked your disciples to cast out the evil spirit, but they couldn't do it."

¹⁹Jesus said to them,* "You faithless people! How long must I be with you? How long must I put up with you? Bring the boy to me."

²⁰So they brought the boy. But when the evil spirit saw Jesus, it threw the child into a violent convulsion, and he fell to the ground, writhing and foaming at the mouth.

²¹"How long has this been happening?" Jesus asked the boy's father.

He replied, "Since he was a little boy. ²²The spirit often throws him into the fire or into water, trying to kill him. Have mercy on us and help us, if you can."

²³"What do you mean, 'If I can'?" Jesus asked. "Anything is possible if a person believes."

²⁴The father instantly cried out, "I do believe, but help me overcome my unbelief!"

²⁵When Jesus saw that the crowd of onlookers was growing, he rebuked the evil* spirit. "Listen, you spirit that makes this boy unable to hear and speak," he said. "I command you to come out of this child and never enter him again!"

²⁶Then the spirit screamed and threw the boy into another violent convulsion and left him. The boy appeared to be dead. A murmur ran through the crowd as people said, "He's dead."
²⁷But Jesus took him by the hand and helped him to his feet, and he stood up.

²⁸Afterward, when Jesus was alone in the house with his disciples, they asked him, "Why couldn't we cast out that evil spirit?"

²⁹Jesus replied, "This kind can be cast out only by prayer.*"

Jesus Again Predicts His Death

³⁰Leaving that region, they traveled through Galilee. Jesus didn't want anyone to know he was there, ³¹for he wanted to spend more time with his disciples and teach them. He said to them, "The Son of Man is going to be betrayed into the hands of his enemies. He will be killed, but three days later he will rise from the dead." ³²They didn't understand what he was saying, however, and they were afraid to ask him what he meant.

The Greatest in the Kingdom

³³After they arrived at Capernaum and settled in a house, Jesus asked his disciples, "What were you discussing out on the

9:19 Or *said to his disciples.*   **9:25** Greek *unclean.*   **9:29** Some manuscripts read *by prayer and fasting.*

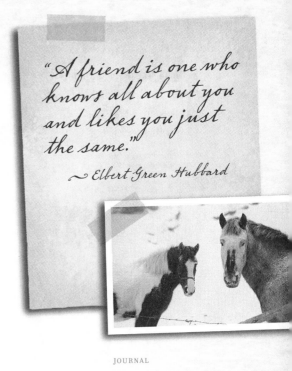

"A friend is one who knows all about you and likes you just the same."

~ Elbert Green Hubbard

JOURNAL

Among those who have a
best friend at church, 87%
say they are very satisfied
with their church.

—from "Friendship and Faith," a Gallup Research Study
Commissioned by Group Publishing, Inc.

JOURNAL

road?" ³⁴But they didn't answer, because they had been arguing about which of them was the greatest. ³⁵He sat down, called the twelve disciples over to him, and said, "Whoever wants to be first must take last place and be the servant of everyone else."

³⁶Then he put a little child among them. Taking the child in his arms, he said to them, ³⁷"Anyone who welcomes a little child like this on my behalf* welcomes me, and anyone who welcomes me welcomes not only me but also my Father who sent me."

Using the Name of Jesus
³⁸John said to Jesus, "Teacher, we saw someone using your name to cast out demons, but we told him to stop because he wasn't in our group."

³⁹"Don't stop him!" Jesus said. "No one who performs a miracle in my name will soon be able to speak evil of me. ⁴⁰Anyone who is not against us is for us. ⁴¹If anyone gives you even a cup of water because you belong to the Messiah, I tell you the truth, that person will surely be rewarded.

⁴²"But if you cause one of these little ones who trusts in me to fall into sin, it would be better for you to be thrown into the sea with a large millstone hung around your neck. ⁴³If your hand causes you to sin, cut it off. It's better to enter eternal life with only one hand than to go into the unquenchable fires of hell* with two hands.* ⁴⁵If your foot causes you to sin, cut it off. It's better to enter eternal life with only one foot than to be thrown into hell with two feet.* ⁴⁷And if your eye causes you to sin, gouge it out. It's better to enter the Kingdom of God with only one eye than to have two eyes and be thrown into hell, ⁴⁸'where the maggots never die and the fire never goes out.'*

⁴⁹"For everyone will be tested with fire.* ⁵⁰Salt is good for seasoning. But if it loses its flavor, how do you make it salty again? You must have the qualities of salt among yourselves and live in peace with each other."

CHAPTER **10**
Discussion about Divorce and Marriage
Then Jesus left Capernaum and went down to the region of Judea and into the area east of the Jordan River. Once again crowds gathered around him, and as usual he was teaching them.

9:37 Greek *in my name.* 9:43a Greek *Gehenna*; also in 9:45, 47. 9:43b Some manuscripts add verse 44, '*where the maggots never die and the fire never goes out.*' See 9:48. 9:45 Some manuscripts add verse 46, '*where the maggots never die and the fire never goes out.*' See 9:48. 9:48 Isa 66:24. 9:49 Greek *salted with fire*; other manuscripts add *and every sacrifice will be salted with salt.*

[2] Some Pharisees came and tried to trap him with this question: "Should a man be allowed to divorce his wife?"

[3] Jesus answered them with a question: "What did Moses say in the law about divorce?"

[4] "Well, he permitted it," they replied. "He said a man can give his wife a written notice of divorce and send her away."*

[5] But Jesus responded, "He wrote this commandment only as a concession to your hard hearts. [6] But 'God made them male and female'* from the beginning of creation. [7] 'This explains why a man leaves his father and mother and is joined to his wife,* [8] and the two are united into one.'* Since they are no longer two but one, [9] let no one split apart what God has joined together."

[10] Later, when he was alone with his disciples in the house, they brought up the subject again. [11] He told them, "Whoever divorces his wife and marries someone else commits adultery against her. [12] And if a woman divorces her husband and marries someone else, she commits adultery."

Jesus Blesses the Children

[13] One day some parents brought their children to Jesus so he could touch and bless them. But the disciples scolded the parents for bothering him.

[14] When Jesus saw what was happening, he was angry with his disciples. He said to them, "Let the children come to me. Don't stop them! For the Kingdom of God belongs to those who are like these children. [15] I tell you the truth, anyone who doesn't receive the Kingdom of God like a child will never enter it." [16] Then he took the children in his arms and placed his hands on their heads and blessed them.

The Rich Man

[17] As Jesus was starting out on his way to Jerusalem, a man came running up to him, knelt down, and asked, "Good Teacher, what must I do to inherit eternal life?"

[18] "Why do you call me good?" Jesus asked. "Only God is truly good. [19] But to answer your question, you know the commandments: 'You must not murder. You must not commit adultery. You must not steal. You must not testify falsely. You must not cheat anyone. Honor your father and mother.'*"

[20] "Teacher," the man replied, "I've obeyed all these commandments since I was young."

10:4 See Deut 24:1.   10:6 Gen 1:27; 5:2.   10:7 Some manuscripts do not include *and is joined to his wife*.   10:7-8 Gen 2:24.   10:19 Exod 20:12-16; Deut 5:16-20.

"How often lately have you felt compassion for people in need? Have you followed up those feelings and actually helped someone by serving them, encouraging them, visiting them, or by expressing love in some other tangible way?"

~ Bill Hybels and Mark Mittelberg

JOURNAL

21 Looking at the man, Jesus felt genuine love for him. "There is still one thing you haven't done," he told him. "Go and sell all your possessions and give the money to the poor, and you will have treasure in heaven. Then come, follow me."

22 At this the man's face fell, and he went away sad, for he had many possessions.

23 Jesus looked around and said to his disciples, "How hard it is for the rich to enter the Kingdom of God!" 24 This amazed them. But Jesus said again, "Dear children, it is very hard* to enter the Kingdom of God. 25 In fact, it is easier for a camel to go through the eye of a needle than for a rich person to enter the Kingdom of God!"

26 The disciples were astounded. "Then who in the world can be saved?" they asked.

27 Jesus looked at them intently and said, "Humanly speaking, it is impossible. But not with God. Everything is possible with God."

28 Then Peter began to speak up. "We've given up everything to follow you," he said.

29 "Yes," Jesus replied, "and I assure you that everyone who has given up house or brothers or sisters or mother or father or children or property, for my sake and for the Good News, 30 will receive now in return a hundred times as many houses, brothers, sisters, mothers, children, and property—along with persecution. And in the world to come that person will have eternal life. 31 But many who are the greatest now will be least important then, and those who seem least important now will be the greatest then.*"

Jesus Again Predicts His Death

32 They were now on the way up to Jerusalem, and Jesus was walking ahead of them. The disciples were filled with awe, and the people following behind were overwhelmed with fear. Taking the twelve disciples aside, Jesus once more began to describe everything that was about to happen to him. 33 "Listen," he said, "we're going up to Jerusalem, where the Son of Man* will be betrayed to the leading priests and the teachers of religious law. They will sentence him to die and hand him over to the Romans.* 34 They will mock him, spit on him, flog him with a whip, and kill him, but after three days he will rise again."

10:24 Some manuscripts read *very hard for those who trust in riches.*   10:31 Greek *But many who are first will be last; and the last, first.*   10:33a "Son of Man" is a title Jesus used for himself. 10:33b Greek *the Gentiles.*

Jesus Teaches about Serving Others

35 Then James and John, the sons of Zebedee, came over and spoke to him. "Teacher," they said, "we want you to do us a favor."

36 "What is your request?" he asked.

37 They replied, "When you sit on your glorious throne, we want to sit in places of honor next to you, one on your right and the other on your left."

38 But Jesus said to them, "You don't know what you are asking! Are you able to drink from the bitter cup of suffering I am about to drink? Are you able to be baptized with the baptism of suffering I must be baptized with?"

39 "Oh yes," they replied, "we are able!"

Then Jesus told them, "You will indeed drink from my bitter cup and be baptized with my baptism of suffering. 40 But I have no right to say who will sit on my right or my left. God has prepared those places for the ones he has chosen."

41 When the ten other disciples heard what James and John had asked, they were indignant. 42 So Jesus called them together and said, "You know that the rulers in this world lord it over their people, and officials flaunt their authority over those under them. 43 But among you it will be different. Whoever wants to be a leader among you must be your servant, 44 and whoever wants to be first among you must be the slave of everyone else. 45 For even the Son of Man came not to be served but to serve others and to give his life as a ransom for many."

Jesus Heals Blind Bartimaeus

46 Then they reached Jericho, and as Jesus and his disciples left town, a large crowd followed him. A blind beggar named Bartimaeus (son of Timaeus) was sitting beside the road. 47 When Bartimaeus heard that Jesus of Nazareth was nearby, he began to shout, "Jesus, Son of David, have mercy on me!"

48 "Be quiet!" many of the people yelled at him.

But he only shouted louder, "Son of David, have mercy on me!"

49 When Jesus heard him, he stopped and said, "Tell him to come here."

So they called the blind man. "Cheer up," they said. "Come on, he's calling you!" 50 Bartimaeus threw aside his coat, jumped up, and came to Jesus.

51 "What do you want me to do for you?" Jesus asked.

WHAT TO SAY
AND
WHAT NOT TO SAY

FRIENDSHIP TYPE: *Jesus*　　　FRIENDSHIP LAYER: *Deepening*

Words of Wisdom

As you seek to deepen your friendship with Jesus, take a cue from some people in Scripture on what not to say and what to say to Jesus…

WHAT NOT TO SAY:

★ "If this man were a prophet, he would know what kind of a woman is touching him. She's a sinner!" (a Pharisee in **Luke 7:39**). *Jesus wants you to show love and compassion to others, no matter who they are or what they've done!*

★ "Lord, first let me return home and bury my father" (a disciple in **Matthew 8:21**). *Jesus is an "action now!" kind of guy.*

★ "Look, your disciples are breaking the law by harvesting grain on the Sabbath" (the Pharisees in **Matthew 12:2**). *Jesus doesn't want his followers to be enslaved by legalism.*

★ "Teacher, we want you to show us a miraculous sign to prove your authority" (the Pharisees and teachers of the Law in **Matthew 12:38**). *Jesus doesn't want to always be proving himself.*

★ "When you sit on your glorious throne, we want to sit in places of honor next to you, one on your right and the other on your left" (James and John in **Mark 10:37**). *Jesus wants you to be more interested in serving him and others than in furthering your own ambitions.*

★ "Heaven forbid, Lord…This will never happen to you!" (Peter in **Matthew 16:22**). *Jesus wants us to follow him, not stop him.*

WHAT TO SAY AND **WHAT NOT TO SAY** *continues on page 92…*

WHAT TO SAY AND WHAT NOT TO SAY *continued from page 91…*

WHAT TO SAY:

★ "Lord…if you are willing, you can heal me and make me clean" (a leper in **Matthew 8:2**). *Jesus wants to make you whole.*

★ "You are the Messiah, the Son of the living God" (Peter in **Matthew 16:16**). *Jesus wants you to recognize who he is.*

★ "Master, you gave me five bags of silver to invest, and I have earned five more" (a servant in Jesus' parable in **Matthew 25:20**). *Jesus wants you to use what you've been given.*

★ "We've left our homes to follow you" (Peter in **Luke 18:28**). *Jesus wants us to follow him, no matter what.*

★ "I will give half my wealth to the poor, Lord, and if I have cheated people on their taxes, I will give them back four times as much!" (Zacchaeus in **Luke 19:8**). *Jesus wants to change our hearts.*

"My rabbi,*" the blind man said, "I want to see!"

⁵²And Jesus said to him, "Go, for your faith has healed you." Instantly the man could see, and he followed Jesus down the road.*

CHAPTER **11**

Jesus' Triumphant Entry

As Jesus and his disciples approached Jerusalem, they came to the towns of Bethphage and Bethany on the Mount of Olives. Jesus sent two of them on ahead. ²"Go into that village over there," he told them. "As soon as you enter it, you will see a young donkey tied there that no one has ever ridden. Untie it and bring it here. ³If anyone asks, 'What are you doing?' just say, 'The Lord needs it and will return it soon.'"

⁴The two disciples left and found the colt standing in the street, tied outside the front door. ⁵As they were untying it, some bystanders demanded, "What are you doing, untying that colt?" ⁶They said what Jesus had told them to say, and they were permitted to take it. ⁷Then they brought the colt to Jesus and threw their garments over it, and he sat on it.

⁸Many in the crowd spread their garments on the road ahead of him, and others spread leafy branches they had cut in the fields. ⁹Jesus was in the center of the procession, and the people all around him were shouting,

"Praise God!*
    Blessings on the one who comes in the name
        of the Lord!
¹⁰ Blessings on the coming Kingdom of our ancestor David!
        Praise God in highest heaven!"*

¹¹So Jesus came to Jerusalem and went into the Temple. After looking around carefully at everything, he left because it was late in the afternoon. Then he returned to Bethany with the twelve disciples.

Jesus Curses the Fig Tree

¹²The next morning as they were leaving Bethany, Jesus was hungry. ¹³He noticed a fig tree in full leaf a little way off, so he went over to see if he could find any figs. But there were only leaves because it was too early in the season for fruit. ¹⁴Then Jesus said to the tree, "May no one ever eat your fruit again!" And the disciples heard him say it.

10:51 Greek uses the Hebrew term *Rabboni.*   **10:52** Or *on the way.*   **11:9** Greek *Hosanna,* an exclamation of praise that literally means "save now"; also in 11:10.   **11:9-10** Pss 118:25-26; 148:1.

Jesus Clears the Temple

15 When they arrived back in Jerusalem, Jesus entered the Temple and began to drive out the people buying and selling animals for sacrifices. He knocked over the tables of the money changers and the chairs of those selling doves, 16 and he stopped everyone from using the Temple as a marketplace.* 17 He said to them, "The Scriptures declare, 'My Temple will be called a house of prayer for all nations,' but you have turned it into a den of thieves."*

18 When the leading priests and teachers of religious law heard what Jesus had done, they began planning how to kill him. But they were afraid of him because the people were so amazed at his teaching.

19 That evening Jesus and the disciples left* the city.

20 The next morning as they passed by the fig tree he had cursed, the disciples noticed it had withered from the roots up. 21 Peter remembered what Jesus had said to the tree on the previous day and exclaimed, "Look, Rabbi! The fig tree you cursed has withered and died!"

22 Then Jesus said to the disciples, "Have faith in God. 23 I tell you the truth, you can say to this mountain, 'May you be lifted up and thrown into the sea,' and it will happen. But you must really believe it will happen and have no doubt in your heart. 24 I tell you, you can pray for anything, and if you believe that you've received it, it will be yours. 25 But when you are praying, first forgive anyone you are holding a grudge against, so that your Father in heaven will forgive your sins, too.*"

The Authority of Jesus Challenged

27 Again they entered Jerusalem. As Jesus was walking through the Temple area, the leading priests, the teachers of religious law, and the elders came up to him. 28 They demanded, "By what authority are you doing all these things? Who gave you the right to do them?"

29 "I'll tell you by what authority I do these things if you answer one question," Jesus replied. 30 "Did John's authority to baptize come from heaven, or was it merely human? Answer me!"

31 They talked it over among themselves. "If we say it was from heaven, he will ask why we didn't believe John. 32 But do we dare say it was merely human?" For they were afraid of what

11:16 Or *from carrying merchandise through the Temple.* 11:17 Isa 56:7; Jer 7:11. 11:19 Greek *they left*; other manuscripts read *he left.* 11:25 Some manuscripts add verse 26, *But if you refuse to forgive, your Father in heaven will not forgive your sins.* Compare Matt 6:15.

the people would do, because everyone believed that John was a prophet. [33] So they finally replied, "We don't know."

And Jesus responded, "Then I won't tell you by what authority I do these things."

CHAPTER 12

Parable of the Evil Farmers

Then Jesus began teaching them with stories: "A man planted a vineyard. He built a wall around it, dug a pit for pressing out the grape juice, and built a lookout tower. Then he leased the vineyard to tenant farmers and moved to another country. [2] At the time of the grape harvest, he sent one of his servants to collect his share of the crop. [3] But the farmers grabbed the servant, beat him up, and sent him back empty-handed. [4] The owner then sent another servant, but they insulted him and beat him over the head. [5] The next servant he sent was killed. Others he sent were either beaten or killed, [6] until there was only one left— his son whom he loved dearly. The owner finally sent him, thinking, 'Surely they will respect my son.'

[7] "But the tenant farmers said to one another, 'Here comes the heir to this estate. Let's kill him and get the estate for ourselves!' [8] So they grabbed him and murdered him and threw his body out of the vineyard.

[9] "What do you suppose the owner of the vineyard will do?" Jesus asked. "I'll tell you—he will come and kill those farmers and lease the vineyard to others. [10] Didn't you ever read this in the Scriptures?

"The stone that the builders rejected
   has now become the cornerstone.
[11] This is the LORD's doing,
   and it is wonderful to see.'*"

[12] The religious leaders* wanted to arrest Jesus because they realized he was telling the story against them—they were the wicked farmers. But they were afraid of the crowd, so they left him and went away.

Taxes for Caesar

[13] Later the leaders sent some Pharisees and supporters of Herod to trap Jesus into saying something for which he could be arrested. [14] "Teacher," they said, "we know how honest you are. You are impartial and don't play favorites. You teach the

12:10-11 Ps 118:22-23.   **12:12** Greek *They.*

way of God truthfully. Now tell us—is it right to pay taxes to Caesar or not? ¹⁵Should we pay them, or shouldn't we?"

Jesus saw through their hypocrisy and said, "Why are you trying to trap me? Show me a Roman coin,* and I'll tell you." ¹⁶When they handed it to him, he asked, "Whose picture and title are stamped on it?"

"Caesar's," they replied.

¹⁷"Well, then," Jesus said, "give to Caesar what belongs to Caesar, and give to God what belongs to God."

His reply completely amazed them.

Discussion about Resurrection

¹⁸Then Jesus was approached by some Sadducees—religious leaders who say there is no resurrection from the dead. They posed this question: ¹⁹"Teacher, Moses gave us a law that if a man dies, leaving a wife without children, his brother should marry the widow and have a child who will carry on the brother's name.* ²⁰Well, suppose there were seven brothers. The oldest one married and then died without children. ²¹So the second brother married the widow, but he also died without children. Then the third brother married her. ²²This continued with all seven of them, and still there were no children. Last of all, the woman also died. ²³So tell us, whose wife will she be in the resurrection? For all seven were married to her."

²⁴Jesus replied, "Your mistake is that you don't know the Scriptures, and you don't know the power of God. ²⁵For when the dead rise, they will neither marry nor be given in marriage. In this respect they will be like the angels in heaven.

²⁶"But now, as to whether the dead will be raised—haven't you ever read about this in the writings of Moses, in the story of the burning bush? Long after Abraham, Isaac, and Jacob had died, God said to Moses,* 'I am the God of Abraham, the God of Isaac, and the God of Jacob.'* ²⁷So he is the God of the living, not the dead. You have made a serious error."

The Most Important Commandment

²⁸One of the teachers of religious law was standing there listening to the debate. He realized that Jesus had answered well, so he asked, "Of all the commandments, which is the most important?"

²⁹Jesus replied, "The most important commandment is this: 'Listen, O Israel! The LORD our God is the one and only LORD.

12:15 Greek *a denarius.*   12:19 See Deut 25:5-6.   12:26a Greek *in the story of the bush? God said to him.*   12:26b Exod 3:6.

FRIENDSHIP EXPERIENCE

FRIENDSHIP TYPE:	FRIENDSHIP LAYER:
Friends	*Acceptance*

Accepting When It Hurts

Accepting someone who is a little different from you often means some sacrifice on your part.

Think of Jesus in **Mark 2:13-17**. Jesus chose to accept Levi as his friend, and the next thing you know, Levi was inviting Jesus over to his house for a party. No one would have blamed Jesus for refusing to come. Consider the implications: There would be lots of "sinners" there—Levi's friends were not exactly the toast of society. Everyone would know Jesus had gone to the party, and his reputation would suffer. The crowds might not respect Jesus' teachings if they knew he was spending his after hours with such wayward company.

But none of that mattered much to Jesus. His reputation wasn't as important as his friendship with Levi. Jesus chose to show love and acceptance to Levi—and Levi's friends—despite the personal sacrifice.

For more examples of Jesus hanging out with "sinners," see **Luke 7:36-50**; **Luke 19:1-10**; **John 4**.

FRIENDSHIP EXPERIENCE *continues on page 96...*

FRIENDSHIP EXPERIENCE *continued from page 95…*

Experience

THE ONE THING YOU CAN DO THIS WEEK — 1

Jesus chose to pursue a friendship with Levi, even at the risk of personal harm. This week, hang out with a new acquaintance, and let your new friend choose the activity! Go along with it, whether it's your kind of thing or not. You might even have fun!

Being a friend of God can often bring trouble to your life. There are plenty of harmful stereotypes that people associate with Christians—and when you have a friendship with God, people will label you with those stereotypes whether you fit them or not. Sometimes simply associating with God or his followers can affect your reputation. But just as Jesus' friendship with Levi was worth all the trouble, your friendship with God is definitely worth whatever trouble it brings (**Philippians 3:7-9**). Spend some time with God this week. Pray, read the Bible, tell others about his love…and don't worry about who might see or hear you!

Reflect

★ How was Jesus' reputation affected by his friendship with Levi? Do you think it mattered?

★ How has your reputation been negatively affected by a friendship? Was it worth it?

★ Why is a friendship with God worth the trouble to you?

30And you must love the LORD your God with all your heart, all your soul, all your mind, and all your strength.'* 31The second is equally important: 'Love your neighbor as yourself.'* No other commandment is greater than these."

32The teacher of religious law replied, "Well said, Teacher. You have spoken the truth by saying that there is only one God and no other. 33And I know it is important to love him with all my heart and all my understanding and all my strength, and to love my neighbor as myself. This is more important than to offer all of the burnt offerings and sacrifices required in the law."

34Realizing how much the man understood, Jesus said to him, "You are not far from the Kingdom of God." And after that, no one dared to ask him any more questions.

Whose Son Is the Messiah?

35Later, as Jesus was teaching the people in the Temple, he asked, "Why do the teachers of religious law claim that the Messiah is the son of David? 36For David himself, speaking under the inspiration of the Holy Spirit, said,

"The LORD said to my Lord,
　Sit in the place of honor at my right hand
　　until I humble your enemies beneath your feet.'*

37Since David himself called the Messiah 'my Lord,' how can the Messiah be his son?" The large crowd listened to him with great delight.

38Jesus also taught: "Beware of these teachers of religious law! For they like to parade around in flowing robes and receive respectful greetings as they walk in the marketplaces. 39And how they love the seats of honor in the synagogues and the head table at banquets. 40Yet they shamelessly cheat widows out of their property and then pretend to be pious by making long prayers in public. Because of this, they will be more severely punished."

The Widow's Offering

41Jesus sat down near the collection box in the Temple and watched as the crowds dropped in their money. Many rich people put in large amounts. 42Then a poor widow came and dropped in two small coins.* 43Jesus called his disciples to him and said, "I tell you the truth, this poor widow has given more than all the others who

12:29-30 Deut 6:4-5.　**12:31** Lev 19:18.　**12:36** Ps 110:1.　**12:42** Greek *two lepta, which is a kodrantes* [i.e., a quadrans].

are making contributions. ⁴⁴For they gave a tiny part of their surplus, but she, poor as she is, has given everything she had to live on."

CHAPTER **13**

Jesus Foretells the Future

As Jesus was leaving the Temple that day, one of his disciples said, "Teacher, look at these magnificent buildings! Look at the impressive stones in the walls."

²Jesus replied, "Yes, look at these great buildings. But they will be completely demolished. Not one stone will be left on top of another!"

³Later, Jesus sat on the Mount of Olives across the valley from the Temple. Peter, James, John, and Andrew came to him privately and asked him, ⁴"Tell us, when will all this happen? What sign will show us that these things are about to be fulfilled?"

⁵Jesus replied, "Don't let anyone mislead you, ⁶for many will come in my name, claiming, 'I am the Messiah.'* They will deceive many. ⁷And you will hear of wars and threats of wars, but don't panic. Yes, these things must take place, but the end won't follow immediately. ⁸Nation will go to war against nation, and kingdom against kingdom. There will be earthquakes in many parts of the world, as well as famines. But this is only the first of the birth pains, with more to come.

⁹"When these things begin to happen, watch out! You will be handed over to the local councils and beaten in the synagogues. You will stand trial before governors and kings because you are my followers. But this will be your opportunity to tell them about me.* ¹⁰For the Good News must first be preached to all nations.* ¹¹But when you are arrested and stand trial, don't worry in advance about what to say. Just say what God tells you at that time, for it is not you who will be speaking, but the Holy Spirit.

¹²"A brother will betray his brother to death, a father will betray his own child, and children will rebel against their parents and cause them to be killed. ¹³And everyone will hate you because you are my followers.* But the one who endures to the end will be saved.

¹⁴"The day is coming when you will see the sacrilegious object that causes desecration* standing where he* should not be." (Reader, pay attention!) "Then those in Judea must flee to

13:6 Greek *claiming, 'I am.'*   **13:9** Or *But this will be your testimony against them.*   **13:10** Or *all peoples.*   **13:13** Greek *on account of my name.*   **13:14a** Greek *the abomination of desolation.* See Dan 9:27; 11:31; 12:11.   **13:14b** Or *it.*

the hills. [15]A person out on the deck of a roof must not go down into the house to pack. [16]A person out in the field must not return even to get a coat. [17]How terrible it will be for pregnant women and for nursing mothers in those days. [18]And pray that your flight will not be in winter. [19]For there will be greater anguish in those days than at any time since God created the world. And it will never be so great again. [20]In fact, unless the Lord shortens that time of calamity, not a single person will survive. But for the sake of his chosen ones he has shortened those days.

[21]"Then if anyone tells you, 'Look, here is the Messiah,' or 'There he is,' don't believe it. [22]For false messiahs and false prophets will rise up and perform signs and wonders so as to deceive, if possible, even God's chosen ones. [23]Watch out! I have warned you about this ahead of time!

[24]"At that time, after the anguish of those days,

the sun will be darkened,
   the moon will give no light,
[25] the stars will fall from the sky,
   and the powers in the heavens will be shaken.*

[26]Then everyone will see the Son of Man* coming on the clouds with great power and glory.* [27]And he will send out his angels to gather his chosen ones from all over the world*—from the farthest ends of the earth and heaven.

[28]"Now learn a lesson from the fig tree. When its branches bud and its leaves begin to sprout, you know that summer is near. [29]In the same way, when you see all these things taking place, you can know that his return is very near, right at the door. [30]I tell you the truth, this generation* will not pass from the scene before all these things take place. [31]Heaven and earth will disappear, but my words will never disappear.

[32]"However, no one knows the day or hour when these things will happen, not even the angels in heaven or the Son himself. Only the Father knows. [33]And since you don't know when that time will come, be on guard! Stay alert*!

[34]"The coming of the Son of Man can be illustrated by the story of a man going on a long trip. When he left home, he gave each of his slaves instructions about the work they were to do, and he told the gatekeeper to watch for his return. [35]You, too, must keep watch! For you don't know when the master of the

13:24-25 See Isa 13:10; 34:4; Joel 2:10.　**13:26a** "Son of Man" is a title Jesus used for himself. **13:26b** See Dan 7:13.　**13:27** Greek *from the four winds.*　**13:30** Or *this age,* or *this nation.* **13:33** Some manuscripts add *and pray.*

household will return—in the evening, at midnight, before dawn, or at daybreak. ³⁶Don't let him find you sleeping when he arrives without warning. ³⁷I say to you what I say to everyone: Watch for him!"

CHAPTER **14**
Jesus Anointed at Bethany

It was now two days before Passover and the Festival of Unleavened Bread. The leading priests and the teachers of religious law were still looking for an opportunity to capture Jesus secretly and kill him. ²"But not during the Passover celebration," they agreed, "or the people may riot."

³Meanwhile, Jesus was in Bethany at the home of Simon, a man who had previously had leprosy. While he was eating,* a woman came in with a beautiful alabaster jar of expensive perfume made from essence of nard. She broke open the jar and poured the perfume over his head.

⁴Some of those at the table were indignant. "Why waste such expensive perfume?" they asked. ⁵"It could have been sold for a year's wages* and the money given to the poor!" So they scolded her harshly.

⁶But Jesus replied, "Leave her alone. Why criticize her for doing such a good thing to me? ⁷You will always have the poor among you, and you can help them whenever you want to. But you will not always have me. ⁸She has done what she could and has anointed my body for burial ahead of time. ⁹I tell you the truth, wherever the Good News is preached throughout the world, this woman's deed will be remembered and discussed."

Judas Agrees to Betray Jesus

¹⁰Then Judas Iscariot, one of the twelve disciples, went to the leading priests to arrange to betray Jesus to them. ¹¹They were delighted when they heard why he had come, and they promised to give him money. So he began looking for an opportunity to betray Jesus.

The Last Supper

¹²On the first day of the Festival of Unleavened Bread, when the Passover lamb is sacrificed, Jesus' disciples asked him, "Where do you want us to go to prepare the Passover meal for you?"

¹³So Jesus sent two of them into Jerusalem with these instructions: "As you go into the city, a man carrying a pitcher of water

14:3 Or *reclining.*   **14:5** Greek *for 300 denarii.* A denarius was equivalent to a laborer's full day's wage.

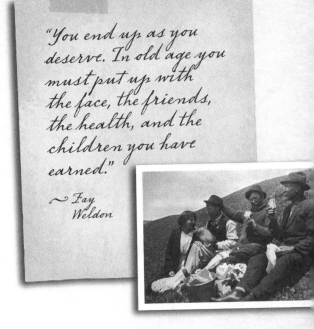

"You end up as you deserve. In old age you must put up with the face, the friends, the health, and the children you have earned."

~ *Fay Weldon*

JOURNAL

Among those who report they are very satisfied with their current church, 77% say they have eaten a meal with people in their congregation in the last year.

—from "Friendship and Faith," a Gallup Research Study Commissioned by Group Publishing, Inc.

JOURNAL

will meet you. Follow him. ¹⁴At the house he enters, say to the owner, 'The Teacher asks: Where is the guest room where I can eat the Passover meal with my disciples?' ¹⁵He will take you upstairs to a large room that is already set up. That is where you should prepare our meal." ¹⁶So the two disciples went into the city and found everything just as Jesus had said, and they prepared the Passover meal there.

¹⁷In the evening Jesus arrived with the twelve disciples.* ¹⁸As they were at the table* eating, Jesus said, "I tell you the truth, one of you eating with me here will betray me."

¹⁹Greatly distressed, each one asked in turn, "Am I the one?"

²⁰He replied, "It is one of you twelve who is eating from this bowl with me. ²¹For the Son of Man* must die, as the Scriptures declared long ago. But how terrible it will be for the one who betrays him. It would be far better for that man if he had never been born!"

²²As they were eating, Jesus took some bread and blessed it. Then he broke it in pieces and gave it to the disciples, saying, "Take it, for this is my body."

²³And he took a cup of wine and gave thanks to God for it. He gave it to them, and they all drank from it. ²⁴And he said to them, "This is my blood, which confirms the covenant* between God and his people. It is poured out as a sacrifice for many. ²⁵I tell you the truth, I will not drink wine again until the day I drink it new in the Kingdom of God."

²⁶Then they sang a hymn and went out to the Mount of Olives.

Jesus Predicts Peter's Denial

²⁷On the way, Jesus told them, "All of you will desert me. For the Scriptures say,

'God will strike* the Shepherd,
    and the sheep will be scattered.'

²⁸But after I am raised from the dead, I will go ahead of you to Galilee and meet you there."

²⁹Peter said to him, "Even if everyone else deserts you, I never will."

³⁰Jesus replied, "I tell you the truth, Peter—this very night, before the rooster crows twice, you will deny three times that you even know me."

³¹"No!" Peter declared emphatically. "Even if I have to die with you, I will never deny you!" And all the others vowed the same.

14:17 Greek *the Twelve.*   14:18 Or *As they reclined.*   14:21 "Son of Man" is a title Jesus used for himself.   14:24 Some manuscripts read *the new covenant.*   14:27 Greek *I will strike.* Zech 13:7.

Jesus Prays in Gethsemane

³²They went to the olive grove called Gethsemane, and Jesus said, "Sit here while I go and pray." ³³He took Peter, James, and John with him, and he became deeply troubled and distressed. ³⁴He told them, "My soul is crushed with grief to the point of death. Stay here and keep watch with me."

³⁵He went on a little farther and fell to the ground. He prayed that, if it were possible, the awful hour awaiting him might pass him by. ³⁶"Abba, Father,"* he cried out, "everything is possible for you. Please take this cup of suffering away from me. Yet I want your will to be done, not mine."

³⁷Then he returned and found the disciples asleep. He said to Peter, "Simon, are you asleep? Couldn't you watch with me even one hour? ³⁸Keep watch and pray, so that you will not give in to temptation. For the spirit is willing, but the body is weak."

³⁹Then Jesus left them again and prayed the same prayer as before. ⁴⁰When he returned to them again, he found them sleeping, for they couldn't keep their eyes open. And they didn't know what to say.

⁴¹When he returned to them the third time, he said, "Go ahead and sleep. Have your rest. But no—the time has come. The Son of Man is betrayed into the hands of sinners. ⁴²Up, let's be going. Look, my betrayer is here!"

Jesus Is Betrayed and Arrested

⁴³And immediately, even as Jesus said this, Judas, one of the twelve disciples, arrived with a crowd of men armed with swords and clubs. They had been sent by the leading priests, the teachers of religious law, and the elders. ⁴⁴The traitor, Judas, had given them a prearranged signal: "You will know which one to arrest when I greet him with a kiss. Then you can take him away under guard." ⁴⁵As soon as they arrived, Judas walked up to Jesus. "Rabbi!" he exclaimed, and gave him the kiss.

⁴⁶Then the others grabbed Jesus and arrested him. ⁴⁷But one of the men with Jesus pulled out his sword and struck the high priest's slave, slashing off his ear.

⁴⁸Jesus asked them, "Am I some dangerous revolutionary, that you come with swords and clubs to arrest me? ⁴⁹Why didn't you arrest me in the Temple? I was there among you teaching every day. But these things are happening to fulfill what the Scriptures say about me."

⁵⁰Then all his disciples deserted him and ran away. ⁵¹One

14:36 *Abba* is an Aramaic term for "father."

young man following behind was clothed only in a long linen shirt. When the mob tried to grab him, 52he slipped out of his shirt and ran away naked.

Jesus before the Council

53They took Jesus to the high priest's home where the leading priests, the elders, and the teachers of religious law had gathered. 54Meanwhile, Peter followed him at a distance and went right into the high priest's courtyard. There he sat with the guards, warming himself by the fire.

55Inside, the leading priests and the entire high council* were trying to find evidence against Jesus, so they could put him to death. But they couldn't find any. 56Many false witnesses spoke against him, but they contradicted each other. 57Finally, some men stood up and gave this false testimony: 58"We heard him say, 'I will destroy this Temple made with human hands, and in three days I will build another, made without human hands.'" 59But even then they didn't get their stories straight!

60Then the high priest stood up before the others and asked Jesus, "Well, aren't you going to answer these charges? What do you have to say for yourself?" 61But Jesus was silent and made no reply. Then the high priest asked him, "Are you the Messiah, the Son of the Blessed One?"

62Jesus said, "I AM.* And you will see the Son of Man seated in the place of power at God's right hand* and coming on the clouds of heaven.*"

63Then the high priest tore his clothing to show his horror and said, "Why do we need other witnesses? 64You have all heard his blasphemy. What is your verdict?"

"Guilty!" they all cried. "He deserves to die!"

65Then some of them began to spit at him, and they blindfolded him and beat him with their fists. "Prophesy to us," they jeered. And the guards slapped him as they took him away.

Peter Denies Jesus

66Meanwhile, Peter was in the courtyard below. One of the servant girls who worked for the high priest came by 67and noticed Peter warming himself at the fire. She looked at him closely and said, "You were one of those with Jesus of Nazareth.*"

14:55 Greek *the Sanhedrin.*   **14:62a** Or *The 'I AM' is here;* or *I am the* LORD. See Exod 3:14.
14:62b Greek *at the right hand of the power.* See Ps 110:1.   **14:62c** See Dan 7:13.   **14:67** Or *Jesus the Nazarene.*

68 But Peter denied it. "I don't know what you're talking about," he said, and he went out into the entryway. Just then, a rooster crowed.*

69 When the servant girl saw him standing there, she began telling the others, "This man is definitely one of them!" 70 But Peter denied it again.

A little later some of the other bystanders confronted Peter and said, "You must be one of them, because you are a Galilean."

71 Peter swore, "A curse on me if I'm lying—I don't know this man you're talking about!" 72 And immediately the rooster crowed the second time.

Suddenly, Jesus' words flashed through Peter's mind: "Before the rooster crows twice, you will deny three times that you even know me." And he broke down and wept. ⚓

CHAPTER 15

Jesus' Trial before Pilate

Very early in the morning the leading priests, the elders, and the teachers of religious law—the entire high council*—met to discuss their next step. They bound Jesus, led him away, and took him to Pilate, the Roman governor.

2 Pilate asked Jesus, "Are you the king of the Jews?"

Jesus replied, "You have said it."

3 Then the leading priests kept accusing him of many crimes, 4 and Pilate asked him, "Aren't you going to answer them? What about all these charges they are bringing against you?" 5 But Jesus said nothing, much to Pilate's surprise.

6 Now it was the governor's custom each year during the Passover celebration to release one prisoner—anyone the people requested. 7 One of the prisoners at that time was Barabbas, a revolutionary who had committed murder in an uprising. 8 The crowd went to Pilate and asked him to release prisoner as usual.

9 "Would you like me to release to you this 'King of the Jews'?" Pilate asked. 10 (For he realized by now that the leading priests had arrested Jesus out of envy.) 11 But at this point the leading priests stirred up the crowd to demand the release of Barabbas instead of Jesus. 12 Pilate asked them,

14:68 Some manuscripts do not include *Just then, a rooster crowed.*   15:1 Greek *the Sanhedrin;* also in 15:43.

Anchor Passage

PASSAGE: Mark 14:66-72

FRIENDSHIP TYPE: *Jesus*   FRIENDSHIP LAYER: *Deepening*

Our Dark Side

In the final *Star Wars* prequel, the friendship of Anakin Skywalker and Obi-Wan Kenobi disintegrates. Anakin's "dark side" drives him away from his friend. Of course, at the beginning of the friendship, Anakin would have said he'd *never* betray Obi-Wan, but then greed and ambition cloud his thinking, and Anakin nearly kills his former friend.

Read **Mark 14:66-72**.

Peter wasn't driven by ambition or greed, but he was driven by fear. And Peter let fear drive him to betray his closest friend.

Peter had spent nearly three years of his life traveling the country with Jesus. He'd seen Jesus perform miracles. He'd heard Jesus teach on the hillsides. He'd declared that Jesus was the Son of God.

Peter was a devoted friend…and yet there he stood around the campfire, only yards away from where Jesus was being tortured, *denying* that he'd ever known Jesus. Not once. Not twice. But *three* times.

Sometimes friendships hit a rough spot. In fact, those hard times are inevitable. But they aren't the end…or, at least, they don't have to be.

Anchor Passage continues on page 104…

Friendship First NEW TESTAMENT

Anchor Passage continued from page 103...

Anakin's dark side destroyed his friendship, but Peter's did not. Peter recognized the ugliness of his betrayal and repented. Jesus forgave Peter (**John 21:15-19**). The friendship continued, deeper than ever. Peter remained faithful to Jesus until the day he died, when he was martyred for his friendship with Jesus.

Experience

THE ONE THING **1** YOU CAN DO THIS WEEK

Most of us start out our friendship with Jesus believing we could never betray our Lord. But then we feel the pressure, our dark sides come out, and we do betray him. We're afraid. We're busy. We're hurting. We're confused. We're rebellious. There are lots of reasons to desert, and at some point, we all do.

But it's not the end. Every friendship has its tough moments, including friendship with Jesus. If they aren't allowed to destroy a friendship, those tough times can deepen the friendship. Write down a time your friendship with Jesus was under attack. How did that time strengthen your friendship?

_____

_____

_____

_____

_____

_____

_____

_____

_____

Anchor Passage continues on page 105...

"Then what should I do with this man you call the king of the Jews?"

[13] They shouted back, "Crucify him!"

[14] "Why?" Pilate demanded. "What crime has he committed?"

But the mob roared even louder, "Crucify him!"

[15] So to pacify the crowd, Pilate released Barabbas to them. He ordered Jesus flogged with a lead-tipped whip, then turned him over to the Roman soldiers to be crucified.

The Soldiers Mock Jesus

[16] The soldiers took Jesus into the courtyard of the governor's headquarters (called the Praetorium) and called out the entire regiment. [17] They dressed him in a purple robe, and they wove thorn branches into a crown and put it on his head. [18] Then they saluted him and taunted, "Hail! King of the Jews!" [19] And they struck him on the head with a reed stick, spit on him, and dropped to their knees in mock worship. [20] When they were finally tired of mocking him, they took off the purple robe and put his own clothes on him again. Then they led him away to be crucified.

The Crucifixion

[21] A passerby named Simon, who was from Cyrene,* was coming in from the countryside just then, and the soldiers forced him to carry Jesus' cross. (Simon was the father of Alexander and Rufus.) [22] And they brought Jesus to a place called Golgotha (which means "Place of the Skull"). [23] They offered him wine drugged with myrrh, but he refused it.

[24] Then the soldiers nailed him to the cross. They divided his clothes and threw dice* to decide who would get each piece. [25] It was nine o'clock in the morning when they crucified him. [26] A sign was fastened to the cross, announcing the charge against him. It read, "The King of the Jews." [27] Two revolutionaries* were crucified with him, one on his right and one on his left.*

[29] The people passing by shouted abuse, shaking their heads in mockery. "Ha! Look at you now!" they yelled at him. "You said you were going to destroy the Temple and rebuild it in three days. [30] Well then, save yourself and come down from the cross!"

[31] The leading priests and teachers of religious law also mocked Jesus. "He saved others," they scoffed, "but he can't

15:21 *Cyrene* was a city in northern Africa. **15:24** Greek *cast lots.* See Ps 22:18. **15:27a** Or *Two criminals.* **15:27b** Some manuscripts add verse 28, *And the Scripture was fulfilled that said, "He was counted among those who were rebels."* See Isa 53:12; also compare Luke 22:37.

save himself! 32 Let this Messiah, this King of Israel, come down
from the cross so we can see it and believe him!" Even the men
who were crucified with Jesus ridiculed him.

The Death of Jesus

33 At noon, darkness fell across the whole land until three o'clock.
34 Then at three o'clock Jesus called out with a loud voice, *"Eloi,
Eloi, lema sabachthani?"* which means "My God, my God, why
have you abandoned me?"*
35 Some of the bystanders misunderstood and thought he was
calling for the prophet Elijah. 36 One of them ran and filled a
sponge with sour wine, holding it up to him on a reed stick so
he could drink. "Wait!" he said. "Let's see whether Elijah comes
to take him down!"
37 Then Jesus uttered another loud cry and breathed his last.
38 And the curtain in the sanctuary of the Temple was torn in
two, from top to bottom.
39 When the Roman officer* who stood facing him* saw how
he had died, he exclaimed, "This man truly was the Son of
God!"
40 Some women were there, watching from a distance, including Mary Magdalene, Mary (the mother of James the younger
and of Joseph*), and Salome. 41 They had been followers of
Jesus and had cared for him while he was in Galilee. Many
other women who had come with him to Jerusalem were also
there.

The Burial of Jesus

42 This all happened on Friday, the day of preparation,* the
day before the Sabbath. As evening approached, 43 Joseph of
Arimathea took a risk and went to Pilate and asked for Jesus'
body. (Joseph was an honored member of the high council,
and he was waiting for the Kingdom of God to come.) 44 Pilate
couldn't believe that Jesus was already dead, so he called for
the Roman officer and asked if he had died yet. 45 The officer
confirmed that Jesus was dead, so Pilate told Joseph he could
have the body. 46 Joseph bought a long sheet of linen cloth.
Then he took Jesus' body down from the cross, wrapped it
in the cloth, and laid it in a tomb that had been carved out
of the rock. Then he rolled a stone in front of the entrance.
47 Mary Magdalene and Mary the mother of Joseph saw where
Jesus' body was laid.

15:34 Ps 22:1. **15:39a** Greek *the centurion;* similarly in 15:44, 45. **15:39b** Some manuscripts add *heard his cry and.* **15:40** Greek *Joses;* also in 15:47. See Matt 27:56. **15:42** Greek *It was the day of preparation.*

Anchor Passage continued from page 104...

Reflect

- ★ When have you denied Jesus?
- ★ What "tough times" have made your friendship with Jesus stronger?
- ★ If you're in the middle of a tough time right now, what can you do to restore your friendship with Jesus?

DIGGING DEEPER

FRIENDSHIP TYPE:	FRIENDSHIP LAYER:
Jesus	*Deepening*

For deepening your friendship with Jesus, check out...

- The Friendship Experience .... on page 75
- The Friendship Story .... on page 337
- What to Say and What Not to Say .... on page 91

JOURNAL

CHAPTER **16**

The Resurrection

Saturday evening, when the Sabbath ended, Mary Magdalene, Mary the mother of James, and Salome went out and purchased burial spices so they could anoint Jesus' body. [2]Very early on Sunday morning,* just at sunrise, they went to the tomb. [3]On the way they were asking each other, "Who will roll away the stone for us from the entrance to the tomb?" [4]But as they arrived, they looked up and saw that the stone, which was very large, had already been rolled aside.

[5]When they entered the tomb, they saw a young man clothed in a white robe sitting on the right side. The women were shocked, [6]but the angel said, "Don't be alarmed. You are looking for Jesus of Nazareth,* who was crucified. He isn't here! He is risen from the dead! Look, this is where they laid his body. [7]Now go and tell his disciples, including Peter, that Jesus is going ahead of you to Galilee. You will see him there, just as he told you before he died."

[8]The women fled from the tomb, trembling and bewildered, and they said nothing to anyone because they were too frightened.*

[Shorter Ending of Mark]

Then they briefly reported all this to Peter and his companions. Afterward Jesus himself sent them out from east to west with the sacred and unfailing message of salvation that gives eternal life. Amen.

[Longer Ending of Mark]

[9]After Jesus rose from the dead early on Sunday morning, the first person who saw him was Mary Magdalene, the woman from whom he had cast out seven demons. [10]She went to the disciples, who were grieving and weeping, and told them what had happened. [11]But when she told them that Jesus was alive and she had seen him, they didn't believe her.

[12]Afterward he appeared in a different form to two of his followers who were walking from Jerusalem into the country. [13]They rushed back to tell the others, but no one believed them.

[14]Still later he appeared to the eleven disciples as they were eating together. He rebuked them for their stubborn unbelief

16:2 Greek *on the first day of the week*; also in 16:9.   **16:6** Or *Jesus the Nazarene.*   **16:8** The most reliable early manuscripts of the Gospel of Mark end at verse 8. Other manuscripts include various endings to the Gospel. A few include both the "shorter ending" and the "longer ending." The majority of manuscripts include the "longer ending" immediately after verse 8.

because they refused to believe those who had seen him after he had been raised from the dead.*

¹⁵And then he told them, "Go into all the world and preach the Good News to everyone. ¹⁶Anyone who believes and is baptized will be saved. But anyone who refuses to believe will be condemned. ¹⁷These miraculous signs will accompany those who believe: They will cast out demons in my name, and they will speak in new languages.* ¹⁸They will be able to handle snakes with safety, and if they drink anything poisonous, it won't hurt them. They will be able to place their hands on the sick, and they will be healed."

¹⁹When the Lord Jesus had finished talking with them, he was taken up into heaven and sat down in the place of honor at God's right hand. ²⁰And the disciples went everywhere and preached, and the Lord worked through them, confirming what they said by many miraculous signs.

16:14 Some early manuscripts add: *And they excused themselves, saying, "This age of lawlessness and unbelief is under Satan, who does not permit God's truth and power to conquer the evil [unclean] spirits. Therefore, reveal your justice now." This is what they said to Christ. And Christ replied to them, "The period of years of Satan's power has been fulfilled, but other dreadful things will happen soon. And I was handed over to death for those who have sinned, so that they may return to the truth and sin no more, and so they may inherit the spiritual, incorruptible, and righteous glory in heaven."* 16:17 Or *new tongues;* some manuscripts omit *new.*

"Oh, the comfort—the inexpressible comfort of feeling safe with a person—having neither to weigh thoughts nor measure words, but pouring them all right out, just as they are, chaff and grain together."

~ Dinah Maria Mulock Craik

Luke

AUTHOR:	DATE WRITTEN:
Luke	About 60 A.D.

CHAPTER 1

Introduction

Many people have set out to write accounts about the events that have been fulfilled among us. [2]They used the eyewitness reports circulating among us from the early disciples.* [3]Having carefully investigated everything from the beginning, I also have decided to write a careful account for you, most honorable Theophilus, [4]so you can be certain of the truth of everything you were taught.

The Birth of John the Baptist Foretold

[5]When Herod was king of Judea, there was a Jewish priest named Zechariah. He was a member of the priestly order of Abijah, and his wife, Elizabeth, was also from the priestly line of Aaron. [6]Zechariah and Elizabeth were righteous in God's eyes, careful to obey all of the Lord's commandments and regulations. [7]They had no children because Elizabeth was unable to conceive, and they were both very old.

[8]One day Zechariah was serving God in the Temple, for his order was on duty that week. [9]As was the custom of the priests, he was chosen by lot to enter the sanctuary of the Lord and burn incense. [10]While the incense was being burned, a great crowd stood outside, praying.

[11]While Zechariah was in the sanctuary, an angel of the Lord appeared to him, standing to the right of the incense altar. [12]Zechariah was shaken and overwhelmed with fear when he saw him. [13]But the angel said, "Don't be afraid, Zechariah! God has heard your prayer. Your wife, Elizabeth, will give you a son, and you are to name him John. [14]You will have great joy and gladness, and many will rejoice at his birth, [15]for he will be great in the eyes of the Lord. He must never touch wine or

1:2 Greek *from those who from the beginning were servants of the word.*

other alcoholic drinks. He will be filled with the Holy Spirit, even before his birth.* ¹⁶And he will turn many Israelites to the Lord their God. ¹⁷He will be a man with the spirit and power of Elijah. He will prepare the people for the coming of the Lord. He will turn the hearts of the fathers to their children,* and he will cause those who are rebellious to accept the wisdom of the godly."

¹⁸Zechariah said to the angel, "How can I be sure this will happen? I'm an old man now, and my wife is also well along in years."

¹⁹Then the angel said, "I am Gabriel! I stand in the very presence of God. It was he who sent me to bring you this good news! ²⁰But now, since you didn't believe what I said, you will be silent and unable to speak until the child is born. For my words will certainly be fulfilled at the proper time."

²¹Meanwhile, the people were waiting for Zechariah to come out of the sanctuary, wondering why he was taking so long. ²²When he finally did come out, he couldn't speak to them. Then they realized from his gestures and his silence that he must have seen a vision in the sanctuary.

²³When Zechariah's week of service in the Temple was over, he returned home. ²⁴Soon afterward his wife, Elizabeth, became pregnant and went into seclusion for five months. ²⁵"How kind the Lord is!" she exclaimed. "He has taken away my disgrace of having no children."

The Birth of Jesus Foretold

²⁶In the sixth month of Elizabeth's pregnancy, God sent the angel Gabriel to Nazareth, a village in Galilee, ²⁷to a virgin named Mary. She was engaged to be married to a man named Joseph, a descendant of King David. ²⁸Gabriel appeared to her and said, "Greetings, favored woman! The Lord is with you!*"

²⁹Confused and disturbed, Mary tried to think what the angel could mean. ³⁰"Don't be afraid, Mary," the angel told her, "for you have found favor with God! ³¹You will conceive and give birth to a son, and you will name him Jesus. ³²He will be very great and will be called the Son of the Most High. The Lord God will give him the throne of his ancestor David. ³³And he will reign over Israel* forever; his Kingdom will never end!"

³⁴Mary asked the angel, "But how can this happen? I am a virgin."

³⁵The angel replied, "The Holy Spirit will come upon you,

1:15 Or *even from birth.*   1:17 See Mal 4:5-6.   1:28 Some manuscripts add *Blessed are you among women.*   1:33 Greek *over the house of Jacob.*

Anchor Passage

PASSAGE: Luke 1:39-45

FRIENDSHIP TYPE: Family

FRIENDSHIP LAYER: Trust

Guess What!

Have you ever had big news? *really* big news? Who did you tell first?

Read **Luke 1:39-45**.

Mary had a secret. A *big* secret. And she couldn't tell just anyone. If the wrong people got wind of it, she'd have trouble, and lots of it.

So what did she do? She made a beeline to her relative's house. She had to share her news with Elizabeth.

Think of the trust it took for Mary to tell Elizabeth she'd seen an *angel*. And that the angel told her she was favored by God. And she was going to have a baby. And not just any baby, but one who would be *great* and would reign on the throne of David *forever* and be called the *Son of the Most High*...Oh right, and she was also still a virgin.

Wow. Do you suppose Mary's stomach did a few flip-flops as Mary wondered how Elizabeth would react? Well, Mary went to the right person. Elizabeth not only believed and accepted her story but also rejoiced with Mary and blessed her.

Trust like that doesn't just happen. It builds over time. You share a little. The other person shares a little. You show each other you're trustworthy. You share a little more. After a while, a new intimacy develops, and a deeper friendship blossoms.

Anchor Passage
continues on page 110...

Anchor Passage continued from page 109...

Trust among family members, as Mary and Elizabeth enjoyed, is worth investing in. Would you race to someone in your family if you wanted to share important news? Why not take the steps that will build up those lifelong relationships and develop them into a haven and treasured camaraderie?

Experience

Look again at the passage, and think what it was like for Mary. What if you were in a situation as dramatic as hers? Who in your family would you depend on to tell such a story to? Call or visit that family member, and share some of what's happening in your life. Consider how much you've shared with this person in the past, and go a step deeper, making yourself a little more vulnerable than before.

Reflect

★ How has trust led to a deeper friendship with someone in your family?

★ What meaningful thing can you share that will demonstrate the trust you have for the other person and will allow you to become more vulnerable?

Anchor Passage continues on page 111...

and the power of the Most High will overshadow you. So the baby to be born will be holy, and he will be called the Son of God. ³⁶What's more, your relative Elizabeth has become pregnant in her old age! People used to say she was barren, but she's now in her sixth month. ³⁷For nothing is impossible with God.*"

³⁸Mary responded, "I am the Lord's servant. May everything you have said about me come true." And then the angel left her.

⚓ Mary Visits Elizabeth

³⁹A few days later Mary hurried to the hill country of Judea, to the town ⁴⁰where Zechariah lived. She entered the house and greeted Elizabeth. ⁴¹At the sound of Mary's greeting, Elizabeth's child leaped within her, and Elizabeth was filled with the Holy Spirit.

⁴²Elizabeth gave a glad cry and exclaimed to Mary, "God has blessed you above all women, and your child is blessed. ⁴³Why am I so honored, that the mother of my Lord should visit me? ⁴⁴When I heard your greeting, the baby in my womb jumped for joy. ⁴⁵You are blessed because you believed that the Lord would do what he said." ⚓

The Magnificat: Mary's Song of Praise

⁴⁶Mary responded,

"Oh, how my soul praises the Lord.
⁴⁷   How my spirit rejoices in God my Savior!
⁴⁸ For he took notice of his lowly servant girl,
       and from now on all generations will call me blessed.
⁴⁹ For the Mighty One is holy,
       and he has done great things for me.
⁵⁰ He shows mercy from generation to generation
       to all who fear him.
⁵¹ His mighty arm has done tremendous things!
       He has scattered the proud and haughty ones.
⁵² He has brought down princes from their thrones
       and exalted the humble.
⁵³ He has filled the hungry with good things
       and sent the rich away with empty hands.

1:37 Some manuscripts read *For the word of God will never fail.*

54 He has helped his servant Israel
    and remembered to be merciful.
55 For he made this promise to our ancestors,
    to Abraham and his children forever."

56 Mary stayed with Elizabeth about three months and then went back to her own home.

The Birth of John the Baptist

57 When it was time for Elizabeth's baby to be born, she gave birth to a son. 58 And when her neighbors and relatives heard that the Lord had been very merciful to her, everyone rejoiced with her.

59 When the baby was eight days old, they all came for the circumcision ceremony. They wanted to name him Zechariah, after his father. 60 But Elizabeth said, "No! His name is John!"

61 "What?" they exclaimed. "There is no one in all your family by that name." 62 So they used gestures to ask the baby's father what he wanted to name him. 63 He motioned for a writing tablet, and to everyone's surprise he wrote, "His name is John." 64 Instantly Zechariah could speak again, and he began praising God.

65 Awe fell upon the whole neighborhood, and the news of what had happened spread throughout the Judean hills. 66 Everyone who heard about it reflected on these events and asked, "What will this child turn out to be?" For the hand of the Lord was surely upon him in a special way.

Zechariah's Prophecy

67 Then his father, Zechariah, was filled with the Holy Spirit and gave this prophecy:

68 "Praise the Lord, the God of Israel,
    because he has visited and redeemed his people.
69 He has sent us a mighty Savior*
    from the royal line of his servant David,
70 just as he promised
    through his holy prophets long ago.
71 Now we will be saved from our enemies
    and from all who hate us.
72 He has been merciful to our ancestors
    by remembering his sacred covenant—
73 the covenant he swore with an oath
    to our ancestor Abraham.

1:69 Greek *has raised up a horn of salvation for us.*

Anchor Passage continued from page 110...

DIGGING DEEPER

FRIENDSHIP TYPE:	FRIENDSHIP LAYER:
Family	*Trust*

For building trust with family, check out...

➤ The Friendship Experience .... on page 113
➤ The Friendship Story .... on page 347
➤ What to Say and What Not to Say .... on page 121

JOURNAL

JOURNAL

74 We have been rescued from our enemies
   so we can serve God without fear,
75 in holiness and righteousness
   for as long as we live.

76 "And you, my little son,
   will be called the prophet of the Most High,
   because you will prepare the way for the Lord.
77 You will tell his people how to find salvation
   through forgiveness of their sins.
78 Because of God's tender mercy,
   the morning light from heaven is about to break upon us,*
79 to give light to those who sit in darkness and in the shadow
      of death,
   and to guide us to the path of peace."

80 John grew up and became strong in spirit. And he lived in the wilderness until he began his public ministry to Israel.

CHAPTER 2

The Birth of Jesus

At that time the Roman emperor, Augustus, decreed that a census should be taken throughout the Roman Empire. 2(This was the first census taken when Quirinius was governor of Syria.) 3All returned to their own ancestral towns to register for this census. 4And because Joseph was a descendant of King David, he had to go to Bethlehem in Judea, David's ancient home. He traveled there from the village of Nazareth in Galilee. 5He took with him Mary, his fiancée, who was now obviously pregnant.

6And while they were there, the time came for her baby to be born. 7She gave birth to her first child, a son. She wrapped him snugly in strips of cloth and laid him in a manger, because there was no lodging available for them.

The Shepherds and Angels

8That night there were shepherds staying in the fields nearby, guarding their flocks of sheep. 9Suddenly, an angel of the Lord appeared among them, and the radiance of the Lord's glory surrounded them. They were terrified, 10but the angel reassured them. "Don't be afraid!" he said. "I bring you good news that will bring great joy to all people. 11The Savior—yes, the Messiah, the Lord—has been born today in Bethlehem, the city of David!

1:78 Or *the Morning Light from Heaven is about to visit us.*

¹²And you will recognize him by this sign: You will find a baby wrapped snugly in strips of cloth, lying in a manger."

¹³Suddenly, the angel was joined by a vast host of others—the armies of heaven—praising God and saying,

¹⁴ "Glory to God in highest heaven,
    and peace on earth to those with whom God is pleased."

¹⁵When the angels had returned to heaven, the shepherds said to each other, "Let's go to Bethlehem! Let's see this thing that has happened, which the Lord has told us about."

¹⁶They hurried to the village and found Mary and Joseph. And there was the baby, lying in the manger. ¹⁷After seeing him, the shepherds told everyone what had happened and what the angel had said to them about this child. ¹⁸All who heard the shepherds' story were astonished, ¹⁹but Mary kept all these things in her heart and thought about them often. ²⁰The shepherds went back to their flocks, glorifying and praising God for all they had heard and seen. It was just as the angel had told them.

Jesus Is Presented in the Temple

²¹Eight days later, when the baby was circumcised, he was named Jesus, the name given him by the angel even before he was conceived.

²²Then it was time for their purification offering, as required by the law of Moses after the birth of a child; so his parents took him to Jerusalem to present him to the Lord. ²³The law of the Lord says, "If a woman's first child is a boy, he must be dedicated to the LORD."* ²⁴So they offered the sacrifice required in the law of the Lord—"either a pair of turtledoves or two young pigeons."*

The Prophecy of Simeon

²⁵At that time there was a man in Jerusalem named Simeon. He was righteous and devout and was eagerly waiting for the Messiah to come and rescue Israel. The Holy Spirit was upon him ²⁶and had revealed to him that he would not die until he had seen the Lord's Messiah. ²⁷That day the Spirit led him to the Temple. So when Mary and Joseph came to present the baby Jesus to the Lord as the law required, ²⁸Simeon was there. He took the child in his arms and praised God, saying,

²⁹ "Sovereign Lord, now let your servant die in peace,
    as you have promised.

2:23 Exod 13:2.   2:24 Lev 12:8.

FRIENDSHIP EXPERIENCE

FRIENDSHIP TYPE:	FRIENDSHIP LAYER:
Family	*Trust*

Family Ties

Often it's much easier to build trust with our friends than with our families. We get to choose our friends, but we inherit our families. We can't trade them in or swap them out. Sometimes we don't even like them, and that can make it pretty hard to get close.

So how do we establish greater trust?

Intentional sharing. Deliberate reliance. Going out on a limb.

OK, so maybe just looking at the limb is the best we can do to start. But that's OK. We start wherever we are and build from there. We need to open up, give them a chance to hold our trust, and be willing to hold their trust.

FRIENDSHIP EXPERIENCE *continues on page 114...*

FRIENDSHIP EXPERIENCE *continued from page 113…*

Experience

Trust grows when we risk depending on one another and the outcome is positive. Think of your life right now. Is there a burden you're carrying on your own? Is there a dream you've never shared with anyone? Could you use someone to baby-sit your kids once in a while? There are lots of ways you can grow trust with a family member. Choose one way, and then contact that family member this week!

Learning to trust God takes intentional effort as well. Tell God what's on your mind. Talk about that burden. Share that dream. Pray about your kids. Don't miss the opportunity to tell God about your life just because you realize he already knows. God wants to hear it from you—he wants to have a conversation with you. Read **Romans 15:13**. Trusting God is hard…but worth it!

THE ONE THING YOU CAN DO THIS WEEK

1

Reflect

★ What did you do to pursue a deeper trust with your family member? How did it go?

★ How did sharing what's important to you deepen the trust with your family member? with God?

★ What can you do to continue building that trust?

30 I have seen your salvation,
31   which you have prepared for all people.
32 He is a light to reveal God to the nations,
        and he is the glory of your people Israel!"

33 Jesus' parents were amazed at what was being said about him. 34 Then Simeon blessed them, and he said to Mary, the baby's mother, "This child is destined to cause many in Israel to fall, but he will be a joy to many others. He has been sent as a sign from God, but many will oppose him. 35 As a result, the deepest thoughts of many hearts will be revealed. And a sword will pierce your very soul."

The Prophecy of Anna

36 Anna, a prophet, was also there in the Temple. She was the daughter of Phanuel from the tribe of Asher, and she was very old. Her husband died when they had been married only seven years. 37 Then she lived as a widow to the age of eighty-four.* She never left the Temple but stayed there day and night, worshiping God with fasting and prayer. 38 She came along just as Simeon was talking with Mary and Joseph, and she began praising God. She talked about the child to everyone who had been waiting expectantly for God to rescue Jerusalem.

39 When Jesus' parents had fulfilled all the requirements of the law of the Lord, they returned home to Nazareth in Galilee. 40 There the child grew up healthy and strong. He was filled with wisdom, and God's favor was on him.

Jesus Speaks with the Teachers

41 Every year Jesus' parents went to Jerusalem for the Passover festival. 42 When Jesus was twelve years old, they attended the festival as usual. 43 After the celebration was over, they started home to Nazareth, but Jesus stayed behind in Jerusalem. His parents didn't miss him at first, 44 because they assumed he was among the other travelers. But when he didn't show up that evening, they started looking for him among their relatives and friends.

45 When they couldn't find him, they went back to Jerusalem to search for him there. 46 Three days later they finally discovered him in the Temple, sitting among the religious teachers, listening to them and asking questions. 47 All who heard him were amazed at his understanding and his answers.

48 His parents didn't know what to think. "Son," his mother

2:37 Or *She had been a widow for eighty-four years.*

said to him, "why have you done this to us? Your father and I have been frantic, searching for you everywhere."

⁴⁹"But why did you need to search?" he asked. "Didn't you know that I must be in my Father's house?"* ⁵⁰But they didn't understand what he meant.

⁵¹Then he returned to Nazareth with them and was obedient to them. And his mother stored all these things in her heart.

⁵²Jesus grew in wisdom and in stature and in favor with God and all the people.

CHAPTER **3**

John the Baptist Prepares the Way

It was now the fifteenth year of the reign of Tiberius, the Roman emperor. Pontius Pilate was governor over Judea; Herod Antipas was ruler* over Galilee; his brother Philip was ruler* over Iturea and Traconitis; Lysanias was ruler over Abilene. ²Annas and Caiaphas were the high priests. At this time a message from God came to John son of Zechariah, who was living in the wilderness. ³Then John went from place to place on both sides of the Jordan River, preaching that people should be baptized to show that they had repented of their sins and turned to God to be forgiven. ⁴Isaiah had spoken of John when he said,

"He is a voice shouting in the wilderness,
'Prepare the way for the LORD's coming!
    Clear the road for him!
⁵ The valleys will be filled,
    and the mountains and hills made level.
The curves will be straightened,
    and the rough places made smooth.
⁶ And then all people will see
    the salvation sent from God.'"*

⁷When the crowds came to John for baptism, he said, "You brood of snakes! Who warned you to flee God's coming wrath? ⁸Prove by the way you live that you have repented of your sins and turned to God. Don't just say to each other, 'We're safe, for we are descendants of Abraham.' That means nothing, for I tell you, God can create children of Abraham from these very stones. ⁹Even now the ax of God's judgment is poised, ready to sever the roots of the trees. Yes, every tree that does not produce good fruit will be chopped down and thrown into the fire."

2:49 Or *"Didn't you realize that I should be involved with my Father's affairs?"* **3:1a** Greek *Herod was tetrarch.* Herod Antipas was a son of King Herod. **3:1b** Greek *tetrarch;* also in 3:1c. **3:4-6** Isa 40:3-5 (Greek version).

[10]The crowds asked, "What should we do?"

[11]John replied, "If you have two shirts, give one to the poor. If you have food, share it with those who are hungry."

[12]Even corrupt tax collectors came to be baptized and asked, "Teacher, what should we do?"

[13]He replied, "Collect no more taxes than the government requires."

[14]"What should we do?" asked some soldiers.

John replied, "Don't extort money or make false accusations. And be content with your pay."

[15]Everyone was expecting the Messiah to come soon, and they were eager to know whether John might be the Messiah. [16]John answered their questions by saying, "I baptize you with* water; but someone is coming soon who is greater than I am—so much greater that I'm not even worthy to be his slave and untie the straps of his sandals. He will baptize you with the Holy Spirit and with fire.* [17]He is ready to separate the chaff from the wheat with his winnowing fork. Then he will clean up the threshing area, gathering the wheat into his barn but burning the chaff with never-ending fire." [18]John used many such warnings as he announced the Good News to the people.

[19]John also publicly criticized Herod Antipas, the ruler of Galilee,* for marrying Herodias, his brother's wife, and for many other wrongs he had done. [20]So Herod put John in prison, adding this sin to his many others.

The Baptism of Jesus

[21]One day when the crowds were being baptized, Jesus himself was baptized. As he was praying, the heavens opened, [22]and the Holy Spirit, in bodily form, descended on him like a dove. And a voice from heaven said, "You are my dearly loved Son, and you bring me great joy.*"

The Ancestors of Jesus

[23]Jesus was about thirty years old when he began his public ministry.

Jesus was known as the son of Joseph.
Joseph was the son of Heli.
[24] Heli was the son of Matthat.
Matthat was the son of Levi.
Levi was the son of Melki.
Melki was the son of Jannai.

3:16a Or *in.* **3:16b** Or *in the Holy Spirit and in fire.* **3:19** Greek *Herod the tetrarch.* **3:22** Some manuscripts read *my Son, and today I have become your Father.*

Jannai was the son of Joseph.
25 Joseph was the son of Mattathias.
Mattathias was the son of Amos.
Amos was the son of Nahum.
Nahum was the son of Esli.
Esli was the son of Naggai.
26 Naggai was the son of Maath.
Maath was the son of Mattathias.
Mattathias was the son of Semein.
Semein was the son of Josech.
Josech was the son of Joda.
27 Joda was the son of Joanan.
Joanan was the son of Rhesa.
Rhesa was the son of Zerubbabel.
Zerubbabel was the son of Shealtiel.
Shealtiel was the son of Neri.
28 Neri was the son of Melki.
Melki was the son of Addi.
Addi was the son of Cosam.
Cosam was the son of Elmadam.
Elmadam was the son of Er.
29 Er was the son of Joshua.
Joshua was the son of Eliezer.
Eliezer was the son of Jorim.
Jorim was the son of Matthat.
Matthat was the son of Levi.
30 Levi was the son of Simeon.
Simeon was the son of Judah.
Judah was the son of Joseph.
Joseph was the son of Jonam.
Jonam was the son of Eliakim.
31 Eliakim was the son of Melea.
Melea was the son of Menna.
Menna was the son of Mattatha.
Mattatha was the son of Nathan.
Nathan was the son of David.
32 David was the son of Jesse.
Jesse was the son of Obed.
Obed was the son of Boaz.
Boaz was the son of Salmon.*
Salmon was the son of Nahshon.
33 Nahshon was the son of Amminadab.

3:32 Greek *Sala,* a variant spelling of Salmon; also in 3:32b. See Ruth 4:22.

Of those respondents who report they are **very satisfied** with their current church, **84%** report that **"the spiritual leaders** of my congregation seem to **care about me."**

—from "Friendship and Faith," a Gallup Research Study Commissioned by Group Publishing, Inc.

JOURNAL

Amminadab was the son of Admin.
Admin was the son of Arni.*
Arni was the son of Hezron.
Hezron was the son of Perez.
Perez was the son of Judah.
34 Judah was the son of Jacob.
Jacob was the son of Isaac.
Isaac was the son of Abraham.
Abraham was the son of Terah.
Terah was the son of Nahor.
35 Nahor was the son of Serug.
Serug was the son of Reu.
Reu was the son of Peleg.
Peleg was the son of Eber.
Eber was the son of Shelah.
36 Shelah was the son of Cainan.
Cainan was the son of Arphaxad.
Arphaxad was the son of Shem.
Shem was the son of Noah.
Noah was the son of Lamech.
37 Lamech was the son of Methuselah.
Methuselah was the son of Enoch.
Enoch was the son of Jared.
Jared was the son of Mahalalel.
Mahalalel was the son of Kenan.
38 Kenan was the son of Enosh.*
Enosh was the son of Seth.
Seth was the son of Adam.
Adam was the son of God.

CHAPTER 4

The Temptation of Jesus

Then Jesus, full of the Holy Spirit, returned from the Jordan River. He was led by the Spirit in the wilderness,* 2where he was tempted by the devil for forty days. Jesus ate nothing all that time and became very hungry.

3Then the devil said to him, "If you are the Son of God, tell this stone to become a loaf of bread."

4But Jesus told him, "No! The Scriptures say, 'People do not live by bread alone.'*"

5Then the devil took him up and revealed to him all the king-

3:33 Some manuscripts read *Amminadab was the son of Aram. Arni* and *Aram* are alternate spellings of Ram. See 1 Chr 2:9-10.   **3:38** Greek *Enos*, a variant spelling of Enosh; also in 3:38b. See Gen 5:6.   **4:1** Some manuscripts read *into the wilderness.*   **4:4** Deut 8:3.

doms of the world in a moment of time. [6]"I will give you the glory of these kingdoms and authority over them," the devil said, "because they are mine to give to anyone I please. [7]I will give it all to you if you will worship me."

[8]Jesus replied, "The Scriptures say,

'You must worship the LORD your God
    and serve only him.'*"

[9]Then the devil took him to Jerusalem, to the highest point of the Temple, and said, "If you are the Son of God, jump off! [10]For the Scriptures say,

'He will order his angels to protect and guard you.
[11] And they will hold you up with their hands
    so you won't even hurt your foot on a stone.'*"

[12]Jesus responded, "The Scriptures also say, 'You must not test the LORD your God.'*"

[13]When the devil had finished tempting Jesus, he left him until the next opportunity came.

Jesus Rejected at Nazareth

[14]Then Jesus returned to Galilee, filled with the Holy Spirit's power. Reports about him spread quickly through the whole region. [15]He taught regularly in their synagogues and was praised by everyone.

[16]When he came to the village of Nazareth, his boyhood home, he went as usual to the synagogue on the Sabbath and stood up to read the Scriptures. [17]The scroll of Isaiah the prophet was handed to him. He unrolled the scroll and found the place where this was written:

[18] "The Spirit of the LORD is upon me,
    for he has anointed me to bring Good News to the poor.
He has sent me to proclaim that captives will be released,
    that the blind will see,
that the oppressed will be set free,
[19]   and that the time of the LORD's favor has come.*"

[20]He rolled up the scroll, handed it back to the attendant, and sat down. All eyes in the synagogue looked at him intently. [21]Then he began to speak to them. "The Scripture you've just heard has been fulfilled this very day!"

[22]Everyone spoke well of him and was amazed by the gracious

4:8 Deut 6:13.   4:10-11 Ps 91:11-12.   4:12 Deut 6:16.   4:18-19 Or *and to proclaim the acceptable year of the LORD.* Isa 61:1-2 (Greek version); 58:6.

"Christ did not lay down his life for us as enemies so that we should remain enemies, but so that he could make us friends."

~ Thomas Aquinas

JOURNAL

words that came from his lips. "How can this be?" they asked. "Isn't this Joseph's son?"

23 Then he said, "You will undoubtedly quote me this proverb: 'Physician, heal yourself'—meaning, 'Do miracles here in your hometown like those you did in Capernaum.' 24 But I tell you the truth, no prophet is accepted in his own hometown.

25 "Certainly there were many needy widows in Israel in Elijah's time, when the heavens were closed for three and a half years, and a severe famine devastated the land. 26 Yet Elijah was not sent to any of them. He was sent instead to a foreigner— a widow of Zarephath in the land of Sidon. 27 And there were many lepers in Israel in the time of the prophet Elisha, but the only one healed was Naaman, a Syrian."

28 When they heard this, the people in the synagogue were furious. 29 Jumping up, they mobbed him and forced him to the edge of the hill on which the town was built. They intended to push him over the cliff, 30 but he passed right through the crowd and went on his way.

Jesus Casts Out a Demon

31 Then Jesus went to Capernaum, a town in Galilee, and taught there in the synagogue every Sabbath day. 32 There, too, the people were amazed at his teaching, for he spoke with authority.

33 Once when he was in the synagogue, a man possessed by a demon—an evil* spirit—began shouting at Jesus, 34 "Go away! Why are you interfering with us, Jesus of Nazareth? Have you come to destroy us? I know who you are—the Holy One sent from God!"

35 Jesus cut him short. "Be quiet! Come out of the man," he ordered. At that, the demon threw the man to the floor as the crowd watched; then it came out of him without hurting him further.

36 Amazed, the people exclaimed, "What authority and power this man's words possess! Even evil spirits obey him, and they flee at his command!" 37 The news about Jesus spread through every village in the entire region.

Jesus Heals Many People

38 After leaving the synagogue that day, Jesus went to Simon's home, where he found Simon's mother-in-law very sick with a high fever. "Please heal her," everyone begged. 39 Standing at her bedside, he rebuked the fever, and it left her. And she got up at once and prepared a meal for them.

4:33 Greek unclean; also in 4:36.

⁴⁰As the sun went down that evening, people throughout the village brought sick family members to Jesus. No matter what their diseases were, the touch of his hand healed every one. ⁴¹Many were possessed by demons; and the demons came out at his command, shouting, "You are the Son of God!" But because they knew he was the Messiah, he rebuked them and refused to let them speak.

Jesus Continues to Preach

⁴²Early the next morning Jesus went out to an isolated place. The crowds searched everywhere for him, and when they finally found him, they begged him not to leave them. ⁴³But he replied, "I must preach the Good News of the Kingdom of God in other towns, too, because that is why I was sent." ⁴⁴So he continued to travel around, preaching in synagogues throughout Judea.*

CHAPTER **5**

The First Disciples

One day as Jesus was preaching on the shore of the Sea of Galilee,* great crowds pressed in on him to listen to the word of God. ²He noticed two empty boats at the water's edge, for the fishermen had left them and were washing their nets. ³Stepping into one of the boats, Jesus asked Simon,* its owner, to push it out into the water. So he sat in the boat and taught the crowds from there.

⁴When he had finished speaking, he said to Simon, "Now go out where it is deeper, and let down your nets to catch some fish."

⁵"Master," Simon replied, "we worked hard all last night and didn't catch a thing. But if you say so, I'll let the nets down again." ⁶And this time their nets were so full of fish they began to tear! ⁷A shout for help brought their partners in the other boat, and soon both boats were filled with fish and on the verge of sinking.

⁸When Simon Peter realized what had happened, he fell to his knees before Jesus and said, "Oh, Lord, please leave me—I'm too much of a sinner to be around you." ⁹For he was awestruck by the number of fish they had caught, as were the others with him. ¹⁰His partners, James and John, the sons of Zebedee, were also amazed.

Jesus replied to Simon, "Don't be afraid! From now on you'll be fishing for people!" ¹¹And as soon as they landed, they left everything and followed Jesus.

4:44 Some manuscripts read *Galilee.*   5:1 Greek *Lake Gennesaret,* another name for the Sea of Galilee.   5:3 *Simon* is called "Peter" in 6:14 and thereafter.

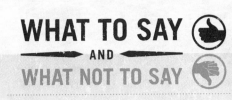

WHAT TO SAY AND **WHAT NOT TO SAY**

| FRIENDSHIP TYPE: *Family* | FRIENDSHIP LAYER: *Trust* |

Get Real, Mr. Spock

OK, so you're not really the emotional type. All that *feelings* stuff makes you want to bolt. You like to think of yourself as *logical* and *reasonable*, and—in your mind—those don't go together with "expressing your feelings."

But it's that time again. That moment in the phone conversation when your brother wants to know how you're doing. He's wondering if you have any prayer requests or if there's anything you want to talk about.

Nope, not really, you think to yourself. *I'm doing just fine, thank you very much.*

But you're not really. There are some problems at work. You're a little worried about money. Your daughter's leaving for college in a few weeks. There's plenty he could pray about…

WHAT NOT TO SAY:

★ "Everything's good with me."
★ "You can pray for my neighbor…"
★ "Oh, you know, you could just pray that I have a good week."
★ "The usual."

Trust starts with vulnerability. You have to open up, show a little emotion. You have to let people know there's a problem before they can help you. Same goes for God. So when that brother (or sister or mom or cousin) asks how you're doing, if you have any prayer requests, go ahead—tell the truth.

WHAT TO SAY AND **WHAT NOT TO SAY** *continues on page 122…*

WHAT TO SAY AND WHAT NOT TO SAY *continued from page 121...*

WHAT TO SAY:

★ "I'm doing all right, but I'm worried about all the layoffs at work…"

★ "My son needs braces, and we have to repair the car this month. Money's a little tight. Can you pray that God would provide for us?"

★ "I'm nervous and sad to let my daughter leave for college. It'd be great if you could pray for me and for her."

(Read about the power of praying for each other in **James 5:13-16**.)

JOURNAL

_____

_____

_____

_____

_____

_____

_____

_____

_____

_____

_____

_____

_____

_____

_____

Jesus Heals a Man with Leprosy

¹²In one of the villages, Jesus met a man with an advanced case of leprosy. When the man saw Jesus, he bowed with his face to the ground, begging to be healed. "Lord," he said, "if you are willing, you can heal me and make me clean."

¹³Jesus reached out and touched him. "I am willing," he said. "Be healed!" And instantly the leprosy disappeared. ¹⁴Then Jesus instructed him not to tell anyone what had happened. He said, "Go to the priest and let him examine you. Take along the offering required in the law of Moses for those who have been healed of leprosy.* This will be a public testimony that you have been cleansed."

¹⁵But despite Jesus' instructions, the report of his power spread even faster, and vast crowds came to hear him preach and to be healed of their diseases. ¹⁶But Jesus often withdrew to the wilderness for prayer.

Jesus Heals a Paralyzed Man

¹⁷One day while Jesus was teaching, some Pharisees and teachers of religious law were sitting nearby. (It seemed that these men showed up from every village in all Galilee and Judea, as well as from Jerusalem.) And the Lord's healing power was strongly with Jesus.

¹⁸Some men came carrying a paralyzed man on a sleeping mat. They tried to take him inside to Jesus, ¹⁹but they couldn't reach him because of the crowd. So they went up to the roof and took off some tiles. Then they lowered the sick man on his mat down into the crowd, right in front of Jesus. ²⁰Seeing their faith, Jesus said to the man, "Young man, your sins are forgiven."

²¹But the Pharisees and teachers of religious law said to themselves, "Who does he think he is? That's blasphemy! Only God can forgive sins!"

²²Jesus knew what they were thinking, so he asked them, "Why do you question this in your hearts? ²³Is it easier to say 'Your sins are forgiven,' or 'Stand up and walk'? ²⁴So I will prove to you that the Son of Man* has the authority on earth to forgive sins." Then Jesus turned to the paralyzed man and said, "Stand up, pick up your mat, and go home!"

²⁵And immediately, as everyone watched, the man jumped up, picked up his mat, and went home praising God. ²⁶Everyone was gripped with great wonder and awe, and they praised God, exclaiming, "We have seen amazing things today!"

5:14 See Lev 14:2-32.   5:24 "Son of Man" is a title Jesus used for himself.

Jesus Calls Levi (Matthew)

27 Later, as Jesus left the town, he saw a tax collector named Levi sitting at his tax collector's booth. "Follow me and be my disciple," Jesus said to him. 28 So Levi got up, left everything, and followed him.

29 Later, Levi held a banquet in his home with Jesus as the guest of honor. Many of Levi's fellow tax collectors and other guests also ate with them. 30 But the Pharisees and their teachers of religious law complained bitterly to Jesus' disciples, "Why do you eat and drink with such scum?*"

31 Jesus answered them, "Healthy people don't need a doctor— sick people do. 32 I have come to call not those who think they are righteous, but those who know they are sinners and need to repent."

A Discussion about Fasting

33 One day some people said to Jesus, "John the Baptist's disciples fast and pray regularly, and so do the disciples of the Pharisees. Why are your disciples always eating and drinking?"

34 Jesus responded, "Do wedding guests fast while celebrating with the groom? Of course not. 35 But someday the groom will be taken away from them, and then they will fast."

36 Then Jesus gave them this illustration: "No one tears a piece of cloth from a new garment and uses it to patch an old garment. For then the new garment would be ruined, and the new patch wouldn't even match the old garment.

37 "And no one puts new wine into old wineskins. For the new wine would burst the wineskins, spilling the wine and ruining the skins. 38 New wine must be stored in new wineskins. 39 But no one who drinks the old wine seems to want the new wine. 'The old is just fine,' they say."

CHAPTER 6

A Discussion about the Sabbath

One Sabbath day as Jesus was walking through some grainfields, his disciples broke off heads of grain, rubbed off the husks in their hands, and ate the grain. 2 But some Pharisees said, "Why are you breaking the law by harvesting grain on the Sabbath?"

3 Jesus replied, "Haven't you read in the Scriptures what David did when he and his companions were hungry? 4 He went into the house of God and broke the law by eating the sacred loaves of bread that only the priests can eat. He also gave some to his

5:30 Greek with tax collectors and sinners?

companions." [5]And Jesus added, "The Son of Man* is Lord, even over the Sabbath."

Jesus Heals on the Sabbath

[6]On another Sabbath day, a man with a deformed right hand was in the synagogue while Jesus was teaching. [7]The teachers of religious law and the Pharisees watched Jesus closely. If he healed the man's hand, they planned to accuse him of working on the Sabbath.

[8]But Jesus knew their thoughts. He said to the man with the deformed hand, "Come and stand in front of everyone." So the man came forward. [9]Then Jesus said to his critics, "I have a question for you. Does the law permit good deeds on the Sabbath, or is it a day for doing evil? Is this a day to save life or to destroy it?"

[10]He looked around at them one by one and then said to the man, "Hold out your hand." So the man held out his hand, and it was restored! [11]At this, the enemies of Jesus were wild with rage and began to discuss what to do with him.

Jesus Chooses the Twelve Apostles

[12]One day soon afterward Jesus went up on a mountain to pray, and he prayed to God all night. [13]At daybreak he called together all of his disciples and chose twelve of them to be apostles. Here are their names:

[14] Simon (whom he named Peter),
Andrew (Peter's brother),
James,
John,
Philip,
Bartholomew,
[15] Matthew,
Thomas,
James (son of Alphaeus),
Simon (who was called the zealot),
[16] Judas (son of James),
Judas Iscariot (who later betrayed him).

Crowds Follow Jesus

[17]When they came down from the mountain, the disciples stood with Jesus on a large, level area, surrounded by many of his followers and by the crowds. There were people from all over Judea and from Jerusalem and from as far north as the

6:5 "Son of Man" is a title Jesus used for himself.

seacoasts of Tyre and Sidon. [18]They had come to hear him and to be healed of their diseases; and those troubled by evil* spirits were healed. [19]Everyone tried to touch him, because healing power went out from him, and he healed everyone.

The Beatitudes

[20]Then Jesus turned to his disciples and said,

"God blesses you who are poor,
for the Kingdom of God is yours.
[21] God blesses you who are hungry now,
for you will be satisfied.
God blesses you who weep now,
for in due time you will laugh.

[22]What blessings await you when people hate you and exclude you and mock you and curse you as evil because you follow the Son of Man. [23]When that happens, be happy! Yes, leap for joy! For a great reward awaits you in heaven. And remember, their ancestors treated the ancient prophets that same way.

Sorrows Foretold

[24] "What sorrow awaits you who are rich,
for you have your only happiness now.
[25] What sorrow awaits you who are fat and prosperous now,
for a time of awful hunger awaits you.
What sorrow awaits you who laugh now,
for your laughing will turn to mourning and sorrow.
[26] What sorrow awaits you who are praised by the crowds,
for their ancestors also praised false prophets.

Love for Enemies

[27]"But to you who are willing to listen, I say, love your enemies! Do good to those who hate you. [28]Bless those who curse you. Pray for those who hurt you. [29]If someone slaps you on one cheek, offer the other cheek also. If someone demands your coat, offer your shirt also. [30]Give to anyone who asks; and when things are taken away from you, don't try to get them back. [31]Do to others as you would like them to do to you.

[32]"If you love only those who love you, why should you get credit for that? Even sinners love those who love them! [33]And if you do good only to those who do good to you, why should you get credit? Even sinners do that much! [34]And if you lend money only to those who can repay you, why should

6:18 Greek *unclean*.

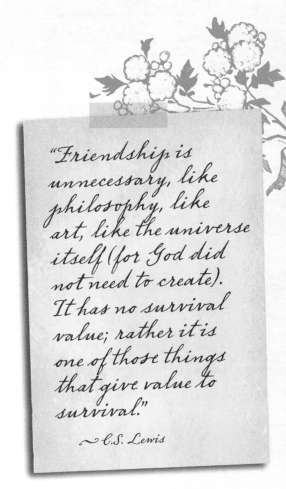

"Friendship is unnecessary, like philosophy, like art, like the universe itself (for God did not need to create). It has no survival value; rather it is one of those things that give value to survival."

~ C.S. Lewis

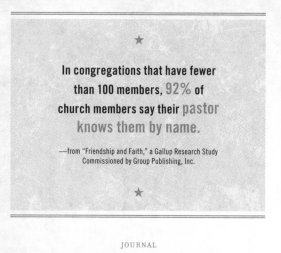

JOURNAL

_____

_____

_____

_____

_____

_____

_____

_____

_____

_____

_____

_____

_____

_____

_____

_____

_____

_____

you get credit? Even sinners will lend to other sinners for a full return.

35 "Love your enemies! Do good to them. Lend to them without expecting to be repaid. Then your reward from heaven will be very great, and you will truly be acting as children of the Most High, for he is kind to those who are unthankful and wicked. 36 You must be compassionate, just as your Father is compassionate.

Do Not Judge Others

37 "Do not judge others, and you will not be judged. Do not condemn others, or it will all come back against you. Forgive others, and you will be forgiven. 38 Give, and you will receive. Your gift will return to you in full—pressed down, shaken together to make room for more, running over, and poured into your lap. The amount you give will determine the amount you get back.*"

39 Then Jesus gave the following illustration: "Can one blind person lead another? Won't they both fall into a ditch? 40 Students* are not greater than their teacher. But the student who is fully trained will become like the teacher.

41 "And why worry about a speck in your friend's eye* when you have a log in your own? 42 How can you think of saying, 'Friend,* let me help you get rid of that speck in your eye,' when you can't see past the log in your own eye? Hypocrite! First get rid of the log in your own eye; then you will see well enough to deal with the speck in your friend's eye.

The Tree and Its Fruit

43 "A good tree can't produce bad fruit, and a bad tree can't produce good fruit. 44 A tree is identified by its fruit. Figs are never gathered from thornbushes, grapes are not picked from bramble bushes. 45 A good person produces good things from the treasury of a good heart, and an evil person produces evil things from the treasury of an evil heart. What you say flows from what is in your heart.

Building on a Solid Foundation

46 "So why do you keep calling me 'Lord, Lord!' when you don't do what I say? 47 I will show you what it's like when someone comes to me, listens to my teaching, and then follows it. 48 It is like a person building a house who digs deep and lays the foundation on solid rock. When the floodwaters rise and break against that house, it stands firm because it is well built. 49 But

6:38 Or *The measure you give will be the measure you get back.*   6:40 Or *Disciples.*   6:41 Greek *your brother's eye*; also in 6:42.   6:42 Greek *Brother.*

anyone who hears and doesn't obey is like a person who builds a house without a foundation. When the floods sweep down against that house, it will collapse into a heap of ruins."

CHAPTER 7

The Faith of a Roman Officer

When Jesus had finished saying all this to the people, he returned to Capernaum. [2] At that time the highly valued slave of a Roman officer* was sick and near death. [3] When the officer heard about Jesus, he sent some respected Jewish elders to ask him to come and heal his slave. [4] So they earnestly begged Jesus to help the man. "If anyone deserves your help, he does," they said, [5] "for he loves the Jewish people and even built a synagogue for us."

[6] So Jesus went with them. But just before they arrived at the house, the officer sent some friends to say, "Lord, don't trouble yourself by coming to my home, for I am not worthy of such an honor. [7] I am not even worthy to come and meet you. Just say the word from where you are, and my servant will be healed. [8] I know this because I am under the authority of my superior officers, and I have authority over my soldiers. I only need to say, 'Go,' and they go, or 'Come,' and they come. And if I say to my slaves, 'Do this,' they do it."

[9] When Jesus heard this, he was amazed. Turning to the crowd that was following him, he said, "I tell you, I haven't seen faith like this in all Israel!" [10] And when the officer's friends returned to his house, they found the slave completely healed.

Jesus Raises a Widow's Son

[11] Soon afterward Jesus went with his disciples to the village of Nain, and a large crowd followed him. [12] A funeral procession was coming out as he approached the village gate. The young man who had died was a widow's only son, and a large crowd from the village was with her. [13] When the Lord saw her, his heart overflowed with compassion. "Don't cry!" he said. [14] Then he walked over to the coffin and touched it, and the bearers stopped. "Young man," he said, "I tell you, get up." [15] Then the dead boy sat up and began to talk! And Jesus gave him back to his mother.

[16] Great fear swept the crowd, and they praised God, saying, "A mighty prophet has risen among us," and "God has visited his people today." [17] And the news about Jesus spread through-out Judea and the surrounding countryside.

7:2 Greek *a centurion;* similarly in 7:6.

Jesus and John the Baptist

[18]The disciples of John the Baptist told John about everything Jesus was doing. So John called for two of his disciples, [19]and he sent them to the Lord to ask him, "Are you the Messiah we've been expecting,* or should we keep looking for someone else?"

[20]John's two disciples found Jesus and said to him, "John the Baptist sent us to ask, 'Are you the Messiah we've been expecting, or should we keep looking for someone else?'"

[21]At that very time, Jesus cured many people of their diseases, illnesses, and evil spirits, and he restored sight to many who were blind. [22]Then he told John's disciples, "Go back to John and tell him what you have seen and heard—the blind see, the lame walk, the lepers are cured, the deaf hear, the dead are raised to life, and the Good News is being preached to the poor. [23]And tell him, 'God blesses those who do not turn away because of me.*'"

[24]After John's disciples left, Jesus began talking about him to the crowds. "What kind of man did you go into the wilderness to see? Was he a weak reed, swayed by every breath of wind? [25]Or were you expecting to see a man dressed in expensive clothes? No, people who wear beautiful clothes and live in luxury are found in palaces. [26]Were you looking for a prophet? Yes, and he is more than a prophet. [27]John is the man to whom the Scriptures refer when they say,

'Look, I am sending my messenger ahead of you,
    and he will prepare your way before you.'*

[28]I tell you, of all who have ever lived, none is greater than John. Yet even the least person in the Kingdom of God is greater than he is!"

[29]When they heard this, all the people—even the tax collectors—agreed that God's way was right,* for they had been baptized by John. [30]But the Pharisees and experts in religious law rejected God's plan for them, for they had refused John's baptism.

[31]"To what can I compare the people of this generation?" Jesus asked. "How can I describe them? [32]They are like children playing a game in the public square. They complain to their friends,

"We played wedding songs,
    and you didn't dance,

7:19 Greek *Are you the one who is coming?* Also in 7:20.   7:23 Or *who are not offended by me.*
7:27 Mal 3:1.   7:29 Or *praised God for his justice.*

so we played funeral songs,
and you didn't weep.'

³³For John the Baptist didn't spend his time eating bread or drinking wine, and you say, 'He's possessed by a demon.' ³⁴The Son of Man,* on the other hand, feasts and drinks, and you say, 'He's a glutton and a drunkard, and a friend of tax collectors and other sinners!' ³⁵But wisdom is shown to be right by the lives of those who follow it.*"

Jesus Anointed by a Sinful Woman

³⁶One of the Pharisees asked Jesus to have dinner with him, so Jesus went to his home and sat down to eat.* ³⁷When a certain immoral woman from that city heard he was eating there, she brought a beautiful alabaster jar filled with expensive perfume. ³⁸Then she knelt behind him at his feet, weeping. Her tears fell on his feet, and she wiped them off with her hair. Then she kept kissing his feet and putting perfume on them.

³⁹When the Pharisee who had invited him saw this, he said to himself, "If this man were a prophet, he would know what kind of woman is touching him. She's a sinner!"

⁴⁰Then Jesus answered his thoughts. "Simon," he said to the Pharisee, "I have something to say to you."

"Go ahead, Teacher," Simon replied.

⁴¹Then Jesus told him this story: "A man loaned money to two people—500 pieces of silver* to one and 50 pieces to the other. ⁴²But neither of them could repay him, so he kindly forgave them both, canceling their debts. Who do you suppose loved him more after that?"

⁴³Simon answered, "I suppose the one for whom he canceled the larger debt."

"That's right," Jesus said. ⁴⁴Then he turned to the woman and said to Simon, "Look at this woman kneeling here. When I entered your home, you didn't offer me water to wash the dust from my feet, but she has washed them with her tears and wiped them with her hair. ⁴⁵You didn't greet me with a kiss, but from the time I first came in, she has not stopped kissing my feet. ⁴⁶You neglected the courtesy of olive oil to anoint my head, but she has anointed my feet with rare perfume.

⁴⁷"I tell you, her sins—and they are many—have been

7:34 "Son of Man" is a title Jesus used for himself.   7:35 Or *But wisdom is justified by all her children.*
7:36 Or *and reclined.*   7:41 Greek *500 denarii.* A denarius was equivalent to a laborer's full day's wage.

FRIENDSHIP EXPERIENCE

FRIENDSHIP TYPE: *Family*   FRIENDSHIP LAYER: *Acceptance*

Remember When

Do you have a family member who is a little "out there"? Maybe someone who has rebelled against family tradition. Or someone who lives far away. Or someone who always talks about things you aren't interested in. Or someone who has a different faith from yours.

It's easy to judge family members. And marginalize them. And dismiss them. Especially when they seem so different from you.

But Jesus calls us to friendship and love. No matter what.

So how *do* you choose to accept and love that oh-so-different family member?

Experience

THE ONE THING 1 YOU CAN DO THIS WEEK

Your family member may not "come to his [or her] senses" as the prodigal son did, but you can still show acceptance and love for that person. After all, God accepted us—"while we were still sinners" (**Romans 5:8**). Surely we can accept our family members…even when they're different from us or we don't always agree with them or we can't understand where they're coming from.

FRIENDSHIP EXPERIENCE *continues on page 130…*

Friendship First NEW TESTAMENT

FRIENDSHIP EXPERIENCE *continued from page 129...*

This week, spend some extra time talking to that family member. Go to a movie, call long-distance, get together to watch the game. And every time you find yourself biting your lip in frustration, think of how God accepted you—shortcomings and all—stop biting your lip, and accept your *friend*.

Reflect

★ How does God's acceptance of you influence your willingness to accept others?

★ How can you show more acceptance and love toward that particularly irritating family member?

★ How did the extra time spent with your family member change your perspective of him or her?

forgiven, so she has shown me much love. But a person who is forgiven little shows only little love." [48]Then Jesus said to the woman, "Your sins are forgiven."

[49]The men at the table said among themselves, "Who is this man, that he goes around forgiving sins?"

[50]And Jesus said to the woman, "Your faith has saved you; go in peace."

CHAPTER **8**

Women Who Followed Jesus

Soon afterward Jesus began a tour of the nearby towns and villages, preaching and announcing the Good News about the Kingdom of God. He took his twelve disciples with him, [2]along with some women who had been cured of evil spirits and diseases. Among them were Mary Magdalene, from whom he had cast out seven demons; [3]Joanna, the wife of Chuza, Herod's business manager; Susanna; and many others who were contributing their own resources to support Jesus and his disciples.

Parable of the Farmer Scattering Seed

[4]One day Jesus told a story in the form of a parable to a large crowd that had gathered from many towns to hear him: [5]"A farmer went out to plant his seed. As he scattered it across his field, some seed fell on a footpath, where it was stepped on, and the birds ate it. [6]Other seed fell among rocks. It began to grow, but the plant soon wilted and died for lack of moisture. [7]Other seed fell among thorns that grew up with it and choked out the tender plants. [8]Still other seed fell on fertile soil. This seed grew and produced a crop that was a hundred times as much as had been planted!" When he had said this, he called out, "Anyone with ears to hear should listen and understand."

[9]His disciples asked him what this parable meant. [10]He replied, "You are permitted to understand the secrets* of the Kingdom of God. But I use parables to teach the others so that the Scriptures might be fulfilled:

"When they look, they won't really see.
    When they hear, they won't understand.'*

[11]"This is the meaning of the parable: The seed is God's word. [12]The seeds that fell on the footpath represent those who hear the message, only to have the devil come and

8:10a Greek *mysteries.*   **8:10b** Isa 6:9 (Greek version).

take it away from their hearts and prevent them from believing and being saved. [13] The seeds on the rocky soil represent those who hear the message and receive it with joy. But since they don't have deep roots, they believe for a while, then they fall away when they face temptation. [14] The seeds that fell among the thorns represent those who hear the message, but all too quickly the message is crowded out by the cares and riches and pleasures of this life. And so they never grow into maturity. [15] And the seeds that fell on the good soil represent honest, good-hearted people who hear God's word, cling to it, and patiently produce a huge harvest.

Parable of the Lamp

[16] "No one lights a lamp and then covers it with a bowl or hides it under a bed. A lamp is placed on a stand, where its light can be seen by all who enter the house. [17] For all that is secret will eventually be brought into the open, and everything that is concealed will be brought to light and made known to all.

[18] "So pay attention to how you hear. To those who listen to my teaching, more understanding will be given. But for those who are not listening, even what they think they understand will be taken away from them."

The True Family of Jesus

[19] Then Jesus' mother and brothers came to see him, but they couldn't get to him because of the crowd. [20] Someone told Jesus, "Your mother and your brothers are outside, and they want to see you."

[21] Jesus replied, "My mother and my brothers are all those who hear God's word and obey it."

Jesus Calms the Storm

[22] One day Jesus said to his disciples, "Let's cross to the other side of the lake." So they got into a boat and started out. [23] As they sailed across, Jesus settled down for a nap. But soon a fierce storm came down on the lake. The boat was filling with water, and they were in real danger.

[24] The disciples went and woke him up, shouting, "Master, Master, we're going to drown!"

When Jesus woke up, he rebuked the wind and the raging waves. Suddenly the storm stopped and all was calm. [25] Then he asked them, "Where is your faith?"

The disciples were terrified and amazed. "Who is this man?"

they asked each other. "When he gives a command, even the wind and waves obey him!"

Jesus Heals a Demon-Possessed Man

26 So they arrived in the region of the Gerasenes,* across the lake from Galilee. 27 As Jesus was climbing out of the boat, a man who was possessed by demons came out to meet him. For a long time he had been homeless and naked, living in a cemetery outside the town.

28 As soon as he saw Jesus, he shrieked and fell down in front of him. Then he screamed, "Why are you interfering with me, Jesus, Son of the Most High God? Please, I beg you, don't torture me!" 29 For Jesus had already commanded the evil* spirit to come out of him. This spirit had often taken control of the man. Even when he was placed under guard and put in chains and shackles, he simply broke them and rushed out into the wilderness, completely under the demon's power.

30 Jesus demanded, "What is your name?"

"Legion," he replied, for he was filled with many demons. 31 The demons kept begging Jesus not to send them into the bottomless pit.*

32 There happened to be a large herd of pigs feeding on the hillside nearby, and the demons begged him to let them enter into the pigs.

So Jesus gave them permission. 33 Then the demons came out of the man and entered the pigs, and the entire herd plunged down the steep hillside into the lake and drowned.

34 When the herdsmen saw it, they fled to the nearby town and the surrounding countryside, spreading the news as they ran. 35 People rushed out to see what had happened. A crowd soon gathered around Jesus, and they saw the man who had been freed from the demons. He was sitting at Jesus' feet, fully clothed and perfectly sane, and they were all afraid. 36 Then those who had seen what happened told the others how the demon-possessed man had been healed. 37 And all the people in the region of the Gerasenes begged Jesus to go away and leave them alone, for a great wave of fear swept over them.

So Jesus returned to the boat and left, crossing back to the other side of the lake. 38 The man who had been freed from the demons begged to go with him. But Jesus sent him home, saying, 39 "No, go back to your family, and tell them

8:26 Other manuscripts read *Gadarenes;* still others read *Gergesenes;* also in 8:37. See Matt 8:28; Mark 5:1. **8:29** Greek *unclean.* **8:31** Or *the abyss,* or *the underworld.*

everything God has done for you." So he went all through the town proclaiming the great things Jesus had done for him.

Jesus Heals in Response to Faith

⁴⁰On the other side of the lake the crowds welcomed Jesus, because they had been waiting for him. ⁴¹Then a man named Jairus, a leader of the local synagogue, came and fell at Jesus' feet, pleading with him to come home with him. ⁴²His only daughter,* who was about twelve years old, was dying.

As Jesus went with him, he was surrounded by the crowds. ⁴³A woman in the crowd had suffered for twelve years with constant bleeding,* and she could find no cure. ⁴⁴Coming up behind Jesus, she touched the fringe of his robe. Immediately, the bleeding stopped.

⁴⁵"Who touched me?" Jesus asked.

Everyone denied it, and Peter said, "Master, this whole crowd is pressing up against you."

⁴⁶But Jesus said, "Someone deliberately touched me, for I felt healing power go out from me." ⁴⁷When the woman realized that she could not stay hidden, she began to tremble and fell to her knees in front of him. The whole crowd heard her explain why she had touched him and that she had been immediately healed. ⁴⁸"Daughter," he said to her, "your faith has made you well. Go in peace."

⁴⁹While he was still speaking to her, a messenger arrived from the home of Jairus, the leader of the synagogue. He told him, "Your daughter is dead. There's no use troubling the Teacher now."

⁵⁰But when Jesus heard what had happened, he said to Jairus, "Don't be afraid. Just have faith, and she will be healed."

⁵¹When they arrived at the house, Jesus wouldn't let anyone go in with him except Peter, John, James, and the little girl's father and mother. ⁵²The house was filled with people weeping and wailing, but he said, "Stop the weeping! She isn't dead; she's only asleep."

⁵³But the crowd laughed at him because they all knew she had died. ⁵⁴Then Jesus took her by the hand and said in a loud voice, "My child, get up!" ⁵⁵And at that moment her life* returned, and she immediately stood up! Then Jesus told them to give her something to eat. ⁵⁶Her parents were overwhelmed, but Jesus insisted that they not tell anyone what had happened.

8:42 Or *His only child, a daughter.* **8:43** Some manuscripts add *having spent everything she had on doctors.* **8:55** Or *her spirit.*

> "Friendship is never established as an understood relation... It is a miracle which requires constant proofs. It is an exercise of the purest imagination and the rarest faith."
>
> ~ Henry David Thoreau

JOURNAL

CHAPTER **9**

Jesus Sends Out the Twelve Disciples

One day Jesus called together his twelve disciples* and gave them power and authority to cast out all demons and to heal all diseases. ²Then he sent them out to tell everyone about the Kingdom of God and to heal the sick. ³"Take nothing for your journey," he instructed them. "Don't take a walking stick, a traveler's bag, food, money,* or even a change of clothes. ⁴Wherever you go, stay in the same house until you leave town. ⁵And if a town refuses to welcome you, shake its dust from your feet as you leave to show that you have abandoned those people to their fate."

⁶So they began their circuit of the villages, preaching the Good News and healing the sick.

Herod's Confusion

⁷When Herod Antipas, the ruler of Galilee,* heard about everything Jesus was doing, he was puzzled. Some were saying that John the Baptist had been raised from the dead. ⁸Others thought Jesus was Elijah or one of the other prophets risen from the dead.

⁹"I beheaded John," Herod said, "so who is this man about whom I hear such stories?" And he kept trying to see him.

Jesus Feeds Five Thousand

¹⁰When the apostles returned, they told Jesus everything they had done. Then he slipped quietly away with them toward the town of Bethsaida. ¹¹But the crowds found out where he was going, and they followed him. He welcomed them and taught them about the Kingdom of God, and he healed those who were sick.

¹²Late in the afternoon the twelve disciples came to him and said, "Send the crowds away to the nearby villages and farms, so they can find food and lodging for the night. There is nothing to eat here in this remote place."

¹³But Jesus said, "You feed them."

"But we have only five loaves of bread and two fish," they answered. "Or are you expecting us to go and buy enough food for this whole crowd?" ¹⁴For there were about 5,000 men there.

Jesus replied, "Tell them to sit down in groups of about fifty each." ¹⁵So the people all sat down. ¹⁶Jesus took the five loaves and two fish, looked up toward heaven, and blessed them. Then,

9:1 Greek *the Twelve;* other manuscripts read *the twelve apostles.*   **9:3** Or *silver coins.*   **9:7** Greek *Herod the tetrarch.* Herod Antipas was a son of King Herod and was ruler over Galilee.

breaking the loaves into pieces, he kept giving the bread and fish to the disciples so they could distribute it to the people. [17] They all ate as much as they wanted, and afterward, the disciples picked up twelve baskets of leftovers!

Peter's Declaration about Jesus

[18] One day Jesus left the crowds to pray alone. Only his disciples were with him, and he asked them, "Who do people say I am?"

[19] "Well," they replied, "some say John the Baptist, some say Elijah, and others say you are one of the other ancient prophets risen from the dead."

[20] Then he asked them, "But who do you say I am?"

Peter replied, "You are the Messiah* sent from God!"

Jesus Predicts His Death

[21] Jesus warned his disciples not to tell anyone who he was. [22] "The Son of Man* must suffer many terrible things," he said. "He will be rejected by the elders, the leading priests, and the teachers of religious law. He will be killed, but on the third day he will be raised from the dead."

[23] Then he said to the crowd, "If any of you wants to be my follower, you must turn from your selfish ways, take up your cross daily, and follow me. [24] If you try to hang on to your life, you will lose it. But if you give up your life for my sake, you will save it. [25] And what do you benefit if you gain the whole world but are yourself lost or destroyed? [26] If anyone is ashamed of me and my message, the Son of Man will be ashamed of that person when he returns in his glory and in the glory of the Father and the holy angels. [27] I tell you the truth, some standing here right now will not die before they see the Kingdom of God."

The Transfiguration

[28] About eight days later Jesus took Peter, John, and James up on a mountain to pray. [29] And as he was praying, the appearance of his face was transformed, and his clothes became dazzling white. [30] Suddenly, two men, Moses and Elijah, appeared and began talking with Jesus. [31] They were glorious to see. And they were speaking about his exodus from this world, which was about to be fulfilled in Jerusalem.

[32] Peter and the others had fallen asleep. When they woke up, they saw Jesus' glory and the two men standing with him. [33] As Moses and Elijah were starting to leave, Peter, not even

9:20 Or *the Christ. Messiah* (a Hebrew term) and *Christ* (a Greek term) both mean "the anointed one." 9:22 "Son of Man" is a title Jesus used for himself.

FRIENDSHIP EXPERIENCE

FRIENDSHIP TYPE: *Neighbors*   FRIENDSHIP LAYER: *Getting Acquainted*

Taking It to the Next Level

It's usually easy to be polite to our neighbors. We say "Hello" and "How are you?" to the man we pass while walking our dog or to the cashier at the grocery store. But if we look at the parable of the good Samaritan in **Luke 10:25-37**, we can see that Jesus calls us to much more than mere politeness. Jesus calls us to true friendship, even with those we would not consider friends.

So how do we go beyond politeness with our neighbors? How do we move into friendship with people we barely know? We begin by getting to know them!

THE ONE THING YOU CAN DO THIS WEEK **1**

Experience

Invite a neighbor or a new acquaintance to join you for coffee or ice cream this week. Your goal is to come away knowing the following details about your new friend and sharing the same details about yourself:

★ hometown
★ job
★ family
★ favorite book or movie
★ dream vacation

While going through this list certainly won't tell you everything about each other, it is a fun and easy way to help you begin to get acquainted!

FRIENDSHIP EXPERIENCE *continues on page 136…*

..

FRIENDSHIP EXPERIENCE *continued from page 135...*

Reflect

★ What did you enjoy about the time you spent getting to know your neighbor?

★ How do you think your friendship was affected by the time you spent getting to know each other?

★ What would it take for you and your neighbor to deepen your friendship?

JOURNAL

knowing what he was saying, blurted out, "Master, it's wonderful for us to be here! Let's make three shelters as memorials*—one for you, one for Moses, and one for Elijah." ³⁴But even as he was saying this, a cloud overshadowed them, and terror gripped them as the cloud covered them.

³⁵Then a voice from the cloud said, "This is my Son, my Chosen One.* Listen to him." ³⁶When the voice finished, Jesus was there alone. They didn't tell anyone at that time what they had seen.

Jesus Heals a Demon-Possessed Boy

³⁷The next day, after they had come down the mountain, a large crowd met Jesus. ³⁸A man in the crowd called out to him, "Teacher, I beg you to look at my son, my only child. ³⁹An evil spirit keeps seizing him, making him scream. It throws him into convulsions so that he foams at the mouth. It batters him and hardly ever leaves him alone. ⁴⁰I begged your disciples to cast out the spirit, but they couldn't do it."

⁴¹Jesus said, "You faithless and corrupt people! How long must I be with you and put up with you?" Then he said to the man, "Bring your son here."

⁴²As the boy came forward, the demon knocked him to the ground and threw him into a violent convulsion. But Jesus rebuked the evil* spirit and healed the boy. Then he gave him back to his father. ⁴³Awe gripped the people as they saw this majestic display of God's power.

Jesus Again Predicts His Death

While everyone was marveling at everything he was doing, Jesus said to his disciples, ⁴⁴"Listen to me and remember what I say. The Son of Man is going to be betrayed into the hands of his enemies." ⁴⁵But they didn't know what he meant. Its significance was hidden from them, so they couldn't understand it, and they were afraid to ask him about it.

The Greatest in the Kingdom

⁴⁶Then his disciples began arguing about which of them was the greatest. ⁴⁷But Jesus knew their thoughts, so he brought a little child to his side. ⁴⁸Then he said to them, "Anyone who welcomes a little child like this on my behalf* welcomes me, and anyone who welcomes me also welcomes my Father who sent me. Whoever is the least among you is the greatest."

9:33 Greek *three tabernacles.* **9:35** Some manuscripts read *This is my dearly loved Son.* **9:42** Greek *unclean.* **9:48** Greek *in my name.*

JOURNAL

Using the Name of Jesus

⁴⁹John said to Jesus, "Master, we saw someone using your name to cast out demons, but we told him to stop because he isn't in our group."

⁵⁰But Jesus said, "Don't stop him! Anyone who is not against you is for you."

Opposition from Samaritans

⁵¹As the time drew near for him to ascend to heaven, Jesus resolutely set out for Jerusalem. ⁵²He sent messengers ahead to a Samaritan village to prepare for his arrival. ⁵³But the people of the village did not welcome Jesus because he was on his way to Jerusalem. ⁵⁴When James and John saw this, they said to Jesus, "Lord, should we call down fire from heaven to burn them up*?" ⁵⁵But Jesus turned and rebuked them.* ⁵⁶So they went on to another village.

The Cost of Following Jesus

⁵⁷As they were walking along, someone said to Jesus, "I will follow you wherever you go."

⁵⁸But Jesus replied, "Foxes have dens to live in, and birds have nests, but the Son of Man has no place even to lay his head."

⁵⁹He said to another person, "Come, follow me."

The man agreed, but he said, "Lord, first let me return home and bury my father."

⁶⁰But Jesus told him, "Let the spiritually dead bury their own dead!* Your duty is to go and preach about the Kingdom of God."

⁶¹Another said, "Yes, Lord, I will follow you, but first let me say good-bye to my family."

⁶²But Jesus told him, "Anyone who puts a hand to the plow and then looks back is not fit for the Kingdom of God."

CHAPTER 10

Jesus Sends Out His Disciples

The Lord now chose seventy-two* other disciples and sent them ahead in pairs to all the towns and places he planned to visit. ²These were his instructions to them: "The harvest is great, but the workers are few. So pray to the Lord who is in charge of the harvest; ask him to send more workers into his fields. ³Now go, and remember that I am sending you out as lambs among wolves. ⁴Don't take any money with you, nor

9:54 Some manuscripts add *as Elijah did.* 9:55 Some manuscripts add an expanded conclusion to verse 55 and an additional sentence in verse 56: *And he said, "You don't realize what your hearts are like.* ⁵⁶*For the Son of Man has not come to destroy people's lives, but to save them."* 9:60 Greek *Let the dead bury their own dead.* 10:1 Some manuscripts read *seventy;* also in 10:17.

a traveler's bag, nor an extra pair of sandals. And don't stop to greet anyone on the road.

5 "Whenever you enter someone's home, first say, 'May God's peace be on this house.' 6 If those who live there are peaceful, the blessing will stand; if they are not, the blessing will return to you. 7 Don't move around from home to home. Stay in one place, eating and drinking what they provide. Don't hesitate to accept hospitality, because those who work deserve their pay.

8 "If you enter a town and it welcomes you, eat whatever is set before you. 9 Heal the sick, and tell them, 'The Kingdom of God is near you now.' 10 But if a town refuses to welcome you, go out into its streets and say, 11 'We wipe even the dust of your town from our feet to show that we have abandoned you to your fate. And know this—the Kingdom of God is near!' 12 I assure you, even wicked Sodom will be better off than such a town on judgment day.

13 "What sorrow awaits you, Korazin and Bethsaida! For if the miracles I did in you had been done in wicked Tyre and Sidon, their people would have repented of their sins long ago, clothing themselves in burlap and throwing ashes on their heads to show their remorse. 14 Yes, Tyre and Sidon will be better off on judgment day than you. 15 And you people of Capernaum, will you be honored in heaven? No, you will go down to the place of the dead.*"

16 Then he said to the disciples, "Anyone who accepts your message is also accepting me. And anyone who rejects you is rejecting me. And anyone who rejects me is rejecting God, who sent me."

17 When the seventy-two disciples returned, they joyfully reported to him, "Lord, even the demons obey us when we use your name!"

18 "Yes," he told them, "I saw Satan fall from heaven like lightning! 19 Look, I have given you authority over all the power of the enemy, and you can walk among snakes and scorpions and crush them. Nothing will injure you. 20 But don't rejoice because evil spirits obey you; rejoice because your names are registered in heaven."

Jesus' Prayer of Thanksgiving

21 At that same time Jesus was filled with the joy of the Holy Spirit, and he said, "O Father, Lord of heaven and earth, thank you for hiding these things from those who think themselves

10:15 Greek *to Hades.*

wise and clever, and for revealing them to the childlike. Yes, Father, it pleased you to do it this way.

22 "My Father has entrusted everything to me. No one truly knows the Son except the Father, and no one truly knows the Father except the Son and those to whom the Son chooses to reveal him."

23 Then when they were alone, he turned to the disciples and said, "Blessed are the eyes that see what you have seen. 24 I tell you, many prophets and kings longed to see what you see, but they didn't see it. And they longed to hear what you hear, but they didn't hear it."

The Most Important Commandment

25 One day an expert in religious law stood up to test Jesus by asking him this question: "Teacher, what should I do to inherit eternal life?"

26 Jesus replied, "What does the law of Moses say? How do you read it?"

27 The man answered, "'You must love the LORD your God with all your heart, all your soul, all your strength, and all your mind.' And, 'Love your neighbor as yourself.'"*

28 "Right!" Jesus told him. "Do this and you will live!"

29 The man wanted to justify his actions, so he asked Jesus, "And who is my neighbor?"

Parable of the Good Samaritan

30 Jesus replied with a story: "A Jewish man was traveling on a trip from Jerusalem to Jericho, and he was attacked by bandits. They stripped him of his clothes, beat him up, and left him half dead beside the road.

31 "By chance a priest came along. But when he saw the man lying there, he crossed to the other side of the road and passed him by. 32 A Temple assistant* walked over and looked at him lying there, but he also passed by on the other side.

33 "Then a despised Samaritan came along, and when he saw the man, he felt compassion for him. 34 Going over to him, the Samaritan soothed his

10:27 Deut 6:5; Lev 19:18. 10:32 Greek A Levite.

Anchor Passage

PASSAGE: Luke 10:25-37

FRIENDSHIP TYPE: Neighbors

FRIENDSHIP LAYER: Getting Acquainted

Overlooked

List your neighbors.

_____

_____

_____

_____

Now read **Luke 10:25-37**.

"Who is my neighbor?"

Jesus answered the question with a story—a story about a man helping a stranger.

Sure, it's easy to read this parable and say, "Well, of course, I would help someone if I saw him robbed and beaten on the side of a road" or to translate the parable into your world and congratulate yourself for stopping to help the woman on the side of the road with the flat tire.

But what about the young man bagging your groceries (his parents are going through a divorce right now), the man you see walking his dog every day (his wife died years ago, and his children live far away), or the telemarketer who calls you in the middle of dinner (she's a first-generation college student just trying to get through her freshman year)? These are the everyday, the overlooked, and they're your neighbors, too.

Anchor Passage continues on
page 140...

Anchor Passage continued from page 139...

Though at first glance they may not appear to be in desperate need, they're the *emotionally* bloodied, the lonely, and the desperate—the neighbors Jesus called you to love and to serve.

You won't see some wounds until you're willing to reach out, open up, and get acquainted with those around you.

Who is your neighbor? The parable of the good Samaritan illustrates that *everyone* is your neighbor. Jesus wants you to recognize that every person you see, walk past, or interact with is a neighbor who needs love and friendship.

Experience

Go back to your list of neighbors. After reading the passage, whom would you add to the list? Think of all the people you met today.

Choose one unlikely person on your list to get acquainted with. See a movie together. Go out for coffee. Invite the person over to watch the game. Think of a specific way to move your friendship forward…and then do it!

Reflect

★ What would make you stop for the people on your list?

★ How can you get to know the people on your list better?

DIGGING DEEPER

FRIENDSHIP TYPE: *Neighbors*   FRIENDSHIP LAYER: *Getting Acquainted*

For getting acquainted with your neighbors, check out…

wounds with olive oil and wine and bandaged them. Then he put the man on his own donkey and took him to an inn, where he took care of him. ³⁵The next day he handed the innkeeper two silver coins,* telling him, "Take care of this man. If his bill runs higher than this, I'll pay you the next time I'm here.'

³⁶"Now which of these three would you say was a neighbor to the man who was attacked by bandits?" Jesus asked.

³⁷The man replied, "The one who showed him mercy."

Then Jesus said, "Yes, now go and do the same." ⚓

Jesus Visits Martha and Mary

³⁸As Jesus and the disciples continued on their way to Jerusalem, they came to a certain village where a woman named Martha welcomed him into her home. ³⁹Her sister, Mary, sat at the Lord's feet, listening to what he taught. ⁴⁰But Martha was distracted by the big dinner she was preparing. She came to Jesus and said, "Lord, doesn't it seem unfair to you that my sister just sits here while I do all the work? Tell her to come and help me."

⁴¹But the Lord said to her, "My dear Martha, you are worried and upset over all these details! ⁴²There is only one thing worth being concerned about. Mary has discovered it, and it will not be taken away from her." ⚓

CHAPTER **11**

Teaching about Prayer

Once Jesus was in a certain place praying. As he finished, one of his disciples came to him and said, "Lord, teach us to pray, just as John taught his disciples."

²Jesus said, "This is how you should pray:*

10:35 Greek *two denarii.* A denarius was equivalent to a laborer's full day's wage.   **11:2** Some manuscripts add additional phrases from the Lord's Prayer as it reads in Matt 6:9-13.

"Father, may your name be kept holy.
    May your Kingdom come soon.
3 Give us each day the food we need,*
4 and forgive us our sins,
    as we forgive those who sin against us.
And don't let us yield to temptation.*"

5 Then, teaching them more about prayer, he used this story: "Suppose you went to a friend's house at midnight, wanting to borrow three loaves of bread. You say to him, 6 'A friend of mine has just arrived for a visit, and I have nothing for him to eat.' 7 And suppose he calls out from his bedroom, 'Don't bother me. The door is locked for the night, and my family and I are all in bed. I can't help you.' 8 But I tell you this—though he won't do it for friendship's sake, if you keep knocking long enough, he will get up and give you whatever you need because of your shameless persistence.*

9 "And so I tell you, keep on asking, and you will receive what you ask for. Keep on seeking, and you will find. Keep on knocking, and the door will be opened to you. 10 For everyone who asks, receives. Everyone who seeks, finds. And to everyone who knocks, the door will be opened.

11 "You fathers—if your children ask* for a fish, do you give them a snake instead? 12 Or if they ask for an egg, do you give them a scorpion? Of course not! 13 So if you sinful people know how to give good gifts to your children, how much more will your heavenly Father give the Holy Spirit to those who ask him."

Jesus and the Prince of Demons

14 One day Jesus cast out a demon from a man who couldn't speak, and when the demon was gone, the man began to speak. The crowds were amazed, 15 but some of them said, "No wonder he can cast out demons. He gets his power from Satan,* the prince of demons." 16 Others, trying to test Jesus, demanded that he show them a miraculous sign from heaven to prove his authority.

17 He knew their thoughts, so he said, "Any kingdom divided by civil war is doomed. A family splintered by feuding will fall apart. 18 You say I am empowered by Satan. But if Satan is divided and fighting against himself, how can his kingdom survive? 19 And if I am empowered by Satan, what about your

11:3 Or *Give us each day our food for the day;* or *Give us each day our food for tomorrow.*   11:4 Or *And keep us from being tested.*   11:8 Or *in order to avoid shame,* or *so his reputation won't be damaged.*
11:11 Some manuscripts add *for bread, do you give them a stone? Or [if they ask.]*   11:15 Greek *Beelzeboul;* also in 11:18, 19. Other manuscripts read *Beezeboul;* Latin version reads *Beelzebub.*

Anchor Passage

PASSAGE: Luke 10:38-42

FRIENDSHIP TYPE: *Jesus*   FRIENDSHIP LAYER: *Companionship*

First Things First

Think about a time you invited friends to your place for dinner—people you enjoyed being with. Got that evening in mind?

Now read **Luke 10:38-42**.

So what did Martha do that was so awful? that earned her a gentle rebuke from her guest of honor?

Martha was dashing around the kitchen, washing figs, gathering up dishes, pulling bread from the oven, when she suddenly realized that her helper—Mary—had deserted the kitchen just when Martha needed Mary most.

You'd have been annoyed, too.

And think how you'd have felt when you heard laughter from the next room and realized Mary was relaxing with the guests.

Martha didn't do anything *wrong*, exactly. She just failed to do what was *right*. She let the demands of the dinner keep her from spending time with Jesus.

Martha busied herself doing good deeds—deeds for Jesus, no less—and she missed out on companionship *with* Jesus.

Think about that dinner with your friends. Was the best part of the evening the time you spent in the kitchen fixing food (or calling the pizza place) or the time spent with your guests? Which fed your friendship?

Anchor Passage continues on page 142...

Anchor Passage continued from page 141...

It's one thing to do good deeds to honor and impress Jesus.

It's another and a far more valuable thing to become his friend and enjoy time with him. Jesus is looking for companionship—not lunch.

Experience

Spending time with Jesus was easy for Martha; she just had to walk into the next room.

Find a quiet spot where you can sit by yourself for a few minutes, but pull up two chairs. Picture Jesus sitting across from you, relaxing with you before dinner. Were he here, what would you say to him? What might he say to you? Spend 10 minutes answering those questions, because if you're talking with him, he's listening.

Reflect

★ How do you think Jesus and his disciples would have felt had Martha joined Mary and there been no meal served at all?

★ In what ways do you choose "busyness" over truly connecting with people? Why do you think you do it?

★ What are the risks of simply spending time with Jesus? the rewards?

DIGGING DEEPER

FRIENDSHIP TYPE:
Jesus

FRIENDSHIP LAYER:
Companionship

For being a companion of Jesus, check out...

➵ The Friendship Experience .... on page 145
➵ The Friendship Story .... on page 364
➵ What to Say and What Not to Say .... on page 361

---

own exorcists? They cast out demons, too, so they will condemn you for what you have said. ²⁰But if I am casting out demons by the power of God,* then the Kingdom of God has arrived among you. ²¹For when a strong man like Satan is fully armed and guards his palace, his possessions are safe—²²until someone even stronger attacks and overpowers him, strips him of his weapons, and carries off his belongings.

²³"Anyone who isn't with me opposes me, and anyone who isn't working with me is actually working against me.

²⁴"When an evil* spirit leaves a person, it goes into the desert, searching for rest. But when it finds none, it says, 'I will return to the person I came from.' ²⁵So it returns and finds that its former home is all swept and in order. ²⁶Then the spirit finds seven other spirits more evil than itself, and they all enter the person and live there. And so that person is worse off than before."

²⁷As he was speaking, a woman in the crowd called out, "God bless your mother—the womb from which you came, and the breasts that nursed you!"

²⁸Jesus replied, "But even more blessed are all who hear the word of God and put it into practice."

The Sign of Jonah

²⁹As the crowd pressed in on Jesus, he said, "This evil generation keeps asking me to show them a miraculous sign. But the only sign I will give them is the sign of Jonah. ³⁰What happened to him was a sign to the people of Nineveh that God had sent him. What happens to the Son of Man* will be a sign to these people that he was sent by God.

³¹"The queen of Sheba* will stand up against this generation on judgment day and condemn it, for she came from a distant land to hear the wisdom of Solomon. Now someone greater than Solomon is here—but you refuse to listen. ³²The people of Nineveh will also stand up against this generation on judgment day and condemn it, for they repented of their sins at the preaching of Jonah. Now someone greater than Jonah is here—but you refuse to repent.

Receiving the Light

³³"No one lights a lamp and then hides it or puts it under a basket.* Instead, a lamp is placed on a stand, where its light can be seen by all who enter the house.

11:20 Greek *by the finger of God.* **11:24** Greek *unclean.* **11:30** "Son of Man" is a title Jesus used for himself. **11:31** Greek *The queen of the south.* **11:33** Some manuscripts omit *or puts it under a basket.*

34 "Your eye is a lamp that provides light for your body. When your eye is good, your whole body is filled with light. But when it is bad, your body is filled with darkness. 35 Make sure that the light you think you have is not actually darkness. 36 If you are filled with light, with no dark corners, then your whole life will be radiant, as though a floodlight were filling you with light."

Jesus Criticizes the Religious Leaders

37 As Jesus was speaking, one of the Pharisees invited him home for a meal. So he went in and took his place at the table.* 38 His host was amazed to see that he sat down to eat without first performing the hand-washing ceremony required by Jewish custom. 39 Then the Lord said to him, "You Pharisees are so careful to clean the outside of the cup and the dish, but inside you are filthy—full of greed and wickedness! 40 Fools! Didn't God make the inside as well as the outside? 41 So clean the inside by giving gifts to the poor, and you will be clean all over.

42 "What sorrow awaits you Pharisees! For you are careful to tithe even the tiniest income from your herb gardens,* but you ignore justice and the love of God. You should tithe, yes, but do not neglect the more important things.

43 "What sorrow awaits you Pharisees! For you love to sit in the seats of honor in the synagogues and receive respectful greetings as you walk in the marketplaces. 44 Yes, what sorrow awaits you! For you are like hidden graves in a field. People walk over them without knowing the corruption they are stepping on."

45 "Teacher," said an expert in religious law, "you have insulted us, too, in what you just said."

46 "Yes," said Jesus, "what sorrow also awaits you experts in religious law! For you crush people with unbearable religious demands, and you never lift a finger to ease the burden. 47 What sorrow awaits you! For you build monuments for the prophets your own ancestors killed long ago. 48 But in fact, you stand as witnesses who agree with what your ancestors did. They killed the prophets, and you join in their crime by building the monuments! 49 This is what God in his wisdom said about you:* 'I will send prophets and apostles to them, but they will kill some and persecute the others.'

50 "As a result, this generation will be held responsible for the murder of all God's prophets from the creation of the world— 51 from the murder of Abel to the murder of Zechariah, who

11:37 Or and reclined.   11:42 Greek tithe the mint, the rue, and every herb.   11:49 Greek Therefore, the wisdom of God said.

JOURNAL

was killed between the altar and the sanctuary. Yes, it will certainly be charged against this generation.

52 "What sorrow awaits you experts in religious law! For you remove the key to knowledge from the people. You don't enter the Kingdom yourselves, and you prevent others from entering."

53 As Jesus was leaving, the teachers of religious law and the Pharisees became hostile and tried to provoke him with many questions. 54 They wanted to trap him into saying something they could use against him.

CHAPTER 12

A Warning against Hypocrisy

Meanwhile, the crowds grew until thousands were milling about and stepping on each other. Jesus turned first to his disciples and warned them, "Beware of the yeast of the Pharisees—their hypocrisy. 2 The time is coming when everything that is covered up will be revealed, and all that is secret will be made known to all. 3 Whatever you have said in the dark will be heard in the light, and what you have whispered behind closed doors will be shouted from the housetops for all to hear!

4 "Dear friends, don't be afraid of those who want to kill your body; they cannot do any more to you after that. 5 But I'll tell you whom to fear. Fear God, who has the power to kill you and then throw you into hell.* Yes, he's the one to fear.

6 "What is the price of five sparrows—two copper coins*? Yet God does not forget a single one of them. 7 And the very hairs on your head are all numbered. So don't be afraid; you are more valuable to God than a whole flock of sparrows.

8 "I tell you the truth, everyone who acknowledges me publicly here on earth, the Son of Man* will also acknowledge in the presence of God's angels. 9 But anyone who denies me here on earth will be denied before God's angels. 10 Anyone who speaks against the Son of Man can be forgiven, but anyone who blasphemes the Holy Spirit will not be forgiven.

11 "And when you are brought to trial in the synagogues and before rulers and authorities, don't worry about how to defend yourself or what to say, 12 for the Holy Spirit will teach you at that time what needs to be said."

Parable of the Rich Fool

13 Then someone called from the crowd, "Teacher, please tell my brother to divide our father's estate with me."

12:5 Greek *Gehenna*. 12:6 Greek *two assaria* [Roman coins equal to 1/16 of a denarius]. 12:8 "Son of Man" is a title Jesus used for himself.

¹⁴Jesus replied, "Friend, who made me a judge over you to decide such things as that?" ¹⁵Then he said, "Beware! Guard against every kind of greed. Life is not measured by how much you own."

¹⁶Then he told them a story: "A rich man had a fertile farm that produced fine crops. ¹⁷He said to himself, 'What should I do? I don't have room for all my crops.' ¹⁸Then he said, 'I know! I'll tear down my barns and build bigger ones. Then I'll have room enough to store all my wheat and other goods. ¹⁹And I'll sit back and say to myself, "My friend, you have enough stored away for years to come. Now take it easy! Eat, drink, and be merry!"'

²⁰"But God said to him, 'You fool! You will die this very night. Then who will get everything you worked for?'

²¹"Yes, a person is a fool to store up earthly wealth but not have a rich relationship with God."

Teaching about Money and Possessions

²²Then, turning to his disciples, Jesus said, "That is why I tell you not to worry about everyday life—whether you have enough food to eat or enough clothes to wear. ²³For life is more than food, and your body more than clothing. ²⁴Look at the ravens. They don't plant or harvest or store food in barns, for God feeds them. And you are far more valuable to him than any birds! ²⁵Can all your worries add a single moment to your life? ²⁶And if worry can't accomplish a little thing like that, what's the use of worrying over bigger things?

²⁷"Look at the lilies and how they grow. They don't work or make their clothing, yet Solomon in all his glory was not dressed as beautifully as they are. ²⁸And if God cares so wonderfully for flowers that are here today and thrown into the fire tomorrow, he will certainly care for you. Why do you have so little faith?

²⁹"And don't be concerned about what to eat and what to drink. Don't worry about such things. ³⁰These things dominate the thoughts of unbelievers all over the world, but your Father already knows your needs. ³¹Seek the Kingdom of God above all else, and he will give you everything you need.

³²"So don't be afraid, little flock. For it gives your Father great happiness to give you the Kingdom.

³³"Sell your possessions and give to those in need. This will store up treasure for you in heaven! And the purses of heaven never get old or develop holes. Your treasure will be safe; no

FRIENDSHIP EXPERIENCE

FRIENDSHIP TYPE:	FRIENDSHIP LAYER:
Jesus	*Companionship*

Hanging Out With God

Friends do things together.

Some friends meet for dinner. Play golf. Go shopping.

But when you hang out with Jesus, you get to change the world.

Cool, huh?

When Jesus recruited his disciples, he told them to follow him—and they did. Jesus taught while on the road, interacting with people. And he's still teaching in places you might not expect to find him: among the poor, the broken, the bitter, the bored. He's still busy bringing the world into a relationship with himself, so companionship with Jesus is an active proposition.

If you want to spend time with him, you have to get with his program. But you—and the world—will never be the same.

FRIENDSHIP EXPERIENCE *continues on page 146...*

FRIENDSHIP EXPERIENCE *continued from page 145...*

Experience

THE ONE THING
1
YOU CAN DO THIS WEEK

Look for where Jesus is working, and go join in.

In a local church, what ministry area could use another volunteer?

In a local church food pantry or homeless shelter, how can you get involved?

In your neighborhood, who's hurting and needing help or comfort?

Think about it: Those are exactly the places Jesus and his followers show up. If you want to hang out with Jesus, doesn't it make sense to go where he is?

Actively serving others isn't the *only* way to be a companion of Jesus; he's just as present when you're sitting quietly as when you're feeding the hungry...but companionship with Jesus also means joining him where he's working.

Your challenge this week: Spend time with Jesus as his companion. First look for where he's working, and then join him!

Reflect

★ Where do you see Jesus working in your church? your neighborhood? your city?

★ How might being a companion of Jesus change you? challenge you?

Friendship First NEW TESTAMENT

---

thief can steal it and no moth can destroy it. ³⁴Wherever your treasure is, there the desires of your heart will also be.

Be Ready for the Lord's Coming

³⁵"Be dressed for service and keep your lamps burning, ³⁶as though you were waiting for your master to return from the wedding feast. Then you will be ready to open the door and let him in the moment he arrives and knocks. ³⁷The servants who are ready and waiting for his return will be rewarded. I tell you the truth, he himself will seat them, put on an apron, and serve them as they sit and eat! ³⁸He may come in the middle of the night or just before dawn.* But whenever he comes, he will reward the servants who are ready.

³⁹"Understand this: If a homeowner knew exactly when a burglar was coming, he would not permit his house to be broken into. ⁴⁰You also must be ready all the time, for the Son of Man will come when least expected."

⁴¹Peter asked, "Lord, is that illustration just for us or for everyone?"

⁴²And the Lord replied, "A faithful, sensible servant is one to whom the master can give the responsibility of managing his other household servants and feeding them. ⁴³If the master returns and finds that the servant has done a good job, there will be a reward. ⁴⁴I tell you the truth, the master will put that servant in charge of all he owns. ⁴⁵But what if the servant thinks, 'My master won't be back for a while,' and he begins beating the other servants, partying, and getting drunk? ⁴⁶The master will return unannounced and unexpected, and he will cut the servant in pieces and banish him with the unfaithful.

⁴⁷"And a servant who knows what the master wants, but isn't prepared and doesn't carry out those instructions, will be severely punished. ⁴⁸But someone who does not know, and then does something wrong, will be punished only lightly. When someone has been given much, much will be required in return; and when someone has been entrusted with much, even more will be required.

Jesus Causes Division

⁴⁹"I have come to set the world on fire, and I wish it were already burning! ⁵⁰I have a terrible baptism of suffering ahead of me, and I am under a heavy burden until it is accomplished. ⁵¹Do you think I have come to bring peace to the earth? No, I have come to divide people against each other! ⁵²From now

12:38 Greek *in the second or third watch.*

on families will be split apart, three in favor of me, and two against—or two in favor and three against.

53 'Father will be divided against son
    and son against father;
mother against daughter
    and daughter against mother;
and mother-in-law against daughter-in-law
    and daughter-in-law against mother-in-law.'*"

54 Then Jesus turned to the crowd and said, "When you see clouds beginning to form in the west, you say, 'Here comes a shower.' And you are right. 55 When the south wind blows, you say, 'Today will be a scorcher.' And it is. 56 You fools! You know how to interpret the weather signs of the earth and sky, but you don't know how to interpret the present times.

57 "Why can't you decide for yourselves what is right? 58 When you are on the way to court with your accuser, try to settle the matter before you get there. Otherwise, your accuser may drag you before the judge, who will hand you over to an officer, who will throw you into prison. 59 And if that happens, you won't be free again until you have paid the very last penny.*"

CHAPTER 13

A Call to Repentance

About this time Jesus was informed that Pilate had murdered some people from Galilee as they were offering sacrifices at the Temple. 2 "Do you think those Galileans were worse sinners than all the other people from Galilee?" Jesus asked. "Is that why they suffered? 3 Not at all! And you will perish, too, unless you repent of your sins and turn to God. 4 And what about the eighteen people who died when the tower in Siloam fell on them? Were they the worst sinners in Jerusalem? 5 No, and I tell you again that unless you repent, you will perish, too."

Parable of the Barren Fig Tree

6 Then Jesus told this story: "A man planted a fig tree in his garden and came again and again to see if there was any fruit on it, but he was always disappointed. 7 Finally, he said to his gardener, 'I've waited three years, and there hasn't been a single fig! Cut it down. It's just taking up space in the garden.'

8 "The gardener answered, 'Sir, give it one more chance. Leave it another year, and I'll give it special attention and

12:53 Mic 7:6.   12:59 Greek last lepton [the smallest Jewish coin].

plenty of fertilizer. [9]If we get figs next year, fine. If not, then you can cut it down.'"

Jesus Heals on the Sabbath

[10]One Sabbath day as Jesus was teaching in a synagogue, [11]he saw a woman who had been crippled by an evil spirit. She had been bent double for eighteen years and was unable to stand up straight. [12]When Jesus saw her, he called her over and said, "Dear woman, you are healed of your sickness!" [13]Then he touched her, and instantly she could stand straight. How she praised God!

[14]But the leader in charge of the synagogue was indignant that Jesus had healed her on the Sabbath day. "There are six days of the week for working," he said to the crowd. "Come on those days to be healed, not on the Sabbath."

[15]But the Lord replied, "You hypocrites! Each of you works on the Sabbath day! Don't you untie your ox or your donkey from its stall on the Sabbath and lead it out for water? [16]This dear woman, a daughter of Abraham, has been held in bondage by Satan for eighteen years. Isn't it right that she be released, even on the Sabbath?"

[17]This shamed his enemies, but all the people rejoiced at the wonderful things he did.

Parable of the Mustard Seed

[18]Then Jesus said, "What is the Kingdom of God like? How can I illustrate it? [19]It is like a tiny mustard seed that a man planted in a garden; it grows and becomes a tree, and the birds make nests in its branches."

Parable of the Yeast

[20]He also asked, "What else is the Kingdom of God like? [21]It is like the yeast a woman used in making bread. Even though she put only a little yeast in three measures of flour, it permeated every part of the dough."

The Narrow Door

[22]Jesus went through the towns and villages, teaching as he went, always pressing on toward Jerusalem. [23]Someone asked him, "Lord, will only a few be saved?"

He replied, [24]"Work hard to enter the narrow door to God's Kingdom, for many will try to enter but will fail. [25]When the master of the house has locked the door, it will be too late. You will stand outside knocking and pleading, 'Lord, open the door for us!' But he will reply, 'I don't know you or where you come from.' ²⁶Then you will say, 'But we ate and drank with you, and you taught in our streets.' ²⁷And he will reply, 'I tell you, I don't know you or where you come from. Get away from me, all you who do evil.'

²⁸"There will be weeping and gnashing of teeth, for you will see Abraham, Isaac, Jacob, and all the prophets in the Kingdom of God, but you will be thrown out. ²⁹And people will come from all over the world—from east and west, north and south—to take their places in the Kingdom of God. ³⁰And note this: Some who seem least important now will be the greatest then, and some who are the greatest now will be least important then.*"

Jesus Grieves over Jerusalem

³¹At that time some Pharisees said to him, "Get away from here if you want to live! Herod Antipas wants to kill you!"

³²Jesus replied, "Go tell that fox that I will keep on casting out demons and healing people today and tomorrow; and the third day I will accomplish my purpose. ³³Yes, today, tomorrow, and the next day I must proceed on my way. For it wouldn't do for a prophet of God to be killed except in Jerusalem!

³⁴"O Jerusalem, Jerusalem, the city that kills the prophets and stones God's messengers! How often I have wanted to gather your children together as a hen protects her chicks beneath her wings, but you wouldn't let me. ³⁵And now, look, your house is abandoned. And you will never see me again until you say, 'Blessings on the one who comes in the name of the LORD!'*"

CHAPTER **14**
Jesus Heals on the Sabbath

One Sabbath day Jesus went to eat dinner in the home of a leader of the Pharisees, and the people were watching him closely. ²There was a man there whose arms and legs were swollen.* ³Jesus asked the Pharisees and experts in religious law, "Is it permitted in the law to heal people on the Sabbath day, or not?" ⁴When they refused to answer, Jesus touched the sick man and healed him and sent him away. ⁵Then he turned to them and said, "Which of you doesn't work on the Sabbath? If your son* or your cow falls into a pit, don't you rush to get him out?" ⁶Again they could not answer.

13:30 Greek *Some are last who will be first, and some are first who will be last.*   **13:35** Ps 118:26.
14:2 Or *who had dropsy.*   **14:5** Some manuscripts read *donkey.*

"A friend is always loyal, and a brother is born to help in time of need."

~ Proverbs 17:17

JOURNAL

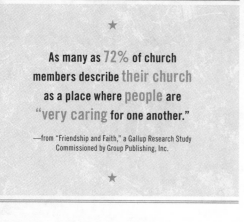

JOURNAL

Jesus Teaches about Humility

7When Jesus noticed that all who had come to the dinner were trying to sit in the seats of honor near the head of the table, he gave them this advice: 8"When you are invited to a wedding feast, don't sit in the seat of honor. What if someone who is more distinguished than you has also been invited? 9The host will come and say, 'Give this person your seat.' Then you will be embarrassed, and you will have to take whatever seat is left at the foot of the table!

10"Instead, take the lowest place at the foot of the table. Then when your host sees you, he will come and say, 'Friend, we have a better place for you!' Then you will be honored in front of all the other guests. 11For those who exalt themselves will be humbled, and those who humble themselves will be exalted."

12Then he turned to his host. "When you put on a luncheon or a banquet," he said, "don't invite your friends, brothers, relatives, and rich neighbors. For they will invite you back, and that will be your only reward. 13Instead, invite the poor, the crippled, the lame, and the blind. 14Then at the resurrection of the righteous, God will reward you for inviting those who could not repay you."

Parable of the Great Feast

15Hearing this, a man sitting at the table with Jesus exclaimed, "What a blessing it will be to attend a banquet* in the Kingdom of God!"

16Jesus replied with this story: "A man prepared a great feast and sent out many invitations. 17When the banquet was ready, he sent his servant to tell the guests, 'Come, the banquet is ready.' 18But they all began making excuses. One said, 'I have just bought a field and must inspect it. Please excuse me.' 19Another said, 'I have just bought five pairs of oxen, and I want to try them out. Please excuse me.' 20Another said, 'I now have a wife, so I can't come.'

21"The servant returned and told his master what they had said. His master was furious and said, 'Go quickly into the streets and alleys of the town and invite the poor, the crippled, the blind, and the lame.' 22After the servant had done this, he reported, 'There is still room for more.' 23So his master said, 'Go out into the country lanes and behind the hedges and urge anyone you find to come, so that the house will be full. 24For none of those I first invited will get even the smallest taste of my banquet.'"

14:15 Greek *to eat bread.*

The Cost of Being a Disciple

25 A large crowd was following Jesus. He turned around and said to them, 26 "If you want to be my disciple, you must hate everyone else by comparison—your father and mother, wife and children, brothers and sisters—yes, even your own life. Otherwise, you cannot be my disciple. 27 And if you do not carry your own cross and follow me, you cannot be my disciple.

28 "But don't begin until you count the cost. For who would begin construction of a building without first calculating the cost to see if there is enough money to finish it? 29 Otherwise, you might complete only the foundation before running out of money, and then everyone would laugh at you. 30 They would say, 'There's the person who started that building and couldn't afford to finish it!'

31 "Or what king would go to war against another king without first sitting down with his counselors to discuss whether his army of 10,000 could defeat the 20,000 soldiers marching against him? 32 And if he can't, he will send a delegation to discuss terms of peace while the enemy is still far away. 33 So you cannot become my disciple without giving up everything you own.

34 "Salt is good for seasoning. But if it loses its flavor, how do you make it salty again? 35 Flavorless salt is good neither for the soil nor for the manure pile. It is thrown away. Anyone with ears to hear should listen and understand!"

CHAPTER 15

Parable of the Lost Sheep

Tax collectors and other notorious sinners often came to listen to Jesus teach. 2 This made the Pharisees and teachers of religious law complain that he was associating with such sinful people—even eating with them!

3 So Jesus told them this story: 4 "If a man has a hundred sheep and one of them gets lost, what will he do? Won't he leave the ninety-nine others in the wilderness and go to search for the one that is lost until he finds it? 5 And when he has found it, he will joyfully carry it home on his shoulders. 6 When he arrives, he will call together his friends and neighbors, saying, 'Rejoice with me because I have found my lost sheep.' 7 In the same way, there is more joy in heaven over one lost sinner who repents and returns to God than over ninety-nine others who are righteous and haven't strayed away!

Parable of the Lost Coin

8"Or suppose a woman has ten silver coins* and loses one. Won't she light a lamp and sweep the entire house and search carefully until she finds it? 9And when she finds it, she will call in her friends and neighbors and say, 'Rejoice with me because I have found my lost coin.' 10In the same way, there is joy in the presence of God's angels when even one sinner repents."

Parable of the Lost Son

11To illustrate the point further, Jesus told them this story: "A man had two sons. 12The younger son told his father, 'I want my share of your estate now before you die.' So his father agreed to divide his wealth between his sons.

13"A few days later this younger son packed all his belongings and moved to a distant land, and there he wasted all his money in wild living. 14About the time his money ran out, a great famine swept over the land, and he began to starve. 15He persuaded a local farmer to hire him, and the man sent him into his fields to feed the pigs. 16The young man became so hungry that even the pods he was feeding the pigs looked good to him. But no one gave him anything.

17"When he finally came to his senses, he said to himself, 'At home even the hired servants have food enough to spare, and here I am dying of hunger! 18I will go home to my father and say, "Father, I have sinned against both heaven and you, 19and I am no longer worthy of being called your son. Please take me on as a hired servant."'

20"So he returned home to his father. And while he was still a long way off, his father saw him coming. Filled with love and compassion, he ran to his son, embraced him, and kissed him. 21His son said to him, 'Father, I have sinned against both heaven and you, and I am no longer worthy of being called your son.*'

22"But his father said to the servants, 'Quick! Bring the finest robe in the house and put it on him. Get a ring for his finger and sandals for his feet. 23And kill the calf we have been fattening. We must celebrate

15:8 Greek ten drachmas. A drachma was the equivalent of a full day's wage. 15:21 Some manuscripts add Please take me on as a hired servant.

with a feast, ²⁴for this son of mine was dead and has now returned to life. He was lost, but now he is found.' So the party began.

²⁵"Meanwhile, the older son was in the fields working. When he returned home, he heard music and dancing in the house, ²⁶and he asked one of the servants what was going on. ²⁷'Your brother is back,' he was told, 'and your father has killed the fattened calf. We are celebrating because of his safe return.'

²⁸"The older brother was angry and wouldn't go in. His father came out and begged him, ²⁹but he replied, 'All these years I've slaved for you and never once refused to do a single thing you told me to. And in all that time you never gave me even one young goat for a feast with my friends. ³⁰Yet when this son of yours comes back after squandering your money on prostitutes, you celebrate by killing the fattened calf!'

³¹"His father said to him, 'Look, dear son, you have always stayed by me, and everything I have is yours. ³²We had to celebrate this happy day. For your brother was dead and has come back to life! He was lost, but now he is found!'" ⚓

CHAPTER **16**
Parable of the Shrewd Manager

Jesus told this story to his disciples: "There was a certain rich man who had a manager handling his affairs. One day a report came that the manager was wasting his employer's money. ²So the employer called him in and said, 'What's this I hear about you? Get your report in order, because you are going to be fired.'

³"The manager thought to himself, 'Now what? My boss has fired me. I don't have the strength to dig ditches, and I'm too proud to beg. ⁴Ah, I know how to ensure that I'll have plenty of friends who will give me a home when I am fired.'

⁵"So he invited each person who owed money to his employer to come and discuss the situation. He asked the first one, 'How much do you owe him?' ⁶The man replied, 'I owe him 800 gallons of olive oil.' So the manager told him, 'Take the bill and quickly change it to 400 gallons.*'

16:6 Greek *100 baths . . . 50 [baths].*

Anchor Passage

PASSAGE: Luke 15:11-32

FRIENDSHIP TYPE: *Family*   FRIENDSHIP LAYER: *Acceptance*

A Different Way of Seeing Things

Is there a family member you just want to *strangle*? Do you sometimes wonder how you could possibly be *related* to that person?

Well, here's a tip to save you some angst: You're both very different.

It might sound simple and trite—a statement of the obvious, even. So why is it that you still find yourself wishing that family member would just see it your way, do it your way, understand your way?

Perhaps you haven't accepted that person.

Read **Luke 15:11-32**.

It's a common family dynamic: the driven and successful father, the typically "responsible" older child, and the rebellious younger child. And, in this case, it was a dynamic that led to conflict and separation.

The youngest ran away.

The father waited and longed for his return.

The oldest continued to work, resentful that his father was paying more attention to his brother's absence than to his presence.

The family was a mess. Everyone was hurting.

So how does a family overcome a situation like that?

Anchor Passage continues on page 154...

Anchor Passage continued from page 153...

Through a *prodigal* response. Large, lavish, extravagant. Big repentance, big acceptance, big tokens of forgiveness, big celebratory parties to say, "You are welcome here!"

These are the kinds of responses that communicate a willingness to break away from our own perspectives, to get beyond our own blind spots, and to create a spaciousness for others to be different from us.

Experience

THE ONE THING
1
YOU CAN DO THIS WEEK

So...that family member you wanted to strangle? This week do something extravagant for that person! Throw a half-birthday party, take him or her to an expensive restaurant, or buy the person an awesome gift. You'll be surprised at how your acceptance can lead to a better relationship...even a friendship!

Having trouble getting out of your habit of expecting the worst from that person? Ask God for his perspective. God can help you see the best in the person and accept him or her—warts and all.

Reflect

★ How did your extravagant actions affect your relationship?

★ What else can you do to show your acceptance of that person?

Anchor Passage continues on page 155...

Friendship First NEW TESTAMENT

7 "'And how much do you owe my employer?' he asked the next man. 'I owe him 1,000 bushels of wheat,' was the reply. 'Here,' the manager said, 'take the bill and change it to 800 bushels.*'

8 "The rich man had to admire the dishonest rascal for being so shrewd. And it is true that the children of this world are more shrewd in dealing with the world around them than are the children of the light. 9 Here's the lesson: Use your worldly resources to benefit others and make friends. Then, when your earthly possessions are gone, they will welcome you to an eternal home.*

10 "If you are faithful in little things, you will be faithful in large ones. But if you are dishonest in little things, you won't be honest with greater responsibilities. 11 And if you are untrustworthy about worldly wealth, who will trust you with the true riches of heaven? 12 And if you are not faithful with other people's things, why should you be trusted with things of your own?

13 "No one can serve two masters. For you will hate one and love the other; you will be devoted to one and despise the other. You cannot serve both God and money."

14 The Pharisees, who dearly loved their money, heard all this and scoffed at him. 15 Then he said to them, "You like to appear righteous in public, but God knows your hearts. What this world honors is detestable in the sight of God.

16 "Until John the Baptist, the law of Moses and the messages of the prophets were your guides. But now the Good News of the Kingdom of God is preached, and everyone is eager to get in.* 17 But that doesn't mean that the law has lost its force. It is easier for heaven and earth to disappear than for the smallest point of God's law to be overturned.

18 "For example, a man who divorces his wife and marries someone else commits adultery. And anyone who marries a woman divorced from her husband commits adultery."

Parable of the Rich Man and Lazarus

19 Jesus said, "There was a certain rich man who was splendidly clothed in purple and fine linen and who lived each day in luxury. 20 At his gate lay a poor man named Lazarus who was covered with sores. 21 As Lazarus lay there longing for scraps from the rich man's table, the dogs would come and lick his open sores.

22 "Finally, the poor man died and was carried by the angels

16:7 Greek *100 korous . . . 80 [korous].*   **16:9** Or *you will be welcomed into eternal homes.*
16:16 Or *everyone is urged to enter in.*

to be with Abraham.* The rich man also died and was buried, 23and his soul went to the place of the dead.* There, in torment, he saw Abraham in the far distance with Lazarus at his side.

24"The rich man shouted, 'Father Abraham, have some pity! Send Lazarus over here to dip the tip of his finger in water and cool my tongue. I am in anguish in these flames.'

25"But Abraham said to him, 'Son, remember that during your lifetime you had everything you wanted, and Lazarus had nothing. So now he is here being comforted, and you are in anguish. 26And besides, there is a great chasm separating us. No one can cross over to you from here, and no one can cross over to us from there.'

27"Then the rich man said, 'Please, Father Abraham, at least send him to my father's home. 28For I have five brothers, and I want him to warn them so they don't end up in this place of torment.'

29"But Abraham said, 'Moses and the prophets have warned them. Your brothers can read what they wrote.'

30"The rich man replied, 'No, Father Abraham! But if someone is sent to them from the dead, then they will repent of their sins and turn to God.'

31"But Abraham said, 'If they won't listen to Moses and the prophets, they won't listen even if someone rises from the dead.'"

CHAPTER 17

Teachings about Forgiveness and Faith

One day Jesus said to his disciples, "There will always be temptations to sin, but what sorrow awaits the person who does the tempting! 2It would be better to be thrown into the sea with a millstone hung around your neck than to cause one of these little ones to fall into sin. 3So watch yourselves!

"If another believer* sins, rebuke that person; then if there is repentance, forgive. 4Even if that person wrongs you seven times a day and each time turns again and asks forgiveness, you must forgive."

5The apostles said to the Lord, "Show us how to increase our faith."

6The Lord answered, "If you had faith even as small as a mustard seed, you could say to this mulberry tree, 'May you be uprooted and thrown into the sea,' and it would obey you!

7"When a servant comes in from plowing or taking care of sheep, does his master say, 'Come in and eat with me'? 8No, he

16:22 Greek *into Abraham's bosom.*   16:23 Greek *to Hades.*   17:3 Greek *If your brother.*

Anchor Passage continued from page 154...

DIGGING DEEPER

FRIENDSHIP TYPE: FRIENDSHIP LAYER:
Family   *Acceptance*

For accepting your family, check out...

➟ The Friendship Experience .... on page 129
➟ The Friendship Story .... on page 381
➟ What to Say and What Not to Say .... on page 384

JOURNAL

says, 'Prepare my meal, put on your apron, and serve me while I eat. Then you can eat later.' ⁹And does the master thank the servant for doing what he was told to do? Of course not. ¹⁰In the same way, when you obey me you should say, 'We are unworthy servants who have simply done our duty.'"

Ten Healed of Leprosy

¹¹As Jesus continued on toward Jerusalem, he reached the border between Galilee and Samaria. ¹²As he entered a village there, ten lepers stood at a distance, ¹³crying out, "Jesus, Master, have mercy on us!"

¹⁴He looked at them and said, "Go show yourselves to the priests."* And as they went, they were cleansed of their leprosy.

¹⁵One of them, when he saw that he was healed, came back to Jesus, shouting, "Praise God!" ¹⁶He fell to the ground at Jesus' feet, thanking him for what he had done. This man was a Samaritan.

¹⁷Jesus asked, "Didn't I heal ten men? Where are the other nine? ¹⁸Has no one returned to give glory to God except this foreigner?" ¹⁹And Jesus said to the man, "Stand up and go. Your faith has healed you.*"

The Coming of the Kingdom

²⁰One day the Pharisees asked Jesus, "When will the Kingdom of God come?"

Jesus replied, "The Kingdom of God can't be detected by visible signs.* ²¹You won't be able to say, 'Here it is!' or 'It's over there!' For the Kingdom of God is already among you.*"

²²Then he said to his disciples, "The time is coming when you will long to see the day when the Son of Man returns,* but you won't see it. ²³People will tell you, 'Look, there is the Son of Man,' or 'Here he is,' but don't go out and follow them. ²⁴For as the lightning flashes and lights up the sky from one end to the other, so it will be on the day when the Son of Man comes. ²⁵But first the Son of Man must suffer terribly* and be rejected by this generation.

²⁶"When the Son of Man returns, it will be like it was in Noah's day. ²⁷In those days, the people enjoyed banquets and parties and weddings right up to the time Noah entered his boat and the flood came and destroyed them all.

²⁸"And the world will be as it was in the days of Lot. People went about their daily business—eating and drinking, buying

17:14 See Lev 14:2-32.   17:19 Or *Your faith has saved you.*   17:20 Or *by your speculations.*
17:21 Or *is within you,* or *is in your grasp.*   17:22 Or *long for even one day with the Son of Man.*
"Son of Man" is a title Jesus used for himself.   17:25 Or *suffer many things.*

and selling, farming and building—²⁹until the morning Lot left Sodom. Then fire and burning sulfur rained down from heaven and destroyed them all. ³⁰Yes, it will be 'business as usual' right up to the day when the Son of Man is revealed. ³¹On that day a person out on the deck of a roof must not go down into the house to pack. A person out in the field must not return home. ³²Remember what happened to Lot's wife! ³³If you cling to your life, you will lose it, and if you let your life go, you will save it. ³⁴That night two people will be asleep in one bed; one will be taken, the other left. ³⁵Two women will be grinding flour together at the mill; one will be taken, the other left.*"

³⁷"Where will this happen, Lord?"* the disciples asked.

Jesus replied, "Just as the gathering of vultures shows there is a carcass nearby, so these signs indicate that the end is near."*

CHAPTER **18**

Parable of the Persistent Widow

One day Jesus told his disciples a story to show that they should always pray and never give up. ²"There was a judge in a certain city," he said, "who neither feared God nor cared about people. ³A widow of that city came to him repeatedly, saying, 'Give me justice in this dispute with my enemy.' ⁴The judge ignored her for a while, but finally he said to himself, 'I don't fear God or care about people, ⁵but this woman is driving me crazy. I'm going to see that she gets justice, because she is wearing me out with her constant requests!'"

⁶Then the Lord said, "Learn a lesson from this unjust judge. ⁷Even he rendered a just decision in the end. So don't you think God will surely give justice to his chosen people who cry out to him day and night? Will he keep putting them off? ⁸I tell you, he will grant justice to them quickly! But when the Son of Man* returns, how many will he find on the earth who have faith?"

Parable of the Pharisee and Tax Collector

⁹Then Jesus told this story to some who had great confidence in their own righteousness and scorned everyone else: ¹⁰"Two men went to the Temple to pray. One was a Pharisee, and the other was a despised tax collector. ¹¹The Pharisee stood by himself and prayed this prayer*: 'I thank you, God, that I am not a sinner like everyone else. For I don't cheat, I don't sin, and I don't

"The proper office of a friend is to side with you when you are in the wrong. Nearly anybody will side with you when you are in the right."

~ Mark Twain

JOURNAL

17:35 Some manuscripts add verse 36, *Two men will be working in the field; one will be taken, the other left.* Compare Matt 24:40. 17:37a Greek *"Where, Lord?"* 17:37b Greek *"Wherever the carcass is, the vultures gather."* 18:8 "Son of Man" is a title Jesus used for himself. 18:11 Some manuscripts read *stood and prayed this prayer to himself.*

commit adultery. I'm certainly not like that tax collector! [12] I fast twice a week, and I give you a tenth of my income.'

[13] "But the tax collector stood at a distance and dared not even lift his eyes to heaven as he prayed. Instead, he beat his chest in sorrow, saying, 'O God, be merciful to me, for I am a sinner.' [14] I tell you, this sinner, not the Pharisee, returned home justified before God. For those who exalt themselves will be humbled, and those who humble themselves will be exalted."

Jesus Blesses the Children

[15] One day some parents brought their little children to Jesus so he could touch and bless them. But when the disciples saw this, they scolded the parents for bothering him.

[16] Then Jesus called for the children and said to the disciples, "Let the children come to me. Don't stop them! For the Kingdom of God belongs to those who are like these children. [17] I tell you the truth, anyone who doesn't receive the Kingdom of God like a child will never enter it."

The Rich Man

[18] Once a religious leader asked Jesus this question: "Good Teacher, what should I do to inherit eternal life?"

[19] "Why do you call me good?" Jesus asked him. "Only God is truly good. [20] But to answer your question, you know the commandments: 'You must not commit adultery. You must not murder. You must not steal. You must not testify falsely. Honor your father and mother.'*"

[21] The man replied, "I've obeyed all these commandments since I was young."

[22] When Jesus heard his answer, he said, "There is still one thing you haven't done. Sell all your possessions and give the money to the poor, and you will have treasure in heaven. Then come, follow me."

[23] But when the man heard this he became very sad, for he was very rich.

[24] When Jesus saw this,* he said, "How hard it is for the rich to enter the Kingdom of God! [25] In fact, it is easier for a camel to go through the eye of a needle than for a rich person to enter the Kingdom of God!"

[26] Those who heard this said, "Then who in the world can be saved?"

18:20 Exod 20:12-16; Deut 5:16-20.   **18:24** Some manuscripts read *When Jesus saw how sad the man was.*

²⁷He replied, "What is impossible for people is possible with God."

²⁸Peter said, "We've left our homes to follow you."

²⁹"Yes," Jesus replied, "and I assure you that everyone who has given up house or wife or brothers or parents or children, for the sake of the Kingdom of God, ³⁰will be repaid many times over in this life, and will have eternal life in the world to come."

Jesus Again Predicts His Death

³¹Taking the twelve disciples aside, Jesus said, "Listen, we're going up to Jerusalem, where all the predictions of the prophets concerning the Son of Man will come true. ³²He will be handed over to the Romans,* and he will be mocked, treated shamefully, and spit upon. ³³They will flog him with a whip and kill him, but on the third day he will rise again."

³⁴But they didn't understand any of this. The significance of his words was hidden from them, and they failed to grasp what he was talking about.

Jesus Heals a Blind Beggar

³⁵As Jesus approached Jericho, a blind beggar was sitting beside the road. ³⁶When he heard the noise of a crowd going past, he asked what was happening. ³⁷They told him that Jesus the Nazarene* was going by. ³⁸So he began shouting, "Jesus, Son of David, have mercy on me!"

³⁹"Be quiet!" the people in front yelled at him.

But he only shouted louder, "Son of David, have mercy on me!"

⁴⁰When Jesus heard him, he stopped and ordered that the man be brought to him. As the man came near, Jesus asked him, ⁴¹"What do you want me to do for you?"

"Lord," he said, "I want to see!"

⁴²And Jesus said, "All right, receive your sight! Your faith has healed you." ⁴³Instantly the man could see, and he followed Jesus, praising God. And all who saw it praised God, too.

CHAPTER **19**
Jesus and Zacchaeus

Jesus entered Jericho and made his way through the town. ²There was a man there named Zacchaeus. He was the chief tax collector in the region, and he had

18:32 Greek *the Gentiles.*   18:37 Or *Jesus of Nazareth.*

Anchor Passage

PASSAGE: Luke 19:1-10

FRIENDSHIP TYPE: *Hard-to-Love People*   FRIENDSHIP LAYER: *Commitment*

Loving the Unlovable

Ever want to see people get what they deserve…or are you content to let difficult people float to the back of the crowd and go unnoticed?

Read **Luke 19:1-10**.

Jesus does something awkward here, something that makes the crowds grumble and complain. Jesus singles out Zacchaeus (hiding up in a tree, no less!) and invites himself over to Zacchaeus' house for dinner. Even though Zacchaeus was a dishonest tax collector. Even though everyone hated Zacchaeus. Even though Zacchaeus was viewed as a traitor because he collected money for the conquering Romans. Despite all that, Jesus chose friendship.

Jesus saw Zacchaeus hanging out up there in that tree, and he knew that Zacchaeus was more than just a tax collector. Jesus called him down and then proceeded to spend the evening with him.

Everyone else saw a hard-to-love person—strike that, an *impossible*-to-love person—but Jesus saw a future friend.

The results were staggering. Instead of getting what he deserved, Zacchaeus became a new man. The first sign of his changed heart was an open hand: He quickly decided to pay back what he had unjustly taken.

Everything inside us might want to get even, but loving hard-to-love people is a far better way of settling the score. In fact, it might make for one less difficult person in the world.

Anchor Passage continues on page 160…

Anchor Passage continued from page 159...

Experience

Think about someone you usually steer clear of. Commit to building a friendship with that person. It may be as simple as talking to someone who people tend to avoid or going further and having dinner with that person—if you have to, take a cue from Jesus, and invite yourself to dinner!

Reflect

★ Why did Jesus pick Zacchaeus?

★ How was the time you spent with your "hard-to-love person"?

★ What difference might your friendship make in that person's life? What difference might that friendship make in your life?

DIGGING DEEPER

FRIENDSHIP TYPE:
Hard-to-Love People

FRIENDSHIP LAYER:
Commitment

For committing to your friendship with hard-to-love people, check out...

➠ The Friendship Experience .... on page 165
➠ The Friendship Story .... on page 173
➠ What to Say and What Not to Say .... on page 367

become very rich. [3] He tried to get a look at Jesus, but he was too short to see over the crowd. [4] So he ran ahead and climbed a sycamore-fig tree beside the road, for Jesus was going to pass that way.

[5] When Jesus came by, he looked up at Zacchaeus and called him by name. "Zacchaeus!" he said. "Quick, come down! I must be a guest in your home today."

[6] Zacchaeus quickly climbed down and took Jesus to his house in great excitement and joy. [7] But the people were displeased. "He has gone to be the guest of a notorious sinner," they grumbled.

[8] Meanwhile, Zacchaeus stood before the Lord and said, "I will give half my wealth to the poor, Lord, and if I have cheated people on their taxes, I will give them back four times as much!"

[9] Jesus responded, "Salvation has come to this home today, for this man has shown himself to be a true son of Abraham. [10] For the Son of Man* came to seek and save those who are lost." ⚓

Parable of the Ten Servants

[11] The crowd was listening to everything Jesus said. And because he was nearing Jerusalem, he told them a story to correct the impression that the Kingdom of God would begin right away. [12] He said, "A nobleman was called away to a distant empire to be crowned king and then return. [13] Before he left, he called together ten of his servants and divided among them ten pounds of silver,* saying, 'Invest this for me while I am gone.' [14] But his people hated him and sent a delegation after him to say, "We do not want him to be our king."

[15] "After he was crowned king, he returned and called in the servants to whom he had given the money. He wanted to find out what their profits were. [16] The first servant reported, 'Master, I invested your money and made ten times the original amount!'

[17] "'Well done!' the king exclaimed. 'You are a good servant. You have been faithful with the little I entrusted to you, so you will be governor of ten cities as your reward.'

[18] "The next servant reported, 'Master, I invested your money and made five times the original amount.'

19:10 "Son of Man" is a title Jesus used for himself.   **19:13** Greek *ten minas;* one mina was worth about three months' wages.

19 "'Well done!' the king said. 'You will be governor over five cities.'

20 "But the third servant brought back only the original amount of money and said, 'Master, I hid your money and kept it safe. 21 I was afraid because you are a hard man to deal with, taking what isn't yours and harvesting crops you didn't plant.'

22 "'You wicked servant!' the king roared. 'Your own words condemn you. If you knew that I'm a hard man who takes what isn't mine and harvests crops I didn't plant, 23 why didn't you deposit my money in the bank? At least I could have gotten some interest on it.'

24 "Then, turning to the others standing nearby, the king ordered, "Take the money from this servant, and give it to the one who has ten pounds.'

25 "'But, master,' they said, 'he already has ten pounds!'

26 "'Yes,' the king replied, 'and to those who use well what they are given, even more will be given. But from those who do nothing, even what little they have will be taken away. 27 And as for these enemies of mine who didn't want me to be their king—bring them in and execute them right here in front of me.'"

Jesus' Triumphant Entry

28 After telling this story, Jesus went on toward Jerusalem, walking ahead of his disciples. 29 As he came to the towns of Bethphage and Bethany on the Mount of Olives, he sent two disciples ahead. 30 "Go into that village over there," he told them. "As you enter it, you will see a young donkey tied there that no one has ever ridden. Untie it and bring it here. 31 If anyone asks, 'Why are you untying that colt?' just say, "The Lord needs it.'"

32 So they went and found the colt, just as Jesus had said. 33 And sure enough, as they were untying it, the owners asked them, "Why are you untying that colt?"

34 And the disciples simply replied, "The Lord needs it." 35 So they brought the colt to Jesus and threw their garments over it for him to ride on.

36 As he rode along, the crowds spread out their garments on the road ahead of him. 37 When he reached the place where the road started down the Mount of Olives, all of his followers began to shout and sing as they walked along, praising God for all the wonderful miracles they had seen.

JOURNAL

38 "Blessings on the King who comes in the name of the LORD!
  Peace in heaven, and glory in highest heaven!"*

39 But some of the Pharisees among the crowd said, "Teacher, rebuke your followers for saying things like that!"

40 He replied, "If they kept quiet, the stones along the road would burst into cheers!"

Jesus Weeps over Jerusalem

41 But as he came closer to Jerusalem and saw the city ahead, he began to weep. 42 "How I wish today that you of all people would understand the way to peace. But now it is too late, and peace is hidden from your eyes. 43 Before long your enemies will build ramparts against your walls and encircle you and close in on you from every side. 44 They will crush you into the ground, and your children with you. Your enemies will not leave a single stone in place, because you did not accept your opportunity for salvation."

Jesus Clears the Temple

45 Then Jesus entered the Temple and began to drive out the people selling animals for sacrifices. 46 He said to them, "The Scriptures declare, 'My Temple will be a house of prayer,' but you have turned it into a den of thieves."*

47 After that, he taught daily in the Temple, but the leading priests, the teachers of religious law, and the other leaders of the people began planning how to kill him. 48 But they could think of nothing, because all the people hung on every word he said.

CHAPTER 20

The Authority of Jesus Challenged

One day as Jesus was teaching the people and preaching the Good News in the Temple, the leading priests, the teachers of religious law, and the elders came up to him. 2 They demanded, "By what authority are you doing all these things? Who gave you the right?"

3 "Let me ask you a question first," he replied. 4 "Did John's authority to baptize come from heaven, or was it merely human?"

5 They talked it over among themselves. "If we say it was from heaven, he will ask why we didn't believe John. 6 But if we say it was merely human, the people will stone us because they are convinced John was a prophet." 7 So they finally replied that they didn't know.

19:38 Pss 118:26; 148:1.   19:46 Isa 56:7; Jer 7:11.

[8]And Jesus responded, "Then I won't tell you by what authority I do these things."

Parable of the Evil Farmers

[9]Now Jesus turned to the people again and told them this story: "A man planted a vineyard, leased it to tenant farmers, and moved to another country to live for several years. [10]At the time of the grape harvest, he sent one of his servants to collect his share of the crop. But the farmers attacked the servant, beat him up, and sent him back empty-handed. [11]So the owner sent another servant, but they also insulted him, beat him up, and sent him away empty-handed. [12]A third man was sent, and they wounded him and chased him away.

[13]"'What will I do?' the owner asked himself. 'I know! I'll send my cherished son. Surely they will respect him.'

[14]"But when the tenant farmers saw his son, they said to each other, 'Here comes the heir to this estate. Let's kill him and get the estate for ourselves!' [15]So they dragged him out of the vineyard and murdered him.

"What do you suppose the owner of the vineyard will do to them?" Jesus asked. [16]"I'll tell you—he will come and kill those farmers and lease the vineyard to others."

"How terrible that such a thing should ever happen," his listeners protested.

[17]Jesus looked at them and said, "Then what does this Scripture mean?

'The stone that the builders rejected
   has now become the cornerstone.'*

[18]Everyone who stumbles over that stone will be broken to pieces, and it will crush anyone it falls on."

[19]The teachers of religious law and the leading priests wanted to arrest Jesus immediately because they realized he was telling the story against them—they were the wicked farmers. But they were afraid of the people's reaction.

Taxes for Caesar

[20]Watching for their opportunity, the leaders sent spies pretending to be honest men. They tried to get Jesus to say something that could be reported to the Roman governor so he would arrest Jesus. [21]"Teacher," they said, "we know that you speak and teach what is right and are not influenced by what others

20:17 Ps 118:22.

"Without friendships no one would choose to live, even if they had all other good things in life."

~ Aristotle

JOURNAL

think. You teach the way of God truthfully. [22] Now tell us—is it right for us to pay taxes to Caesar or not?"

[23] He saw through their trickery and said, [24] "Show me a Roman coin.* Whose picture and title are stamped on it?"

"Caesar's," they replied.

[25] "Well then," he said, "give to Caesar what belongs to Caesar, and give to God what belongs to God."

[26] So they failed to trap him by what he said in front of the people. Instead, they were amazed by his answer, and they became silent.

Discussion about Resurrection

[27] Then Jesus was approached by some Sadducees—religious leaders who say there is no resurrection from the dead. [28] They posed this question: "Teacher, Moses gave us a law that if a man dies, leaving a wife but no children, his brother should marry the widow and have a child who will carry on the brother's name.* [29] Well, suppose there were seven brothers. The oldest one married and then died without children. [30] So the second brother married the widow, but he also died. [31] Then the third brother married her. This continued with all seven of them, who died without children. [32] Finally, the woman also died. [33] So tell us, whose wife will she be in the resurrection? For all seven were married to her!"

[34] Jesus replied, "Marriage is for people here on earth. [35] But in the age to come, those worthy of being raised from the dead will neither marry nor be given in marriage. [36] And they will never die again. In this respect they will be like angels. They are children of God and children of the resurrection.

[37] "But now, as to whether the dead will be raised—even Moses proved this when he wrote about the burning bush. Long after Abraham, Isaac, and Jacob had died, he referred to the Lord* as 'the God of Abraham, the God of Isaac, and the God of Jacob.'* [38] So he is the God of the living, not the dead, for they are all alive to him."

[39] "Well said, Teacher!" remarked some of the teachers of religious law who were standing there. [40] And then no one dared to ask him any more questions.

Whose Son Is the Messiah?

[41] Then Jesus presented them with a question. "Why is it," he asked, "that the Messiah is said to be the son of David? [42] For David himself wrote in the book of Psalms:

20:24 Greek *a denarius.* 20:28 See Deut 25:5-6. 20:37a Greek *when he wrote about the bush. He referred to the Lord.* 20:37b Exod 3:6.

'The LORD said to my Lord,
　　Sit in the place of honor at my right hand
43 until I humble your enemies,
　　making them a footstool under your feet.'*

44Since David called the Messiah 'Lord,' how can the Messiah be his son?"

45Then, with the crowds listening, he turned to his disciples and said, 46"Beware of these teachers of religious law! For they like to parade around in flowing robes and love to receive respectful greetings as they walk in the marketplaces. And how they love the seats of honor in the synagogues and the head table at banquets. 47Yet they shamelessly cheat widows out of their property and then pretend to be pious by making long prayers in public. Because of this, they will be severely punished."

CHAPTER 21
The Widow's Offering

While Jesus was in the Temple, he watched the rich people dropping their gifts in the collection box. 2Then a poor widow came by and dropped in two small coins.*

3"I tell you the truth," Jesus said, "this poor widow has given more than all the rest of them. 4For they have given a tiny part of their surplus, but she, poor as she is, has given everything she has."

Jesus Foretells the Future

5Some of his disciples began talking about the majestic stonework of the Temple and the memorial decorations on the walls. But Jesus said, 6"The time is coming when all these things will be completely demolished. Not one stone will be left on top of another!"

7"Teacher," they asked, "when will all this happen? What sign will show us that these things are about to take place?"

8He replied, "Don't let anyone mislead you, for many will come in my name, claiming, 'I am the Messiah,'* and saying, 'The time has come!' But don't believe them. 9And when you hear of wars and insurrections, don't panic. Yes, these things must take place first, but the end won't follow immediately."

10Then he added, "Nation will go to war against nation, and kingdom against kingdom. 11There will be great earthquakes, and there will be famines and plagues in many lands, and there will be terrifying things and great miraculous signs from heaven.

20:42-43 Ps 110:1.　21:2 Greek *two lepta* [the smallest of Jewish coins].　21:8 Greek *claiming, 'I am.'*

FRIENDSHIP EXPERIENCE

FRIENDSHIP TYPE: *Hard-to-Love People*　　FRIENDSHIP LAYER: *Commitment*

I Don't Have Time!

Being a committed friend to a hard-to-love person may seem like just one more demand in an already demanding lifestyle. How are you supposed to make time for one more person when you barely have enough time for those you love?

It isn't easy. Jesus knew that. Yet he stopped in the middle of a busy day—when he was surrounded by devoted followers and friends—and committed to a friendship with someone else. Why would he do that? Why wouldn't he have just gone to dinner with one of those people in the crowd? You know, someone who *deserved* to have dinner with Jesus?

Because Jesus knew that Zacchaeus *needed* his friendship. Jesus had once told the Pharisees, "Healthy people don't need a doctor—sick people do. I have come to call not those who think they are righteous, but those who know they are sinners and need to repent" (**Luke 5:31-32**).

FRIENDSHIP EXPERIENCE *continues on page 166...*

FRIENDSHIP EXPERIENCE *continued from page 165...*

Experience

Is there anyone who might *need* your friendship? Perhaps a co-worker who just moved here and hasn't met many people. Or maybe an elderly acquaintance whose family lives far away. Take a cue from this story, and invite the person over to your house for dinner. You might even make a good friend who will be there someday when *you* need someone!

Talk about a busy schedule! God is the master of the universe, he commands the heavens, and yet he wants to spend time with all of us—no matter who we are or what we've done. God is the master of the universe *and* the master of committing to friendships with hard-to-love people. How can you show your commitment to God this week, even when it's hard? Maybe you could read your Bible at a certain time each day, pray daily with a friend, or volunteer at your church or a local shelter.

THE ONE THING YOU CAN DO THIS WEEK **1**

Reflect

★ How can you make time for friendships with hard-to-love people?

★ Why is staying committed to God a challenge?

★ How is committing to a hard-to-love person similar to committing to God? How is it different?

¹²"But before all this occurs, there will be a time of great persecution. You will be dragged into synagogues and prisons, and you will stand trial before kings and governors because you are my followers. ¹³But this will be your opportunity to tell them about me.* ¹⁴So don't worry in advance about how to answer the charges against you, ¹⁵for I will give you the right words and such wisdom that none of your opponents will be able to reply or refute you! ¹⁶Even those closest to you—your parents, brothers, relatives, and friends—will betray you. They will even kill some of you. ¹⁷And everyone will hate you because you are my followers.* ¹⁸But not a hair of your head will perish! ¹⁹By standing firm, you will win your souls.

²⁰"And when you see Jerusalem surrounded by armies, then you will know that the time of its destruction has arrived. ²¹Then those in Judea must flee to the hills. Those in Jerusalem must get out, and those out in the country should not return to the city. ²²For those will be days of God's vengeance, and the prophetic words of the Scriptures will be fulfilled. ²³How terrible it will be for pregnant women and for nursing mothers in those days. For there will be disaster in the land and great anger against this people. ²⁴They will be killed by the sword or sent away as captives to all the nations of the world. And Jerusalem will be trampled down by the Gentiles until the period of the Gentiles comes to an end.

²⁵"And there will be strange signs in the sun, moon, and stars. And here on earth the nations will be in turmoil, perplexed by the roaring seas and strange tides. ²⁶People will be terrified at what they see coming upon the earth, for the powers in the heavens will be shaken. ²⁷Then everyone will see the Son of Man* coming on a cloud with power and great glory.* ²⁸So when all these things begin to happen, stand and look up, for your salvation is near!"

²⁹Then he gave them this illustration: "Notice the fig tree, or any other tree. ³⁰When the leaves come out, you know without being told that summer is near. ³¹In the same way, when you see all these things taking place, you can know that the Kingdom of God is near. ³²I tell you the truth, this generation will not pass from the scene until all these things have taken place. ³³Heaven and earth will disappear, but my words will never disappear.

³⁴"Watch out! Don't let your hearts be dulled by carousing and drunkenness, and by the worries of this life. Don't let that

21:13 Or *This will be your testimony against them.*   **21:17** Greek *on account of my name.*
21:27a "Son of Man" is a title Jesus used for himself.   **21:27b** See Dan 7:13.

day catch you unaware, [35]like a trap. For that day will come upon everyone living on the earth. [36]Keep alert at all times. And pray that you might be strong enough to escape these coming horrors and stand before the Son of Man."

[37]Every day Jesus went to the Temple to teach, and each evening he returned to spend the night on the Mount of Olives. [38]The crowds gathered at the Temple early each morning to hear him.

CHAPTER 22

Judas Agrees to Betray Jesus

The Festival of Unleavened Bread, which is also called Passover, was approaching. [2]The leading priests and teachers of religious law were plotting how to kill Jesus, but they were afraid of the people's reaction.

[3]Then Satan entered into Judas Iscariot, who was one of the twelve disciples, [4]and he went to the leading priests and captains of the Temple guard to discuss the best way to betray Jesus to them. [5]They were delighted, and they promised to give him money. [6]So he agreed and began looking for an opportunity to betray Jesus so they could arrest him when the crowds weren't around.

The Last Supper

[7]Now the Festival of Unleavened Bread arrived, when the Passover lamb is sacrificed. [8]Jesus sent Peter and John ahead and said, "Go and prepare the Passover meal, so we can eat it together."

[9]"Where do you want us to prepare it?" they asked him.

[10]He replied, "As soon as you enter Jerusalem, a man carrying a pitcher of water will meet you. Follow him. At the house he enters, [11]say to the owner, 'The Teacher asks: Where is the guest room where I can eat the Passover meal with my disciples?' [12]He will take you upstairs to a large room that is already set up. That is where you should prepare our meal." [13]They went off to the city and found everything just as Jesus had said, and they prepared the Passover meal there.

[14]When the time came, Jesus and the apostles sat down together at the table.* [15]Jesus said, "I have been very eager to eat this Passover meal with you before my suffering begins. [16]For I tell you now that I won't eat this meal again until its meaning is fulfilled in the Kingdom of God."

[17]Then he took a cup of wine and gave thanks to God for it.

22:14 Or *reclined together.*

JOURNAL

Then he said, "Take this and share it among yourselves. [18] For I will not drink wine again until the Kingdom of God has come."

[19] He took some bread and gave thanks to God for it. Then he broke it in pieces and gave it to the disciples, saying, "This is my body, which is given for you. Do this to remember me."

[20] After supper he took another cup of wine and said, "This cup is the new covenant between God and his people—an agreement confirmed with my blood, which is poured out as a sacrifice for you.*

[21] "But here at this table, sitting among us as a friend, is the man who will betray me. [22] For it has been determined that the Son of Man* must die. But what sorrow awaits the one who betrays him." [23] The disciples began to ask each other which of them would ever do such a thing.

[24] Then they began to argue among themselves about who would be the greatest among them. [25] Jesus told them, "In this world the kings and great men lord it over their people, yet they are called 'friends of the people.' [26] But among you it will be different. Those who are the greatest among you should take the lowest rank, and the leader should be like a servant. [27] Who is more important, the one who sits at the table or the one who serves? The one who sits at the table, of course. But not here! For I am among you as one who serves.

[28] "You have stayed with me in my time of trial. [29] And just as my Father has granted me a Kingdom, I now grant you the right [30] to eat and drink at my table in my Kingdom. And you will sit on thrones, judging the twelve tribes of Israel.

Jesus Predicts Peter's Denial

[31] "Simon, Simon, Satan has asked to sift each of you like wheat. [32] But I have pleaded in prayer for you, Simon, that your faith should not fail. So when you have repented and turned to me again, strengthen your brothers."

[33] Peter said, "Lord, I am ready to go to prison with you, and even to die with you."

[34] But Jesus said, "Peter, let me tell you something. Before the rooster crows tomorrow morning, you will deny three times that you even know me."

[35] Then Jesus asked them, "When I sent you out to preach the Good News and you did not have money, a traveler's bag, or extra clothing, did you need anything?"

"No," they replied.

22:19-20 Some manuscripts omit 22:19b-20, *which is given for you . . . which is poured out as a sacrifice for you.*   **22:22** "Son of Man" is a title Jesus used for himself.

36 "But now," he said, "take your money and a traveler's bag. And if you don't have a sword, sell your cloak and buy one! 37 For the time has come for this prophecy about me to be fulfilled: 'He was counted among the rebels.'* Yes, everything written about me by the prophets will come true."

38 "Look, Lord," they replied, "we have two swords among us."

"That's enough," he said.

Jesus Prays on the Mount of Olives

39 Then, accompanied by the disciples, Jesus left the upstairs room and went as usual to the Mount of Olives. 40 There he told them, "Pray that you will not give in to temptation."

41 He walked away, about a stone's throw, and knelt down and prayed, 42 "Father, if you are willing, please take this cup of suffering away from me. Yet I want your will to be done, not mine." 43 Then an angel from heaven appeared and strengthened him. 44 He prayed more fervently, and he was in such agony of spirit that his sweat fell to the ground like great drops of blood.*

45 At last he stood up again and returned to the disciples, only to find them asleep, exhausted from grief. 46 "Why are you sleeping?" he asked them. "Get up and pray, so that you will not give in to temptation."

Jesus Is Betrayed and Arrested

47 But even as Jesus said this, a crowd approached, led by Judas, one of the twelve disciples. Judas walked over to Jesus to greet him with a kiss. 48 But Jesus said, "Judas, would you betray the Son of Man with a kiss?"

49 When the other disciples saw what was about to happen, they exclaimed, "Lord, should we fight? We brought the swords!" 50 And one of them struck at the high priest's slave, slashing off his right ear.

51 But Jesus said, "No more of this." And he touched the man's ear and healed him.

52 Then Jesus spoke to the leading priests, the captains of the Temple guard, and the elders who had come for him. "Am I some dangerous revolutionary," he asked, "that you come with swords and clubs to arrest me? 53 Why didn't you arrest me in the Temple? I was there every day. But this is your moment, the time when the power of darkness reigns."

22:37 Isa 53:12.   22:43-44 Verses 43 and 44 are not included in many ancient manuscripts.

"If siblings are able to graduate from siblinghood to friendship, this relationship has the potential for evolving into one of the strongest life can bring."

~ Joseph Leininger Wheeler

Peter Denies Jesus

54So they arrested him and led him to the high priest's home. And Peter followed at a distance. 55The guards lit a fire in the middle of the courtyard and sat around it, and Peter joined them there. 56A servant girl noticed him in the firelight and began staring at him. Finally she said, "This man was one of Jesus' followers!"

57But Peter denied it. "Woman," he said, "I don't even know him!"

58After a while someone else looked at him and said, "You must be one of them!"

"No, man, I'm not!" Peter retorted.

59About an hour later someone else insisted, "This must be one of them, because he is a Galilean, too."

60But Peter said, "Man, I don't know what you are talking about." And immediately, while he was still speaking, the rooster crowed. 61At that moment the Lord turned and looked at Peter. Suddenly, the Lord's words flashed through Peter's mind: "Before the rooster crows tomorrow morning, you will deny three times that you even know me." 62And Peter left the courtyard, weeping bitterly.

63The guards in charge of Jesus began mocking and beating him. 64They blindfolded him and said, "Prophesy to us! Who hit you that time?" 65And they hurled all sorts of terrible insults at him.

Jesus before the Council

66At daybreak all the elders of the people assembled, including the leading priests and the teachers of religious law. Jesus was led before this high council,* 67and they said, "Tell us, are you the Messiah?"

But he replied, "If I tell you, you won't believe me. 68And if I ask you a question, you won't answer. 69But from now on the Son of Man will be seated in the place of power at God's right hand.*"

70They all shouted, "So, are you claiming to be the Son of God?"

And he replied, "You say that I am."

71"Why do we need other witnesses?" they said. "We ourselves heard him say it."

CHAPTER **23**

Jesus' Trial before Pilate

Then the entire council took Jesus to Pilate, the Roman governor. 2They began to state their case: "This man has been leading

22:66 Greek *before their Sanhedrin.*   **22:69** See Ps 110:1.

our people astray by telling them not to pay their taxes to the Roman government and by claiming he is the Messiah, a king."

3 So Pilate asked him, "Are you the king of the Jews?"

Jesus replied, "You have said it."

4 Pilate turned to the leading priests and to the crowd and said, "I find nothing wrong with this man!"

5 Then they became insistent. "But he is causing riots by his teaching wherever he goes—all over Judea, from Galilee to Jerusalem!"

6 "Oh, is he a Galilean?" Pilate asked. 7 When they said that he was, Pilate sent him to Herod Antipas, because Galilee was under Herod's jurisdiction, and Herod happened to be in Jerusalem at the time.

8 Herod was delighted at the opportunity to see Jesus, because he had heard about him and had been hoping for a long time to see him perform a miracle. 9 He asked Jesus question after question, but Jesus refused to answer. 10 Meanwhile, the leading priests and the teachers of religious law stood there shouting their accusations. 11 Then Herod and his soldiers began mocking and ridiculing Jesus. Finally, they put a royal robe on him and sent him back to Pilate. 12 (Herod and Pilate, who had been enemies before, became friends that day.)

13 Then Pilate called together the leading priests and other religious leaders, along with the people, 14 and he announced his verdict. "You brought this man to me, accusing him of leading a revolt. I have examined him thoroughly on this point in your presence and find him innocent. 15 Herod came to the same conclusion and sent him back to us. Nothing this man has done calls for the death penalty. 16 So I will have him flogged, and then I will release him."*

18 Then a mighty roar rose from the crowd, and with one voice they shouted, "Kill him, and release Barabbas to us!" 19 (Barabbas was in prison for taking part in an insurrection in Jerusalem against the government, and for murder.) 20 Pilate argued with them, because he wanted to release Jesus. 21 But they kept shouting, "Crucify him! Crucify him!"

22 For the third time he demanded, "Why? What crime has he committed? I have found no reason to sentence him to death. So I will have him flogged, and then I will release him."

23 But the mob shouted louder and louder, demanding that Jesus be crucified, and their voices prevailed. 24 So Pilate sentenced Jesus to die as they demanded. 25 As they had requested,

23:16 Some manuscripts add verse 17, *Now it was necessary for him to release one prisoner to them during the Passover celebration.* Compare Matt 27:15; Mark 15:6; John 18:39.

A full 75% of church members describe their church as "very friendly."

—from "Friendship and Faith," a Gallup Research Study Commissioned by Group Publishing, Inc.

JOURNAL

he released Barabbas, the man in prison for insurrection and murder. But he turned Jesus over to them to do as they wished.

The Crucifixion

26As they led Jesus away, a man named Simon, who was from Cyrene,* happened to be coming in from the countryside. The soldiers seized him and put the cross on him and made him carry it behind Jesus. 27A large crowd trailed behind, including many grief-stricken women. 28But Jesus turned and said to them, "Daughters of Jerusalem, don't weep for me, but weep for yourselves and for your children. 29For the days are coming when they will say, 'Fortunate indeed are the women who are childless, the wombs that have not borne a child and the breasts that have never nursed.' 30People will beg the mountains, 'Fall on us,' and plead with the hills, 'Bury us.'* 31For if these things are done when the tree is green, what will happen when it is dry?*"

32Two others, both criminals, were led out to be executed with him. 33When they came to a place called The Skull,* they nailed him to the cross. And the criminals were also crucified— one on his right and one on his left.

34Jesus said, "Father, forgive them, for they don't know what they are doing."* And the soldiers gambled for his clothes by throwing dice.*

35The crowd watched and the leaders scoffed. "He saved others," they said, "let him save himself if he is really God's Messiah, the Chosen One." 36The soldiers mocked him, too, by offering him a drink of sour wine. 37They called out to him, "If you are the King of the Jews, save yourself!" 38A sign was fastened to the cross above him with these words: "This is the King of the Jews."

39One of the criminals hanging beside him scoffed, "So you're the Messiah, are you? Prove it by saving yourself—and us, too, while you're at it!"

40But the other criminal protested, "Don't you fear God even when you have been sentenced to die? 41We deserve to die for our crimes, but this man hasn't done anything wrong." 42Then he said, "Jesus, remember me when you come into your Kingdom."

43And Jesus replied, "I assure you, today you will be with me in paradise."

23:26 *Cyrene* was a city in northern Africa.   **23:30** Hos 10:8.   **23:31** Or *If these things are done to me, the living tree, what will happen to you, the dry tree?*   **23:33** Sometimes rendered *Calvary,* which comes from the Latin word for "skull."   **23:34a** This sentence is not included in many ancient manuscripts.   **23:34b** Greek *by casting lots.* See Ps 22:18.

The Death of Jesus

⁴⁴By this time it was noon, and darkness fell across the whole land until three o'clock. ⁴⁵The light from the sun was gone. And suddenly, the curtain in the sanctuary of the Temple was torn down the middle. ⁴⁶Then Jesus shouted, "Father, I entrust my spirit into your hands!"* And with those words he breathed his last.

⁴⁷When the Roman officer* overseeing the execution saw what had happened, he worshiped God and said, "Surely this man was innocent.*" ⁴⁸And when all the crowd that came to see the crucifixion saw what had happened, they went home in deep sorrow.* ⁴⁹But Jesus' friends, including the women who had followed him from Galilee, stood at a distance watching.

The Burial of Jesus

⁵⁰Now there was a good and righteous man named Joseph. He was a member of the Jewish high council, ⁵¹but he had not agreed with the decision and actions of the other religious leaders. He was from the town of Arimathea in Judea, and he was waiting for the Kingdom of God to come. ⁵²He went to Pilate and asked for Jesus' body. ⁵³Then he took the body down from the cross and wrapped it in a long sheet of linen cloth and laid it in a new tomb that had been carved out of rock. ⁵⁴This was done late on Friday afternoon, the day of preparation,* as the Sabbath was about to begin.

⁵⁵As his body was taken away, the women from Galilee followed and saw the tomb where his body was placed. ⁵⁶Then they went home and prepared spices and ointments to anoint his body. But by the time they were finished the Sabbath had begun, so they rested as required by the law.

CHAPTER 24

The Resurrection

But very early on Sunday morning* the women went to the tomb, taking the spices they had prepared. ²They found that the stone had been rolled away from the entrance. ³So they went in, but they didn't find the body of the Lord Jesus. ⁴As they stood there puzzled, two men suddenly appeared to them, clothed in dazzling robes.

⁵The women were terrified and bowed with their faces to the ground. Then the men asked, "Why are you looking among the

23:46 Ps 31:5.   23:47a Greek the centurion.   23:47b Or righteous.   23:48 Greek went home beating their breasts.   23:54 Greek It was the day of preparation.   24:1 Greek But on the first day of the week, very early in the morning.

No. 05-FA-173

FRIENDSHIP STORY

FRIENDSHIP TYPE: *Hard-to-Love People*

FRIENDSHIP LAYER: *Commitment*

FROM THE ARCHIVES

An Adopted Mom

C.S. Lewis: powerful writer, renowned Christian thinker, visionary…caregiver. Most people don't know it, of course, but C.S. Lewis was in fact a caregiver—to a very hard-to-love person.

As a younger man, during World War I, Lewis and his friend Paddy Moore pledged to take care of one another's families should one of them die. The war did take Paddy's life, and Lewis returned home to Paddy's mother.

No one liked her. She was difficult at every turn. She was needy, demanding, emotionally draining, and tedious to be with. She would demand that he do her household chores, despite the obvious fact that he was trying to write. She didn't like his friends, and they didn't like her.

Yet despite all that, Lewis adopted her as his own mom. He took care of her needs every day, even when it interfered with his own freedom. When, late in life, she was hospitalized, he visited her daily.

He didn't have to. Sometimes he probably didn't want to. But Lewis knew that acts of friendship and commitment could change a person, so he persevered and hoped.

Lewis lived out a committed friendship, even to the most difficult of people…and it made a difference. Before her death, she thanked him. And that was enough.

FRIENDSHIP STORY

continues on page 174…

FRIENDSHIP STORY *continued from page 173...*

Experience

Is there anyone you know who no one would want to be around? Maybe that person is in need of the kind of unflinching love that Lewis showed to Mrs. Moore. It's the same love that Jesus offered to Zacchaeus in **Luke 19:1-10**. How can you show that kind of committed love? Perhaps you could invite the person to lunch weekly. Or maybe you could offer to do a weekly chore for him or her. Think of something that will show you're not going to abandon the person when things get difficult.

THE ONE THING YOU CAN DO THIS WEEK **1**

Reflect

★ Why did Lewis stay committed to Mrs. Moore despite her challenges?

★ How can you commit to long-term friendship with a hard-to-love person?

★ Who has shown love to you even at a time you were hard to love?

dead for someone who is alive? ⁶He isn't here! He is risen from the dead! Remember what he told you back in Galilee, ⁷that the Son of Man* must be betrayed into the hands of sinful men and be crucified, and that he would rise again on the third day."

⁸Then they remembered that he had said this. ⁹So they rushed back from the tomb to tell his eleven disciples—and everyone else—what had happened. ¹⁰It was Mary Magdalene, Joanna, Mary the mother of James, and several other women who told the apostles what had happened. ¹¹But the story sounded like nonsense to the men, so they didn't believe it. ¹²However, Peter jumped up and ran to the tomb to look. Stooping, he peered in and saw the empty linen wrappings; then he went home again, wondering what had happened.

The Walk to Emmaus

¹³That same day two of Jesus' followers were walking to the village of Emmaus, seven miles* from Jerusalem. ¹⁴As they walked along they were talking about everything that had happened. ¹⁵As they talked and discussed these things, Jesus himself suddenly came and began walking with them. ¹⁶But God kept them from recognizing him.

¹⁷He asked them, "What are you discussing so intently as you walk along?"

They stopped short, sadness written across their faces. ¹⁸Then one of them, Cleopas, replied, "You must be the only person in Jerusalem who hasn't heard about all the things that have happened there the last few days."

¹⁹"What things?" Jesus asked.

"The things that happened to Jesus, the man from Nazareth," they said. "He was a prophet who did powerful miracles, and he was a mighty teacher in the eyes of God and all the people. ²⁰But our leading priests and other religious leaders handed him over to be condemned to death, and they crucified him. ²¹We had hoped he was the Messiah who had come to rescue Israel. This all happened three days ago.

²²"Then some women from our group of his followers were at his tomb early this morning, and they came back with an amazing report. ²³They said his body was missing, and they had seen angels who told them Jesus is alive! ²⁴Some of our men ran out to see, and sure enough, his body was gone, just as the women had said."

²⁵Then Jesus said to them, "You foolish people! You find it so

24:7 "Son of Man" is a title Jesus used for himself.   24:13 Greek *60 stadia* [11.1 kilometers].

hard to believe all that the prophets wrote in the Scriptures. [26]Wasn't it clearly predicted that the Messiah would have to suffer all these things before entering his glory?" [27]Then Jesus took them through the writings of Moses and all the prophets, explaining from all the Scriptures the things concerning himself.

[28]By this time they were nearing Emmaus and the end of their journey. Jesus acted as if he were going on, [29]but they begged him, "Stay the night with us, since it is getting late." So he went home with them. [30]As they sat down to eat,* he took the bread and blessed it. Then he broke it and gave it to them. [31]Suddenly, their eyes were opened, and they recognized him. And at that moment he disappeared!

[32]They said to each other, "Didn't our hearts burn within us as he talked with us on the road and explained the Scriptures to us?" [33]And within the hour they were on their way back to Jerusalem. There they found the eleven disciples and the others who had gathered with them, [34]who said, "The Lord has really risen! He appeared to Peter.*"

Jesus Appears to the Disciples

[35]Then the two from Emmaus told their story of how Jesus had appeared to them as they were walking along the road, and how they had recognized him as he was breaking the bread. [36]And just as they were telling about it, Jesus himself was suddenly standing there among them. "Peace be with you," he said. [37]But the whole group was startled and frightened, thinking they were seeing a ghost!

[38]"Why are you frightened?" he asked. "Why are your hearts filled with doubt? [39]Look at my hands. Look at my feet. You can see that it's really me. Touch me and make sure that I am not a ghost, because ghosts don't have bodies, as you see that I do." [40]As he spoke, he showed them his hands and his feet.

[41]Still they stood there in disbelief, filled with joy and wonder. Then he asked them, "Do you have anything here to eat?" [42]They gave him a piece of broiled fish, [43]and he ate it as they watched.

[44]Then he said, "When I was with you before, I told you that everything written about me in the law of Moses and the prophets and in the Psalms must be fulfilled." [45]Then he opened their minds to understand the Scriptures. [46]And he said, "Yes, it was written long ago that the Messiah would suffer

24:30 Or *As they reclined.*   **24:34** Greek *Simon.*

and die and rise from the dead on the third day. [47] It was also written that this message would be proclaimed in the authority of his name to all the nations,* beginning in Jerusalem: 'There is forgiveness of sins for all who repent.' [48] You are witnesses of all these things.

[49] "And now I will send the Holy Spirit, just as my Father promised. But stay here in the city until the Holy Spirit comes and fills you with power from heaven."

The Ascension

[50] Then Jesus led them to Bethany, and lifting his hands to heaven, he blessed them. [51] While he was blessing them, he left them and was taken up to heaven.* [52] So they worshiped him and then returned to Jerusalem filled with great joy. [53] And they spent all of their time in the Temple, praising God.

24:47 Or *all peoples.*   24:51 Some manuscripts do not include *and was taken up to heaven.*

John

AUTHOR:	DATE WRITTEN:
John (The Apostle)	Approximately A.D. 85–90

CHAPTER **1**

Prologue: Christ, the Eternal Word

¹ In the beginning the Word already existed.
  The Word was with God,
  and the Word was God.
² He existed in the beginning with God.
³ God created everything through him,
  and nothing was created except through him.
⁴ The Word gave life to everything that was created,*
  and his life brought light to everyone.
⁵ The light shines in the darkness,
  and the darkness can never extinguish it.*

⁶God sent a man, John the Baptist,* ⁷to tell about the light so that everyone might believe because of his testimony. ⁸John himself was not the light; he was simply a witness to tell about the light. ⁹The one who is the true light, who gives light to everyone, was coming into the world.

¹⁰He came into the very world he created, but the world didn't recognize him. ¹¹He came to his own people, and even they rejected him. ¹²But to all who believed him and accepted him, he gave the right to become children of God. ¹³They are reborn—not with a physical birth resulting from human passion or plan, but a birth that comes from God.

¹⁴So the Word became human* and made his home among us. He was full of unfailing love and faithfulness.* And we have seen his glory, the glory of the Father's one and only Son. ☩

1:3-4 Or *and nothing that was created was created except through him. The Word gave life to everything.* 1:5 Or *and the darkness has not understood it.* 1:6 Greek *a man named John.* 1:14a Greek *became flesh.* 1:14b Or *grace and truth;* also in 1:17.

The Offer

Read **John 1:10-14**.

The night before it happened, goldfish jumped out of their bowls. People saw strange lights in the sky. Dogs barked incessantly, and chickens refused to eat. Most of the people of Tangshan were asleep when the quake struck. An estimated 80,000 people died in the first shock of the 1976 earthquake. And in the aftershocks and weeks that followed, thousands more people lost their lives. Many estimate the final death toll at nearly half a million.

Quickly, the international community mobilized relief efforts to find survivors trapped in the rubble and to help China rebuild the metropolis of Tangshan. But China refused all efforts of help.

Anchor Passage continues on page 178...

Anchor Passage continued from page 177...

To refuse help in the face of such disaster may seem outrageous and appalling, but it shouldn't be surprising. Since the very beginning, people have been refusing help—full of pride and trying to go it alone.

But God has always been there, ready and willing to help.

"To all who believed him and accepted him, he gave the right to become children of God." Jesus, God's Son, became human and came to earth to help us. He *died* so we could be forgiven—so we could know God, become God's children, and live eternally. Many have rejected him. Many have chosen to refuse his help. But the offer still stands, for any who will take it. All you have to do is believe in Jesus and accept him as a friend...and Savior.

Experience

Do you know Jesus as a friend? as a Savior?

If not, what's stopping you? Write it down. Then, if you're willing, ask God to answer your questions and help you believe.

_____

_____

_____

If you already know Jesus as your friend, write down an area of your life in which you haven't accepted Jesus' help. Maybe it's with a problem at work, a conflict with a friend, or an addiction you're fighting. Whatever the problem, Jesus is your friend, who not only wants to help but actually *can* help. Why not ask for his help now?

_____

_____

_____

Anchor Passage continues on page 179...

¹⁵John testified about him when he shouted to the crowds, "This is the one I was talking about when I said, 'Someone is coming after me who is far greater than I am, for he existed long before me.'"

¹⁶From his abundance we have all received one gracious blessing after another.* ¹⁷For the law was given through Moses, but God's unfailing love and faithfulness came through Jesus Christ. ¹⁸No one has ever seen God. But the unique One, who is himself God,* is near to the Father's heart. He has revealed God to us.

The Testimony of John the Baptist

¹⁹This was John's testimony when the Jewish leaders sent priests and Temple assistants* from Jerusalem to ask John, "Who are you?" ²⁰He came right out and said, "I am not the Messiah."

²¹"Well then, who are you?" they asked. "Are you Elijah?"

"No," he replied.

"Are you the Prophet we are expecting?"*

"No."

²²"Then who are you? We need an answer for those who sent us. What do you have to say about yourself?"

²³John replied in the words of the prophet Isaiah:

"I am a voice shouting in the wilderness,
   'Clear the way for the LORD's coming!'"*

²⁴Then the Pharisees who had been sent ²⁵asked him, "If you aren't the Messiah or Elijah or the Prophet, what right do you have to baptize?"

²⁶John told them, "I baptize with* water, but right here in the crowd is someone you do not recognize. ²⁷Though his ministry follows mine, I'm not even worthy to be his slave and untie the straps of his sandal."

²⁸This encounter took place in Bethany, an area east of the Jordan River, where John was baptizing.

Jesus, the Lamb of God

²⁹The next day John saw Jesus coming toward him and said, "Look! The Lamb of God who takes away the sin of the world! ³⁰He is the one I was talking about when I said, 'A man is coming after me who is far greater than I am, for he existed long before me.' ³¹I did not recognize him as the Messiah, but I have been baptizing with water so that he might be revealed to Israel."

1:16 Or *received the grace of Christ rather than the grace of the law;* Greek reads *received grace upon grace.* 1:18 Some manuscripts read *But the one and only Son.* 1:19 Greek *and Levites.* 1:21 Greek *Are you the Prophet?* See Deut 18:15, 18; Mal 4:5-6. 1:23 Isa 40:3. 1:26 Or *in;* also in 1:31, 33.

[32]Then John testified, "I saw the Holy Spirit descending like a dove from heaven and resting upon him. [33]I didn't know he was the one, but when God sent me to baptize with water, he told me, 'The one on whom you see the Spirit descend and rest is the one who will baptize with the Holy Spirit.' [34]I saw this happen to Jesus, so I testify that he is the Chosen One of God.*"

The First Disciples

[35]The following day John was again standing with two of his disciples. [36]As Jesus walked by, John looked at him and declared, "Look! There is the Lamb of God!" [37]When John's two disciples heard this, they followed Jesus.

[38]Jesus looked around and saw them following. "What do you want?" he asked them.

They replied, "Rabbi" (which means "Teacher"), "where are you staying?"

[39]"Come and see," he said. It was about four o'clock in the afternoon when they went with him to the place where he was staying, and they remained with him the rest of the day.

[40]Andrew, Simon Peter's brother, was one of these men who heard what John said and then followed Jesus. [41]Andrew went to find his brother, Simon, and told him, "We have found the Messiah" (which means "Christ"*).

[42]Then Andrew brought Simon to meet Jesus. Looking intently at Simon, Jesus said, "Your name is Simon, son of John—but you will be called Cephas" (which means "Peter"*).

[43]The next day Jesus decided to go to Galilee. He found Philip and said to him, "Come, follow me." [44]Philip was from Bethsaida, Andrew and Peter's hometown.

[45]Philip went to look for Nathanael and told him, "We have found the very person Moses* and the prophets wrote about! His name is Jesus, the son of Joseph from Nazareth."

[46]"Nazareth!" exclaimed Nathanael. "Can anything good come from Nazareth?"

1:34 Some manuscripts read *the Son of God.*　1:41 *Messiah* (a Hebrew term) and *Christ* (a Greek term) both mean "the anointed one."　1:42 The names *Cephas* (from Aramaic) and *Peter* (from Greek) both mean "rock."　1:45 Greek *Moses in the law.*

Anchor Passage continued from page 178...

Reflect

★ What does it mean to accept Jesus as a friend?

★ What is the difference between believing in a friend and accepting a friend? Can you be in a true friendship that excludes one or the other?

★ Where are you in your friendship with Jesus? Do you believe what he says about himself?

DIGGING DEEPER

FRIENDSHIP TYPE:	FRIENDSHIP LAYER:
Jesus	*Acceptance*

For accepting Jesus, check out...

➤ The Friendship Experience .... on page 193
➤ The Friendship Story .... on page 489
➤ What to Say and What Not to Say .... on page 481

Anchor Passage

PASSAGE: **John 1:35-51**

FRIENDSHIP TYPE: *Friends* FRIENDSHIP LAYER: *Getting Acquainted*

From Strangers to Friends

Think of a close friend. Do you remember when you first met? What was your first impression?

Read **John 1:35-51**.

How do strangers become friends? They begin with a smile, a nod, a conversation. They find out that they have some common experiences; they like the same things; they share an opinion.

They get acquainted.

Friends don't just start out as friends; there's always a moment when they first meet, when they begin getting to know each other.

Jesus got acquainted with his closest friends through a shared afternoon and an invitation to hang out.

He got to know them. Asked them questions. Invited them to stay with him. Told them about himself. He didn't just introduce himself, make small talk, and then move on. Instead he started friendships that would last for years.

And those friends invited more friends to get to know Jesus.

Friends of mine have a sign on their front door that reads, "There are no strangers here, only friends we have not met." But strangers won't become friends until you take that first step, move beyond formalities, and begin getting acquainted.

Anchor Passage continues on page 181...

"Come and see for yourself," Philip replied.

47 As they approached, Jesus said, "Now here is a genuine son of Israel—a man of complete integrity."

48 "How do you know about me?" Nathanael asked.

Jesus replied, "I could see you under the fig tree before Philip found you."

49 Then Nathanael exclaimed, "Rabbi, you are the Son of God—the King of Israel!"

50 Jesus asked him, "Do you believe this just because I told you I had seen you under the fig tree? You will see greater things than this." 51 Then he said, "I tell you the truth, you will all see heaven open and the angels of God going up and down on the Son of Man, the one who is the stairway between heaven and earth.*" ⚓

CHAPTER **2**

The Wedding at Cana

The next day* there was a wedding celebration in the village of Cana in Galilee. Jesus' mother was there, 2 and Jesus and his disciples were also invited to the celebration. 3 The wine supply ran out during the festivities, so Jesus' mother told him, "They have no more wine."

4 "Dear woman, that's not our problem," Jesus replied. "My time has not yet come."

5 But his mother told the servants, "Do whatever he tells you."

6 Standing nearby were six stone water jars, used for Jewish ceremonial washing. Each could hold twenty to thirty gallons.* 7 Jesus told the servants, "Fill the jars with water." When the jars had been filled, 8 he said, "Now dip some out, and take it to the master of ceremonies." So the servants followed his instructions.

9 When the master of ceremonies tasted the water that was now wine, not knowing where it had come from (though, of course, the servants knew), he called the bridegroom over. 10 "A host always serves the best wine first," he said. "Then, when everyone has had a lot to drink, he brings out the less expensive wine. But you have kept the best until now!"

11 This miraculous sign at Cana in Galilee was the first time Jesus revealed his glory. And his disciples believed in him.

12 After the wedding he went to Capernaum for a few days with his mother, his brothers, and his disciples.

1:51 Greek *going up and down on the Son of Man*; see Gen 28:10-17. "Son of Man" is a title Jesus used for himself. 2:1 Greek *On the third day*; see 1:35, 43. 2:6 Greek *2 or 3 measures* [75 to 113 liters].

Jesus Clears the Temple

¹³It was nearly time for the Jewish Passover celebration, so Jesus went to Jerusalem. ¹⁴In the Temple area he saw merchants selling cattle, sheep, and doves for sacrifices; he also saw dealers at tables exchanging foreign money. ¹⁵Jesus made a whip from some ropes and chased them all out of the Temple. He drove out the sheep and cattle, scattered the money changers' coins over the floor, and turned over their tables. ¹⁶Then, going over to the people who sold doves, he told them, "Get these things out of here. Stop turning my Father's house into a marketplace!"

¹⁷Then his disciples remembered this prophecy from the Scriptures: "Passion for God's house will consume me."*

¹⁸But the Jewish leaders demanded, "What are you doing? If God gave you authority to do this, show us a miraculous sign to prove it."

¹⁹"All right," Jesus replied. "Destroy this temple, and in three days I will raise it up."

²⁰"What!" they exclaimed. "It has taken forty-six years to build this Temple, and you can rebuild it in three days?" ²¹But when Jesus said "this temple," he meant his own body. ²²After he was raised from the dead, his disciples remembered he had said this, and they believed both the Scriptures and what Jesus had said.

Jesus and Nicodemus

²³Because of the miraculous signs Jesus did in Jerusalem at the Passover celebration, many began to trust in him. ²⁴But Jesus didn't trust them, because he knew human nature. ²⁵No one needed to tell him what mankind is really like.

CHAPTER **3**

There was a man named Nicodemus, a Jewish religious leader who was a Pharisee. ²After dark one evening, he came to speak with Jesus. "Rabbi," he said, "we all know that God has sent you to teach us. Your miraculous signs are evidence that God is with you."

³Jesus replied, "I tell you the truth, unless you are born again,* you cannot see the Kingdom of God."

⁴"What do you mean?" exclaimed Nicodemus. "How can an old man go back into his mother's womb and be born again?"

⁵Jesus replied, "I assure you, no one can enter the Kingdom of God without being born of water and the Spirit.* ⁶Humans

2:17 Or *"Concern for God's house will be my undoing."* Ps 69:9.   **3:3** Or *born from above; also in 3:7.*
3:5 Or *and spirit.* The Greek word for *Spirit* can also be translated *wind; see 3:8.*

Anchor Passage continued from page 180...

Experience

Think of a person you see regularly but don't know very well. What steps could you take to make that person a friend instead of a stranger? A dinner invitation? Conversation over coffee? List three ideas, and put them into action this week.

_____

_____

_____

Reflect

★ What did Jesus do to become acquainted with the disciples? How can you follow Jesus' example when you meet new people?

★ How did it go with your new friend? What's the next step in your friendship?

DIGGING DEEPER

FRIENDSHIP TYPE: *Friends*

FRIENDSHIP LAYER: *Getting Acquainted*

For getting acquainted with friends, check out...

➡ The Friendship Experience .... on page 203
➡ The Friendship Story .... on page 311
➡ What to Say and What Not to Say .... on page 314

Friendship First NEW TESTAMENT

JOURNAL

can reproduce only human life, but the Holy Spirit gives birth to spiritual life.* ⁷So don't be surprised when I say, 'You* must be born again.' ⁸The wind blows wherever it wants. Just as you can hear the wind but can't tell where it comes from or where it is going, so you can't explain how people are born of the Spirit."

⁹"How are these things possible?" Nicodemus asked.

¹⁰Jesus replied, "You are a respected Jewish teacher, and yet you don't understand these things? ¹¹I assure you, we tell you what we know and have seen, and yet you won't believe our testimony. ¹²But if you don't believe me when I tell you about earthly things, how can you possibly believe if I tell you about heavenly things? ¹³No one has ever gone to heaven and returned. But the Son of Man* has come down from heaven. ¹⁴And as Moses lifted up the bronze snake on a pole in the wilderness, so the Son of Man must be lifted up, ¹⁵so that everyone who believes in him will have eternal life.*

¹⁶"For God loved the world so much that he gave his one and only Son, so that everyone who believes in him will not perish but have eternal life. ¹⁷God sent his Son into the world not to judge the world, but to save the world through him.

¹⁸"There is no judgment against anyone who believes in him. But anyone who does not believe in him has already been judged for not believing in God's one and only Son. ¹⁹And the judgment is based on this fact: God's light came into the world, but people loved the darkness more than the light, for their actions were evil. ²⁰All who do evil hate the light and refuse to go near it for fear their sins will be exposed. ²¹But those who do what is right come to the light so others can see that they are doing what God wants.*"

John the Baptist Exalts Jesus

²²Then Jesus and his disciples left Jerusalem and went into the Judean countryside. Jesus spent some time with them there, baptizing people.

²³At this time John the Baptist was baptizing at Aenon, near Salim, because there was plenty of water there; and people kept coming to him for baptism. ²⁴(This was before John was thrown into prison.) ²⁵A debate broke out between John's disciples and a certain Jew* over ceremonial cleansing. ²⁶So John's disciples came to him and said, "Rabbi, the man you met on the other

3:6 Greek *what is born of the Spirit is spirit.*   3:7 The Greek word for *you* is plural; also in 3:12.
3:13 Some manuscripts add *who lives in heaven.* "Son of Man" is a title Jesus used for himself.
3:15 Or *everyone who believes will have eternal life in him.*   3:21 Or *can see God at work in what he is doing.*   3:25 Some manuscripts read *some Jews.*

side of the Jordan River, the one you identified as the Messiah, is also baptizing people. And everybody is going to him instead of coming to us."

²⁷ John replied, "No one can receive anything unless God gives it from heaven. ²⁸ You yourselves know how plainly I told you, 'I am not the Messiah. I am only here to prepare the way for him.' ²⁹ It is the bridegroom who marries the bride, and the best man is simply glad to stand with him and hear his vows. Therefore, I am filled with joy at his success. ³⁰ He must become greater and greater, and I must become less and less.

³¹ "He has come from above and is greater than anyone else. We are of the earth, and we speak of earthly things, but he has come from heaven and is greater than anyone else.* ³² He testifies about what he has seen and heard, but how few believe what he tells them! ³³ Anyone who accepts his testimony can affirm that God is true. ³⁴ For he is sent by God. He speaks God's words, for God gives him the Spirit without limit. ³⁵ The Father loves his Son and has put everything into his hands. ³⁶ And anyone who believes in God's Son has eternal life. Anyone who doesn't obey the Son will never experience eternal life but remains under God's angry judgment."

CHAPTER 4
Jesus and the Samaritan Woman

Jesus* knew the Pharisees had heard that he was baptizing and making more disciples than John ²(though Jesus himself didn't baptize them—his disciples did). ³ So he left Judea and returned to Galilee.

⁴ He had to go through Samaria on the way. ⁵ Eventually he came to the Samaritan village of Sychar, near the field that Jacob gave to his son Joseph. ⁶ Jacob's well was there; and Jesus, tired from the long walk, sat wearily beside the well about noontime. ⁷ Soon a Samaritan woman came to draw water, and Jesus said to her, "Please give me a drink." ⁸ He was alone at the time because his disciples had gone into the village to buy some food.

⁹ The woman was surprised, for Jews refuse to have anything to do with Samaritans.* She said to Jesus,

3:31 Some manuscripts omit *and is greater than anyone else.* 4:1 Some manuscripts read *The Lord.*
4:9 Some manuscripts omit this sentence.

Anchor Passage

PASSAGE: **John 4:1-30**

FRIENDSHIP TYPE: *Jesus* FRIENDSHIP LAYER: *Getting Acquainted*

A Thirst Quenched

Go get a nice, tall glass of water, and drink every drop. Ahhh…

Now read **John 4:1-30**.

Imagine it's over 100 degrees and you're in the middle of the desert. You just walked 20 miles. You're hot, sweaty, tired, and *thirsty*. All you want is a drink of water and a place to rest. That's probably how Jesus felt when he sat down on the well next to the Samaritan woman. The two were all alone, and the woman probably wasn't too happy to see Jesus—her questionable lifestyle didn't make her too popular.

To make matters worse, Jesus was Jewish and the woman was a Samaritan—two groups that just didn't get along. She likely braced for the worst.

But instead of judgment, Jesus offered warm friendship, tender understanding, and a valuable gift. He offered her living water, the kind that would quench her thirst forever. The woman knew a good thing when she saw it. She didn't hesitate to drink the water Jesus offered. And it made all the difference—her thirst was quenched, and her joy overflowed.

Anchor Passage continues on page 184…

Anchor Passage continued from page 183...

Experience

Tired and thirsty, Jesus still took the time to get acquainted with the woman at the well. It's the same with you—Jesus is always ready to strike up a friendship.

Get to know Jesus this week. Find out why he's called the "living water." (Read this passage again, and check out **Revelation 21:5-6**.) Write down why Jesus is like water.

_____

_____

_____

_____

_____

When you reach for a glass of water this week, think of the ways Jesus quenches your thirst.

THE ONE THING ★ YOU CAN DO THIS WEEK ★
1

Reflect

★ Why did Jesus even stop to talk to the woman? Why is he so interested in getting acquainted with you?

★ How could becoming better acquaintances with Jesus change your life?

DIGGING DEEPER

FRIENDSHIP TYPE:
Jesus

FRIENDSHIP LAYER:
Getting Acquainted

For getting acquainted with Jesus, check out...

➥ The Friendship Experience .... on page 189
➥ The Friendship Story .... on page 425
➥ What to Say and What Not to Say .... on page 430

"You are a Jew, and I am a Samaritan woman. Why are you asking me for a drink?"

[10] Jesus replied, "If you only knew the gift God has for you and who you are speaking to, you would ask me, and I would give you living water."

[11] "But sir, you don't have a rope or a bucket," she said, "and this well is very deep. Where would you get this living water? [12] And besides, do you think you're greater than our ancestor Jacob, who gave us this well? How can you offer better water than he and his sons and his animals enjoyed?"

[13] Jesus replied, "Anyone who drinks this water will soon become thirsty again. [14] But those who drink the water I give will never be thirsty again. It becomes a fresh, bubbling spring within them, giving them eternal life."

[15] "Please, sir," the woman said, "give me this water! Then I'll never be thirsty again, and I won't have to come here to get water."

[16] "Go and get your husband," Jesus told her.

[17] "I don't have a husband," the woman replied.

Jesus said, "You're right! You don't have a husband—[18] for you have had five husbands, and you aren't even married to the man you're living with now. You certainly spoke the truth!"

[19] "Sir," the woman said, "you must be a prophet. [20] So tell me, why is it that you Jews insist that Jerusalem is the only place of worship, while we Samaritans claim it is here at Mount Gerizim,* where our ancestors worshiped?"

[21] Jesus replied, "Believe me, dear woman, the time is coming when it will no longer matter whether you worship the Father on this mountain or in Jerusalem. [22] You Samaritans know very little about the one you worship, while we Jews know all about him, for salvation comes through the Jews. [23] But the time is coming—indeed it's here now—when true worshipers will worship the Father in spirit and in truth. The Father is looking for those who will worship him that way. [24] For God is Spirit, so those who worship him must worship in spirit and in truth."

4:20 Greek *on this mountain.*

25The woman said, "I know the Messiah is coming—the one who is called Christ. When he comes, he will explain everything to us."

26Then Jesus told her, "I AM the Messiah!"*

27Just then his disciples came back. They were shocked to find him talking to a woman, but none of them had the nerve to ask, "What do you want with her?" or "Why are you talking to her?" 28The woman left her water jar beside the well and ran back to the village, telling everyone, 29"Come and see a man who told me everything I ever did! Could he possibly be the Messiah?" 30So the people came streaming from the village to see him. ⚓

31Meanwhile, the disciples were urging Jesus, "Rabbi, eat something."

32But Jesus replied, "I have a kind of food you know nothing about."

33"Did someone bring him food while we were gone?" the disciples asked each other.

34Then Jesus explained: "My nourishment comes from doing the will of God, who sent me, and from finishing his work. 35You know the saying, 'Four months between planting and harvest.' But I say, wake up and look around. The fields are already ripe* for harvest. 36The harvesters are paid good wages, and the fruit they harvest is people brought to eternal life. What joy awaits both the planter and the harvester alike! 37You know the saying, 'One plants and another harvests.' And it's true. 38I sent you to harvest where you didn't plant; others had already done the work, and now you will get to gather the harvest."

Many Samaritans Believe

39Many Samaritans from the village believed in Jesus because the woman had said, "He told me everything I ever did!" 40When they came out to see him, they begged him to stay in their village. So he stayed for two days, 41long enough for many more to hear his message and believe. 42Then they said to the woman, "Now we believe, not just because of what you told us, but because we have heard him ourselves. Now we know that he is indeed the Savior of the world."

4:26 Or "The 'I AM' is here"; or "I am the LORD"; Greek reads "I am, the one speaking to you." See Exod 3:14.   4:35 Greek white.

JOURNAL

Jesus Heals an Official's Son

⁴³At the end of the two days, Jesus went on to Galilee. ⁴⁴He himself had said that a prophet is not honored in his own hometown. ⁴⁵Yet the Galileans welcomed him, for they had been in Jerusalem at the Passover celebration and had seen everything he did there.

⁴⁶As he traveled through Galilee, he came to Cana, where he had turned the water into wine. There was a government official in nearby Capernaum whose son was very sick. ⁴⁷When he heard that Jesus had come from Judea to Galilee, he went and begged Jesus to come to Capernaum to heal his son, who was about to die.

⁴⁸Jesus asked, "Will you never believe in me unless you see miraculous signs and wonders?"

⁴⁹The official pleaded, "Lord, please come now before my little boy dies."

⁵⁰Then Jesus told him, "Go back home. Your son will live!" And the man believed what Jesus said and started home.

⁵¹While the man was on his way, some of his servants met him with the news that his son was alive and well. ⁵²He asked them when the boy had begun to get better, and they replied, "Yesterday afternoon at one o'clock his fever suddenly disappeared!" ⁵³Then the father realized that that was the very time Jesus had told him, "Your son will live." And he and his entire household believed in Jesus. ⁵⁴This was the second miraculous sign Jesus did in Galilee after coming from Judea.

CHAPTER **5**

Jesus Heals a Lame Man

Afterward Jesus returned to Jerusalem for one of the Jewish holy days. ²Inside the city, near the Sheep Gate, was the pool of Bethesda,* with five covered porches. ³Crowds of sick people— blind, lame, or paralyzed—lay on the porches.* ⁵One of the men lying there had been sick for thirty-eight years. ⁶When Jesus saw him and knew he had been ill for a long time, he asked him, "Would you like to get well?"

⁷"I can't, sir," the sick man said, "for I have no one to put me into the pool when the water bubbles up. Someone else always gets there ahead of me."

⁸Jesus told him, "Stand up, pick up your mat, and walk!"

5:2 Other manuscripts read *Beth-zatha;* still others read *Bethsaida.* 5:3 Some manuscripts add an expanded conclusion to verse 3 and all of verse 4: *waiting for a certain movement of the water,* ⁴*for an angel of the Lord came from time to time and stirred up the water. And the first person to step in after the water was stirred was healed of whatever disease he had.*

[9] Instantly, the man was healed! He rolled up his sleeping mat and began walking! But this miracle happened on the Sabbath, [10] so the Jewish leaders objected. They said to the man who was cured, "You can't work on the Sabbath! The law doesn't allow you to carry that sleeping mat!"

[11] But he replied, "The man who healed me told me, 'Pick up your mat and walk.'"

[12] "Who said such a thing as that?" they demanded.

[13] The man didn't know, for Jesus had disappeared into the crowd. [14] But afterward Jesus found him in the Temple and told him, "Now you are well; so stop sinning, or something even worse may happen to you." [15] Then the man went and told the Jewish leaders that it was Jesus who had healed him.

Jesus Claims to Be the Son of God

[16] So the Jewish leaders began harassing* Jesus for breaking the Sabbath rules. [17] But Jesus replied, "My Father is always working, and so am I." [18] So the Jewish leaders tried all the harder to find a way to kill him. For he not only broke the Sabbath, he called God his Father, thereby making himself equal with God.

[19] So Jesus explained, "I tell you the truth, the Son can do nothing by himself. He does only what he sees the Father doing. Whatever the Father does, the Son also does. [20] For the Father loves the Son and shows him everything he is doing. In fact, the Father will show him how to do even greater works than healing this man. Then you will truly be astonished. [21] For just as the Father gives life to those he raises from the dead, so the Son gives life to anyone he wants. [22] In addition, the Father judges no one. Instead, he has given the Son absolute authority to judge, [23] so that everyone will honor the Son, just as they honor the Father. Anyone who does not honor the Son is certainly not honoring the Father who sent him.

[24] "I tell you the truth, those who listen to my message and believe in God who sent me have eternal life. They will never be condemned for their sins, but they have already passed from death into life.

[25] "And I assure you that the time is coming, indeed it's here now, when the dead will hear my voice—the voice of the Son of God. And those who listen will live. [26] The Father has life in himself, and he has granted that same life-giving power to his Son. [27] And he has given him authority to judge everyone because he is the Son of Man.* [28] Don't be so surprised! Indeed,

5:16 Or *persecuting.*   5:27 "Son of Man" is a title Jesus used for himself.

"I must feel pride in my friend's accomplishments as if they were mine."
~ Ralph Waldo Emerson

"The best mirror
is an old friend."
~ English Proverb

JOURNAL

the time is coming when all the dead in their graves will hear the voice of God's Son, 29and they will rise again. Those who have done good will rise to experience eternal life, and those who have continued in evil will rise to experience judgment. 30I can do nothing on my own. I judge as God tells me. Therefore, my judgment is just, because I carry out the will of the one who sent me, not my own will.

Witnesses to Jesus

31"If I were to testify on my own behalf, my testimony would not be valid. 32But someone else is also testifying about me, and I assure you that everything he says about me is true. 33In fact, you sent investigators to listen to John the Baptist, and his testimony about me was true. 34Of course, I have no need of human witnesses, but I say these things so you might be saved. 35John was like a burning and shining lamp, and you were excited for a while about his message. 36But I have a greater witness than John—my teachings and my miracles. The Father gave me these works to accomplish, and they prove that he sent me. 37And the Father who sent me has testified about me himself. You have never heard his voice or seen him face to face, 38and you do not have his message in your hearts, because you do not believe me—the one he sent to you.

39"You search the Scriptures because you think they give you eternal life. But the Scriptures point to me! 40Yet you refuse to come to me to receive this life.

41"Your approval means nothing to me, 42because I know you don't have God's love within you. 43For I have come to you in my Father's name, and you have rejected me. Yet if others come in their own name, you gladly welcome them. 44No wonder you can't believe! For you gladly honor each other, but you don't care about the honor that comes from the one who alone is God.*

45"Yet it isn't I who will accuse you before the Father. Moses will accuse you! Yes, Moses, in whom you put your hopes. 46If you really believed Moses, you would believe me, because he wrote about me. 47But since you don't believe what he wrote, how will you believe what I say?"

CHAPTER 6
Jesus Feeds Five Thousand

After this, Jesus crossed over to the far side of the Sea of Galilee, also known as the Sea of Tiberias. 2A huge crowd kept following him wherever he went, because they saw his miraculous signs as

5:44 Some manuscripts read *from the only One.*

he healed the sick. ³Then Jesus climbed a hill and sat down with his disciples around him. ⁴(It was nearly time for the Jewish Passover celebration.) ⁵Jesus soon saw a huge crowd of people coming to look for him. Turning to Philip, he asked, "Where can we buy bread to feed all these people?" ⁶He was testing Philip, for he already knew what he was going to do.

⁷Philip replied, "Even if we worked for months, we wouldn't have enough money* to feed them!"

⁸Then Andrew, Simon Peter's brother, spoke up. ⁹"There's a young boy here with five barley loaves and two fish. But what good is that with this huge crowd?"

¹⁰"Tell everyone to sit down," Jesus said. So they all sat down on the grassy slopes. (The men alone numbered about 5,000.) ¹¹Then Jesus took the loaves, gave thanks to God, and distributed them to the people. Afterward he did the same with the fish. And they all ate as much as they wanted. ¹²After everyone was full, Jesus told his disciples, "Now gather the leftovers, so that nothing is wasted." ¹³So they picked up the pieces and filled twelve baskets with scraps left by the people who had eaten from the five barley loaves.

¹⁴When the people saw him* do this miraculous sign, they exclaimed, "Surely, he is the Prophet we have been expecting!"* ¹⁵When Jesus saw that they were ready to force him to be their king, he slipped away into the hills by himself.

Jesus Walks on Water

¹⁶That evening Jesus' disciples went down to the shore to wait for him. ¹⁷But as darkness fell and Jesus still hadn't come back, they got into the boat and headed across the lake toward Capernaum. ¹⁸Soon a gale swept down upon them, and the sea grew very rough. ¹⁹They had rowed three or four miles* when suddenly they saw Jesus walking on the water toward the boat. They were terrified, ²⁰but he called out to them, "Don't be afraid. I am here!*" ²¹Then they were eager to let him in the boat, and immediately they arrived at their destination!

Jesus, the Bread of Life

²²The next day the crowd that had stayed on the far shore saw that the disciples had taken the only boat, and they realized Jesus had not gone with them. ²³Several boats from Tiberias landed near the place where the Lord had blessed the bread and the people had eaten. ²⁴So when the crowd saw that neither

6:7 Greek *Two hundred denarii would not be enough.* A denarius was equivalent to a laborer's full day's wage.   6:14a Some manuscripts read *Jesus.*   6:14b See Deut 18:15, 18; Mal 4:5-6.   6:19 Greek *25 or 30 stadia* [4.6 or 5.5 kilometers].   6:20 Or *The 'I Am' is here;* Greek reads *I am.* See Exod 3:14.

FRIENDSHIP TYPE: *Jesus*   FRIENDSHIP LAYER: *Getting Acquainted*

Getting to Know the Real Jesus

It's hard to live in our society without hearing something about Jesus. Everyone has an opinion. But really, how accurate are those opinions? The woman at the well in **John 4:1-30** just assumed that Jesus wouldn't like her simply because he was a Jew and she was a sinful Samaritan woman.

But when she got to know Jesus, she realized that he wasn't there to judge her; he was there to love her, no matter who she was or what she'd done.

It's easy for misconceptions about Jesus—about his life and death, his ministry, his followers—to creep in. We need to get past what we *think* we know about Jesus and get to know the *real* Jesus.

Experience

THE ONE THING 1 YOU CAN DO THIS WEEK

Get to know the real Jesus this week. Set aside a couple of hours for the read of a lifetime. Read the Gospel of **John** straight through. It won't take more than a couple of hours. As you read, ask yourself, "What would it have been like to know this man when he walked the earth?" Then spend some time talking to Jesus about what you discovered when you were reading. Jot your discoveries on the journal pages throughout John.

FRIENDSHIP EXPERIENCE *continues on page 190...*

FRIENDSHIP EXPERIENCE *continued from page 189...*

Reflect

★ What new insights did you get from reading about Jesus' life?

★ How did spending time with Jesus and learning about him clear up misconceptions you had?

★ What can you do to get to know Jesus even better?

JOURNAL

Jesus nor his disciples were there, they got into the boats and went across to Capernaum to look for him. ²⁵They found him on the other side of the lake and asked, "Rabbi, when did you get here?"

²⁶Jesus replied, "I tell you the truth, you want to be with me because I fed you, not because you understood the miraculous signs. ²⁷But don't be so concerned about perishable things like food. Spend your energy seeking the eternal life that the Son of Man* can give you. For God the Father has given me the seal of his approval."

²⁸They replied, "We want to perform God's works, too. What should we do?"

²⁹Jesus told them, "This is the only work God wants from you: Believe in the one he has sent."

³⁰They answered, "Show us a miraculous sign if you want us to believe in you. What can you do? ³¹After all, our ancestors ate manna while they journeyed through the wilderness! The Scriptures say, 'Moses gave them bread from heaven to eat.'*"

³²Jesus said, "I tell you the truth, Moses didn't give you bread from heaven. My Father did. And now he offers you the true bread from heaven. ³³The true bread of God is the one who comes down from heaven and gives life to the world."

³⁴"Sir," they said, "give us that bread every day."

³⁵Jesus replied, "I am the bread of life. Whoever comes to me will never be hungry again. Whoever believes in me will never be thirsty. ³⁶But you haven't believed in me even though you have seen me. ³⁷However, those the Father has given me will come to me, and I will never reject them. ³⁸For I have come down from heaven to do the will of God who sent me, not to do my own will. ³⁹And this is the will of God, that I should not lose even one of all those he has given me, but that I should raise them up at the last day. ⁴⁰For it is my Father's will that all who see his Son and believe in him should have eternal life. I will raise them up at the last day."

⁴¹Then the people* began to murmur in disagreement because he had said, "I am the bread that came down from heaven." ⁴²They said, "Isn't this Jesus, the son of Joseph? We know his father and mother. How can he say, 'I came down from heaven'?"

⁴³But Jesus replied, "Stop complaining about what I said. ⁴⁴For no one can come to me unless the Father who sent me

6:27 "Son of Man" is a title Jesus used for himself.   6:31 Exod 16:4; Ps 78:24.   6:41 Greek *Jewish people*; also in 6:52.

draws them to me, and at the last day I will raise them up. [45]As it is written in the Scriptures,* 'They will all be taught by God.' Everyone who listens to the Father and learns from him comes to me. [46](Not that anyone has ever seen the Father; only I, who was sent from God, have seen him.)

[47]"I tell you the truth, anyone who believes has eternal life. [48]Yes, I am the bread of life! [49]Your ancestors ate manna in the wilderness, but they all died. [50]Anyone who eats the bread from heaven, however, will never die. [51]I am the living bread that came down from heaven. Anyone who eats this bread will live forever; and this bread, which I will offer so the world may live, is my flesh."

[52]Then the people began arguing with each other about what he meant. "How can this man give us his flesh to eat?" they asked.

[53]So Jesus said again, "I tell you the truth, unless you eat the flesh of the Son of Man and drink his blood, you cannot have eternal life within you. [54]But anyone who eats my flesh and drinks my blood has eternal life, and I will raise that person at the last day. [55]For my flesh is true food, and my blood is true drink. [56]Anyone who eats my flesh and drinks my blood remains in me, and I in him. [57]I live because of the living Father who sent me; in the same way, anyone who feeds on me will live because of me. [58]I am the true bread that came down from heaven. Anyone who eats this bread will not die as your ancestors did (even though they ate the manna) but will live forever."

[59]He said these things while he was teaching in the synagogue in Capernaum.

Many Disciples Desert Jesus

[60]Many of his disciples said, "This is very hard to understand. How can anyone accept it?"

[61]Jesus was aware that his disciples were complaining, so he said to them, "Does this offend you? [62]Then what will you think if you see the Son of Man ascend to heaven again? [63]The Spirit alone gives eternal life. Human effort accomplishes nothing. And the very words I have spoken to you are spirit and life. [64]But some of you do not believe me." (For Jesus knew from the beginning which ones didn't believe, and he knew who would betray him.) [65]Then he said, "That is why I said that people can't come to me unless the Father gives them to me."

[66]At this point many of his disciples turned away and deserted him. [67]Then Jesus turned to the Twelve and asked, "Are you also going to leave?"

6:45 Greek *in the prophets.* Isa 54:13.

JOURNAL

68 Simon Peter replied, "Lord, to whom would we go? You have the words that give eternal life. 69 We believe, and we know you are the Holy One of God.*"

70 Then Jesus said, "I chose the twelve of you, but one is a devil." 71 He was speaking of Judas, son of Simon Iscariot, one of the Twelve, who would later betray him.

CHAPTER 7

Jesus and His Brothers

After this, Jesus traveled around Galilee. He wanted to stay out of Judea, where the Jewish leaders were plotting his death. 2 But soon it was time for the Jewish Festival of Shelters, 3 and Jesus' brothers said to him, "Leave here and go to Judea, where your followers can see your miracles! 4 You can't become famous if you hide like this! If you can do such wonderful things, show yourself to the world!" 5 For even his brothers didn't believe in him.

6 Jesus replied, "Now is not the right time for me to go, but you can go anytime. 7 The world can't hate you, but it does hate me because I accuse it of doing evil. 8 You go on. I'm not going* to this festival, because my time has not yet come." 9 After saying these things, Jesus remained in Galilee.

Jesus Teaches Openly at the Temple

10 But after his brothers left for the festival, Jesus also went, though secretly, staying out of public view. 11 The Jewish leaders tried to find him at the festival and kept asking if anyone had seen him. 12 There was a lot of grumbling about him among the crowds. Some argued, "He's a good man," but others said, "He's nothing but a fraud who deceives the people." 13 But no one had the courage to speak favorably about him in public, for they were afraid of getting in trouble with the Jewish leaders.

14 Then, midway through the festival, Jesus went up to the Temple and began to teach. 15 The people* were surprised when they heard him. "How does he know so much when he hasn't been trained?" they asked.

16 So Jesus told them, "My message is not my own; it comes from God who sent me. 17 Anyone who wants to do the will of God will know whether my teaching is from God or is merely my own. 18 Those who speak for themselves want glory only for themselves, but a person who seeks to honor the one who sent

6:69 Other manuscripts read *you are the Christ, the Holy One of God;* still others read *you are the Christ, the Son of God;* and still others read *you are the Christ, the Son of the living God.* 7:8 Some manuscripts read *not yet going.* 7:15 Greek *Jewish people.*

him speaks truth, not lies. ¹⁹Moses gave you the law, but none of you obeys it! In fact, you are trying to kill me."

²⁰The crowd replied, "You're demon possessed! Who's trying to kill you?"

²¹Jesus replied, "I did one miracle on the Sabbath, and you were amazed. ²²But you work on the Sabbath, too, when you obey Moses' law of circumcision. (Actually, this tradition of circumcision began with the patriarchs, long before the law of Moses.) ²³For if the correct time for circumcising your son falls on the Sabbath, you go ahead and do it so as not to break the law of Moses. So why should you be angry with me for healing a man on the Sabbath? ²⁴Look beneath the surface so you can judge correctly."

Is Jesus the Messiah?

²⁵Some of the people who lived in Jerusalem started to ask each other, "Isn't this the man they are trying to kill? ²⁶But here he is, speaking in public, and they say nothing to him. Could our leaders possibly believe that he is the Messiah? ²⁷But how could he be? For we know where this man comes from. When the Messiah comes, he will simply appear; no one will know where he comes from."

²⁸While Jesus was teaching in the Temple, he called out, "Yes, you know me, and you know where I come from. But I'm not here on my own. The one who sent me is true, and you don't know him. ²⁹But I know him because I come from him, and he sent me to you." ³⁰Then the leaders tried to arrest him; but no one laid a hand on him, because his time* had not yet come.

³¹Many among the crowds at the Temple believed in him. "After all," they said, "would you expect the Messiah to do more miraculous signs than this man has done?"

³²When the Pharisees heard that the crowds were whispering such things, they and the leading priests sent Temple guards to arrest Jesus. ³³But Jesus told them, "I will be with you only a little longer. Then I will return to the one who sent me. ³⁴You will search for me but not find me. And you cannot go where I am going."

³⁵The Jewish leaders were puzzled by this statement. "Where is he planning to go?" they asked. "Is he thinking of leaving the country and going to the Jews in other lands?* Maybe he will even teach the Greeks! ³⁶What does he mean when he says, 'You will search for me but not find me,' and 'You cannot go where I am going'?"

7:30 Greek *his hour.*   7:35 Or *the Jews who live among the Greeks?*

FRIENDSHIP EXPERIENCE

FRIENDSHIP TYPE: *Jesus*   FRIENDSHIP LAYER: *Acceptance*

Join the Club

Have you ever been part of a group, club, or social organization? They can be a lot of fun, right? The camaraderie. The common interests. The good times together.

But have you ever been excluded from a group? Not so fun. It hurts…a lot. You feel left out. You feel unwanted. You feel rejected.

There is one who will not reject you, one who wants to accept you. Jesus has already accepted you as a friend; he is only waiting for you to accept him (**John 1:12**).

And being in Jesus' circle of friends? Well, it's a great place to be!

THE ONE THING 1 **YOU CAN DO THIS WEEK**

Experience

What do you love to do? What's a hobby you've dreamed of mastering? Investigate a group or club that's connected with that interest or hobby. Do you like motorcycles? Then find out what it takes to be part of a riding group. Into music? Check out a music club. Want to make a splash? Research a swim club. You get the idea. If you like what you see, join the group. It's a great way to make new friends!

FRIENDSHIP EXPERIENCE *continues on page 194…*

Friendship First NEW TESTAMENT

FRIENDSHIP EXPERIENCE *continued from page 193...*

Every group offers a benefit to you and requires something of you. A lot of groups require money. Many simply require your participation. Some require you to do work outside group meetings. You put up with the requirements because you believe it's worth the benefits.

Have you ever considered the benefits of being in God's "group"?

★ Eternal life in heaven
★ Peace
★ Wisdom
★ Purpose
★ Freedom from sin and guilt
★ Unconditional love

Is belonging worth it to you?

Reflect

★ What did you like about the group you researched? What didn't you like?
★ What has it cost you to be Jesus' friend? What have you gained?

Jesus Promises Living Water

37 On the last day, the climax of the festival, Jesus stood and shouted to the crowds, "Anyone who is thirsty may come to me! 38 Anyone who believes in me may come and drink! For the Scriptures declare, 'Rivers of living water will flow from his heart.'"* 39 (When he said "living water," he was speaking of the Spirit, who would be given to everyone believing in him. But the Spirit had not yet been given,* because Jesus had not yet entered into his glory.)

Division and Unbelief

40 When the crowds heard him say this, some of them declared, "Surely this man is the Prophet we've been expecting."* 41 Others said, "He is the Messiah." Still others said, "But he can't be! Will the Messiah come from Galilee? 42 For the Scriptures clearly state that the Messiah will be born of the royal line of David, in Bethlehem, the village where King David was born."* 43 So the crowd was divided about him. 44 Some even wanted him arrested, but no one laid a hand on him.

45 When the Temple guards returned without having arrested Jesus, the leading priests and Pharisees demanded, "Why didn't you bring him in?"

46 "We have never heard anyone speak like this!" the guards responded.

47 "Have you been led astray, too?" the Pharisees mocked. 48 "Is there a single one of us rulers or Pharisees who believes in him? 49 This foolish crowd follows him, but they are ignorant of the law. God's curse is on them!"

50 Then Nicodemus, the leader who had met with Jesus earlier, spoke up. 51 "Is it legal to convict a man before he is given a hearing?" he asked.

52 They replied, "Are you from Galilee, too? Search the Scriptures and see for yourself—no prophet ever comes* from Galilee!"

[*The most ancient Greek manuscripts do not include John 7:53–8:11.*]

53 Then the meeting broke up, and everybody went home.

7:37-38 Or *"Let anyone who is thirsty come to me and drink.* 38 *For the Scriptures declare, 'Rivers of living water will flow from the heart of anyone who believes in me.'"* 7:39 Some manuscripts read *But as yet there was no Spirit.* Still others read *But as yet there was no Holy Spirit.* 7:40 See Deut 18:15, 18; Mal 4:5-6. 7:42 See Mic 5:2. 7:52 Some manuscripts read *the prophet does not come.*

CHAPTER 8

A Woman Caught in Adultery

Jesus returned to the Mount of Olives, [2]but early the next morning he was back again at the Temple. A crowd soon gathered, and he sat down and taught them. [3]As he was speaking, the teachers of religious law and the Pharisees brought a woman who had been caught in the act of adultery. They put her in front of the crowd.

[4]"Teacher," they said to Jesus, "this woman was caught in the act of adultery. [5]The law of Moses says to stone her. What do you say?"

[6]They were trying to trap him into saying something they could use against him, but Jesus stooped down and wrote in the dust with his finger. [7]They kept demanding an answer, so he stood up again and said, "All right, but let the one who has never sinned throw the first stone!" [8]Then he stooped down again and wrote in the dust.

[9]When the accusers heard this, they slipped away one by one, beginning with the oldest, until only Jesus was left in the middle of the crowd with the woman. [10]Then Jesus stood up again and said to the woman, "Where are your accusers? Didn't even one of them condemn you?"

[11]"No, Lord," she said.

And Jesus said, "Neither do I. Go and sin no more."

Jesus, the Light of the World

[12]Jesus spoke to the people once more and said, "I am the light of the world. If you follow me, you won't have to walk in darkness, because you will have the light that leads to life."

[13]The Pharisees replied, "You are making those claims about yourself! Such testimony is not valid."

[14]Jesus told them, "These claims are valid even though I make them about myself. For I know where I came from and where I am going, but you don't know this about me. [15]You judge me by human standards, but I do not judge anyone. [16]And if I did, my judgment would be correct in every respect because I am not alone. The Father* who sent me is with me. [17]Your own law says that if two people agree about something, their witness is accepted as fact.* [18]I am one witness, and my Father who sent me is the other."

[19]"Where is your father?" they asked.

8:16 Some manuscripts read *The One*.   **8:17** See Deut 19:15.

A full 80% of respondents say they developed most of their church friendships during fellowship or fun times.

—from "Friendship and Faith," a Gallup Research Study Commissioned by Group Publishing, Inc.

JOURNAL

Jesus answered, "Since you don't know who I am, you don't know who my Father is. If you knew me, you would also know my Father." [20] Jesus made these statements while he was teaching in the section of the Temple known as the Treasury. But he was not arrested, because his time* had not yet come.

The Unbelieving People Warned

[21] Later Jesus said to them again, "I am going away. You will search for me but will die in your sin. You cannot come where I am going."

[22] The people* asked, "Is he planning to commit suicide? What does he mean, 'You cannot come where I am going'?"

[23] Jesus continued, "You are from below; I am from above. You belong to this world; I do not. [24] That is why I said that you will die in your sins; for unless you believe that I AM who I claim to be,* you will die in your sins."

[25] "Who are you?" they demanded.

Jesus replied, "The one I have always claimed to be.* [26] I have much to say about you and much to condemn, but I won't. For I say only what I have heard from the one who sent me, and he is completely truthful." [27] But they still didn't understand that he was talking about his Father.

[28] So Jesus said, "When you have lifted up the Son of Man on the cross, then you will understand that I AM he.* I do nothing on my own but say only what the Father taught me. [29] And the one who sent me is with me—he has not deserted me. For I always do what pleases him." [30] Then many who heard him say these things believed in him.

Jesus and Abraham

[31] Jesus said to the people who believed in him, "You are truly my disciples if you remain faithful to my teachings. [32] And you will know the truth, and the truth will set you free."

[33] "But we are descendants of Abraham," they said. "We have never been slaves to anyone. What do you mean, 'You will be set free'?"

[34] Jesus replied, "I tell you the truth, everyone who sins is a slave of sin. [35] A slave is not a permanent member of the family, but a son is part of the family forever. [36] So if the Son sets you free, you are truly free. [37] Yes, I realize that you are descendants of Abraham. And yet some of you are trying to kill me because

8:20 Greek *his hour.*   8:22 Greek *Jewish people;* also in 8:31, 48, 52, 57.   8:24 Greek *unless you believe that I am.* See Exod 3:14.   8:25 Or *Why do I speak to you at all?*   8:28 Greek *When you have lifted up the Son of Man, then you will know that I am.* "Son of Man" is a title Jesus used for himself.

there's no room in your hearts for my message. 38I am telling you what I saw when I was with my Father. But you are following the advice of your father."

39"Our father is Abraham!" they declared.

"No," Jesus replied, "for if you were really the children of Abraham, you would follow his example.* 40Instead, you are trying to kill me because I told you the truth, which I heard from God. Abraham never did such a thing. 41No, you are imitating your real father."

They replied, "We aren't illegitimate children! God himself is our true Father."

42Jesus told them, "If God were your Father, you would love me, because I have come to you from God. I am not here on my own, but he sent me. 43Why can't you understand what I am saying? It's because you can't even hear me! 44For you are the children of your father the devil, and you love to do the evil things he does. He was a murderer from the beginning. He has always hated the truth, because there is no truth in him. When he lies, it is consistent with his character; for he is a liar and the father of lies. 45So when I tell the truth, you just naturally don't believe me! 46Which of you can truthfully accuse me of sin? And since I am telling you the truth, why don't you believe me? 47Anyone who belongs to God listens gladly to the words of God. But you don't listen because you don't belong to God."

48The people retorted, "You Samaritan devil! Didn't we say all along that you were possessed by a demon?"

49"No," Jesus said, "I have no demon in me. For I honor my Father—and you dishonor me. 50And though I have no wish to glorify myself, God is going to glorify me. He is the true judge. 51I tell you the truth, anyone who obeys my teaching will never die!"

52The people said, "Now we know you are possessed by a demon. Even Abraham and the prophets died, but you say, 'Anyone who obeys my teaching will never die!' 53Are you greater than our father Abraham? He died, and so did the prophets. Who do you think you are?"

54Jesus answered, "If I want glory for myself, it doesn't count. But it is my Father who will glorify me. You say, 'He is our God,*' 55but you don't even know him. I know him. If I said otherwise, I would be as great a liar as you! But I do know him

8:39 Some manuscripts read *if you are really the children of Abraham, follow his example.* 8:54 Some manuscripts read *your God.*

FRIENDSHIP EXPERIENCE

FRIENDSHIP TYPE: *Friends*   FRIENDSHIP LAYER: *Commitment*

Loving As Jesus Loved

"Love each other in the same way I have loved you" (**John 15:12**).

What does it look like to love the way Jesus loved?

★ Serve even when you're tired (**Mark 6:30-34**).

★ Accept someone, even when others don't (**Mark 2:13-17**).

★ Feed the hungry (**Matthew 14:15-21**).

★ Love the unlovable (**Luke 19:1-10**).

★ Forgive even when you're deeply wounded (**Luke 23:34**).

★ Defend the defenseless (**John 8:1-11**).

★ Pray for your friends—and the world (**John 17**).

★ Lay down your life (**Romans 5:6-11**).

THE ONE THING 1 YOU CAN DO THIS WEEK

Experience

Jesus knew what it took to be a committed friend, and he lived it out. Following his example is the best way to develop a committed friendship. This week love as Jesus loved: serve someone, even when you're tired; accept a friend others don't; feed a hungry friend; love that unlovable person; forgive a friend who has hurt you; defend a defenseless friend; or pray for a hurting friend. In all these things, you are laying down your life for a friend.

FRIENDSHIP EXPERIENCE *continues on page 198...*

FRIENDSHIP EXPERIENCE *continued from page 197...*

Make a commitment, and write it here:

_____

_____

_____

_____

_____

Have you ever heard the phrase "That's to die for"? Well, Jesus thought you were to die for. **Romans 5:11** says Jesus *died* for you so you could be a friend of God. How can you be a committed friend of God? In the same ways you are a committed friend to others! Perhaps you could serve God by volunteering at a youth center or working in a food pantry. You could "defend" God by standing up for Christians or by telling others about your friendship with God. You could pray for the people God loves.

Make a commitment, and write it in the space below.

_____

_____

_____

_____

Reflect

★ How did your friend respond to your act of commitment?

★ How has your friendship with God changed as a result of your commitment to him?

and obey him. 56 Your father Abraham rejoiced as he looked forward to my coming. He saw it and was glad."

57 The people said, "You aren't even fifty years old. How can you say you have seen Abraham?*"

58 Jesus answered, "I tell you the truth, before Abraham was even born, I AM!*" 59 At that point they picked up stones to throw at him. But Jesus was hidden from them and left the Temple.

CHAPTER **9**

Jesus Heals a Man Born Blind

As Jesus was walking along, he saw a man who had been blind from birth. 2 "Rabbi," his disciples asked him, "why was this man born blind? Was it because of his own sins or his parents' sins?"

3 "It was not because of his sins or his parents' sins," Jesus answered. "This happened so the power of God could be seen in him. 4 We must quickly carry out the tasks assigned us by the one who sent us.* The night is coming, and then no one can work. 5 But while I am here in the world, I am the light of the world."

6 Then he spit on the ground, made mud with the saliva, and spread the mud over the blind man's eyes. 7 He told him, "Go wash yourself in the pool of Siloam" (Siloam means "sent"). So the man went and washed and came back seeing!

8 His neighbors and others who knew him as a blind beggar asked each other, "Isn't this the man who used to sit and beg?" 9 Some said he was, and others said, "No, he just looks like him!"

But the beggar kept saying, "Yes, I am the same one!"

10 They asked, "Who healed you? What happened?"

11 He told them, "The man they call Jesus made mud and spread it over my eyes and told me, 'Go to the pool of Siloam and wash yourself.' So I went and washed, and now I can see!"

12 "Where is he now?" they asked.

"I don't know," he replied.

13 Then they took the man who had been blind to the Pharisees, 14 because it was on the Sabbath that Jesus had made the mud and healed him. 15 The Pharisees asked the man all about it. So he told them, "He put the mud over my eyes, and when I washed it away, I could see!"

16 Some of the Pharisees said, "This man Jesus is not from God, for he is working on the Sabbath." Others said, "But how

8:57 Some manuscripts read *How can you say Abraham has seen you?* **8:58** Or *before Abraham was even born, I have always been alive;* Greek reads *before Abraham was, I am.* See Exod 3:14. **9:4** Other manuscripts read *I must quickly carry out the tasks assigned me by the one who sent me;* still others read *We must quickly carry out the tasks assigned us by the one who sent me.*

could an ordinary sinner do such miraculous signs?" So there was a deep division of opinion among them.

17 Then the Pharisees again questioned the man who had been blind and demanded, "What's your opinion about this man who healed you?"

The man replied, "I think he must be a prophet."

18 The Jewish leaders still refused to believe the man had been blind and could now see, so they called in his parents. 19 They asked them, "Is this your son? Was he born blind? If so, how can he now see?"

20 His parents replied, "We know this is our son and that he was born blind, 21 but we don't know how he can see or who healed him. Ask him. He is old enough to speak for himself." 22 His parents said this because they were afraid of the Jewish leaders, who had announced that anyone saying Jesus was the Messiah would be expelled from the synagogue. 23 That's why they said, "He is old enough. Ask him."

24 So for the second time they called in the man who had been blind and told him, "God should get the glory for this,* because we know this man Jesus is a sinner."

25 "I don't know whether he is a sinner," the man replied. "But I know this: I was blind, and now I can see!"

26 "But what did he do?" they asked. "How did he heal you?"

27 "Look!" the man exclaimed. "I told you once. Didn't you listen? Why do you want to hear it again? Do you want to become his disciples, too?"

28 Then they cursed him and said, "You are his disciple, but we are disciples of Moses! 29 We know God spoke to Moses, but we don't even know where this man comes from."

30 "Why, that's very strange!" the man replied. "He healed my eyes, and yet you don't know where he comes from? 31 We know that God doesn't listen to sinners, but he is ready to hear those who worship him and do his will. 32 Ever since the world began, no one has been able to open the eyes of someone born blind. 33 If this man were not from God, he couldn't have done it."

34 "You were born a total sinner!" they answered. "Are you trying to teach us?" And they threw him out of the synagogue.

Spiritual Blindness

35 When Jesus heard what had happened, he found the man and asked, "Do you believe in the Son of Man?*"

9:24 Or *Give glory to God, not to Jesus;* Greek reads *Give glory to God.*   9:35 Some manuscripts read *the Son of God?* "Son of Man" is a title Jesus used for himself.

³⁶The man answered, "Who is he, sir? I want to believe in him."

³⁷"You have seen him," Jesus said, "and he is speaking to you!"

³⁸"Yes, Lord, I believe!" the man said. And he worshiped Jesus.

³⁹Then Jesus told him,* "I entered this world to render judgment—to give sight to the blind and to show those who think they see* that they are blind."

⁴⁰Some Pharisees who were standing nearby heard him and asked, "Are you saying we're blind?"

⁴¹"If you were blind, you wouldn't be guilty," Jesus replied. "But you remain guilty because you claim you can see.

CHAPTER **10**

The Good Shepherd and His Sheep

"I tell you the truth, anyone who sneaks over the wall of a sheepfold, rather than going through the gate, must surely be a thief and a robber! ²But the one who enters through the gate is the shepherd of the sheep. ³The gatekeeper opens the gate for him, and the sheep recognize his voice and come to him. He calls his own sheep by name and leads them out. ⁴After he has gathered his own flock, he walks ahead of them, and they follow him because they know his voice. ⁵They won't follow a stranger; they will run from him because they don't know his voice."

⁶Those who heard Jesus use this illustration didn't understand what he meant, ⁷so he explained it to them: "I tell you the truth, I am the gate for the sheep. ⁸All who came before me* were thieves and robbers. But the true sheep did not listen to them. ⁹Yes, I am the gate. Those who come in through me will be saved.* They will come and go freely and will find good pastures. ¹⁰The thief's purpose is to steal and kill and destroy. My purpose is to give them a rich and satisfying life.

¹¹"I am the good shepherd. The good shepherd sacrifices his life for the sheep. ¹²A hired hand will run when he sees a wolf coming. He will abandon the sheep because they don't belong to him and he isn't their shepherd. And so the wolf attacks them and scatters the flock. ¹³The hired hand runs away because he's working only for the money and doesn't really care about the sheep.

¹⁴"I am the good shepherd; I know my own sheep, and they know me, ¹⁵just as my Father knows me and I know the Father. So I sacrifice my life for the sheep. ¹⁶I have other sheep, too, that are not in this sheepfold. I must bring them also. They

9:38-39a Some manuscripts do not include *"Yes, Lord, I believe!" the man said. And he worshiped Jesus. Then Jesus told him.*   **9:39b** Greek *those who see.*   **10:8** Some manuscripts do not include *before me.*   **10:9** Or *will find safety.*

will listen to my voice, and there will be one flock with one shepherd.

17 "The Father loves me because I sacrifice my life so I may take it back again. 18 No one can take my life from me. I sacrifice it voluntarily. For I have the authority to lay it down when I want to and also to take it up again. For this is what my Father has commanded."

19 When he said these things, the people* were again divided in their opinions about him. 20 Some said, "He's demon possessed and out of his mind. Why listen to a man like that?" 21 Others said, "This doesn't sound like a man possessed by a demon! Can a demon open the eyes of the blind?"

Jesus Claims to Be the Son of God

22 It was now winter, and Jesus was in Jerusalem at the time of Hanukkah, the Festival of Dedication. 23 He was in the Temple, walking through the section known as Solomon's Colonnade. 24 The people surrounded him and asked, "How long are you going to keep us in suspense? If you are the Messiah, tell us plainly."

25 Jesus replied, "I have already told you, and you don't believe me. The proof is the work I do in my Father's name. 26 But you don't believe me because you are not my sheep. 27 My sheep listen to my voice; I know them, and they follow me. 28 I give them eternal life, and they will never perish. No one can snatch them away from me, 29 for my Father has given them to me, and he is more powerful than anyone else.* No one can snatch them from the Father's hand. 30 The Father and I are one."

31 Once again the people picked up stones to kill him. 32 Jesus said, "At my Father's direction I have done many good works. For which one are you going to stone me?"

33 They replied, "We're stoning you not for any good work, but for blasphemy! You, a mere man, claim to be God."

34 Jesus replied, "It is written in your own Scriptures* that God said to certain leaders of the people, 'I say, you are gods!'* 35 And you know that the Scriptures cannot be altered. So if those people who received God's message were called 'gods,' 36 why do you call it blasphemy when I say, 'I am the Son of God'? After all, the Father set me apart and sent me into the world. 37 Don't believe me unless I carry out my Father's work. 38 But if I do his work, believe in the evidence of the miraculous

"The Friendship is not a reward for our discrimination and good taste in finding one another out. It is the instrument by which God reveals to each the beauties of all the others."

~ C.S. Lewis

JOURNAL

10:19 Greek *Jewish people;* also in 10:24, 31.   10:29 Other manuscripts read *for what my Father has given me is more powerful than anything;* still others read *for regarding that which my Father has given me, he is greater than all.*   10:34a Greek *your own law.*   10:34b Ps 82:6.

works I have done, even if you don't believe me. Then you will know and understand that the Father is in me, and I am in the Father."

³⁹Once again they tried to arrest him, but he got away and left them. ⁴⁰He went beyond the Jordan River near the place where John was first baptizing and stayed there awhile. ⁴¹And many followed him. "John didn't perform miraculous signs," they remarked to one another, "but everything he said about this man has come true." ⁴²And many who were there believed in Jesus.

CHAPTER **11**

The Raising of Lazarus

A man named Lazarus was sick. He lived in Bethany with his sisters, Mary and Martha. ²This is the Mary who later poured the expensive perfume on the Lord's feet and wiped them with her hair.* Her brother, Lazarus, was sick. ³So the two sisters sent a message to Jesus telling him, "Lord, your dear friend is very sick."

⁴But when Jesus heard about it he said, "Lazarus's sickness will not end in death. No, it happened for the glory of God so that the Son of God will receive glory from this." ⁵So although Jesus loved Martha, Mary, and Lazarus, ⁶he stayed where he was for the next two days. ⁷Finally, he said to his disciples, "Let's go back to Judea."

⁸But his disciples objected. "Rabbi," they said, "only a few days ago the people* in Judea were trying to stone you. Are you going there again?"

⁹Jesus replied, "There are twelve hours of daylight every day. During the day people can walk safely. They can see because they have the light of this world. ¹⁰But at night there is danger of stumbling because they have no light." ¹¹Then he said, "Our friend Lazarus has fallen asleep, but now I will go and wake him up."

¹²The disciples said, "Lord, if he is sleeping, he will soon get better!" ¹³They thought Jesus meant Lazarus was simply sleeping, but Jesus meant Lazarus had died.

¹⁴So he told them plainly, "Lazarus is dead. ¹⁵And for your sakes, I'm glad I wasn't there, for now you will really believe. Come, let's go see him."

¹⁶Thomas, nicknamed the Twin,* said to his fellow disciples, "Let's go, too—and die with Jesus."

11:2 This incident is recorded in chapter 12.   11:8 Greek *Jewish people;* also in 11:19, 31, 33, 36, 45, 54.
11:16 Greek *Thomas, who was called Didymus.*

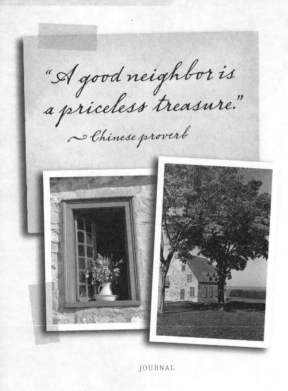

"A good neighbor is a priceless treasure."
~ Chinese proverb

JOURNAL

¹⁷When Jesus arrived at Bethany, he was told that Lazarus had already been in his grave for four days. ¹⁸Bethany was only a few miles* down the road from Jerusalem, ¹⁹and many of the people had come to console Martha and Mary in their loss. ²⁰When Martha got word that Jesus was coming, she went to meet him. But Mary stayed in the house. ²¹Martha said to Jesus, "Lord, if only you had been here, my brother would not have died. ²²But even now I know that God will give you whatever you ask."

²³Jesus told her, "Your brother will rise again."

²⁴"Yes," Martha said, "he will rise when everyone else rises, at the last day."

²⁵Jesus told her, "I am the resurrection and the life.* Anyone who believes in me will live, even after dying. ²⁶Everyone who lives in me and believes in me will never ever die. Do you believe this, Martha?"

²⁷"Yes, Lord," she told him. "I have always believed you are the Messiah, the Son of God, the one who has come into the world from God." ²⁸Then she returned to Mary. She called Mary aside from the mourners and told her, "The Teacher is here and wants to see you." ²⁹So Mary immediately went to him.

³⁰Jesus had stayed outside the village, at the place where Martha met him. ³¹When the people who were at the house consoling Mary saw her leave so hastily, they assumed she was going to Lazarus's grave to weep. So they followed her there. ³²When Mary arrived and saw Jesus, she fell at his feet and said, "Lord, if only you had been here, my brother would not have died."

³³When Jesus saw her weeping and saw the other people wailing with her, a deep anger welled up within him,* and he was deeply troubled. ³⁴"Where have you put him?" he asked them.

They told him, "Lord, come and see." ³⁵Then Jesus wept. ³⁶The people who were standing nearby said, "See how much he loved him!" ³⁷But some said, "This man healed a blind man. Couldn't he have kept Lazarus from dying?"

³⁸Jesus was still angry as he arrived at the tomb, a cave with a stone rolled across its entrance. ³⁹"Roll the stone aside," Jesus told them.

But Martha, the dead man's sister, protested, "Lord, he has been dead for four days. The smell will be terrible."

⁴⁰Jesus responded, "Didn't I tell you that you would see God's glory if you believe?" ⁴¹So they rolled the stone aside. Then Jesus looked up to heaven and said, "Father, thank you for hearing me.

11:18 Greek *was about 15 stadia* [about 2.8 kilometers].   11:25 Some manuscripts do not include *and the life.*   11:33 Or *he was angry in his spirit.*

FRIENDSHIP EXPERIENCE

FRIENDSHIP TYPE:	FRIENDSHIP LAYER:
Friends	Getting Acquainted

More Than Small Talk

"Hi, how are you?"
"Good. How are you?"
"Fine, thanks."

A common American conversation. And after it's finished? The two walk away without another word.

"Hi, how are you?" It's not so much a question of inquiry about another's welfare as it is a casual greeting. So often we don't really even care how the other person is doing; we're just being polite, making small talk. And it says something about the way we view those we bump into every day. We're not really looking to get to know people or invest in their lives. We're simply passing by.

In **John 1:35-50**, Jesus was more than just passing by; he wanted to make friends! He got to know the people who followed him; he asked them questions; he spent time with them; he told them things about himself. He invited them to join his mission.

Experience

This week, get to know someone better. Stop yourself from just saying, "How are you?" and instead ask a more specific question: "How is your family?" or "How are things going at work?" or "Where are you from?" Engage in the conversation, dig a little deeper, share something about yourself. And don't just stop with that conversation. Set up a lunch date, invite the person over to watch the game, or schedule a round of golf together.

FRIENDSHIP EXPERIENCE *continues on page 204…*

FRIENDSHIP EXPERIENCE *continued from page 203...*

Now get to know God better. Stop yourself from just hurriedly thanking God for a meal or sending up a quick prayer before bed. Instead, have a *meaningful* conversation with God. Tell God how you're doing. Ask God to show you how he's working in your life. Read **John 1**, and ask God to help you know him better through that passage. God wants you to be more than just a casual passerby; God wants you to be a true friend.

Reflect

★ What was it like to take time to get to know someone better? What did you learn about yourself? about the other person?

★ What else can you do to get to know people better? What about God?

42 You always hear me, but I said it out loud for the sake of all these people standing here, so that they will believe you sent me." 43 Then Jesus shouted, "Lazarus, come out!" 44 And the dead man came out, his hands and feet bound in graveclothes, his face wrapped in a headcloth. Jesus told them, "Unwrap him and let him go!"

The Plot to Kill Jesus

45 Many of the people who were with Mary believed in Jesus when they saw this happen. 46 But some went to the Pharisees and told them what Jesus had done. 47 Then the leading priests and Pharisees called the high council* together. "What are we going to do?" they asked each other. "This man certainly performs many miraculous signs. 48 If we allow him to go on like this, soon everyone will believe in him. Then the Roman army will come and destroy both our Temple* and our nation."

49 Caiaphas, who was high priest at that time,* said, "You don't know what you're talking about! 50 You don't realize that it's better for you that one man should die for the people than for the whole nation to be destroyed."

51 He did not say this on his own; as high priest at that time he was led to prophesy that Jesus would die for the entire nation. 52 And not only for that nation, but to bring together and unite all the children of God scattered around the world.

53 So from that time on, the Jewish leaders began to plot Jesus' death. 54 As a result, Jesus stopped his public ministry among the people and left Jerusalem. He went to a place near the wilderness, to the village of Ephraim, and stayed there with his disciples.

55 It was now almost time for the Jewish Passover celebration, and many people from all over the country arrived in Jerusalem several days early so they could go through the purification ceremony before Passover began. 56 They kept looking for Jesus, but as they stood around in the Temple, they said to each other, "What do you think? He won't come for Passover, will he?" 57 Meanwhile, the leading priests and Pharisees had publicly ordered that anyone seeing Jesus must report it immediately so they could arrest him.

CHAPTER **12**

Jesus Anointed at Bethany

Six days before the Passover celebration began, Jesus arrived in Bethany, the home of Lazarus—the man he had raised from the

11:47 Greek *the Sanhedrin.* **11:48** Or *our position;* Greek reads *our place.* **11:49** Greek *that year;* also in 11:51.

dead. ²A dinner was prepared in Jesus' honor. Martha served, and Lazarus was among those who ate* with him. ³Then Mary took a twelve-ounce jar* of expensive perfume made from essence of nard, and she anointed Jesus' feet with it, wiping his feet with her hair. The house was filled with the fragrance.

⁴But Judas Iscariot, the disciple who would soon betray him, said, ⁵"That perfume was worth a year's wages.* It should have been sold and the money given to the poor." ⁶Not that he cared for the poor—he was a thief, and since he was in charge of the disciples' money, he often stole some for himself.

⁷Jesus replied, "Leave her alone. She did this in preparation for my burial. ⁸You will always have the poor among you, but you will not always have me."

⁹When all the people* heard of Jesus' arrival, they flocked to see him and also to see Lazarus, the man Jesus had raised from the dead. ¹⁰Then the leading priests decided to kill Lazarus, too, ¹¹for it was because of him that many of the people had deserted them* and believed in Jesus.

Jesus' Triumphant Entry

¹²The next day, the news that Jesus was on the way to Jerusalem swept through the city. A large crowd of Passover visitors ¹³took palm branches and went down the road to meet him. They shouted,

"Praise God!*
Blessings on the one who comes in the name of the Lord!
Hail to the King of Israel!"*

¹⁴Jesus found a young donkey and rode on it, fulfilling the prophecy that said:

¹⁵ "Don't be afraid, people of Jerusalem.*
Look, your King is coming,
    riding on a donkey's colt."*

¹⁶His disciples didn't understand at the time that this was a fulfillment of prophecy. But after Jesus entered into his glory, they remembered what had happened and realized that these things had been written about him.

¹⁷Many in the crowd had seen Jesus call Lazarus from the tomb, raising him from the dead, and they were telling others*

JOURNAL

12:2 Or *who reclined.*   **12:3** Greek *took 1 litra* [327 grams].   **12:5** Greek *worth 300 denarii.* A denarius was equivalent to a laborer's full day's wage.   **12:9** Greek *Jewish people;* also in 12:11.   **12:11** Or *had deserted their traditions;* Greek reads *had deserted.*   **12:13a** Greek *Hosanna,* an exclamation of praise adapted from a Hebrew expression that means "save now."   **12:13b** Ps 118:25-26; Zeph 3:15.
12:15a Greek *daughter of Zion.*   **12:15b** Zech 9:9.   **12:17** Greek *were testifying.*

JOURNAL

about it. [18] That was the reason so many went out to meet him—because they had heard about this miraculous sign. [19] Then the Pharisees said to each other, "There's nothing we can do. Look, everyone* has gone after him!"

Jesus Predicts His Death

[20] Some Greeks who had come to Jerusalem for the Passover celebration [21] paid a visit to Philip, who was from Bethsaida in Galilee. They said, "Sir, we want to meet Jesus." [22] Philip told Andrew about it, and they went together to ask Jesus.

[23] Jesus replied, "Now the time has come for the Son of Man* to enter into his glory. [24] I tell you the truth, unless a kernel of wheat is planted in the soil and dies, it remains alone. But its death will produce many new kernels—a plentiful harvest of new lives. [25] Those who love their life in this world will lose it. Those who care nothing for their life in this world will keep it for eternity. [26] Anyone who wants to be my disciple must follow me, because my servants must be where I am. And the Father will honor anyone who serves me.

[27] "Now my soul is deeply troubled. Should I pray, 'Father, save me from this hour'? But this is the very reason I came! [28] Father, bring glory to your name."

Then a voice spoke from heaven, saying, "I have already brought glory to my name, and I will do so again." [29] When the crowd heard the voice, some thought it was thunder, while others declared an angel had spoken to him.

[30] Then Jesus told them, "The voice was for your benefit, not mine. [31] The time for judging this world has come, when Satan, the ruler of this world, will be cast out. [32] And when I am lifted up from the earth, I will draw everyone to myself." [33] He said this to indicate how he was going to die.

[34] The crowd responded, "We understood from Scripture* that the Messiah would live forever. How can you say the Son of Man will die? Just who is this Son of Man, anyway?"

[35] Jesus replied, "My light will shine for you just a little longer. Walk in the light while you can, so the darkness will not overtake you. Those who walk in the darkness cannot see where they are going. [36] Put your trust in the light while there is still time; then you will become children of the light."

After saying these things, Jesus went away and was hidden from them.

12:19 Greek *the world.*   **12:23** "Son of Man" is a title Jesus used for himself.   **12:34** Greek *from the law.*

The Unbelief of the People

37 But despite all the miraculous signs Jesus had done, most of the people still did not believe in him. 38 This is exactly what Isaiah the prophet had predicted:

"LORD, who has believed our message?
To whom has the LORD revealed his powerful arm?"*

39 But the people couldn't believe, for as Isaiah also said,

40 "The Lord has blinded their eyes
and hardened their hearts—
so that their eyes cannot see,
and their hearts cannot understand,
and they cannot turn to me
and have me heal them."*

41 Isaiah was referring to Jesus when he said this, because he saw the future and spoke of the Messiah's glory. 42 Many people did believe in him, however, including some of the Jewish leaders. But they wouldn't admit it for fear that the Pharisees would expel them from the synagogue. 43 For they loved human praise more than the praise of God.

44 Jesus shouted to the crowds, "If you trust me, you are trusting not only me, but also God who sent me. 45 For when you see me, you are seeing the one who sent me. 46 I have come as a light to shine in this dark world, so that all who put their trust in me will no longer remain in the dark. 47 I will not judge those who hear me but don't obey me, for I have come to save the world and not to judge it. 48 But all who reject me and my message will be judged on the day of judgment by the truth I have spoken. 49 I don't speak on my own authority. The Father who sent me has commanded me what to say and how to say it. 50 And I know his commands lead to eternal life; so I say whatever the Father tells me to say."

CHAPTER **13**

Jesus Washes His Disciples' Feet

Before the Passover celebration, Jesus knew that his hour had come to leave this world and return to his Father. He had loved his disciples during his ministry on earth, and now he loved them to the very end.*

12:38 Isa 53:1.   12:40 Isa 6:10.   13:1 Or *he showed them the full extent of his love.*

Anchor Passage

PASSAGE: **John 13:1-17**

FRIENDSHIP TYPE: *Friends*

FRIENDSHIP LAYER: *Companionship*

Celebrate!

You're in a restaurant with your closest friends. Laughter rings out from those sitting around you. Your friend is sharing a story from his day at work. Everyone is smiling, sharing food, laughing. These are good times, and you know it. You sit there filled up with the moment, and you don't want it to end.

Companionship. What do you think of? What comes to mind?

Read **John 13:1-17**, a powerful story of companionship. Jesus and his closest friends are eating together, enjoying one another's company, but at the heart of this celebration is something deeper and more significant.

Jesus knows he is about to die, and he knows one of his own disciples—one of the very men eating at the table—is going to betray him.

Doesn't sound like such a great memory in the making…and then Jesus takes a towel and a basin of water, and he washes their feet. In a stunning, remarkable demonstration of love and servanthood, Jesus shows the disciples how much he cares for them.

Anchor Passage continues on page 208…

Anchor Passage continued from page 207…

Here, at the Last Supper, is ultimate companionship: Jesus and his friends experiencing a time of celebration, love, and life-changing memories. Jesus told them to live out this same love and companionship with others. And we have the same challenge: to experience companionship through rich times of celebration and memory-making…with Jesus and with our friends.

Experience

THE ONE THING
1
YOU CAN DO THIS WEEK

Spend time experiencing companionship with a friend. Make great memories and simply celebrate your friendship. Be lighthearted. Be serious. Go to a movie together, and talk about what the movie meant to you. Take a road trip together, and share favorite stories. Or wash each other's feet as Jesus did, and pray together that God would strengthen your friendship. Whatever you do, make it a time of celebration!

Reflect

★ Imagine you were sitting at the table with the disciples. What's going through your head as Jesus washes your feet? Why?

★ How have times of companionship and celebration strengthened your friendships?

Anchor Passage continues on page 209…

²It was time for supper, and the devil had already prompted Judas,* son of Simon Iscariot, to betray Jesus. ³Jesus knew that the Father had given him authority over everything and that he had come from God and would return to God. ⁴So he got up from the table, took off his robe, wrapped a towel around his waist, ⁵and poured water into a basin. Then he began to wash the disciples' feet, drying them with the towel he had around him.

⁶When Jesus came to Simon Peter, Peter said to him, "Lord, are you going to wash my feet?"

⁷Jesus replied, "You don't understand now what I am doing, but someday you will."

⁸"No," Peter protested, "you will never ever wash my feet!"

Jesus replied, "Unless I wash you, you won't belong to me."

⁹Simon Peter exclaimed, "Then wash my hands and head as well, Lord, not just my feet!"

¹⁰Jesus replied, "A person who has bathed all over does not need to wash, except for the feet,* to be entirely clean. And you disciples are clean, but not all of you." ¹¹For Jesus knew who would betray him. That is what he meant when he said, "Not all of you are clean."

¹²After washing their feet, he put on his robe again and sat down and asked, "Do you understand what I was doing? ¹³You call me 'Teacher' and 'Lord,' and you are right, because that's what I am. ¹⁴And since I, your Lord and Teacher, have washed your feet, you ought to wash each other's feet. ¹⁵I have given you an example to follow. Do as I have done to you. ¹⁶I tell you the truth, slaves are not greater than their master. Nor is the messenger more important than the one who sends the message. ¹⁷Now that you know these things, God will bless you for doing them. ⚓

Jesus Predicts His Betrayal

¹⁸"I am not saying these things to all of you; I know the ones I have chosen. But this fulfills the Scripture that says, "The one

13:2 Or *the devil had already intended for Judas.* **13:10** Some manuscripts do not include *except for the feet.*

who eats my food has turned against me.'* [19] I tell you this beforehand, so that when it happens you will believe that I Aᴍ the Messiah.* [20] I tell you the truth, anyone who welcomes my messenger is welcoming me, and anyone who welcomes me is welcoming the Father who sent me."

[21] Now Jesus was deeply troubled,* and he exclaimed, "I tell you the truth, one of you will betray me!"

[22] The disciples looked at each other, wondering whom he could mean. [23] The disciple Jesus loved was sitting next to Jesus at the table.* [24] Simon Peter motioned to him to ask, "Who's he talking about?" [25] So that disciple leaned over to Jesus and asked, "Lord, who is it?"

[26] Jesus responded, "It is the one to whom I give the bread I dip in the bowl." And when he had dipped it, he gave it to Judas, son of Simon Iscariot. [27] When Judas had eaten the bread, Satan entered into him. Then Jesus told him, "Hurry and do what you're going to do." [28] None of the others at the table knew what Jesus meant. [29] Since Judas was their treasurer, some thought Jesus was telling him to go and pay for the food or to give some money to the poor. [30] So Judas left at once, going out into the night.

Jesus Predicts Peter's Denial

[31] As soon as Judas left the room, Jesus said, "The time has come for the Son of Man* to enter into his glory, and God will be glorified because of him. [32] And since God receives glory because of the Son,* he will soon give glory to the Son. [33] Dear children, I will be with you only a little longer. And as I told the Jewish leaders, you will search for me, but you can't come where I am going. [34] So now I am giving you a new commandment: Love each other. Just as I have loved you, you should love each other. [35] Your love for one another will prove to the world that you are my disciples."

[36] Simon Peter asked, "Lord, where are you going?"

And Jesus replied, "You can't go with me now, but you will follow me later."

[37] "But why can't I come now, Lord?" he asked. "I'm ready to die for you."

[38] Jesus answered, "Die for me? I tell you the truth, Peter—before the rooster crows tomorrow morning, you will deny three times that you even know me.

13:18 Ps 41:9.   13:19 Or that the 'I Aᴍ' has come; or that I am the Loʀᴅ; Greek reads that I am. See Exod 3:14.   13:21 Greek was troubled in his spirit.   13:23 Greek was reclining on Jesus' bosom. The "disciple Jesus loved" was probably John.   13:31 "Son of Man" is a title Jesus used for himself. 13:32 Some manuscripts omit And since God receives glory because of the Son.

Anchor Passage continued from page 208...

DIGGING DEEPER

FRIENDSHIP TYPE:	FRIENDSHIP LAYER:
Friends	*Companionship*

For being a companion of your friends, check out...

➼ The Friendship Experience .... on page 223
➼ The Friendship Story .... on page 433
➼ What to Say and What Not to Say .... on page 438

JOURNAL

CHAPTER **14**

Jesus, the Way to the Father

"Don't let your hearts be troubled. Trust in God, and trust also in me. [2]There is more than enough room in my Father's home.* If this were not so, would I have told you that I am going to prepare a place for you?* [3]When everything is ready, I will come and get you, so that you will always be with me where I am. [4]And you know the way to where I am going."

[5]"No, we don't know, Lord," Thomas said. "We have no idea where you are going, so how can we know the way?"

[6]Jesus told him, "I am the way, the truth, and the life. No one can come to the Father except through me. [7]If you had really known me, you would know who my Father is.* From now on, you do know him and have seen him!"

[8]Philip said, "Lord, show us the Father, and we will be satisfied."

[9]Jesus replied, "Have I been with you all this time, Philip, and yet you still don't know who I am? Anyone who has seen me has seen the Father! So why are you asking me to show him to you? [10]Don't you believe that I am in the Father and the Father is in me? The words I speak are not my own, but my Father who lives in me does his work through me. [11]Just believe that I am in the Father and the Father is in me. Or at least believe because of the work you have seen me do.

[12]"I tell you the truth, anyone who believes in me will do the same works I have done, and even greater works, because I am going to be with the Father. [13]You can ask for anything in my name, and I will do it, so that the Son can bring glory to the Father. [14]Yes, ask me for anything in my name, and I will do it!

Jesus Promises the Holy Spirit

[15]"If you love me, obey* my commandments. [16]And I will ask the Father, and he will give you another Advocate,* who will never leave you. [17]He is the Holy Spirit, who leads into all truth. The world cannot receive him, because it isn't looking for him and doesn't recognize him. But you know him, because he lives with you now and later will be in you.* [18]No, I will not abandon you as orphans—I will come to you. [19]Soon the world will no longer see me, but you will see me. Since I live, you also will live. [20]When I am raised to life again, you will know that I am in my Father, and you are in me, and I am

14:2a Or *There are many rooms in my Father's house.*   14:2b Or *If this were not so, I would have told you that I am going to prepare a place for you.* Some manuscripts read *If this were not so, I would have told you. I am going to prepare a place for you.*   14:7 Some manuscripts read *If you have really known me, you will know who my Father is.*   14:15 Other manuscripts read *you will obey;* still others read *you should obey.*   14:16 Or *Comforter,* or *Encourager,* or *Counselor.* Greek reads *Paraclete;* also in 14:26.   14:17 Some manuscripts read *and is in you.*

in you. ²¹Those who accept my commandments and obey them are the ones who love me. And because they love me, my Father will love them. And I will love them and reveal myself to each of them."

²²Judas (not Judas Iscariot, but the other disciple with that name) said to him, "Lord, why are you going to reveal yourself only to us and not to the world at large?"

²³Jesus replied, "All who love me will do what I say. My Father will love them, and we will come and make our home with each of them. ²⁴Anyone who doesn't love me will not obey me. And remember, my words are not my own. What I am telling you is from the Father who sent me. ²⁵I am telling you these things now while I am still with you. ²⁶But when the Father sends the Advocate as my representative—that is, the Holy Spirit—he will teach you everything and will remind you of everything I have told you.

²⁷"I am leaving you with a gift—peace of mind and heart. And the peace I give is a gift the world cannot give. So don't be troubled or afraid. ²⁸Remember what I told you: I am going away, but I will come back to you again. If you really loved me, you would be happy that I am going to the Father, who is greater than I am. ²⁹I have told you these things before they happen so that when they do happen, you will believe.

³⁰"I don't have much more time to talk to you, because the ruler of this world approaches. He has no power over me, ³¹but I will do what the Father requires of me, so that the world will know that I love the Father. Come, let's be going.

CHAPTER 15

Jesus, the True Vine

"I am the true grapevine, and my Father is the gardener. ²He cuts off every branch of mine that doesn't produce fruit, and he prunes the branches that do bear fruit so they will produce even more. ³You have already been pruned and purified by the message I have given you. ⁴Remain in me, and I will remain in you. For a branch cannot produce fruit if it is severed from the vine, and you cannot be fruitful unless you remain in me.

⁵"Yes, I am the vine; you are the branches. Those who remain in me, and I in them, will produce much fruit. For apart from me you can do nothing. ⁶Anyone who does not remain in me is thrown away like a useless branch and withers. Such branches are gathered into a pile to be burned. ⁷But if you remain in me and my words remain in you, you may ask for anything you

"How is fellowship with other Christians related to fellowship with God?

We are united with Him so intimately that our identity and even our life depend on Him. We have fellowship with each other because we are branches of the same vine, limbs of the same body, and children of the same Father."

~ Karen Lee-Thorp

Fig. 12.

want, and it will be granted! ⁸When you produce much fruit, you are my true disciples. This brings great glory to my Father.

⁹"I have loved you even as the Father has loved me. Remain in my love. ¹⁰When you obey my commandments, you remain in my love, just as I obey my Father's commandments and remain in his love. ¹¹I have told you these things so that you will be filled with my joy. Yes, your joy will overflow!

¹²This is my commandment: Love each other in the same way I have loved you. ¹³There is no greater love than to lay down one's life for one's friends. ¹⁴You are my friends if you do what I command. ¹⁵I no longer call you slaves, because a master doesn't confide in his slaves. Now you are my friends, since I have told you everything the Father told me. ¹⁶You didn't choose me. I chose you. I appointed you to go and produce lasting fruit, so that the Father will give you whatever you ask for, using my name. ¹⁷This is my command: Love each other.   ⚓

The World's Hatred

¹⁸"If the world hates you, remember that it hated me first. ¹⁹The world would love you as one of its own if you belonged to it, but you are no longer part of the world. I chose you to come out of the world, so it hates you. ²⁰Do you remember what I told you? 'A slave is not greater than the master.' Since they persecuted me, naturally they will persecute you. And if they had listened to me, they would listen to you. ²¹They will do all this to you because of me, for they have rejected the One who sent me. ²²They would not be guilty if I had not come and spoken to them. But now they have no excuse for their sin. ²³Anyone who hates me also hates my Father. ²⁴If I hadn't done such miraculous signs among them that no one else could do, they would not be guilty. But as it is, they have seen everything I did, yet they still hate me and my Father. ²⁵This fulfills what is written in their Scriptures*: 'They hated me without cause.'

²⁶"But I will send you the Advocate*—the Spirit of truth. He will come to you from the Father and will testify all about me.

15:25 Greek *in their law.* Pss 35:19; 69:4.   15:26 Or *Comforter,* or *Encourager,* or *Counselor.* Greek reads *Paraclete.*

²⁷And you must also testify about me because you have been with me from the beginning of my ministry.

CHAPTER **16**

"I have told you these things so that you won't abandon your faith. ²For you will be expelled from the synagogues, and the time is coming when those who kill you will think they are doing a holy service for God. ³This is because they have never known the Father or me. ⁴Yes, I'm telling you these things now, so that when they happen, you will remember my warning. I didn't tell you earlier because I was going to be with you for a while longer.

The Work of the Holy Spirit

⁵"But now I am going away to the One who sent me, and not one of you is asking where I am going. ⁶Instead, you grieve because of what I've told you. ⁷But in fact, it is best for you that I go away, because if I don't, the Advocate* won't come. If I do go away, then I will send him to you. ⁸And when he comes, he will convict the world of its sin, and of God's righteousness, and of the coming judgment. ⁹The world's sin is that it refuses to believe in me. ¹⁰Righteousness is available because I go to the Father, and you will see me no more. ¹¹Judgment will come because the ruler of this world has already been judged.

¹²"There is so much more I want to tell you, but you can't bear it now. ¹³When the Spirit of truth comes, he will guide you into all truth. He will not speak on his own but will tell you what he has heard. He will tell you about the future. ¹⁴He will bring me glory by telling you whatever he receives from me. ¹⁵All that belongs to the Father is mine; this is why I said, 'The Spirit will tell you whatever he receives from me.'

Sadness Will Be Turned to Joy

¹⁶"In a little while you won't see me anymore. But a little while after that, you will see me again."

¹⁷Some of the disciples asked each other, "What does he mean when he says, 'In a little while you won't see me, but then you will see me,' and 'I am going to the Father'? ¹⁸And what does he mean by 'a little while'? We don't understand."

¹⁹Jesus realized they wanted to ask him about it, so he said, "Are you asking yourselves what I meant? I said in a little while you won't see me, but a little while after that you will see me again. ²⁰I tell you the truth, you will weep and mourn over what

16:7 Or *Comforter,* or *Encourager,* or *Counselor.* Greek reads *Paraclete.*

Anchor Passage

PASSAGE: John 15:12-17

FRIENDSHIP TYPE: *Friends*   FRIENDSHIP LAYER: *Commitment*

Lay Down Your Life

Read **John 15:12-17**.

"There is no greater love," Jesus said, "than to lay down one's life for one's friends."

It's easy to read this passage and think, "Absolutely, I would die for my friends. I love them. I'd give up my life for them." Dying for a friend—it sounds so noble...and it is. But there are other ways to give your life for your friends—not-so-glorious ways, small ways, *everyday* ways.

Like when your friend needs money, and you happen to have some saved up. Sure, you've been saving that money for a motorcycle, but now your friend's in trouble. You could lay down your life and give up that money.

Or what about when another friend desperately needs you to baby-sit on Friday night? You have plans—you've had plans for weeks—but you could change them. You could lay down your life and give up your Friday night.

Laying down your life doesn't always seem noble or glorious...or fun. But it's what a committed friendship is all about.

Anchor Passage continues on page 214...

Anchor Passage continued from page 213...

Experience

THE ONE THING 1 YOU CAN DO THIS WEEK

Choose to lay down your life for a friend this week—in a big way or a small way.

Maybe you'll give up your Saturday to help a friend move. Maybe you'll let your friend choose the restaurant when you go out together. Maybe you'll buy your friend a present instead of getting something for yourself.

Whatever you do, notice your friend's need, and put it above your own. Sacrifice something. Give something up to help your friend.

Reflect

★ How have you laid down your life for a friend in the past? How did that act affect your friendship?

★ How has a friend laid down his or her life for you?

★ Why is laying down your life for one another important in a committed friendship?

DIGGING DEEPER

FRIENDSHIP TYPE: *Friends*   FRIENDSHIP LAYER: *Commitment*

For committing to your friends, check out...
➼ The Friendship Experience............. on page 197
➼ The Friendship Story...................... on page 293
➼ What to Say and What Not to Say .... on page 289

is going to happen to me, but the world will rejoice. You will grieve, but your grief will suddenly turn to wonderful joy. 21 It will be like a woman suffering the pains of labor. When her child is born, her anguish gives way to joy because she has brought a new baby into the world. 22 So you have sorrow now, but I will see you again; then you will rejoice, and no one can rob you of that joy. 23 At that time you won't need to ask me for anything. I tell you the truth, you will ask the Father directly, and he will grant your request because you use my name. 24 You haven't done this before. Ask, using my name, and you will receive, and you will have abundant joy.

25 "I have spoken of these matters in figures of speech, but soon I will stop speaking figuratively and will tell you plainly all about the Father. 26 Then you will ask in my name. I'm not saying I will ask the Father on your behalf, 27 for the Father himself loves you dearly because you love me and believe that I came from God.* 28 Yes, I came from the Father into the world, and now I will leave the world and return to the Father."

29 Then his disciples said, "At last you are speaking plainly and not figuratively. 30 Now we understand that you know everything, and there's no need to question you. From this we believe that you came from God."

31 Jesus asked, "Do you finally believe? 32 But the time is coming—indeed it's here now—when you will be scattered, each one going his own way, leaving me alone. Yet I am not alone because the Father is with me. 33 I have told you all this so that you may have peace in me. Here on earth you will have many trials and sorrows. But take heart, because I have overcome the world."

CHAPTER **17**

The Prayer of Jesus

After saying all these things, Jesus looked up to heaven and said, "Father, the hour has come. Glorify your Son so he can give glory back to you. 2 For you have given him authority over everyone. He gives eternal life to each one you have given him. 3 And this is the way to have eternal life—to know you, the only true God, and Jesus Christ, the one you sent to earth. 4 I brought glory to you here on earth by completing the work you gave me to do. 5 Now, Father, bring me into the glory we shared before the world began.

6 "I have revealed you* to the ones you gave me from this

16:27 Some manuscripts read *from the Father.*   17:6 Greek *have revealed your name*; also in 17:26.

world. They were always yours. You gave them to me, and they have kept your word. [7] Now they know that everything I have is a gift from you, [8] for I have passed on to them the message you gave me. They accepted it and know that I came from you, and they believe you sent me.

[9] "My prayer is not for the world, but for those you have given me, because they belong to you. [10] All who are mine belong to you, and you have given them to me, so they bring me glory. [11] Now I am departing from the world; they are staying in this world, but I am coming to you. Holy Father, you have given me your name;* now protect them by the power of your name so that they will be united just as we are. [12] During my time here, I protected them by the power of the name you gave me.* I guarded them so that not one was lost, except the one headed for destruction, as the Scriptures foretold.

[13] "Now I am coming to you. I told them many things while I was with them in this world so they would be filled with my joy. [14] I have given them your word. And the world hates them because they do not belong to the world, just as I do not belong to the world. [15] I'm not asking you to take them out of the world, but to keep them safe from the evil one. [16] They do not belong to this world any more than I do. [17] Make them holy by your truth; teach them your word, which is truth. [18] Just as you sent me into the world, I am sending them into the world. [19] And I give myself as a holy sacrifice for them so they can be made holy by your truth.

[20] "I am praying not only for these disciples but also for all who will ever believe in me through their message. [21] I pray that they will all be one, just as you and I are one—as you are in me, Father, and I am in you. And may they be in us so that the world will believe you sent me.

[22] "I have given them the glory you gave me, so they may be one as we are one. [23] I am in them and you are in me. May they experience such perfect unity that the world will know that you sent me and that you love them as much as you love me. [24] Father, I want these whom you have given me to be with me where I am. Then they can see all the glory you gave me because you loved me even before the world began!

[25] "O righteous Father, the world doesn't know you, but I do; and these disciples know you sent me. [26] I have revealed you to them, and I will continue to do so. Then your love for me will be in them, and I will be in them."

17:11 Some manuscripts read *you have given me these [disciples].* 17:12 Some manuscripts read *I protected those you gave me, by the power of your name.*

JOURNAL

CHAPTER 18

Jesus Is Betrayed and Arrested

After saying these things, Jesus crossed the Kidron Valley with his disciples and entered a grove of olive trees. ²Judas, the betrayer, knew this place, because Jesus had often gone there with his disciples. ³The leading priests and Pharisees had given Judas a contingent of Roman soldiers and Temple guards to accompany him. Now with blazing torches, lanterns, and weapons, they arrived at the olive grove.

⁴Jesus fully realized all that was going to happen to him, so he stepped forward to meet them. "Who are you looking for?" he asked.

⁵"Jesus the Nazarene,"* they replied.

"I Am he,"* Jesus said. (Judas, who betrayed him, was standing with them.) ⁶As Jesus said "I Am he," they all drew back and fell to the ground! ⁷Once more he asked them, "Who are you looking for?"

And again they replied, "Jesus the Nazarene."

⁸"I told you that I Am he," Jesus said. "And since I am the one you want, let these others go." ⁹He did this to fulfill his own statement: "I did not lose a single one of those you have given me."*

¹⁰Then Simon Peter drew a sword and slashed off the right ear of Malchus, the high priest's slave. ¹¹But Jesus said to Peter, "Put your sword back into its sheath. Shall I not drink from the cup of suffering the Father has given me?"

Jesus at the High Priest's House

¹²So the soldiers, their commanding officer, and the Temple guards arrested Jesus and tied him up. ¹³First they took him to Annas, the father-in-law of Caiaphas, the high priest at that time.* ¹⁴Caiaphas was the one who had told the other Jewish leaders, "It's better that one man should die for the people."

Peter's First Denial

¹⁵Simon Peter followed Jesus, as did another of the disciples. That other disciple was acquainted with the high priest, so he was allowed to enter the high priest's courtyard with Jesus. ¹⁶Peter had to stay outside the gate. Then the disciple who knew the high priest spoke to the woman watching at the gate, and she let Peter in. ¹⁷The woman asked Peter, "You're not one of that man's disciples, are you?"

"No," he said, "I am not."

18:5a Or *Jesus of Nazareth;* also in 18:7.   18:5b Or *"The 'I Am' is here";* or *"I am the Lord";* Greek reads *I am;* also in 18:6, 8. See Exod 3:14.   18:9 See John 6:39 and 17:12.   18:13 Greek *that year.*

[18]Because it was cold, the household servants and the guards had made a charcoal fire. They stood around it, warming themselves, and Peter stood with them, warming himself.

The High Priest Questions Jesus

[19]Inside, the high priest began asking Jesus about his followers and what he had been teaching them. [20]Jesus replied, "Everyone knows what I teach. I have preached regularly in the synagogues and the Temple, where the people* gather. I have not spoken in secret. [21]Why are you asking me this question? Ask those who heard me. They know what I said."

[22]Then one of the Temple guards standing nearby slapped Jesus across the face. "Is that the way to answer the high priest?" he demanded.

[23]Jesus replied, "If I said anything wrong, you must prove it. But if I'm speaking the truth, why are you beating me?"

[24]Then Annas bound Jesus and sent him to Caiaphas, the high priest.

Peter's Second and Third Denials

[25]Meanwhile, as Simon Peter was standing by the fire warming himself, they asked him again, "You're not one of his disciples, are you?"

He denied it, saying, "No, I am not."

[26]But one of the household slaves of the high priest, a relative of the man whose ear Peter had cut off, asked, "Didn't I see you out there in the olive grove with Jesus?" [27]Again Peter denied it. And immediately a rooster crowed.

Jesus' Trial before Pilate

[28]Jesus' trial before Caiaphas ended in the early hours of the morning. Then he was taken to the headquarters of the Roman governor.* His accusers didn't go inside because it would defile them, and they wouldn't be allowed to celebrate the Passover. [29]So Pilate, the governor, went out to them and asked, "What is your charge against this man?"

[30]"We wouldn't have handed him over to you if he weren't a criminal!" they retorted.

[31]"Then take him away and judge him by your own law," Pilate told them.

"Only the Romans are permitted to execute someone," the Jewish leaders replied. [32](This fulfilled Jesus' prediction about the way he would die.*)

18:20 Greek *Jewish people;* also in 18:38.   **18:28** Greek *to the Praetorium;* also in 18:33.   **18:32** See John 12:32-33.

"One should keep old roads and old friends."
~*German proverb*

JOURNAL

★

About 74% of church members who worship with a best friend are very likely to describe their spiritual lives as a friendship with God. This is 14 percentage points higher than those who do not have a best friend at church!

—from "Friendship and Faith," a Gallup Research Study Commissioned by Group Publishing, Inc.

★

JOURNAL

33Then Pilate went back into his headquarters and called for
Jesus to be brought to him. "Are you the king of the Jews?" he
asked him.
34Jesus replied, "Is this your own question, or did others tell
you about me?"
35"Am I a Jew?" Pilate retorted. "Your own people and their
leading priests brought you to me for trial. Why? What have you
done?"
36Jesus answered, "My Kingdom is not an earthly kingdom.
If it were, my followers would fight to keep me from being
handed over to the Jewish leaders. But my Kingdom is not of
this world."
37Pilate said, "So you are a king?"

Jesus responded, "You say I am a king. Actually, I was born and came into the world to testify to the truth. All who love the truth recognize that what I say is true."

38"What is truth?" Pilate asked. Then he went out again to the
people and told them, "He is not guilty of any crime. 39But you
have a custom of asking me to release one prisoner each year at
Passover. Would you like me to release this 'King of the Jews'?"
40But they shouted back, "No! Not this man. We want Barabbas!" (Barabbas was a revolutionary.)

CHAPTER 19

Jesus Sentenced to Death

Then Pilate had Jesus flogged with a lead-tipped whip. 2The
soldiers wove a crown of thorns and put it on his head, and they
put a purple robe on him. 3"Hail! King of the Jews!" they mocked,
as they slapped him across the face.
4Pilate went outside again and said to the people, "I am going to
bring him out to you now, but understand clearly that I find him
not guilty." 5Then Jesus came out wearing the crown of thorns and
the purple robe. And Pilate said, "Look, here is the man!"
6When they saw him, the leading priests and Temple guards
began shouting, "Crucify him! Crucify him!"

"Take him yourselves and crucify him," Pilate said. "I find him not guilty."

7The Jewish leaders replied, "By our law he ought to die
because he called himself the Son of God."
8When Pilate heard this, he was more frightened than ever.
9He took Jesus back into the headquarters* again and asked
him, "Where are you from?" But Jesus gave no answer. 10"Why

19:9 Greek *the Praetorium.*

don't you talk to me?" Pilate demanded. "Don't you realize that I have the power to release you or crucify you?"

¹¹Then Jesus said, "You would have no power over me at all unless it were given to you from above. So the one who handed me over to you has the greater sin."

¹²Then Pilate tried to release him, but the Jewish leaders shouted, "If you release this man, you are no 'friend of Caesar.'* Anyone who declares himself a king is a rebel against Caesar."

¹³When they said this, Pilate brought Jesus out to them again. Then Pilate sat down on the judgment seat on the platform that is called the Stone Pavement (in Hebrew, *Gabbatha*). ¹⁴It was now about noon on the day of preparation for the Passover. And Pilate said to the people,* "Look, here is your king!"

¹⁵"Away with him," they yelled. "Away with him! Crucify him!"

"What? Crucify your king?" Pilate asked.

"We have no king but Caesar," the leading priests shouted back. ¹⁶Then Pilate turned Jesus over to them to be crucified.

The Crucifixion

So they took Jesus away. ¹⁷Carrying the cross by himself, he went to the place called Place of the Skull (in Hebrew, *Golgotha*). ¹⁸There they nailed him to the cross. Two others were crucified with him, one on either side, with Jesus between them. ¹⁹And Pilate posted a sign over him that read, "Jesus of Nazareth,* the King of the Jews." ²⁰The place where Jesus was crucified was near the city, and the sign was written in Hebrew, Latin, and Greek, so that many people could read it. ²¹Then the leading priests objected and said to Pilate, "Change it from 'The King of the Jews' to 'He said, I am King of the Jews.'"

²²Pilate replied, "No, what I have written, I have written."

²³When the soldiers had crucified Jesus, they divided his clothes among the four of them. They also took his robe, but it was seamless, woven in one piece from top to bottom. ²⁴So they said, "Rather than tearing it apart, let's throw dice* for it." This fulfilled the Scripture that says, "They divided my garments among themselves and threw dice for my clothing."* So that is what they did.

²⁵Standing near the cross were Jesus' mother, and his mother's sister, Mary (the wife of Clopas), and Mary Magdalene. ²⁶When Jesus saw his mother standing there beside the disciple he loved, he said to her, "Dear woman, here is your son." ²⁷And he said to this disciple, "Here is your mother." And from then on this disciple took her into his home.

19:12 "Friend of Caesar" is a technical term that refers to an ally of the emperor.   19:14 Greek *Jewish people*; also in 19:20.   19:19 Or *Jesus the Nazarene*.   19:24a Greek *cast lots*.   19:24b Ps 22:18.

JOURNAL

The Death of Jesus

28 Jesus knew that his mission was now finished, and to fulfill Scripture he said, "I am thirsty."* 29 A jar of sour wine was sitting there, so they soaked a sponge in it, put it on a hyssop branch, and held it up to his lips. 30 When Jesus had tasted it, he said, "It is finished!" Then he bowed his head and released his spirit.

31 It was the day of preparation, and the Jewish leaders didn't want the bodies hanging there the next day, which was the Sabbath (and a very special Sabbath, because it was the Passover). So they asked Pilate to hasten their deaths by ordering that their legs be broken. Then their bodies could be taken down. 32 So the soldiers came and broke the legs of the two men crucified with Jesus. 33 But when they came to Jesus, they saw that he was already dead, so they didn't break his legs. 34 One of the soldiers, however, pierced his side with a spear, and immediately blood and water flowed out. 35 (This report is from an eyewitness giving an accurate account. He speaks the truth so that you also can believe.*) 36 These things happened in fulfillment of the Scriptures that say, "Not one of his bones will be broken,"* 37 and "They will look on the one they pierced."*

The Burial of Jesus

38 Afterward Joseph of Arimathea, who had been a secret disciple of Jesus (because he feared the Jewish leaders), asked Pilate for permission to take down Jesus' body. When Pilate gave permission, Joseph came and took the body away. 39 With him came Nicodemus, the man who had come to Jesus at night. He brought seventy-five pounds* of perfumed ointment made from myrrh and aloes. 40 Following Jewish burial custom, they wrapped Jesus' body with the spices in long sheets of linen cloth. 41 The place of crucifixion was near a garden, where there was a new tomb, never used before. 42 And so, because it was the day of preparation for the Jewish Passover* and since the tomb was close at hand, they laid Jesus there.

CHAPTER **20**

The Resurrection

Early on Sunday morning,* while it was still dark, Mary Magdalene came to the tomb and found that the stone had been rolled away from the entrance. 2 She ran and found Simon Peter and the other disciple, the one whom Jesus loved. She said, "They

19:28 See Pss 22:15; 69:21. **19:35** Some manuscripts read *can continue to believe.* **19:36** Exod 12:46; Num 9:12; Ps 34:20. **19:37** Zech 12:10. **19:39** Greek *100 litras* [32.7 kilograms]. **19:42** Greek *because of the Jewish day of preparation.* **20:1** Greek *On the first day of the week.*

have taken the Lord's body out of the tomb, and we don't know where they have put him!"

³Peter and the other disciple started out for the tomb. ⁴They were both running, but the other disciple outran Peter and reached the tomb first. ⁵He stooped and looked in and saw the linen wrappings lying there, but he didn't go in. ⁶Then Simon Peter arrived and went inside. He also noticed the linen wrappings lying there, ⁷while the cloth that had covered Jesus' head was folded up and lying apart from the other wrappings. ⁸Then the disciple who had reached the tomb first also went in, and he saw and believed—⁹for until then they still hadn't understood the Scriptures that said Jesus must rise from the dead. ¹⁰Then they went home.

Jesus Appears to Mary Magdalene

¹¹Mary was standing outside the tomb crying, and as she wept, she stooped and looked in. ¹²She saw two white-robed angels, one sitting at the head and the other at the foot of the place where the body of Jesus had been lying. ¹³"Dear woman, why are you crying?" the angels asked her.

"Because they have taken away my Lord," she replied, "and I don't know where they have put him."

¹⁴She turned to leave and saw someone standing there. It was Jesus, but she didn't recognize him. ¹⁵"Dear woman, why are you crying?" Jesus asked her. "Who are you looking for?"

She thought he was the gardener. "Sir," she said, "if you have taken him away, tell me where you have put him, and I will go and get him."

¹⁶"Mary!" Jesus said.

She turned to him and cried out, "Rabboni!" (which is Hebrew for "Teacher").

¹⁷"Don't cling to me," Jesus said, "for I haven't yet ascended to the Father. But go find my brothers and tell them, 'I am ascending to my Father and your Father, to my God and your God.'"

¹⁸Mary Magdalene found the disciples and told them, "I have seen the Lord!" Then she gave them his message.

Jesus Appears to His Disciples

¹⁹That Sunday evening* the disciples were meeting behind locked doors because they were afraid of the Jewish leaders. Suddenly, Jesus was standing there among them! "Peace be with you," he said. ²⁰As he spoke, he showed them the wounds in his hands and his side. They were filled with joy when they saw the

20:19 Greek *In the evening of that day, the first day of the week.*

"A friend is someone who understands your past, believes in your future, and accepts you today just the way you are. A friend is someone with whom you dare to be yourself."

~ C. Raymond Beran

JOURNAL

Lord! [21]Again he said, "Peace be with you. As the Father has sent me, so I am sending you." [22]Then he breathed on them and said, "Receive the Holy Spirit. [23]If you forgive anyone's sins, they are forgiven. If you do not forgive them, they are not forgiven."

Jesus Appears to Thomas

[24]One of the twelve disciples, Thomas (nicknamed the Twin),* was not with the others when Jesus came. [25]They told him, "We have seen the Lord!"

But he replied, "I won't believe it unless I see the nail wounds in his hands, put my fingers into them, and place my hand into the wound in his side."

[26]Eight days later the disciples were together again, and this time Thomas was with them. The doors were locked; but suddenly, as before, Jesus was standing among them. "Peace be with you," he said. [27]Then he said to Thomas, "Put your finger here, and look at my hands. Put your hand into the wound in my side. Don't be faithless any longer. Believe!"

[28]"My Lord and my God!" Thomas exclaimed.

[29]Then Jesus told him, "You believe because you have seen me. Blessed are those who believe without seeing me."

Purpose of the Book

[30]The disciples saw Jesus do many other miraculous signs in addition to the ones recorded in this book. [31]But these are written so that you may continue to believe* that Jesus is the Messiah, the Son of God, and that by believing in him you will have life by the power of his name.

CHAPTER 21

Epilogue: Jesus Appears to Seven Disciples

Later, Jesus appeared again to the disciples beside the Sea of Galilee.* This is how it happened. [2]Several of the disciples were there—Simon Peter, Thomas (nicknamed the Twin),* Nathanael from Cana in Galilee, the sons of Zebedee, and two other disciples.

[3]Simon Peter said, "I'm going fishing."

"We'll come, too," they all said. So they went out in the boat, but they caught nothing all night.

[4]At dawn Jesus was standing on the beach, but the disciples couldn't see who he was. [5]He called out, "Fellows,* have you caught any fish?"

20:24 Greek *Thomas, who was called Didymus.*   **20:31** Some manuscripts read *that you may believe.*   **21:1** Greek *Sea of Tiberias,* another name for the Sea of Galilee.   **21:2** Greek *Thomas, who was called Didymus.*   **21:5** Greek *Children.*

"No," they replied.

⁶Then he said, "Throw out your net on the right-hand side of the boat, and you'll get some!" So they did, and they couldn't haul in the net because there were so many fish in it.

⁷Then the disciple Jesus loved said to Peter, "It's the Lord!" When Simon Peter heard that it was the Lord, he put on his tunic (for he had stripped for work), jumped into the water, and headed to shore. ⁸The others stayed with the boat and pulled the loaded net to the shore, for they were only about a hundred yards* from shore. ⁹When they got there, they found breakfast waiting for them—fish cooking over a charcoal fire, and some bread.

¹⁰"Bring some of the fish you've just caught," Jesus said. ¹¹So Simon Peter went aboard and dragged the net to the shore. There were 153 large fish, and yet the net hadn't torn.

¹²"Now come and have some breakfast!" Jesus said. None of the disciples dared to ask him, "Who are you?" They knew it was the Lord. ¹³Then Jesus served them the bread and the fish. ¹⁴This was the third time Jesus had appeared to his disciples since he had been raised from the dead.

¹⁵After breakfast Jesus asked Simon Peter, "Simon son of John, do you love me more than these?*"

"Yes, Lord," Peter replied, "you know I love you."

"Then feed my lambs," Jesus told him.

¹⁶Jesus repeated the question: "Simon son of John, do you love me?"

"Yes, Lord," Peter said, "you know I love you."

"Then take care of my sheep," Jesus said.

¹⁷A third time he asked him, "Simon son of John, do you love me?"

Peter was hurt that Jesus asked the question a third time. He said, "Lord, you know everything. You know that I love you."

Jesus said, "Then feed my sheep.

¹⁸"I tell you the truth, when you were young, you were able to do as you liked; you dressed yourself and went wherever you wanted to go. But when you are old, you will stretch out your hands, and others* will dress you and take you where you don't want to go." ¹⁹Jesus said this to let him know by what kind of death he would glorify God. Then Jesus told him, "Follow me."

²⁰Peter turned around and saw behind them the disciple Jesus loved—the one who had leaned over to Jesus during supper and asked, "Lord, who will betray you?" ²¹Peter asked Jesus, "What about him, Lord?"

21:8 Greek 200 cubits [90 meters].   21:15 Or more than these others do?   21:18 Some manuscripts read and another one.

FRIENDSHIP EXPERIENCE

FRIENDSHIP TYPE: *Friends*   FRIENDSHIP LAYER: *Companionship*

Just Hanging Out

Companionship is time spent together, celebrating a friendship—sweet memories being created between two people. Companionship draws friends closer, strengthens the connection between them, and makes the friendship itself more valuable and so much richer.

And the beauty of companionship is that it can happen in so many different ways. It's friends laughing together, crying together, working together, playing together, talking together, or being together without saying a word.

We can experience companionship—in all its wonderful variety—with God. And just like in a friendship with a person, these times of celebration with God build a richer friendship with him.

THE ONE THING 1 YOU CAN DO THIS WEEK

Experience

Choose one object that represents how you'll build a richer friendship with someone through companionship—for example, a sketch pad, photo, Frisbee, cookbook, or CD. Write on a sticky note how you'll celebrate this friendship through time spent together. You might write "cook dinner together," "go to an art museum together," "listen to music together," or "play Frisbee together." Attach this sticky note to the object, and the next time you see your friend, arrange a time to hang out.

FRIENDSHIP EXPERIENCE *continues on page 224...*

FRIENDSHIP EXPERIENCE *continued from page 223...*

Now choose another object that represents how you'll grow as a companion of God—for example, a journal, Bible, clock, or even a towel (see Jesus' selfless love in **John 13:1-17!**).

Write on a sticky note how you'll celebrate your friendship with God through time spent together. You might write "journal my thoughts to God," "memorize a Bible passage," "spend time praying," "read Jesus' life story in the Bible," or "serve my family." Attach this sticky note to the object. Hold the object, and pray that God will make your friendship richer as you spend time with him.

Reflect

★ When have you experienced the best times of companionship with friends? What made those times so special?

★ How was your planned time of companionship with your friend? with God? How did it affect your friendship?

²²Jesus replied, "If I want him to remain alive until I return, what is that to you? As for you, follow me." ²³So the rumor spread among the community of believers* that this disciple wouldn't die. But that isn't what Jesus said at all. He only said, "If I want him to remain alive until I return, what is that to you?"

²⁴This disciple is the one who testifies to these events and has recorded them here. And we know that his account of these things is accurate.

²⁵Jesus also did many other things. If they were all written down, I suppose the whole world could not contain the books that would be written.

21:23 Greek *the brothers.*

Acts

AUTHOR:	DATE WRITTEN:
Luke	Between A.D. 63–70

CHAPTER 1

The Promise of the Holy Spirit

In my first book* I told you, Theophilus, about everything Jesus began to do and teach ²until the day he was taken up to heaven after giving his chosen apostles further instructions through the Holy Spirit. ³During the forty days after his crucifixion, he appeared to the apostles from time to time, and he proved to them in many ways that he was actually alive. And he talked to them about the Kingdom of God.

⁴Once when he was eating with them, he commanded them, "Do not leave Jerusalem until the Father sends you the gift he promised, as I told you before. ⁵John baptized with* water, but in just a few days you will be baptized with the Holy Spirit."

The Ascension of Jesus

⁶So when the apostles were with Jesus, they kept asking him, "Lord, has the time come for you to free Israel and restore our kingdom?"

⁷He replied, "The Father alone has the authority to set those dates and times, and they are not for you to know. ⁸But you will receive power when the Holy Spirit comes upon you. And you will be my witnesses, telling people about me everywhere—in Jerusalem, throughout Judea, in Samaria, and to the ends of the earth."

⁹After saying this, he was taken up into a cloud while they were watching, and they could no longer see him. ¹⁰As they strained to see him rising into heaven, two white-robed men suddenly stood among them. ¹¹"Men of Galilee," they said, "why are you standing here staring into heaven? Jesus has been taken from you into heaven, but someday he will return from heaven in the same way you saw him go!"

1:1 The reference is to the Gospel of Luke. **1:5** Or *in;* also in 1:5b.

JOURNAL

Matthias Replaces Judas

12 Then the apostles returned to Jerusalem from the Mount of Olives, a distance of half a mile.* 13 When they arrived, they went to the upstairs room of the house where they were staying.

Here are the names of those who were present: Peter, John, James, Andrew, Philip, Thomas, Bartholomew, Matthew, James (son of Alphaeus), Simon (the Zealot), and Judas (son of James). 14 They all met together and were constantly united in prayer, along with Mary the mother of Jesus, several other women, and the brothers of Jesus.

15 During this time, when about 120 believers* were together in one place, Peter stood up and addressed them. 16 "Brothers," he said, "the Scriptures had to be fulfilled concerning Judas, who guided those who arrested Jesus. This was predicted long ago by the Holy Spirit, speaking through King David. 17 Judas was one of us and shared in the ministry with us."

18 (Judas had bought a field with the money he received for his treachery. Falling headfirst there, his body split open, spilling out all his intestines. 19 The news of his death spread to all the people of Jerusalem, and they gave the place the Aramaic name *Akeldama,* which means "Field of Blood.")

20 Peter continued, "This was written in the book of Psalms, where it says, 'Let his home become desolate, with no one living in it.' It also says, 'Let someone else take his position.'*

21 "So now we must choose a replacement for Judas from among the men who were with us the entire time we were traveling with the Lord Jesus—22 from the time he was baptized by John until the day he was taken from us. Whoever is chosen will join us as a witness of Jesus' resurrection."

23 So they nominated two men: Joseph called Barsabbas (also known as Justus) and Matthias. 24 Then they all prayed, "O Lord, you know every heart. Show us which of these men you have chosen 25 as an apostle to replace Judas in this ministry, for he has deserted us and gone where he belongs." 26 Then they cast lots, and Matthias was selected to become an apostle with the other eleven.

CHAPTER 2

The Holy Spirit Comes

On the day of Pentecost* all the believers were meeting together in one place. 2 Suddenly, there was a sound from heaven like the

1:12 Greek *a Sabbath day's journey.* 1:15 Greek *brothers.* 1:20 Pss 69:25; 109:8. 2:1 The Festival of Pentecost came 50 days after Passover (when Jesus was crucified).

roaring of a mighty windstorm, and it filled the house where they were sitting. ³Then, what looked like flames or tongues of fire appeared and settled on each of them. ⁴And everyone present was filled with the Holy Spirit and began speaking in other languages,* as the Holy Spirit gave them this ability.

⁵At that time there were devout Jews from every nation living in Jerusalem. ⁶When they heard the loud noise, everyone came running, and they were bewildered to hear their own languages being spoken by the believers.

⁷They were completely amazed. "How can this be?" they exclaimed. "These people are all from Galilee, ⁸and yet we hear them speaking in our own native languages! ⁹Here we are— Parthians, Medes, Elamites, people from Mesopotamia, Judea, Cappadocia, Pontus, the province of Asia, ¹⁰Phrygia, Pamphylia, Egypt, and the areas of Libya around Cyrene, visitors from Rome ¹¹(both Jews and converts to Judaism), Cretans, and Arabs. And we all hear these people speaking in our own languages about the wonderful things God has done!" ¹²They stood there amazed and perplexed. "What can this mean?" they asked each other.

¹³But others in the crowd ridiculed them, saying, "They're just drunk, that's all!"

Peter Preaches to the Crowd

¹⁴Then Peter stepped forward with the eleven other apostles and shouted to the crowd, "Listen carefully, all of you, fellow Jews and residents of Jerusalem! Make no mistake about this. ¹⁵These people are not drunk, as some of you are assuming. Nine o'clock in the morning is much too early for that. ¹⁶No, what you see was predicted long ago by the prophet Joel:

¹⁷ 'In the last days,' God says,
　　'I will pour out my Spirit upon all people.
　Your sons and daughters will prophesy.
　　　Your young men will see visions,
　　　and your old men will dream dreams.
¹⁸ In those days I will pour out my Spirit
　　　even on my servants—men and women alike—
　　　and they will prophesy.
¹⁹ And I will cause wonders in the heavens above
　　　and signs on the earth below—
　　　blood and fire and clouds of smoke.
²⁰ The sun will become dark,

2:4 Or *in other tongues.*

FRIENDSHIP TYPE: *Hard-to-Love People*　　**FRIENDSHIP LAYER:** *Acceptance*

Tag Team

You want to accept a hard-to-love person? You have to find common ground. It's pretty easy to spot your differences; now try to find your similarities, your shared values, your mutual hobbies.

But you don't have to do it alone. It doesn't have to be a solo adventure. Team up with a close friend you already trust…

THE ONE THING 1 YOU CAN DO THIS WEEK

Experience

Plan a fun day with a close friend—go skiing, see a movie, shop. But *before* you set a date, invite that hard-to-love person to join you.

As you hang out together, talk through these questions:
★ What's the craziest thing you've ever done?
★ What's one thing you feel you can do really well?
★ What's one thing you usually struggle with?
★ What's the nicest thing someone has ever done for you?
★ What's the one thing you're most thankful for in your life?

These questions will help you understand and get to know each other.

You have to admit: Sometimes all of us can be hard to love. Yet God loves us despite our faults and weaknesses. Read **Romans 8:35-39** to get an idea of God's unflinching—and unfailing—love for us.

FRIENDSHIP EXPERIENCE *continues on page 228…*

FRIENDSHIP EXPERIENCE *continued from page 227…*

Reflect

★ How did your perceptions of that hard-to-love person change after you spent time getting to know him or her?

★ What about you do you think God would find hard to love? How do you feel knowing that God loves you no matter what?

JOURNAL

and the moon will turn blood red
before that great and glorious day of the Lord arrives.
²¹ But everyone who calls on the name of the Lord
will be saved.'*

²² "People of Israel, listen! God publicly endorsed Jesus the Nazarene* by doing powerful miracles, wonders, and signs through him, as you well know. ²³ But God knew what would happen, and his prearranged plan was carried out when Jesus was betrayed. With the help of lawless Gentiles, you nailed him to a cross and killed him. ²⁴ But God released him from the horrors of death and raised him back to life, for death could not keep him in its grip. ²⁵ King David said this about him:

'I see that the Lord is always with me.
I will not be shaken, for he is right beside me.
²⁶ No wonder my heart is glad,
and my tongue shouts his praises!
My body rests in hope.
²⁷ For you will not leave my soul among the dead*
or allow your Holy One to rot in the grave.
²⁸ You have shown me the way of life,
and you will fill me with the joy of your presence.'*

²⁹ "Dear brothers, think about this! You can be sure that the patriarch David wasn't referring to himself, for he died and was buried, and his tomb is still here among us. ³⁰ But he was a prophet, and he knew God had promised with an oath that one of David's own descendants would sit on his throne. ³¹ David was looking into the future and speaking of the Messiah's resurrection. He was saying that God would not leave him among the dead or allow his body to rot in the grave.

³² "God raised Jesus from the dead, and we are all witnesses of this. ³³ Now he is exalted to the place of highest honor in heaven, at God's right hand. And the Father, as he had promised, gave him the Holy Spirit to pour out upon us, just as you see and hear today. ³⁴ For David himself never ascended into heaven, yet he said,

'The Lord said to my Lord,
"Sit in the place of honor at my right hand
³⁵ until I humble your enemies,
making them a footstool under your feet."'*

2:17-21 Joel 2:28-32. **2:22** Or *Jesus of Nazareth.* **2:27** Greek *in Hades;* also in 2:31. **2:25-28** Ps 16:8-11 (Greek version). **2:34-35** Ps 110:1.

36 "So let everyone in Israel know for certain that God has made this Jesus, whom you crucified, to be both Lord and Messiah!"

37 Peter's words pierced their hearts, and they said to him and to the other apostles, "Brothers, what should we do?"

38 Peter replied, "Each of you must repent of your sins and turn to God, and be baptized in the name of Jesus Christ for the forgiveness of your sins. Then you will receive the gift of the Holy Spirit. 39 This promise is to you, and to your children, and even to the Gentiles*—all who have been called by the Lord our God." 40 Then Peter continued preaching for a long time, strongly urging all his listeners, "Save yourselves from this crooked generation!"

41 Those who believed what Peter said were baptized and added to the church that day—about 3,000 in all.

The Believers Form a Community

42 All the believers devoted themselves to the apostles' teaching, and to fellowship, and to sharing in meals (including the Lord's Supper*), and to prayer.

43 A deep sense of awe came over them all, and the apostles performed many miraculous signs and wonders. 44 And all the believers met together in one place and shared everything they had. 45 They sold their property and possessions and shared the money with those in need. 46 They worshiped together at the Temple each day, met in homes for the Lord's Supper, and shared their meals with great joy and generosity*—47 all the while praising God and enjoying the goodwill of all the people. And each day the Lord added to their fellowship those who were being saved.

CHAPTER **3**

Peter Heals a Crippled Beggar

Peter and John went to the Temple one afternoon to take part in the three o'clock prayer service. 2 As they approached the Temple, a man lame from birth was being carried in. Each day he was put beside the Temple gate, the one called the Beautiful Gate, so he could beg from the people going into the Temple. 3 When he saw Peter and John about to enter, he asked them for some money.

4 Peter and John looked at him intently, and Peter said, "Look at us!" 5 The lame man looked at them eagerly, expecting some

"This is the most profound spiritual truth I know: that even when we're most sure that love can't conquer all, it seems to anyway. It goes down into the rat hole with us, in the guise of our friends, and there it swells and comforts."

~ Anne Lamott

2:39 Or *and to people far in the future;* Greek reads *and to those far away.* 2:42 Greek *the breaking of bread;* also in 2:46. 2:46 Or *and sincere hearts.*

JOURNAL

money. 6 But Peter said, "I don't have any silver or gold for you. But I'll give you what I have. In the name of Jesus Christ the Nazarene,* get up and* walk!"

7 Then Peter took the lame man by the right hand and helped him up. And as he did, the man's feet and ankles were instantly healed and strengthened. 8 He jumped up, stood on his feet, and began to walk! Then, walking, leaping, and praising God, he went into the Temple with them.

9 All the people saw him walking and heard him praising God. 10 When they realized he was the lame beggar they had seen so often at the Beautiful Gate, they were absolutely astounded! 11 They all rushed out in amazement to Solomon's Colonnade, where the man was holding tightly to Peter and John.

Peter Preaches in the Temple

12 Peter saw his opportunity and addressed the crowd. "People of Israel," he said, "what is so surprising about this? And why stare at us as though we had made this man walk by our own power or godliness? 13 For it is the God of Abraham, Isaac, and Jacob—the God of all our ancestors—who has brought glory to his servant Jesus by doing this. This is the same Jesus whom you handed over and rejected before Pilate, despite Pilate's decision to release him. 14 You rejected this holy, righteous one and instead demanded the release of a murderer. 15 You killed the author of life, but God raised him from the dead. And we are witnesses of this fact!

16 "Through faith in the name of Jesus, this man was healed—and you know how crippled he was before. Faith in Jesus' name has healed him before your very eyes.

17 "Friends,* I realize that what you and your leaders did to Jesus was done in ignorance. 18 But God was fulfilling what all the prophets had foretold about the Messiah—that he must suffer these things. 19 Now repent of your sins and turn to God, so that your sins may be wiped away. 20 Then times of refreshment will come from the presence of the Lord, and he will again send you Jesus, your appointed Messiah. 21 For he must remain in heaven until the time for the final restoration of all things, as God promised long ago through his holy prophets. 22 Moses said, 'The LORD your God will raise up for you a Prophet like me from among your own people. Listen carefully to everything he tells you.'* 23 Then Moses said, 'Anyone who will not listen to that Prophet will be completely cut off from God's people.'*

3:6a Or *Jesus Christ of Nazareth.*   3:6b Some manuscripts omit *get up and.*   3:17 Greek *Brothers.*
3:22 Deut 18:15.   3:23 Deut 18:19; Lev 23:29.

24"Starting with Samuel, every prophet spoke about what is happening today. 25You are the children of those prophets, and you are included in the covenant God promised to your ancestors. For God said to Abraham, 'Through your descendants* all the families on earth will be blessed.' 26When God raised up his servant, Jesus, he sent him first to you people of Israel, to bless you by turning each of you back from your sinful ways."

CHAPTER **4**

Peter and John before the Council

While Peter and John were speaking to the people, they were confronted by the priests, the captain of the Temple guard, and some of the Sadducees. 2These leaders were very disturbed that Peter and John were teaching the people that through Jesus there is a resurrection of the dead. 3They arrested them and, since it was already evening, put them in jail until morning. 4But many of the people who heard their message believed it, so the number of believers now totaled about 5,000 men, not counting women and children.*

5The next day the council of all the rulers and elders and teachers of religious law met in Jerusalem. 6Annas the high priest was there, along with Caiaphas, John, Alexander, and other relatives of the high priest. 7They brought in the two disciples and demanded, "By what power, or in whose name, have you done this?"

8Then Peter, filled with the Holy Spirit, said to them, "Rulers and elders of our people, 9are we being questioned today because we've done a good deed for a crippled man? Do you want to know how he was healed? 10Let me clearly state to all of you and to all the people of Israel that he was healed by the powerful name of Jesus Christ the Nazarene,* the man you crucified but whom God raised from the dead. 11For Jesus is the one referred to in the Scriptures, where it says,

'The stone that you builders rejected
    has now become the cornerstone.'*

12There is salvation in no one else! God has given no other name under heaven by which we must be saved."

13The members of the council were amazed when they saw the boldness of Peter and John, for they could see that they were ordinary men with no special training in the Scriptures. They also recognized them as men who had been with Jesus. 14But

3:25 Greek *your seed;* see Gen 12:3; 22:18.   **4:4** Greek *5,000 adult males.*   **4:10** Or *Jesus Christ of Nazareth.*   **4:11** Ps 118:22.

No. 06-TE-231

FRIENDSHIP STORY

FRIENDSHIP TYPE: *Hard-to-Love People*   FRIENDSHIP LAYER: *Getting Acquainted*

BASED ON TRUE EVENTS

Reaching Out to a Drug Trafficker

Antonio* was the most notorious drug trafficker in the worst crime neighborhood of Belo Horizonte, Brazil. Rumor was that he'd killed more than 100 people. Which would explain why Pastor Jefferson wasn't all that excited to see Antonio in his church one Sunday. Pastor Jefferson had come to this barrio to help the poor and to give them the hope that comes through Jesus Christ. But Antonio was one of the bad guys—somebody he was trying to protect his church *from.*

Still, what could he do? Scared as he was, Pastor Jefferson knew that God had called him to share the gospel with those who needed it, and who needed it more than Antonio?

Many of Pastor Jefferson's church members, however, didn't want Antonio at their church. They said they weren't going to sit with their families next to a murdering drug trafficker. But Pastor Jefferson kept inviting Antonio to come back, even when many in his congregation stopped coming because of it.

Then one day a miracle happened. With tears streaming down his face, Antonio, the feared drug trafficker and murderer, began a friendship with Jesus. He asked Jesus to forgive him. He asked the congregation to forgive him. That day Antonio experienced God's love...and he changed.

FRIENDSHIP STORY *continues on page 232...*

*This story is true, but the name is fictional.

FRIENDSHIP STORY *continued from page 231...*

He put drug trafficking behind him. He got rid of his guns. He moved to a different city to be away from his gangs. He joined the church of another minister whom Pastor Jefferson knew. Soon he was leading a cell group in that church. Even months later when Antonio's brother was murdered in a drug war, Antonio refused to pick up his guns and join his gang as they sought revenge. He told Pastor Jefferson that he wanted to bring hope—not violence—to his barrio.

After his brother's death, Antonio moved back and rejoined Pastor Jefferson's church. Within four years the little barrio church had grown from 77 members to more than 900. More than 200 of those members were former drug traffickers. A barrio that was rated the worst in Belo Horizonte in virtually every violent crime category had dropped to number 20 in the city. And it all started with one hard-to-love person and a pastor who was willing to trust God and reach out.

Experience

THE ONE THING 1 YOU CAN DO THIS WEEK

You don't need to risk your life to reach out to a hard-to-love person. However, you could reach out to someone others keep at arm's length. Invite that person out for coffee or dinner. Just start by asking about the person's story, and then listen. If you're uncertain at first, remember Ananias (**Acts 9:10-19a**)—God gave him strength and wisdom, and God will do the same for you.

Reflect

★ How do you balance a legitimate safety concern and the desire to reach out to "dangerous" people?

★ What did you learn about the person you spent time with? yourself? God?

since they could see the man who had been healed standing right there among them, there was nothing the council could say. [15]So they ordered Peter and John out of the council chamber* and conferred among themselves.

[16]"What should we do with these men?" they asked each other. "We can't deny that they have performed a miraculous sign, and everybody in Jerusalem knows about it. [17]But to keep them from spreading their propaganda any further, we must warn them not to speak to anyone in Jesus' name again." [18]So they called the apostles back in and commanded them never again to speak or teach in the name of Jesus.

[19]But Peter and John replied, "Do you think God wants us to obey you rather than him? [20]We cannot stop telling about everything we have seen and heard."

[21]The council then threatened them further, but they finally let them go because they didn't know how to punish them without starting a riot. For everyone was praising God [22]for this miraculous sign—the healing of a man who had been lame for more than forty years.

The Believers Pray for Courage

[23]As soon as they were freed, Peter and John returned to the other believers and told them what the leading priests and elders had said. [24]When they heard the report, all the believers lifted their voices together in prayer to God: "O Sovereign Lord, Creator of heaven and earth, the sea, and everything in them—[25]you spoke long ago by the Holy Spirit through our ancestor David, your servant, saying,

'Why were the nations so angry?
    Why did they waste their time with futile plans?
[26] The kings of the earth prepared for battle;
    the rulers gathered together
against the LORD
    and against his Messiah.'*

[27]"In fact, this has happened here in this very city! For Herod Antipas, Pontius Pilate the governor, the Gentiles, and the people of Israel were all united against Jesus, your holy servant, whom you anointed. [28]But everything they did was determined beforehand according to your will. [29]And now, O Lord, hear their threats, and give us, your servants, great boldness in preaching your word. [30]Stretch out your hand

4:15 Greek *the Sanhedrin.*   **4:25-26** Or *his anointed one;* or *his Christ.* Ps 2:1-2.

with healing power; may miraculous signs and wonders be done through the name of your holy servant Jesus."

[31]After this prayer, the meeting place shook, and they were all filled with the Holy Spirit. Then they preached the word of God with boldness.

The Believers Share Their Possessions

[32]All the believers were united in heart and mind. And they felt that what they owned was not their own, so they shared everything they had. [33]The apostles testified powerfully to the resurrection of the Lord Jesus, and God's great blessing was upon them all. [34]There were no needy people among them, because those who owned land or houses would sell them [35]and bring the money to the apostles to give to those in need.

[36]For instance, there was Joseph, the one the apostles nicknamed Barnabas (which means "Son of Encouragement"). He was from the tribe of Levi and came from the island of Cyprus. [37]He sold a field he owned and brought the money to the apostles.

CHAPTER **5**

Ananias and Sapphira

But there was a certain man named Ananias who, with his wife, Sapphira, sold some property. [2]He brought part of the money to the apostles, claiming it was the full amount. With his wife's consent, he kept the rest.

[3]Then Peter said, "Ananias, why have you let Satan fill your heart? You lied to the Holy Spirit, and you kept some of the money for yourself. [4]The property was yours to sell or not sell, as you wished. And after selling it, the money was also yours to give away. How could you do a thing like this? You weren't lying to us but to God!"

[5]As soon as Ananias heard these words, he fell to the floor and died. Everyone who heard about it was terrified. [6]Then some young men got up, wrapped him in a sheet, and took him out and buried him.

[7]About three hours later his wife came in, not knowing what had happened. [8]Peter asked her, "Was this the price you and your husband received for your land?"

"Yes," she replied, "that was the price."

[9]And Peter said, "How could the two of you even think of conspiring to test the Spirit of the Lord like this? The young men who buried your husband are just outside the door, and they will carry you out, too."

"*Frodo sat, eating, drinking, and talking with delight....He knew a little of the elf-speech and listened eagerly. Now and again he spoke to those that served him and thanked them in their own language. They smiled at him and said laughing: 'Here is a jewel among hobbits!'*"

~ *J.R.R. Tolkien*

JOURNAL

[10] Instantly, she fell to the floor and died. When the young men came in and saw that she was dead, they carried her out and buried her beside her husband. [11] Great fear gripped the entire church and everyone else who heard what had happened.

The Apostles Heal Many

[12] The apostles were performing many miraculous signs and wonders among the people. And all the believers were meeting regularly at the Temple in the area known as Solomon's Colonnade. [13] But no one else dared to join them, even though all the people had high regard for them. [14] Yet more and more people believed and were brought to the Lord—crowds of both men and women. [15] As a result of the apostles' work, sick people were brought out into the streets on beds and mats so that Peter's shadow might fall across some of them as he went by. [16] Crowds came from the villages around Jerusalem, bringing their sick and those possessed by evil* spirits, and they were all healed.

The Apostles Meet Opposition

[17] The high priest and his officials, who were Sadducees, were filled with jealousy. [18] They arrested the apostles and put them in the public jail. [19] But an angel of the Lord came at night, opened the gates of the jail, and brought them out. Then he told them, [20] "Go to the Temple and give the people this message of life!"

[21] So at daybreak the apostles entered the Temple, as they were told, and immediately began teaching.

When the high priest and his officials arrived, they convened the high council*—the full assembly of the elders of Israel. Then they sent for the apostles to be brought from the jail for trial. [22] But when the Temple guards went to the jail, the men were gone. So they returned to the council and reported, [23] "The jail was securely locked, with the guards standing outside, but when we opened the gates, no one was there!"

[24] When the captain of the Temple guard and the leading priests heard this, they were perplexed, wondering where it would all end. [25] Then someone arrived with startling news: "The men you put in jail are standing in the Temple, teaching the people!"

[26] The captain went with his Temple guards and arrested the apostles, but without violence, for they were afraid the people would stone them. [27] Then they brought the apostles before the high council, where the high priest confronted them. [28] "Didn't we tell you never again to teach in this man's name?"

5:16 Greek *unclean*.   **5:21** Greek *Sanhedrin*; also in 5:27, 41.

he demanded. "Instead, you have filled all Jerusalem with your teaching about him, and you want to make us responsible for his death!"

²⁹But Peter and the apostles replied, "We must obey God rather than any human authority. ³⁰The God of our ancestors raised Jesus from the dead after you killed him by hanging him on a cross.* ³¹Then God put him in the place of honor at his right hand as Prince and Savior. He did this so the people of Israel would repent of their sins and be forgiven. ³²We are witnesses of these things and so is the Holy Spirit, who is given by God to those who obey him."

³³When they heard this, the high council was furious and decided to kill them. ³⁴But one member, a Pharisee named Gamaliel, who was an expert in religious law and respected by all the people, stood up and ordered that the men be sent outside the council chamber for a while. ³⁵Then he said to his colleagues, "Men of Israel, take care what you are planning to do to these men! ³⁶Some time ago there was that fellow Theudas, who pretended to be someone great. About 400 others joined him, but he was killed, and all his followers went their various ways. The whole movement came to nothing. ³⁷After him, at the time of the census, there was Judas of Galilee. He got people to follow him, but he was killed, too, and all his followers were scattered.

³⁸"So my advice is, leave these men alone. Let them go. If they are planning and doing these things merely on their own, it will soon be overthrown. ³⁹But if it is from God, you will not be able to overthrow them. You may even find yourselves fighting against God!"

⁴⁰The others accepted his advice. They called in the apostles and had them flogged. Then they ordered them never again to speak in the name of Jesus, and they let them go.

⁴¹The apostles left the high council rejoicing that God had counted them worthy to suffer disgrace for the name of Jesus.* ⁴²And every day, in the Temple and from house to house, they continued to teach and preach this message: "Jesus is the Messiah."

CHAPTER **6**

Seven Men Chosen to Serve

But as the believers* rapidly multiplied, there were rumblings of discontent. The Greek-speaking believers complained about the

5:30 Greek *on a tree.*   **5:41** Greek *for the name.*   **6:1** Greek *disciples;* also in 6:2, 7.

FRIENDSHIP
EXPERIENCE

FRIENDSHIP TYPE: *Hard-to-Love People*   FRIENDSHIP LAYER: *Getting Acquainted*

Moving Beyond Reputation

Reputation isn't always a reliable indicator of what a person is like. After all, reputation is really nothing more than a person seen through the eyes of other imperfect people.

There were some who considered Jesus a glutton and a drunkard (**Matthew 11:19**). If people hadn't been willing to look beyond that reputation, would they ever have listened? Saul had a reputation as a violent man who was not to be trusted. If Ananias hadn't been willing—with God's help—to look beyond reputation, who would have helped Saul (**Acts 9:10-19a**)?

The truth is, hard-to-love people aren't always that hard to love. Sometimes it's just their reputation getting in the way.

Experience

Who has a bad reputation in your area? A certain racial or religious group? The employees of a particular company? People who live on the other side of town?

Think of an individual or family from that group, and reach out. Invite them into your home, or visit theirs. Talk about what you have in common—and what you don't. Get past reputations, and get to know one another... for real.

FRIENDSHIP EXPERIENCE *continues on page 236...*

FRIENDSHIP EXPERIENCE *continued from page 235...*

You can't get to know anyone by reputation alone, and that includes God. For some people, God has a bad reputation. They see God as judgmental because they've met judgmental Christians. They think God is boring because church was boring. Maybe that's how you think about God. It takes personal experience to know God...for real. This week get beyond God's "reputation," and get to know God personally.

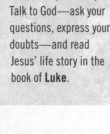

Talk to God—ask your questions, express your doubts—and read Jesus' life story in the book of **Luke**.

Reflect

★ What surprised you most during your time getting to know the person? God?

★ What are the differences between God's reputation and the experiences you've had with him?

Hebrew-speaking believers, saying that their widows were being discriminated against in the daily distribution of food.

[2] So the Twelve called a meeting of all the believers. They said, "We apostles should spend our time teaching the word of God, not running a food program. [3] And so, brothers, select seven men who are well respected and are full of the Spirit and wisdom. We will give them this responsibility. [4] Then we apostles can spend our time in prayer and teaching the word."

[5] Everyone liked this idea, and they chose the following: Stephen (a man full of faith and the Holy Spirit), Philip, Procorus, Nicanor, Timon, Parmenas, and Nicolas of Antioch (an earlier convert to the Jewish faith). [6] These seven were presented to the apostles, who prayed for them as they laid their hands on them.

[7] So God's message continued to spread. The number of believers greatly increased in Jerusalem, and many of the Jewish priests were converted, too.

Stephen Is Arrested

[8] Stephen, a man full of God's grace and power, performed amazing miracles and signs among the people. [9] But one day some men from the Synagogue of Freed Slaves, as it was called, started to debate with him. They were Jews from Cyrene, Alexandria, Cilicia, and the province of Asia. [10] None of them could stand against the wisdom and the Spirit with which Stephen spoke.

[11] So they persuaded some men to lie about Stephen, saying, "We heard him blaspheme Moses, and even God." [12] This roused the people, the elders, and the teachers of religious law. So they arrested Stephen and brought him before the high council.*

[13] The lying witnesses said, "This man is always speaking against the holy Temple and against the law of Moses. [14] We have heard him say that this Jesus of Nazareth* will destroy the Temple and change the customs Moses handed down to us."

[15] At this point everyone in the high council stared at Stephen, because his face became as bright as an angel's.

CHAPTER **7**
Stephen Addresses the Council

Then the high priest asked Stephen, "Are these accusations true?"

6:12 Greek *Sanhedrin;* also in **6:15**.   **6:14** Or *Jesus the Nazarene.*

²This was Stephen's reply: "Brothers and fathers, listen to me. Our glorious God appeared to our ancestor Abraham in Mesopotamia before he settled in Haran.* ³God told him, 'Leave your native land and your relatives, and come into the land that I will show you.'* ⁴So Abraham left the land of the Chaldeans and lived in Haran until his father died. Then God brought him here to the land where you now live.

⁵"But God gave him no inheritance here, not even one square foot of land. God did promise, however, that eventually the whole land would belong to Abraham and his descendants—even though he had no children yet. ⁶God also told him that his descendants would live in a foreign land, where they would be oppressed as slaves for 400 years. ⁷'But I will punish the nation that enslaves them,' God said, 'and in the end they will come out and worship me here in this place.'*

⁸"God also gave Abraham the covenant of circumcision at that time. So when Abraham became the father of Isaac, he circumcised him on the eighth day. And the practice was continued when Isaac became the father of Jacob, and when Jacob became the father of the twelve patriarchs of the Israelite nation.

⁹"These patriarchs were jealous of their brother Joseph, and they sold him to be a slave in Egypt. But God was with him ¹⁰and rescued him from all his troubles. And God gave him favor before Pharaoh, king of Egypt. God also gave Joseph unusual wisdom, so that Pharaoh appointed him governor over all of Egypt and put him in charge of the palace.

¹¹"But a famine came upon Egypt and Canaan. There was great misery, and our ancestors ran out of food. ¹²Jacob heard that there was still grain in Egypt, so he sent his sons—our ancestors—to buy some. ¹³The second time they went, Joseph revealed his identity to his brothers,* and they were introduced to Pharaoh. ¹⁴Then Joseph sent for his father, Jacob, and all his relatives to come to Egypt, seventy-five persons in all. ¹⁵So Jacob went to Egypt. He died there, as did our ancestors. ¹⁶Their bodies were taken to Shechem and buried in the tomb Abraham had bought for a certain price from Hamor's sons in Shechem.

¹⁷"As the time drew near when God would fulfill his promise to Abraham, the number of our people in Egypt greatly increased. ¹⁸But then a new king came to the throne of Egypt who knew nothing about Joseph. ¹⁹This king exploited our

JOURNAL

7:2 Mesopotamia was the region now called Iraq. Haran was a city in what is now called Syria. 7:3 Gen 12:1. 7:5-7 Gen 12:7; 15:13-14; Exod 3:12. 7:13 Other manuscripts read Joseph was recognized by his brothers.

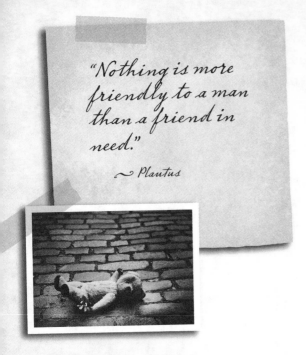

"Nothing is more friendly to a man than a friend in need."

~ Plautus

JOURNAL

people and oppressed them, forcing parents to abandon their newborn babies so they would die.

20 "At that time Moses was born—a beautiful child in God's eyes. His parents cared for him at home for three months. 21 When they had to abandon him, Pharaoh's daughter adopted him and raised him as her own son. 22 Moses was taught all the wisdom of the Egyptians, and he was powerful in both speech and action.

23 "One day when Moses was forty years old, he decided to visit his relatives, the people of Israel. 24 He saw an Egyptian mistreating an Israelite. So Moses came to the man's defense and avenged him, killing the Egyptian. 25 Moses assumed his fellow Israelites would realize that God had sent him to rescue them, but they didn't.

26 "The next day he visited them again and saw two men of Israel fighting. He tried to be a peacemaker. 'Men,' he said, 'you are brothers. Why are you fighting each other?'

27 "But the man in the wrong pushed Moses aside. 'Who made you a ruler and judge over us?' he asked. 28 'Are you going to kill me as you killed that Egyptian yesterday?' 29 When Moses heard that, he fled the country and lived as a foreigner in the land of Midian. There his two sons were born.

30 "Forty years later, in the desert near Mount Sinai, an angel appeared to Moses in the flame of a burning bush. 31 When Moses saw it, he was amazed at the sight. As he went to take a closer look, the voice of the LORD called out to him, 32 'I am the God of your ancestors—the God of Abraham, Isaac, and Jacob.' Moses shook with terror and did not dare to look.

33 "Then the LORD said to him, 'Take off your sandals, for you are standing on holy ground. 34 I have certainly seen the oppression of my people in Egypt. I have heard their groans and have come down to rescue them. Now go, for I am sending you back to Egypt.'*

35 "So God sent back the same man his people had previously rejected when they demanded, 'Who made you a ruler and judge over us?' Through the angel who appeared to him in the burning bush, God sent Moses to be their ruler and savior. 36 And by means of many wonders and miraculous signs, he led them out of Egypt, through the Red Sea, and through the wilderness for forty years.

37 "Moses himself told the people of Israel, 'God will raise up for you a Prophet like me from among your own people.'*

7:31-34 Exod 3:5-10.   7:37 Deut 18:15.

38 Moses was with our ancestors, the assembly of God's people in the wilderness, when the angel spoke to him at Mount Sinai. And there Moses received life-giving words to pass on to us.*

39 "But our ancestors refused to listen to Moses. They rejected him and wanted to return to Egypt. 40 They told Aaron, 'Make us some gods who can lead us, for we don't know what has become of this Moses, who brought us out of Egypt.' 41 So they made an idol shaped like a calf, and they sacrificed to it and celebrated over this thing they had made. 42 Then God turned away from them and abandoned them to serve the stars of heaven as their gods! In the book of the prophets it is written,

'Was it to me you were bringing sacrifices and offerings
    during those forty years in the wilderness, Israel?
43 No, you carried your pagan gods—
    the shrine of Molech,
    the star of your god Rephan,
    and the images you made to worship them.
So I will send you into exile
    as far away as Babylon.'*

44 "Our ancestors carried the Tabernacle* with them through the wilderness. It was constructed according to the plan God had shown to Moses. 45 Years later, when Joshua led our ancestors in battle against the nations that God drove out of this land, the Tabernacle was taken with them into their new territory. And it stayed there until the time of King David.

46 "David found favor with God and asked for the privilege of building a permanent Temple for the God of Jacob.* 47 But it was Solomon who actually built it. 48 However, the Most High doesn't live in temples made by human hands. As the prophet says,

49 'Heaven is my throne,
    and the earth is my footstool.
Could you build me a temple as good as that?'
    asks the LORD.
'Could you build me such a resting place?
50   Didn't my hands make both heaven and earth?'*

51 "You stubborn people! You are heathen* at heart and deaf to the truth. Must you forever resist the Holy Spirit? That's what your ancestors did, and so do you! 52 Name one prophet your ancestors didn't persecute! They even killed the ones who

7:38 Some manuscripts read *to you.* 7:42-43 Amos 5:25-27 (Greek version). 7:44 Greek *the tent of witness.* 7:46 Some manuscripts read *the house of Jacob.* 7:49-50 Isa 66:1-2. 7:51 Greek *uncircumcised.*

WHAT TO SAY
AND
WHAT NOT TO SAY

FRIENDSHIP TYPE: *Hard-to-Love People*   FRIENDSHIP LAYER: *Getting Acquainted*

A Matter of Perspective

Who really is hard to love? You might be surprised to learn that you're on someone else's list—perhaps someone reading this will be contacting you! It's all a matter of perspective. With that in mind, it would be best to avoid saying the following as you're getting acquainted with a hard-to-love person:

 WHAT NOT TO SAY:

★ "I bet you never thought someone like me would ever be friends with someone like you."
★ "Gosh! I don't understand why everyone else thinks you're so annoying!"
★ "OK, this has been better than I thought, but if my real friends come along, would you mind laying low?"

Jesus told a parable about a tax collector and a Pharisee (**Luke 18:9-14**). The Pharisee, full of pride, assumed that God loved him more than the tax collector. Jesus gave a far different perspective: It was the modest and humble tax collector who had become a closer friend of God. So take a lesson from the tax collector, and be humble as you get acquainted with a hard-to-love person.

 WHAT TO SAY:

★ "I'm glad we've had this chance to learn more about each other."
★ "We should do this again sometime."
★ "I would like to introduce you to some of my other friends so they can get to know you the way I do."

predicted the coming of the Righteous One—the Messiah whom you betrayed and murdered. ⁵³ You deliberately disobeyed God's law, even though you received it from the hands of angels."

⁵⁴ The Jewish leaders were infuriated by Stephen's accusation, and they shook their fists at him in rage.* ⁵⁵ But Stephen, full of the Holy Spirit, gazed steadily into heaven and saw the glory of God, and he saw Jesus standing in the place of honor at God's right hand. ⁵⁶ And he told them, "Look, I see the heavens opened and the Son of Man standing in the place of honor at God's right hand!"

⁵⁷ Then they put their hands over their ears and began shouting. They rushed at him ⁵⁸ and dragged him out of the city and began to stone him. His accusers took off their coats and laid them at the feet of a young man named Saul.*

⁵⁹ As they stoned him, Stephen prayed, "Lord Jesus, receive my spirit." ⁶⁰ He fell to his knees, shouting, "Lord, don't charge them with this sin!" And with that, he died.

CHAPTER **8**

Saul was one of the witnesses, and he agreed completely with the killing of Stephen.

Persecution Scatters the Believers

A great wave of persecution began that day, sweeping over the church in Jerusalem; and all the believers except the apostles were scattered through the regions of Judea and Samaria. ² (Some devout men came and buried Stephen with great mourning.) ³ But Saul was going everywhere to destroy the church. He went from house to house, dragging out both men and women to throw them into prison.

Philip Preaches in Samaria

⁴ But the believers who were scattered preached the Good News about Jesus wherever they went. ⁵ Philip, for example, went to the city of Samaria and told the people there about the Messiah. ⁶ Crowds listened intently to Philip because they were eager to hear his message and see the miraculous signs he did. ⁷ Many evil* spirits were cast out, screaming as they left their victims. And many who had been paralyzed or lame were healed. ⁸ So there was great joy in that city.

⁹ A man named Simon had been a sorcerer there for many

7:54 Greek *they were grinding their teeth against him.*   **7:58** *Saul* is later called *Paul*; see 13:9. **8:7** Greek *unclean.*

years, amazing the people of Samaria and claiming to be some-one great. [10]Everyone, from the least to the greatest, often spoke of him as "the Great One—the Power of God." [11]They listened closely to him because for a long time he had astounded them with his magic.

[12]But now the people believed Philip's message of Good News concerning the Kingdom of God and the name of Jesus Christ. As a result, many men and women were baptized. [13]Then Simon himself believed and was baptized. He began following Philip wherever he went, and he was amazed by the signs and great miracles Philip performed.

[14]When the apostles in Jerusalem heard that the people of Samaria had accepted God's message, they sent Peter and John there. [15]As soon as they arrived, they prayed for these new believers to receive the Holy Spirit. [16]The Holy Spirit had not yet come upon any of them, for they had only been baptized in the name of the Lord Jesus. [17]Then Peter and John laid their hands upon these believers, and they received the Holy Spirit.

[18]When Simon saw that the Spirit was given when the apostles laid their hands on people, he offered them money to buy this power. [19]"Let me have this power, too," he exclaimed, "so that when I lay my hands on people, they will receive the Holy Spirit!"

[20]But Peter replied, "May your money be destroyed with you for thinking God's gift can be bought! [21]You can have no part in this, for your heart is not right with God. [22]Repent of your wickedness and pray to the Lord. Perhaps he will forgive your evil thoughts, [23]for I can see that you are full of bitter jealousy and are held captive by sin."

[24]"Pray to the Lord for me," Simon exclaimed, "that these terrible things you've said won't happen to me!"

[25]After testifying and preaching the word of the Lord in Samaria, Peter and John returned to Jerusalem. And they stopped in many Samaritan villages along the way to preach the Good News.

Philip and the Ethiopian Eunuch

[26]As for Philip, an angel of the Lord said to him, "Go south* down the desert road that runs from Jerusalem to Gaza." [27]So he started out, and he met the treasurer of Ethiopia, a eunuch of great authority under the Kandake, the queen of Ethiopia. The eunuch had gone to Jerusalem to worship, [28]and he was

8:26 Or *Go at noon.*

"There is always an intangible something which makes a friend, it is not what he does, but what he is."

~ Oswald Chambers

JOURNAL

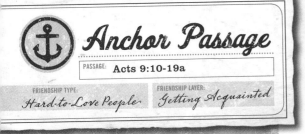

PASSAGE: Acts 9:10-19a

FRIENDSHIP TYPE: Hard-to-Love People

FRIENDSHIP LAYER: Getting Acquainted

A Man With a Bad Reputation

When most people today think of Saul (better known as Paul), they don't think of him as a hard-to-love person. After all, he did write the "love chapter" (check it out in **1 Corinthians 13**). But from the perspective of most early Christians, Saul was the bad guy.

The Bible says Saul "was going everywhere to destroy the church. He went from house to house, dragging out both men and women to throw them into prison" (**Acts 8:3**). And he "was uttering threats with every breath and was eager to kill the Lord's followers" (**Acts 9:1**).

But on the way to Damascus, Saul's life changed forever. Jesus called to him in a vision, and Saul, blinded by this vision, went to Damascus looking for help.

Read **Acts 9:10-19a**.

Ananias wasn't too happy with God's message: "But Lord…I've heard many people talk about the terrible things this man has done to the believers in Jerusalem!" Fear almost kept Ananias from Saul. But Ananias chose to obey God's command and meet with Saul, despite the dangers. Ananias trusted God to help him and care for him as he met with Saul.

Sometimes God specifically calls us to love a hard-to-love person. Even when we don't want to. Even when it seems crazy and foolish. We can take a lesson from Ananias and trust God's plan.

Anchor Passage continues on page 243…

now returning. Seated in his carriage, he was reading aloud from the book of the prophet Isaiah.

29 The Holy Spirit said to Philip, "Go over and walk along beside the carriage."

30 Philip ran over and heard the man reading from the prophet Isaiah. Philip asked, "Do you understand what you are reading?"

31 The man replied, "How can I, unless someone instructs me?" And he urged Philip to come up into the carriage and sit with him.

32 The passage of Scripture he had been reading was this:

"He was led like a sheep to the slaughter.
    And as a lamb is silent before the shearers,
        he did not open his mouth.
33 He was humiliated and received no justice.
    Who can speak of his descendants?
    For his life was taken from the earth."*

34 The eunuch asked Philip, "Tell me, was the prophet talking about himself or someone else?" 35 So beginning with this same Scripture, Philip told him the Good News about Jesus.

36 As they rode along, they came to some water, and the eunuch said, "Look! There's some water! Why can't I be baptized?"* 38 He ordered the carriage to stop, and they went down into the water, and Philip baptized him.

39 When they came up out of the water, the Spirit of the Lord snatched Philip away. The eunuch never saw him again but went on his way rejoicing. 40 Meanwhile, Philip found himself farther north at the town of Azotus. He preached the Good News there and in every town along the way until he came to Caesarea.

CHAPTER **9**

Saul's Conversion

Meanwhile, Saul was uttering threats with every breath and was eager to kill the Lord's followers.* So he went to the high priest. 2 He requested letters addressed to the synagogues in Damascus, asking for their cooperation in the arrest of any followers of the Way he found there. He wanted to bring them—both men and women—back to Jerusalem in chains.

3 As he was approaching Damascus on this mission, a light from heaven suddenly shone down around him. 4 He fell to the

8:32-33 Isa 53:7-8 (Greek version).   8:36 Some manuscripts add verse 37, "You can," Philip answered, "if you believe with all your heart." And the eunuch replied, "I believe that Jesus Christ is the Son of God."   9:1 Greek *disciples*.

ground and heard a voice saying to him, "Saul! Saul! Why are you persecuting me?"

⁵"Who are you, lord?" Saul asked.

And the voice replied, "I am Jesus, the one you are persecuting! ⁶Now get up and go into the city, and you will be told what you must do."

⁷The men with Saul stood speechless, for they heard the sound of someone's voice but saw no one! ⁸Saul picked himself up off the ground, but when he opened his eyes he was blind. So his companions led him by the hand to Damascus. ⁹He remained there blind for three days and did not eat or drink.

¹⁰Now there was a believer* in Damascus named Ananias. The Lord spoke to him in a vision, calling, "Ananias!"

"Yes, Lord!" he replied.

¹¹The Lord said, "Go over to Straight Street, to the house of Judas. When you get there, ask for a man from Tarsus named Saul. He is praying to me right now. ¹²I have shown him a vision of a man named Ananias coming in and laying hands on him so he can see again."

¹³"But Lord," exclaimed Ananias, "I've heard many people talk about the terrible things this man has done to the believers* in Jerusalem! ¹⁴And he is authorized by the leading priests to arrest everyone who calls upon your name."

¹⁵But the Lord said, "Go, for Saul is my chosen instrument to take my message to the Gentiles and to kings, as well as to the people of Israel. ¹⁶And I will show him how much he must suffer for my name's sake."

¹⁷So Ananias went and found Saul. He laid his hands on him and said, "Brother Saul, the Lord Jesus, who appeared to you on the road, has sent me so that you might regain your sight and be filled with the Holy Spirit." ¹⁸Instantly something like scales fell from Saul's eyes, and he regained his sight. Then he got up and was baptized. ¹⁹Afterward he ate some food and regained his strength. ⚓

9:10 Greek *disciple*; also in 9:26, 36. 9:13 Greek *God's holy people*; also in 9:32, 41.

Anchor Passage continued from page 242...

"But the Lord said, 'Go, for Saul is my chosen instrument to take my message to the Gentiles and to kings, as well as to the people of Israel.' "

THE ONE THING
1
YOU CAN DO THIS WEEK

Experience

Who is the most hard-to-love person you know—a co-worker, family member, neighbor? Pray for that person. Not necessarily that God changes that person but that God changes your attitude toward that person. Then watch for changes in *both* of you!

Reflect

★ Who is a hard-to-love person God has put in your life? What's one way you can be a friend to that person this week?

★ How does Jesus change the lives of dangerous or hard-to-love people today?

DIGGING DEEPER

FRIENDSHIP TYPE:
Hard-to-Love People

FRIENDSHIP LAYER:
Getting Acquainted

For getting acquainted with hard-to-love people, check out...

➼ The Friendship Experience .... on page 235
➼ The Friendship Story .... on page 231
➼ What to Say and What Not to Say .... on page 239

JOURNAL

Saul in Damascus and Jerusalem

Saul stayed with the believers* in Damascus for a few days. 20And immediately he began preaching about Jesus in the synagogues, saying, "He is indeed the Son of God!"

21All who heard him were amazed. "Isn't this the same man who caused such devastation among Jesus' followers in Jerusalem?" they asked. "And didn't he come here to arrest them and take them in chains to the leading priests?"

22Saul's preaching became more and more powerful, and the Jews in Damascus couldn't refute his proofs that Jesus was indeed the Messiah. 23After a while some of the Jews plotted together to kill him. 24They were watching for him day and night at the city gate so they could murder him, but Saul was told about their plot. 25So during the night, some of the other believers* lowered him in a large basket through an opening in the city wall.

26When Saul arrived in Jerusalem, he tried to meet with the believers, but they were all afraid of him. They did not believe he had truly become a believer! 27Then Barnabas brought him to the apostles and told them how Saul had seen the Lord on the way to Damascus and how the Lord had spoken to Saul. He also told them that Saul had preached boldly in the name of Jesus in Damascus.

28So Saul stayed with the apostles and went all around Jerusalem with them, preaching boldly in the name of the Lord. ⚓

29He debated with some Greek-speaking Jews, but they tried to murder him. 30When the believers* heard about this, they took him down to Caesarea and sent him away to Tarsus, his hometown.

31The church then had peace throughout Judea, Galilee, and Samaria, and it became stronger as the believers lived in the fear of the Lord. And with the encouragement of the Holy Spirit, it also grew in numbers.

9:19 Greek *disciples;* also in 9:26, 38. **9:25** Greek *his disciples.* **9:30** Greek *brothers.*

Peter Heals Aeneas and Raises Dorcas

³²Meanwhile, Peter traveled from place to place, and he came down to visit the believers in the town of Lydda. ³³There he met a man named Aeneas, who had been paralyzed and bedridden for eight years. ³⁴Peter said to him, "Aeneas, Jesus Christ heals you! Get up, and roll up your sleeping mat!" And he was healed instantly. ³⁵Then the whole population of Lydda and Sharon saw Aeneas walking around, and they turned to the Lord.

³⁶There was a believer in Joppa named Tabitha (which in Greek is Dorcas*). She was always doing kind things for others and helping the poor. ³⁷About this time she became ill and died. Her body was washed for burial and laid in an upstairs room. ³⁸But the believers had heard that Peter was nearby at Lydda, so they sent two men to beg him, "Please come as soon as possible!"

³⁹So Peter returned with them; and as soon as he arrived, they took him to the upstairs room. The room was filled with widows who were weeping and showing him the coats and other clothes Dorcas had made for them. ⁴⁰But Peter asked them all to leave the room; then he knelt and prayed. Turning to the body he said, "Get up, Tabitha." And she opened her eyes! When she saw Peter, she sat up! ⁴¹He gave her his hand and helped her up. Then he called in the widows and all the believers, and he presented her to them alive.

⁴²The news spread through the whole town, and many believed in the Lord. ⁴³And Peter stayed a long time in Joppa, living with Simon, a tanner of hides.

CHAPTER **10**

Cornelius Calls for Peter

In Caesarea there lived a Roman army officer* named Cornelius, who was a captain of the Italian Regiment. ²He was a devout, God-fearing man, as was everyone in his household. He gave generously to the poor and prayed regularly to God. ³One afternoon about three o'clock, he had a vision in which he saw an angel of God coming toward him. "Cornelius!" the angel said.

⁴Cornelius stared at him in terror. "What is it, sir?" he asked the angel.

And the angel replied, "Your prayers and gifts to the poor have been received by God as an offering! ⁵Now send some men to Joppa, and summon a man named Simon Peter. ⁶He is staying with Simon, a tanner who lives near the seashore."

9:36 The names *Tabitha* in Aramaic and *Dorcas* in Greek both mean "gazelle." 10:1 Greek *a centurion;* similarly in 10:22.

Anchor Passage

PASSAGE: Acts 9:19b-28

FRIENDSHIP TYPE: *Hard-to-Love People*

FRIENDSHIP LAYER: *Acceptance*

The Harder They Come

It's easy to notice when something's different or out of place. It takes only a second to spot the wilted piece of lettuce in your salad. You probably wouldn't have remembered what shirt your friend was wearing if it hadn't been for that stain on the sleeve. And who can forget that awful smell in your brother's car?

It's even easier to spot people who are different or seem out of place. We make quick assumptions about a person's "lovability" with only a glance.

Read **Acts 9:19b-28**.

The Christians in Damascus made some assumptions about Saul, most of which were true. It's understandable why they were wary of accepting a guy like Saul. In fact, he was probably the last person in the world you'd expect Christians to accept, much less love. He was, after all, *out to kill them.*

Thankfully, though, Barnabas chose to look past all that and accept Saul in spite of what everyone else thought…and Saul turned out to be one of the most influential Christians of all time.

Anchor Passage continues on page 246…

Anchor Passage continued from page 245...

All of us—*all of us*—have people in our lives who are hard to love. For one reason or another, those people just rub us the wrong way. We keep our distance. We look the other way. But despite their differences, every one of those people has something in common with us. And every one of those people has a need for acceptance…just like us.

What's more, all of us—*all of us*—can be hard to love at one time or another. Thankfully there are people like Barnabas in our lives who are willing to look past the rough spots and accept us anyway.

So now it's your turn to be a Barnabas—to accept someone who is hard to love…and to offer your friendship.

Experience

THE ONE THING 1 YOU CAN DO THIS WEEK

Pick up today's newspaper and a red marker. From cover to cover, circle the photos of people you'd consider hard to love—criminals, politicians, celebrities, anyone. What would it take for you to accept each of those people?

Now think of a person in your life who's difficult to love. God doesn't wait for us to get our act together before he loves us, and you shouldn't either. Do something nice for that hard-to-love person *now*…Don't wait!

Reflect

★ Why do you think it's important to accept hard-to-love people?

★ How can doing something nice for an unlovable person change your perspective of that person?

Anchor Passage continues on page 247...

7 As soon as the angel was gone, Cornelius called two of his household servants and a devout soldier, one of his personal attendants. 8 He told them what had happened and sent them off to Joppa.

Peter Visits Cornelius

9 The next day as Cornelius's messengers were nearing the town, Peter went up on the flat roof to pray. It was about noon, 10 and he was hungry. But while a meal was being prepared, he fell into a trance. 11 He saw the sky open, and something like a large sheet was let down by its four corners. 12 In the sheet were all sorts of animals, reptiles, and birds. 13 Then a voice said to him, "Get up, Peter; kill and eat them."

14 "No, Lord," Peter declared. "I have never eaten anything that our Jewish laws have declared impure and unclean.*"

15 But the voice spoke again: "Do not call something unclean if God has made it clean." 16 The same vision was repeated three times. Then the sheet was suddenly pulled up to heaven.

17 Peter was very perplexed. What could the vision mean? Just then the men sent by Cornelius found Simon's house. Standing outside the gate, 18 they asked if a man named Simon Peter was staying there.

19 Meanwhile, as Peter was puzzling over the vision, the Holy Spirit said to him, "Three men have come looking for you. 20 Get up, go downstairs, and go with them without hesitation. Don't worry, for I have sent them."

21 So Peter went down and said, "I'm the man you are looking for. Why have you come?"

22 They said, "We were sent by Cornelius, a Roman officer. He is a devout and God-fearing man, well respected by all the Jews. A holy angel instructed him to summon you to his house so that he can hear your message." 23 So Peter invited the men to stay for the night. The next day he went with them, accompanied by some of the brothers from Joppa.

24 They arrived in Caesarea the following day. Cornelius was waiting for them and had called together his relatives and close friends. 25 As Peter entered his home, Cornelius fell at his feet and worshiped him. 26 But Peter pulled him up and said, "Stand up! I'm a human being just like you!" 27 So they talked together and went inside, where many others were assembled.

28 Peter told them, "You know it is against our laws for a Jewish man to enter a Gentile home like this or to associate with

10:14 Greek *anything common and unclean.*

you. But God has shown me that I should no longer think of anyone as impure or unclean. ²⁹So I came without objection as soon as I was sent for. Now tell me why you sent for me."

³⁰Cornelius replied, "Four days ago I was praying in my house about this same time, three o'clock in the afternoon. Suddenly, a man in dazzling clothes was standing in front of me. ³¹He told me, 'Cornelius, your prayer has been heard, and your gifts to the poor have been noticed by God! ³²Now send messengers to Joppa, and summon a man named Simon Peter. He is staying in the home of Simon, a tanner who lives near the seashore.' ³³So I sent for you at once, and it was good of you to come. Now we are all here, waiting before God to hear the message the Lord has given you."

The Gentiles Hear the Good News

³⁴Then Peter replied, "I see very clearly that God shows no favoritism. ³⁵In every nation he accepts those who fear him and do what is right. ³⁶This is the message of Good News for the people of Israel—that there is peace with God through Jesus Christ, who is Lord of all. ³⁷You know what happened throughout Judea, beginning in Galilee, after John began preaching his message of baptism. ³⁸And you know that God anointed Jesus of Nazareth with the Holy Spirit and with power. Then Jesus went around doing good and healing all who were oppressed by the devil, for God was with him.

³⁹"And we apostles are witnesses of all he did throughout Judea and in Jerusalem. They put him to death by hanging him on a cross,* ⁴⁰but God raised him to life on the third day. Then God allowed him to appear, ⁴¹not to the general public,* but to us whom God had chosen in advance to be his witnesses. We were those who ate and drank with him after he rose from the dead. ⁴²And he ordered us to preach everywhere and to testify that Jesus is the one appointed by God to be the judge of all—the living and the dead. ⁴³He is the one all the prophets testified about, saying that everyone who believes in him will have their sins forgiven through his name."

The Gentiles Receive the Holy Spirit

⁴⁴Even as Peter was saying these things, the Holy Spirit fell upon all who were listening to the message. ⁴⁵The Jewish believers* who came with Peter were amazed that the gift of the Holy Spirit had been poured out on the Gentiles, too. ⁴⁶For they heard them speaking in tongues and praising God.

10:39 Greek *on a tree.*   **10:41** Greek *the people.*   **10:45** Greek *The faithful ones of the circumcision.*

Anchor Passage continued from page 246...

DIGGING DEEPER

FRIENDSHIP TYPE:
Hard-to-Love People

FRIENDSHIP LAYER:
Acceptance

For accepting hard-to-love people, check out...
➡ The Friendship Experience .... on page 227
➡ The Friendship Story .... on page 251
➡ What to Say and What Not to Say .... on page 418

JOURNAL

Then Peter asked, [47]"Can anyone object to their being baptized, now that they have received the Holy Spirit just as we did?" [48]So he gave orders for them to be baptized in the name of Jesus Christ. Afterward Cornelius asked him to stay with them for several days.

CHAPTER 11

Peter Explains His Actions

Soon the news reached the apostles and other believers* in Judea that the Gentiles had received the word of God. [2]But when Peter arrived back in Jerusalem, the Jewish believers* criticized him. [3]"You entered the home of Gentiles* and even ate with them!" they said.

[4]Then Peter told them exactly what had happened. [5]"I was in the town of Joppa," he said, "and while I was praying, I went into a trance and saw a vision. Something like a large sheet was let down by its four corners from the sky. And it came right down to me. [6]When I looked inside the sheet, I saw all sorts of small animals, wild animals, reptiles, and birds. [7]And I heard a voice say, 'Get up, Peter; kill and eat them.'

[8]"'No, Lord,' I replied. 'I have never eaten anything that our Jewish laws have declared impure or unclean.*'

[9]"But the voice from heaven spoke again: 'Do not call something unclean if God has made it clean.' [10]This happened three times before the sheet and all it contained was pulled back up to heaven.

[11]"Just then three men who had been sent from Caesarea arrived at the house where we were staying. [12]The Holy Spirit told me to go with them and not to worry that they were Gentiles. These six brothers here accompanied me, and we soon entered the home of the man who had sent for us. [13]He told us how an angel had appeared to him in his home and had told him, 'Send messengers to Joppa, and summon a man named Simon Peter. [14]He will tell you how you and everyone in your household can be saved!'

[15]"As I began to speak," Peter continued, "the Holy Spirit fell on them, just as he fell on us at the beginning. [16]Then I thought of the Lord's words when he said, 'John baptized with* water, but you will be baptized with the Holy Spirit.' [17]And since God gave these Gentiles the same gift he gave us when we believed in the Lord Jesus Christ, who was I to stand in God's way?"

11:1 Greek *brothers.*   11:2 Greek *those of the circumcision.*   11:3 Greek *of uncircumcised men.*
11:8 Greek *anything common or unclean.*   11:16 Or *in;* also in 11:16b.

[18] When the others heard this, they stopped objecting and began praising God. They said, "We can see that God has also given the Gentiles the privilege of repenting of their sins and receiving eternal life."

The Church in Antioch of Syria

[19] Meanwhile, the believers who had been scattered during the persecution after Stephen's death traveled as far as Phoenicia, Cyprus, and Antioch of Syria. They preached the word of God, but only to Jews. [20] However, some of the believers who went to Antioch from Cyprus and Cyrene began preaching to the Gentiles* about the Lord Jesus. [21] The power of the Lord was with them, and a large number of these Gentiles believed and turned to the Lord.

[22] When the church at Jerusalem heard what had happened, they sent Barnabas to Antioch. [23] When he arrived and saw this evidence of God's blessing, he was filled with joy, and he encouraged the believers to stay true to the Lord. [24] Barnabas was a good man, full of the Holy Spirit and strong in faith. And many people were brought to the Lord.

[25] Then Barnabas went on to Tarsus to look for Saul. [26] When he found him, he brought him back to Antioch. Both of them stayed there with the church for a full year, teaching large crowds of people. (It was at Antioch that the believers* were first called Christians.)

[27] During this time some prophets traveled from Jerusalem to Antioch. [28] One of them named Agabus stood up in one of the meetings and predicted by the Spirit that a great famine was coming upon the entire Roman world. (This was fulfilled during the reign of Claudius.) [29] So the believers in Antioch decided to send relief to the brothers and sisters* in Judea, everyone giving as much as they could. [30] This they did, entrusting their gifts to Barnabas and Saul to take to the elders of the church in Jerusalem.

CHAPTER **12**

James Is Killed and Peter Is Imprisoned

About that time King Herod Agrippa* began to persecute some believers in the church. [2] He had the apostle James (John's brother) killed with a sword. [3] When Herod saw how much this pleased the Jewish people, he also arrested Peter. (This took place during the Passover celebration.*) [4] Then he imprisoned

11:20 Greek *the Hellenists* (i.e., those who speak Greek); other manuscripts read *the Greeks.*
11:26 Greek *disciples;* also in 11:29.   11:29 Greek *the brothers.*   12:1 Greek *Herod the king.* He was the nephew of Herod Antipas and a grandson of Herod the Great.   12:3 Greek *the days of unleavened bread.*

"Treat your friends as you do your pictures, and place them in their best light."

~ Jennie Jerome Churchill (Winston Churchill's mother)

JOURNAL

him, placing him under the guard of four squads of four soldiers each. Herod intended to bring Peter out for public trial after the Passover. [5]But while Peter was in prison, the church prayed very earnestly for him.

Peter's Miraculous Escape from Prison

[6]The night before Peter was to be placed on trial, he was asleep, fastened with two chains between two soldiers. Others stood guard at the prison gate. [7]Suddenly, there was a bright light in the cell, and an angel of the Lord stood before Peter. The angel struck him on the side to awaken him and said, "Quick! Get up!" And the chains fell off his wrists. [8]Then the angel told him, "Get dressed and put on your sandals." And he did. "Now put on your coat and follow me," the angel ordered.

[9]So Peter left the cell, following the angel. But all the time he thought it was a vision. He didn't realize it was actually happening. [10]They passed the first and second guard posts and came to the iron gate leading to the city, and this opened for them all by itself. So they passed through and started walking down the street, and then the angel suddenly left him.

[11]Peter finally came to his senses. "It's really true!" he said. "The Lord has sent his angel and saved me from Herod and from what the Jewish leaders* had planned to do to me!"

[12]When he realized this, he went to the home of Mary, the mother of John Mark, where many were gathered for prayer. [13]He knocked at the door in the gate, and a servant girl named Rhoda came to open it. [14]When she recognized Peter's voice, she was so overjoyed that, instead of opening the door, she ran back inside and told everyone, "Peter is standing at the door!"

[15]"You're out of your mind!" they said. When she insisted, they decided, "It must be his angel."

[16]Meanwhile, Peter continued knocking. When they finally opened the door and saw him, they were amazed. [17]He motioned for them to quiet down and told them how the Lord had led him out of prison. "Tell James and the other brothers what happened," he said. And then he went to another place.

[18]At dawn there was a great commotion among the soldiers about what had happened to Peter. [19]Herod Agrippa ordered a thorough search for him. When he couldn't be found, Herod interrogated the guards and sentenced them to death. Afterward Herod left Judea to stay in Caesarea for a while.

12:11 Or *the Jewish people.*

The Death of Herod Agrippa

²⁰Now Herod was very angry with the people of Tyre and Sidon. So they sent a delegation to make peace with him because their cities were dependent upon Herod's country for food. The delegates won the support of Blastus, Herod's personal assistant, ²¹and an appointment with Herod was granted. When the day arrived, Herod put on his royal robes, sat on his throne, and made a speech to them. ²²The people gave him a great ovation, shouting, "It's the voice of a god, not of a man!"

²³Instantly, an angel of the Lord struck Herod with a sickness, because he accepted the people's worship instead of giving the glory to God. So he was consumed with worms and died.

²⁴Meanwhile, the word of God continued to spread, and there were many new believers.

²⁵When Barnabas and Saul had finished their mission to Jerusalem, they returned,* taking John Mark with them.

CHAPTER **13**

Barnabas and Saul Are Commissioned

Among the prophets and teachers of the church at Antioch of Syria were Barnabas, Simeon (called "the black man"*), Lucius (from Cyrene), Manaen (the childhood companion of King Herod Antipas*), and Saul. ²One day as these men were worshiping the Lord and fasting, the Holy Spirit said, "Dedicate Barnabas and Saul for the special work to which I have called them." ³So after more fasting and prayer, the men laid their hands on them and sent them on their way.

Paul's First Missionary Journey

⁴So Barnabas and Saul were sent out by the Holy Spirit. They went down to the seaport of Seleucia and then sailed for the island of Cyprus. ⁵There, in the town of Salamis, they went to the Jewish synagogues and preached the word of God. John Mark went with them as their assistant.

⁶Afterward they traveled from town to town across the entire island until finally they reached Paphos, where they met a Jewish sorcerer, a false prophet named Bar-Jesus. ⁷He had attached himself to the governor, Sergius Paulus, who was an intelligent man. The governor invited Barnabas and Saul to visit him, for he wanted to hear the word of God. ⁸But Elymas, the sorcerer (as his name means in Greek), interfered and urged the governor

12:25 Or *mission, they returned to Jerusalem.* Other manuscripts read *mission, they returned from Jerusalem;* still others read *mission, they returned from Jerusalem to Antioch.*   13:1a Greek *who was called Niger.*   13:1b Greek *Herod the tetrarch.*

No. 07-FS-251

FRIENDSHIP STORY

FRIENDSHIP TYPE: *Hard-to-Love People*   FRIENDSHIP LAYER: *Acceptance*

FOUND IN SCRIPTURE

Jacob's Broken Ladder

If there's one guy in the Bible who doesn't seem to deserve all the blessings he received, it's probably Jacob. It'd be easy—and correct—to call him a lying, deceiving, unscrupulous swindler. More often than not, his hands were clenched into fists, not folded in prayer. He fought with his brother, his in-laws, even one of God's angels. Jacob was hardheaded, and it wasn't because he actually used a rock as a pillow. He was the kind of guy only a mother could love...

The very beginning of Jacob's life was a sign of things to come. When he and his twin brother were born, Jacob came out second...with his hand clamped firmly around twin Esau's ankle.

They definitely were not identical twins. As they grew up, it was obvious there was *nothing* identical about them. Esau, a hairy, tough-looking outdoorsman, spent his days hunting away from home. Jacob, on the other hand, preferred to stay

at home and spend his time in the kitchen. With so little in common, it must have been hard for them to accept each other, much less love each other.

Now, it's hard to love someone who cheats you once. But it can be nearly impossible to love someone who tricks you twice. Jacob first cheated Esau out of his inheritance, and then he lied and stole Esau's blessing from their father, Isaac. Esau hated Jacob and vowed to kill him. So Jacob ran far, far away.

FRIENDSHIP STORY *continues on page 252...*

FRIENDSHIP STORY *continued from page 251...*

Fortunately, Jacob and Esau's story has a happy ending. Jacob recognized all the wrong things he'd done and wanted to make peace. He eventually returned to Esau's ranch, and, despite everything, they embraced and forgave each other. No matter their painful past, they chose to accept—and love—each other. Jacob summed it up perfectly when he told Esau, "What a relief it is to see your friendly smile. It is like seeing the smile of God!"

Read the whole story in Genesis 25; 27; 32; and 33.

Experience

THE ONE THING 1 YOU CAN DO THIS WEEK

Whom do you find hard to love? When Jacob went to make peace with Esau, he did two things: He gave Esau gifts, and he introduced Esau to his family. Think about that person you need to accept. Find some point of common ground between the two of you—some shared interest or perhaps a food you both like. Then get that person a small gift. Say something such as, "I noticed that you really like coffee, so I thought you might like this coffeehouse gift certificate." You might also consider introducing that person to a close friend or family member, just as Jacob introduced Esau to his family. You'll be amazed at how even a small gesture like that can break down barriers.

Reflect

★ What happened when you introduced your hard-to-love friend to one of your close friends or family members?

★ Read **Romans 13:10**. How does this verse apply to your relationship with that hard-to-love person?

to pay no attention to what Barnabas and Saul said. He was trying to keep the governor from believing.

⁹Saul, also known as Paul, was filled with the Holy Spirit, and he looked the sorcerer in the eye. ¹⁰Then he said, "You son of the devil, full of every sort of deceit and fraud, and enemy of all that is good! Will you never stop perverting the true ways of the Lord? ¹¹Watch now, for the Lord has laid his hand of punishment upon you, and you will be struck blind. You will not see the sunlight for some time." Instantly mist and darkness came over the man's eyes, and he began groping around begging for someone to take his hand and lead him.

¹²When the governor saw what had happened, he became a believer, for he was astonished at the teaching about the Lord.

Paul Preaches in Antioch of Pisidia

¹³Paul and his companions then left Paphos by ship for Pamphylia, landing at the port town of Perga. There John Mark left them and returned to Jerusalem. ¹⁴But Paul and Barnabas traveled inland to Antioch of Pisidia.*

On the Sabbath they went to the synagogue for the services. ¹⁵After the usual readings from the books of Moses* and the prophets, those in charge of the service sent them this message: "Brothers, if you have any word of encouragement for the people, come and give it."

¹⁶So Paul stood, lifted his hand to quiet them, and started speaking. "Men of Israel," he said, "and you God-fearing Gentiles, listen to me.

¹⁷"The God of this nation of Israel chose our ancestors and made them multiply and grow strong during their stay in Egypt. Then with a powerful arm he led them out of their slavery. ¹⁸He put up with them* through forty years of wandering in the wilderness. ¹⁹Then he destroyed seven nations in Canaan and gave their land to Israel as an inheritance. ²⁰All this took about 450 years.

"After that, God gave them judges to rule until the time of Samuel the prophet. ²¹Then the people begged for a king, and God gave them Saul son of Kish, a man of the tribe of Benjamin, who reigned for forty years. ²²But God removed Saul and replaced him with David, a man about whom God said, 'I have found David son of Jesse, a man after my own heart. He will do everything I want him to do.'*

²³"And it is one of King David's descendants, Jesus, who is

13:13-14 *Pamphylia* and *Pisidia* were districts in what is now Turkey.   13:15 Greek *from the law.* 13:18 Some manuscripts read *He cared for them;* compare Deut 1:31.   13:22 1 Sam 13:14.

God's promised Savior of Israel! ²⁴Before he came, John the Baptist preached that all the people of Israel needed to repent of their sins and turn to God and be baptized. ²⁵As John was finishing his ministry he asked, 'Do you think I am the Messiah? No, I am not! But he is coming soon—and I'm not even worthy to be his slave and untie the sandals on his feet.'

²⁶"Brothers—you sons of Abraham, and also you God-fearing Gentiles—this message of salvation has been sent to us! ²⁷The people in Jerusalem and their leaders did not recognize Jesus as the one the prophets had spoken about. Instead, they condemned him, and in doing this they fulfilled the prophets' words that are read every Sabbath. ²⁸They found no legal reason to execute him, but they asked Pilate to have him killed anyway.

²⁹"When they had done all that the prophecies said about him, they took him down from the cross* and placed him in a tomb. ³⁰But God raised him from the dead! ³¹And over a period of many days he appeared to those who had gone with him from Galilee to Jerusalem. They are now his witnesses to the people of Israel.

³²"And now we are here to bring you this Good News. The promise was made to our ancestors, ³³and God has now fulfilled it for us, their descendants, by raising Jesus. This is what the second psalm says about Jesus:

'You are my Son.
  Today I have become your Father.*'

³⁴For God had promised to raise him from the dead, not leaving him to rot in the grave. He said, 'I will give you the sacred blessings I promised to David.'* ³⁵Another psalm explains it more fully: 'You will not allow your Holy One to rot in the grave.'* ³⁶This is not a reference to David, for after David had done the will of God in his own generation, he died and was buried with his ancestors, and his body decayed. ³⁷No, it was a reference to someone else—someone whom God raised and whose body did not decay.

³⁸*"Brothers, listen! We are here to proclaim that through this man Jesus there is forgiveness for your sins. ³⁹Everyone who believes in him is declared right with God—something the law of Moses could never do. ⁴⁰Be careful! Don't let the prophets' words apply to you. For they said,

⁴¹ 'Look, you mockers,
  be amazed and die!

13:29 Greek *from the tree.*   13:33 Or *Today I reveal you as my Son.* Ps 2:7.   13:34 Isa 55:3.
13:35 Ps 16:10.   13:38 English translations divide verses 38 and 39 in various ways.

"God is our chief friend."
~ St. Thomas Aquinas

JOURNAL

JOURNAL

For I am doing something in your own day,
    something you wouldn't believe
    even if someone told you about it.'*"

42As Paul and Barnabas left the synagogue that day, the people begged them to speak about these things again the next week. 43Many Jews and devout converts to Judaism followed Paul and Barnabas, and the two men urged them to continue to rely on the grace of God.

Paul Turns to the Gentiles

44The following week almost the entire city turned out to hear them preach the word of the Lord. 45But when some of the Jews saw the crowds, they were jealous; so they slandered Paul and argued against whatever he said.

46Then Paul and Barnabas spoke out boldly and declared, "It was necessary that we first preach the word of God to you Jews. But since you have rejected it and judged yourselves unworthy of eternal life, we will offer it to the Gentiles. 47For the Lord gave us this command when he said,

'I have made you a light to the Gentiles,
    to bring salvation to the farthest corners of the earth.'*"

48When the Gentiles heard this, they were very glad and thanked the Lord for his message; and all who were chosen for eternal life became believers. 49So the Lord's message spread throughout that region.

50Then the Jews stirred up the influential religious women and the leaders of the city, and they incited a mob against Paul and Barnabas and ran them out of town. 51So they shook the dust from their feet as a sign of rejection and went to the town of Iconium. 52And the believers* were filled with joy and with the Holy Spirit.

CHAPTER **14**

Paul and Barnabas in Iconium

The same thing happened in Iconium.* Paul and Barnabas went to the Jewish synagogue and preached with such power that a great number of both Jews and Greeks became believers. 2Some of the Jews, however, spurned God's message and poisoned the minds of the Gentiles against Paul and Barnabas. 3But the apostles stayed there a long time, preaching boldly

13:41 Hab 1:5 (Greek version). **13:47** Isa 49:6. **13:52** Greek *the disciples.* **14:1** *Iconium,* as well as *Lystra* and *Derbe* (14:6), were towns in what is now Turkey.

about the grace of the Lord. And the Lord proved their message was true by giving them power to do miraculous signs and wonders. [4]But the people of the town were divided in their opinion about them. Some sided with the Jews, and some with the apostles.

[5]Then a mob of Gentiles and Jews, along with their leaders, decided to attack and stone them. [6]When the apostles learned of it, they fled to the region of Lycaonia—to the towns of Lystra and Derbe and the surrounding area. [7]And there they preached the Good News.

Paul and Barnabas in Lystra and Derbe

[8]While they were at Lystra, Paul and Barnabas came upon a man with crippled feet. He had been that way from birth, so he had never walked. He was sitting [9]and listening as Paul preached. Looking straight at him, Paul realized he had faith to be healed. [10]So Paul called to him in a loud voice, "Stand up!" And the man jumped to his feet and started walking.

[11]When the crowd saw what Paul had done, they shouted in their local dialect, "These men are gods in human form!" [12]They decided that Barnabas was the Greek god Zeus and that Paul was Hermes, since he was the chief speaker. [13]Now the temple of Zeus was located just outside the town. So the priest of the temple and the crowd brought bulls and wreaths of flowers to the town gates, and they prepared to offer sacrifices to the apostles.

[14]But when the apostles Barnabas and Paul heard what was happening, they tore their clothing in dismay and ran out among the people, shouting, [15]"Friends,* why are you doing this? We are merely human beings—just like you! We have come to bring you the Good News that you should turn from these worthless things and turn to the living God, who made heaven and earth, the sea, and everything in them. [16]In the past he permitted all the nations to go their own ways, [17]but he never left them without evidence of himself and his goodness. For instance, he sends you rain and good crops and gives you food and joyful hearts." [18]But even with these words, Paul and Barnabas could scarcely restrain the people from sacrificing to them.

[19]Then some Jews arrived from Antioch and Iconium and won the crowds to their side. They stoned Paul and dragged him out of town, thinking he was dead. [20]But as the believers*

14:15 Greek *Men.* 14:20 Greek *disciples;* also in 14:22, 28.

WHAT TO SAY
AND
WHAT NOT TO SAY

FRIENDSHIP TYPE: *Neighbors*   FRIENDSHIP LAYER: *Trust*

Five Neighbor Trust-Builders

 WHAT TO SAY:

★ "Hi. My name is _____, and I'm your neighbor."

★ "I noticed you could use some help carrying that bag of groceries out to the car. I'd be glad to help you."

★ "I'm organizing a block party next Saturday. We'd love to have you come."

★ "I'll take care of it. I promise."

★ "I heard your father died. May I pray for you?"

Five Neighbor Trust-Busters

 WHAT NOT TO SAY:

★ "Hello? Oh, hi. Sure, I remember I said I'd feed your dog while you're on vacation. What? You were gone *last* week?"

★ "You need a stamp? And you want to borrow one? Well…if you'll leave a deposit…"

★ "I'd love to talk, but there's that *Friends* rerun on channel 11…"

★ "I really don't have room in my life for any new friends right now."

★ "Did you hear about that guy over in Accounting? I promised I wouldn't say anything, but you have to *hear* this…"

"*Dear George,
Remember no man
is a failure who has
friends. Thanks for
the wings!
Love,
Clarence.*"

~ *It's a Wonderful Life*

JOURNAL

gathered around him, he got up and went back into the town. The next day he left with Barnabas for Derbe.

Paul and Barnabas Return to Antioch of Syria

21After preaching the Good News in Derbe and making many disciples, Paul and Barnabas returned to Lystra, Iconium, and Antioch of Pisidia, 22where they strengthened the believers. They encouraged them to continue in the faith, reminding them that we must suffer many hardships to enter the Kingdom of God. 23Paul and Barnabas also appointed elders in every church. With prayer and fasting, they turned the elders over to the care of the Lord, in whom they had put their trust. 24Then they traveled back through Pisidia to Pamphylia. 25They preached the word in Perga, then went down to Attalia.

26Finally, they returned by ship to Antioch of Syria, where their journey had begun. The believers there had entrusted them to the grace of God to do the work they had now completed. 27Upon arriving in Antioch, they called the church together and reported everything God had done through them and how he had opened the door of faith to the Gentiles, too. 28And they stayed there with the believers for a long time.

CHAPTER **15**

The Council at Jerusalem

While Paul and Barnabas were at Antioch of Syria, some men from Judea arrived and began to teach the believers*: "Unless you are circumcised as required by the law of Moses, you cannot be saved." 2Paul and Barnabas disagreed with them, arguing vehemently. Finally, the church decided to send Paul and Barnabas to Jerusalem, accompanied by some local believers, to talk to the apostles and elders about this question. 3The church sent the delegates to Jerusalem, and they stopped along the way in Phoenicia and Samaria to visit the believers. They told them— much to everyone's joy—that the Gentiles, too, were being converted.

4When they arrived in Jerusalem, Barnabas and Paul were welcomed by the whole church, including the apostles and elders. They reported everything God had done through them. 5But then some of the believers who belonged to the sect of the Pharisees stood up and insisted, "The Gentile converts must be circumcised and required to follow the law of Moses."

6So the apostles and elders met together to resolve this issue.

15:1 Greek *brothers;* also in 15:3, 23, 32, 33, 36, 40.

7At the meeting, after a long discussion, Peter stood and addressed them as follows: "Brothers, you all know that God chose me from among you some time ago to preach to the Gentiles so that they could hear the Good News and believe. 8God knows people's hearts, and he confirmed that he accepts Gentiles by giving them the Holy Spirit, just as he did to us. 9He made no distinction between us and them, for he cleansed their hearts through faith. 10So why are you now challenging God by burdening the Gentile believers* with a yoke that neither we nor our ancestors were able to bear? 11We believe that we are all saved the same way, by the undeserved grace of the Lord Jesus."

12Everyone listened quietly as Barnabas and Paul told about the miraculous signs and wonders God had done through them among the Gentiles.

13When they had finished, James stood and said, "Brothers, listen to me. 14Peter* has told you about the time God first visited the Gentiles to take from them a people for himself. 15And this conversion of Gentiles is exactly what the prophets predicted. As it is written:

16 'Afterward I will return
      and restore the fallen house* of David.
    I will rebuild its ruins
      and restore it,
17 so that the rest of humanity might seek the LORD,
      including the Gentiles—
      all those I have called to be mine.
    The LORD has spoken—
18   he who made these things known so long ago.'*

19"And so my judgment is that we should not make it difficult for the Gentiles who are turning to God. 20Instead, we should write and tell them to abstain from eating food offered to idols, from sexual immorality, from eating the meat of strangled animals, and from consuming blood. 21For these laws of Moses have been preached in Jewish synagogues in every city on every Sabbath for many generations."

The Letter for Gentile Believers

22Then the apostles and elders together with the whole church in Jerusalem chose delegates, and they sent them to Antioch of Syria with Paul and Barnabas to report on this decision. The

15:10 Greek *disciples.*   **15:14** Greek *Symeon.*   **15:16** Or *kingdom;* Greek reads *tent.*   **15:16-18** Amos 9:11-12 (Greek version); Isa 45:21.

men chosen were two of the church leaders*—Judas (also called Barsabbas) and Silas. ²³This is the letter they took with them:

"This letter is from the apostles and elders, your brothers in Jerusalem. It is written to the Gentile believers in Antioch, Syria, and Cilicia. Greetings!

²⁴"We understand that some men from here have troubled you and upset you with their teaching, but we did not send them! ²⁵So we decided, having come to complete agreement, to send you official representatives, along with our beloved Barnabas and Paul, ²⁶who have risked their lives for the name of our Lord Jesus Christ. ²⁷We are sending Judas and Silas to confirm what we have decided concerning your question.

²⁸"For it seemed good to the Holy Spirit and to us to lay no greater burden on you than these few requirements: ²⁹You must abstain from eating food offered to idols, from consuming blood or the meat of strangled animals, and from sexual immorality. If you do this, you will do well. Farewell."

³⁰The messengers went at once to Antioch, where they called a general meeting of the believers and delivered the letter. ³¹And there was great joy throughout the church that day as they read this encouraging message.

³²Then Judas and Silas, both being prophets, spoke at length to the believers, encouraging and strengthening their faith. ³³They stayed for a while, and then the believers sent them back to the church in Jerusalem with a blessing of peace.* ³⁵Paul and Barnabas stayed in Antioch. They and many others taught and preached the word of the Lord there.

Paul and Barnabas Separate

³⁶After some time Paul said to Barnabas, "Let's go back and visit each city where we previously preached the word of the Lord, to see how the new believers are doing." ³⁷Barnabas agreed and wanted to take along John Mark. ³⁸But Paul disagreed strongly, since John Mark had deserted them in Pamphylia and had not continued with them in their work. ³⁹Their disagreement was so sharp that they separated. Barnabas took John Mark with him and sailed for Cyprus. ⁴⁰Paul chose Silas, and as he left, the believers entrusted him

15:22 Greek *were leaders among the brothers.*   15:33 Some manuscripts add verse 34, *But Silas decided to stay there.*

to the Lord's gracious care. ⁴¹Then he traveled throughout Syria and Cilicia, strengthening the churches there. ⚓

CHAPTER 16

Paul's Second Missionary Journey

Paul went first to Derbe and then to Lystra, where there was a young disciple named Timothy. His mother was a Jewish believer, but his father was a Greek. ²Timothy was well thought of by the believers* in Lystra and Iconium, ³so Paul wanted him to join them on their journey. In deference to the Jews of the area, he arranged for Timothy to be circumcised before they left, for everyone knew that his father was a Greek. ⁴Then they went from town to town, instructing the believers to follow the decisions made by the apostles and elders in Jerusalem. ⁵So the churches were strengthened in their faith and grew larger every day.

A Call from Macedonia

⁶Next Paul and Silas traveled through the area of Phrygia and Galatia, because the Holy Spirit had prevented them from preaching the word in the province of Asia at that time. ⁷Then coming to the borders of Mysia, they headed north for the province of Bithynia,* but again the Spirit of Jesus did not allow them to go there. ⁸So instead, they went on through Mysia to the seaport of Troas.

⁹That night Paul had a vision: A man from Macedonia in northern Greece was standing there, pleading with him, "Come over to Macedonia and help us!" ¹⁰So we* decided to leave for Macedonia at once, having concluded that God was calling us to preach the Good News there.

Lydia of Philippi Believes in Jesus

¹¹We boarded a boat at Troas and sailed straight across to the island of Samothrace, and the next day we landed at Neapolis. ¹²From there we reached Philippi, a major city of that district of Macedonia and a Roman colony. And we stayed there several days.

¹³On the Sabbath we went a little way outside the city to a riverbank, where we thought people would be meeting for

16:2 Greek *brothers;* also in 16:40. 16:6-7 *Phrygia, Galatia, Asia, Mysia,* and *Bithynia* were all districts in what is now Turkey. 16:10 Luke, the writer of this book, here joined Paul and accompanied him on his journey.

Anchor Passage

PASSAGE: Acts 15:36-41

FRIENDSHIP TYPE: *Friends* FRIENDSHIP LAYER: *Deepening*

Divide and Conquer

Have you ever had a disagreement with a close friend? What was it like?

Read **Acts 15:36-41**.

Sometimes a friendship seems so good, as if nothing could ever go wrong. You'll be friends forever…and then something happens. Some small thing gets in the way, and suddenly you're fighting. You can't figure out what happened; everything was going so well.

Conflict is a necessary part of friendships. The truth is, a friendship wouldn't mature without some conflict.

Take a look at Paul and Barnabas—two of the most famous Christian leaders of all time. Even they went head-to-head now and then. They were good friends, serving God together, and they still argued with one another.

Healthy friendships go through times of discord. It's inevitable…and important. Conflict disrupts the norm; it shakes you and causes you to reflect on the friendship. Conflict forces you to decide if a friendship is worth the effort it takes to get through the tough times. And when you decide the friendship is worth it…and you work through the conflict…well, that's taking friendship to a whole new level!

Anchor Passage continues on page 260…

Friendship First NEW TESTAMENT

Anchor Passage continued from page 259...

Paul and Barnabas worked through their conflict and remained friends (**1 Corinthians 9:6**). Though we don't know all the details, we do know that Paul and Barnabas maintained a deep friendship in spite of—maybe because of—their differences.

Experience

Think of a conflict you've recently had with a friend. How might God use your differences to deepen the friendship? Think of ways to discuss the conflict with your friend. Write down aspects of your character (pride, cynicism, impatience) or words you used that might have contributed to the conflict. As tough as it might be, talk to your friend. Then take responsibility for whatever you can in the conflict—without taking the opportunity to blame the rest on your friend! Try to work through the conflict together.

THE ONE THING YOU CAN DO THIS WEEK
1

Reflect

★ How have disagreements deepened your friendships in the past?

★ What's the value of your friendship? Why is it worth working through tough times?

★ How did your friend respond to your offer of reconciliation?

DIGGING DEEPER

FRIENDSHIP TYPE:	FRIENDSHIP LAYER:
Friends	*Deepening*

For deepening your friendships, check out...

➻ The Friendship Experience.............. on page 263
➻ The Friendship Story....................... on page 269
➻ What to Say and What Not to Say .... on page 400

prayer, and we sat down to speak with some women who had gathered there. [14] One of them was Lydia from Thyatira, a merchant of expensive purple cloth, who worshiped God. As she listened to us, the Lord opened her heart, and she accepted what Paul was saying. [15] She was baptized along with other members of her household, and she asked us to be her guests. "If you agree that I am a true believer in the Lord," she said, "come and stay at my home." And she urged us until we agreed.

Paul and Silas in Prison

[16] One day as we were going down to the place of prayer, we met a demon-possessed slave girl. She was a fortune-teller who earned a lot of money for her masters. [17] She followed Paul and the rest of us, shouting, "These men are servants of the Most High God, and they have come to tell you how to be saved."

[18] This went on day after day until Paul got so exasperated that he turned and said to the demon within her, "I command you in the name of Jesus Christ to come out of her." And instantly it left her.

[19] Her masters' hopes of wealth were now shattered, so they grabbed Paul and Silas and dragged them before the authorities at the marketplace. [20] "The whole city is in an uproar because of these Jews!" they shouted to the city officials. [21] "They are teaching customs that are illegal for us Romans to practice."

[22] A mob quickly formed against Paul and Silas, and the city officials ordered them stripped and beaten with wooden rods. [23] They were severely beaten, and then they were thrown into prison. The jailer was ordered to make sure they didn't escape. [24] So the jailer put them into the inner dungeon and clamped their feet in the stocks.

[25] Around midnight Paul and Silas were praying and singing hymns to God, and the other prisoners were listening. [26] Suddenly, there was a massive earthquake, and the prison was shaken to its foundations. All the doors immediately flew open, and the chains of every prisoner fell off! [27] The jailer woke up to see the prison doors wide open. He assumed the prisoners had escaped, so he drew his sword to kill himself. [28] But Paul shouted to him, "Stop! Don't kill yourself! We are all here!"

[29] The jailer called for lights and ran to the dungeon and fell down trembling before Paul and Silas. [30] Then he brought them out and asked, "Sirs, what must I do to be saved?"

[31] They replied, "Believe in the Lord Jesus and you will be

saved, along with everyone in your household." 32And they shared the word of the Lord with him and with all who lived in his household. 33Even at that hour of the night, the jailer cared for them and washed their wounds. Then he and everyone in his household were immediately baptized. 34He brought them into his house and set a meal before them, and he and his entire household rejoiced because they all believed in God.

35The next morning the city officials sent the police to tell the jailer, "Let those men go!" 36So the jailer told Paul, "The city officials have said you and Silas are free to leave. Go in peace."

37But Paul replied, "They have publicly beaten us without a trial and put us in prison—and we are Roman citizens. So now they want us to leave secretly? Certainly not! Let them come themselves to release us!"

38When the police reported this, the city officials were alarmed to learn that Paul and Silas were Roman citizens. 39So they came to the jail and apologized to them. Then they brought them out and begged them to leave the city. 40When Paul and Silas left the prison, they returned to the home of Lydia. There they met with the believers and encouraged them once more. Then they left town.

CHAPTER 17

Paul Preaches in Thessalonica

Paul and Silas then traveled through the towns of Amphipolis and Apollonia and came to Thessalonica, where there was a Jewish synagogue. 2As was Paul's custom, he went to the synagogue service, and for three Sabbaths in a row he used the Scriptures to reason with the people. 3He explained the prophecies and proved that the Messiah must suffer and rise from the dead. He said, "This Jesus I'm telling you about is the Messiah." 4Some of the Jews who listened were persuaded and joined Paul and Silas, along with many God-fearing Greek men and quite a few prominent women.*

5But some of the Jews were jealous, so they gathered some troublemakers from the marketplace to form a mob and start a riot. They attacked the home of Jason, searching for Paul and Silas so they could drag them out to the crowd.* 6Not finding them there, they dragged out Jason and some of the other believers* instead and took them before the city council. "Paul and Silas have caused trouble all over the world," they shouted,

17:4 Some manuscripts read *quite a few of the wives of the leading men.*   17:5 Or *the city council.*
17:6 Greek *brothers;* also in 17:10, 14.

★

Among church members, 70% of those with church friendships that go beyond weekly worship services say others in their sphere of influence would say the members love God. This is 26 percentage points higher than members whose church-based friendships are not as deep.

—from "Friendship and Faith," a Gallup Research Study Commissioned by Group Publishing, Inc.

★

JOURNAL

"and now they are here disturbing our city, too. 7And Jason has
welcomed them into his home. They are all guilty of treason
against Caesar, for they profess allegiance to another king,
named Jesus."
8The people of the city, as well as the city council, were
thrown into turmoil by these reports. 9So the officials forced
Jason and the other believers to post bond, and then they
released them.

Paul and Silas in Berea

10That very night the believers sent Paul and Silas to Berea.
When they arrived there, they went to the Jewish synagogue.
11And the people of Berea were more open-minded than those
in Thessalonica, and they listened eagerly to Paul's message.
They searched the Scriptures day after day to see if Paul and
Silas were teaching the truth. 12As a result, many Jews believed,
as did many of the prominent Greek women and men.
13But when some Jews in Thessalonica learned that Paul was
preaching the word of God in Berea, they went there and stirred
up trouble. 14The believers acted at once, sending Paul on to
the coast, while Silas and Timothy remained behind. 15Those
escorting Paul went with him all the way to Athens; then they
returned to Berea with instructions for Silas and Timothy to
hurry and join him.

Paul Preaches in Athens

16While Paul was waiting for them in Athens, he was deeply
troubled by all the idols he saw everywhere in the city. 17He
went to the synagogue to reason with the Jews and the God-
fearing Gentiles, and he spoke daily in the public square to all
who happened to be there.
18He also had a debate with some of the Epicurean and Stoic
philosophers. When he told them about Jesus and his resurrection, they said, "What's this babbler trying to say with these
strange ideas he's picked up?" Others said, "He seems to be
preaching about some foreign gods."
19Then they took him to the high council of the city.* "Come
and tell us about this new teaching," they said. 20"You are saying
some rather strange things, and we want to know what it's all
about." 21(It should be explained that all the Athenians as well
as the foreigners in Athens seemed to spend all their time discussing the latest ideas.)

17:19 Or *the most learned society of philosophers in the city.* Greek reads *the Areopagus.*

²²So Paul, standing before the council,* addressed them as follows: "Men of Athens, I notice that you are very religious in every way, ²³for as I was walking along I saw your many shrines. And one of your altars had this inscription on it: 'To an Unknown God.' This God, whom you worship without knowing, is the one I'm telling you about.

²⁴"He is the God who made the world and everything in it. Since he is Lord of heaven and earth, he doesn't live in man-made temples, ²⁵and human hands can't serve his needs—for he has no needs. He himself gives life and breath to everything, and he satisfies every need. ²⁶From one man* he created all the nations throughout the whole earth. He decided beforehand when they should rise and fall, and he determined their boundaries.

²⁷"His purpose was for the nations to seek after God and perhaps feel their way toward him and find him—though he is not far from any one of us. ²⁸For in him we live and move and exist. As some of your* own poets have said, 'We are his offspring.' ²⁹And since this is true, we shouldn't think of God as an idol designed by craftsmen from gold or silver or stone.

³⁰"God overlooked people's ignorance about these things in earlier times, but now he commands everyone everywhere to repent of their sins and turn to him. ³¹For he has set a day for judging the world with justice by the man he has appointed, and he proved to everyone who this is by raising him from the dead."

³²When they heard Paul speak about the resurrection of the dead, some laughed in contempt, but others said, "We want to hear more about this later." ³³That ended Paul's discussion with them, ³⁴but some joined him and became believers. Among them were Dionysius, a member of the council,* a woman named Damaris, and others with them.

CHAPTER **18**

Paul Meets Priscilla and Aquila in Corinth

Then Paul left Athens and went to Corinth.* ²There he became acquainted with a Jew named Aquila, born in Pontus, who had recently arrived from Italy with his wife, Priscilla. They had left Italy when Claudius Caesar deported all Jews from Rome. ³Paul lived and worked with them, for they were tentmakers* just as he was.

17:22 Traditionally rendered *standing in the middle of Mars Hill;* Greek reads *standing in the middle of the Areopagus.*   17:26 Greek *From one;* other manuscripts read *From one blood.*   17:28 Some manuscripts read *our.*   17:34 Greek *an Areopagite.*   18:1 *Athens* and *Corinth* were major cities in Achaia, the region in the southern portion of the Greek peninsula.   18:3 Or *leather-workers.*

FRIENDSHIP
EXPERIENCE

FRIENDSHIP TYPE: *Friends*   FRIENDSHIP LAYER: *Deepening*

The Old Couch

When you keep a piece of furniture in the same place day in and day out, you start to forget about it. You sit on it, you throw things on it, you walk past it, but you don't really *notice* it. You don't think about what color it is, how it looks in that space, or how much you liked it when you bought it.

Sometimes our friendships get to be the same way. If you see your friend each and every day in the same context, you may stop noticing the person and start taking him or her for granted! You talk to one another, maybe you carpool together or have dinner together every Friday, but you quit really noticing each other. You don't think about what you value in your friend, how much your friendship means to you, or why you became friends in the first place.

Sometimes it takes a bit of a disruption to make you notice each other again.

FRIENDSHIP EXPERIENCE *continues on page 264...*

Friendship First NEW TESTAMENT

FRIENDSHIP EXPERIENCE *continued from page 263…*

Experience

See your friend in a new context. This week, do something with a friend that you've never done together. Go camping with a friend from work; volunteer with a friend from your neighborhood; go to a movie with a friend from church.

A friendship with God works the same way. God can become like a piece of familiar furniture in your life. You go to church every week. You pray every morning. You go to a Bible study on Wednesdays. And the rest of the week? God's there, but you don't really notice.

Disrupt that pattern: Think of something *different* you can do with God, something to help you experience your friendship with him in a new way. Go for a nature walk as you pray. Climb to the highest point in your area, and praise God. Ask some friends to tell you about their experiences with God. You'll start to see God in a new light (**Acts 17:27**).

THE ONE THING YOU CAN DO THIS WEEK

1

Reflect

★ Think of a friendship. How have you let it grow too familiar?

★ What can you regularly do to "disrupt" the familiarity in your friendships?

★ What did you learn about your friend and about God when you did something new together?

4 Each Sabbath found Paul at the synagogue, trying to convince the Jews and Greeks alike. 5 And after Silas and Timothy came down from Macedonia, Paul spent all his time preaching the word. He testified to the Jews that Jesus was the Messiah. 6 But when they opposed and insulted him, Paul shook the dust from his clothes and said, "Your blood is upon your own heads—I am innocent. From now on I will go preach to the Gentiles."

7 Then he left and went to the home of Titius Justus, a Gentile who worshiped God and lived next door to the synagogue. 8 Crispus, the leader of the synagogue, and everyone in his household believed in the Lord. Many others in Corinth also heard Paul, became believers, and were baptized.

9 One night the Lord spoke to Paul in a vision and told him, "Don't be afraid! Speak out! Don't be silent! 10 For I am with you, and no one will attack and harm you, for many people in this city belong to me." 11 So Paul stayed there for the next year and a half, teaching the word of God.

12 But when Gallio became governor of Achaia, some Jews rose up together against Paul and brought him before the governor for judgment. 13 They accused Paul of "persuading people to worship God in ways that are contrary to our law."

14 But just as Paul started to make his defense, Gallio turned to Paul's accusers and said, "Listen, you Jews, if this were a case involving some wrongdoing or a serious crime, I would have a reason to accept your case. 15 But since it is merely a question of words and names and your Jewish law, take care of it yourselves. I refuse to judge such matters." 16 And he threw them out of the courtroom.

17 The crowd* then grabbed Sosthenes, the leader of the synagogue, and beat him right there in the courtroom. But Gallio paid no attention.

Paul Returns to Antioch of Syria

18 Paul stayed in Corinth for some time after that, then said good-bye to the brothers and sisters* and went to nearby Cenchrea. There he shaved his head according to Jewish custom, marking the end of a vow. Then he set sail for Syria, taking Priscilla and Aquila with him.

19 They stopped first at the port of Ephesus, where Paul left the others behind. While he was there, he went to the synagogue to reason with the Jews. 20 They asked him to stay longer, but he declined. 21 As he left, however, he said, "I will come back

18:17 Greek *Everyone;* other manuscripts read *All the Greeks.*   **18:18** Greek *brothers;* also in 18:27.

later,* God willing." Then he set sail from Ephesus. [22]The next stop was at the port of Caesarea. From there he went up and visited the church at Jerusalem* and then went back to Antioch.

[23]After spending some time in Antioch, Paul went back through Galatia and Phrygia, visiting and strengthening all the believers.*

Apollos Instructed at Ephesus

[24]Meanwhile, a Jew named Apollos, an eloquent speaker who knew the Scriptures well, had arrived in Ephesus from Alexandria in Egypt. [25]He had been taught the way of the Lord, and he taught others about Jesus with an enthusiastic spirit* and with accuracy. However, he knew only about John's baptism. [26]When Priscilla and Aquila heard him preaching boldly in the synagogue, they took him aside and explained the way of God even more accurately.

[27]Apollos had been thinking about going to Achaia, and the brothers and sisters in Ephesus encouraged him to go. They wrote to the believers in Achaia, asking them to welcome him. When he arrived there, he proved to be of great benefit to those who, by God's grace, had believed. [28]He refuted the Jews with powerful arguments in public debate. Using the Scriptures, he explained to them that Jesus was the Messiah.

CHAPTER **19**

Paul's Third Missionary Journey

While Apollos was in Corinth, Paul traveled through the interior regions until he reached Ephesus, on the coast, where he found several believers.* [2]"Did you receive the Holy Spirit when you believed?" he asked them.

"No," they replied, "we haven't even heard that there is a Holy Spirit."

[3]"Then what baptism did you experience?" he asked.

And they replied, "The baptism of John."

[4]Paul said, "John's baptism called for repentance from sin. But John himself told the people to believe in the one who would come later, meaning Jesus."

[5]As soon as they heard this, they were baptized in the name of the Lord Jesus. [6]Then when Paul laid his hands on them, the Holy Spirit came on them, and they spoke in other tongues and prophesied. [7]There were about twelve men in all.

18:21 Some manuscripts read *"I must by all means be at Jerusalem for the upcoming festival, but I will come back later."* **18:22** Greek *the church.* **18:23** Greek *disciples;* also in 18:27. **18:25** Or *with enthusiasm in the Spirit.* **19:1** Greek *disciples;* also in 19:9, 30.

JOURNAL

"Between friends differences in taste or opinion are irritating in direct proportion to their triviality."

~ W. H. Auden

Paul Ministers in Ephesus

8 Then Paul went to the synagogue and preached boldly for the next three months, arguing persuasively about the Kingdom of God. 9 But some became stubborn, rejecting his message and publicly speaking against the Way. So Paul left the synagogue and took the believers with him. Then he held daily discussions at the lecture hall of Tyrannus. 10 This went on for the next two years, so that people throughout the province of Asia—both Jews and Greeks—heard the word of the Lord.

11 God gave Paul the power to perform unusual miracles. 12 When handkerchiefs or aprons that had merely touched his skin were placed on sick people, they were healed of their diseases, and evil spirits were expelled.

13 A group of Jews was traveling from town to town casting out evil spirits. They tried to use the name of the Lord Jesus in their incantation, saying, "I command you in the name of Jesus, whom Paul preaches, to come out!" 14 Seven sons of Sceva, a leading priest, were doing this. 15 But one time when they tried it, the evil spirit replied, "I know Jesus, and I know Paul, but who are you?" 16 Then the man with the evil spirit leaped on them, overpowered them, and attacked them with such violence that they fled from the house, naked and battered.

17 The story of what happened spread quickly all through Ephesus, to Jews and Greeks alike. A solemn fear descended on the city, and the name of the Lord Jesus was greatly honored. 18 Many who became believers confessed their sinful practices. 19 A number of them who had been practicing sorcery brought their incantation books and burned them at a public bonfire. The value of the books was several million dollars.* 20 So the message about the Lord spread widely and had a powerful effect.

21 Afterward Paul felt compelled by the Spirit* to go over to Macedonia and Achaia before going to Jerusalem. "And after that," he said, "I must go on to Rome!" 22 He sent his two assistants, Timothy and Erastus, ahead to Macedonia while he stayed awhile longer in the province of Asia.

The Riot in Ephesus

23 About that time, serious trouble developed in Ephesus concerning the Way. 24 It began with Demetrius, a silversmith who had a large business manufacturing silver shrines of the Greek goddess Artemis.* He kept many craftsmen busy. 25 He called

19:19 Greek *50,000 pieces of silver,* each of which was the equivalent of a day's wage. 19:21 Or *decided in his spirit.* 19:24 *Artemis* is otherwise known as Diana.

them together, along with others employed in similar trades, and addressed them as follows:

"Gentlemen, you know that our wealth comes from this business. [26]But as you have seen and heard, this man Paul has persuaded many people that handmade gods aren't really gods at all. And he's done this not only here in Ephesus but throughout the entire province! [27]Of course, I'm not just talking about the loss of public respect for our business. I'm also concerned that the temple of the great goddess Artemis will lose its influence and that Artemis—this magnificent goddess worshiped throughout the province of Asia and all around the world—will be robbed of her great prestige!"

[28]At this their anger boiled, and they began shouting, "Great is Artemis of the Ephesians!" [29]Soon the whole city was filled with confusion. Everyone rushed to the amphitheater, dragging along Gaius and Aristarchus, who were Paul's traveling companions from Macedonia. [30]Paul wanted to go in, too, but the believers wouldn't let him. [31]Some of the officials of the province, friends of Paul, also sent a message to him, begging him not to risk his life by entering the amphitheater.

[32]Inside, the people were all shouting, some one thing and some another. Everything was in confusion. In fact, most of them didn't even know why they were there. [33]The Jews in the crowd pushed Alexander forward and told him to explain the situation. He motioned for silence and tried to speak. [34]But when the crowd realized he was a Jew, they started shouting again and kept it up for two hours: "Great is Artemis of the Ephesians! Great is Artemis of the Ephesians!"

[35]At last the mayor was able to quiet them down enough to speak. "Citizens of Ephesus," he said. "Everyone knows that Ephesus is the official guardian of the temple of the great Artemis, whose image fell down to us from heaven. [36]Since this is an undeniable fact, you should stay calm and not do anything rash. [37]You have brought these men here, but they have stolen nothing from the temple and have not spoken against our goddess.

[38]"If Demetrius and the craftsmen have a case against them, the courts are in session and the officials can hear the case at once. Let them make formal charges. [39]And if there are complaints about other matters, they can be settled in a legal assembly. [40]I am afraid we are in danger of being charged with rioting by the Roman government, since there is no cause for all this commotion. And if Rome demands an

---

★

A full **74%** of church members who worship with a **best friend** (not a family member) say their faith is involved in **every aspect** of their lives—20 percentage points higher than those who worship without a best friend at church.

—from "Friendship and Faith," a Gallup Research Study Commissioned by Group Publishing, Inc.

★

JOURNAL

JOURNAL

explanation, we won't know what to say." [41] *Then he dismissed them, and they dispersed.

CHAPTER 20

Paul Goes to Macedonia and Greece

When the uproar was over, Paul sent for the believers* and encouraged them. Then he said good-bye and left for Macedonia. [2] While there, he encouraged the believers in all the towns he passed through. Then he traveled down to Greece, [3] where he stayed for three months. He was preparing to sail back to Syria when he discovered a plot by some Jews against his life, so he decided to return through Macedonia.

[4] Several men were traveling with him. They were Sopater son of Pyrrhus from Berea; Aristarchus and Secundus from Thessalonica; Gaius from Derbe; Timothy; and Tychicus and Trophimus from the province of Asia. [5] They went on ahead and waited for us at Troas. [6] After the Passover* ended, we boarded a ship at Philippi in Macedonia and five days later joined them in Troas, where we stayed a week.

Paul's Final Visit to Troas

[7] On the first day of the week, we gathered with the local believers to share in the Lord's Supper.* Paul was preaching to them, and since he was leaving the next day, he kept talking until midnight. [8] The upstairs room where we met was lighted with many flickering lamps. [9] As Paul spoke on and on, a young man named Eutychus, sitting on the windowsill, became very drowsy. Finally, he fell sound asleep and dropped three stories to his death below. [10] Paul went down, bent over him, and took him into his arms. "Don't worry," he said, "he's alive!" [11] Then they all went back upstairs, shared in the Lord's Supper,* and ate together. Paul continued talking to them until dawn, and then he left. [12] Meanwhile, the young man was taken home unhurt, and everyone was greatly relieved.

Paul Meets the Ephesian Elders

[13] Paul went by land to Assos, where he had arranged for us to join him, while we traveled by ship. [14] He joined us there, and we sailed together to Mitylene. [15] The next day we sailed past the island of Kios. The following day we crossed to the island of Samos, and* a day later we arrived at Miletus.

19:41 Some translations include verse 41 as part of verse 40.   **20:1** Greek *disciples*.   **20:6** Greek *the days of unleavened bread*.   **20:7** Greek *to break bread*.   **20:11** Greek *broke the bread*.   **20:15** Some manuscripts read *and having stayed at Trogyllium*.

¹⁶Paul had decided to sail on past Ephesus, for he didn't want to spend any more time in the province of Asia. He was hurrying to get to Jerusalem, if possible, in time for the Festival of Pentecost. ¹⁷But when we landed at Miletus, he sent a message to the elders of the church at Ephesus, asking them to come and meet him.

¹⁸When they arrived he declared, "You know that from the day I set foot in the province of Asia until now ¹⁹I have done the Lord's work humbly and with many tears. I have endured the trials that came to me from the plots of the Jews. ²⁰I never shrank back from telling you what you needed to hear, either publicly or in your homes. ²¹I have had one message for Jews and Greeks alike—the necessity of repenting from sin and turning to God, and of having faith in our Lord Jesus.

²²"And now I am bound by the Spirit* to go to Jerusalem. I don't know what awaits me, ²³except that the Holy Spirit tells me in city after city that jail and suffering lie ahead. ²⁴But my life is worth nothing to me unless I use it for finishing the work assigned me by the Lord Jesus—the work of telling others the Good News about the wonderful grace of God.

²⁵"And now I know that none of you to whom I have preached the Kingdom will ever see me again. ²⁶I declare today that I have been faithful. If anyone suffers eternal death, it's not my fault,* ²⁷for I didn't shrink from declaring all that God wants you to know.

²⁸"So guard yourselves and God's people. Feed and shepherd God's flock—his church, purchased with his own blood*—over which the Holy Spirit has appointed you as elders.* ²⁹I know that false teachers, like vicious wolves, will come in among you after I leave, not sparing the flock. ³⁰Even some men from your own group will rise up and distort the truth in order to draw a following. ³¹Watch out! Remember the three years I was with you—my constant watch and care over you night and day, and my many tears for you.

³²"And now I entrust you to God and the message of his grace that is able to build you up and give you an inheritance with all those he has set apart for himself.

³³"I have never coveted anyone's silver or gold or fine clothes. ³⁴You know that these hands of mine have worked to supply my own needs and even the needs of those who were with me. ³⁵And I have been a constant example of how you can help

20:22 Or *by my spirit,* or *by an inner compulsion;* Greek reads *by the spirit.* **20:26** Greek *I am innocent of the blood of all.* **20:28a** Or *with the blood of his own [Son].* **20:28b** Greek *overseers.*

No. 08-FS-269

FRIENDSHIP STORY

FRIENDSHIP TYPE: *Friends*

FRIENDSHIP LAYER: *Deepening*

FOUND IN SCRIPTURE

Carried Away

Imagine this: You're walking with a close friend, just hanging out, when your friend is suddenly swept away by a chariot of fire. No, really. And if that isn't crazy enough, the chariot pulls your friend *up into the sky* in a tornadolike, whirlwind storm thing. What are you feeling? Scared, amazed, regretful?

Well, how about if it weren't a surprise, and you *knew* your friend was about to be taken away into heaven—and this was the last time you were going to be together on Earth? What would you say? What kinds of things would you tell your friend? What would you want to do together?

Seems like a taking-it-to-the-next-level, deepening moment in a friendship. Second Kings tells us about Elijah and Elisha, two prophets who experienced this exact next-level moment in their friendship. Elijah and Elisha had been traveling and doing the prophet thing for years together. They were undoubtedly close. But not close in the "a chariot of fire is carrying one of us away as we speak" close.

Not until one day when Elisha found out the big news: Elijah wasn't going to be around much longer. Like, for good. Perhaps to make the parting easier, Elijah gave his friend the option to avoid the scene: "Stay here, man, because God is telling me to go to another town." Elisha's strong, immediate response? "I won't leave you." He was basically letting his friend and mentor know his feelings: "I care about you, and I want to be with you until the end."

FRIENDSHIP STORY *continues on page 270...*

FRIENDSHIP STORY *continued from page 269...*

Deepening a friendship means being open and vulnerable. It means showing affection when it may be uncomfortable. It means sharing emotions you don't normally expose...and asking questions that are tough to ask.

Speaking of tough questions, right when Elijah was about to be carried up into heaven, Elisha asked if he could be Elijah's successor and inherit a double share of Elijah's spirit...a powerful, God-given spirit. Wow, talk about a big request. And what a risk. But a risk that paid off—Elisha was granted his wish.

This scene is a clear picture of two friends going deeper in their friendship. And as a result of his vulnerability and courage to ask the difficult question, Elisha also went deeper in his friendship with God. After Elijah's grand exit, the Bible immediately tells us about a miracle God performed through Elisha. You have to be pretty close to God for that...

Opening up, showing emotion and affection, and asking the tough questions. Which of these risks will you take to go deeper with a friend and with Jesus?

Read the entire story in 1 Kings 19 and 2 Kings 2, in the Old Testament.

FRIENDSHIP STORY *continues on page 271...*

those in need by working hard. You should remember the words of the Lord Jesus: 'It is more blessed to give than to receive.'"

36When he had finished speaking, he knelt and prayed with them. 37They all cried as they embraced and kissed him good-bye. 38They were sad most of all because he had said that they would never see him again. Then they escorted him down to the ship.

CHAPTER 21

Paul's Journey to Jerusalem

After saying farewell to the Ephesian elders, we sailed straight to the island of Cos. The next day we reached Rhodes and then went to Patara. 2There we boarded a ship sailing for Phoenicia. 3We sighted the island of Cyprus, passed it on our left, and landed at the harbor of Tyre, in Syria, where the ship was to unload its cargo.

4We went ashore, found the local believers,* and stayed with them a week. These believers prophesied through the Holy Spirit that Paul should not go on to Jerusalem. 5When we returned to the ship at the end of the week, the entire congregation, including women* and children, left the city and came down to the shore with us. There we knelt, prayed, 6and said our farewells. Then we went aboard, and they returned home.

7The next stop after leaving Tyre was Ptolemais, where we greeted the brothers and sisters* and stayed for one day. 8The next day we went on to Caesarea and stayed at the home of Philip the Evangelist, one of the seven men who had been chosen to distribute food. 9He had four unmarried daughters who had the gift of prophecy.

10Several days later a man named Agabus, who also had the gift of prophecy, arrived from Judea. 11He came over, took Paul's belt, and bound his own feet and hands with it. Then he said, "The Holy Spirit declares, 'So shall the owner of this belt be bound by the Jewish leaders in Jerusalem and turned over to the Gentiles.'" 12When we heard this, we and the local believers all begged Paul not to go on to Jerusalem.

13But he said, "Why all this weeping? You are breaking my heart! I am ready not only to be jailed at Jerusalem but even to die for the sake of the Lord Jesus." 14When it was clear that we couldn't persuade him, we gave up and said, "The Lord's will be done."

21:4 Greek *disciples;* also in 21:16. **21:5** Or *wives.* **21:7** Greek *brothers;* also in 21:17.

Paul Arrives at Jerusalem

¹⁵After this we packed our things and left for Jerusalem. ¹⁶Some believers from Caesarea accompanied us, and they took us to the home of Mnason, a man originally from Cyprus and one of the early believers. ¹⁷When we arrived, the brothers and sisters in Jerusalem welcomed us warmly.

¹⁸The next day Paul went with us to meet with James, and all the elders of the Jerusalem church were present. ¹⁹After greeting them, Paul gave a detailed account of the things God had accomplished among the Gentiles through his ministry.

²⁰After hearing this, they praised God. And then they said, "You know, dear brother, how many thousands of Jews have also believed, and they all follow the law of Moses very seriously. ²¹But the Jewish believers here in Jerusalem have been told that you are teaching all the Jews who live among the Gentiles to turn their backs on the laws of Moses. They've heard that you teach them not to circumcise their children or follow other Jewish customs. ²²What should we do? They will certainly hear that you have come.

²³"Here's what we want you to do. We have four men here who have completed their vow. ²⁴Go with them to the Temple and join them in the purification ceremony, paying for them to have their heads ritually shaved. Then everyone will know that the rumors are all false and that you yourself observe the Jewish laws.

²⁵"As for the Gentile believers, they should do what we already told them in a letter: They should abstain from eating food offered to idols, from consuming blood or the meat of strangled animals, and from sexual immorality."

Paul Is Arrested

²⁶So Paul went to the Temple the next day with the other men. They had already started the purification ritual, so he publicly announced the date when their vows would end and sacrifices would be offered for each of them.

²⁷The seven days were almost ended when some Jews from the province of Asia saw Paul in the Temple and roused a mob against him. They grabbed him, ²⁸yelling, "Men of Israel, help us! This is the man who preaches against our people everywhere and tells everybody to disobey the Jewish laws. He speaks against the Temple—and even defiles this holy place by bringing in Gentiles.*" ²⁹(For earlier that day they had seen

21:28 Greek *Greeks.*

FRIENDSHIP STORY *continued from page 270…*

THE ONE THING 1 YOU CAN DO THIS WEEK

Experience

Hang out one-on-one with a friend, and intentionally talk to that friend as if you may not see him or her again. And if that seems a little dramatic…well, OK. You may end up saying some dramatic stuff. But the risk will be worth it. You might share a feeling or thought you never would have dared to before, such as "I want you to know how grateful I am for the ways you encourage me." Or you may ask your friend a question you've been too scared to ask, such as "Could you try to do a better job listening to me?" And if you get into a sticky disagreement, read **Acts 15:36-41** for a glimpse into conflict between another set of friends. No matter what happens, it's worth the risk to deepen your friendship and go to that next level of intimacy and trust.

Reflect

★ If you and your best friend were about to part forever, what would you say or do? Why is that perspective important to your friendship now?

★ What risks will you take to go deeper in your friendships?

him in the city with Trophimus, a Gentile from Ephesus,* and they assumed Paul had taken him into the Temple.)

³⁰ The whole city was rocked by these accusations, and a great riot followed. Paul was grabbed and dragged out of the Temple, and immediately the gates were closed behind him. ³¹ As they were trying to kill him, word reached the commander of the Roman regiment that all Jerusalem was in an uproar. ³² He immediately called out his soldiers and officers* and ran down among the crowd. When the mob saw the commander and the troops coming, they stopped beating Paul.

³³ Then the commander arrested him and ordered him bound with two chains. He asked the crowd who he was and what he had done. ³⁴ Some shouted one thing and some another. Since he couldn't find out the truth in all the uproar and confusion, he ordered that Paul be taken to the fortress. ³⁵ As Paul reached the stairs, the mob grew so violent the soldiers had to lift him to their shoulders to protect him. ³⁶ And the crowd followed behind, shouting, "Kill him, kill him!"

Paul Speaks to the Crowd

³⁷ As Paul was about to be taken inside, he said to the commander, "May I have a word with you?"

"Do you know Greek?" the commander asked, surprised. ³⁸ "Aren't you the Egyptian who led a rebellion some time ago and took 4,000 members of the Assassins out into the desert?"

³⁹ "No," Paul replied, "I am a Jew and a citizen of Tarsus in Cilicia, which is an important city. Please, let me talk to these people." ⁴⁰ The commander agreed, so Paul stood on the stairs and motioned to the people to be quiet. Soon a deep silence enveloped the crowd, and he addressed them in their own language, Aramaic.*

CHAPTER **22**

"Brothers and esteemed fathers," Paul said, "listen to me as I offer my defense." ² When they heard him speaking in their own language,* the silence was even greater.

³ Then Paul said, "I am a Jew, born in Tarsus, a city in Cilicia, and I was brought up and educated here in Jerusalem under Gamaliel. As his student, I was carefully trained in our Jewish laws and customs. I became very zealous to honor God in everything I did, just like all of you today. ⁴ And I persecuted the followers of the Way, hounding some to death, arresting

21:29 Greek *Trophimus, the Ephesian.*   21:32 Greek *centurions.*   21:40 Or *Hebrew.*   22:2 Greek *in Aramaic,* or *in Hebrew.*

both men and women and throwing them in prison. ⁵The high priest and the whole council of elders can testify that this is so. For I received letters from them to our Jewish brothers in Damascus, authorizing me to bring the Christians from there to Jerusalem, in chains, to be punished.

⁶"As I was on the road, approaching Damascus about noon, a very bright light from heaven suddenly shone down around me. ⁷I fell to the ground and heard a voice saying to me, 'Saul, Saul, why are you persecuting me?'

⁸"'Who are you, lord?' I asked.

"And the voice replied, 'I am Jesus the Nazarene,* the one you are persecuting.' ⁹The people with me saw the light but didn't understand the voice speaking to me.

¹⁰"I asked, 'What should I do, Lord?'

"And the Lord told me, 'Get up and go into Damascus, and there you will be told everything you are to do.'

¹¹"I was blinded by the intense light and had to be led by the hand to Damascus by my companions. ¹²A man named Ananias lived there. He was a godly man, deeply devoted to the law, and well regarded by all the Jews of Damascus. ¹³He came and stood beside me and said, 'Brother Saul, regain your sight.' And that very moment I could see him!

¹⁴"Then he told me, 'The God of our ancestors has chosen you to know his will and to see the Righteous One and hear him speak. ¹⁵For you are to be his witness, telling everyone what you have seen and heard. ¹⁶What are you waiting for? Get up and be baptized. Have your sins washed away by calling on the name of the Lord.'

¹⁷"After I returned to Jerusalem, I was praying in the Temple and fell into a trance. ¹⁸I saw a vision of Jesus* saying to me, 'Hurry! Leave Jerusalem, for the people here won't accept your testimony about me.'

¹⁹"'But Lord,' I argued, 'they certainly know that in every synagogue I imprisoned and beat those who believed in you. ²⁰And I was in complete agreement when your witness Stephen was killed. I stood by and kept the coats they took off when they stoned him.'

²¹"But the Lord said to me, 'Go, for I will send you far away to the Gentiles!'"

²²The crowd listened until Paul said that word. Then they all began to shout, "Away with such a fellow! He isn't fit to live!" ²³They yelled, threw off their coats, and tossed handfuls of dust into the air.

22:8 Or *Jesus of Nazareth.*   22:18 Greek *him.*

FRIENDSHIP EXPERIENCE

FRIENDSHIP TYPE:	FRIENDSHIP LAYER:
Neighbors	*Trust*

Welcome to the Neighborhood...Sorta

They live on your street, but you don't know their names.

They've been in the next apartment for three months, but you've never actually seen them. You only hear muffled conversations through the wall.

They're your neighbors...sorta.

You hear them clicking away on keyboards in a neighboring cube. They drop off your paper and pick up your interoffice mail.

They're your neighbors...sorta.

But so what? Really, who cares?

When you need to borrow a drill bit, *you'll* care. When your neighbor needs someone to lend a hand, your *neighbor* will care.

If you want to trust—or be trusted by—people who live and work near you, there's no skipping the get-to-know-you step.

And here's the truth: The process can be an absolute joy.

FRIENDSHIP EXPERIENCE *continues on page 274...*

Friendship First NEW TESTAMENT

FRIENDSHIP EXPERIENCE *continued from page 273...*

Experience

Create a neighborhood directory, and then distribute it.

When Jim started his neighborhood directory project, he had ulterior motives for knocking on the doors of his neighbors. "I hoped I'd find teenage girls who might baby-sit my kids," he says. But he found more than just that.

He discovered that his neighbors didn't know each other—or know how to get to know each other. Jim's offer to type up a directory listing each person's name, address, and anything they wanted their neighbors to know was met with enthusiasm.

The cost? A few evenings and some photocopies.

The benefit? What had been a collection of houses became more of a neighborhood. And even better: Jim's neighbors all knew and trusted him.

Consider creating a directory of *your* neighborhood...or the other students on your floor of the dorm...or the cubicles near yours at work.

FRIENDSHIP EXPERIENCE *continues on page 275...*

Paul Reveals His Roman Citizenship

24 The commander brought Paul inside and ordered him lashed with whips to make him confess his crime. He wanted to find out why the crowd had become so furious. 25 When they tied Paul down to lash him, Paul said to the officer* standing there, "Is it legal for you to whip a Roman citizen who hasn't even been tried?"

26 When the officer heard this, he went to the commander and asked, "What are you doing? This man is a Roman citizen!"

27 So the commander went over and asked Paul, "Tell me, are you a Roman citizen?"

"Yes, I certainly am," Paul replied.

28 "I am, too," the commander muttered, "and it cost me plenty!" Paul answered, "But I am a citizen by birth!"

29 The soldiers who were about to interrogate Paul quickly withdrew when they heard he was a Roman citizen, and the commander was frightened because he had ordered him bound and whipped.

Paul before the High Council

30 The next day the commander ordered the leading priests into session with the Jewish high council.* He wanted to find out what the trouble was all about, so he released Paul to have him stand before them.

CHAPTER **23**

Gazing intently at the high council,* Paul began: "Brothers, I have always lived before God with a clear conscience!"

2 Instantly Ananias the high priest commanded those close to Paul to slap him on the mouth. 3 But Paul said to him, "God will slap you, you corrupt hypocrite!* What kind of judge are you to break the law yourself by ordering me struck like that?"

4 Those standing near Paul said to him, "Do you dare to insult God's high priest?"

5 "I'm sorry, brothers. I didn't realize he was the high priest," Paul replied, "for the Scriptures say, 'You must not speak evil of any of your rulers.'*"

6 Paul realized that some members of the high council were Sadducees and some were Pharisees, so he shouted, "Brothers, I am a Pharisee, as were my ancestors! And I am on trial because my hope is in the resurrection of the dead!"

7 This divided the council—the Pharisees against the Saddu-

22:25 Greek *the centurion;* also in 22:26. 22:30 Greek *Sanhedrin.* 23:1 Greek *Sanhedrin;* also in 23:6, 15, 20, 28. 23:3 Greek *you whitewashed wall.* 23:5 Exod 22:28.

cees—[8] for the Sadducees say there is no resurrection or angels or spirits, but the Pharisees believe in all of these. [9] So there was a great uproar. Some of the teachers of religious law who were Pharisees jumped up and began to argue forcefully. "We see nothing wrong with him," they shouted. "Perhaps a spirit or an angel spoke to him." [10] As the conflict grew more violent, the commander was afraid they would tear Paul apart. So he ordered his soldiers to go and rescue him by force and take him back to the fortress.

[11] That night the Lord appeared to Paul and said, "Be encouraged, Paul. Just as you have been a witness to me here in Jerusalem, you must preach the Good News in Rome as well."

The Plan to Kill Paul

[12] The next morning a group of Jews* got together and bound themselves with an oath not to eat or drink until they had killed Paul. [13] There were more than forty of them in the conspiracy. [14] They went to the leading priests and elders and told them, "We have bound ourselves with an oath to eat nothing until we have killed Paul. [15] So you and the high council should ask the commander to bring Paul back to the council again. Pretend you want to examine his case more fully. We will kill him on the way."

[16] But Paul's nephew—his sister's son—heard of their plan and went to the fortress and told Paul. [17] Paul called for one of the Roman officers* and said, "Take this young man to the commander. He has something important to tell him."

[18] So the officer did, explaining, "Paul, the prisoner, called me over and asked me to bring this young man to you because he has something to tell you."

[19] The commander took his hand, led him aside, and asked, "What is it you want to tell me?"

[20] Paul's nephew told him, "Some Jews are going to ask you to bring Paul before the high council tomorrow, pretending they want to get some more information. [21] But don't do it! There are more than forty men hiding along the way ready to ambush him. They have vowed not to eat or drink anything until they have killed him. They are ready now, just waiting for your consent."

[22] "Don't let anyone know you told me this," the commander warned the young man.

Paul Is Sent to Caesarea

[23] Then the commander called two of his officers and ordered, "Get 200 soldiers ready to leave for Caesarea at nine o'clock

23:12 Greek *the Jews.*   23:17 Greek *centurions;* also in 23:23.

FRIENDSHIP EXPERIENCE *continued from page 274...*

Reflect

★ How well do you trust your neighbors? What interferes with your trusting them more?

★ What might change if you reached out to your neighbors with a directory or other service project?

★ If you were designing your own directory entry right now, what would you want your neighbors to know about you?

JOURNAL

tonight. Also take 200 spearmen and 70 mounted troops. [24] Provide horses for Paul to ride, and get him safely to Governor Felix." [25] Then he wrote this letter to the governor:

[26] "From Claudius Lysias, to his Excellency, Governor Felix: Greetings!

[27] "This man was seized by some Jews, and they were about to kill him when I arrived with the troops. When I learned that he was a Roman citizen, I removed him to safety. [28] Then I took him to their high council to try to learn the basis of the accusations against him. [29] I soon discovered the charge was something regarding their religious law—certainly nothing worthy of imprisonment or death. [30] But when I was informed of a plot to kill him, I immediately sent him on to you. I have told his accusers to bring their charges before you."

[31] So that night, as ordered, the soldiers took Paul as far as Antipatris. [32] They returned to the fortress the next morning, while the mounted troops took him on to Caesarea. [33] When they arrived in Caesarea, they presented Paul and the letter to Governor Felix. [34] He read it and then asked Paul what province he was from. "Cilicia," Paul answered.

[35] "I will hear your case myself when your accusers arrive," the governor told him. Then the governor ordered him kept in the prison at Herod's headquarters.*

CHAPTER 24

Paul Appears before Felix

Five days later Ananias, the high priest, arrived with some of the Jewish elders and the lawyer* Tertullus, to present their case against Paul to the governor. [2] When Paul was called in, Tertullus presented the charges against Paul in the following address to the governor:

"Your Excellency, you have provided a long period of peace for us Jews and with foresight have enacted reforms for us. [3] For all of this we are very grateful to you. [4] But I don't want to bore you, so please give me your attention for only a moment. [5] We have found this man to be a troublemaker who is constantly stirring up riots among the Jews all over the world. He is a ringleader of the cult known as the Nazarenes. [6] Furthermore, he was trying to desecrate the Temple when we arrested him.* [8] You can find out

23:35 Greek *Herod's Praetorium.* 24:1 Greek *some elders and an orator.* 24:6 Some manuscripts add an expanded conclusion to verse 6, all of verse 7, and an additional phrase in verse 8: *We would have judged him by our law,* [7] *but Lysias, the commander of the garrison, came and violently took him away from us,* [8] *commanding his accusers to come before you.*

the truth of our accusations by examining him yourself." ⁹Then the other Jews chimed in, declaring that everything Tertullus said was true.

¹⁰The governor then motioned for Paul to speak. Paul said, "I know, sir, that you have been a judge of Jewish affairs for many years, so I gladly present my defense before you. ¹¹You can quickly discover that I arrived in Jerusalem no more than twelve days ago to worship at the Temple. ¹²My accusers never found me arguing with anyone in the Temple, nor stirring up a riot in any synagogue or on the streets of the city. ¹³These men cannot prove the things they accuse me of doing.

¹⁴"But I admit that I follow the Way, which they call a cult. I worship the God of our ancestors, and I firmly believe the Jewish law and everything written in the prophets. ¹⁵I have the same hope in God that these men have, that he will raise both the righteous and the unrighteous. ¹⁶Because of this, I always try to maintain a clear conscience before God and all people.

¹⁷"After several years away, I returned to Jerusalem with money to aid my people and to offer sacrifices to God. ¹⁸My accusers saw me in the Temple as I was completing a purification ceremony. There was no crowd around me and no rioting. ¹⁹But some Jews from the province of Asia were there—and they ought to be here to bring charges if they have anything against me! ²⁰Ask these men here what crime the Jewish high council* found me guilty of, ²¹except for the one time I shouted out, 'I am on trial before you today because I believe in the resurrection of the dead!'"

²²At that point Felix, who was quite familiar with the Way, adjourned the hearing and said, "Wait until Lysias, the garrison commander, arrives. Then I will decide the case." ²³He ordered an officer* to keep Paul in custody but to give him some freedom and allow his friends to visit him and take care of his needs.

²⁴A few days later Felix came back with his wife, Drusilla, who was Jewish. Sending for Paul, they listened as he told them about faith in Christ Jesus. ²⁵As he reasoned with them about righteousness and self-control and the coming day of judgment, Felix became frightened. "Go away for now," he replied. "When it is more convenient, I'll call for you again." ²⁶He also hoped that Paul would bribe him, so he sent for him quite often and talked with him.

²⁷After two years went by in this way, Felix was succeeded by

24:20 Greek *Sanhedrin.* 24:23 Greek *a centurion.*

"Distant relatives are not as important as nearby neighbors."
~ Chinese proverb

JOURNAL

Porcius Festus. And because Felix wanted to gain favor with the Jewish people, he left Paul in prison.

CHAPTER **25**

Paul Appears before Festus

Three days after Festus arrived in Caesarea to take over his new responsibilities, he left for Jerusalem, [2]where the leading priests and other Jewish leaders met with him and made their accusations against Paul. [3]They asked Festus as a favor to transfer Paul to Jerusalem (planning to ambush and kill him on the way). [4]But Festus replied that Paul was at Caesarea and he himself would be returning there soon. [5]So he said, "Those of you in authority can return with me. If Paul has done anything wrong, you can make your accusations."

[6]About eight or ten days later Festus returned to Caesarea, and on the following day he took his seat in court and ordered that Paul be brought in. [7]When Paul arrived, the Jewish leaders from Jerusalem gathered around and made many serious accusations they couldn't prove.

[8]Paul denied the charges. "I am not guilty of any crime against the Jewish laws or the Temple or the Roman government," he said.

[9]Then Festus, wanting to please the Jews, asked him, "Are you willing to go to Jerusalem and stand trial before me there?"

[10]But Paul replied, "No! This is the official Roman court, so I ought to be tried right here. You know very well I am not guilty of harming the Jews. [11]If I have done something worthy of death, I don't refuse to die. But if I am innocent, no one has a right to turn me over to these men to kill me. I appeal to Caesar!"

[12]Festus conferred with his advisers and then replied, "Very well! You have appealed to Caesar, and to Caesar you will go!"

[13]A few days later King Agrippa arrived with his sister, Bernice,* to pay their respects to Festus. [14]During their stay of several days, Festus discussed Paul's case with the king. "There is a prisoner here," he told him, "whose case was left for me by Felix. [15]When I was in Jerusalem, the leading priests and Jewish elders pressed charges against him and asked me to condemn him. [16]I pointed out to them that Roman law does not convict people without a trial. They must be given an opportunity to confront their accusers and defend themselves. [17]"When his accusers came here for the trial, I didn't delay.

25:13 Greek *Agrippa the king and Bernice arrived.*

I called the case the very next day and ordered Paul brought in. ¹⁸But the accusations made against him weren't any of the crimes I expected. ¹⁹Instead, it was something about their religion and a dead man named Jesus, who Paul insists is alive. ²⁰I was at a loss to know how to investigate these things, so I asked him whether he would be willing to stand trial on these charges in Jerusalem. ²¹But Paul appealed to have his case decided by the emperor. So I ordered that he be held in custody until I could arrange to send him to Caesar."

²²"I'd like to hear the man myself," Agrippa said.

And Festus replied, "You will—tomorrow!"

Paul Speaks to Agrippa

²³So the next day Agrippa and Bernice arrived at the auditorium with great pomp, accompanied by military officers and prominent men of the city. Festus ordered that Paul be brought in. ²⁴Then Festus said, "King Agrippa and all who are here, this is the man whose death is demanded by all the Jews, both here and in Jerusalem. ²⁵But in my opinion he has done nothing deserving death. However, since he appealed his case to the emperor, I have decided to send him to Rome.

²⁶"But what shall I write the emperor? For there is no clear charge against him. So I have brought him before all of you, and especially you, King Agrippa, so that after we examine him, I might have something to write. ²⁷For it makes no sense to send a prisoner to the emperor without specifying the charges against him!"

CHAPTER **26**

Then Agrippa said to Paul, "You may speak in your defense."

So Paul, gesturing with his hand, started his defense: ²"I am fortunate, King Agrippa, that you are the one hearing my defense today against all these accusations made by the Jewish leaders, ³for I know you are an expert on all Jewish customs and controversies. Now please listen to me patiently!

⁴"As the Jewish leaders are well aware, I was given a thorough Jewish training from my earliest childhood among my own people and in Jerusalem. ⁵If they would admit it, they know that I have been a member of the Pharisees, the strictest sect of our religion. ⁶Now I am on trial because of my hope in the fulfillment of God's promise made to our ancestors. ⁷In fact, that is why the twelve tribes of Israel zealously worship God night and day, and they share the same hope I have. Yet, Your Majesty,

---

No. 09-TE-279

FRIENDSHIP STORY

FRIENDSHIP TYPE: *Neighbors*   FRIENDSHIP LAYER: *Trust*

BASED ON TRUE EVENTS

Moment of Truth

Terry sat in the rented moving truck, fuming. In 20 seconds he needed to quit blocking traffic and back the truck into a narrow driveway—one clearly *not* built to accommodate 26-foot trucks. Too far to the left, and he'd scrape against the brick wall of his new house. Too far to the right, and he'd rip out his new neighbor's fence. And to make matters worse, in his right rearview mirror, a buddy was gesturing that Terry should crank the wheel to the right. In his left rearview mirror, another of his helpers was urging him to crank the wheel left.

That's when Jack leapt up on the running board.

"Forget what they're saying," Jack said. "Follow my directions."

Terry shot Jack a frustrated glare. "Why should I trust *your* directions?"

"Because *I'm* hanging on the side of the truck. If I mess up, you'll be smearing my backside all over the house."

Terry followed Jack's instructions exactly, and everyone survived: Terry, the truck, the house, the fence…and Jack's posterior.

Two lessons Terry learned about trust that moving day: First, kindhearted people aren't necessarily trustworthy. Terry's friends who gave him contradictory directions meant Terry no harm—they thought they were doing him a favor. But at least one of them was wrong. Maybe both.

FRIENDSHIP STORY
continues on page 280…

FRIENDSHIP STORY *continued from page 279...*

And second, it's easier to trust people who are invested in the outcome.

Want to build trust with your neighbor? Invest something in the outcome by investing in the relationship. Then, when the time comes, climb up on the side of the truck.

Experience

THE ONE THING
1
YOU CAN DO THIS WEEK

Giving good advice from a safe distance is easy. Getting involved is tough…but it builds trust.

In your neighborhood, school, church, or workplace, who needs encouragement or help?

Maybe it's the family whose last child just left for college…or the couple moving in two doors down who need to muscle a sofa up the stairs…or the young mother who looks exhausted.

Your challenge this week: Invest in a neighbor or co-worker by offering practical, easy-to-accept help. Baby-sit. Mow a yard. Grab a paintbrush. Give a hug. Offer something *specific*, and then follow through.

Reflect

★ When's a time a neighbor came to your rescue with encouragement, a ride to work, or another practical act of compassion? How did that act impact your friendship with that neighbor?

★ What might need to change in your life before your neighbors or co-workers consider you trustworthy?

they accuse me for having this hope! ⁸Why does it seem incredible to any of you that God can raise the dead?

⁹"I used to believe that I ought to do everything I could to oppose the very name of Jesus the Nazarene.* ¹⁰Indeed, I did just that in Jerusalem. Authorized by the leading priests, I caused many believers* there to be sent to prison. And I cast my vote against them when they were condemned to death. ¹¹Many times I had them punished in the synagogues to get them to curse Jesus.* I was so violently opposed to them that I even chased them down in foreign cities.

¹²"One day I was on such a mission to Damascus, armed with the authority and commission of the leading priests. ¹³About noon, Your Majesty, as I was on the road, a light from heaven brighter than the sun shone down on me and my companions. ¹⁴We all fell down, and I heard a voice saying to me in Aramaic,* 'Saul, Saul, why are you persecuting me? It is useless for you to fight against my will.*'

¹⁵"'Who are you, lord?' I asked.

"And the Lord replied, 'I am Jesus, the one you are persecuting. ¹⁶Now get to your feet! For I have appeared to you to appoint you as my servant and witness. You are to tell the world what you have seen and what I will show you in the future. ¹⁷And I will rescue you from both your own people and the Gentiles. Yes, I am sending you to the Gentiles ¹⁸to open their eyes, so they may turn from darkness to light and from the power of Satan to God. Then they will receive forgiveness for their sins and be given a place among God's people, who are set apart by faith in me.'

¹⁹"And so, King Agrippa, I obeyed that vision from heaven. ²⁰I preached first to those in Damascus, then in Jerusalem and throughout all Judea, and also to the Gentiles, that all must repent of their sins and turn to God—and prove they have changed by the good things they do. ²¹Some Jews arrested me in the Temple for preaching this, and they tried to kill me. ²²But God has protected me right up to this present time so I can testify to everyone, from the least to the greatest. I teach nothing except what the prophets and Moses said would happen—²³that the Messiah would suffer and be the first to rise from the dead, and in this way announce God's light to Jews and Gentiles alike."

²⁴Suddenly, Festus shouted, "Paul, you are insane. Too much study has made you crazy!"

26:9 Or *Jesus of Nazareth.*   26:10 Greek *many of God's holy people.*   26:11 Greek *to blaspheme.*
26:14a Or *Hebrew.*   26:14b Greek *It is hard for you to kick against the oxgoads.*

25But Paul replied, "I am not insane, Most Excellent Festus. What I am saying is the sober truth. 26And King Agrippa knows about these things. I speak boldly, for I am sure these events are all familiar to him, for they were not done in a corner! 27King Agrippa, do you believe the prophets? I know you do—"

28Agrippa interrupted him. "Do you think you can persuade me to become a Christian so quickly?"*

29Paul replied, "Whether quickly or not, I pray to God that both you and everyone here in this audience might become the same as I am, except for these chains."

30Then the king, the governor, Bernice, and all the others stood and left. 31As they went out, they talked it over and agreed, "This man hasn't done anything to deserve death or imprisonment."

32And Agrippa said to Festus, "He could have been set free if he hadn't appealed to Caesar."

CHAPTER 27
Paul Sails for Rome

When the time came, we set sail for Italy. Paul and several other prisoners were placed in the custody of a Roman officer* named Julius, a captain of the Imperial Regiment. 2Aristarchus, a Macedonian from Thessalonica, was also with us. We left on a ship whose home port was Adramyttium on the northwest coast of the province of Asia;* it was scheduled to make several stops at ports along the coast of the province.

3The next day when we docked at Sidon, Julius was very kind to Paul and let him go ashore to visit with friends so they could provide for his needs. 4Putting out to sea from there, we encountered strong headwinds that made it difficult to keep the ship on course, so we sailed north of Cyprus between the island and the mainland. 5Keeping to the open sea, we passed along the coast of Cilicia and Pamphylia, landing at Myra, in the province of Lycia. 6There the commanding officer found an Egyptian ship from Alexandria that was bound for Italy, and he put us on board.

7We had several days of slow sailing, and after great difficulty we finally neared Cnidus. But the wind was against us, so we sailed across to Crete and along the sheltered coast of the island, past the cape of Salmone. 8We struggled along the coast with great difficulty and finally arrived at Fair Havens, near the town

26:28 Or "A little more, and your arguments would make me a Christian." 27:1 Greek centurion; similarly in 27:6, 11, 31, 43. 27:2 Asia was a Roman province in what is now western Turkey.

"Love prospers when a fault is forgiven, but dwelling on it separates close friends."
~ Proverbs 17:9

JOURNAL

of Lasea. ⁹We had lost a lot of time. The weather was becoming dangerous for sea travel because it was so late in the fall,* and Paul spoke to the ship's officers about it.

¹⁰"Men," he said, "I believe there is trouble ahead if we go on—shipwreck, loss of cargo, and danger to our lives as well." ¹¹But the officer in charge of the prisoners listened more to the ship's captain and the owner than to Paul. ¹²And since Fair Havens was an exposed harbor—a poor place to spend the winter—most of the crew wanted to go on to Phoenix, farther up the coast of Crete, and spend the winter there. Phoenix was a good harbor with only a southwest and northwest exposure.

The Storm at Sea

¹³When a light wind began blowing from the south, the sailors thought they could make it. So they pulled up anchor and sailed close to the shore of Crete. ¹⁴But the weather changed abruptly, and a wind of typhoon strength (called a "northeaster") burst across the island and blew us out to sea. ¹⁵The sailors couldn't turn the ship into the wind, so they gave up and let it run before the gale.

¹⁶We sailed along the sheltered side of a small island named Cauda,* where with great difficulty we hoisted aboard the lifeboat being towed behind us. ¹⁷Then the sailors bound ropes around the hull of the ship to strengthen it. They were afraid of being driven across to the sandbars of Syrtis off the African coast, so they lowered the sea anchor to slow the ship and were driven before the wind.

¹⁸The next day, as gale-force winds continued to batter the ship, the crew began throwing the cargo overboard. ¹⁹The following day they even took some of the ship's gear and threw it overboard. ²⁰The terrible storm raged for many days, blotting out the sun and the stars, until at last all hope was gone.

²¹No one had eaten for a long time. Finally, Paul called the crew together and said, "Men, you should have listened to me in the first place and not left Crete. You would have avoided all this damage and loss. ²²But take courage! None of you will lose your

27:9 Greek *because the fast was now already gone by.* This fast was associated with the Day of Atonement (*Yom Kippur*), which occurred in late September or early October.   27:16 Some manuscripts read *Clauda.*

lives, even though the ship will go down. ²³For last night an angel of the God to whom I belong and whom I serve stood beside me, ²⁴and he said, 'Don't be afraid, Paul, for you will surely stand trial before Caesar! What's more, God in his goodness has granted safety to everyone sailing with you.' ²⁵So take courage! For I believe God. It will be just as he said. ²⁶But we will be shipwrecked on an island."

The Shipwreck

²⁷About midnight on the fourteenth night of the storm, as we were being driven across the Sea of Adria,* the sailors sensed land was near. ²⁸They dropped a weighted line and found that the water was 120 feet deep. But a little later they measured again and found it was only 90 feet deep.* ²⁹At this rate they were afraid we would soon be driven against the rocks along the shore, so they threw out four anchors from the back of the ship and prayed for daylight.

³⁰Then the sailors tried to abandon the ship; they lowered the lifeboat as though they were going to put out anchors from the front of the ship. ³¹But Paul said to the commanding officer and the soldiers, "You will all die unless the sailors stay aboard." ³²So the soldiers cut the ropes to the lifeboat and let it drift away.

³³Just as day was dawning, Paul urged everyone to eat. "You have been so worried that you haven't touched food for two weeks," he said. ³⁴"Please eat something now for your own good. For not a hair of your heads will perish." ³⁵Then he took some bread, gave thanks to God before them all, and broke off a piece and ate it. ³⁶Then everyone was encouraged and began to eat—³⁷all 276 of us who were on board. ³⁸After eating, the crew lightened the ship further by throwing the cargo of wheat overboard.

³⁹When morning dawned, they didn't recognize the coastline, but they saw a bay with a beach and wondered if they could get to shore by running the ship aground. ⁴⁰So they cut off the anchors and left them in the sea. Then they lowered the rudders, raised the

Anchor Passage

PASSAGE **Acts 27:13-44**

FRIENDSHIP TYPE: *Neighbors*   FRIENDSHIP LAYER: *Trust*

Welcome Aboard

Read **Acts 27:13-44**.

If you'd been in that ship's crew, you wouldn't have considered Paul an especially trustworthy shipmate.

For starters, Paul was a *prisoner*—dead weight on a ship where there was more than enough work to keep everyone busy.

The crew tolerated Paul…until the storm sent waves slamming against the ship, shredding sails, splitting timbers, shoving the ship miles off course.

Then the crew treated Paul with respect. The soldiers on board trusted Paul so thoroughly that, at Paul's urging, they ditched the only lifeboat on what the crew believed was a sinking ship.

But why the trust? Because the storm proved Paul right?

Maybe…but there was something else.

Notice that Paul didn't cower down below in the hold, safe from the waves. Instead, he scampered across the tilting deck, reassuring his shipmates that God would keep them safe. He encouraged the crew to eat. He prayed.

When trouble came, Paul lived out the definition of *neighbor* that Jesus suggested in the parable of the good Samaritan: anyone who was nearby. Anyone who was in trouble. In short, everyone on the ship.

Anchor Passage
continues on page 284…

27:27 The *Sea of Adria* includes the central portion of the Mediterranean.   **27:28** Greek *20 fathoms . . . 15 fathoms* [37 meters . . . 27 meters].

Anchor Passage continued from page 283...

Do you show up when *your* neighbors are in trouble? Every neighbor drops by when there's a picnic; few come when there's rain.

If you want to build trust with a neighbor, *be there*—even when the hurricanes hit.

Experience

THE ONE THING
★ 1 ★
YOU CAN DO THIS WEEK

Take inventory: How approachable are you to your neighbors?

If all they ever see of you is when you pull your car into the garage or silently climb in and out of an elevator, it's going to be hard to strike up a conversation.

This week, decide to be accessible. Sit out on the front steps. Knock on the next apartment's door, and take along a dozen cookies. Hang out in the employee cafeteria, and strike up a conversation with some people you recognize but whose names you don't yet know.

Paul earned trust through relationship. That's still how it happens.

Reflect

★ Who are the neighbors you trust most? What's made them trustworthy?

★ What's scary about building trust with neighbors? What are you afraid might happen?

★ What are the rewards that come with having a trusting relationship with neighbors?

Anchor Passage continues on page 285...

foresail, and headed toward shore. ⁴¹But they hit a shoal and ran the ship aground too soon. The bow of the ship stuck fast, while the stern was repeatedly smashed by the force of the waves and began to break apart.

⁴²The soldiers wanted to kill the prisoners to make sure they didn't swim ashore and escape. ⁴³But the commanding officer wanted to spare Paul, so he didn't let them carry out their plan. Then he ordered all who could swim to jump overboard first and make for land. ⁴⁴The others held onto planks or debris from the broken ship.* So everyone escaped safely to shore.   ⚓

CHAPTER **28**
Paul on the Island of Malta

Once we were safe on shore, we learned that we were on the island of Malta. ²The people of the island were very kind to us. It was cold and rainy, so they built a fire on the shore to welcome us.

³As Paul gathered an armful of sticks and was laying them on the fire, a poisonous snake, driven out by the heat, bit him on the hand. ⁴The people of the island saw it hanging from his hand and said to each other, "A murderer, no doubt! Though he escaped the sea, justice will not permit him to live." ⁵But Paul shook off the snake into the fire and was unharmed. ⁶The people waited for him to swell up or suddenly drop dead. But when they had waited a long time and saw that he wasn't harmed, they changed their minds and decided he was a god.

⁷Near the shore where we landed was an estate belonging to Publius, the chief official of the island. He welcomed us and treated us kindly for three days. ⁸As it happened, Publius's father was ill with fever and dysentery. Paul went in and prayed for him, and laying his hands on him, he healed him. ⁹Then all the other sick people on the island came and were healed. ¹⁰As a result we were showered with honors, and when the time came to sail, people supplied us with everything we would need for the trip.

Paul Arrives at Rome

¹¹It was three months after the shipwreck that we set sail on another ship that had wintered at the island—an Alexandrian

27:44 Or *or were helped by members of the ship's crew.*

ship with the twin gods* as its figurehead. ¹²Our first stop was Syracuse,* where we stayed three days. ¹³From there we sailed across to Rhegium.* A day later a south wind began blowing, so the following day we sailed up the coast to Puteoli. ¹⁴There we found some believers,* who invited us to spend a week with them. And so we came to Rome.

¹⁵The brothers and sisters* in Rome had heard we were coming, and they came to meet us at the Forum* on the Appian Way. Others joined us at The Three Taverns.* When Paul saw them, he was encouraged and thanked God.

¹⁶When we arrived in Rome, Paul was permitted to have his own private lodging, though he was guarded by a soldier.

Paul Preaches at Rome under Guard

¹⁷Three days after Paul's arrival, he called together the local Jewish leaders. He said to them, "Brothers, I was arrested in Jerusalem and handed over to the Roman government, even though I had done nothing against our people or the customs of our ancestors. ¹⁸The Romans tried me and wanted to release me, because they found no cause for the death sentence. ¹⁹But when the Jewish leaders protested the decision, I felt it necessary to appeal to Caesar, even though I had no desire to press charges against my own people. ²⁰I asked you to come here today so we could get acquainted and so I could explain to you that I am bound with this chain because I believe that the hope of Israel—the Messiah—has already come."

²¹They replied, "We have had no letters from Judea or reports against you from anyone who has come here. ²²But we want to hear what you believe, for the only thing we know about this movement is that it is denounced everywhere."

²³So a time was set, and on that day a large number of people came to Paul's lodging. He explained and testified about the Kingdom of God and tried to persuade them about Jesus from the Scriptures. Using the law of Moses and the books of the prophets, he spoke to them from morning until evening. ²⁴Some were persuaded by the things he said, but others did not believe. ²⁵And after they had argued back and forth among themselves, they left with this final word from Paul: "The Holy Spirit was right when he said to your ancestors through Isaiah the prophet,

28:11 The *twin gods* were the Roman gods Castor and Pollux. 28:12 *Syracuse* was on the island of Sicily. 28:13 *Rhegium* was on the southern tip of Italy. 28:14 Greek *brothers.* 28:15a Greek *brothers.* 28:15b *The Forum* was about 43 miles (70 kilometers) from Rome. 28:15c *The Three Taverns* was about 35 miles (57 kilometers) from Rome.

Anchor Passage continued from page 284...

DIGGING DEEPER

FRIENDSHIP TYPE:
Neighbors

FRIENDSHIP LAYER:
Trust

For building trust with your neighbors, check out...

➡ The Friendship Experience.............. on page 273
➡ The Friendship Story....................... on page 279
➡ What to Say and What Not to Say .... on page 255

JOURNAL

> "I truly feel that if there is, in this world, <u>one</u> person whom we can touch totally, unabashedly and unashamedly, we will never die of loneliness. One person!...someone you can go to and lay it on the line with, who will listen. Someone you don't have to hide from."
>
> ~ Leo Buscaglia

²⁶ 'Go and say to this people:
When you hear what I say,
  you will not understand.
When you see what I do,
  you will not comprehend.
²⁷ For the hearts of these people are hardened,
  and their ears cannot hear,
  and they have closed their eyes—
so their eyes cannot see,
  and their ears cannot hear,
  and their hearts cannot understand,
and they cannot turn to me
  and let me heal them.'*

²⁸ So I want you to know that this salvation from God has also been offered to the Gentiles, and they will accept it."*

³⁰ For the next two years, Paul lived in Rome at his own expense.* He welcomed all who visited him, ³¹ boldly proclaiming the Kingdom of God and teaching about the Lord Jesus Christ. And no one tried to stop him.

28:26-27 Isa 6:9-10 (Greek version).   28:28 Some manuscripts add verse 29, *And when he had said these words, the Jews departed, greatly disagreeing with each other.*   28:30 Or *in his own rented quarters.*

Romans

AUTHOR:	DATE WRITTEN:
Paul	About A.D. 57

CHAPTER 1

Greetings from Paul

This letter is from Paul, a slave of Christ Jesus, chosen by God to be an apostle and sent out to preach his Good News. 2God promised this Good News long ago through his prophets in the holy Scriptures. 3The Good News is about his Son. In his earthly life he was born into King David's family line, 4and he was shown to be* the Son of God when he was raised from the dead by the power of the Holy Spirit.* He is Jesus Christ our Lord. 5Through Christ, God has given us the privilege* and authority as apostles to tell Gentiles everywhere what God has done for them, so that they will believe and obey him, bringing glory to his name.

6And you are included among those Gentiles who have been called to belong to Jesus Christ. 7I am writing to all of you in Rome who are loved by God and are called to be his own holy people.

May God our Father and the Lord Jesus Christ give you grace and peace.

God's Good News

8Let me say first that I thank my God through Jesus Christ for all of you, because your faith in him is being talked about all over the world. 9God knows how often I pray for you. Day and night I bring you and your needs in prayer to God, whom I serve with all my heart* by spreading the Good News about his Son.

10One of the things I always pray for is the opportunity, God willing, to come at last to see you. 11For I long to visit you so I can bring you some spiritual gift that will help you grow strong in the Lord. 12When we get together, I want to encourage you in your faith, but I also want to be encouraged by yours.

1:4a Or *and was designated.*   1:4b Or *by the Spirit of holiness; or in the new realm of the Spirit.*
1:5 Or *the grace.*   1:9 Or *in my spirit.*

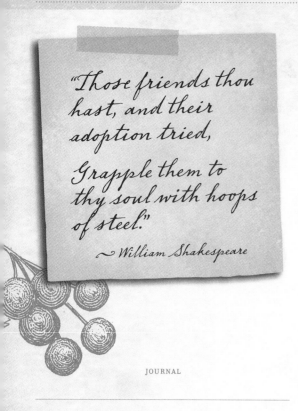

"Those friends thou hast, and their adoption tried,

Grapple them to thy soul with hoops of steel."

~ William Shakespeare

JOURNAL

_____

_____

_____

_____

_____

_____

_____

_____

_____

_____

_____

_____

_____

_____

_____

_____

_____

¹³I want you to know, dear brothers and sisters,* that I planned many times to visit you, but I was prevented until now. I want to work among you and see spiritual fruit, just as I have seen among other Gentiles. ¹⁴For I have a great sense of obligation to people in both the civilized world and the rest of the world,* to the educated and uneducated alike. ¹⁵So I am eager to come to you in Rome, too, to preach the Good News.

¹⁶For I am not ashamed of this Good News about Christ. It is the power of God at work, saving everyone who believes—the Jew first and also the Gentile.* ¹⁷This Good News tells us how God makes us right in his sight. This is accomplished from start to finish by faith. As the Scriptures say, "It is through faith that a righteous person has life."*

God's Anger at Sin

¹⁸But God shows his anger from heaven against all sinful, wicked people who suppress the truth by their wickedness.* ¹⁹They know the truth about God because he has made it obvious to them. ²⁰For ever since the world was created, people have seen the earth and sky. Through everything God made, they can clearly see his invisible qualities—his eternal power and divine nature. So they have no excuse for not knowing God.

²¹Yes, they knew God, but they wouldn't worship him as God or even give him thanks. And they began to think up foolish ideas of what God was like. As a result, their minds became dark and confused. ²²Claiming to be wise, they instead became utter fools. ²³And instead of worshiping the glorious, ever-living God, they worshiped idols made to look like mere people and birds and animals and reptiles.

²⁴So God abandoned them to do whatever shameful things their hearts desired. As a result, they did vile and degrading things with each other's bodies. ²⁵They traded the truth about God for a lie. So they worshiped and served the things God created instead of the Creator himself, who is worthy of eternal praise! Amen. ²⁶That is why God abandoned them to their shameful desires. Even the women turned against the natural way to have sex and instead indulged in sex with each other. ²⁷And the men, instead of having normal sexual relations with women, burned with lust for each other. Men did shameful things with other men, and as a result of this sin, they suffered within themselves the penalty they deserved.

1:13 Greek *brothers.*   1:14 Greek *to Greeks and barbarians.*   1:16 Greek *also the Greek.*   1:17 Or *"The righteous will live by faith."* Hab 2:4.   1:18 Or *who, by their wickedness, prevent the truth from being known.*

²⁸Since they thought it foolish to acknowledge God, he abandoned them to their foolish thinking and let them do things that should never be done. ²⁹Their lives became full of every kind of wickedness, sin, greed, hate, envy, murder, quarreling, deception, malicious behavior, and gossip. ³⁰They are backstabbers, haters of God, insolent, proud, and boastful. They invent new ways of sinning, and they disobey their parents. ³¹They refuse to understand, break their promises, are heartless, and have no mercy. ³²They know God's justice requires that those who do these things deserve to die, yet they do them anyway. Worse yet, they encourage others to do them, too.

CHAPTER 2
God's Judgment of Sin

You may think you can condemn such people, but you are just as bad, and you have no excuse! When you say they are wicked and should be punished, you are condemning yourself, for you who judge others do these very same things. ²And we know that God, in his justice, will punish anyone who does such things. ³Since you judge others for doing these things, why do you think you can avoid God's judgment when you do the same things? ⁴Don't you see how wonderfully kind, tolerant, and patient God is with you? Does this mean nothing to you? Can't you see that his kindness is intended to turn you from your sin?

⁵But because you are stubborn and refuse to turn from your sin, you are storing up terrible punishment for yourself. For a day of anger is coming, when God's righteous judgment will be revealed. ⁶He will judge everyone according to what they have done. ⁷He will give eternal life to those who keep on doing good, seeking after the glory and honor and immortality that God offers. ⁸But he will pour out his anger and wrath on those who live for themselves, who refuse to obey the truth and instead live lives of wickedness. ⁹There will be trouble and calamity for everyone who keeps on doing what is evil—for the Jew first and also for the Gentile.* ¹⁰But there will be glory and honor and peace from God for all who do good—for the Jew first and also for the Gentile. ¹¹For God does not show favoritism.

¹²When the Gentiles sin, they will be destroyed, even though they never had God's written law. And the Jews, who do have God's law, will be judged by that law when they fail to obey it. ¹³For merely listening to the law doesn't make us right with God. It is obeying the law that makes us right in his sight.

2:9 Greek *also for the Greek;* also in 2:10.

WHAT TO SAY AND WHAT NOT TO SAY

FRIENDSHIP TYPE:	FRIENDSHIP LAYER:
Friends	*Commitment*

No Excuses

A committed friendship means sacrifice, service, and being there when you're needed. It's not always fun. It's not always easy. Sometimes you'd honestly rather be somewhere else. But, in the end, a committed friendship is always worth your time.

So take our advice: Avoid the excuses, and grab hold of any and every opportunity to serve your friend.

1. **A close friend of yours is moving. He needs help loading his moving truck. But if there's one thing you hate, it's moving. Putting all that stuff into boxes. Wrapping dishes. Lifting heavy stuff. You've done it before, and you hate all of it.**

 WHAT NOT TO SAY: "Oh man, you caught me just going out. I promise I'll help you next time…"

 WHAT TO SAY: "Hey, let's make a party of it. I'll get some of the guys I know from my softball team. We'll all come over. We can order out for pizza."

2. **A friend invites you and your wife over to play board games with a few other couples. But you hate board games…in fact, you're pretty sure they're really called "*bored* games."**

 WHAT NOT TO SAY: "Ugh, I hate board games. Can't we do something else instead? Why do we *always* have to do something I don't like?"

 WHAT TO SAY: "Sure, we'll come over. Thanks for inviting us; we always enjoy hanging out with you guys. Maybe next time we'll have everyone over to our house for a movie night!"

WHAT TO SAY AND **WHAT NOT TO SAY** *continues on page 290…*

WHAT TO SAY AND **WHAT NOT TO SAY** *continued from page 289...*

3. A friend who is taking classes asks you to help her study for a final. It's a subject she just doesn't get, and she knows you're good at it. But you have kids to put to bed, and a house to clean.

 WHAT NOT TO SAY: "I'm really busy tonight. You know the stuff well, just wing it…you'll do fine! That's what I did in school."

 WHAT TO SAY: "Come on over. We'll fit it in. I'll put the kids to bed, and then we can study."

Jesus wasn't exactly thrilled to go to the cross (**Luke 22:39-46**). But he was a committed friend, and he knew what was needed of him. He didn't make excuses or shrink from the sacrifice…he committed to his friendship with us and gave himself fully for the sake of that friendship.

¹⁴Even Gentiles, who do not have God's written law, show that they know his law when they instinctively obey it, even without having heard it. ¹⁵They demonstrate that God's law is written in their hearts, for their own conscience and thoughts either accuse them or tell them they are doing right. ¹⁶And this is the message I proclaim—that the day is coming when God, through Christ Jesus, will judge everyone's secret life.

The Jews and the Law

¹⁷You who call yourselves Jews are relying on God's law, and you boast about your special relationship with him. ¹⁸You know what he wants; you know what is right because you have been taught his law. ¹⁹You are convinced that you are a guide for the blind and a light for people who are lost in darkness. ²⁰You think you can instruct the ignorant and teach children the ways of God. For you are certain that God's law gives you complete knowledge and truth.

²¹Well then, if you teach others, why don't you teach yourself? You tell others not to steal, but do you steal? ²²You say it is wrong to commit adultery, but do you commit adultery? You condemn idolatry, but do you use items stolen from pagan temples?* ²³You are so proud of knowing the law, but you dishonor God by breaking it. ²⁴No wonder the Scriptures say, "The Gentiles blaspheme the name of God because of you."*

²⁵The Jewish ceremony of circumcision has value only if you obey God's law. But if you don't obey God's law, you are no better off than an uncircumcised Gentile. ²⁶And if the Gentiles obey God's law, won't God declare them to be his own people? ²⁷In fact, uncircumcised Gentiles who keep God's law will condemn you Jews who are circumcised and possess God's law but don't obey it.

²⁸For you are not a true Jew just because you were born of Jewish parents or because you have gone through the ceremony of circumcision. ²⁹No, a true Jew is one whose heart is right with God. And true circumcision is not merely obeying the letter of the law; rather, it is a change of heart produced by God's Spirit. And a person with a changed heart seeks praise* from God, not from people.

CHAPTER **3**
God Remains Faithful

Then what's the advantage of being a Jew? Is there any value in the ceremony of circumcision? ²Yes, there are great benefits!

2:22 Greek *do you steal from temples?* **2:24** Isa 52:5 (Greek version). **2:29** Or *receives praise.*

First of all, the Jews were entrusted with the whole revelation of God.*

³True, some of them were unfaithful; but just because they were unfaithful, does that mean God will be unfaithful? ⁴Of course not! Even if everyone else is a liar, God is true. As the Scriptures say about him,

"You will be proved right in what you say,
     and you will win your case in court."*

⁵"But," some might say, "our sinfulness serves a good purpose, for it helps people see how righteous God is. Isn't it unfair, then, for him to punish us?" (This is merely a human point of view.) ⁶Of course not! If God were not entirely fair, how would he be qualified to judge the world? ⁷"But," someone might still argue, "how can God condemn me as a sinner if my dishonesty highlights his truthfulness and brings him more glory?" ⁸And some people even slander us by claiming that we say, "The more we sin, the better it is!" Those who say such things deserve to be condemned.

All People Are Sinners

⁹Well then, should we conclude that we Jews are better than others? No, not at all, for we have already shown that all people, whether Jews or Gentiles,* are under the power of sin. ¹⁰As the Scriptures say,

"No one is righteous—
     not even one.
¹¹ No one is truly wise;
     no one is seeking God.
¹² All have turned away;
     all have become useless.
No one does good,
     not a single one."*
¹³ "Their talk is foul, like the stench from an open grave.
     Their tongues are filled with lies."
"Snake venom drips from their lips."*
¹⁴   "Their mouths are full of cursing and bitterness."*
¹⁵ "They rush to commit murder.
¹⁶   Destruction and misery always follow them.
¹⁷ They don't know where to find peace."*
¹⁸   "They have no fear of God at all."*

3:2 Greek *the oracles of God.*   3:4 Ps 51:4 (Greek version).   3:9 Greek *or Greeks.*   3:10-12 Pss 14:1-3; 53:1-3 (Greek version).   3:13 Pss 5:9 (Greek version); 140:3.   3:14 Ps 10:7 (Greek version). 3:15-17 Isa 59:7-8.   3:18 Ps 36:1.

Church members who have a best friend at church are much more likely to report attending church at least once a week: 72% compared to only 51% of those who don't have a best friend at their church.

—from "Friendship and Faith," a Gallup Research Study Commissioned by Group Publishing, Inc.

JOURNAL

[19] Obviously, the law applies to those to whom it was given, for its purpose is to keep people from having excuses, and to show that the entire world is guilty before God. [20] For no one can ever be made right with God by doing what the law commands. The law simply shows us how sinful we are.

Christ Took Our Punishment

[21] But now God has shown us a way to be made right with him without keeping the requirements of the law, as was promised in the writings of Moses* and the prophets long ago. [22] We are made right with God by placing our faith in Jesus Christ. And this is true for everyone who believes, no matter who we are.

[23] For everyone has sinned; we all fall short of God's glorious standard. [24] Yet God, with undeserved kindness, declares that we are righteous. He did this through Christ Jesus when he freed us from the penalty for our sins. [25] For God presented Jesus as the sacrifice for sin. People are made right with God when they believe that Jesus sacrificed his life, shedding his blood. This sacrifice shows that God was being fair when he held back and did not punish those who sinned in times past, [26] for he was looking ahead and including them in what he would do in this present time. God did this to demonstrate his righteousness, for he himself is fair and just, and he declares sinners to be right in his sight when they believe in Jesus.

[27] Can we boast, then, that we have done anything to be accepted by God? No, because our acquittal is not based on obeying the law. It is based on faith. [28] So we are made right with God through faith and not by obeying the law.

[29] After all, is God the God of the Jews only? Isn't he also the God of the Gentiles? Of course he is. [30] There is only one God, and he makes people right with himself only by faith, whether they are Jews or Gentiles.* [31] Well then, if we emphasize faith, does this mean that we can forget about the law? Of course not! In fact, only when we have faith do we truly fulfill the law.

CHAPTER **4**

The Faith of Abraham

Abraham was, humanly speaking, the founder of our Jewish nation. What did he discover about being made right with God? [2] If his good deeds had made him acceptable to God, he would

3:21 Greek *in the law.*   **3:30** Greek *whether they are circumcised or uncircumcised.*

have had something to boast about. But that was not God's way. ³For the Scriptures tell us, "Abraham believed God, and God counted him as righteous because of his faith."*

⁴When people work, their wages are not a gift, but something they have earned. ⁵But people are counted as righteous, not because of their work, but because of their faith in God who forgives sinners. ⁶David also spoke of this when he described the happiness of those who are declared righteous without working for it:

⁷ "Oh, what joy for those
  whose disobedience is forgiven,
  whose sins are put out of sight.
⁸ Yes, what joy for those
  whose record the LORD has cleared of sin."*

⁹Now, is this blessing only for the Jews, or is it also for uncircumcised Gentiles?* Well, we have been saying that Abraham was counted as righteous by God because of his faith. ¹⁰But how did this happen? Was he counted as righteous only after he was circumcised, or was it before he was circumcised? Clearly, God accepted Abraham before he was circumcised!

¹¹Circumcision was a sign that Abraham already had faith and that God had already accepted him and declared him to be righteous—even before he was circumcised. So Abraham is the spiritual father of those who have faith but have not been circumcised. They are counted as righteous because of their faith. ¹²And Abraham is also the spiritual father of those who have been circumcised, but only if they have the same kind of faith Abraham had before he was circumcised.

¹³Clearly, God's promise to give the whole earth to Abraham and his descendants was based not on his obedience to God's law, but on a right relationship with God that comes by faith. ¹⁴If God's promise is only for those who obey the law, then faith is not necessary and the promise is pointless. ¹⁵For the law always brings punishment on those who try to obey it. (The only way to avoid breaking the law is to have no law to break!)

¹⁶So the promise is received by faith. It is given as a free gift. And we are all certain to receive it, whether or not we live according to the law of Moses, if we have faith like Abraham's. For Abraham is the father of all who believe. ¹⁷That is what the Scriptures mean when God told him, "I have made you the father of many nations."* This happened because Abraham

4:3 Gen 15:6.   4:7-8 Ps 32:1-2 (Greek version).   4:9 Greek *is this blessing only for the circumcised, or is it also for the uncircumcised?*   4:17 Gen 17:5.

No. 10-FS-293

FRIENDSHIP
STORY

FRIENDSHIP TYPE: *Friends*   FRIENDSHIP LAYER: *Commitment*

FOUND IN SCRIPTURE

Always Reliable

Most of us have had a friend or two our family didn't like…but have you ever had a friend who your family wanted to *kill?*

Well, Jonathan did. His father, Saul, disliked Jonathan's friend David so intensely that Saul tried over and over again to kill David.

But David wasn't some no-good kid with a bad reputation and a penchant for leading his friends astray. David was God's chosen king of Israel; David was a man after God's own heart.

And Jonathan was in a tight spot…he had to choose between his father (the current king of Israel), and his best friend, David (the future king of Israel). Not to mention that, in truth, David was usurping Jonathan's rightful spot as the future king. All in all, it was a tough call.

But Jonathan was a committed friend, and he certainly wasn't going to let any of that stand in the way of his friendship with David. And he didn't. Despite his father's increasing dislike of David, and despite the obvious—and growing—public sentiment toward David as the next king, Jonathan remained a faithful friend.

David and Jonathan rank as one of the Bible's greatest friendships. But what was it about this friendship that was so compelling, so endearing, so inspiring?

FRIENDSHIP STORY *continues on page 294…*

FRIENDSHIP STORY *continued from page 293...*

Well, they were fast friends: there was "an immediate bond of love between them" (**1 Samuel 18:1**), and they made a solemn pact of friendship.

They were also companions. They fought side by side; they shared meals; they served in court together.

But what else? Many would say it was their loyalty and enduring faithfulness to one another, their *commitment*…against all odds.

Jonathan went against his father's will and saved David's life—more than once.

The two swore an oath of loyalty to each other and to their families: "The LORD is the witness of a bond between us and our children forever" (**1 Samuel 20:42**).

After Jonathan was killed in battle, David searched the land for Jonathan's relatives. He found Mephibosheth, Jonathan's crippled son, and brought the terrified man to eat from David's own table. Mephibosheth remained at David's house for the rest of his life.

Jonathan and David's commitment to one another has led the ages to remember their friendship as one of the great friendships of all

time. They were loyal, kind, good, gentle, faithful, and loving to each other always. For that reason, their relationship was one of joy and peace (**Galatians 5:22-23**).

To read the whole story of Jonathan and David's friendship, check out **1 Samuel 18–20** in the Old Testament.

FRIENDSHIP STORY *continues on page 295...*

believed in the God who brings the dead back to life and who creates new things out of nothing.

¹⁸Even when there was no reason for hope, Abraham kept hoping—believing that he would become the father of many nations. For God had said to him, "That's how many descendants you will have!"* ¹⁹And Abraham's faith did not weaken, even though, at about 100 years of age, he figured his body was as good as dead—and so was Sarah's womb.

²⁰Abraham never wavered in believing God's promise. In fact, his faith grew stronger, and in this he brought glory to God. ²¹He was fully convinced that God is able to do whatever he promises. ²²And because of Abraham's faith, God counted him as righteous. ²³And when God counted him as righteous, it wasn't just for Abraham's benefit. It was recorded ²⁴for our benefit, too, assuring us that God will also count us as righteous if we believe in him, the one who raised Jesus our Lord from the dead. ²⁵He was handed over to die because of our sins, and he was raised to life to make us right with God.

CHAPTER **5**
Faith Brings Joy

Therefore, since we have been made right in God's sight by faith, we have peace with God because of what Jesus Christ our Lord has done for us. ²Because of our faith, Christ has brought us into this place of undeserved privilege where we now stand, and we confidently and joyfully look forward to sharing God's glory.

³We can rejoice, too, when we run into problems and trials, for we know that they help us develop endurance. ⁴And endurance develops strength of character, and character strengthens our confident hope of salvation. ⁵And this hope will not lead to disappointment. For we know how dearly God loves us, because he has given us the Holy Spirit to fill our hearts with his love.

⁶When we were utterly helpless, Christ came at just the right time and died for us sinners. ⁷Now, most people would not be willing to die for an upright person, though someone might perhaps be willing to die for a person who is especially good. ⁸But God showed his great love for us by sending Christ to die for us while we were still sinners. ⁹And since we have been made right in God's sight by the blood of Christ, he will certainly save us from God's condemnation. ¹⁰For since our friendship with God was restored by the death of his Son while we

4:18 Gen 15:5.

were still his enemies, we will certainly be saved through the life of his Son. [11]So now we can rejoice in our wonderful new relationship with God because our Lord Jesus Christ has made us friends of God.

Adam and Christ Contrasted

[12]When Adam sinned, sin entered the world. Adam's sin brought death, so death spread to everyone, for everyone sinned. [13]Yes, people sinned even before the law was given. But it was not counted as sin because there was not yet any law to break. [14]Still, everyone died—from the time of Adam to the time of Moses— even those who did not disobey an explicit commandment of God, as Adam did. Now Adam is a symbol, a representation of Christ, who was yet to come. [15]But there is a great difference between Adam's sin and God's gracious gift. For the sin of this one man, Adam, brought death to many. But even greater is God's wonderful grace and his gift of forgiveness to many through this other man, Jesus Christ. [16]And the result of God's gracious gift is very different from the result of that one man's sin. For Adam's sin led to condemnation, but God's free gift leads to our being made right with God, even though we are guilty of many sins. [17]For the sin of this one man, Adam, caused death to rule over many. But even greater is God's wonderful grace and his gift of righteousness, for all who receive it will live in triumph over sin and death through this one man, Jesus Christ.

[18]Yes, Adam's one sin brings condemnation for everyone, but Christ's one act of righteousness brings a right relationship with God and new life for everyone. [19]Because one person disobeyed God, many became sinners. But because one other person obeyed God, many will be made righteous.

[20]God's law was given so that all people could see how sinful they were. But as people sinned more and more, God's wonderful grace became more abundant. [21]So just as sin ruled over all people and brought them to death, now God's wonderful grace rules instead, giving us right standing with God and resulting in eternal life through Jesus Christ our Lord.

CHAPTER **6**

Sin's Power Is Broken

Well then, should we keep on sinning so that God can show us more and more of his wonderful grace? [2]Of course not! Since we have died to sin, how can we continue to live in it? [3]Or have you forgotten that when we were joined with Christ Jesus in

FRIENDSHIP STORY *continued from page 294...*

Experience

David and Jonathan sealed their friendship with gifts and an oath of loyalty. This oath bound the two friends together and revealed the commitment between them.

Think of your closest friend: How can you seal your friendship? Perhaps you can write an oath of friendship together. Or maybe you can exchange meaningful gifts that will symbolize your commitment to one another. Come up with your own unique way to seal the friendship and do it this week!

Reflect

★ Why is commitment such an important part of friendship? How is commitment evident in your closest friendships?

★ What can you do to emphasize commitment in your friendships?

JOURNAL

_____

_____

_____

_____

_____

_____

_____

_____

Among those whose church friendships **extend beyond** weekly worship, **70%** report that **others** would say that they **love God**...but **only 44%** of those whose church friendships exist only at the **weekly** worship would say the same thing.

—from "Friendship and Faith," a Gallup Research Study Commissioned by Group Publishing, Inc.

JOURNAL

baptism, we joined him in his death? [4] For we died and were buried with Christ by baptism. And just as Christ was raised from the dead by the glorious power of the Father, now we also may live new lives.

[5] Since we have been united with him in his death, we will also be raised to life as he was. [6] We know that our old sinful selves were crucified with Christ so that sin might lose its power in our lives. We are no longer slaves to sin. [7] For when we died with Christ we were set free from the power of sin. [8] And since we died with Christ, we know we will also live with him. [9] We are sure of this because Christ was raised from the dead, and he will never die again. Death no longer has any power over him. [10] When he died, he died once to break the power of sin. But now that he lives, he lives for the glory of God. [11] So you also should consider yourselves to be dead to the power of sin and alive to God through Christ Jesus.

[12] Do not let sin control the way you live;* do not give in to sinful desires. [13] Do not let any part of your body become an instrument of evil to serve sin. Instead, give yourselves completely to God, for you were dead, but now you have new life. So use your whole body as an instrument to do what is right for the glory of God. [14] Sin is no longer your master, for you no longer live under the requirements of the law. Instead, you live under the freedom of God's grace.

[15] Well then, since God's grace has set us free from the law, does that mean we can go on sinning? Of course not! [16] Don't you realize that you become the slave of whatever you choose to obey? You can be a slave to sin, which leads to death, or you can choose to obey God, which leads to righteous living. [17] Thank God! Once you were slaves of sin, but now you wholeheartedly obey this teaching we have given you. [18] Now you are free from your slavery to sin, and you have become slaves to righteous living.

[19] Because of the weakness of your human nature, I am using the illustration of slavery to help you understand all this. Previously, you let yourselves be slaves to impurity and lawlessness, which led ever deeper into sin. Now you must give yourselves to be slaves to righteous living so that you will become holy.

[20] When you were slaves to sin, you were free from the obligation to do right. [21] And what was the result? You are now ashamed of the things you used to do, things that end in eternal doom. [22] But now you are free from the power of sin and

6:12 Or *Do not let sin reign in your body, which is subject to death.*

have become slaves of God. Now you do those things that lead to holiness and result in eternal life. ²³For the wages of sin is death, but the free gift of God is eternal life through Christ Jesus our Lord.

CHAPTER 7
No Longer Bound to the Law

Now, dear brothers and sisters*—you who are familiar with the law—don't you know that the law applies only while a person is living? ²For example, when a woman marries, the law binds her to her husband as long as he is alive. But if he dies, the laws of marriage no longer apply to her. ³So while her husband is alive, she would be committing adultery if she married another man. But if her husband dies, she is free from that law and does not commit adultery when she remarries.

⁴So, my dear brothers and sisters, this is the point: You died to the power of the law when you died with Christ. And now you are united with the one who was raised from the dead. As a result, we can produce a harvest of good deeds for God. ⁵When we were controlled by our old nature,* sinful desires were at work within us, and the law aroused these evil desires that produced a harvest of sinful deeds, resulting in death. ⁶But now we have been released from the law, for we died to it and are no longer captive to its power. Now we can serve God, not in the old way of obeying the letter of the law, but in the new way of living in the Spirit.

God's Law Reveals Our Sin

⁷Well then, am I suggesting that the law of God is sinful? Of course not! In fact, it was the law that showed me my sin. I would never have known that coveting is wrong if the law had not said, "You must not covet."* ⁸But sin used this command to arouse all kinds of covetous desires within me! If there were no law, sin would not have that power. ⁹At one time I lived without understanding the law. But when I learned the command not to covet, for instance, the power of sin came to life, ¹⁰and I died. So I discovered that the law's commands, which were supposed to bring life, brought spiritual death instead. ¹¹Sin took advantage of those commands and deceived me; it used the commands to kill me. ¹²But still, the law itself is holy, and its commands are holy and right and good.

¹³But how can that be? Did the law, which is good, cause my

7:1 Greek *brothers*; also in 7:4.   7:5 Greek *When we were in the flesh.*   7:7 Exod 20:17; Deut 5:21.

WHAT TO SAY AND WHAT NOT TO SAY

FRIENDSHIP TYPE:	FRIENDSHIP LAYER:
Neighbors	Companionship

Hospitality Avenue: A Two-Way Street

When she traveled east, old friends of Ursula's family offered to host her. Though the hosts were kind, open, and patient, several hours into the visit, even a fly on the wall recognized that this was going to be a trying time. Listen to some of the things the fly heard:

WHAT NOT TO SAY:

★ Ursula: *(At dinner)* I can't have pasta—I'm on a wheat-free diet. Anyhow, when I did eat it, I always made my own.

★ Ursula: *(At breakfast, when the hosts inquire about Ursula's night)* I slept horribly! That bed was so hard! Plus, the water pressure in the shower is really weak. Maybe if you didn't have so much stuff cluttering up your life, you'd get time to fix it.

★ Ursula: *(Looking at the breakfast food)* What!? You drink *whole* milk!?

Needless to say, the fly on the wall was appalled at Ursula's behavior. You see, hospitality is a two-way street. The hosts must be gracious, of course, but it's equally important—perhaps more so—that the guests be gracious, too. So, next time you're a guest, don't follow Ursula's example. Instead, try the following suggestions.

WHAT TO SAY AND WHAT NOT TO SAY *continues on page 298...*

WHAT TO SAY AND WHAT NOT TO SAY *continued from page 297...*

WHAT TO SAY:

★ Don't mention any special diet you're on, especially if the food served to you conflicts with the diet. Be gracious—people are more important than food.

★ If you're severely allergic to certain foods, tell your host graciously—perhaps even privately—in the kitchen.

★ Be aware that every household has its own culture—enjoy it!

★ Keep your comments about the surroundings positive.

★ Most importantly, review **Romans 12:9-18**. Practice being peaceful, patient, and honoring.

JOURNAL

_____

_____

_____

_____

_____

_____

_____

_____

_____

_____

_____

_____

_____

death? Of course not! Sin used what was good to bring about my condemnation to death. So we can see how terrible sin really is. It uses God's good commands for its own evil purposes.

Struggling with Sin

14 So the trouble is not with the law, for it is spiritual and good. The trouble is with me, for I am all too human, a slave to sin. 15 I don't really understand myself, for I want to do what is right, but I don't do it. Instead, I do what I hate. 16 But if I know that what I am doing is wrong, this shows that I agree that the law is good. 17 So I am not the one doing wrong; it is sin living in me that does it.

18 And I know that nothing good lives in me, that is, in my sinful nature.* I want to do what is right, but I can't. 19 I want to do what is good, but I don't. I don't want to do what is wrong, but I do it anyway. 20 But if I do what I don't want to do, I am not really the one doing wrong; it is sin living in me that does it.

21 I have discovered this principle of life—that when I want to do what is right, I inevitably do what is wrong. 22 I love God's law with all my heart. 23 But there is another power* within me that is at war with my mind. This power makes me a slave to the sin that is still within me. 24 Oh, what a miserable person I am! Who will free me from this life that is dominated by sin and death? 25 Thank God! The answer is in Jesus Christ our Lord. So you see how it is: In my mind I really want to obey God's law, but because of my sinful nature I am a slave to sin.

CHAPTER **8**
Life in the Spirit

So now there is no condemnation for those who belong to Christ Jesus. 2 And because you belong to him, the power* of the life-giving Spirit has freed you* from the power of sin that leads to death. 3 The law of Moses was unable to save us because of the weakness of our sinful nature.* So God did what the law could not do. He sent his own Son in a body like the bodies we sinners have. And in that body God declared an end to sin's control over us by giving his Son as a sacrifice for our sins. 4 He did this so that the just requirement of the law would be fully satisfied for us, who no longer follow our sinful nature but instead follow the Spirit.

5 Those who are dominated by the sinful nature think about sinful things, but those who are controlled by the Holy Spirit

7:18 Greek *my flesh;* also in 7:25.   **7:23** Greek *law;* also in 7:23b.   **8:2a** Greek *the law;* also in 8:2b.
8:2b Some manuscripts read *me.*   **8:3** Greek *our flesh;* similarly in 8:4, 5, 6, 7, 8, 9, 12.

think about things that please the Spirit. [6]So letting your sinful nature control your mind leads to death. But letting the Spirit control your mind leads to life and peace. [7]For the sinful nature is always hostile to God. It never did obey God's laws, and it never will. [8]That's why those who are still under the control of their sinful nature can never please God.

[9]But you are not controlled by your sinful nature. You are controlled by the Spirit if you have the Spirit of God living in you. (And remember that those who do not have the Spirit of Christ living in them do not belong to him at all.) [10]And Christ lives within you, so even though your body will die because of sin, the Spirit gives you life* because you have been made right with God. [11]The Spirit of God, who raised Jesus from the dead, lives in you. And just as God raised Christ Jesus from the dead, he will give life to your mortal bodies by this same Spirit living within you.

[12]Therefore, dear brothers and sisters,* you have no obligation to do what your sinful nature urges you to do. [13]For if you live by its dictates, you will die. But if through the power of the Spirit you put to death the deeds of your sinful nature,* you will live. [14]For all who are led by the Spirit of God are children* of God.

[15]So you have not received a spirit that makes you fearful slaves. Instead, you received God's Spirit when he adopted you as his own children.* Now we call him, "Abba, Father."* [16]For his Spirit joins with our spirit to affirm that we are God's children. [17]And since we are his children, we are his heirs. In fact, together with Christ we are heirs of God's glory. But if we are to share his glory, we must also share his suffering.

The Future Glory

[18]Yet what we suffer now is nothing compared to the glory he will reveal to us later. [19]For all creation is waiting eagerly for that future day when God will reveal who his children really are. [20]Against its will, all creation was subjected to God's curse. But with eager hope, [21]the creation looks forward to the day when it will join God's children in glorious freedom from death and decay. [22]For we know that all creation has been groaning as in the pains of childbirth right up to the present time. [23]And we believers also groan, even though we have the Holy Spirit within us as a foretaste of future glory, for we long

"How wonderful and pleasant it is when brothers live together in harmony!"
~ Psalm 133:1

JOURNAL

8:10 Or *your spirit is alive.*   8:12 Greek *brothers;* also in 8:29.   8:13 Greek *deeds of the body.*
8:14 Greek *sons;* also in 8:19.   8:15a Greek *you received a spirit of sonship.*   8:15b *Abba* is an Aramaic term for "father."

for our bodies to be released from sin and suffering. We, too, wait with eager hope for the day when God will give us our full rights as his adopted children,* including the new bodies he has promised us. 24 We were given this hope when we were saved. (If we already have something, we don't need to hope* for it. 25 But if we look forward to something we don't yet have, we must wait patiently and confidently.)

26 And the Holy Spirit helps us in our weakness. For example, we don't know what God wants us to pray for. But the Holy Spirit prays for us with groanings that cannot be expressed in words. 27 And the Father who knows all hearts knows what the Spirit is saying, for the Spirit pleads for us believers* in harmony with God's own will. 28 And we know that God causes everything to work together* for the good of those who love God and are called according to his purpose for them. 29 For God knew his people in advance, and he chose them to become like his Son, so that his Son would be the firstborn among many brothers and sisters. 30 And having chosen them, he called them to come to him. And having called them, he gave them right standing with himself. And having given them right standing, he gave them his glory.

Nothing Can Separate Us from God's Love

31 What shall we say about such wonderful things as these? If God is for us, who can ever be against us? 32 Since he did not spare even his own Son but gave him up for us all, won't he also give us everything else? 33 Who dares accuse us whom God has chosen for his own? No one—for God himself has given us right standing with himself. 34 Who then will condemn us? No one—for Christ Jesus died for us and was raised to life for us, and he is sitting in the place of honor at God's right hand, pleading for us.

35 Can anything ever separate us from Christ's love? Does it mean he no longer loves us if we have trouble or calamity, or are persecuted, or hungry, or destitute, or in danger, or threatened with death? 36 (As the Scriptures say, "For your sake we are killed every day; we are being slaughtered like sheep."*) 37 No, despite all these things, overwhelming victory is ours through Christ, who loved us.

38 And I am convinced that nothing can ever separate us from God's love. Neither death nor life, neither angels nor demons,*

8:23 Greek *wait anxiously for sonship.*   8:24 Some manuscripts read *wait.*   8:27 Greek *for God's holy people.*   8:28 Some manuscripts read *And we know that everything works together.*   8:36 Ps 44:22. 8:38 Greek *nor rulers.*

neither our fears for today nor our worries about tomorrow—not even the powers of hell can separate us from God's love. ³⁹No power in the sky above or in the earth below—indeed, nothing in all creation will ever be able to separate us from the love of God that is revealed in Christ Jesus our Lord.

CHAPTER 9
God's Selection of Israel

With Christ as my witness, I speak with utter truthfulness. My conscience and the Holy Spirit confirm it. ²My heart is filled with bitter sorrow and unending grief ³for my people, my Jewish brothers and sisters.* I would be willing to be forever cursed—cut off from Christ!—if that would save them. ⁴They are the people of Israel, chosen to be God's adopted children.* God revealed his glory to them. He made covenants with them and gave them his law. He gave them the privilege of worshiping him and receiving his wonderful promises. ⁵Abraham, Isaac, and Jacob are their ancestors, and Christ himself was an Israelite as far as his human nature is concerned. And he is God, the one who rules over everything and is worthy of eternal praise! Amen.*

⁶Well then, has God failed to fulfill his promise to Israel? No, for not all who are born into the nation of Israel are truly members of God's people! ⁷Being descendants of Abraham doesn't make them truly Abraham's children. For the Scriptures say, "Isaac is the son through whom your descendants will be counted,"* though Abraham had other children, too. ⁸This means that Abraham's physical descendants are not necessarily children of God. Only the children of the promise are considered to be Abraham's children. ⁹For God had promised, "I will return about this time next year, and Sarah will have a son."*

¹⁰This son was our ancestor Isaac. When he married Rebekah, she gave birth to twins.* ¹¹But before they were born, before they had done anything good or bad, she received a message from God. (This message shows that God chooses people according to his own purposes; ¹²he calls people, but not according to their good or bad works.) She was told, "Your older son will serve your younger son."* ¹³In the words of the Scriptures, "I loved Jacob, but I rejected Esau."*

¹⁴Are we saying, then, that God was unfair? Of course not! ¹⁵For God said to Moses,

9:3 Greek *my brothers.*   9:4 Greek *chosen for sonship.*   9:5 Or *May God, the one who rules over everything, be praised forever. Amen.*   9:7 Gen 21:12.   9:9 Gen 18:10, 14.   9:10 Greek *she conceived children through this one man.*   9:12 Gen 25:23.   9:13 Mal 1:2-3.

FRIENDSHIP EXPERIENCE

FRIENDSHIP TYPE:	FRIENDSHIP LAYER:
Neighbors	*Companionship*

Happy and Happy or Sad and Sad

Who has been a good neighbor to you? Did someone let you "borrow" a cup of sugar? Or lend you a lawn mower when yours wasn't working? In **Romans 12:9-18**, Paul gives some relational advice that's a definitive "good neighbor" checklist!

Being a good neighbor isn't easy—it requires work, self-discipline, and a holy motivation to love—but it's what's necessary in order to become a closer companion to your neighbors.

And critical to being a good neighbor is to "be happy with those who are happy, and weep with those who weep." When the clerk at the grocery store looks sad, ask her if she is OK. If someone is smiling a little more than usual, say, "You look like you're having a great day. What happened?" People *like* to share their stories. And people *love* it when someone empathizes with them—when someone experiences those emotions *with* them. That's what Paul's talking about.

FRIENDSHIP EXPERIENCE *continues on page 302...*

FRIENDSHIP EXPERIENCE *continued from page 301...*

Experience

Call a neighbor, and invite him or her to your house for a simple meal. Don't stress yourself out making cheesecake and a roasted chicken—eat something simple, such as grilled cheese sandwiches and tomato soup…or just order a pizza! As you eat together, listen to your neighbor. Ask questions. Empathize. Laugh together. Remember, it's all about empathy, not about impressing your neighbor with a clean house, fancy cooking, or clever conversation.

THE ONE THING ★ 1 ★ YOU CAN DO THIS WEEK

Companionship with Jesus is the same way. Read **Luke 22:39-53**. Imagine Jesus telling you this story. How would you empathize with him? Practicing hospitality with Jesus is just like practicing hospitality with neighbors—you can't wait until your house is clean and you're prepared to show him your best side. With Jesus you have to be real, and if you wait until you're "ready," you'll never meet with him. Think of an urgent task you need to do—now, instead of doing the task right away, spend a little time talking with Jesus. Whatever you tell him…you can be sure he's empathizing!

FRIENDSHIP EXPERIENCE *continues on page 303...*

"I will show mercy to anyone I choose,
    and I will show compassion to anyone I choose."*

¹⁶So it is God who decides to show mercy. We can neither choose it nor work for it.

¹⁷For the Scriptures say that God told Pharaoh, "I have appointed you for the very purpose of displaying my power in you and to spread my fame throughout the earth."* ¹⁸So you see, God chooses to show mercy to some, and he chooses to harden the hearts of others so they refuse to listen.

¹⁹Well then, you might say, "Why does God blame people for not responding? Haven't they simply done what he makes them do?"

²⁰No, don't say that. Who are you, a mere human being, to argue with God? Should the thing that was created say to the one who created it, "Why have you made me like this?" ²¹When a potter makes jars out of clay, doesn't he have a right to use the same lump of clay to make one jar for decoration and another to throw garbage into? ²²In the same way, even though God has the right to show his anger and his power, he is very patient with those on whom his anger falls, who are destined for destruction. ²³He does this to make the riches of his glory shine even brighter on those to whom he shows mercy, who were prepared in advance for glory. ²⁴And we are among those whom he selected, both from the Jews and from the Gentiles.

²⁵Concerning the Gentiles, God says in the prophecy of Hosea,

"Those who were not my people,
    I will now call my people.
And I will love those
    whom I did not love before."*

²⁶And,

"Then, at the place where they were told,
    'You are not my people,'
there they will be called
    'children of the living God.'"*

²⁷And concerning Israel, Isaiah the prophet cried out,

"Though the people of Israel are as numerous as the sand
    of the seashore,
    only a remnant will be saved.

9:15 Exod 33:19. **9:17** Exod 9:16 (Greek version). **9:25** Hos 2:23. **9:26** Greek *sons of the living God.* Hos 1:10.

28 For the LORD will carry out his sentence upon the earth
 quickly and with finality. "*

29 And Isaiah said the same thing in another place:

"If the LORD of Heaven's Armies
 had not spared a few of our children,
we would have been wiped out like Sodom,
 destroyed like Gomorrah. "*

Israel's Unbelief

30 What does all this mean? Even though the Gentiles were not
trying to follow God's standards, they were made right with
God. And it was by faith that this took place. 31 But the people
of Israel, who tried so hard to get right with God by keeping
the law, never succeeded. 32 Why not? Because they were trying
to get right with God by keeping the law* instead of by trusting
in him. They stumbled over the great rock in their path. 33 God
warned them of this in the Scriptures when he said,

"I am placing a stone in Jerusalem* that makes people
 stumble,
 a rock that makes them fall.
But anyone who trusts in him
 will never be disgraced. "*

CHAPTER 10

Dear brothers and sisters,* the longing of my heart and my
prayer to God is for the people of Israel to be saved. 2 I know
what enthusiasm they have for God, but it is misdirected zeal.
3 For they don't understand God's way of making people right
with himself. Refusing to accept God's way, they cling to their
own way of getting right with God by trying to keep the law.
4 For Christ has already accomplished the purpose for which
the law was given.* As a result, all who believe in him are made
right with God.

Salvation Is for Everyone

5 For Moses writes that the law's way of making a person right
with God requires obedience to all of its commands.* 6 But
faith's way of getting right with God says, "Don't say in your
heart, 'Who will go up to heaven' (to bring Christ down to
earth). 7 And don't say, 'Who will go down to the place of the
dead' (to bring Christ back to life again)." 8 In fact, it says,

9:27-28 Isa 10:22-23 (Greek version).   **9:29** Isa 1:9.   **9:32** Greek *by works.*   **9:33a** Greek *in Zion.*
9:33b Isa 8:14; 28:16 (Greek version).   **10:1** Greek *Brothers.*   **10:4** Or *For Christ is the end of the law.*
10:5 See Lev 18:5.

FRIENDSHIP EXPERIENCE *continued from page 302...*

Reflect

★ How does it feel when someone empathizes
 with you?
★ How did showing empathy toward your neighbor
 affect your friendship?
★ What "priorities" keep you from meeting with
 your neighbors? with Jesus?

JOURNAL

"The message is very close at hand;
    it is on your lips and in your heart."*

And that message is the very message about faith that we preach: ⁹If you confess with your mouth that Jesus is Lord and believe in your heart that God raised him from the dead, you will be saved. ¹⁰For it is by believing in your heart that you are made right with God, and it is by confessing with your mouth that you are saved. ¹¹As the Scriptures tell us, "Anyone who trusts in him will never be disgraced."* ¹²Jew and Gentile* are the same in this respect. They have the same Lord, who gives generously to all who call on him. ¹³For "Everyone who calls on the name of the LORD will be saved."*

¹⁴But how can they call on him to save them unless they believe in him? And how can they believe in him if they have never heard about him? And how can they hear about him unless someone tells them? ¹⁵And how will anyone go and tell them without being sent? That is why the Scriptures say, "How beautiful are the feet of messengers who bring good news!"*

¹⁶But not everyone welcomes the Good News, for Isaiah the prophet said, "LORD, who has believed our message?"* ¹⁷So faith comes from hearing, that is, hearing the Good News about Christ. ¹⁸But I ask, have the people of Israel actually heard the message? Yes, they have:

"The message has gone throughout the earth,
    and the words to all the world."*

¹⁹But I ask, did the people of Israel really understand? Yes, they did, for even in the time of Moses, God said,

"I will rouse your jealousy through people who are not even
        a nation.
    I will provoke your anger through the foolish Gentiles."*

²⁰And later Isaiah spoke boldly for God, saying,

"I was found by people who were not looking for me.
    I showed myself to those who were not asking for me."*

²¹But regarding Israel, God said,

"All day long I opened my arms to them,
    but they were disobedient and rebellious."*

10:6-8 Deut 30:12-14. 10:11 Isa 28:16 (Greek version). 10:12 Greek *and Greek*. 10:13 Joel 2:32.
10:15 Isa 52:7. 10:16 Isa 53:1. 10:18 Ps 19:4. 10:19 Deut 32:21. 10:20 Isa 65:1 (Greek version).
10:21 Isa 65:2 (Greek version).

> "Any friend of God is called to faithfully embody the ways of God in the world, even to the point of suffering on account of them. There may be grace and glory in being a friend of God, but there is also clearly a cost."
>
> ~ Paul J. Wadell

CHAPTER **11**
God's Mercy on Israel

I ask, then, has God rejected his own people, the nation of Israel? Of course not! I myself am an Israelite, a descendant of Abraham and a member of the tribe of Benjamin.

²No, God has not rejected his own people, whom he chose from the very beginning. Do you realize what the Scriptures say about this? Elijah the prophet complained to God about the people of Israel and said, ³"LORD, they have killed your prophets and torn down your altars. I am the only one left, and now they are trying to kill me, too."*

⁴And do you remember God's reply? He said, "No, I have 7,000 others who have never bowed down to Baal!"*

⁵It is the same today, for a few of the people of Israel* have remained faithful because of God's grace—his undeserved kindness in choosing them. ⁶And since it is through God's kindness, then it is not by their good works. For in that case, God's grace would not be what it really is—free and undeserved.

⁷So this is the situation: Most of the people of Israel have not found the favor of God they are looking for so earnestly. A few have—the ones God has chosen—but the hearts of the rest were hardened. ⁸As the Scriptures say,

"God has put them into a deep sleep.
To this day he has shut their eyes so they do not see,
　and closed their ears so they do not hear."*

⁹Likewise, David said,

"Let their bountiful table become a snare,
　a trap that makes them think all is well.
Let their blessings cause them to stumble,
　and let them get what they deserve.
¹⁰ Let their eyes go blind so they cannot see,
　and let their backs be bent forever."*

¹¹Did God's people stumble and fall beyond recovery? Of course not! They were disobedient, so God made salvation available to the Gentiles. But he wanted his own people to become jealous and claim it for themselves. ¹²Now if the Gentiles were enriched because the people of Israel turned down God's offer of salvation, think how much greater a blessing the world will share when they finally accept it.

11:3 1 Kgs 19:10, 14.　**11:4** 1 Kgs 19:18.　**11:5** Greek *for a remnant.*　**11:8** Isa 29:10; Deut 29:4.
11:9-10 Ps 69:22-23 (Greek version).

No. 11-FA-305
FRIENDSHIP STORY

FRIENDSHIP TYPE: *Neighbors*　　FRIENDSHIP LAYER: *Companionship*

FROM THE ARCHIVES

Friends Despite Doctrinal Differences

It wasn't so much that he didn't like what George Whitefield was saying—that was all well and good, if not a little *dramatically* spoken, and it was theologically sound and inspiring—but it was more that John Wesley really didn't care for people's reactions to the words. There was just so much *emotion* involved—people weeping and collapsing on the floor, the loud cries for forgiveness, the sudden leaps into the air and loud declarations of joy…such lack of *dignity*. Wesley would have preferred a little more solemnity, a little more *respect*.

But he couldn't deny the results, people were responding to what Whitefield had to say. So Wesley agreed to work with him, and the two neighbors began holding revivals throughout England.

And it worked…for a while. Eventually Wesley even admitted that those seemingly undignified responses appeared to be *genuine* and heartfelt… that they were really a struggle between Satan and the Holy Spirit and that he shouldn't get in the way of the work of God. But after a time, Whitefield and Wesley parted company. We don't know exactly how it happened, but the two began to have some disagreements.

FRIENDSHIP STORY *continues on page 306…*

Friendship First NEW TESTAMENT

FRIENDSHIP STORY *continued from page 305...*

Oh, they were probably mild at first, simply conversations about tough issues that would occasionally end in an argument. After a time, though, the arguments became more frequent… and more heated. They even exchanged public letters in which they debated. Whitefield believed strongly in predestination, arguing that God knew and *chose* those who would believe in him. Wesley could not agree—he held firmly to the belief that men had absolute choice in whether or not to believe in God.

It may seem like a small thing, but eventually the two chose to part because of it. They decided they simply could not work together when they disagreed on such a fundamental point.

For some time the two had nothing to do with one another. But after a time they met again… and decided that being companions was more important than any disagreement. Though they never worked together again, they did share a friendship that lasted through their lives.

Experience

THE ONE THING
1
YOU CAN DO THIS WEEK

Is there a disagreement you're having with someone that would be best to set aside? Remember that sometimes no one has to win! Consider what Paul writes in **Romans 12**: Don't think you know it all! Sometimes, in order to maintain a relationship, it's vital to set aside an issue of disagreement. Talk about other things. Discover what you agree about! Identify a relationship you're in that needs this type of healing. Call the person. Talk about other things. Agree to disagree. Talk about something else.

(Remember: This doesn't mean you'll never argue about this again, nor does it mean that you have to agree with your friend. It may even be that you feel you can't work with the person as a result of your disagreement. But disagreement or not, you can still be friends.)

FRIENDSHIP STORY *continues on page 307...*

[13] I am saying all this especially for you Gentiles. God has appointed me as the apostle to the Gentiles. I stress this, [14] for I want somehow to make the people of Israel jealous of what you Gentiles have, so I might save some of them. [15] For since their rejection meant that God offered salvation to the rest of the world, their acceptance will be even more wonderful. It will be life for those who were dead! [16] And since Abraham and the other patriarchs were holy, their descendants will also be holy—just as the entire batch of dough is holy because the portion given as an offering is holy. For if the roots of the tree are holy, the branches will be, too.

[17] But some of these branches from Abraham's tree—some of the people of Israel—have been broken off. And you Gentiles, who were branches from a wild olive tree, have been grafted in. So now you also receive the blessing God has promised Abraham and his children, sharing in the rich nourishment from the root of God's special olive tree. [18] But you must not brag about being grafted in to replace the branches that were broken off. You are just a branch, not the root.

[19] "Well," you may say, "those branches were broken off to make room for me." [20] Yes, but remember—those branches were broken off because they didn't believe in Christ, and you are there because you do believe. So don't think highly of yourself, but fear what could happen. [21] For if God did not spare the original branches, he won't* spare you either.

[22] Notice how God is both kind and severe. He is severe toward those who disobeyed, but kind to you if you continue to trust in his kindness. But if you stop trusting, you also will be cut off. [23] And if the people of Israel turn from their unbelief, they will be grafted in again, for God has the power to graft them back into the tree. [24] You, by nature, were a branch cut from a wild olive tree. So if God was willing to do something contrary to nature by grafting you into his cultivated tree, he will be far more eager to graft the original branches back into the tree where they belong.

God's Mercy Is for Everyone

[25] I want you to understand this mystery, dear brothers and sisters,* so that you will not feel proud about yourselves. Some of the people of Israel have hard hearts, but this will last only until the full number of Gentiles comes to Christ. [26] And so all Israel will be saved. As the Scriptures say,

11:21 Some manuscripts read *perhaps he won't.*   11:25 Greek *brothers.*

"The one who rescues will come from Jerusalem,*
   and he will turn Israel* away from ungodliness.
²⁷ And this is my covenant with them,
   that I will take away their sins."*

²⁸Many of the people of Israel are now enemies of the Good News, and this benefits you Gentiles. Yet they are still the people he loves because he chose their ancestors Abraham, Isaac, and Jacob. ²⁹For God's gifts and his call can never be withdrawn. ³⁰Once, you Gentiles were rebels against God, but when the people of Israel rebelled against him, God was merciful to you instead. ³¹Now they are the rebels, and God's mercy has come to you so that they, too, will share* in God's mercy. ³²For God has imprisoned everyone in disobedience so he could have mercy on everyone.

³³Oh, how great are God's riches and wisdom and knowledge! How impossible it is for us to understand his decisions and his ways!

³⁴ For who can know the LORD's thoughts?
   Who knows enough to give him advice?*
³⁵ And who has given him so much
   that he needs to pay it back?*

³⁶For everything comes from him and exists by his power and is intended for his glory. All glory to him forever! Amen.

CHAPTER **12**

A Living Sacrifice to God

And so, dear brothers and sisters,* I plead with you to give your bodies to God because of all he has done for you. Let them be a living and holy sacrifice—the kind he will find acceptable. This is truly the way to worship him.* ²Don't copy the behavior and customs of this world, but let God transform you into a new person by changing the way you think. Then you will learn to know God's will for you, which is good and pleasing and perfect.

³Because of the privilege and authority* God has given me, I give each of you this warning: Don't think you are better than you really are. Be honest in your evaluation of yourselves, measuring yourselves by the faith God has given us.* ⁴Just as our bodies have many parts and each part has a special function,

---

FRIENDSHIP STORY *continued from page 306...*

Reflect

★ Why do you think it was significant for Whitefield and Wesley to set aside their theological differences?

★ What relationships can you repair by "agreeing to disagree"?

★ How does this teach you humility? How does this teach you peace?

JOURNAL

11:26a Greek *from Zion.* **11:26b** Greek *Jacob.* **11:26-27** Isa 59:20-21; 27:9 (Greek version).
11:31 Other manuscripts read *will now share;* still others read *will someday share.* **11:34** Isa 40:13
(Greek version). **11:35** See Job 41:11. **12:1a** Greek *brothers.* **12:1b** Or *This is your spiritual
worship;* or *This is your reasonable service.* **12:3a** Or *Because of the grace;* compare 1:5.
12:3b Or *by the faith God has given you;* or *by the standard of our God-given faith.*

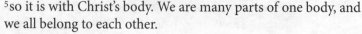

Anchor Passage

PASSAGE: **Romans 12:9-18**

FRIENDSHIP TYPE: *Neighbors*

FRIENDSHIP LAYER: *Companionship*

Relational Checklist

Imagine one or two of your neighbors as you read **Romans 12:9-18**.

It's quite a list...seems like one command after another. And, in fact, it is—there are over 19 total commands in the passage. And many of them are nearly impossible.

So how are you supposed to follow them all? It's hard enough to try to love others with genuine affection—but to bless those who persecute you? To *always* be ready to help? What about when you're tired or sick? It's almost enough to make you crawl back into bed and sleep the rest of your life!

Well then, it's a good thing Paul didn't leave it at that. It's a good thing he also mentioned that you don't have to do any of that on your own. It's a good thing he included the part about God transforming you into a new person...the kind of person who's a bit more like God. It's a little easier to look at all those commands when you know God has given you certain gifts to help you live in peace with everyone (**Romans 12:1-8**).

So next time you see those neighbors, take comfort knowing that God will help you to live in companionship as neighbors...to "love each other with genuine affection, and take delight in honoring each other."

Anchor Passage continues on page 309...

⁵so it is with Christ's body. We are many parts of one body, and we all belong to each other.

⁶In his grace, God has given us different gifts for doing certain things well. So if God has given you the ability to prophesy, speak out with as much faith as God has given you. ⁷If your gift is serving others, serve them well. If you are a teacher, teach well. ⁸If your gift is to encourage others, be encouraging. If it is giving, give generously. If God has given you leadership ability, take the responsibility seriously. And if you have a gift for showing kindness to others, do it gladly.

⁹Don't just pretend to love others. Really love them. Hate what is wrong. Hold tightly to what is good. ¹⁰Love each other with genuine affection,* and take delight in honoring each other. ¹¹Never be lazy, but work hard and serve the Lord enthusiastically.* ¹²Rejoice in our confident hope. Be patient in trouble, and keep on praying. ¹³When God's people are in need, be ready to help them. Always be eager to practice hospitality.

¹⁴Bless those who persecute you. Don't curse them; pray that God will bless them. ¹⁵Be happy with those who are happy, and weep with those who weep. ¹⁶Live in harmony with each other. Don't be too proud to enjoy the company of ordinary people. And don't think you know it all!

¹⁷Never pay back evil with more evil. Do things in such a way that everyone can see you are honorable. ¹⁸Do all that you can to live in peace with everyone. ⚓

¹⁹Dear friends, never take revenge. Leave that to the righteous anger of God. For the Scriptures say,

"I will take revenge;
    I will pay them back,"*
    says the LORD.

²⁰Instead,

"If your enemies are hungry, feed them.
    If they are thirsty, give them something to drink.

12:10 Greek *with brotherly love.*   **12:11** Or *but serve the Lord with a zealous spirit;* or *but let the Spirit excite you as you serve the Lord.*   **12:19** Deut 32:35.

In doing this, you will heap
burning coals of shame on their heads."*

²¹ Don't let evil conquer you, but conquer evil by doing good.

CHAPTER 13
Respect for Authority

Everyone must submit to governing authorities. For all authority comes from God, and those in positions of authority have
been placed there by God. ²So anyone who rebels against
authority is rebelling against what God has instituted, and they
will be punished. ³For the authorities do not strike fear in people who are doing right, but in those who are doing wrong.
Would you like to live without fear of the authorities? Do what
is right, and they will honor you. ⁴The authorities are God's servants, sent for your good. But if you are doing wrong, of course
you should be afraid, for they have the power to punish you.
They are God's servants, sent for the very purpose of punishing
those who do what is wrong. ⁵So you must submit to them, not
only to avoid punishment, but also to keep a clear conscience.

⁶Pay your taxes, too, for these same reasons. For government
workers need to be paid. They are serving God in what they do.
⁷Give to everyone what you owe them: Pay your taxes and government fees to those who collect them, and give respect and
honor to those who are in authority.

Love Fulfills God's Requirements

⁸Owe nothing to anyone—except for your obligation to love one
another. If you love your neighbor, you will fulfill the requirements of God's law. ⁹For the commandments say, "You must not
commit adultery. You must not murder. You must not steal. You
must not covet."* These—and other such commandments—are
summed up in this one commandment: "Love your neighbor as
yourself."* ¹⁰Love does no wrong to others, so love fulfills the
requirements of God's law.

¹¹This is all the more urgent, for you know how late it is; time
is running out. Wake up, for our salvation is nearer now than
when we first believed. ¹²The night is almost gone; the day of
salvation will soon be here. So remove your dark deeds like
dirty clothes, and put on the shining armor of right living.
¹³Because we belong to the day, we must live decent lives for
all to see. Don't participate in the darkness of wild parties and
drunkenness, or in sexual promiscuity and immoral living, or

12:20 Prov 25:21-22.   **13:9a** Exod 20:13-15, 17.   **13:9b** Lev 19:18.

Anchor Passage continued from page 308...

THE ONE THING
1
YOU CAN DO THIS WEEK

Experience

Read through Romans 12:9-
18 again. Circle, highlight, or
underline one of those commands
in the passage—choose the one
that you want to do for a neighbor this week.
Perhaps you know a neighbor who just had a
baby and is in need. How can you help? Offer to
baby-sit; give her your child's old crib; drive her
to the doctor. Or maybe you know a neighbor
who is having unexpected guests; be hospitable
and help out by delivering a homemade meal or
box of chicken from your favorite chicken joint.
Once you've chosen your "command" to follow,
ask God to help you follow through.

Reflect

★ How would you summarize Paul's list of
commands in one sentence?

★ When has someone followed a command on this
list and reached out to you in friendship? How did
that action make you feel?

★ Reflect on Paul's list again. What good habits
do you already have that correspond to this list?
(Don't think of your failures here—think about
how God has helped transform you into a new
person!)

★ How did your chosen command help you become a
closer companion to your neighbor?

DIGGING DEEPER

FRIENDSHIP TYPE:
Neighbors

FRIENDSHIP LAYER:
Companionship

For being a companion of your neighbors, find...

➥ The Friendship Experience .... on page 301
➥ The Friendship Story .... on page 305
➥ What to Say and What Not to Say .... on page 297

in quarreling and jealousy. ¹⁴Instead, clothe yourself with the presence of the Lord Jesus Christ. And don't let yourself think about ways to indulge your evil desires.

CHAPTER **14**

The Danger of Criticism

Accept other believers who are weak in faith, and don't argue with them about what they think is right or wrong. ²For instance, one person believes it's all right to eat anything. But another believer with a sensitive conscience will eat only vegetables. ³Those who feel free to eat anything must not look down on those who don't. And those who don't eat certain foods must not condemn those who do, for God has accepted them. ⁴Who are you to condemn someone else's servants? They are responsible to the Lord, so let him judge whether they are right or wrong. And with the Lord's help, they will do what is right and will receive his approval.

⁵In the same way, some think one day is more holy than another day, while others think every day is alike. You should each be fully convinced that whichever day you choose is acceptable. ⁶Those who worship the Lord on a special day do it to honor him. Those who eat any kind of food do so to honor the Lord, since they give thanks to God before eating. And those who refuse to eat certain foods also want to please the Lord and give thanks to God. ⁷For we don't live for ourselves or die for ourselves. ⁸If we live, it's to honor the Lord. And if we die, it's to honor the Lord. So whether we live or die, we belong to the Lord. ⁹Christ died and rose again for this very purpose—to be Lord both of the living and of the dead.

¹⁰So why do you condemn another believer*? Why do you look down on another believer? Remember, we will all stand before the judgment seat of God. ¹¹For the Scriptures say,

> "'As surely as I live,' says the LORD,
> 'every knee will bend to me,
>   and every tongue will confess and give praise to God.*'"

¹²Yes, each of us will give a personal account to God. ¹³So let's stop condemning each other. Decide instead to live in such a way that you will not cause another believer to stumble and fall.

¹⁴I know and am convinced on the authority of the Lord Jesus that no food, in and of itself, is wrong to eat. But if some-

14:10 Greek *your brother;* also in 14:10b, 13, 15, 21.   **14:11** Or *confess allegiance to God.* Isa 49:18; 45:23 (Greek version).

one believes it is wrong, then for that person it is wrong. ¹⁵And if another believer is distressed by what you eat, you are not acting in love if you eat it. Don't let your eating ruin someone for whom Christ died. ¹⁶Then you will not be criticized for doing something you believe is good. ¹⁷For the Kingdom of God is not a matter of what we eat or drink, but of living a life of goodness and peace and joy in the Holy Spirit. ¹⁸If you serve Christ with this attitude, you will please God, and others will approve of you, too. ¹⁹So then, let us aim for harmony in the church and try to build each other up.

²⁰Don't tear apart the work of God over what you eat. Remember, all foods are acceptable, but it is wrong to eat something if it makes another person stumble. ²¹It is better not to eat meat or drink wine or do anything else if it might cause another believer to stumble. ²²You may believe there's nothing wrong with what you are doing, but keep it between yourself and God. Blessed are those who don't feel guilty for doing something they have decided is right. ²³But if you have doubts about whether or not you should eat something, you are sinning if you go ahead and do it. For you are not following your convictions. If you do anything you believe is not right, you are sinning.

CHAPTER 15
Living to Please Others

We who are strong must be considerate of those who are sensitive about things like this. We must not just please ourselves. ²We should help others do what is right and build them up in the Lord. ³For even Christ didn't live to please himself. As the Scriptures say, "The insults of those who insult you, O God, have fallen on me."* ⁴Such things were written in the Scriptures long ago to teach us. And the Scriptures give us hope and encouragement as we wait patiently for God's promises to be fulfilled.

⁵May God, who gives this patience and encouragement, help you live in complete harmony with each other, as is fitting for followers of Christ Jesus. ⁶Then all of you can join together with one voice, giving praise and glory to God, the Father of our Lord Jesus Christ.

⁷Therefore, accept each other just as Christ has accepted you so that God will be given glory. ⁸Remember that Christ came as a servant to the Jews* to show that God is true to the promises he made to their ancestors. ⁹He also came so that the Gentiles

15:3 Greek *who insult you have fallen on me.* Ps 69:9. **15:8** Greek *servant of circumcision.*

No. 12-TE-311

FRIENDSHIP
STORY

FRIENDSHIP TYPE:	FRIENDSHIP LAYER:
Friends	*Getting Acquainted*

BASED ON TRUE EVENTS

Friendship Shows You Really Care

It wasn't an easy life. Divorced and taking care of his little boy, Jason was a busy man, and he certainly didn't have time for any extras in his life. And church was definitely an "extra" in his mind. In fact, he couldn't even remember the last time he'd been to church. Well, maybe he could remember…it was that time his mother had forced him to go as a teenager. And then the other teens were rude to him. And that was that. If Christians were going to act that way, then he certainly wasn't going to put himself out going back to church. Hypocrites.

So why was he agreeing to go now? Why was he standing here nodding his head as Tom explained the directions to the church? What had made him change his mind?

Jason knew the answer before he asked the question: Tom. Tom was the reason he would go.

Tom made him question his original take on Christians. Tom wasn't a hypocrite. Tom wasn't rude. Tom didn't try to force Jason to change. Tom listened to how Jason felt without judgment or easy answers. Ever since they'd met—in the bleachers at their sons' first baseball game—Tom had simply been his friend.

FRIENDSHIP STORY

continues on page 312…

FRIENDSHIP STORY *continued from page 311...*

And Jason trusted Tom; he trusted Tom enough to put his bad church experiences aside and try again. After all, they had a lot in common—if Tom liked this church-thing and the people that went there, then maybe he would, too.

And the following Sunday, when Jason and his son slowly climbed the stairs to the entrance of the church…Tom was there to meet them.

Experience

Tom and Jason's friendship didn't start at church—it started at a baseball game. Through the process of getting acquainted and becoming friends, Tom and Jason shared their lives with one another…and eventually, because of Tom's friendship, Jason was willing to try church—and God—again.

Get acquainted with someone outside of church this week. Don't do it just so you can invite them to church, either. Do it because you want to be friends. Do it because you're interested in growing that friendship and in sharing your life with that person. Do it because getting acquainted with a new friend can change your life…and your friend's.

Reflect

★ Tom didn't have an agenda when he got to know Jason—he simply wanted to be friends. Why is that distinction so important?

★ Have you ever had an agenda when you got to know someone? How did that affect your friendship?

★ Jason trusted Tom, and that's why he went to church. Trust is key in friendship, and it's won (or lost) from Day One of that friendship. How can you build trust with the friend you just met?

might give glory to God for his mercies to them. That is what the psalmist meant when he wrote:

"For this, I will praise you among the Gentiles;
  I will sing praises to your name."*

¹⁰And in another place it is written,

"Rejoice with his people,
  you Gentiles."*

¹¹And yet again,

"Praise the LORD, all you Gentiles.
  Praise him, all you people of the earth."*

¹²And in another place Isaiah said,

"The heir to David's throne* will come,
  and he will rule over the Gentiles.
They will place their hope on him."*

¹³I pray that God, the source of hope, will fill you completely with joy and peace because you trust in him. Then you will overflow with confident hope through the power of the Holy Spirit.

Paul's Reason for Writing

¹⁴I am fully convinced, my dear brothers and sisters,* that you are full of goodness. You know these things so well you can teach each other all about them. ¹⁵Even so, I have been bold enough to write about some of these points, knowing that all you need is this reminder. For by God's grace, ¹⁶I am a special messenger from Christ Jesus to you Gentiles. I bring you the Good News so that I might present you as an acceptable offering to God, made holy by the Holy Spirit. ¹⁷So I have reason to be enthusiastic about all Christ Jesus has done through me in my service to God. ¹⁸Yet I dare not boast about anything except what Christ has done through me, bringing the Gentiles to God by my message and by the way I worked among them. ¹⁹They were convinced by the power of miraculous signs and wonders and by the power of God's Spirit.* In this way, I have fully presented the Good News of Christ from Jerusalem all the way to Illyricum.* ²⁰My ambition has always been to preach the Good News

15:9 Ps 18:49. 15:10 Deut 32:43. 15:11 Ps 117:1. 15:12a Greek *The root of Jesse.* David was the son of Jesse. 15:12b Isa 11:10 (Greek version). 15:14 Greek *brothers;* also in 15:30. 15:19a Other manuscripts read *the Spirit;* still others read *the Holy Spirit.* 15:19b *Illyricum* was a region northeast of Italy.

where the name of Christ has never been heard, rather than where a church has already been started by someone else. ²¹I have been following the plan spoken of in the Scriptures, where it says,

> "Those who have never been told about him will see,
>   and those who have never heard of him will understand."*

²²In fact, my visit to you has been delayed so long because I have been preaching in these places.

Paul's Travel Plans

²³But now I have finished my work in these regions, and after all these long years of waiting, I am eager to visit you. ²⁴I am planning to go to Spain, and when I do, I will stop off in Rome. And after I have enjoyed your fellowship for a little while, you can provide for my journey.

²⁵But before I come, I must go to Jerusalem to take a gift to the believers* there. ²⁶For you see, the believers in Macedonia and Achaia* have eagerly taken up an offering for the poor among the believers in Jerusalem. ²⁷They were glad to do this because they feel they owe a real debt to them. Since the Gentiles received the spiritual blessings of the Good News from the believers in Jerusalem, they feel the least they can do in return is to help them financially. ²⁸As soon as I have delivered this money and completed this good deed of theirs, I will come to see you on my way to Spain. ²⁹And I am sure that when I come, Christ will richly bless our time together.

³⁰Dear brothers and sisters, I urge you in the name of our Lord Jesus Christ to join in my struggle by praying to God for me. Do this because of your love for me, given to you by the Holy Spirit. ³¹Pray that I will be rescued from those in Judea who refuse to obey God. Pray also that the believers there will be willing to accept the donation* I am taking to Jerusalem. ³²Then, by the will of God, I will be able to come to you with a joyful heart, and we will be an encouragement to each other.

³³And now may God, who gives us his peace, be with you all. Amen.*

CHAPTER 16

Paul Greets His Friends

I commend to you our sister Phoebe, who is a deacon in the church in Cenchrea. ²Welcome her in the Lord as one who is

"First time strangers; second time friends."
~ Chinese proverb

JOURNAL

15:21 Isa 52:15 (Greek version).   15:25 Greek *God's holy people;* also in 15:26, 31.   15:26 *Macedonia* and *Achaia* were the northern and southern regions of Greece.   15:31 Greek *the ministry;* other manuscripts read *the gift.*   15:33 Some manuscripts omit *Amen.* One very early manuscript places 16:25-27 here.

WHAT TO SAY AND WHAT NOT TO SAY

FRIENDSHIP TYPE: *Friends* **FRIENDSHIP LAYER:** *Getting Acquainted*

We Have Another Friend!

You've got a new person in your group. He's a bit shy—unsure of himself. He only knows one person there, the person who invited him, and everyone seems a little uncomfortable around him…it's been awhile since you've had a new person. But, this is what you're all about, right? Meeting new people. Having fun together. Becoming better friends with one another and with God.

This is where the rubber meets the road for your group, and if you want to make your new friend comfortable and welcome, here's a few things to avoid:

WHAT NOT TO SAY:

★ "Welcome to the group. We've all been friends for a very long time…well, let's hope you fit in."
★ "You're using the wrong Bible translation. You'll have to buy the right one in order to keep up."
★ "You're a little late, and we don't have time to talk right now. We need to get on with our study for tonight."

WHAT TO SAY:

"Jesus looked around and saw them following. 'What do you want?' he asked them…They went with him to the place where he was staying, and they remained with him the rest of the day" (**John 1:38-39**). Jesus made everyone feel welcome—take his example, and do the same.

WHAT TO SAY AND WHAT NOT TO SAY *continues on page 315…*

worthy of honor among God's people. Help her in whatever she needs, for she has been helpful to many, and especially to me.

³Give my greetings to Priscilla and Aquila, my co-workers in the ministry of Christ Jesus. ⁴In fact, they once risked their lives for me. I am thankful to them, and so are all the Gentile churches. ⁵Also give my greetings to the church that meets in their home.

Greet my dear friend Epenetus. He was the first person from the province of Asia to become a follower of Christ. ⁶Give my greetings to Mary, who has worked so hard for your benefit. ⁷Greet Andronicus and Junia,* my fellow Jews,* who were in prison with me. They are highly respected among the apostles and became followers of Christ before I did. ⁸Greet Ampliatus, my dear friend in the Lord. ⁹Greet Urbanus, our co-worker in Christ, and my dear friend Stachys.

¹⁰Greet Apelles, a good man whom Christ approves. And give my greetings to the believers from the household of Aristobulus. ¹¹Greet Herodion, my fellow Jew.* Greet the Lord's people from the household of Narcissus. ¹²Give my greetings to Tryphena and Tryphosa, the Lord's workers, and to dear Persis, who has worked so hard for the Lord. ¹³Greet Rufus, whom the Lord picked out to be his very own; and also his dear mother, who has been a mother to me.

¹⁴Give my greetings to Asyncritus, Phlegon, Hermes, Patrobas, Hermas, and the brothers and sisters* who meet with them. ¹⁵Give my greetings to Philologus, Julia, Nereus and his sister, and to Olympas and all the believers* who meet with them. ¹⁶Greet each other in Christian love.* All the churches of Christ send you their greetings.

Paul's Final Instructions

¹⁷And now I make one more appeal, my dear brothers and sisters. Watch out for people who cause divisions and upset people's faith by teaching things contrary to what you have been taught. Stay away from them. ¹⁸Such people are not serving Christ our Lord; they are serving their own personal interests. By smooth talk and glowing words they deceive innocent people. ¹⁹But everyone knows that you are obedient to the Lord. This makes me very happy. I want you to be wise in doing right and to stay innocent of any wrong. ²⁰The God of peace will soon crush Satan under your feet. May the grace of our Lord Jesus* be with you.

16:7a *Junia* is a feminine name. Some late manuscripts accent the word so it reads *Junias,* a masculine name; still others read *Julia* (feminine). **16:7b** Or *compatriots;* also in 16:21. **16:11** Or *compatriot.* **16:14** Greek *brothers;* also in 16:17. **16:15** Greek *all of God's holy people.* **16:16** Greek *with a sacred kiss.* **16:20** Some manuscripts read *Lord Jesus Christ.*

²¹Timothy, my fellow worker, sends you his greetings, as do Lucius, Jason, and Sosipater, my fellow Jews.

²²I, Tertius, the one writing this letter for Paul, send my greetings, too, as one of the Lord's followers.

²³Gaius says hello to you. He is my host and also serves as host to the whole church. Erastus, the city treasurer, sends you his greetings, and so does our brother Quartus.*

²⁵Now all glory to God, who is able to make you strong, just as my Good News says. This message about Jesus Christ has revealed his plan for you Gentiles, a plan kept secret from the beginning of time. ²⁶But now as the prophets* foretold and as the eternal God has commanded, this message is made known to all Gentiles everywhere, so that they too might believe and obey him. ²⁷All glory to the only wise God, through Jesus Christ, forever. Amen.

16:23 Some manuscripts add verse 24, *May the grace of our Lord Jesus Christ be with you all. Amen.* Still others add this sentence after verse 27.   16:26 Greek *the prophetic writings.*

WHAT TO SAY AND WHAT NOT TO SAY *continued from page 314...*

★ "We're so glad that you came to our group. It's always good to have someone new."

★ "It's great that you have a different Bible translation…it'll give us another way of looking at things."

★ "Hey, maybe a few of us can go out for a cup of coffee after this and get to know each other better."

JOURNAL

"Never let loyalty and kindness leave you!
Tie them around your neck as a reminder.
Write them deep within your heart.
Then you will find favor with both God and people, and you will earn a good reputation."
~ Proverbs 3:3-4

1 Corinthians

AUTHOR:	DATE WRITTEN:
Paul	Approximately A.D. 55

CHAPTER 1

Greetings from Paul

This letter is from Paul, chosen by the will of God to be an apostle of Christ Jesus, and from our brother Sosthenes.

²I am writing to God's church in Corinth,* to you who have been called by God to be his own holy people. He made you holy by means of Christ Jesus,* just as he did for all people everywhere who call on the name of our Lord Jesus Christ, their Lord and ours.

³May God our Father and the Lord Jesus Christ give you grace and peace.

Paul Gives Thanks to God

⁴I always thank my God for you and for the gracious gifts he has given you, now that you belong to Christ Jesus. ⁵Through him, God has enriched your church in every way—with all of your eloquent words and all of your knowledge. ⁶This confirms that what I told you about Christ is true. ⁷Now you have every spiritual gift you need as you eagerly wait for the return of our Lord Jesus Christ. ⁸He will keep you strong to the end so that you will be free from all blame on the day when our Lord Jesus Christ returns. ⁹God will do this, for he is faithful to do what he says, and he has invited you into partnership with his Son, Jesus Christ our Lord.

Divisions in the Church

¹⁰I appeal to you, dear brothers and sisters,* by the authority of our Lord Jesus Christ, to live in harmony with each other. Let there be no divisions in the church. Rather, be of one mind, united in thought and purpose. ¹¹For some members of Chloe's household have told me about your quarrels, my dear brothers

1:2a *Corinth* was the capital city of Achaia, the southern region of the Greek peninsula.   1:2b Or *because you belong to Christ Jesus.*   1:10 Greek *brothers;* also in 1:11, 26.

and sisters. [12]Some of you are saying, "I am a follower of Paul." Others are saying, "I follow Apollos," or "I follow Peter,*" or "I follow only Christ."

[13]Has Christ been divided into factions? Was I, Paul, crucified for you? Were any of you baptized in the name of Paul? Of course not! [14]I thank God that I did not baptize any of you except Crispus and Gaius, [15]for now no one can say they were baptized in my name. [16](Oh yes, I also baptized the household of Stephanas, but I don't remember baptizing anyone else.) [17]For Christ didn't send me to baptize, but to preach the Good News—and not with clever speech, for fear that the cross of Christ would lose its power.

The Wisdom of God

[18]The message of the cross is foolish to those who are headed for destruction! But we who are being saved know it is the very power of God. [19]As the Scriptures say,

> "I will destroy the wisdom of the wise
>   and discard the intelligence of the intelligent."*

[20]So where does this leave the philosophers, the scholars, and the world's brilliant debaters? God has made the wisdom of this world look foolish. [21]Since God in his wisdom saw to it that the world would never know him through human wisdom, he has used our foolish preaching to save those who believe. [22]It is foolish to the Jews, who ask for signs from heaven. And it is foolish to the Greeks, who seek human wisdom. [23]So when we preach that Christ was crucified, the Jews are offended and the Gentiles say it's all nonsense.

[24]But to those called by God to salvation, both Jews and Gentiles,* Christ is the power of God and the wisdom of God. [25]This foolish plan of God is wiser than the wisest of human plans, and God's weakness is stronger than the greatest of human strength.

[26]Remember, dear brothers and sisters, that few of you were wise in the world's eyes or powerful or wealthy* when God called you. [27]Instead, God chose things the world considers foolish in order to shame those who think they are wise. And he chose things that are powerless to shame those who are powerful. [28]God chose things despised by the world,* things counted as nothing at all, and used them to bring to nothing what the world considers important. [29]As a result, no one can ever boast in the presence of God.

1:12 Greek *Cephas.*   1:19 Isa 29:14.   1:24 Greek *and Greeks.*   1:26 Or *high born.*   1:28 Or *God chose those who are low born.*

FRIENDSHIP STORY

No. 13-FS-317

FRIENDSHIP TYPE: *Neighbors*

FRIENDSHIP LAYER: *Commitment*

FOUND IN SCRIPTURE

Building Up

Malkijah and his sons live two doors down from me and my family. We've seen a lot of each other lately. We've been working together to rebuild the wall that surrounds our city. It's been lying in heaps too long. It's time to change that. A new man in town, a wise man named Nehemiah, is motivating my people to do something about our city and its crumbling defensive wall. But it certainly hasn't been easy!

Day in, day out, dawn to dusk, we labor to put the stones back in their places, to lift the doors, sink the bolts, and set the bars into their proper alignment. My neighbor, Malkijah, is a diligent worker. He works with me constantly to raise our assigned portion of the wall. I'm glad he works with me…he's so dedicated to the work. We also work near the daughters of Shallum who show care for the work, care for the rest of our people, and commitment to our cause and to us.

FRIENDSHIP STORY *continues on page 318…*

FRIENDSHIP STORY *continued from page 317...*

Opposition has risen to the project by some outsiders. They make fun of us, and call us feeble Jews. I even heard them say that if a fox climbed upon our work it would come tumbling down—how wrong they are! They don't realize that daily we cry out to our God, the God of Abraham, and he hears us. God gives us strength even when we think we can go on no longer. When Malkijah sags beneath the burden of his load, I find the strength to go to him and help. When I think I can no longer lift my burden, others around me come to my side and help me lift my arms.

There is rumor of attack. We can't ignore the possibility, so we have prepared. When Malkijah and his sons toil on my right, and my other neighbor Shallum and his daughters work on my left, I carry my spear and shield and watch over them. I will do everything I can to protect them! And when it's my turn to carry the mortar and trowel, I know they're watching my back. We work together to build the wall around our city. Together, we'll accomplish this task.

The stars are out now. I'm on duty as guard. I struggle to keep my heavy lids open. I stand tall,

holding my weapon at all times. The wall is nearly complete, but I will *not* slack in my duty. And when we're done, we will celebrate! We'll worship our God and feast together. For without each other, we couldn't have come this far. It's because of our commitment to each other and to our God that now the wall around our city is nearly complete.

Read the whole story in **Nehemiah 1–6:16** *in the Old Testament.*

FRIENDSHIP STORY *continues on page 319...*

³⁰God has united you with Christ Jesus. For our benefit God made him to be wisdom itself. Christ made us right with God; he made us pure and holy, and he freed us from sin. ³¹Therefore, as the Scriptures say, "If you want to boast, boast only about the LORD."*

CHAPTER 2

Paul's Message of Wisdom

When I first came to you, dear brothers and sisters,* I didn't use lofty words and impressive wisdom to tell you God's secret plan.* ²For I decided that while I was with you I would forget everything except Jesus Christ, the one who was crucified. ³I came to you in weakness—timid and trembling. ⁴And my message and my preaching were very plain. Rather than using clever and persuasive speeches, I relied only on the power of the Holy Spirit. ⁵I did this so you would trust not in human wisdom but in the power of God.

⁶Yet when I am among mature believers, I do speak with words of wisdom, but not the kind of wisdom that belongs to this world or to the rulers of this world, who are soon forgotten. ⁷No, the wisdom we speak of is the mystery of God*—his plan that was previously hidden, even though he made it for our ultimate glory before the world began. ⁸But the rulers of this world have not understood it; if they had, they would not have crucified our glorious Lord. ⁹That is what the Scriptures mean when they say,

"No eye has seen, no ear has heard,
   and no mind has imagined
what God has prepared
   for those who love him."*

¹⁰But* it was to us that God revealed these things by his Spirit. For his Spirit searches out everything and shows us God's deep secrets. ¹¹No one can know a person's thoughts except that person's own spirit, and no one can know God's thoughts except God's own Spirit. ¹²And we have received God's Spirit (not the world's spirit), so we can know the wonderful things God has freely given us.

¹³When we tell you these things, we do not use words that come from human wisdom. Instead, we speak words given to us by the Spirit, using the Spirit's words to explain spiritual truths.*

1:31 Jer 9:24.   **2:1a** Greek *brothers.*   **2:1b** Greek *God's mystery;* other manuscripts read *God's testimony.*   **2:7** Greek *But we speak God's wisdom in a mystery.*   **2:9** Isa 64:4.   **2:10** Some manuscripts read *For.*   **2:13** Or *explaining spiritual truths in spiritual language,* or *explaining spiritual truths to spiritual people.*

14But people who aren't spiritual* can't receive these truths from God's Spirit. It all sounds foolish to them and they can't understand it, for only those who are spiritual can understand what the Spirit means. 15Those who are spiritual can evaluate all things, but they themselves cannot be evaluated by others. 16For,

"Who can know the LORD's thoughts?
Who knows enough to teach him?"*

But we understand these things, for we have the mind of Christ.

CHAPTER 3

Paul and Apollos, Servants of Christ

Dear brothers and sisters,* when I was with you I couldn't talk to you as I would to spiritual people.* I had to talk as though you belonged to this world or as though you were infants in the Christian life.* 2I had to feed you with milk, not with solid food, because you weren't ready for anything stronger. And you still aren't ready, 3for you are still controlled by your sinful nature. You are jealous of one another and quarrel with each other. Doesn't that prove you are controlled by your sinful nature? Aren't you living like people of the world? 4When one of you says, "I am a follower of Paul," and another says, "I follow Apollos," aren't you acting just like people of the world?

5After all, who is Apollos? Who is Paul? We are only God's servants through whom you believed the Good News. Each of us did the work the Lord gave us. 6I planted the seed in your hearts, and Apollos watered it, but it was God who made it grow. 7It's not important who does the planting, or who does the watering. What's important is that God makes the seed grow. 8The one who plants and the one who waters work together with the same purpose. And both will be rewarded for their own hard work. 9For we are both God's workers. And you are God's field. You are God's building.

10Because of God's grace to me, I have laid the foundation like an expert builder. Now others are building on it. But whoever is building on this foundation must be very careful. 11For no one can lay any foundation other than the one we already have—Jesus Christ.

12Anyone who builds on that foundation may use a variety of materials—gold, silver, jewels, wood, hay, or straw. 13But on the judgment day, fire will reveal what kind of work each builder

2:14 Or who don't have the Spirit; or who have only physical life.   2:16 Isa 40:13 (Greek version).
3:1a Greek Brothers.   3:1b Or to people who have the Spirit.   3:1c Greek in Christ.

FRIENDSHIP STORY continued from page 318...

Experience

Get together with others in your neighborhood and surrounding area. During your meeting, plan a way that you can "build up" your neighborhood together. Perhaps you can begin an after-school tutorial program for kids in your area, or maybe you can all get together and build a playground, or replace those cracked sidewalks. Whatever you decide to do, make a timeline during your meeting and make plans for completing the project!

Reflect

★ What can you do to make your neighborhood a more friendly and cooperative place?
★ What words would you use to describe a good neighborhood?
★ How can you make those words a reality in your neighborhood?

JOURNAL

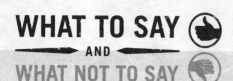

WHAT TO SAY 👍 AND WHAT NOT TO SAY 👎

FRIENDSHIP TYPE: *Neighbors*   FRIENDSHIP LAYER: *Commitment*

Test Your Commitment

Answer the following questions to see how committed you are to your neighbors!

1. A certain fellow walks his dog by your house every day and allows his animal to do its business on your lawn. You would:

a. Follow him home to learn where he lives, and deliver his dog's "business" on his front porch when he isn't looking.

b. Leave a container of plastic bags near the sidewalk with a sign that yells, "CLEAN UP AFTER YOUR BEAST!!"

c. Get to know the fellow by visiting with him when he passes by. Treat him with the respect you'd like him to show you, with the hope of one day growing a friendship.

2. Your child plays on a sports team with another child whose parent yells at all the other players to get with it, win the game or else! You would:

a. Send around a petition to get the parent kicked off the field.

b. Ask the screaming parent to step out back and see who's really tough and who's all hot air.

c. Ask God to help you have patience and love for the parent, and attempt to sit near the parent at games to offer kind, calm words and a gentle example.

WHAT TO SAY AND WHAT NOT TO SAY *continues on page 321…*

has done. The fire will show if a person's work has any value. [14]If the work survives, that builder will receive a reward. [15]But if the work is burned up, the builder will suffer great loss. The builder will be saved, but like someone barely escaping through a wall of flames.

[16]Don't you realize that all of you together are the temple of God and that the Spirit of God lives in* you? [17]God will destroy anyone who destroys this temple. For God's temple is holy, and you are that temple.

[18]Stop deceiving yourselves. If you think you are wise by this world's standards, you need to become a fool to be truly wise. [19]For the wisdom of this world is foolishness to God. As the Scriptures say,

"He traps the wise
    in the snare of their own cleverness."*

[20]And again,

"The LORD knows the thoughts of the wise;
    he knows they are worthless."*

[21]So don't boast about following a particular human leader. For everything belongs to you—[22]whether Paul or Apollos or Peter,* or the world, or life and death, or the present and the future. Everything belongs to you, [23]and you belong to Christ, and Christ belongs to God.

CHAPTER **4**

Paul's Relationship with the Corinthians

So look at Apollos and me as mere servants of Christ who have been put in charge of explaining God's mysteries. [2]Now, a person who is put in charge as a manager must be faithful. [3]As for me, it matters very little how I might be evaluated by you or by any human authority. I don't even trust my own judgment on this point. [4]My conscience is clear, but that doesn't prove I'm right. It is the Lord himself who will examine me and decide.

[5]So don't make judgments about anyone ahead of time—before the Lord returns. For he will bring our darkest secrets to light and will reveal our private motives. Then God will give to each one whatever praise is due.

[6]Dear brothers and sisters,* I have used Apollos and myself to illustrate what I've been saying. If you pay attention to what I have quoted from the Scriptures,* you won't be proud of one

3:16 Or *among.*   **3:19** Job 5:13.   **3:20** Ps 94:11.   **3:22** Greek *Cephas.*   **4:6a** Greek *Brothers.*
4:6b Or *If you learn not to go beyond "what is written."*

of your leaders at the expense of another. [7]For what gives you the right to make such a judgment? What do you have that God hasn't given you? And if everything you have is from God, why boast as though it were not a gift?

[8]You think you already have everything you need. You think you are already rich. You have begun to reign in God's kingdom without us! I wish you really were reigning already, for then we would be reigning with you. [9]Instead, I sometimes think God has put us apostles on display, like prisoners of war at the end of a victor's parade, condemned to die. We have become a spectacle to the entire world—to people and angels alike.

[10]Our dedication to Christ makes us look like fools, but you claim to be so wise in Christ! We are weak, but you are so powerful! You are honored, but we are ridiculed. [11]Even now we go hungry and thirsty, and we don't have enough clothes to keep warm. We are often beaten and have no home. [12]We work wearily with our own hands to earn our living. We bless those who curse us. We are patient with those who abuse us. [13]We appeal gently when evil things are said about us. Yet we are treated like the world's garbage, like everybody's trash—right up to the present moment.

[14]I am not writing these things to shame you, but to warn you as my beloved children. [15]For even if you had ten thousand others to teach you about Christ, you have only one spiritual father. For I became your father in Christ Jesus when I preached the Good News to you. [16]So I urge you to imitate me.

[17]That's why I have sent Timothy, my beloved and faithful child in the Lord. He will remind you of how I follow Christ Jesus, just as I teach in all the churches wherever I go.

[18]Some of you have become arrogant, thinking I will not visit you again. [19]But I will come—and soon—if the Lord lets me, and then I'll find out whether these arrogant people just give pretentious speeches or whether they really have God's power. [20]For the Kingdom of God is not just a lot of talk; it is living by God's power. [21]Which do you choose? Should I come with a rod to punish you, or should I come with love and a gentle spirit?

CHAPTER **5**

Paul Condemns Spiritual Pride

I can hardly believe the report about the sexual immorality going on among you—something that even pagans don't do. I am told that a man in your church is living in sin with his

WHAT TO SAY AND **WHAT NOT TO SAY** *continued from page 320…*

3. **Your co-worker keeps eating your lunch. You even found the empty wrappers in the trash can by the culprit's desk. The best thing to do would be:**

a. Draw and hang up a picture of a pig with an arrow pointing toward the thief.

b. Confront the co-worker in front of everyone, producing the evidence from the trash can to prove your point.

c. Bring extra, and offer some to your co-worker.

WHAT NOT TO SAY:

★ If you answered A or B to the questions, then you'd best go read **1 Corinthians 13:1-7** a few more times. If you wanted to answer A or B, but knew C was best…well, then you're on your way to knowing how to show love to your neighbors.

WHAT TO SAY:

★ If it was a cinch to go with C every time, then great job! Keep up the good work—go out there and show 'em how to love one another as God calls you to!

stepmother.* ²You are so proud of yourselves, but you should be mourning in sorrow and shame. And you should remove this man from your fellowship.

³Even though I am not with you in person, I am with you in the Spirit.* And as though I were there, I have already passed judgment on this man ⁴in the name of the Lord Jesus. You must call a meeting of the church.* I will be present with you in spirit, and so will the power of our Lord Jesus. ⁵Then you must throw this man out and hand him over to Satan so that his sinful nature will be destroyed* and he himself* will be saved on the day the Lord* returns.

⁶Your boasting about this is terrible. Don't you realize that this sin is like a little yeast that spreads through the whole batch of dough? ⁷Get rid of the old "yeast" by removing this wicked person from among you. Then you will be like a fresh batch of dough made without yeast, which is what you really are. Christ, our Passover Lamb, has been sacrificed for us.* ⁸So let us celebrate the festival, not with the old bread* of wickedness and evil, but with the new bread* of sincerity and truth.

⁹When I wrote to you before, I told you not to associate with people who indulge in sexual sin. ¹⁰But I wasn't talking about unbelievers who indulge in sexual sin, or are greedy, or cheat people, or worship idols. You would have to leave this world to avoid people like that. ¹¹I meant that you are not to associate with anyone who claims to be a believer* yet indulges in sexual sin, or is greedy, or worships idols, or is abusive, or is a drunkard, or cheats people. Don't even eat with such people.

¹²It isn't my responsibility to judge outsiders, but it certainly is your responsibility to judge those inside the church who are sinning. ¹³God will judge those on the outside; but as the Scriptures say, "You must remove the evil person from among you."*

CHAPTER **6**

Avoiding Lawsuits with Christians

When one of you has a dispute with another believer, how dare you file a lawsuit and ask a secular court to decide the matter instead of taking it to other believers*! ²Don't you realize that someday we believers will judge the world? And since you are going to judge the world, can't you decide even these little

5:1 Greek *his father's wife.*   5:3 Or *in spirit.*   5:4 Or *In the name of the Lord Jesus, you must call a meeting of the church.*   5:5a Or *so that his body will be destroyed;* Greek reads *for the destruction of the flesh.*   5:5b Greek *and the spirit.*   5:5c Other manuscripts read *the Lord Jesus;* still others read *our Lord Jesus Christ.*   5:7 Greek *has been sacrificed.*   5:8a Greek *not with old leaven.*   5:8b Greek *but with unleavened [bread].*   5:11 Greek *a brother.*   5:13 Deut 17:7.   6:1 Greek *God's holy people;* also in 6:2.

"If you truly want to help the soul of your neighbor, you should approach God first with all your heart. Ask him simply to fill you with charity, the greatest of all virtues; with it you can accomplish what you desire."

~ *St. Vincent Ferrer*

JOURNAL

things among yourselves? [3]Don't you realize that we will judge angels? So you should surely be able to resolve ordinary disputes in this life. [4]If you have legal disputes about such matters, why go to outside judges who are not respected by the church? [5]I am saying this to shame you. Isn't there anyone in all the church who is wise enough to decide these issues? [6]But instead, one believer* sues another—right in front of unbelievers!

[7]Even to have such lawsuits with one another is a defeat for you. Why not just accept the injustice and leave it at that? Why not let yourselves be cheated? [8]Instead, you yourselves are the ones who do wrong and cheat even your fellow believers.*

[9]Don't you realize that those who do wrong will not inherit the Kingdom of God? Don't fool yourselves. Those who indulge in sexual sin, or who worship idols, or commit adultery, or are male prostitutes, or practice homosexuality, [10]or are thieves, or greedy people, or drunkards, or are abusive, or cheat people—none of these will inherit the Kingdom of God. [11]Some of you were once like that. But you were cleansed; you were made holy; you were made right with God by calling on the name of the Lord Jesus Christ and by the Spirit of our God.

Avoiding Sexual Sin

[12]You say, "I am allowed to do anything"—but not everything is good for you. And even though "I am allowed to do anything," I must not become a slave to anything. [13]You say, "Food was made for the stomach, and the stomach for food." (This is true, though someday God will do away with both of them.) But you can't say that our bodies were made for sexual immorality. They were made for the Lord, and the Lord cares about our bodies. [14]And God will raise us from the dead by his power, just as he raised our Lord from the dead.

[15]Don't you realize that your bodies are actually parts of Christ? Should a man take his body, which is part of Christ, and join it to a prostitute? Never! [16]And don't you realize that if a man joins himself to a prostitute, he becomes one body with her? For the Scriptures say, "The two are united into one."* [17]But the person who is joined to the Lord is one spirit with him.

[18]Run from sexual sin! No other sin so clearly affects the body as this one does. For sexual immorality is a sin against your own body. [19]Don't you realize that your body is the temple of the Holy Spirit, who lives in you and was given to you by God? You do not

6:6 Greek *one brother.*   6:8 Greek *even the brothers.*   6:16 Gen 2:24.

No. 14-TE-323

FRIENDSHIP STORY

FRIENDSHIP TYPE: *Neighbors*   FRIENDSHIP LAYER: *Getting Acquainted*

BASED ON TRUE EVENTS

Scenes From Dancing Horse Drive

Dean and Kim are the new kids on the block. One day Hank from across the street lumbers over saying, "Guess it's time to meet the new neighbors." Hank and his wife, Jennifer, are expecting their first child. Dean and Kim have a 6-month-old daughter. The couples bond over baby talk.

It's movie night. Dean and Hank attend a "guy" movie, as Kim and Jennifer stay home with their baby girls and watch *Pride and Prejudice* together. The two women hatch the idea of having a weekly neighborhood get-together and Bible study.

Hank—a military man—is transferred. Dean and Kim help them pack up their things and load the moving truck. Through tears and hugs, the couples promise to keep in touch. Weeks later Wayne, a JAG officer, moves into the empty house. Dean and Kim walk across the street and introduce themselves. Wayne joins them for dinner that evening.

Wayne receives temporary orders to Saudi Arabia. He asks Dean and Kim to take care of his cat while he is away. They do—for three months. Wayne returns with gifts of appreciation: small animal statues made in Saudi Arabia…a tradition is born. Every time Wayne is called to overseas duty, Dean and Kim watch his cat, and Wayne returns with a new "Noah's ark" statue for their growing collection.

FRIENDSHIP STORY *continues on page 324…*

FRIENDSHIP STORY *continued from page 323...*

New families move to the court. Dean and Kim's kids race to bring fresh-baked goodies to each new neighbor. The weekly neighborhood get-together and Bible study continues to grow. Almost the entire neighborhood gathers together for a Christmas party, treats, holiday stories, and caroling.

Brett and Ruth move in next door to Dean and Kim. Dean comes home from work and offers to help the new couple unload their heavy furniture. As he's helping, he invites them to dinner that evening. At the dinner table, Brett admits that he and his wife have been living apart...and this move is their last attempt to "make the marriage work." Brett asks if Dean and Kim would help them as they work through the struggles that are killing their marriage.

Brett and Ruth begin attending the weekly neighborhood get-together and Bible study. They also hang out regularly with Dean and Kim. The friendships grow quickly. Brett and Ruth join Dean and Kim for church one Sunday and love it. A year goes by, and Brett and Ruth are still together... and happy.

Dean and Kim receive a family update from Hank and Jennifer. The two are doing well—their kids are growing up. Jennifer writes in her letter: "Kim, I just want to thank you so much for investing your life in me...it's made such a difference in our entire family."

Dean shuts out the lights in his house but leaves his porch light on. Just as he does every night...a personal reminder that he and Kim are committed to letting their "good deeds shine out for all to see, so that everyone will praise [their] heavenly Father" (**Matthew 5:16**). He looks out his window at the shining lights of his neighbors' houses...and he smiles thinking of his friends who live there.

FRIENDSHIP STORY *continues on page 325...*

belong to yourself, [20] for God bought you with a high price. So you must honor God with your body.

CHAPTER 7

Instruction on Marriage

Now regarding the questions you asked in your letter. Yes, it is good to live a celibate life.* [2] But because there is so much sexual immorality, each man should have his own wife, and each woman should have her own husband.

[3] The husband should fulfill his wife's sexual needs, and the wife should fulfill her husband's needs. [4] The wife gives authority over her body to her husband, and the husband gives authority over his body to his wife.

[5] Do not deprive each other of sexual relations, unless you both agree to refrain from sexual intimacy for a limited time so you can give yourselves more completely to prayer. Afterward, you should come together again so that Satan won't be able to tempt you because of your lack of self-control. [6] I say this as a concession, not as a command. [7] But I wish everyone were single, just as I am. But God gives to some the gift of marriage, and to others the gift of singleness.

[8] So I say to those who aren't married and to widows—it's better to stay unmarried, just as I am. [9] But if they can't control themselves, they should go ahead and marry. It's better to marry than to burn with lust.

[10] But for those who are married, I have a command that comes not from me, but from the Lord.* A wife must not leave her husband. [11] But if she does leave him, let her remain single or else be reconciled to him. And the husband must not leave his wife.

[12] Now, I will speak to the rest of you, though I do not have a direct command from the Lord. If a Christian man* has a wife who is not a believer and she is willing to continue living with him, he must not leave her. [13] And if a Christian woman has a husband who is not a believer and he is willing to continue living with her, she must not leave him. [14] For the Christian wife brings holiness to her marriage, and the Christian husband* brings holiness to his marriage. Otherwise, your children would not be holy, but now they are holy. [15] (But if the husband or wife who isn't a believer insists on leaving, let them go. In such cases the Christian husband or wife* is no longer bound to the other, for God has called you* to live in peace.) [16] Don't you wives realize

7:1 Greek *It is good for a man not to touch a woman.*   7:10 See Matt 5:32; 19:9; Mark 10:11-12; Luke 16:18.   7:12 Greek *a brother.*   7:14 Greek *the brother.*   7:15a Greek *the brother or sister.* 7:15b Some manuscripts read *us.*

that your husbands might be saved because of you? And don't you husbands realize that your wives might be saved because of you?

¹⁷Each of you should continue to live in whatever situation the Lord has placed you, and remain as you were when God first called you. This is my rule for all the churches. ¹⁸For instance, a man who was circumcised before he became a believer should not try to reverse it. And the man who was uncircumcised when he became a believer should not be circumcised now. ¹⁹For it makes no difference whether or not a man has been circumcised. The important thing is to keep God's commandments.

²⁰Yes, each of you should remain as you were when God called you. ²¹Are you a slave? Don't let that worry you—but if you get a chance to be free, take it. ²²And remember, if you were a slave when the Lord called you, you are now free in the Lord. And if you were free when the Lord called you, you are now a slave of Christ. ²³God paid a high price for you, so don't be enslaved by the world.* ²⁴Each of you, dear brothers and sisters,* should remain as you were when God first called you.

²⁵Now regarding your question about the young women who are not yet married. I do not have a command from the Lord for them. But the Lord in his mercy has given me wisdom that can be trusted, and I will share it with you. ²⁶Because of the present crisis,* I think it is best to remain as you are. ²⁷If you have a wife, do not seek to end the marriage. If you do not have a wife, do not seek to get married. ²⁸But if you do get married, it is not a sin. And if a young woman gets married, it is not a sin. However, those who get married at this time will have troubles, and I am trying to spare you those problems.

²⁹But let me say this, dear brothers and sisters: The time that remains is very short. So from now on, those with wives should not focus only on their marriage. ³⁰Those who weep or who rejoice or who buy things should not be absorbed by their weeping or their joy or their possessions. ³¹Those who use the things of the world should not become attached to them. For this world as we know it will soon pass away.

³²I want you to be free from the concerns of this life. An unmarried man can spend his time doing the Lord's work and thinking how to please him. ³³But a married man has to think about his earthly responsibilities and how to please his wife. ³⁴His interests are divided. In the same way, a woman who is no

7:23 Greek *don't become slaves of people.*   7:24 Greek *brothers;* also in 7:29.   7:26 Or *the pressures of life.*

FRIENDSHIP STORY *continued from page 324...*

Experience

Sometimes you don't know the impact you're having in a neighborhood, just being neighbors who care. Dean and Kim once heard the quote, "Preach the gospel always, and if necessary, use words," and truth be told that's what they've attempted to live out in their community.

Use your actions and love to preach the Gospel in your neighborhood. Commit to welcoming each new member in your community with a fresh-baked goodie, surprise an old member of the community with a gift, or offer a dinner invitation to a neighbor you don't know well.

Reflect

★ Getting acquainted—and becoming friends— with your neighbors is a matter of taking the first step. What steps can you take with your neighbors to better your friendships?

★ St. Francis is credited as saying, "Preach the gospel always, and if necessary, use words." How can you make that a reality in your neighborhood?

> *"I speak a word. My friend speaks back. Then I again, then he, and thus we make a bridge of words so each may fetch across the ditch that lies between what's in his heart."*
>
> ~ *Frederick Buechner*

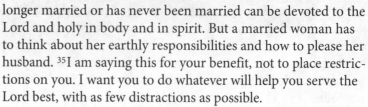

JOURNAL

longer married or has never been married can be devoted to the Lord and holy in body and in spirit. But a married woman has to think about her earthly responsibilities and how to please her husband. ³⁵I am saying this for your benefit, not to place restrictions on you. I want you to do whatever will help you serve the Lord best, with as few distractions as possible.

³⁶But if a man thinks that he's treating his fiancée improperly and will inevitably give in to his passion, let him marry her as he wishes. It is not a sin. ³⁷But if he has decided firmly not to marry and there is no urgency and he can control his passion, he does well not to marry. ³⁸So the person who marries his fiancée does well, and the person who doesn't marry does even better.

³⁹A wife is bound to her husband as long as he lives. If her husband dies, she is free to marry anyone she wishes, but only if he loves the Lord.* ⁴⁰But in my opinion it would be better for her to stay single, and I think I am giving you counsel from God's Spirit when I say this.

CHAPTER **8**

Food Sacrificed to Idols

Now regarding your question about food that has been offered to idols. Yes, we know that "we all have knowledge" about this issue. But while knowledge makes us feel important, it is love that strengthens the church. ²Anyone who claims to know all the answers doesn't really know very much. ³But the person who loves God is the one whom God recognizes.*

⁴So, what about eating meat that has been offered to idols? Well, we all know that an idol is not really a god and that there is only one God. ⁵There may be so-called gods both in heaven and on earth, and some people actually worship many gods and many lords. ⁶But we know that there is only one God, the Father, who created everything, and we live for him. And there is only one Lord, Jesus Christ, through whom God made everything and through whom we have been given life.

⁷However, not all believers know this. Some are accustomed to thinking of idols as being real, so when they eat food that has been offered to idols, they think of it as the worship of real gods, and their weak consciences are violated. ⁸It's true that we can't win God's approval by what we eat. We don't lose anything if we don't eat it, and we don't gain anything if we do.

⁹But you must be careful so that your freedom does not cause

7:39 Greek *but only in the Lord.*   **8:3** Some manuscripts read *the person who loves has full knowledge.*

others with a weaker conscience to stumble. ¹⁰For if others see you—with your "superior knowledge"—eating in the temple of an idol, won't they be encouraged to violate their conscience by eating food that has been offered to an idol? ¹¹So because of your superior knowledge, a weak believer* for whom Christ died will be destroyed. ¹²And when you sin against other believers* by encouraging them to do something they believe is wrong, you are sinning against Christ. ¹³So if what I eat causes another believer to sin, I will never eat meat again as long as I live—for I don't want to cause another believer to stumble.

CHAPTER **9**

Paul Gives Up His Rights

Am I not as free as anyone else? Am I not an apostle? Haven't I seen Jesus our Lord with my own eyes? Isn't it because of my work that you belong to the Lord? ²Even if others think I am not an apostle, I certainly am to you. You yourselves are proof that I am the Lord's apostle.

³This is my answer to those who question my authority.* ⁴Don't we have the right to live in your homes and share your meals? ⁵Don't we have the right to bring a Christian wife with us as the other apostles and the Lord's brothers do, and as Peter* does? ⁶Or is it only Barnabas and I who have to work to support ourselves?

⁷What soldier has to pay his own expenses? What farmer plants a vineyard and doesn't have the right to eat some of its fruit? What shepherd cares for a flock of sheep and isn't allowed to drink some of the milk? ⁸Am I expressing merely a human opinion, or does the law say the same thing? ⁹For the law of Moses says, "You must not muzzle an ox to keep it from eating as it treads out the grain."* Was God thinking only about oxen when he said this? ¹⁰Wasn't he actually speaking to us? Yes, it was written for us, so that the one who plows and the one who threshes the grain might both expect a share of the harvest.

¹¹Since we have planted spiritual seed among you, aren't we entitled to a harvest of physical food and drink? ¹²If you support others who preach to you, shouldn't we have an even greater right to be supported? But we have never used this right. We would rather put up with anything than be an obstacle to the Good News about Christ.

¹³Don't you realize that those who work in the temple get

8:11 Greek *brother;* also in 8:13. **8:12** Greek *brothers.* **9:3** Greek *those who examine me.* **9:5** Greek *Cephas.* **9:9** Deut 25:4.

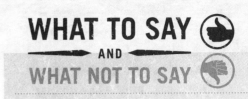

WHAT TO SAY AND WHAT NOT TO SAY

FRIENDSHIP TYPE: *Neighbors* FRIENDSHIP LAYER: *Getting Acquainted*

 THE TOP 10 THINGS NOT TO SAY

...*when introducing yourself to the new neighbors:*

10. What possessed you to move into *this* neighborhood?
9. What's for supper?
8. I know you're unloading the moving truck, but tell me all about yourselves!
7. Man, I'd love to help unpack, but the game's just about to start.
6. The people before you let their dog do its business on our lawn!
5. You don't have teenagers, do you?
4. Looks like your new home could use a fresh coat of paint.
3. Whoa—nice car! I guess I know where to come if I need to borrow some cash.
2. Whatever you do, keep your kids outta my yard.
1. What time shall I pick you up for church on Sunday?

 THE TOP 10 THINGS TO SAY

...*when introducing yourself to the new neighbors:*

10. Welcome to the neighborhood!
9. Here's a fresh-baked goodie.
8. I look forward to getting to know you a bit better when you get settled.
7. Can I lend a hand with anything?
6. Hey, what's your dog's name?
5. I notice you have kids—what are their ages?
4. You're gonna love your new home!
3. Just drop by any time if you need something.
2. There's a really cool park just around the corner, the kids'll love it!
1. If you need some tips on schools, shopping, churches—just let me know!

JOURNAL

their meals from the offerings brought to the temple? And those who serve at the altar get a share of the sacrificial offerings. [14] In the same way, the Lord ordered that those who preach the Good News should be supported by those who benefit from it. [15] Yet I have never used any of these rights. And I am not writing this to suggest that I want to start now. In fact, I would rather die than lose my right to boast about preaching without charge. [16] Yet preaching the Good News is not something I can boast about. I am compelled by God to do it. How terrible for me if I didn't preach the Good News!

[17] If I were doing this on my own initiative, I would deserve payment. But I have no choice, for God has given me this sacred trust. [18] What then is my pay? It is the opportunity to preach the Good News without charging anyone. That's why I never demand my rights when I preach the Good News.

[19] Even though I am a free man with no master, I have become a slave to all people to bring many to Christ. [20] When I was with the Jews, I lived like a Jew to bring the Jews to Christ. When I was with those who follow the Jewish law, I too lived under that law. Even though I am not subject to the law, I did this so I could bring to Christ those who are under the law. [21] When I am with the Gentiles who do not follow the Jewish law,* I too live apart from that law so I can bring them to Christ. But I do not ignore the law of God; I obey the law of Christ.

[22] When I am with those who are weak, I share their weakness, for I want to bring the weak to Christ. Yes, I try to find common ground with everyone, doing everything I can to save some. [23] I do everything to spread the Good News and share in its blessings.

[24] Don't you realize that in a race everyone runs, but only one person gets the prize? So run to win! [25] All athletes are disciplined in their training. They do it to win a prize that will fade away, but we do it for an eternal prize. [26] So I run with purpose in every step. I am not just shadowboxing. [27] I discipline my body like an athlete, training it to do what it should. Otherwise, I fear that after preaching to others I myself might be disqualified.

CHAPTER **10**

Lessons from Israel's Idolatry

I don't want you to forget, dear brothers and sisters,* about our ancestors in the wilderness long ago. All of them were guided by a cloud that moved ahead of them, and all of them walked through the sea on dry ground. [2] In the cloud and in the sea, all

9:21 Greek *those without the law.*   10:1 Greek *brothers.*

JOURNAL

of them were baptized as followers of Moses. [3]All of them ate the same spiritual food, [4]and all of them drank the same spiritual water. For they drank from the spiritual rock that traveled with them, and that rock was Christ. [5]Yet God was not pleased with most of them, and their bodies were scattered in the wilderness.

[6]These things happened as a warning to us, so that we would not crave evil things as they did, [7]or worship idols as some of them did. As the Scriptures say, "The people celebrated with feasting and drinking, and they indulged in pagan revelry."* [8]And we must not engage in sexual immorality as some of them did, causing 23,000 of them to die in one day.

[9]Nor should we put Christ* to the test, as some of them did and then died from snakebites. [10]And don't grumble as some of them did, and then were destroyed by the angel of death. [11]These things happened to them as examples for us. They were written down to warn us who live at the end of the age.

[12]If you think you are standing strong, be careful not to fall. [13]The temptations in your life are no different from what others experience. And God is faithful. He will not allow the temptation to be more than you can stand. When you are tempted, he will show you a way out so that you can endure.

[14]So, my dear friends, flee from the worship of idols. [15]You are reasonable people. Decide for yourselves if what I am saying is true. [16]When we bless the cup at the Lord's Table, aren't we sharing in the blood of Christ? And when we break the bread, aren't we sharing in the body of Christ? [17]And though we are many, we all eat from one loaf of bread, showing that we are one body. [18]Think about the people of Israel. Weren't they united by eating the sacrifices at the altar?

[19]What am I trying to say? Am I saying that food offered to idols has some significance, or that idols are real gods? [20]No, not at all. I am saying that these sacrifices are offered to demons, not to God. And I don't want you to participate with demons. [21]You cannot drink from the cup of the Lord and from the cup of demons, too. You cannot eat at the Lord's Table and at the table of demons, too. [22]What? Do we dare to rouse the Lord's jealousy? Do you think we are stronger than he is?

[23]You say, "I am allowed to do anything"*—but not everything is good for you. You say, "I am allowed to do anything"—but not everything is beneficial. [24]Don't be concerned for your own good but for the good of others.

10:7 Exod 32:6.   10:9 Some manuscripts read *the Lord*.   10:23 Greek *All things are lawful*; also in 10:23b.

"Do not withhold good from those who deserve it when it's in your power to help them.

If you can help your neighbor now, don't say, 'Come back tomorrow, and then I'll help you.'"

~ Proverbs 3:27-28

JOURNAL

25So you may eat any meat that is sold in the marketplace without raising questions of conscience. 26For "the earth is the LORD's, and everything in it."*

27If someone who isn't a believer asks you home for dinner, accept the invitation if you want to. Eat whatever is offered to you without raising questions of conscience. 28(But suppose someone tells you, "This meat was offered to an idol." Don't eat it, out of consideration for the conscience of the one who told you. 29It might not be a matter of conscience for you, but it is for the other person.) For why should my freedom be limited by what someone else thinks? 30If I can thank God for the food and enjoy it, why should I be condemned for eating it?

31So whether you eat or drink, or whatever you do, do it all for the glory of God. 32Don't give offense to Jews or Gentiles* or the church of God. 33I, too, try to please everyone in everything I do. I don't just do what is best for me; I do what is best for others so that many may be saved. 11:1And you should imitate me, just as I imitate Christ.

CHAPTER 11

Instructions for Public Worship

2I am so glad that you always keep me in your thoughts, and that you are following the teachings I passed on to you. 3But there is one thing I want you to know: The head of every man is Christ, the head of woman is man, and the head of Christ is God.* 4A man dishonors his head* if he covers his head while praying or prophesying. 5But a woman dishonors her head* if she prays or prophesies without a covering on her head, for this is the same as shaving her head. 6Yes, if she refuses to wear a head covering, she should cut off all her hair! But since it is shameful for a woman to have her hair cut or her head shaved, she should wear a covering.*

7A man should not wear anything on his head when worshiping, for man is made in God's image and reflects God's glory. And woman reflects man's glory. 8For the first man didn't come from woman, but the first woman came from man. 9And man was not made for woman, but woman was made for man. 10For this reason, and because the angels are watching, a woman should wear a covering on her head to show she is under authority.*

11But among the Lord's people, women are not independent of

10:26 Ps 24:1.   10:32 Greek or Greeks.   11:3 Or to know: The source of every man is Christ, the source of woman is man, and the source of Christ is God. Or to know: Every man is responsible to Christ, a woman is responsible to her husband, and Christ is responsible to God.   11:4 Or dishonors Christ.   11:5 Or dishonors her husband.   11:6 Or should have long hair.   11:10 Greek should have an authority on her head.

men, and men are not independent of women. ¹²For although the first woman came from man, every other man was born from a woman, and everything comes from God.

¹³Judge for yourselves. Is it right for a woman to pray to God in public without covering her head? ¹⁴Isn't it obvious that it's disgraceful for a man to have long hair? ¹⁵And isn't long hair a woman's pride and joy? For it has been given to her as a covering. ¹⁶But if anyone wants to argue about this, I simply say that we have no other custom than this, and neither do God's other churches.

Order at the Lord's Supper

¹⁷But in the following instructions, I cannot praise you. For it sounds as if more harm than good is done when you meet together. ¹⁸First, I hear that there are divisions among you when you meet as a church, and to some extent I believe it. ¹⁹But, of course, there must be divisions among you so that you who have God's approval will be recognized!

²⁰When you meet together, you are not really interested in the Lord's Supper. ²¹For some of you hurry to eat your own meal without sharing with others. As a result, some go hungry while others get drunk. ²²What? Don't you have your own homes for eating and drinking? Or do you really want to disgrace God's church and shame the poor? What am I supposed to say? Do you want me to praise you? Well, I certainly will not praise you for this!

²³For I pass on to you what I received from the Lord himself. On the night when he was betrayed, the Lord Jesus took some bread ²⁴and gave thanks to God for it. Then he broke it in pieces and said, "This is my body, which is given for you.* Do this to remember me." ²⁵In the same way, he took the cup of wine after supper, saying, "This cup is the new covenant between God and his people—an agreement confirmed with my blood. Do this to remember me as often as you drink it." ²⁶For every time you eat this bread and drink this cup, you are announcing the Lord's death until he comes again.

²⁷So anyone who eats this bread or drinks this cup of the Lord unworthily is guilty of sinning against* the body and blood of the Lord. ²⁸That is why you should examine yourself before eating the bread and drinking the cup. ²⁹For if you eat the bread or drink the cup without honoring the body of Christ,* you are eating and drinking God's judgment upon yourself. ³⁰That is why many of you are weak and sick and some have even died.

11:24 Greek *which is for you;* other manuscripts read *which is broken for you.*   11:27 Or *is responsible for.*   11:29 Greek *the body;* other manuscripts read *the Lord's body.*

FRIENDSHIP EXPERIENCE

FRIENDSHIP TYPE:	FRIENDSHIP LAYER:
Neighbors	*Commitment*

Love Is a Commitment

How do you live out a committed friendship with your neighbors when your neighbors are so many different people—the grocery clerk one day, the office receptionist the next, and the little old lady across the street on yet another day?

By being patient. By being kind. By avoiding jealousy, boastfulness, or pride. By being polite instead of rude. By serving instead of demanding. By swallowing irritation and forgetting past hurts. By rejoicing when they rejoice…and not when they weep. By never giving up on them or losing faith in them. By remaining hopeful. By enduring as a friend through thick and thin.

So what does that look like? Well, when you're standing in line behind the slowest person *in the world*, it means offering an encouraging word, a smile, and your time. When the teen across the street seems lonely, or the mail carrier seems harried, or a co-worker just seems too busy to make eye contact, it means taking the time to ask a question, offer your help, say a kind word.

FRIENDSHIP EXPERIENCE

continues on page 332…

FRIENDSHIP EXPERIENCE *continued from page 331…*

Jesus never avoided people just because he was too busy or too tired or too irritated. He was always an available friend and a helper to those in need.

Experience

As you go through your week, look for an opportunity to show love to your neighbor. It's OK if it costs you some of your time or convenience. That shows real commitment.

Maybe you know someone who needs a baby sitter but can't afford one. Or someone who needs help with a house project. Or someone who recently lost a family member and could use some extra encouragement.

1 Corinthians 10:31 says to do everything for the glory of God. So as you take a meal to a neighbor who just had surgery, invite a couple over for an evening game, or help a family fix their fence, do it as though your neighbors were Jesus. It's a pretty safe bet you'll want to do a great job…and what an encouragement you'll be!

THE ONE THING
1
YOU CAN DO THIS WEEK

Reflect

★ How do you usually treat the people you encounter through your day?

★ When has someone unexpectedly treated you with love? How did you feel?

★ How does showing a commitment to love others reflect a commitment to love God?

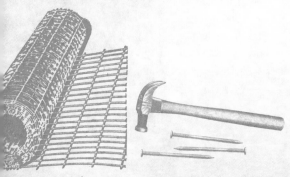

Friendship First NEW TESTAMENT

³¹But if we would examine ourselves, we would not be judged by God in this way. ³²Yet when we are judged by the Lord, we are being disciplined so that we will not be condemned along with the world.

³³So, my dear brothers and sisters,* when you gather for the Lord's Supper, wait for each other. ³⁴If you are really hungry, eat at home so you won't bring judgment upon yourselves when you meet together. I'll give you instructions about the other matters after I arrive.

CHAPTER **12**

Spiritual Gifts

Now, dear brothers and sisters,* regarding your question about the special abilities the Spirit gives us. I don't want you to misunderstand this. ²You know that when you were still pagans, you were led astray and swept along in worshiping speechless idols. ³So I want you to know that no one speaking by the Spirit of God will curse Jesus, and no one can say Jesus is Lord, except by the Holy Spirit.

⁴There are different kinds of spiritual gifts, but the same Spirit is the source of them all. ⁵There are different kinds of service, but we serve the same Lord. ⁶God works in different ways, but it is the same God who does the work in all of us.

⁷A spiritual gift is given to each of us so we can help each other. ⁸To one person the Spirit gives the ability to give wise advice*; to another the same Spirit gives a message of special knowledge.* ⁹The same Spirit gives great faith to another, and to someone else the one Spirit gives the gift of healing. ¹⁰He gives one person the power to perform miracles, and another the ability to prophesy. He gives someone else the ability to discern whether a message is from the Spirit of God or from another spirit. Still another person is given the ability to speak in unknown languages,* while another is given the ability to interpret what is being said. ¹¹It is the one and only Spirit who distributes all these gifts. He alone decides which gift each person should have.

One Body with Many Parts

¹²The human body has many parts, but the many parts make up one whole body. So it is with the body of Christ. ¹³Some of us are Jews, some are Gentiles,* some are slaves, and some are free.

11:33 Greek *brothers.*   **12:1** Greek *brothers.*   **12:8a** Or *gives a word of wisdom.*   **12:8b** Or *gives a word of knowledge.*   **12:10** Or *in various tongues;* also in 12:28, 30.   **12:13a** Greek *some are Greeks.* **12:13b** Greek *we were all given one Spirit to drink.*

But we have all been baptized into one body by one Spirit, and we all share the same Spirit.*

¹⁴ Yes, the body has many different parts, not just one part. ¹⁵ If the foot says, "I am not a part of the body because I am not a hand," that does not make it any less a part of the body. ¹⁶ And if the ear says, "I am not part of the body because I am not an eye," would that make it any less a part of the body? ¹⁷ If the whole body were an eye, how would you hear? Or if your whole body were an ear, how would you smell anything?

¹⁸ But our bodies have many parts, and God has put each part just where he wants it. ¹⁹ How strange a body would be if it had only one part! ²⁰ Yes, there are many parts, but only one body. ²¹ The eye can never say to the hand, "I don't need you." The head can't say to the feet, "I don't need you."

²² In fact, some parts of the body that seem weakest and least important are actually the most necessary. ²³ And the parts we regard as less honorable are those we clothe with the greatest care. So we carefully protect those parts that should not be seen, ²⁴ while the more honorable parts do not require this special care. So God has put the body together such that extra honor and care are given to those parts that have less dignity. ²⁵ This makes for harmony among the members, so that all the members care for each other. ²⁶ If one part suffers, all the parts suffer with it, and if one part is honored, all the parts are glad.

²⁷ All of you together are Christ's body, and each of you is a part of it. ²⁸ Here are some of the parts God has appointed for the church:

> first are apostles,
> second are prophets,
> third are teachers,
> then those who do miracles,
> those who have the gift of healing,
> those who can help others,
> those who have the gift of leadership,
> those who speak in unknown languages.

²⁹ Are we all apostles? Are we all prophets? Are we all teachers? Do we all have the power to do miracles? ³⁰ Do we all have the gift of healing? Do we all have the ability to speak in unknown languages? Do we all have the ability to interpret unknown languages? Of course not! ³¹ So you should earnestly desire the most helpful gifts.

But now let me show you a way of life that is best of all.

"It is a sin to belittle one's neighbor; blessed are those who help the poor."

~ Proverbs 14:21

JOURNAL

Anchor Passage

PASSAGE: **1 Corinthians 13:1-7**

FRIENDSHIP TYPE:
Neighbors

FRIENDSHIP LAYER:
Commitment

Committed to Love

Read **1 Corinthians 13:1-7**.

It's a popular wedding passage, but it's not just for lovers. It's often quoted on Mother's Day or Father's Day, but it's not just for family members. You see it on cards meant for best friends, but it's not just for your friends.

This passage is for everyone. *This* is how you're supposed to love everyone…*this* is how you're supposed to love your neighbors.

Patiently. Kindly. Without jealousy or pride. Filled with hope. Enduringly.

Living out this passage *is* living out a committed friendship with your neighbors.

And…just in case you thought running out and doing a lot of nice things for your neighbors is the way to live out this passage…well, take a closer look at the first three verses.

Good deeds and kind actions *are* great, but only if they're done out of genuine love. When they're done out of guilt, obligation or fear, they mean nothing— they are, according to this passage, little more than a "noisy gong or a clanging cymbal."

So in the spirit of this passage: Go out and share the love!

Anchor Passage continues on page 335…

Friendship First NEW TESTAMENT

CHAPTER 13
Love Is the Greatest

If I could speak all the languages of earth and of angels, but didn't love others, I would only be a noisy gong or a clanging cymbal. [2] If I had the gift of prophecy, and if I understood all of God's secret plans and possessed all knowledge, and if I had such faith that I could move mountains, but didn't love others, I would be nothing. [3] If I gave everything I have to the poor and even sacrificed my body, I could boast about it;* but if I didn't love others, I would have gained nothing.

[4] Love is patient and kind. Love is not jealous or boastful or proud [5] or rude. It does not demand its own way. It is not irritable, and it keeps no record of being wronged. [6] It does not rejoice about injustice but rejoices whenever the truth wins out. [7] Love never gives up, never loses faith, is always hopeful, and endures through every circumstance.

[8] Prophecy and speaking in unknown languages* and special knowledge will become useless. But love will last forever! [9] Now our knowledge is partial and incomplete, and even the gift of prophecy reveals only part of the whole picture! [10] But when full understanding comes, these partial things will become useless.

[11] When I was a child, I spoke and thought and reasoned as a child. But when I grew up, I put away childish things. [12] Now we see things imperfectly as in a cloudy mirror, but then we will see everything with perfect clarity.* All that I know now is partial and incomplete, but then I will know everything completely, just as God now knows me completely.

[13] Three things will last forever—faith, hope, and love—and the greatest of these is love.

CHAPTER 14
Tongues and Prophecy

Let love be your highest goal! But you should also desire the special abilities the Spirit gives—especially the ability to prophesy. [2] For if you have the ability to speak in tongues,* you will be talking only to God, since people won't be able to understand

13:3 Some manuscripts read *sacrificed my body to be burned.*   **13:8** Or *in tongues.*   **13:12** Greek *see face to face.*   **14:2** Or *in unknown languages;* also in 14:4, 5, 13, 14, 18, 22, 26, 27, 28, 39.

you. You will be speaking by the power of the Spirit, but it will all be mysterious. ³But one who prophesies strengthens others, encourages them, and comforts them. ⁴A person who speaks in tongues is strengthened personally, but one who speaks a word of prophecy strengthens the entire church.

⁵I wish you could all speak in tongues, but even more I wish you could all prophesy. For prophecy is greater than speaking in tongues, unless someone interprets what you are saying so that the whole church will be strengthened.

⁶Dear brothers and sisters,* if I should come to you speaking in an unknown language,* how would that help you? But if I bring you a revelation or some special knowledge or prophecy or teaching, that will be helpful. ⁷Even lifeless instruments like the flute or the harp must play the notes clearly, or no one will recognize the melody. ⁸And if the bugler doesn't sound a clear call, how will the soldiers know they are being called to battle?

⁹It's the same for you. If you speak to people in words they don't understand, how will they know what you are saying? You might as well be talking into empty space.

¹⁰There are many different languages in the world, and every language has meaning. ¹¹But if I don't understand a language, I will be a foreigner to someone who speaks it, and the one who speaks it will be a foreigner to me. ¹²And the same is true for you. Since you are so eager to have the special abilities the Spirit gives, seek those that will strengthen the whole church.

¹³So anyone who speaks in tongues should pray also for the ability to interpret what has been said. ¹⁴For if I pray in tongues, my spirit is praying, but I don't understand what I am saying.

¹⁵Well then, what shall I do? I will pray in the spirit,* and I will also pray in words I understand. I will sing in the spirit, and I will also sing in words I understand. ¹⁶For if you praise God only in the spirit, how can those who don't understand you praise God along with you? How can they join you in giving thanks when they don't understand what you are saying? ¹⁷You will be giving thanks very well, but it won't strengthen the people who hear you.

¹⁸I thank God that I speak in tongues more than any of you. ¹⁹But in a church meeting I would rather speak five understandable words to help others than ten thousand words in an unknown language.

²⁰Dear brothers and sisters, don't be childish in your under-

14:6a Greek *brothers;* also in 14:20, 26, 39.   14:6b Or *in tongues;* also in 14:19, 23.   14:15 Or *in the Spirit;* also in 14:15b, 16.

Anchor Passage continued from page 334…

THE ONE THING · 1 · YOU CAN DO THIS WEEK

Experience

Think of the people around you—your neighbors. Those you encounter as you go about your day. Be a committed friend to them this week…*love them*!

Choose one of the traits described in the passage, and make a determined effort to live out that trait as you interact with your neighbors this week. For example, if you choose "Love is not jealous" and you find yourself feeling jealous as you talk to your neighbor about his new sports car, make a conscious effort to feel happy for the person's success instead of jealous. If you choose "[Love] is not irritable" and you find yourself getting irritated when the cashier at the register pronounces your name wrong or the woman at the tollbooth takes too long counting your change, stop and take a breath and remember that love is not irritable.

Reflect

★ Why aren't actions without love enough?

★ When do you find yourself simply performing good deeds out of guilt or obligation instead of out of love? How can you change your attitude?

DIGGING DEEPER

FRIENDSHIP TYPE:
Neighbors

FRIENDSHIP LAYER:
Commitment

For committing to friendship with your neighbors, find…

➼ The Friendship Experience .... on page 331

➼ The Friendship Story .... on page 317

➼ What to Say and What Not to Say .... on page 320

> "When we claim and constantly reclaim God as the source of all love, we will discover love as God's gift to God's people."
>
> ~ *Henri J. M. Nouwen*

JOURNAL

standing of these things. Be innocent as babies when it comes to evil, but be mature in understanding matters of this kind. ²¹It is written in the Scriptures*:

> "I will speak to my own people
>   through strange languages
>   and through the lips of foreigners.
> But even then, they will not listen to me,"*
>   says the LORD.

²²So you see that speaking in tongues is a sign, not for believers, but for unbelievers. Prophecy, however, is for the benefit of believers, not unbelievers. ²³Even so, if unbelievers or people who don't understand these things come into your church meeting and hear everyone speaking in an unknown language, they will think you are crazy. ²⁴But if all of you are prophesying, and unbelievers or people who don't understand these things come into your meeting, they will be convicted of sin and judged by what you say. ²⁵As they listen, their secret thoughts will be exposed, and they will fall to their knees and worship God, declaring, "God is truly here among you."

A Call to Orderly Worship

²⁶Well, my brothers and sisters, let's summarize. When you meet together, one will sing, another will teach, another will tell some special revelation God has given, one will speak in tongues, and another will interpret what is said. But everything that is done must strengthen all of you.

²⁷No more than two or three should speak in tongues. They must speak one at a time, and someone must interpret what they say. ²⁸But if no one is present who can interpret, they must be silent in your church meeting and speak in tongues to God privately.

²⁹Let two or three people prophesy, and let the others evaluate what is said. ³⁰But if someone is prophesying and another person receives a revelation from the Lord, the one who is speaking must stop. ³¹In this way, all who prophesy will have a turn to speak, one after the other, so that everyone will learn and be encouraged. ³²Remember that people who prophesy are in control of their spirit and can take turns. ³³For God is not a God of disorder but of peace, as in all the meetings of God's holy people.*

³⁴Women should be silent during the church meetings. It is

14:21a Greek *in the law.*   14:21b Isa 28:11-12.   14:33 The phrase *as in all the meetings of God's holy people* could instead be joined to the beginning of 14:34.

not proper for them to speak. They should be submissive, just as the law says. ³⁵If they have any questions, they should ask their husbands at home, for it is improper for women to speak in church meetings.*

³⁶Or do you think God's word originated with you Corinthians? Are you the only ones to whom it was given? ³⁷If you claim to be a prophet or think you are spiritual, you should recognize that what I am saying is a command from the Lord himself. ³⁸But if you do not recognize this, you yourself will not be recognized.*

³⁹So, my dear brothers and sisters, be eager to prophesy, and don't forbid speaking in tongues. ⁴⁰But be sure that everything is done properly and in order.

CHAPTER 15

The Resurrection of Christ

Let me now remind you, dear brothers and sisters,* of the Good News I preached to you before. You welcomed it then, and you still stand firm in it. ²It is this Good News that saves you if you continue to believe the message I told you—unless, of course, you believed something that was never true in the first place.*

³I passed on to you what was most important and what had also been passed on to me. Christ died for our sins, just as the Scriptures said. ⁴He was buried, and he was raised from the dead on the third day, just as the Scriptures said. ⁵He was seen by Peter* and then by the Twelve. ⁶After that, he was seen by more than 500 of his followers* at one time, most of whom are still alive, though some have died. ⁷Then he was seen by James and later by all the apostles. ⁸Last of all, as though I had been born at the wrong time, I also saw him. ⁹For I am the least of all the apostles. In fact, I'm not even worthy to be called an apostle after the way I persecuted God's church.

¹⁰But whatever I am now, it is all because God poured out his special favor on me—and not without results. For I have worked harder than any of the other apostles; yet it was not I but God who was working through me by his grace. ¹¹So it makes no difference whether I preach or they preach, for we all preach the same message you have already believed.

The Resurrection of the Dead

¹²But tell me this—since we preach that Christ rose from the dead, why are some of you saying there will be no resurrection

14:35 Some manuscripts place verses 34-35 after 14:40.   14:38 Some manuscripts read *If you are ignorant of this, stay in your ignorance.*   15:1 Greek *brothers;* also in 15:31, 50, 58.   15:2 Or *unless you never believed it in the first place.*   15:5 Greek *Cephas.*   15:6 Greek *the brothers.*

No. 15-FA-337

FRIENDSHIP STORY

FRIENDSHIP TYPE: *Jesus*   FRIENDSHIP LAYER: *Deepening*

FROM THE ARCHIVES

The King of Youth

There is no other way to say it: Francis Bernardone was a playboy. His father was one of the wealthiest men in his city, and Francis was more than willing to take advantage of the perks wealth brought him. Francis' home was regularly filled with the young and glamorous of the city—the parties almost never stopped.

One observer of the time wrote of Francis, "more advanced in frivolity than all his comrades, he became the master of their revels, prompting them to do evil and vying with them in foolishness…In other respects an exquisite youth, he attracted to himself a whole retinue of young people addicted to evil and accustomed to vice."

His city and home became known for drunken orgies. His friends called him "the king of youth."

It wasn't that Francis didn't know better. He'd been raised to follow Christ, been taught the Lord's Prayer, recited the various creeds of the church. But his selfish and indulgent lifestyle betrayed that friendship. He wasn't interested in living a pure life, in giving to the poor, or in deepening his friendship with Christ.

But then something happened. Francis woke up one day and wondered about his life…in that mood, he wandered into a ruined chapel, and looked at the crucifix. As Francis stared at the crucified Christ, he fell to his knees.

FRIENDSHIP STORY *continues on page 338…*

Friendship First NEW TESTAMENT

FRIENDSHIP STORY *continued from page 337...*

Francis later said that he suddenly realized—in a way he never had before—what it meant that Jesus had died *for him*. He knew suddenly and completely that it wasn't just some abstract theological principle, but a personal act of love. Jesus had become a sacrifice for him.

Francis' life took on a new mission; he gave up all of his worldly wealth and took on the simple garb of the poor. He wandered the roads of Italy, preaching with joy the good news of Christ...and his country responded. Large joyful crowds followed him across the hills of Umbria, praising God. Many followed his example and turned away from selfish pursuits to dedicate themselves to Christ's mission and his people.

It was 1208, and Francis Bernardone had become Francis of Assisi...later known as *Saint Francis of Assisi*. The king of youth had become a friend of the King of Heaven.

Experience

Both Francis and Peter (**Mark 14:66-72**), denied Jesus. But both of them also came back to their friendship with Jesus. And because they'd been through trial and hardship, their friendship was deeper and stronger. They devoted themselves to Christ's mission and to his people.

Think of a way you can show the depth of your friendship to Jesus by serving others. In the spirit of Francis of Assisi, it might be especially appropriate to do something for the poor: Serve at a feeding ministry; collect warm blankets for those on the street; volunteer at a local orphanage. Pray and ask Jesus where you are most needed.

THE ONE THING YOU CAN DO THIS WEEK 1

FRIENDSHIP STORY *continues on page 339...*

of the dead? [13]For if there is no resurrection of the dead, then Christ has not been raised either. [14]And if Christ has not been raised, then all our preaching is useless, and your faith is useless. [15]And we apostles would all be lying about God—for we have said that God raised Christ from the grave. But that can't be true if there is no resurrection of the dead. [16]And if there is no resurrection of the dead, then Christ has not been raised. [17]And if Christ has not been raised, then your faith is useless and you are still guilty of your sins. [18]In that case, all who have died believing in Christ are lost! [19]And if our hope in Christ is only for this life, we are more to be pitied than anyone in the world.

[20]But in fact, Christ has been raised from the dead. He is the first of a great harvest of all who have died.

[21]So you see, just as death came into the world through a man, now the resurrection from the dead has begun through another man. [22]Just as everyone dies because we all belong to Adam, everyone who belongs to Christ will be given new life. [23]But there is an order to this resurrection: Christ was raised as the first of the harvest; then all who belong to Christ will be raised when he comes back.

[24]After that the end will come, when he will turn the Kingdom over to God the Father, having destroyed every ruler and authority and power. [25]For Christ must reign until he humbles all his enemies beneath his feet. [26]And the last enemy to be destroyed is death. [27]For the Scriptures say, "God has put all things under his authority."* (Of course, when it says "all things are under his authority," that does not include God himself, who gave Christ his authority.) [28]Then, when all things are under his authority, the Son will put himself under God's authority, so that God, who gave his Son authority over all things, will be utterly supreme over everything everywhere.

[29]If the dead will not be raised, what point is there in people being baptized for those who are dead? Why do it unless the dead will someday rise again?

[30]And why should we ourselves risk our lives hour by hour? [31]For I swear, dear brothers and sisters, that I face death daily. This is as certain as my pride in what Christ Jesus our Lord has done in you. [32]And what value was there in fighting wild beasts—those people of Ephesus*—if there will be no resurrection from the dead? And if there is no resurrection, "Let's feast and drink, for tomorrow we die!"* [33]Don't be fooled by those who say such things, for "bad company corrupts good charac-

15:27 Ps 8:6.   15:32a Greek *fighting wild beasts in Ephesus.*   15:32b Isa 22:13.

ter." ³⁴Think carefully about what is right, and stop sinning. For to your shame I say that some of you don't know God at all.

The Resurrection Body

³⁵But someone may ask, "How will the dead be raised? What kind of bodies will they have?" ³⁶What a foolish question! When you put a seed into the ground, it doesn't grow into a plant unless it dies first. ³⁷And what you put in the ground is not the plant that will grow, but only a bare seed of wheat or whatever you are planting. ³⁸Then God gives it the new body he wants it to have. A different plant grows from each kind of seed. ³⁹Similarly there are different kinds of flesh—one kind for humans, another for animals, another for birds, and another for fish.

⁴⁰There are also bodies in the heavens and bodies on the earth. The glory of the heavenly bodies is different from the glory of the earthly bodies. ⁴¹The sun has one kind of glory, while the moon and stars each have another kind. And even the stars differ from each other in their glory.

⁴²It is the same way with the resurrection of the dead. Our earthly bodies are planted in the ground when we die, but they will be raised to live forever. ⁴³Our bodies are buried in brokenness, but they will be raised in glory. They are buried in weakness, but they will be raised in strength. ⁴⁴They are buried as natural human bodies, but they will be raised as spiritual bodies. For just as there are natural bodies, there are also spiritual bodies.

⁴⁵The Scriptures tell us, "The first man, Adam, became a living person."* But the last Adam—that is, Christ—is a life-giving Spirit. ⁴⁶What comes first is the natural body, then the spiritual body comes later. ⁴⁷Adam, the first man, was made from the dust of the earth, while Christ, the second man, came from heaven. ⁴⁸Earthly people are like the earthly man, and heavenly people are like the heavenly man. ⁴⁹Just as we are now like the earthly man, we will someday be like* the heavenly man.

⁵⁰What I am saying, dear brothers and sisters, is that our physical bodies cannot inherit the Kingdom of God. These dying bodies cannot inherit what will last forever.

⁵¹But let me reveal to you a wonderful secret. We will not all die, but we will all be transformed! ⁵²It will happen in a moment, in the blink of an eye, when the last trumpet is blown. For when the trumpet sounds, those who have died will be raised to live forever. And we who are living will also be transformed. ⁵³For our

15:45 Gen 2:7.   **15:49** Some manuscripts read *let us be like.*

FRIENDSHIP STORY *continued from page 338...*

Reflect

★ In what ways have *you* denied Christ—by what you have done and not done, by what you have said and not said?

★ How can serving the church and those in need deepen your friendship with Jesus?

JOURNAL

_____

_____

_____

_____

_____

_____

_____

_____

_____

_____

_____

_____

_____

_____

_____

_____

WHAT TO SAY 👍 AND WHAT NOT TO SAY 👎

FRIENDSHIP TYPE: *Friends*

FRIENDSHIP LAYER: *Acceptance*

To Accept or Not to Accept?

Take this quiz to discover how you're doing in the "acceptance" category!

1. You can't stand your friend's spouse. You...

a. Take every opportunity to let your friend know this.

b. Change the subject when your friend talks about this person.

c. Try to see the person through your friend's eyes.

2. Your friend brings up the same problem he or she has complained about for 10 years. You...

a. Say you've heard this song before and you're sick of the tune.

b. Point out that you've given advice on this subject before.

c. Listen again as if it's the first time, looking for the nuance in the problem that's keeping it fresh in your friend's mind.

3. Your friend has a disgusting habit, such as chewing with his or her mouth open. You...

a. Point out the behavior and say, "You're so gross!"

b. Try your best to look away and not notice.

c. Ask God to help you focus on your friend's words instead of actions. (And, if the time is right, say, "You may not realize it, but when you chew with your mouth open, it's hard for me to pay full attention to what you're saying.")

WHAT TO SAY AND WHAT NOT TO SAY *continues on page 341...*

Friendship First NEW TESTAMENT

---

dying bodies must be transformed into bodies that will never die; our mortal bodies must be transformed into immortal bodies.

54 Then, when our dying bodies have been transformed into bodies that will never die,* this Scripture will be fulfilled:

"Death is swallowed up in victory.*
55 O death, where is your victory?
O death, where is your sting?*"

56 For sin is the sting that results in death, and the law gives sin its power. 57 But thank God! He gives us victory over sin and death through our Lord Jesus Christ.

58 So, my dear brothers and sisters, be strong and immovable. Always work enthusiastically for the Lord, for you know that nothing you do for the Lord is ever useless.

CHAPTER **16**

The Collection for Jerusalem

Now regarding your question about the money being collected for God's people in Jerusalem. You should follow the same procedure I gave to the churches in Galatia. 2 On the first day of each week, you should each put aside a portion of the money you have earned. Don't wait until I get there and then try to collect it all at once. 3 When I come, I will write letters of recommendation for the messengers you choose to deliver your gift to Jerusalem. 4 And if it seems appropriate for me to go along, they can travel with me.

Paul's Final Instructions

5 I am coming to visit you after I have been to Macedonia,* for I am planning to travel through Macedonia. 6 Perhaps I will stay awhile with you, possibly all winter, and then you can send me on my way to my next destination. 7 This time I don't want to make just a short visit and then go right on. I want to come and stay awhile, if the Lord will let me. 8 In the meantime, I will be staying here at Ephesus until the Festival of Pentecost. 9 There is a wide-open door for a great work here, although many oppose me.

10 When Timothy comes, don't intimidate him. He is doing the Lord's work, just as I am. 11 Don't let anyone treat him with contempt. Send him on his way with your blessing when he returns to me. I expect him to come with the other believers.*

15:54a Some manuscripts add *and our mortal bodies have been transformed into immortal bodies.* 15:54b Isa 25:8. 15:55 Hos 13:14 (Greek version). 16:5 *Macedonia* was in the northern region of Greece. 16:11 Greek *with the brothers;* also in 16:12.

12Now about our brother Apollos—I urged him to visit you with the other believers, but he was not willing to go right now. He will see you later when he has the opportunity.

13Be on guard. Stand firm in the faith. Be courageous.* Be strong. 14And do everything with love.

15You know that Stephanas and his household were the first of the harvest of believers in Greece,* and they are spending their lives in service to God's people. I urge you, dear brothers and sisters,* 16to submit to them and others like them who serve with such devotion. 17I am very glad that Stephanas, Fortunatus, and Achaicus have come here. They have been providing the help you weren't here to give me. 18They have been a wonderful encouragement to me, as they have been to you. You must show your appreciation to all who serve so well.

Paul's Final Greetings

19The churches here in the province of Asia* send greetings in the Lord, as do Aquila and Priscilla* and all the others who gather in their home for church meetings. 20All the brothers and sisters here send greetings to you. Greet each other with Christian love.*

21HERE IS MY GREETING IN MY OWN HANDWRITING—PAUL.

22If anyone does not love the Lord, that person is cursed. Our Lord, come!*

23May the grace of the Lord Jesus be with you.

24My love to all of you in Christ Jesus.*

16:13 Greek *Be men.*   16:15a Greek *in Achaia,* the southern region of the Greek peninsula.
16:15b Greek *brothers;* also in 16:20.   16:19a *Asia* was a Roman province in what is now western Turkey.   16:19b Greek *Prisca.*   16:20 Greek *with a sacred kiss.*   16:22 From Aramaic, *Marana tha.* Some manuscripts read *Maran atha, "Our Lord has come."*   16:24 Some manuscripts add *Amen.*

WHAT TO SAY AND WHAT NOT TO SAY *continued from page 340...*

4. Your friend claims to be a Christian, but he or she doesn't agree with your opinion on moral issues. You...

a. Refuse to affiliate with this person, who obviously doesn't know anything about God's truth.

b. Pray that God will show the person how wrong he or she is and help the person come around to your way of thinking.

c. Listen to your friend's perspective, and if you can't find common ground, *agreeably* agree to disagree.

YOU GET THE IDEA!

★ Give yourself 25 points for every C you've chosen; 10 for every B you've chosen; and 0 for every A. (Check out **1 Corinthians 1:10**.)

JOURNAL

2 Corinthians

AUTHOR:	DATE WRITTEN:
Paul	Approximately A.D. 55-57

CHAPTER 1

Greetings from Paul

This letter is from Paul, chosen by the will of God to be an apostle of Christ Jesus, and from our brother Timothy.

I am writing to God's church in Corinth and to all of his holy people throughout Greece.*

2 May God our Father and the Lord Jesus Christ give you grace and peace.

God Offers Comfort to All

3 All praise to God, the Father of our Lord Jesus Christ. God is our merciful Father and the source of all comfort. 4 He comforts us in all our troubles so that we can comfort others. When they are troubled, we will be able to give them the same comfort God has given us. 5 For the more we suffer for Christ, the more God will shower us with his comfort through Christ. 6 Even when we are weighed down with troubles, it is for your comfort and salvation! For when we ourselves are comforted, we will certainly comfort you. Then you can patiently endure the same things we suffer. 7 We are confident that as you share in our sufferings, you will also share in the comfort God gives us.

8 We think you ought to know, dear brothers and sisters,* about the trouble we went through in the province of Asia. We were crushed and overwhelmed beyond our ability to endure, and we thought we would never live through it. 9 In fact, we expected to die. But as a result, we stopped relying on ourselves and learned to rely only on God, who raises the dead. 10 And he did rescue us from mortal danger, and he will rescue us again. We have placed our confidence in him, and he will continue to rescue us. 11 And you are helping us by praying for us. Then many people will give thanks because God has graciously answered so many prayers for our safety.

1:1 Greek *Achaia*, the southern region of the Greek peninsula.   1:8 Greek *brothers*.

Paul's Change of Plans

12 We can say with confidence and a clear conscience that we have lived with a God-given holiness* and sincerity in all our dealings. We have depended on God's grace, not on our own human wisdom. That is how we have conducted ourselves before the world, and especially toward you. 13 Our letters have been straightforward, and there is nothing written between the lines and nothing you can't understand. I hope someday you will fully understand us, 14 even if you don't understand us now. Then on the day when the Lord Jesus* returns, you will be proud of us in the same way we are proud of you.

15 Since I was so sure of your understanding and trust, I wanted to give you a double blessing by visiting you twice—16 first on my way to Macedonia and again when I returned from Macedonia.* Then you could send me on my way to Judea.

17 You may be asking why I changed my plan. Do you think I make my plans carelessly? Do you think I am like people of the world who say "Yes" when they really mean "No"? 18 As surely as God is faithful, my word to you does not waver between "Yes" and "No." 19 For Jesus Christ, the Son of God, does not waver between "Yes" and "No." He is the one whom Silas,* Timothy, and I preached to you, and as God's ultimate "Yes," he always does what he says. 20 For all of God's promises have been fulfilled in Christ with a resounding "Yes!" And through Christ, our "Amen" (which means "Yes") ascends to God for his glory.

21 It is God who enables us, along with you, to stand firm for Christ. He has commissioned us, 22 and he has identified us as his own by placing the Holy Spirit in our hearts as the first installment that guarantees everything he has promised us.

23 Now I call upon God as my witness that I am telling the truth. The reason I didn't return to Corinth was to spare you from a severe rebuke. 24 But that does not mean we want to dominate you by telling you how to put your faith into practice. We want to work together with you so you will be full of joy, for it is by your own faith that you stand firm.

CHAPTER **2**

So I decided that I would not bring you grief with another painful visit. 2 For if I cause you grief, who will make me glad? Certainly not someone I have grieved. 3 That is why I wrote to you

1:12 Some manuscripts read *honesty.* 1:14 Some manuscripts read *our Lord Jesus.* 1:16 *Macedonia was in the northern region of Greece.* 1:19 Greek *Silvanus.*

Anchor Passage

PASSAGE: 2 Corinthians 2:5-11

FRIENDSHIP TYPE: Hard-to-Love People   FRIENDSHIP LAYER: Companionship

Release

Think of someone who has offended you. Read **2 Corinthians 2:5-11**.

Whatever he did, it must've been pretty bad. Maybe he tried to embezzle money from the church. Maybe he initiated secret meetings to remove the pastor. Maybe he spread rumors and lies that caused confused church members to leave for good. The Bible doesn't say what the man in 2 Corinthians 2:5-11 did. It appears that Paul, the author of 2 Corinthians, was the chief target of the man's behavior. And we know that his behavior affected nearly everyone at the church of Corinth in some way. The truth had come out, and the church was hurt and angry. The church in Corinth was known for its generous giving, but at this moment it was struggling to give forgiveness.

Paul's solution showed tremendous insight and compassion for everyone involved. The answer to their healing was so simple, yet likely so difficult: Forgive him. Through forgiveness the offender could find comfort, healing, and companionship. Through forgiveness the church could close the door to the destructive attitudes of bitterness, hate, and judgment. And they could regain companionship with a friend who was otherwise hard to love. The man desperately needed to be forgiven, just as the church desperately needed to forgive.

Anchor Passage continues on page 344...

Friendship First NEW TESTAMENT

Anchor Passage continued from page 343...

Experience

Ask God to bring to mind one friend who is hard to love because you feel angry with him or her. Ask God to help you forgive that person. You may not want to forgive, but it's important to remember that you need to forgive others just like God has forgiven you. Check out pages 351-352 for some practical tips on how to forgive.

Make a list of all the good things that could come about by forgiving that person...such as being able to hang out together again, talking about movies, and going golfing on nice days.

If you're ready, go ahead and give the person a call!

Reflect

★ How does an unwillingness to forgive hurt the person who has offended or wronged someone else?

★ How does an unwillingness to forgive hurt the person who has been offended or wronged?

★ Why is forgiveness so powerful? How does it restore companionship?

DIGGING DEEPER

FRIENDSHIP TYPE:
Hard-to-Love People

FRIENDSHIP LAYER:
Companionship

For being a companion of hard-to-love people, check out...

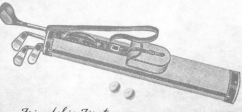

Friendship First NEW TESTAMENT

---

as I did, so that when I do come, I won't be grieved by the very ones who ought to give me the greatest joy. Surely you all know that my joy comes from your being joyful. ⁴I wrote that letter in great anguish, with a troubled heart and many tears. I didn't want to grieve you, but I wanted to let you know how much love I have for you.

⚓ Forgiveness for the Sinner

⁵I am not overstating it when I say that the man who caused all the trouble hurt all of you more than he hurt me. ⁶Most of you opposed him, and that was punishment enough. ⁷Now, however, it is time to forgive and comfort him. Otherwise he may be overcome by discouragement. ⁸So I urge you now to reaffirm your love for him.

⁹I wrote to you as I did to test you and see if you would fully comply with my instructions. ¹⁰When you forgive this man, I forgive him, too. And when I forgive whatever needs to be forgiven, I do so with Christ's authority for your benefit, ¹¹so that Satan will not outsmart us. For we are familiar with his evil schemes. ⚓

¹²When I came to the city of Troas to preach the Good News of Christ, the Lord opened a door of opportunity for me. ¹³But I had no peace of mind because my dear brother Titus hadn't yet arrived with a report from you. So I said good-bye and went on to Macedonia to find him.

Ministers of the New Covenant

¹⁴But thank God! He has made us his captives and continues to lead us along in Christ's triumphal procession. Now he uses us to spread the knowledge of Christ everywhere, like a sweet perfume. ¹⁵Our lives are a Christ-like fragrance rising up to God. But this fragrance is perceived differently by those who are being saved and by those who are perishing. ¹⁶To those who are perishing, we are a dreadful smell of death and doom. But to those who are being saved, we are a life-giving perfume. And who is adequate for such a task as this?

¹⁷You see, we are not like the many hucksters* who preach

2:17 Some manuscripts read *the rest of the hucksters.*

for personal profit. We preach the word of God with sincerity and with Christ's authority, knowing that God is watching us.

CHAPTER 3

Are we beginning to praise ourselves again? Are we like others, who need to bring you letters of recommendation, or who ask you to write such letters on their behalf? Surely not! 2The only letter of recommendation we need is you yourselves. Your lives are a letter written in our* hearts; everyone can read it and recognize our good work among you. 3Clearly, you are a letter from Christ showing the result of our ministry among you. This "letter" is written not with pen and ink, but with the Spirit of the living God. It is carved not on tablets of stone, but on human hearts.

4We are confident of all this because of our great trust in God through Christ. 5It is not that we think we are qualified to do anything on our own. Our qualification comes from God. 6He has enabled us to be ministers of his new covenant. This is a covenant not of written laws, but of the Spirit. The old written covenant ends in death; but under the new covenant, the Spirit gives life.

The Glory of the New Covenant

7The old way,* with laws etched in stone, led to death, though it began with such glory that the people of Israel could not bear to look at Moses' face. For his face shone with the glory of God, even though the brightness was already fading away. 8Shouldn't we expect far greater glory under the new way, now that the Holy Spirit is giving life? 9If the old way, which brings condemnation, was glorious, how much more glorious is the new way, which makes us right with God! 10In fact, that first glory was not glorious at all compared with the overwhelming glory of the new way. 11So if the old way, which has been replaced, was glorious, how much more glorious is the new, which remains forever!

12Since this new way gives us such confidence, we can be very bold. 13We are not like Moses, who put a veil over his face so the people of Israel would not see the glory, even though it was destined to fade away. 14But the people's minds were hardened, and to this day whenever the old covenant is being read, the same veil covers their minds so they cannot understand the truth. And this veil can be removed only by believing in Christ.

3:2 Some manuscripts read your.   3:7 Or ministry; also in 3:8, 9, 10, 11, 12.

> *"Friendship with God introduces us into God's universal friendship, in which we are commanded to love every person as our neighbor."*
>
> ~ Liz Carmichael

JOURNAL

[15] Yes, even today when they read Moses' writings, their hearts are covered with that veil, and they do not understand.

[16] But whenever someone turns to the Lord, the veil is taken away. [17] For the Lord is the Spirit, and wherever the Spirit of the Lord is, there is freedom. [18] So all of us who have had that veil removed can see and reflect the glory of the Lord. And the Lord—who is the Spirit—makes us more and more like him as we are changed into his glorious image.

CHAPTER **4**

Treasure in Fragile Clay Jars

Therefore, since God in his mercy has given us this new way,* we never give up. [2] We reject all shameful deeds and underhanded methods. We don't try to trick anyone or distort the word of God. We tell the truth before God, and all who are honest know this.

[3] If the Good News we preach is hidden behind a veil, it is hidden only from people who are perishing. [4] Satan, who is the god of this world, has blinded the minds of those who don't believe. They are unable to see the glorious light of the Good News. They don't understand this message about the glory of Christ, who is the exact likeness of God.

[5] You see, we don't go around preaching about ourselves. We preach that Jesus Christ is Lord, and we ourselves are your servants for Jesus' sake. [6] For God, who said, "Let there be light in the darkness," has made this light shine in our hearts so we could know the glory of God that is seen in the face of Jesus Christ.

[7] We now have this light shining in our hearts, but we ourselves are like fragile clay jars containing this great treasure.* This makes it clear that our great power is from God, not from ourselves.

[8] We are pressed on every side by troubles, but we are not crushed. We are perplexed, but not driven to despair. [9] We are hunted down, but never abandoned by God. We get knocked down, but we are not destroyed. [10] Through suffering, our bodies continue to share in the death of Jesus so that the life of Jesus may also be seen in our bodies.

[11] Yes, we live under constant danger of death because we serve Jesus, so that the life of Jesus will be evident in our dying bodies. [12] So we live in the face of death, but this has resulted in eternal life for you.

[13] But we continue to preach because we have the same kind of faith the psalmist had when he said, "I believed in God, so I

4:1 Or *ministry.*   4:7 Greek *We now have this treasure in clay jars.*

spoke."* ¹⁴We know that God, who raised the Lord Jesus,* will also raise us with Jesus and present us to himself together with you. ¹⁵All of this is for your benefit. And as God's grace reaches more and more people, there will be great thanksgiving, and God will receive more and more glory.

¹⁶That is why we never give up. Though our bodies are dying, our spirits are* being renewed every day. ¹⁷For our present troubles are small and won't last very long. Yet they produce for us a glory that vastly outweighs them and will last forever! ¹⁸So we don't look at the troubles we can see now; rather, we fix our gaze on things that cannot be seen. For the things we see now will soon be gone, but the things we cannot see will last forever.

CHAPTER 5

New Bodies

For we know that when this earthly tent we live in is taken down (that is, when we die and leave this earthly body), we will have a house in heaven, an eternal body made for us by God himself and not by human hands. ²We grow weary in our present bodies, and we long to put on our heavenly bodies like new clothing. ³For we will put on heavenly bodies; we will not be spirits without bodies.* ⁴While we live in these earthly bodies, we groan and sigh, but it's not that we want to die and get rid of these bodies that clothe us. Rather, we want to put on our new bodies so that these dying bodies will be swallowed up by life. ⁵God himself has prepared us for this, and as a guarantee he has given us his Holy Spirit.

⁶So we are always confident, even though we know that as long as we live in these bodies we are not at home with the Lord. ⁷For we live by believing and not by seeing. ⁸Yes, we are fully confident, and we would rather be away from these earthly bodies, for then we will be at home with the Lord. ⁹So whether we are here in this body or away from this body, our goal is to please him. ¹⁰For we must all stand before Christ to be judged. We will each receive whatever we deserve for the good or evil we have done in this earthly body.

We Are God's Ambassadors

¹¹Because we understand our fearful responsibility to the Lord, we work hard to persuade others. God knows we are sincere, and

4:13 Ps 116:10. 4:14 Some manuscripts read *who raised Jesus.* 4:16 Greek *our inner being is.*
5:3 Greek *we will not be naked.*

No. 16-TE-347

FRIENDSHIP STORY

FRIENDSHIP TYPE:	FRIENDSHIP LAYER:
Family	*Trust*

BASED ON TRUE EVENTS

Hard Hat Area: Other Shoes Dropping

Kelly took a deep breath and prepared for the inevitable fallout. Man, she wished someone else could be in her place for a day. Or about nine-bazillion days. This time was going to be *bad*!

Jill—her older, *perfect* sister—sat there, yammering away like everything in the world was peachy. Kelly struggled to open her mouth, interrupt Jill, and spill it. But it wouldn't come out. Not yet. Not with that knot tied in her windpipe. She'd have to somehow get it untangled if she ever hoped to fess up.

As Jill's loose jaw hinge flapped on and on, Kelly's mind left the room and wandered back to a time years before when she'd decided to let Jill in on a little secret. She'd shown Jill her newly pierced bellybutton. She did it partially out of spite; to prove to Jill not everyone saw things like she did. And partly to test Jill to see if Jill really meant it when she'd promised her love was unconditional. *Nobody's* love was really unconditional.

Jill's eyes had opened a bit wider when Kelly unveiled the piercing. But she didn't say anything. She just seemed to think for a while. Kelly could see the gears grinding behind her eyes as she tried to come up with some sermon about it all. Kelly felt satisfaction; knowing Jill had been struck dumb.

FRIENDSHIP STORY
continues on page 348...

continues on page 348...

Friendship First NEW TESTAMENT

FRIENDSHIP STORY *continued from page 347...*

But when Jill finally said something, it wasn't what Kelly expected.

"Your skin's so perfect. I wish you hadn't done that. With all my scars from the surgeries, if I could have skin like yours again, I'd take it in a minute."

Kelly suddenly realized the other shoe never dropped on that one. Their parents never found out. The sermon never came. And Jill never shunned her. Maybe today Jill wouldn't hate her after all. Maybe there was a chance Jill would find a way to eventually speak to her and care about her again.

"I have something to tell you," Kelly blurted. The knot squeezed in her throat, but she made herself speak. "I'm pregnant." Then she braced herself.

Jill was quiet for a long time. A *really* long time. Then she smiled...not a mean, judging smile as Kelly had feared, but a kind smile. And then Jill asked what Kelly thought, how she felt.

How she felt? She'd been devastated. Excited. Terror-stricken. Filled with wonder. Overwhelmed. She opened her mouth to express some of it, but instead of sensible words, sobs spilled out. Jill wrapped her arms around Kelly and let her cry till her mascara smeared all over Jill's shoulder.

Experience

Kelly chose to share this big secret with Jill because she remembered that Jill had been trustworthy with a small secret. Mary probably felt the same way when she chose to trust her relative Elizabeth with such a big secret in **Luke 1:39-45**.

Trust doesn't happen overnight, it's built one confidence at a time. Is there someone in your family who has proven trustworthy over time? Call the person up this week, and thank him or her for being that trusted confidant whom you know you can always go to.

FRIENDSHIP STORY *continues on page 349...*

(THE ONE THING YOU CAN DO THIS WEEK — 1)

I hope you know this, too. [12]Are we commending ourselves to you again? No, we are giving you a reason to be proud of us,* so you can answer those who brag about having a spectacular ministry rather than having a sincere heart. [13]If it seems we are crazy, it is to bring glory to God. And if we are in our right minds, it is for your benefit. [14]Either way, Christ's love controls us.* Since we believe that Christ died for all, we also believe that we have all died to our old life.* [15]He died for everyone so that those who receive his new life will no longer live for themselves. Instead, they will live for Christ, who died and was raised for them.

[16]So we have stopped evaluating others from a human point of view. At one time we thought of Christ merely from a human point of view. How differently we know him now! [17]This means that anyone who belongs to Christ has become a new person. The old life is gone; a new life has begun!

[18]And all of this is a gift from God, who brought us back to himself through Christ. And God has given us this task of reconciling people to him. [19]For God was in Christ, reconciling the world to himself, no longer counting people's sins against them. And he gave us this wonderful message of reconciliation. [20]So we are Christ's ambassadors; God is making his appeal through us. We speak for Christ when we plead, "Come back to God!" [21]For God made Christ, who never sinned, to be the offering for our sin,* so that we could be made right with God through Christ.

CHAPTER **6**

As God's partners,* we beg you not to accept this marvelous gift of God's kindness and then ignore it. [2]For God says,

"At just the right time, I heard you.
On the day of salvation, I helped you."*

Indeed, the "right time" is now. Today is the day of salvation.

Paul's Hardships

[3]We live in such a way that no one will stumble because of us, and no one will find fault with our ministry. [4]In everything we do, we show that we are true ministers of God. We patiently endure troubles and hardships and calamities of every kind. [5]We have been beaten, been put in prison, faced angry mobs, worked to exhaustion, endured sleepless nights, and gone without food. [6]We prove ourselves by our purity, our understanding,

5:12 Some manuscripts read *proud of yourselves.* **5:14a** Or *urges us on.* **5:14b** Greek *Since one died for all, then all died.* **5:21** Or *to become sin itself.* **6:1** Or *As we work together.* **6:2** Isa 49:8 (Greek version).

our patience, our kindness, by the Holy Spirit within us,* and by our sincere love. ⁷We faithfully preach the truth. God's power is working in us. We use the weapons of righteousness in the right hand for attack and the left hand for defense. ⁸We serve God whether people honor us or despise us, whether they slander us or praise us. We are honest, but they call us impostors. ⁹We are ignored, even though we are well known. We live close to death, but we are still alive. We have been beaten, but we have not been killed. ¹⁰Our hearts ache, but we always have joy. We are poor, but we give spiritual riches to others. We own nothing, and yet we have everything.

¹¹Oh, dear Corinthian friends! We have spoken honestly with you, and our hearts are open to you. ¹²There is no lack of love on our part, but you have withheld your love from us. ¹³I am asking you to respond as if you were my own children. Open your hearts to us!

The Temple of the Living God

¹⁴Don't team up with those who are unbelievers. How can righteousness be a partner with wickedness? How can light live with darkness? ¹⁵What harmony can there be between Christ and the devil*? How can a believer be a partner with an unbeliever? ¹⁶And what union can there be between God's temple and idols? For we are the temple of the living God. As God said:

"I will live in them
    and walk among them.
I will be their God,
    and they will be my people.*
¹⁷ Therefore, come out from among unbelievers,
    and separate yourselves from them, says the LORD.
Don't touch their filthy things,
    and I will welcome you.*
¹⁸ And I will be your Father,
    and you will be my sons and daughters,
    says the LORD Almighty.*"

CHAPTER **7**

Because we have these promises, dear friends, let us cleanse ourselves from everything that can defile our body or spirit. And let us work toward complete holiness because we fear God.

²Please open your hearts to us. We have not done wrong to

6:6 Or *by our holiness of spirit.* 6:15 Greek *Beliar;* various other manuscripts render this proper name of the devil as *Belian, Beliab,* or *Belial.* 6:16 Lev 26:12; Ezek 37:27. 6:17 Isa 52:11; Ezek 20:34 (Greek version). 6:18 2 Sam 7:14.

FRIENDSHIP STORY *continued from page 348...*

Reflect

★ What made Kelly decide to share her secret with Jill?

★ In what ways can you grow as a trusted friend to others?

★ When has God revealed he is a trustworthy friend to you?

trust (trŭst) *v.*
To expect with assurance...To believe.
To place in the care of another; entrust.

Friendship First NEW TESTAMENT

> *"As iron sharpens iron, so a friend sharpens a friend."*
>
> ~ Proverbs 27:17

JOURNAL

anyone, nor led anyone astray, nor taken advantage of anyone. ³I'm not saying this to condemn you. I said before that you are in our hearts, and we live or die together with you. ⁴I have the highest confidence in you, and I take great pride in you. You have greatly encouraged me and made me happy despite all our troubles.

Paul's Joy at the Church's Repentance

⁵When we arrived in Macedonia, there was no rest for us. We faced conflict from every direction, with battles on the outside and fear on the inside. ⁶But God, who encourages those who are discouraged, encouraged us by the arrival of Titus. ⁷His presence was a joy, but so was the news he brought of the encouragement he received from you. When he told us how much you long to see me, and how sorry you are for what happened, and how loyal you are to me, I was filled with joy!

⁸I am not sorry that I sent that severe letter to you, though I was sorry at first, for I know it was painful to you for a little while. ⁹Now I am glad I sent it, not because it hurt you, but because the pain caused you to repent and change your ways. It was the kind of sorrow God wants his people to have, so you were not harmed by us in any way. ¹⁰For the kind of sorrow God wants us to experience leads us away from sin and results in salvation. There's no regret for that kind of sorrow. But worldly sorrow, which lacks repentance, results in spiritual death.

¹¹Just see what this godly sorrow produced in you! Such earnestness, such concern to clear yourselves, such indignation, such alarm, such longing to see me, such zeal, and such a readiness to punish wrong. You showed that you have done everything necessary to make things right. ¹²My purpose, then, was not to write about who did the wrong or who was wronged. I wrote to you so that in the sight of God you could see for yourselves how loyal you are to us. ¹³We have been greatly encouraged by this.

In addition to our own encouragement, we were especially delighted to see how happy Titus was about the way all of you welcomed him and set his mind* at ease. ¹⁴I had told him how proud I was of you—and you didn't disappoint me. I have always told you the truth, and now my boasting to Titus has also proved true! ¹⁵Now he cares for you more than ever when he remembers the way all of you obeyed him and welcomed him with such fear and deep respect. ¹⁶I am very happy now because I have complete confidence in you.

7:13 Greek *his spirit.*

CHAPTER **8**

A Call to Generous Giving

Now I want you to know, dear brothers and sisters,* what God in his kindness has done through the churches in Macedonia. ²They are being tested by many troubles, and they are very poor. But they are also filled with abundant joy, which has overflowed in rich generosity.

³For I can testify that they gave not only what they could afford, but far more. And they did it of their own free will. ⁴They begged us again and again for the privilege of sharing in the gift for the believers* in Jerusalem. ⁵They even did more than we had hoped, for their first action was to give themselves to the Lord and to us, just as God wanted them to do.

⁶So we have urged Titus, who encouraged your giving in the first place, to return to you and encourage you to finish this ministry of giving. ⁷Since you excel in so many ways—in your faith, your gifted speakers, your knowledge, your enthusiasm, and your love from us*—I want you to excel also in this gracious act of giving.

⁸I am not commanding you to do this. But I am testing how genuine your love is by comparing it with the eagerness of the other churches.

⁹You know the generous grace of our Lord Jesus Christ. Though he was rich, yet for your sakes he became poor, so that by his poverty he could make you rich.

¹⁰Here is my advice: It would be good for you to finish what you started a year ago. Last year you were the first who wanted to give, and you were the first to begin doing it. ¹¹Now you should finish what you started. Let the eagerness you showed in the beginning be matched now by your giving. Give in proportion to what you have. ¹²Whatever you give is acceptable if you give it eagerly. And give according to what you have, not what you don't have. ¹³Of course, I don't mean your giving should make life easy for others and hard for yourselves. I only mean that there should be some equality. ¹⁴Right now you have plenty and can help those who are in need. Later, they will have plenty and can share with you when you need it. In this way, things will be equal. ¹⁵As the Scriptures say,

> "Those who gathered a lot had nothing left over,
>   and those who gathered only a little had
>   enough."*

8:1 Greek *brothers.*   **8:4** Greek *for God's holy people.*   **8:7** Some manuscripts read *your love for us.*
8:15 Exod 16:18.

FRIENDSHIP EXPERIENCE

FRIENDSHIP TYPE: *Hard-to-Love People*   FRIENDSHIP LAYER: *Companionship*

Let It Go

There are some things you just know you have to forgive: that hard-to-love co-worker who seems to offend you just about every time you see him, the former best friend you've put on ice for months, your sister who borrowed money and hasn't paid you back.

But what about the more subtle—and lingering—things you haven't forgiven? A good friend who didn't call when you were in pain. A close companion who drifted away and made you feel you were no longer worth the effort. A hurtful comment made in jest that you just can't seem to forget. You don't hate the person, and you might even still call the person your friend. But there's bitterness there, just under the surface…and it's affecting your companionship.

Whether you're in an all-out war with someone or there just seems to be an intangible distance between you and a close friend—it's probably time for you to work through forgiveness.

THE ONE THING 1 YOU CAN DO THIS WEEK

Experience

God has probably already brought the person to mind, now work through the process of forgiveness—and restoring companionship. That's right, forgiveness is a process—not a feeling! Here are some steps you can take right now:

1. Ask God to help you forgive. If you could do it all on your own, you likely would've already done it.

FRIENDSHIP EXPERIENCE *continues on page 352…*

FRIENDSHIP EXPERIENCE *continued from page 351...*

2. Apologize for your unforgiving attitude. Yep, the Bible makes it clear that having an unforgiving heart is a sin. Start by simply telling God you're sorry for being unforgiving… and that you *want* to forgive.

3. Ask God to bring specific hurts to mind. Forgiving Bill for being a jerk doesn't really get you anywhere. What specific jerk-like things did Bill do?

4. Choose to forgive. It may sound strange, but say it out loud (maybe in a closet or your car). "I forgive Bill for…" You may not feel all "forgive-y" inside, but you just made a choice when you said it.

5. Pray for the person or do something kind to the person you just forgave. You'll start to feel your heart change toward the person.

6. Repeat as needed and as new specific hurts come to mind.

7. As you move through these steps, God may bring to mind things for which you need to ask forgiveness. Read **1 John 1:9**. Tell God—and the person—that you're sorry…and know that God has completely forgiven you!

Reflect

★ How has an unforgiving attitude colored your views of people and affected your companionship with that person?

★ Which step of forgiveness is hardest for you? Why?

★ How can you rely on God to help you forgive that hard-to-love person?

Titus and His Companions

¹⁶But thank God! He has given Titus the same enthusiasm for you that I have. ¹⁷Titus welcomed our request that he visit you again. In fact, he himself was very eager to go and see you. ¹⁸We are also sending another brother with Titus. All the churches praise him as a preacher of the Good News. ¹⁹He was appointed by the churches to accompany us as we take the offering to Jerusalem*—a service that glorifies the Lord and shows our eagerness to help.

²⁰We are traveling together to guard against any criticism for the way we are handling this generous gift. ²¹We are careful to be honorable before the Lord, but we also want everyone else to see that we are honorable.

²²We are also sending with them another of our brothers who has proven himself many times and has shown on many occasions how eager he is. He is now even more enthusiastic because of his great confidence in you. ²³If anyone asks about Titus, say that he is my partner who works with me to help you. And the brothers with him have been sent by the churches,* and they bring honor to Christ. ²⁴So show them your love, and prove to all the churches that our boasting about you is justified.

CHAPTER **9**

The Collection for Christians in Jerusalem

I really don't need to write to you about this ministry of giving for the believers in Jerusalem.* ²For I know how eager you are to help, and I have been boasting to the churches in Macedonia that you in Greece* were ready to send an offering a year ago. In fact, it was your enthusiasm that stirred up many of the Macedonian believers to begin giving.

³But I am sending these brothers to be sure you really are ready, as I have been telling them, and that your money is all collected. I don't want to be wrong in my boasting about you. ⁴We would be embarrassed—not to mention your own embarrassment—if some Macedonian believers came with me and found that you weren't ready after all I had told them! ⁵So I thought I should send these brothers ahead of me to make sure the gift you promised is ready. But I want it to be a willing gift, not one given grudgingly.

⁶Remember this—a farmer who plants only a few seeds will get a small crop. But the one who plants generously will get a

8:19 See 1 Cor 16:3-4.   8:23 Greek *are apostles of the churches.*   9:1 Greek *about the offering for God's holy people.*   9:2 Greek *in Achaia,* the southern region of the Greek peninsula. *Macedonia* was in the northern region of Greece.

generous crop. [7]You must each decide in your heart how much to give. And don't give reluctantly or in response to pressure. "For God loves a person who gives cheerfully."* [8]And God will generously provide all you need. Then you will always have everything you need and plenty left over to share with others. [9]As the Scriptures say,

> "They share freely and give generously to the poor.
>   Their good deeds will be remembered forever."*

[10]For God is the one who provides seed for the farmer and then bread to eat. In the same way, he will provide and increase your resources and then produce a great harvest of generosity* in you.

[11]Yes, you will be enriched in every way so that you can always be generous. And when we take your gifts to those who need them, they will thank God. [12]So two good things will result from this ministry of giving—the needs of the believers in Jerusalem* will be met, and they will joyfully express their thanks to God.

[13]As a result of your ministry, they will give glory to God. For your generosity to them and to all believers will prove that you are obedient to the Good News of Christ. [14]And they will pray for you with deep affection because of the overflowing grace God has given to you. [15]Thank God for this gift* too wonderful for words!

CHAPTER 10
Paul Defends His Authority

Now I, Paul, appeal to you with the gentleness and kindness of Christ—though I realize you think I am timid in person and bold only when I write from far away. [2]Well, I am begging you now so that when I come I won't have to be bold with those who think we act from human motives.

[3]We are human, but we don't wage war as humans do. [4]*We use God's mighty weapons, not worldly weapons, to knock down the strongholds of human reasoning and to destroy false arguments. [5]We destroy every proud obstacle that keeps people from knowing God. We capture their rebellious thoughts and teach them to obey Christ. [6]And after you have become fully obedient, we will punish everyone who remains disobedient.

[7]Look at the obvious facts.* Those who say they belong to

9:7 See footnote on Prov 22:8.   9:9 Ps 112:9.   9:10 Greek *righteousness*.   9:12 Greek *of God's holy people*.   9:15 Greek *his gift*.   10:4 English translations divide verses 4 and 5 in various ways. 10:7 Or *You look at things only on the basis of appearance*.

WHAT TO SAY
AND
WHAT NOT TO SAY

Thoughts on Forgiveness

It takes a lot of grace and a lot of forgiveness to turn a hard-to-love person into a companion or to restore companionship with a friend who has become hard to love. Forgiving and loving someone like that seems nearly impossible. Before you throw in the towel though, consider the following about forgiveness:

WHAT IT ISN'T:

★ **Forgiveness isn't saying what the person did was OK.** You've been hurt, and that's not OK. Behavior from hard-to-love people often isn't acceptable. You don't have to pretend their behavior is acceptable to forgive them.

★ **Forgiveness isn't forgetting.** Only God can completely forgive and forget. No matter how thoroughly you've forgiven someone, often you'll still remember what happened.

★ **Forgiveness isn't denying or sweeping things under the rug.** Working through conflict with a hard-to-love person turns that person into a companion. Avoiding the conflict destroys the friendship. Sometimes you need to talk through your hurt or frustration with the hard-to-love person to start the forgiveness process. Sometimes you have to work it through on your own first. But you should never pretend to forgive.

★ **Forgiveness isn't choosing to put yourself in harm's way.** If the person is a threat to your safety or continues to hurt you, you need to keep forgiving, but you also need to set some safe boundaries—forgiving doesn't mean staying in an unsafe situation.

WHAT TO SAY AND WHAT NOT TO SAY *continues on page 355...*

Friendship First NEW TESTAMENT

Christ must recognize that we belong to Christ as much as they do. [8]I may seem to be boasting too much about the authority given to us by the Lord. But our authority builds you up; it doesn't tear you down. So I will not be ashamed of using my authority.

[9]I'm not trying to frighten you by my letters. [10]For some say, "Paul's letters are demanding and forceful, but in person he is weak, and his speeches are worthless!" [11]Those people should realize that our actions when we arrive in person will be as forceful as what we say in our letters from far away.

[12]Oh, don't worry; we wouldn't dare say that we are as wonderful as these other men who tell you how important they are! But they are only comparing themselves with each other, using themselves as the standard of measurement. How ignorant!

[13]We will not boast about things done outside our area of authority. We will boast only about what has happened within the boundaries of the work God has given us, which includes our working with you. [14]We are not reaching beyond these boundaries when we claim authority over you, as if we had never visited you. For we were the first to travel all the way to Corinth with the Good News of Christ.

[15]Nor do we boast and claim credit for the work someone else has done. Instead, we hope that your faith will grow so that the boundaries of our work among you will be extended. [16]Then we will be able to go and preach the Good News in other places far beyond you, where no one else is working. Then there will be no question of our boasting about work done in someone else's territory. [17]As the Scriptures say, "If you want to boast, boast only about the LORD."*

[18]When people commend themselves, it doesn't count for much. The important thing is for the Lord to commend them.

CHAPTER **11**

Paul and the False Apostles

I hope you will put up with a little more of my foolishness. Please bear with me. [2]For I am jealous for you with the jealousy of God himself. I promised you as a pure bride* to one husband—Christ. [3]But I fear that somehow your pure and undivided devotion to Christ will be corrupted, just as Eve was deceived by the cunning ways of the serpent. [4]You happily put up with whatever anyone tells you, even if they preach a different Jesus than the one we preach, or a different kind of Spirit

10:17 Jer 9:24.   **11:2** Greek *a virgin.*

than the one you received, or a different kind of gospel than the one you believed.

5But I don't consider myself inferior in any way to these "super apostles" who teach such things. 6I may be unskilled as a speaker, but I'm not lacking in knowledge. We have made this clear to you in every possible way.

7Was I wrong when I humbled myself and honored you by preaching God's Good News to you without expecting anything in return? 8I "robbed" other churches by accepting their contributions so I could serve you at no cost. 9And when I was with you and didn't have enough to live on, I did not become a financial burden to anyone. For the brothers who came from Macedonia brought me all that I needed. I have never been a burden to you, and I never will be. 10As surely as the truth of Christ is in me, no one in all of Greece* will ever stop me from boasting about this. 11Why? Because I don't love you? God knows that I do.

12But I will continue doing what I have always done. This will undercut those who are looking for an opportunity to boast that their work is just like ours. 13These people are false apostles. They are deceitful workers who disguise themselves as apostles of Christ. 14But I am not surprised! Even Satan disguises himself as an angel of light. 15So it is no wonder that his servants also disguise themselves as servants of righteousness. In the end they will get the punishment their wicked deeds deserve.

Paul's Many Trials

16Again I say, don't think that I am a fool to talk like this. But even if you do, listen to me, as you would to a foolish person, while I also boast a little. 17Such boasting is not from the Lord, but I am acting like a fool. 18And since others boast about their human achievements, I will, too. 19After all, you think you are so wise, but you enjoy putting up with fools! 20You put up with it when someone enslaves you, takes everything you have, takes advantage of you, takes control of everything, and slaps you in the face. 21I'm ashamed to say that we've been too "weak" to do that!

But whatever they dare to boast about—I'm talking like a fool again—I dare to boast about it, too. 22Are they Hebrews? So am I. Are they Israelites? So am I. Are they descendants of Abraham? So am I. 23Are they servants of Christ? I know I sound like a madman, but I have served him far more! I have worked harder, been put in prison more often, been

11:10 Greek *Achaia*, the southern region of the Greek peninsula.

WHAT TO SAY AND WHAT NOT TO SAY *continued from page 354…*

WHAT IT IS:

★ Mostly, forgiveness is letting go—letting go of your right to hate, your right to be bitter, and your right to get revenge. And forgiveness is grabbing a hold of *love.* God loves us so much that he sacrificed his Son in order to forgive us…that love should inspire us to forgive the people around us.

★ Forgiveness is ending the power the offense had over you. When you refuse to forgive, the anger and hurt you feel takes control of your emotions. How much better it is to be full of forgiveness and love rather than anger and bitterness!

★ Forgiveness is a process. You don't have to feel forgiveness to start forgiving. Rather, start forgiving, and you'll begin to feel forgiveness. It takes time, persistence, and work. But it's worth it—and it's essential for true companionship. Check out some tips on pages 351-352 to discover how you can get the ball rolling.

"Don't rejoice when your enemies fall; don't be happy when they stumble."

~ *Proverbs 24:17*

Friendship First NEW TESTAMENT

JOURNAL

whipped times without number, and faced death again and again. 24Five different times the Jewish leaders gave me thirty-nine lashes. 25Three times I was beaten with rods. Once I was stoned. Three times I was shipwrecked. Once I spent a whole night and a day adrift at sea. 26I have traveled on many long journeys. I have faced danger from rivers and from robbers. I have faced danger from my own people, the Jews, as well as from the Gentiles. I have faced danger in the cities, in the deserts, and on the seas. And I have faced danger from men who claim to be believers but are not.* 27I have worked hard and long, enduring many sleepless nights. I have been hungry and thirsty and have often gone without food. I have shivered in the cold, without enough clothing to keep me warm.

28Then, besides all this, I have the daily burden of my concern for all the churches. 29Who is weak without my feeling that weakness? Who is led astray, and I do not burn with anger?

30If I must boast, I would rather boast about the things that show how weak I am. 31God, the Father of our Lord Jesus, who is worthy of eternal praise, knows I am not lying. 32When I was in Damascus, the governor under King Aretas kept guards at the city gates to catch me. 33I had to be lowered in a basket through a window in the city wall to escape from him.

CHAPTER 12

Paul's Vision and His Thorn in the Flesh

This boasting will do no good, but I must go on. I will reluctantly tell about visions and revelations from the Lord. 2I* was caught up to the third heaven fourteen years ago. Whether I was in my body or out of my body, I don't know—only God knows. 3Yes, only God knows whether I was in my body or outside my body. But I do know 4that I was caught up* to paradise and heard things so astounding that they cannot be expressed in words, things no human is allowed to tell.

5That experience is worth boasting about, but I'm not going to do it. I will boast only about my weaknesses. 6If I wanted to boast, I would be no fool in doing so, because I would be telling the truth. But I won't do it, because I don't want anyone to give me credit beyond what they can see in my life or hear in my message, 7even though I have received such wonderful revelations from God. So to keep me from becoming proud, I was given a thorn in my flesh, a messenger from Satan to torment me and keep me from becoming proud.

11:26 Greek *from false brothers.* 12:2 Greek *I know a man in Christ who.* 12:3-4 Greek *But I know such a man, 4that he was caught up.*

8 Three different times I begged the Lord to take it away. 9 Each time he said, "My grace is all you need. My power works best in weakness." So now I am glad to boast about my weaknesses, so that the power of Christ can work through me. 10 That's why I take pleasure in my weaknesses, and in the insults, hardships, persecutions, and troubles that I suffer for Christ. For when I am weak, then I am strong.

Paul's Concern for the Corinthians

11 You have made me act like a fool—boasting like this.* You ought to be writing commendations for me, for I am not at all inferior to these "super apostles," even though I am nothing at all. 12 When I was with you, I certainly gave you proof that I am an apostle. For I patiently did many signs and wonders and miracles among you. 13 The only thing I failed to do, which I do in the other churches, was to become a financial burden to you. Please forgive me for this wrong!

14 Now I am coming to you for the third time, and I will not be a burden to you. I don't want what you have—I want you. After all, children don't provide for their parents. Rather, parents provide for their children. 15 I will gladly spend myself and all I have for you, even though it seems that the more I love you, the less you love me.

16 Some of you admit I was not a burden to you. But others still think I was sneaky and took advantage of you by trickery. 17 But how? Did any of the men I sent to you take advantage of you? 18 When I urged Titus to visit you and sent our other brother with him, did Titus take advantage of you? No! For we have the same spirit and walk in each other's steps, doing things the same way.

19 Perhaps you think we're saying these things just to defend ourselves. No, we tell you this as Christ's servants, and with God as our witness. Everything we do, dear friends, is to strengthen you. 20 For I am afraid that when I come I won't like what I find, and you won't like my response. I am afraid that I will find quarreling, jealousy, anger, selfishness, slander, gossip, arrogance, and disorderly behavior. 21 Yes, I am afraid that when I come again, God will humble me in your presence. And I will be grieved because many of you have not given up your old sins. You have not repented of your impurity, sexual immorality, and eagerness for lustful pleasure.

12:11 Some manuscripts omit *boasting like this.*

No. 17-FS-331

FRIENDSHIP
STORY

FRIENDSHIP TYPE: *Hard-to-Love People*   FRIENDSHIP LAYER: *Companionship*

FOUND IN SCRIPTURE

Impossible Love

It was the ultimate betrayal. Hosea obviously loved Gomer and was certainly a loving father to their three children. There's no evidence that Hosea was inattentive or even rude. But Gomer had an appetite for more. She abandoned her husband and family to chase after her own desires for pleasure and indulgence.

Gomer willingly gave herself to multiple lovers who shared her mindset to exploit and use others for personal amusement. Not surprisingly, Gomer's selfish pursuits began a downward spiral. Gomer's lovers became more elusive as she became more "used up" and desperate. Money ran out and friends slipped away. Prostitution was the natural and logical next step as the need for survival starved Gomer's appetite for gratification.

Hosea's hurt, sense of betrayal, and embarrassment were overwhelming. Forgiveness seemed impossible…let alone *love*. But with God *all things* are possible (**Mark 10:27**), and when God asked Hosea to find his wife, forgive her, bring her home—and love her again—Hosea obeyed and trusted that God would help him do this impossible thing.

FRIENDSHIP STORY *continues on page 358…*

Friendship First NEW TESTAMENT

FRIENDSHIP STORY *continued from page 357...*

When Hosea found Gomer, she was destitute. Her poverty had forced her into slavery and left her abused and broken. Despite his pain, Hosea didn't act in anger. He didn't act in pity. Instead, Hosea acted in love. He bought Gomer out of slavery, forgave her, and took her back into his home. Hosea didn't punish Gomer or hold the betrayal against her. Instead he made Gomer his companion inviting her to live in purity, faithfulness, and love with him for the rest of their lives.

Read the whole story in the Old Testament book of Hosea.

Experience

God used the story of Hosea and Gomer as a picture of Israel's unfaithfulness to God...and God's passion for forgiving and restoring them. Read the first three chapters of the Old Testament book of Hosea to find out how God feels about people who turn their backs on him. (If you don't have a Bible, look it up online at www.biblegateway.com.) As you read, underline the words or images that you find moving or even surprising. Now just look at the underlined words. What do they say about God's desire to have companionship with us even when we're hard to love?

THE ONE THING
1
YOU CAN DO THIS WEEK

Reflect

★ What would you have done if you were Hosea? Gomer?

★ Why is forgiveness so powerful? Why is it necessary for companionship?

★ Who has hurt you deeply? How can you forgive that person?

Friendship First NEW TESTAMENT

CHAPTER **13**
Paul's Final Advice

This is the third time I am coming to visit you (and as the Scriptures say, "The facts of every case must be established by the testimony of two or three witnesses"*). ²I have already warned those who had been sinning when I was there on my second visit. Now I again warn them and all others, just as I did before, that next time I will not spare them.

³I will give you all the proof you want that Christ speaks through me. Christ is not weak when he deals with you; he is powerful among you. ⁴Although he was crucified in weakness, he now lives by the power of God. We, too, are weak, just as Christ was, but when we deal with you we will be alive with him and will have God's power.

⁵Examine yourselves to see if your faith is genuine. Test yourselves. Surely you know that Jesus Christ is among you*; if not, you have failed the test of genuine faith. ⁶As you test yourselves, I hope you will recognize that we have not failed the test of apostolic authority.

⁷We pray to God that you will not do what is wrong by refusing our correction. I hope we won't need to demonstrate our authority when we arrive. Do the right thing before we come—even if that makes it look like we have failed to demonstrate our authority. ⁸For we cannot oppose the truth, but must always stand for the truth. ⁹We are glad to seem weak if it helps show that you are actually strong. We pray that you will become mature.

¹⁰I am writing this to you before I come, hoping that I won't need to deal severely with you when I do come. For I want to use the authority the Lord has given me to strengthen you, not to tear you down.

Paul's Final Greetings

¹¹Dear brothers and sisters,* I close my letter with these last words: Be joyful. Grow to maturity. Encourage each other. Live in harmony and peace. Then the God of love and peace will be with you.

¹²Greet each other with Christian love.* ¹³All of God's people here send you their greetings.

¹⁴*May the grace of the Lord Jesus Christ, the love of God, and the fellowship of the Holy Spirit be with you all.

13:1 Deut 19:15. **13:5** Or *in you.* **13:11** Greek *Brothers.* **13:12** Greek *with a sacred kiss.*
13:14 Some English translations include verse 13 as part of verse 12, and then verse 14 becomes verse 13.

Galatians

AUTHOR:	DATE WRITTEN:
Paul	Approximately A.D. 49

CHAPTER **1**

Greetings from Paul

This letter is from Paul, an apostle. I was not appointed by any group of people or any human authority, but by Jesus Christ himself and by God the Father, who raised Jesus from the dead.

²All the brothers and sisters* here join me in sending this letter to the churches of Galatia.

³May God our Father and the Lord Jesus Christ* give you grace and peace. ⁴Jesus gave his life for our sins, just as God our Father planned, in order to rescue us from this evil world in which we live. ⁵All glory to God forever and ever! Amen.

There Is Only One Good News

⁶I am shocked that you are turning away so soon from God, who called you to himself through the loving mercy of Christ.* You are following a different way that pretends to be the Good News ⁷but is not the Good News at all. You are being fooled by those who deliberately twist the truth concerning Christ.

⁸Let God's curse fall on anyone, including us or even an angel from heaven, who preaches a different kind of Good News than the one we preached to you. ⁹I say again what we have said before: If anyone preaches any other Good News than the one you welcomed, let that person be cursed.

¹⁰Obviously, I'm not trying to win the approval of people, but of God. If pleasing people were my goal, I would not be Christ's servant.

Paul's Message Comes from Christ

¹¹Dear brothers and sisters, I want you to understand that the gospel message I preach is not based on mere human reasoning. ¹²I received my message from no human source, and no

1:2 Greek *brothers;* also in 1:11.   **1:3** Some manuscripts read *God the Father and our Lord Jesus Christ.*   **1:6** Some manuscripts read *through loving mercy.*

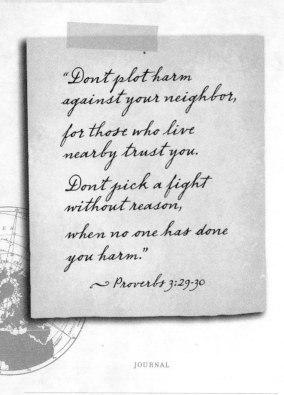

"Don't plot harm against your neighbor, for those who live nearby trust you. Don't pick a fight without reason, when no one has done you harm."

~ Proverbs 3:29-30

JOURNAL

one taught me. Instead, I received it by direct revelation from Jesus Christ.*

[13] You know what I was like when I followed the Jewish religion—how I violently persecuted God's church. I did my best to destroy it. [14] I was far ahead of my fellow Jews in my zeal for the traditions of my ancestors.

[15] But even before I was born, God chose me and called me by his marvelous grace. Then it pleased him [16] to reveal his Son to me* so that I would proclaim the Good News about Jesus to the Gentiles.

When this happened, I did not rush out to consult with any human being.* [17] Nor did I go up to Jerusalem to consult with those who were apostles before I was. Instead, I went away into Arabia, and later I returned to the city of Damascus.

[18] Then three years later I went to Jerusalem to get to know Peter,* and I stayed with him for fifteen days. [19] The only other apostle I met at that time was James, the Lord's brother. [20] I declare before God that what I am writing to you is not a lie.

[21] After that visit I went north into the provinces of Syria and Cilicia. [22] And still the Christians in the churches in Judea didn't know me personally. [23] All they knew was that people were saying, "The one who used to persecute us is now preaching the very faith he tried to destroy!" [24] And they praised God because of me.

CHAPTER 2

The Apostles Accept Paul

Then fourteen years later I went back to Jerusalem again, this time with Barnabas; and Titus came along, too. [2] I went there because God revealed to me that I should go. While I was there I met privately with those considered to be leaders of the church and shared with them the message I had been preaching to the Gentiles. I wanted to make sure that we were in agreement, for fear that all my efforts had been wasted and I was running the race for nothing. [3] And they supported me and did not even demand that my companion Titus be circumcised, though he was a Gentile.*

[4] Even that question came up only because of some so-called Christians there—false ones, really*—who were secretly brought in. They sneaked in to spy on us and take away the freedom we have in Christ Jesus. They wanted to enslave us and force us to

1:12 Or *by the revelation of Jesus Christ.* 1:16a Or *in me.* 1:16b Greek *with flesh and blood.*
1:18 Greek *Cephas.* 2:3 Greek *a Greek.* 2:4 Greek *some false brothers.*

follow their Jewish regulations. ⁵But we refused to give in to them for a single moment. We wanted to preserve the truth of the gospel message for you.

⁶And the leaders of the church had nothing to add to what I was preaching. (By the way, their reputation as great leaders made no difference to me, for God has no favorites.) ⁷Instead, they saw that God had given me the responsibility of preaching the gospel to the Gentiles, just as he had given Peter the responsibility of preaching to the Jews. ⁸For the same God who worked through Peter as the apostle to the Jews also worked through me as the apostle to the Gentiles.

⁹In fact, James, Peter,* and John, who were known as pillars of the church, recognized the gift God had given me, and they accepted Barnabas and me as their co-workers. They encouraged us to keep preaching to the Gentiles, while they continued their work with the Jews. ¹⁰Their only suggestion was that we keep on helping the poor, which I have always been eager to do.

Paul Confronts Peter

¹¹But when Peter came to Antioch, I had to oppose him to his face, for what he did was very wrong. ¹²When he first arrived, he ate with the Gentile Christians, who were not circumcised. But afterward, when some friends of James came, Peter wouldn't eat with the Gentiles anymore. He was afraid of criticism from these people who insisted on the necessity of circumcision. ¹³As a result, other Jewish Christians followed Peter's hypocrisy, and even Barnabas was led astray by their hypocrisy.

¹⁴When I saw that they were not following the truth of the gospel message, I said to Peter in front of all the others, "Since you, a Jew by birth, have discarded the Jewish laws and are living like a Gentile, why are you now trying to make these Gentiles follow the Jewish traditions?

¹⁵"You and I are Jews by birth, not 'sinners' like the Gentiles. ¹⁶Yet we know that a person is made right with God by faith in Jesus Christ, not by obeying the law. And we have believed in Christ Jesus, so that we might be made right with God because of our faith in Christ, not because we have obeyed the law. For no one will ever be made right with God by obeying the law."*

¹⁷But suppose we seek to be made right with God through faith in Christ and then we are found guilty because we have abandoned the law. Would that mean Christ has led us into sin? Absolutely not! ¹⁸Rather, I am a sinner if I rebuild the old

2:9 Greek *Cephas*; also in 2:11, 14.   2:16 Some translators hold that the quotation extends through verse 14; others through verse 16; and still others through verse 21.

WHAT TO SAY 👍
AND
WHAT NOT TO SAY 👎

FRIENDSHIP TYPE: *Jesus*   FRIENDSHIP LAYER: *Companionship*

Say a Prayer

 WHAT NOT TO SAY:

4 Things to *Avoid* Saying if You Want to Be a Companion of Jesus

★ **Oh, Lord, thou dost know 'tis I, thy companion, who now dost cometh unto thee…**
Like you'd ever talk with your *other* friends that way. Talk with Jesus the same way you talk with any other friend—honestly, openly, from the heart.

★ **Um, let's not discuss that thing that happened…**
News flash: Read **Matthew 10:29-31**, and you'll discover that Jesus *already* knows what you've said, what Web pages you've visited, and what arguments you've had with your spouse. So be *transparent* in your friendship with Jesus—he knows and loves you no matter what.

★ **I have a list for you, Jesus. First, I could use a raise. Second, I could use a new car. Third…**
If you called your other friends only when you wanted something, how long would your friendships last? Jesus wants a *relationship* with you—not to be an all-season stand-in for Santa. Talk about more than your wish list.

★ **Now I lay me down to sleep. I pray the Lord my soul to keep. If I should…if I should…*yawn*…if I…*zzzzzzz*…**
Nobody likes friends falling asleep midconversation. If you're praying, do so when you're wide awake and fully engaged…and able to listen as well as talk.

 WHAT TO SAY:

And 1 Thing You *Should* Say

★ **I'm listening, Jesus.**

"No government, no matter how well-intentioned, can take the place of the family in the scheme of things."

~ Gerald R. Ford, U.S. president

system of law I already tore down. ¹⁹For when I tried to keep the law, it condemned me. So I died to the law—I stopped trying to meet all its requirements—so that I might live for God. ²⁰My old self has been crucified with Christ.* It is no longer I who live, but Christ lives in me. So I live in this earthly body by trusting in the Son of God, who loved me and gave himself for me. ²¹I do not treat the grace of God as meaningless. For if keeping the law could make us right with God, then there was no need for Christ to die.

CHAPTER 3

The Law and Faith in Christ

Oh, foolish Galatians! Who has cast an evil spell on you? For the meaning of Jesus Christ's death was made as clear to you as if you had seen a picture of his death on the cross. ²Let me ask you this one question: Did you receive the Holy Spirit by obeying the law of Moses? Of course not! You received the Spirit because you believed the message you heard about Christ. ³How foolish can you be? After starting your Christian lives in the Spirit, why are you now trying to become perfect by your own human effort? ⁴Have you experienced* so much for nothing? Surely it was not in vain, was it?

⁵I ask you again, does God give you the Holy Spirit and work miracles among you because you obey the law? Of course not! It is because you believe the message you heard about Christ.

⁶In the same way, "Abraham believed God, and God counted him as righteous because of his faith."* ⁷The real children of Abraham, then, are those who put their faith in God.

⁸What's more, the Scriptures looked forward to this time when God would declare the Gentiles to be righteous because of their faith. God proclaimed this good news to Abraham long ago when he said, "All nations will be blessed through you."* ⁹So all who put their faith in Christ share the same blessing Abraham received because of his faith.

¹⁰But those who depend on the law to make them right with God are under his curse, for the Scriptures say, "Cursed is everyone who does not observe and obey all the commands that are written in God's Book of the Law."* ¹¹So it is clear that no one can be made right with God by trying to keep the law. For the Scriptures say, "It is through faith that a righteous person has life."* ¹²This way of faith is very different from the way

2:20 Some English translations put this sentence in verse 19.   3:4 Or *Have you suffered.*   3:6 Gen 15:6.   3:8 Gen 12:3; 18:18; 22:18.   3:10 Deut 27:26.   3:11 Hab 2:4.

of law, which says, "It is through obeying the law that a person has life."*

¹³But Christ has rescued us from the curse pronounced by the law. When he was hung on the cross, he took upon himself the curse for our wrongdoing. For it is written in the Scriptures, "Cursed is everyone who is hung on a tree."* ¹⁴Through Christ Jesus, God has blessed the Gentiles with the same blessing he promised to Abraham, so that we who are believers might receive the promised* Holy Spirit through faith.

The Law and God's Promise

¹⁵Dear brothers and sisters,* here's an example from everyday life. Just as no one can set aside or amend an irrevocable agreement, so it is in this case. ¹⁶God gave the promises to Abraham and his child.* And notice that the Scripture doesn't say "to his children,*" as if it meant many descendants. Rather, it says "to his child"—and that, of course, means Christ. ¹⁷This is what I am trying to say: The agreement God made with Abraham could not be canceled 430 years later when God gave the law to Moses. God would be breaking his promise. ¹⁸For if the inheritance could be received by keeping the law, then it would not be the result of accepting God's promise. But God graciously gave it to Abraham as a promise.

¹⁹Why, then, was the law given? It was given alongside the promise to show people their sins. But the law was designed to last only until the coming of the child who was promised. God gave his law through angels to Moses, who was the mediator between God and the people. ²⁰Now a mediator is helpful if more than one party must reach an agreement. But God, who is one, did not use a mediator when he gave his promise to Abraham.

²¹Is there a conflict, then, between God's law and God's promises?* Absolutely not! If the law could give us new life, we could be made right with God by obeying it. ²²But the Scriptures declare that we are all prisoners of sin, so we receive God's promise of freedom only by believing in Jesus Christ.

God's Children through Faith

²³Before the way of faith in Christ was available to us, we were placed under guard by the law. We were kept in protective custody, so to speak, until the way of faith was revealed.

²⁴Let me put it another way. The law was our guardian until

3:12 Lev 18:5.   3:13 Deut 21:23 (Greek version).   3:14 Some manuscripts read *the blessing of the.*
3:15 Greek *Brothers.*   3:16a Greek *seed;* also in 3:16c, 19. See notes on Gen 12:7 and 13:15.
3:16b Greek *seeds.*   3:21 Some manuscripts read *and the promises?*

No. 18-FA-364

FRIENDSHIP STORY

FRIENDSHIP TYPE: *Jesus*   FRIENDSHIP LAYER: *Companionship*

FROM THE ARCHIVES

When Jesus Rubs Off on You

To say Ben was on a fast track is an understatement.

The son of minor nobility, Ben grew up with every advantage he could desire. He was well-connected, his future was wide open with possibilities, and he was receiving a first-rate classical education in the capital of the empire. Ben was going places.

So why did he drop out of school? Why would a young man accustomed to comfort and companionship choose solitary confinement in a remote cave at the far end of a rocky Italian ravine?

What was *wrong* with this guy?

Nothing, actually.

Ben walked away from his easy life to seek companionship with Jesus, far away from the temptations and distractions of fifth-century Rome. And the several years he spent in prayer and companionship with Jesus changed Ben.

He moved into the cave a confused young man, escaping an overwhelming world.

He emerged sure of who he was in Christ and secure in his friendship with Jesus.

Ben—we now know him as St. Benedict—spent enough time with Jesus that he started viewing life as Jesus viewed it. The scrambling for wealth and influence in Rome? Meaningless. His education? Ben saw that knowledge without wisdom wasn't worth much.

Ben summed up his learning in the *Benedictine Rule*, which inspires and informs millions to this day.

What changed Ben into St. Benedict? Companionship—with Jesus.

FRIENDSHIP STORY *continues on page 365...*

Christ came; it protected us until we could be made right with God through faith. 25And now that the way of faith has come, we no longer need the law as our guardian.

26For you are all children* of God through faith in Christ Jesus. 27And all who have been united with Christ in baptism have put on Christ, like putting on new clothes.* 28There is no longer Jew or Gentile,* slave or free, male and female. For you are all one in Christ Jesus. 29And now that you belong to Christ, you are the true children* of Abraham. You are his heirs, and God's promise to Abraham belongs to you.

CHAPTER **4**

Think of it this way. If a father dies and leaves an inheritance for his young children, those children are not much better off than slaves until they grow up, even though they actually own everything their father had. 2They have to obey their guardians until they reach whatever age their father set. 3And that's the way it was with us before Christ came. We were like children; we were slaves to the basic spiritual principles* of this world.

4But when the right time came, God sent his Son, born of a woman, subject to the law. 5God sent him to buy freedom for us who were slaves to the law, so that he could adopt us as his very own children.* 6And because we* are his children, God has sent the Spirit of his Son into our hearts, prompting us to call out, "Abba, Father."* 7Now you are no longer a slave but God's own child.* And since you are his child, God has made you his heir.

Paul's Concern for the Galatians

8Before you Gentiles knew God, you were slaves to so-called gods that do not even exist. 9So now that you know God (or should I say, now that God knows you), why do you want to go back again and become slaves once more to the weak and useless spiritual principles of this world? 10You are trying to earn favor with God by observing certain days or months or seasons or years. 11I fear for you. Perhaps all my hard work with you was for nothing. 12Dear brothers and sisters,* I plead with you to live as I do in freedom from these things, for I have become like you Gentiles—free from those laws.

You did not mistreat me when I first preached to you. 13Surely you remember that I was sick when I first brought you the Good News. 14But even though my condition tempted

3:26 Greek *sons.* 3:27 Greek *have put on Christ.* 3:28 Greek *Jew or Greek.* 3:29 Greek *seed.* 4:3 Or *powers;* also in 4:9. 4:5 Greek *sons;* also in 4:6. 4:6a Greek *you.* 4:6b *Abba* is an Aramaic term for "father." 4:7 Greek *son;* also in 4:7b. 4:12 Greek *brothers;* also in 4:28, 31.

you to reject me, you did not despise me or turn me away. No, you took me in and cared for me as though I were an angel from God or even Christ Jesus himself. ¹⁵Where is that joyful and grateful spirit you felt then? I am sure you would have taken out your own eyes and given them to me if it had been possible. ¹⁶Have I now become your enemy because I am telling you the truth?

¹⁷Those false teachers are so eager to win your favor, but their intentions are not good. They are trying to shut you off from me so that you will pay attention only to them. ¹⁸If someone is eager to do good things for you, that's all right; but let them do it all the time, not just when I'm with you.

¹⁹Oh, my dear children! I feel as if I'm going through labor pains for you again, and they will continue until Christ is fully developed in your lives. ²⁰I wish I were with you right now so I could change my tone. But at this distance I don't know how else to help you.

Abraham's Two Children

²¹Tell me, you who want to live under the law, do you know what the law actually says? ²²The Scriptures say that Abraham had two sons, one from his slave wife and one from his freeborn wife.* ²³The son of the slave wife was born in a human attempt to bring about the fulfillment of God's promise. But the son of the freeborn wife was born as God's own fulfillment of his promise.

²⁴These two women serve as an illustration of God's two covenants. The first woman, Hagar, represents Mount Sinai where people received the law that enslaved them. ²⁵And now Jerusalem is just like Mount Sinai in Arabia,* because she and her children live in slavery to the law. ²⁶But the other woman, Sarah, represents the heavenly Jerusalem. She is the free woman, and she is our mother. ²⁷As Isaiah said,

"Rejoice, O childless woman,
    you who have never given birth!
Break into a joyful shout,
    you who have never been in labor!
For the desolate woman now has more children
    than the woman who lives with her husband!"*

²⁸And you, dear brothers and sisters, are children of the promise, just like Isaac. ²⁹But you are now being persecuted

4:22 See Gen 16:15; 21:2-3.   4:25 Greek *And Hagar, which is Mount Sinai in Arabia, is now like Jerusalem;* other manuscripts read *And Mount Sinai in Arabia is now like Jerusalem.*   4:27 Isa 54:1.

FRIENDSHIP STORY *continued from page 364...*

THE ONE THING YOU CAN DO THIS WEEK — 1

Experience

Companions check in with each other often. This week do the same with Jesus by using these reminders: When you stop at a red light, ask Jesus what you should be praying about, and use that time to pray. When you hang up a phone, ask Jesus to help you see people the way he sees them, and treat them accordingly. When you touch a doorknob, quickly ask Jesus how he wants to use you in the next five minutes, and look for his leading.

Let Jesus rub off on you; it'll make for an interesting week.

Reflect

★ What actions or attitudes in your life show a new acquaintance that you've been spending time with Jesus?

★ In what ways do you regularly spend time with Jesus? What's hard about making that happen?

★ What's the best thing that could happen if you were a companion of Jesus? What's the worst? What do you expect to happen between you and Jesus?

by those who want you to keep the law, just as Ishmael, the child born by human effort, persecuted Isaac, the child born by the power of the Spirit.

³⁰But what do the Scriptures say about that? "Get rid of the slave and her son, for the son of the slave woman will not share the inheritance with the free woman's son."* ³¹So, dear brothers and sisters, we are not children of the slave woman; we are children of the free woman.

CHAPTER 5

Freedom in Christ

So Christ has truly set us free. Now make sure that you stay free, and don't get tied up again in slavery to the law.

²Listen! I, Paul, tell you this: If you are counting on circumcision to make you right with God, then Christ will be of no benefit to you. ³I'll say it again. If you are trying to find favor with God by being circumcised, you must obey every regulation in the whole law of Moses. ⁴For if you are trying to make yourselves right with God by keeping the law, you have been cut off from Christ! You have fallen away from God's grace.

⁵But we who live by the Spirit eagerly wait to receive by faith the righteousness God has promised to us. ⁶For when we place our faith in Christ Jesus, there is no benefit in being circumcised or being uncircumcised. What is important is faith expressing itself in love.

⁷You were running the race so well. Who has held you back from following the truth? ⁸It certainly isn't God, for he is the one who called you to freedom. ⁹This false teaching is like a little yeast that spreads through the whole batch of dough! ¹⁰I am trusting the Lord to keep you from believing false teachings. God will judge that person, whoever he is, who has been confusing you.

¹¹Dear brothers and sisters,* if I were still preaching that you must be circumcised—as some say I do—why am I still being persecuted? If I were no longer preaching salvation through the cross of Christ, no one would be offended. ¹²I just wish that those troublemakers who want to mutilate you by circumcision would mutilate themselves.*

¹³For you have been called to live in freedom, my brothers and sisters. But don't use your freedom to satisfy your sinful nature. Instead, use your freedom to serve one another in love.

4:30 Gen 21:10.   **5:11** Greek *Brothers;* similarly in 5:13.   **5:12** Or *castrate themselves,* or *cut themselves off from you;* Greek reads *cut themselves off.*

14For the whole law can be summed up in this one command: "Love your neighbor as yourself."* 15But if you are always biting and devouring one another, watch out! Beware of destroying one another.

Living by the Spirit's Power

16So I say, let the Holy Spirit guide your lives. Then you won't be doing what your sinful nature craves. 17The sinful nature wants to do evil, which is just the opposite of what the Spirit wants. And the Spirit gives us desires that are the opposite of what the sinful nature desires. These two forces are constantly fighting each other, so you are not free to carry out your good intentions. 18But when you are directed by the Spirit, you are not under obligation to the law of Moses.

19When you follow the desires of your sinful nature, the results are very clear: sexual immorality, impurity, lustful pleasures, 20idolatry, sorcery, hostility, quarreling, jealousy, outbursts of anger, selfish ambition, dissension, division, 21envy, drunkenness, wild parties, and other sins like these. Let me tell you again, as I have before, that anyone living that sort of life will not inherit the Kingdom of God.

22But the Holy Spirit produces this kind of fruit in our lives: love, joy, peace, patience, kindness, goodness, faithfulness, 23gentleness, and self-control. There is no law against these things!

24Those who belong to Christ Jesus have nailed the passions and desires of their sinful nature to his cross and crucified them there. 25Since we are living by the Spirit, let us follow the Spirit's leading in every part of our lives. 26Let us not become conceited, or provoke one another, or be jealous of one another.

CHAPTER 6
We Harvest What We Plant

Dear brothers and sisters, if another believer* is overcome by some sin, you who are godly* should gently and humbly help that person back onto the right path. And be careful not to fall into the same temptation yourself. 2Share each other's burdens, and in this way obey the law of Christ. 3If you think you are too important to help someone, you are only fooling yourself. You are not that important.

4Pay careful attention to your own work, for then you will get the satisfaction of a job well done, and you won't need to

5:14 Lev 19:18.   6:1a Greek *Brothers, if a man.*   6:1b Greek *spiritual.*

WHAT TO SAY
AND
WHAT NOT TO SAY

FRIENDSHIP TYPE: *Hard-to-Love People*   FRIENDSHIP LAYER: *Commitment*

Mr. Candid

Inside our brains there is a production department and a marketing department. The production department decides what we're going to say. The marketing department decides how to say it. Imagine not having a marketing department. Though some people think being completely candid is the best route, saying *everything* you're thinking is probably not the best thing…that is, unless you're perfect. But for the rest of us, that marketing department is critical.

Brutal honesty is highly overrated.

And it's *never* an excuse for being a jerk.

If you're trying to commit to friendship with a hard-to-love person, then it's probably a good idea to frequently check in with your marketing department. For example…

1. Your friend is picking his teeth in public *again*.

 WHAT NOT TO SAY: "Oooh, gross! Can you go to the bathroom?"

 WHAT TO SAY: *Nothing.*

2. Your friend is really down on one of your co-workers.

 WHAT NOT TO SAY: "Well, it's not like you're perfect, either. You are…" (and then launch into a list of your friend's flaws).

 WHAT TO SAY: "You know, I really like Sarah. Have you had a chance to spend any time with her?"

WHAT TO SAY AND WHAT NOT TO SAY *continues on page 368…*

WHAT TO SAY AND WHAT NOT TO SAY *continued from page 367...*

2. Your friend is telling you all about a recent show she watched on television…a show about the life cycle of army ants. You're not interested. You don't like insects. Besides, you listened yesterday when she told you.

WHAT NOT TO SAY: "Yeah, yeah, I know—you told me yesterday. How can you stand to watch that kind of thing anyway? It's so boring."

WHAT TO SAY: "I never knew that about army ants. You sure can learn a lot from watching TV."

What would Jesus want you to do in these situations? Well, see for yourself in **Luke 6:31**; it's a commonly known "rule."

compare yourself to anyone else. ⁵For we are each responsible for our own conduct.

⁶Those who are taught the word of God should provide for their teachers, sharing all good things with them.

⁷Don't be misled—you cannot mock the justice of God. You will always harvest what you plant. ⁸Those who live only to satisfy their own sinful nature will harvest decay and death from that sinful nature. But those who live to please the Spirit will harvest everlasting life from the Spirit. ⁹So let's not get tired of doing what is good. At just the right time we will reap a harvest of blessing if we don't give up. ¹⁰Therefore, whenever we have the opportunity, we should do good to everyone—especially to those in the family of faith.

Paul's Final Advice

¹¹NOTICE WHAT LARGE LETTERS I USE AS I WRITE THESE CLOSING WORDS IN MY OWN HANDWRITING.

¹²Those who are trying to force you to be circumcised want to look good to others. They don't want to be persecuted for teaching that the cross of Christ alone can save. ¹³And even those who advocate circumcision don't keep the whole law themselves. They only want you to be circumcised so they can boast about it and claim you as their disciples.

¹⁴As for me, may I never boast about anything except the cross of our Lord Jesus Christ. Because of that cross,* my interest in this world has been crucified, and the world's interest in me has also died. ¹⁵It doesn't matter whether we have been circumcised or not. What counts is whether we have been transformed into a new creation. ¹⁶May God's peace and mercy be upon all who live by this principle; they are the new people of God.*

¹⁷From now on, don't let anyone trouble me with these things. For I bear on my body the scars that show I belong to Jesus.

¹⁸Dear brothers and sisters,* may the grace of our Lord Jesus Christ be with your spirit. Amen.

6:14 Or *Because of him.*   6:16 Greek *this principle, and upon the Israel of God.*   6:18 Greek *Brothers.*

Ephesians

AUTHOR:	DATE WRITTEN:
Paul	Approximately A.D. 60

CHAPTER 1

Greetings from Paul

This letter is from Paul, chosen by the will of God to be an apostle of Christ Jesus.

I am writing to God's holy people in Ephesus,* who are faithful followers of Christ Jesus.

²May God our Father and the Lord Jesus Christ give you grace and peace.

Spiritual Blessings

³All praise to God, the Father of our Lord Jesus Christ, who has blessed us with every spiritual blessing in the heavenly realms because we are united with Christ. ⁴Even before he made the world, God loved us and chose us in Christ to be holy and without fault in his eyes. ⁵God decided in advance to adopt us into his own family by bringing us to himself through Jesus Christ. This is what he wanted to do, and it gave him great pleasure. ⁶So we praise God for the glorious grace he has poured out on us who belong to his dear Son.* ⁷He is so rich in kindness and grace that he purchased our freedom with the blood of his Son and forgave our sins. ⁸He has showered his kindness on us, along with all wisdom and understanding.

⁹God has now revealed to us his mysterious plan regarding Christ, a plan to fulfill his own good pleasure. ¹⁰And this is the plan: At the right time he will bring everything together under the authority of Christ—everything in heaven and on earth. ¹¹Furthermore, because we are united with Christ, we have received an inheritance from God,* for he chose us in advance, and he makes everything work out according to his plan.

¹²God's purpose was that we Jews who were the first to trust in Christ would bring praise and glory to God. ¹³And now you

1:1 The most ancient manuscripts do not include *in Ephesus.* 1:6 Greek *to us in the beloved.*
1:11 Or *we have become God's inheritance.*

> "To speak of friendship
> with God can sound so cozy
> and consoling, as if we are
> all snuggling up to God;
> however, there is no riskier
> vulnerability than to live in
> friendship with God, because
> every friendship changes
> us, because friends have
> expectations of each other, and
> because friends are said to be
> committed to the same things..."
>
> ~ Paul J. Wadell

JOURNAL

Gentiles have also heard the truth, the Good News that God saves you. And when you believed in Christ, he identified you as his own* by giving you the Holy Spirit, whom he promised long ago. 14The Spirit is God's guarantee that he will give us the inheritance he promised and that he has purchased us to be his own people. He did this so we would praise and glorify him.

Paul's Prayer for Spiritual Wisdom

15Ever since I first heard of your strong faith in the Lord Jesus and your love for God's people everywhere,* 16I have not stopped thanking God for you. I pray for you constantly, 17asking God, the glorious Father of our Lord Jesus Christ, to give you spiritual wisdom* and insight so that you might grow in your knowledge of God. 18I pray that your hearts will be flooded with light so that you can understand the confident hope he has given to those he called—his holy people who are his rich and glorious inheritance.*

19I also pray that you will understand the incredible greatness of God's power for us who believe him. This is the same mighty power 20that raised Christ from the dead and seated him in the place of honor at God's right hand in the heavenly realms. 21Now he is far above any ruler or authority or power or leader or anything else—not only in this world but also in the world to come. 22God has put all things under the authority of Christ and has made him head over all things for the benefit of the church. 23And the church is his body; it is made full and complete by Christ, who fills all things everywhere with himself.

CHAPTER **2**

Made Alive with Christ

Once you were dead because of your disobedience and your many sins. 2You used to live in sin, just like the rest of the world, obeying the devil—the commander of the powers in the unseen world.* He is the spirit at work in the hearts of those who refuse to obey God. 3All of us used to live that way, following the passionate desires and inclinations of our sinful nature. By our very nature we were subject to God's anger, just like everyone else.

4But God is so rich in mercy, and he loved us so much, 5that even though we were dead because of our sins, he gave us life when he raised Christ from the dead. (It is only by God's grace that you have been saved!) 6For he raised us from the dead

1:13 Or *he put his seal on you.*   1:15 Some manuscripts read *your faithfulness to the Lord Jesus and to God's people everywhere.*   1:17 Or *to give you the Spirit of wisdom.*   1:18 Or *called, and the rich and glorious inheritance he has given to his holy people.*   2:2 Greek *obeying the commander of the power of the air.*

along with Christ and seated us with him in the heavenly realms because we are united with Christ Jesus. ⁷So God can point to us in all future ages as examples of the incredible wealth of his grace and kindness toward us, as shown in all he has done for us who are united with Christ Jesus.

⁸God saved you by his grace when you believed. And you can't take credit for this; it is a gift from God. ⁹Salvation is not a reward for the good things we have done, so none of us can boast about it. ¹⁰For we are God's masterpiece. He has created us anew in Christ Jesus, so we can do the good things he planned for us long ago.

Oneness and Peace in Christ

¹¹Don't forget that you Gentiles used to be outsiders. You were called "uncircumcised heathens" by the Jews, who were proud of their circumcision, even though it affected only their bodies and not their hearts. ¹²In those days you were living apart from Christ. You were excluded from citizenship among the people of Israel, and you did not know the covenant promises God had made to them. You lived in this world without God and without hope. ¹³But now you have been united with Christ Jesus. Once you were far away from God, but now you have been brought near to him through the blood of Christ.

¹⁴For Christ himself has brought peace to us. He united Jews and Gentiles into one people when, in his own body on the cross, he broke down the wall of hostility that separated us. ¹⁵He did this by ending the system of law with its commandments and regulations. He made peace between Jews and Gentiles by creating in himself one new people from the two groups. ¹⁶Together as one body, Christ reconciled both groups to God by means of his death on the cross, and our hostility toward each other was put to death.

¹⁷He brought this Good News of peace to you Gentiles who were far away from him, and peace to the Jews who were near. ¹⁸Now all of us can come to the Father through the same Holy Spirit because of what Christ has done for us.

Anchor Passage

PASSAGE: Ephesians 2:11-22

FRIENDSHIP TYPE: Hard-to-Love People

FRIENDSHIP LAYER: Trust

Easier Said Than Done

Picture the sort of person you find hardest to love, whom you'd least like your child, friend, or sibling to date—a *category* of person you view with suspicion and maybe prejudice.

Now imagine how you'd feel if that person moved in as a member of your family. And even better, *you're* expected to hand over the TV remote and your favorite chair so that person feels welcome and at home.

Read **Ephesians 2:11-22**.

Paul's words here stunned his Jewish readers. They'd been trained to *despise* Gentiles. Hadn't God himself told his people to steer clear of non-believing nations? Gentiles weren't to be trusted and certainly weren't to be loved. They were *pagans*. They weren't even allowed in the Temple's inner court.

Yet here's Paul saying that, in Christ, Jews and Gentiles are equals. No—worse than that. He's saying they're *family*. Unthinkable!

Except that what drew Jewish and Gentile converts together in Christ was stronger than any suspicion, culture, or prejudice that separated them. Paul proclaimed that in Jesus there was unity—like it or not.

Anchor Passage continues on page 372...

Friendship First NEW TESTAMENT

Anchor Passage continued from page 371...

At the foot of the cross, it's a level playing field. Anyone who comes does so as a sinner needing forgiveness. There's no preferred seating for Jews and standing room only for Gentiles. We're in this forgiveness thing together, no matter how difficult we've found it to like or trust each other in the past.

The barriers are down. The blockades have been lifted. Those hard-to-love people are now family.

So...now what?

Experience

Connect with someone like the person you imagined above. Share an elevator, strike up a conversation while waiting in line to order coffee, or take a seat on the subway next to someone you've been trained to distrust or dislike

because of skin color, religion, age, or status. You probably won't become best buddies during one casual conversation, but you may walk away seeing the person as just that: a *person*, not a *category*.

Reflect

★ Why do you think you view some categories of people with suspicion or distrust? Where does that bias come from?

★ What is it about this category of people that makes it hard for you to appreciate and love them?

★ What might you be missing because of your distrust?

Anchor Passage continues on page 373...

A Temple for the Lord

¹⁹So now you Gentiles are no longer strangers and foreigners. You are citizens along with all of God's holy people. You are members of God's family. ²⁰Together, we are his house, built on the foundation of the apostles and the prophets. And the cornerstone is Christ Jesus himself. ²¹We are carefully joined together in him, becoming a holy temple for the Lord. ²²Through him you Gentiles are also being made part of this dwelling where God lives by his Spirit. ⚓

CHAPTER **3**

God's Mysterious Plan Revealed

When I think of all this, I, Paul, a prisoner of Christ Jesus for the benefit of you Gentiles* . . . ²assuming, by the way, that you know God gave me the special responsibility of extending his grace to you Gentiles. ³As I briefly wrote earlier, God himself revealed his mysterious plan to me. ⁴As you read what I have written, you will understand my insight into this plan regarding Christ. ⁵God did not reveal it to previous generations, but now by his Spirit he has revealed it to his holy apostles and prophets.

⁶And this is God's plan: Both Gentiles and Jews who believe the Good News share equally in the riches inherited by God's children. Both are part of the same body, and both enjoy the promise of blessings because they belong to Christ Jesus.* ⁷By God's grace and mighty power, I have been given the privilege of serving him by spreading this Good News.

⁸Though I am the least deserving of all God's people, he graciously gave me the privilege of telling the Gentiles about the endless treasures available to them in Christ. ⁹I was chosen to explain to everyone* this mysterious plan that God, the Creator of all things, had kept secret from the beginning.

¹⁰God's purpose in all this was to use the church to display his wisdom in its rich variety to all the unseen rulers and authorities in the heavenly places. ¹¹This was his eternal plan, which he carried out through Christ Jesus our Lord.

¹²Because of Christ and our faith in him,* we can now come boldly and confidently into God's presence. ¹³So please don't lose heart because of my trials here. I am suffering for you, so you should feel honored.

3:1 Paul resumes this thought in verse 14: "When I think of all this, I fall to my knees and pray to the Father." **3:6** Or *because they are united with Christ Jesus.* **3:9** Some manuscripts omit *to everyone.* **3:12** Or *Because of Christ's faithfulness.*

Paul's Prayer for Spiritual Growth

14When I think of all this, I fall to my knees and pray to the Father,* 15the Creator of everything in heaven and on earth.* 16I pray that from his glorious, unlimited resources he will empower you with inner strength through his Spirit. 17Then Christ will make his home in your hearts as you trust in him. Your roots will grow down into God's love and keep you strong. 18And may you have the power to understand, as all God's people should, how wide, how long, how high, and how deep his love is. 19May you experience the love of Christ, though it is too great to understand fully. Then you will be made complete with all the fullness of life and power that comes from God.

20Now all glory to God, who is able, through his mighty power at work within us, to accomplish infinitely more than we might ask or think. 21Glory to him in the church and in Christ Jesus through all generations forever and ever! Amen.

CHAPTER **4**

Unity in the Body

Therefore I, a prisoner for serving the Lord, beg you to lead a life worthy of your calling, for you have been called by God. 2Always be humble and gentle. Be patient with each other, making allowance for each other's faults because of your love. 3Make every effort to keep yourselves united in the Spirit, binding yourselves together with peace. 4For there is one body and one Spirit, just as you have been called to one glorious hope for the future. 5There is one Lord, one faith, one baptism, 6and one God and Father, who is over all and in all and living through all.

7However, he has given each one of us a special gift* through the generosity of Christ. 8That is why the Scriptures say,

"When he ascended to the heights,
    he led a crowd of captives
    and gave gifts to his people."*

9Notice that it says "he ascended." This clearly means that Christ also descended to our lowly world.* 10And the same one who descended is the one who ascended higher than all the heavens, so that he might fill the entire universe with himself.

11Now these are the gifts Christ gave to the church: the apostles, the prophets, the evangelists, and the pastors and teachers. 12Their responsibility is to equip God's people to do his work

3:14 Some manuscripts read *the Father of our Lord Jesus Christ.* 3:15 Or *from whom every family in heaven and on earth takes its name.* 4:7 Greek *a grace.* 4:8 Ps 68:18. 4:9 Or *to the lowest parts of the earth.*

Anchor Passage continued from page 372…

DIGGING DEEPER

FRIENDSHIP TYPE:
Hard-to-Love People

FRIENDSHIP LAYER:
Trust

For building trust with hard-to-love people, check out…

➡ The Friendship Experience .... on page 507
➡ The Friendship Story .... on page 483
➡ What to Say and What Not to Say .... on page 486

JOURNAL

Anchor Passage

PASSAGE: Ephesians 4:25-32

FRIENDSHIP TYPE:
Neighbors

FRIENDSHIP LAYER:
Deepening

Getting Messy

Write on a piece of paper five things that could break a relationship apart.

Remember the old parental adage "if you can't say something nice, don't say anything at all"? Good advice, but not God's advice. **Ephesians 4:25-32** is God's advice—go ahead, read it right now.

At first glance this passage may sound like a parent's laundry list of the "don'ts" for proper behavior. Don't lie, don't be angry, and stop saying bad things! Your heavenly Father *is* trying to teach you the don'ts, but his real desire is to teach you the do's: *Do* be useful to others, *do* be kind and compassionate, and *do* forgive others as Christ has forgiven you!

Great advice...but hard to do in the heat of an argument, when your emotions are on high and your judgment is, well...at a low. It's during those times, though, that you have your greatest opportunity for *building* that friendship...or destroying it.

In order to build it, you have to really dig in and learn to love as God loves—even when it's tough. You have to forgive as he forgives. You have to build others up instead of tearing them down. You have to bless them instead of cursing them. You have to be tenderhearted instead of hardhearted. And here's the good news: God's power can help you do these tough things.

When it comes to deepening in friendship with your neighbors, you can't always avoid the messes. But there's a reward for getting your hands dirty and learning to work through the conflicts: a deeper friendship that lasts!

Anchor Passage continues on page 375...

and build up the church, the body of Christ. [13] This will continue until we all come to such unity in our faith and knowledge of God's Son that we will be mature in the Lord, measuring up to the full and complete standard of Christ.

[14] Then we will no longer be immature like children. We won't be tossed and blown about by every wind of new teaching. We will not be influenced when people try to trick us with lies so clever they sound like the truth. [15] Instead, we will speak the truth in love, growing in every way more and more like Christ, who is the head of his body, the church. [16] He makes the whole body fit together perfectly. As each part does its own special work, it helps the other parts grow, so that the whole body is healthy and growing and full of love.

Living as Children of Light

[17] With the Lord's authority I say this: Live no longer as the Gentiles do, for they are hopelessly confused. [18] Their minds are full of darkness; they wander far from the life God gives because they have closed their minds and hardened their hearts against him. [19] They have no sense of shame. They live for lustful pleasure and eagerly practice every kind of impurity.

[20] But that isn't what you learned about Christ. [21] Since you have heard about Jesus and have learned the truth that comes from him, [22] throw off your old sinful nature and your former way of life, which is corrupted by lust and deception. [23] Instead, let the Spirit renew your thoughts and attitudes. [24] Put on your new nature, created to be like God—truly righteous and holy.

[25] So stop telling lies. Let us tell our neighbors the truth, for we are all parts of the same body. [26] And "don't sin by letting anger control you."* Don't let the sun go down while you are still angry, [27] for anger gives a foothold to the devil.

[28] If you are a thief, quit stealing. Instead, use your hands for good hard work, and then give generously to others in need. [29] Don't use foul or abusive language. Let everything you say be good and helpful, so that your words will be an encouragement to those who hear them.

[30] And do not bring sorrow to God's Holy Spirit

4:26 Ps 4:4.

by the way you live. Remember, he has identified you as his own,* guaranteeing that you will be saved on the day of redemption.

31 Get rid of all bitterness, rage, anger, harsh words, and slander, as well as all types of evil behavior. 32 Instead, be kind to each other, tenderhearted, forgiving one another, just as God through Christ has forgiven you. ⚓

CHAPTER **5**
Living in the Light

Imitate God, therefore, in everything you do, because you are his dear children. 2 Live a life filled with love, following the example of Christ. He loved us* and offered himself as a sacrifice for us, a pleasing aroma to God.

3 Let there be no sexual immorality, impurity, or greed among you. Such sins have no place among God's people. 4 Obscene stories, foolish talk, and coarse jokes—these are not for you. Instead, let there be thankfulness to God. 5 You can be sure that no immoral, impure, or greedy person will inherit the Kingdom of Christ and of God. For a greedy person is an idolater, worshiping the things of this world.

6 Don't be fooled by those who try to excuse these sins, for the anger of God will fall on all who disobey him. 7 Don't participate in the things these people do. 8 For once you were full of darkness, but now you have light from the Lord. So live as people of light! 9 For this light within you produces only what is good and right and true.

10 Carefully determine what pleases the Lord. 11 Take no part in the worthless deeds of evil and darkness; instead, expose them. 12 It is shameful even to talk about the things that ungodly people do in secret. 13 But their evil intentions will be exposed when the light shines on them, 14 for the light makes everything visible. This is why it is said,

> "Awake, O sleeper,
>   rise up from the dead,
>   and Christ will give you light."

Living by the Spirit's Power

15 So be careful how you live. Don't live like fools, but like those who are wise. 16 Make the most of every opportunity in these

4:30 Or *has put his seal on you.*   5:2 Some manuscripts read *loved you.*

Anchor Passage continued from page 374...

THE ONE THING **1** YOU CAN DO THIS WEEK

Experience

Take your list of things that could break apart a relationship, and tear it into pieces. Use tape to reassemble the pieces in the shape of a building. As you build, identify each piece of tape as something that could repair a friendship.

Choose a neighbor in your life whom you've had trouble getting along with but would like to deepen your relationship with. Pick one of the do's from **Ephesians 4:25-32** that would help you build that deeper friendship...and do it! (And don't be afraid of making a mess!)

Reflect

★ What friendship troubles are you having right now?

★ Underline the specific things from the Scripture passage that can help you deal with the relationship messes in your life. How can those words help you deepen your friendships?

DIGGING DEEPER

FRIENDSHIP TYPE:
Neighbors

FRIENDSHIP LAYER:
Deepening

For deepening in friendship with your neighbors, check out...

➜ The Friendship Experience .... on page 387
➜ The Friendship Story .... on page 502
➜ What to Say and What Not to Say .... on page 391

> ★
>
> About 59% of U.S. church members spend a portion of every day in prayer or worship. That number drops to 46% among members who don't have deep friendships at church.
>
> —from "Friendship and Faith," a Gallup Research Study Commissioned by Group Publishing, Inc.
>
> ★

JOURNAL

_____

_____

_____

_____

_____

_____

_____

_____

_____

_____

_____

_____

_____

_____

_____

_____

_____

evil days. ¹⁷Don't act thoughtlessly, but understand what the Lord wants you to do. ¹⁸Don't be drunk with wine, because that will ruin your life. Instead, be filled with the Holy Spirit, ¹⁹singing psalms and hymns and spiritual songs among yourselves, and making music to the Lord in your hearts. ²⁰And give thanks for everything to God the Father in the name of our Lord Jesus Christ.

Spirit-Guided Relationships: Wives and Husbands

²¹And further, submit to one another out of reverence for Christ.

²²For wives, this means submit to your husbands as to the Lord. ²³For a husband is the head of his wife as Christ is the head of the church. He is the Savior of his body, the church. ²⁴As the church submits to Christ, so you wives should submit to your husbands in everything.

²⁵For husbands, this means love your wives, just as Christ loved the church. He gave up his life for her ²⁶to make her holy and clean, washed by the cleansing of God's word.* ²⁷He did this to present her to himself as a glorious church without a spot or wrinkle or any other blemish. Instead, she will be holy and without fault. ²⁸In the same way, husbands ought to love their wives as they love their own bodies. For a man who loves his wife actually shows love for himself. ²⁹No one hates his own body but feeds and cares for it, just as Christ cares for the church. ³⁰And we are members of his body.

³¹As the Scriptures say, "A man leaves his father and mother and is joined to his wife, and the two are united into one."* ³²This is a great mystery, but it is an illustration of the way Christ and the church are one. ³³So again I say, each man must love his wife as he loves himself, and the wife must respect her husband.

CHAPTER 6
Children and Parents

Children, obey your parents because you belong to the Lord,* for this is the right thing to do. ²"Honor your father and mother." This is the first commandment with a promise: ³If you honor your father and

5:26 Greek *washed by water with the word.* 5:31 Gen 2:24. 6:1 Or *Children, obey your parents who belong to the Lord;* some manuscripts read simply *Children, obey your parents.*

mother, "things will go well for you, and you will have a long life on the earth."*

⁴Fathers, do not provoke your children to anger by the way you treat them. Rather, bring them up with the discipline and instruction that comes from the Lord. ⚓

Slaves and Masters

⁵Slaves, obey your earthly masters with deep respect and fear. Serve them sincerely as you would serve Christ. ⁶Try to please them all the time, not just when they are watching you. As slaves of Christ, do the will of God with all your heart. ⁷Work with enthusiasm, as though you were working for the Lord rather than for people. ⁸Remember that the Lord will reward each one of us for the good we do, whether we are slaves or free.

⁹Masters, treat your slaves in the same way. Don't threaten them; remember, you both have the same Master in heaven, and he has no favorites.

The Whole Armor of God

¹⁰A final word: Be strong in the Lord and in his mighty power. ¹¹Put on all of God's armor so that you will be able to stand firm against all strategies of the devil. ¹²For we* are not fighting against flesh-and-blood enemies, but against evil rulers and authorities of the unseen world, against mighty powers in this dark world, and against evil spirits in the heavenly places. ¹³Therefore, put on every piece of God's armor so you will be able to resist the enemy in the time of evil. Then after the battle you will still be standing firm. ¹⁴Stand your ground, putting on the belt of truth and the body armor of God's righteousness. ¹⁵For shoes, put on the peace that comes from the Good News so that you will be fully prepared.* ¹⁶In addition to all of these, hold up the shield of faith to stop the fiery arrows of the devil.* ¹⁷Put on salvation as your helmet, and take the sword of the Spirit, which is the word of God.

¹⁸Pray in the Spirit at all times and on every occasion. Stay alert and be persistent in your prayers for all believers everywhere.*

¹⁹And pray for me, too. Ask God to give me the right words

6:2-3 Exod 20:12; Deut 5:16.   6:12 Some manuscripts read you.   6:15 Or For shoes, put on the readiness to preach the Good News of peace with God.   6:16 Greek the evil one.   6:18 Greek all of God's holy people.

Anchor Passage

PASSAGE: Ephesians 5:31–6:4

FRIENDSHIP TYPE: Family

FRIENDSHIP LAYER: Companionship

Making Friends and Family One

Draw a family tree—but not a traditional one. Instead of organizing it by parent-child relationships, organize it by friendships. Do you have the closest friendship with your cousin? Put her name close to yours. Are you feeling emotionally distant from your parents right now? Then put their names far from yours. There is no right or wrong way to do this; it's just an exercise to help you consider your friendships with family members.

Now read **Ephesians 5:31–6:4**. Notice the give-and-take in family relationships. It's not just the wife who's commanded to do something; the husband has responsibility to the relationship, too. And rather than children being held accountable for their relationship with mom and dad, the parents are instructed not to do things that would cause their children frustration.

Being in a close relationship with family members—a spouse, parents, or even that third cousin from California you can't even figure out how you're related to—takes time and effort...from both people. Family relationships certainly aren't always the easiest, but sometimes they can be the most rewarding, especially when family members move from being relatives to being companions.

Anchor Passage
continues on page 378...

Anchor Passage continued from page 377…

Experience

THE ONE THING
1
YOU CAN DO THIS WEEK

Look back at your family tree of friendship. After reading **Ephesians 5:31–6:4**, consider the different relationships on your tree. Choose a family member you placed far away from you on the tree. How could you become closer to that person? If you live close enough, call the person and ask to meet for breakfast, a round of golf, or a movie. If you're far away, send a letter or e-mail expressing your desire to become better friends. But before you do, pray and ask God to inspire your companionship.

Reflect

★ Which of your family relationships are give and take? Which ones aren't?

★ Who's listed on your family tree whom you do not desire to get to know more? Why is that? Pray for God's guidance with that relationship.

DIGGING DEEPER

FRIENDSHIP TYPE:
Family

FRIENDSHIP LAYER:
Companionship

For being a companion with your family, check out…

➡ The Friendship Experience .... on page 493
➡ The Friendship Story .... on page 497
➡ What to Say and What Not to Say .... on page 500

so I can boldly explain God's mysterious plan that the Good News is for Jews and Gentiles alike.* [20] I am in chains now, still preaching this message as God's ambassador. So pray that I will keep on speaking boldly for him, as I should.

Final Greetings

[21] To bring you up to date, Tychicus will give you a full report about what I am doing and how I am getting along. He is a beloved brother and faithful helper in the Lord's work. [22] I have sent him to you for this very purpose—to let you know how we are doing and to encourage you.

[23] Peace be with you, dear brothers and sisters,* and may God the Father and the Lord Jesus Christ give you love with faithfulness. [24] May God's grace be eternally upon all who love our Lord Jesus Christ.

6:19 Greek *explain the mystery of the Good News;* some manuscripts read simply *explain the mystery.*
6:23 Greek *brothers.*

Philippians

AUTHOR:	DATE WRITTEN:
Paul	Approximately A.D. 61

JOURNAL

Greetings from Paul

This letter is from Paul and Timothy, slaves of Christ Jesus.

I am writing to all of God's holy people in Philippi who belong to Christ Jesus, including the elders* and deacons.

²May God our Father and the Lord Jesus Christ give you grace and peace.

Paul's Thanksgiving and Prayer

³Every time I think of you, I give thanks to my God. ⁴Whenever I pray, I make my requests for all of you with joy, ⁵for you have been my partners in spreading the Good News about Christ from the time you first heard it until now. ⁶And I am certain that God, who began the good work within you, will continue his work until it is finally finished on the day when Christ Jesus returns.

⁷So it is right that I should feel as I do about all of you, for you have a special place in my heart. You share with me the special favor of God, both in my imprisonment and in defending and confirming the truth of the Good News. ⁸God knows how much I love you and long for you with the tender compassion of Christ Jesus.

⁹I pray that your love will overflow more and more, and that you will keep on growing in knowledge and understanding. ¹⁰For I want you to understand what really matters, so that you may live pure and blameless lives until the day of Christ's return. ¹¹May you always be filled with the fruit of your salvation—the righteous character produced in your life by Jesus Christ*—for this will bring much glory and praise to God.

Paul's Joy That Christ Is Preached

¹²And I want you to know, my dear brothers and sisters,* that everything that has happened to me here has helped to spread

1:1 Or *overseers; or bishops.*   1:11 Greek *with the fruit of righteousness through Jesus Christ.*
1:12 Greek *brothers.*

the Good News. [13] For everyone here, including the whole palace guard,* knows that I am in chains because of Christ. [14] And because of my imprisonment, most of the believers* here have gained confidence and boldly speak God's message* without fear.

[15] It's true that some are preaching out of jealousy and rivalry. But others preach about Christ with pure motives. [16] They preach because they love me, for they know I have been appointed to defend the Good News. [17] Those others do not have pure motives as they preach about Christ. They preach with selfish ambition, not sincerely, intending to make my chains more painful to me. [18] But that doesn't matter. Whether their motives are false or genuine, the message about Christ is being preached either way, so I rejoice. And I will continue to rejoice. [19] For I know that as you pray for me and the Spirit of Jesus Christ helps me, this will lead to my deliverance.

Paul's Life for Christ

[20] For I fully expect and hope that I will never be ashamed, but that I will continue to be bold for Christ, as I have been in the past. And I trust that my life will bring honor to Christ, whether I live or die. [21] For to me, living means living for Christ, and dying is even better. [22] But if I live, I can do more fruitful work for Christ. So I really don't know which is better. [23] I'm torn between two desires: I long to go and be with Christ, which would be far better for me. [24] But for your sakes, it is better that I continue to live.

[25] Knowing this, I am convinced that I will remain alive so I can continue to help all of you grow and experience the joy of your faith. [26] And when I come to you again, you will have even more reason to take pride in Christ Jesus because of what he is doing through me.

Live as Citizens of Heaven

[27] Above all, you must live as citizens of heaven, conducting yourselves in a manner worthy of the Good News about Christ. Then, whether I come and see you again or only hear about you, I will know that you are standing together with one spirit and one purpose, fighting together for the faith, which is the Good News. [28] Don't be intimidated in any way by your enemies. This will be a sign to them that they are going to be destroyed, but that you are going to be saved, even by God himself. [29] For you have been given not only the privilege of trusting in Christ but

1:13 Greek *including all the Praetorium.*   **1:14a** Greek *brothers in the Lord.*   **1:14b** Some manuscripts read *speak the message.*

also the privilege of suffering for him. ³⁰We are in this struggle together. You have seen my struggle in the past, and you know that I am still in the midst of it.

CHAPTER **2**

Have the Attitude of Christ

Is there any encouragement from belonging to Christ? Any comfort from his love? Any fellowship together in the Spirit? Are your hearts tender and compassionate? ²Then make me truly happy by agreeing wholeheartedly with each other, loving one another, and working together with one mind and purpose.

³Don't be selfish; don't try to impress others. Be humble, thinking of others as better than yourselves. ⁴Don't look out only for your own interests, but take an interest in others, too.

⁵You must have the same attitude that Christ Jesus had.

⁶ Though he was God,*
  he did not think of equality with God
  as something to cling to.
⁷ Instead, he gave up his divine privileges*;
  he took the humble position of a slave*
  and was born as a human being.
 When he appeared in human form,*
⁸ he humbled himself in obedience to God
  and died a criminal's death on a cross.

⁹ Therefore, God elevated him to the place of highest honor
  and gave him the name above all other names,
¹⁰ that at the name of Jesus every knee should bow,
  in heaven and on earth and under the earth,
¹¹ and every tongue confess that Jesus Christ is Lord,
  to the glory of God the Father.

Shine Brightly for Christ

¹²Dear friends, you always followed my instructions when I was with you. And now that I am away, it is even more important. Work hard to show the results of your salvation, obeying God with deep reverence and fear. ¹³For God is working in you, giving you the desire and the power to do what pleases him.

¹⁴Do everything without complaining and arguing, ¹⁵so that no one can criticize you. Live clean, innocent lives as children of God, shining like bright lights in a world full of crooked and perverse people. ¹⁶Hold firmly to the word of life; then, on the

2:6 Or *Being in the form of God.*   2:7a Greek *he emptied himself.*   2:7b Or *the form of a slave.*
2:7c Some English translations put this phrase in verse 8.

No. 19-TE-381

FRIENDSHIP
STORY

FRIENDSHIP TYPE:	FRIENDSHIP LAYER:
Family	*Acceptance*

BASED ON TRUE EVENTS

Somewhere on the Spectrum

"Autistic spectrum disorder."

Craig sat rigidly as the doctor's words echoed in his head. *"Autistic spectrum disorder."* Craig glanced at his young daughter. How could this beautiful little girl have such a terrible sounding *disorder*? And yet, Craig knew it was true. He and his wife, Christine, had been noticing the symptoms for months now. Neither he nor Christine had experienced the same intimacy with baby Claire as they had with their two sons. They'd never been able to connect to Claire in the same way. In fact, this beautiful baby girl seemed to look right through Craig, his wife, and everyone else. Claire didn't respond to verbal directions, didn't name objects around her. She'd developed a fascination with some toys while hardly seeming to notice others.

"Autistic spectrum disorder." Craig knew it was true even as he tried to deny it.

In the months that followed, Craig and Christine spun between denial and deep disappointment. They knew they had to accept that Claire might never enter her family's world, might never engage in a real conversation with her family, might never become independent…but some days were better than others.

FRIENDSHIP STORY *continues on page 382…*

FRIENDSHIP STORY *continued from page 381...*

And yet, Claire was so precious, so beautiful, and her laugh…it could melt the hardest heart.

Their shock gradually gave way to acceptance and a desire for knowledge. Craig and Christine learned everything they could about the disorder and how to cope. This information gradually led to training as Craig and Christine learned how to care for and support Claire and to help her grow.

Craig and Christine's dreams for their daughter began to take shape around Claire and her own potential rather than some obscure ideal of having a little girl.

At a recent small-group gathering, Christine said this about her daughter: "Claire is the daughter I always wanted. She is traveling her own path in her own way. We take delight in every accomplishment. Every mom can hardly wait to hear that first ma-ma sound, but for me the delight was doubly sweet because I had to wait so long and work so hard for it. We're trying hard not to focus on what she doesn't do and to focus instead on what she brings to us and the work God is doing in our lives through her."

Experience

Life is full of challenges— whether in the form of disease, unemployment, death, or even natural disaster. Think about someone in your family who is facing a temporary or long-term challenge. Have a photo taken of the two of you together (or, if you live far away, just use a photo of the person). Put the photo somewhere you'll see it often, and use it as a reminder to stand by your family member during this hard time. (If a photo isn't practical, just write the person's name on a piece of paper and hang it up.)

THE ONE THING YOU CAN DO THIS WEEK 1

FRIENDSHIP STORY *continues on page 383...*

day of Christ's return, I will be proud that I did not run the race in vain and that my work was not useless. [17] But I will rejoice even if I lose my life, pouring it out like a liquid offering to God,* just like your faithful service is an offering to God. And I want all of you to share that joy. [18] Yes, you should rejoice, and I will share your joy.

Paul Commends Timothy

[19] If the Lord Jesus is willing, I hope to send Timothy to you soon for a visit. Then he can cheer me up by telling me how you are getting along. [20] I have no one else like Timothy, who genuinely cares about your welfare. [21] All the others care only for themselves and not for what matters to Jesus Christ. [22] But you know how Timothy has proved himself. Like a son with his father, he has served with me in preaching the Good News. [23] I hope to send him to you just as soon as I find out what is going to happen to me here. [24] And I have confidence from the Lord that I myself will come to see you soon.

Paul Commends Epaphroditus

[25] Meanwhile, I thought I should send Epaphroditus back to you. He is a true brother, co-worker, and fellow soldier. And he was your messenger to help me in my need. [26] I am sending him because he has been longing to see you, and he was very distressed that you heard he was ill. [27] And he certainly was ill; in fact, he almost died. But God had mercy on him—and also on me, so that I would not have one sorrow after another.

[28] So I am all the more anxious to send him back to you, for I know you will be glad to see him, and then I will not be so worried about you. [29] Welcome him with Christian love* and with great joy, and give him the honor that people like him deserve. [30] For he risked his life for the work of Christ, and he was at the point of death while doing for me what you couldn't do from far away.

CHAPTER **3**

The Priceless Value of Knowing Christ

Whatever happens, my dear brothers and sisters,* rejoice in the Lord. I never get tired of telling you these things, and I do it to safeguard your faith.

[2] Watch out for those dogs, those people who do evil, those mutilators who say you must be circumcised to be saved. [3] For

2:17 Greek *I will rejoice even if I am to be poured out as a liquid offering.*   **2:29** Greek *in the Lord.*
3:1 Greek *brothers;* also in 3:13, 17.

we who worship by the Spirit of God* are the ones who are truly circumcised. We rely on what Christ Jesus has done for us. We put no confidence in human effort, ⁴though I could have confidence in my own effort if anyone could. Indeed, if others have reason for confidence in their own efforts, I have even more!

⁵I was circumcised when I was eight days old. I am a pure-blooded citizen of Israel and a member of the tribe of Benjamin—a real Hebrew if there ever was one! I was a member of the Pharisees, who demand the strictest obedience to the Jewish law. ⁶I was so zealous that I harshly persecuted the church. And as for righteousness, I obeyed the law without fault.

⁷I once thought these things were valuable, but now I consider them worthless because of what Christ has done. ⁸Yes, everything else is worthless when compared with the infinite value of knowing Christ Jesus my Lord. For his sake I have discarded everything else, counting it all as garbage, so that I could gain Christ ⁹and become one with him. I no longer count on my own righteousness through obeying the law; rather, I become righteous through faith in Christ.* For God's way of making us right with himself depends on faith. ¹⁰I want to know Christ and experience the mighty power that raised him from the dead. I want to suffer with him, sharing in his death, ¹¹so that one way or another I will experience the resurrection from the dead!

Pressing toward the Goal

¹²I don't mean to say that I have already achieved these things or that I have already reached perfection. But I press on to possess that perfection for which Christ Jesus first possessed me. ¹³No, dear brothers and sisters, I have not achieved it,* but I focus on this one thing: Forgetting the past and looking forward to what lies ahead, ¹⁴I press on to reach the end of the race and receive the heavenly prize for which God, through Christ Jesus, is calling us.

¹⁵Let all who are spiritually mature agree on these things. If you disagree on some point, I believe God will make it plain to you. ¹⁶But we must hold on to the progress we have already made.

¹⁷Dear brothers and sisters, pattern your lives after mine, and learn from those who follow our example. ¹⁸For I have told you often before, and I say it again with tears in my eyes, that there are many whose conduct shows they are really enemies of the

3:3 Some manuscripts read *worship God in spirit*; one early manuscript reads *worship in spirit.*
3:9 Or *through the faithfulness of Christ.*   3:13 Some manuscripts read *not yet achieved it.*

FRIENDSHIP STORY *continued from page 382...*

Reflect

★ **Romans 8:28** says God causes everything to work together for the good of those who love God. How has God used your family member's challenge for good?

★ In what practical ways can you "stand by" your family member?

JOURNAL

WHAT TO SAY 👍
AND
WHAT NOT TO SAY 👎

FRIENDSHIP TYPE:	FRIENDSHIP LAYER:
Family	*Acceptance*

How to "Short Circuit" Acceptance in 5 Easy Steps

👎 WHAT NOT TO SAY:

★ Pretend differences don't exist.
★ Refuse to make eye contact—act as though your family member is invisible.
★ Beg, plead, threaten, and bribe your loved one to do things your way.
★ Shove the issue aside. Deal with the mess later.
★ Hang a poster of the "hear no evil, speak no evil, see no evil" monkeys on your door.

👍 WHAT TO SAY:

If you want to communicate acceptance, follow what's modeled in the story of the prodigal son (Luke 15:11-32)...

★ Acknowledge the person's need to explore options you don't value (verse 12).
★ Look into the distance (the future), hoping for something good to happen (verse 20).
★ Acknowledge your own grief and loss about the choices being made (verse 24).
★ Celebrate all steps toward reconciliation (verses 21-22).
★ Confront undermining criticisms with love (verses 31-32).

cross of Christ. ¹⁹They are headed for destruction. Their god is their appetite, they brag about shameful things, and they think only about this life here on earth. ²⁰But we are citizens of heaven, where the Lord Jesus Christ lives. And we are eagerly waiting for him to return as our Savior. ²¹He will take our weak mortal bodies and change them into glorious bodies like his own, using the same power with which he will bring everything under his control.

CHAPTER **4**

Therefore, my dear brothers and sisters,* stay true to the Lord. I love you and long to see you, dear friends, for you are my joy and the crown I receive for my work.

Words of Encouragement

²Now I appeal to Euodia and Syntyche. Please, because you belong to the Lord, settle your disagreement. ³And I ask you, my true partner,* to help these two women, for they worked hard with me in telling others the Good News. They worked along with Clement and the rest of my co-workers, whose names are written in the Book of Life.

⁴Always be full of joy in the Lord. I say it again—rejoice! ⁵Let everyone see that you are considerate in all you do. Remember, the Lord is coming soon.

⁶Don't worry about anything; instead, pray about everything. Tell God what you need, and thank him for all he has done. ⁷Then you will experience God's peace, which exceeds anything we can understand. His peace will guard your hearts and minds as you live in Christ Jesus.

⁸And now, dear brothers and sisters, one final thing. Fix your thoughts on what is true, and honorable, and right, and pure, and lovely, and admirable. Think about things that are excellent and worthy of praise. ⁹Keep putting into practice all you learned and received from me—everything you heard from me and saw me doing. Then the God of peace will be with you.

Paul's Thanks for Their Gifts

¹⁰How I praise the Lord that you are concerned about me again. I know you have always been concerned for me, but you didn't have the chance to help me. ¹¹Not that I was ever in need, for I have learned how to be content with whatever I have. ¹²I know how to live on almost nothing or with everything. I have learned the secret of living in every situation, whether it is with

4:1 Greek *brothers;* also in 4:8. **4:3** Or *loyal Syzygus.*

a full stomach or empty, with plenty or little. ¹³For I can do everything through Christ,* who gives me strength. ¹⁴Even so, you have done well to share with me in my present difficulty.

¹⁵As you know, you Philippians were the only ones who gave me financial help when I first brought you the Good News and then traveled on from Macedonia. No other church did this. ¹⁶Even when I was in Thessalonica you sent help more than once. ¹⁷I don't say this because I want a gift from you. Rather, I want you to receive a reward for your kindness.

¹⁸At the moment I have all I need—and more! I am generously supplied with the gifts you sent me with Epaphroditus. They are a sweet-smelling sacrifice that is acceptable and pleasing to God. ¹⁹And this same God who takes care of me will supply all your needs from his glorious riches, which have been given to us in Christ Jesus.

²⁰Now all glory to God our Father forever and ever! Amen.

Paul's Final Greetings

²¹Give my greetings to each of God's holy people—all who belong to Christ Jesus. The brothers who are with me send you their greetings. ²²And all the rest of God's people send you greetings, too, especially those in Caesar's household.

²³May the grace of the Lord Jesus Christ be with your spirit.

4:13 Greek *through the one.*

"The solution to a fight, argument, difference of opinion, unthoughtfulness on the part of another person, unfair treatment, selfishness, egoism, disregard for another person's rights, is <u>not</u> splitting up and finding other human beings to live with... understanding must be taught, time after time, through seeking to find solutions which are not perfect, but which are possible."

~ Edith Schaeffer

Colossians

AUTHOR:	DATE WRITTEN:
Paul	Approximately A.D. 60

CHAPTER 1

Greetings from Paul

This letter is from Paul, chosen by the will of God to be an apostle of Christ Jesus, and from our brother Timothy.

²We are writing to God's holy people in the city of Colosse, who are faithful brothers and sisters* in Christ.

May God our Father give you grace and peace.

Paul's Thanksgiving and Prayer

³We always pray for you, and we give thanks to God, the Father of our Lord Jesus Christ. ⁴For we have heard of your faith in Christ Jesus and your love for all of God's people, ⁵which come from your confident hope of what God has reserved for you in heaven. You have had this expectation ever since you first heard the truth of the Good News.

⁶This same Good News that came to you is going out all over the world. It is bearing fruit everywhere by changing lives, just as it changed your lives from the day you first heard and understood the truth about God's wonderful grace.

⁷You learned about the Good News from Epaphras, our beloved co-worker. He is Christ's faithful servant, and he is helping us on your behalf.* ⁸He has told us about the love for others that the Holy Spirit has given you.

⁹So we have not stopped praying for you since we first heard about you. We ask God to give you complete knowledge of his will and to give you spiritual wisdom and understanding. ¹⁰Then the way you live will always honor and please the Lord, and your lives will produce every kind of good fruit. All the while, you will grow as you learn to know God better and better.

¹¹We also pray that you will be strengthened with all his

1:2 Greek *faithful brothers.*   1:7 Or *he is ministering on your behalf;* some manuscripts read *he is ministering on our behalf.*

glorious power so you will have all the endurance and patience you need. May you be filled with joy,* [12] always thanking the Father. He has enabled you to share in the inheritance that belongs to his people, who live in the light. [13] For he has rescued us from the kingdom of darkness and transferred us into the Kingdom of his dear Son, [14] who purchased our freedom* and forgave our sins.

Christ Is Supreme

[15] Christ is the visible image of the invisible God.
>   He existed before anything was created and is supreme
>   over all creation,*
[16] for through him God created everything
>   in the heavenly realms and on earth.
> He made the things we can see
>   and the things we can't see—
> such as thrones, kingdoms, rulers, and authorities in the
>   unseen world.
> Everything was created through him and for him.
[17] He existed before anything else,
>   and he holds all creation together.
[18] Christ is also the head of the church,
>   which is his body.
> He is the beginning,
>   supreme over all who rise from the dead.*
>   So he is first in everything.
[19] For God in all his fullness
>   was pleased to live in Christ,
[20] and through him God reconciled
>   everything to himself.
> He made peace with everything in heaven and on earth
>   by means of Christ's blood on the cross.

[21] This includes you who were once far away from God. You were his enemies, separated from him by your evil thoughts and actions. [22] Yet now he has reconciled you to himself through the death of Christ in his physical body. As a result, he has brought you into his own presence, and you are holy and blameless as you stand before him without a single fault.

[23] But you must continue to believe this truth and stand firmly in it. Don't drift away from the assurance you received when you heard the Good News. The Good News has been preached

1:11 Or *all the patience and endurance you need with joy.* 1:14 Some manuscripts add *with his blood.*
1:15 Or *He is the firstborn of all creation.* 1:18 Or *the firstborn from the dead.*

FRIENDSHIP EXPERIENCE

FRIENDSHIP TYPE: *Neighbors*   FRIENDSHIP LAYER: *Deepening*

No Fences

It wasn't as if David didn't like his neighbor, Will. In fact, he thought Will was a pretty nice guy. It was more that David just wasn't all that interested in building a friendship with the guy. What with work and church and his baseball team, David figured he had enough friends for now. David even semi-joked with his wife that they should stop introducing themselves to new people because they just really didn't need any more friends.

Then one day Will invited David over to watch a football game—Will had just gotten a new TV, and he wanted to show it off a little. David couldn't think of any excuses, and besides, he really did want to check out the new TV, so he agreed to come. After a few hours of watching football, talking about work, and discussing fishing (a mutual hobby), David had changed his mind about Will. He decided there might be room for another friend in his life after all.

What kind of relationship do you have with your neighbors?

Perhaps you see each other at work, at the grocery store, or across the fence. You know a lot about what the other person is *doing*, but do you really *know* the person?

FRIENDSHIP EXPERIENCE *continues on page 388...*

FRIENDSHIP EXPERIENCE *continued from page 387...*

Maybe you like living parallel lives—seeing each other, saying "hi" occasionally, but never actually crossing paths. It's comfortable that way. You don't have to give anything, they don't have to give anything…nobody has to work very hard, nobody gets hurt.

But you're missing out! Deepening your relationship with neighbors can lead to great and rewarding friendships. Don't overlook friendship with your neighbors just because you have friends elsewhere. God has placed those neighbors in your life for a reason!

Experience

THE ONE THING 1 YOU CAN DO THIS WEEK

Going deeper doesn't mean you always have to get "deep" and serious in your times together. David and Will developed a friendship over football. Breaking down the barriers and learning to be friends with your neighbors can happen anytime!

Invite your neighbor to an activity you enjoy together: Watch a football game, rent a documentary, or go fishing together. Express to your new friend how much you enjoy the company. Share with your neighbor some of the reasons you like him or her; build the person up **(Ephesians 4:29)**.

Do the same things to deepen your friendship with God. God's with you 24/7 anyway! Just like your friend, God wants to feel your expressions of love toward him. Jot down the things you love about God and what you enjoy about God's company. Then read **Matthew 5:1-16**, and receive his loving words toward you.

FRIENDSHIP EXPERIENCE *continues on page 389...*

all over the world, and I, Paul, have been appointed as God's servant to proclaim it.

Paul's Work for the Church

[24] I am glad when I suffer for you in my body, for I am participating in the sufferings of Christ that continue for his body, the church. [25] God has given me the responsibility of serving his church by proclaiming his entire message to you. [26] This message was kept secret for centuries and generations past, but now it has been revealed to God's people. [27] For God wanted them to know that the riches and glory of Christ are for you Gentiles, too. And this is the secret: Christ lives in you. This gives you assurance of sharing his glory.

[28] So we tell others about Christ, warning everyone and teaching everyone with all the wisdom God has given us. We want to present them to God, perfect* in their relationship to Christ. [29] That's why I work and struggle so hard, depending on Christ's mighty power that works within me.

CHAPTER **2**

I want you to know how much I have agonized for you and for the church at Laodicea, and for many other believers who have never met me personally. [2] I want them to be encouraged and knit together by strong ties of love. I want them to have complete confidence that they understand God's mysterious plan, which is Christ himself. [3] In him lie hidden all the treasures of wisdom and knowledge.

[4] I am telling you this so no one will deceive you with well-crafted arguments. [5] For though I am far away from you, my heart is with you. And I rejoice that you are living as you should and that your faith in Christ is strong.

Freedom from Rules and New Life in Christ

[6] And now, just as you accepted Christ Jesus as your Lord, you must continue to follow him. [7] Let your roots grow down into him, and let your lives be built on him. Then your faith will grow strong in the truth you were taught, and you will overflow with thankfulness.

[8] Don't let anyone capture you with empty philosophies and high-sounding nonsense that come from human thinking and from the spiritual powers* of this world, rather than from Christ. [9] For in Christ lives all the fullness of God in a human body.*

1:28 Or *mature.*   **2:8** Or *the spiritual principles;* also in 2:20.   **2:9** Or *in him dwells all the completeness of the Godhead bodily.*

¹⁰So you also are complete through your union with Christ, who is the head over every ruler and authority.

¹¹When you came to Christ, you were "circumcised," but not by a physical procedure. Christ performed a spiritual circumcision—the cutting away of your sinful nature.* ¹²For you were buried with Christ when you were baptized. And with him you were raised to new life because you trusted the mighty power of God, who raised Christ from the dead.

¹³You were dead because of your sins and because your sinful nature was not yet cut away. Then God made you alive with Christ, for he forgave all our sins. ¹⁴He canceled the record of the charges against us and took it away by nailing it to the cross. ¹⁵In this way, he disarmed* the spiritual rulers and authorities. He shamed them publicly by his victory over them on the cross.

¹⁶So don't let anyone condemn you for what you eat or drink, or for not celebrating certain holy days or new moon ceremonies or Sabbaths. ¹⁷For these rules are only shadows of the reality yet to come. And Christ himself is that reality. ¹⁸Don't let anyone condemn you by insisting on pious self-denial or the worship of angels,* saying they have had visions about these things. Their sinful minds have made them proud, ¹⁹and they are not connected to Christ, the head of the body. For he holds the whole body together with its joints and ligaments, and it grows as God nourishes it.

²⁰You have died with Christ, and he has set you free from the spiritual powers of this world. So why do you keep on following the rules of the world, such as, ²¹"Don't handle! Don't taste! Don't touch!"? ²²Such rules are mere human teachings about things that deteriorate as we use them. ²³These rules may seem wise because they require strong devotion, pious self-denial, and severe bodily discipline. But they provide no help in conquering a person's evil desires.

CHAPTER 3

Living the New Life

Since you have been raised to new life with Christ, set your sights on the realities of heaven, where Christ sits in the place of honor at God's right hand. ²Think about the things of heaven, not the things of earth. ³For you died to this life, and your real life is hidden with Christ in God. ⁴And when Christ, who is your* life, is revealed to the whole world, you will share in all his glory.

2:11 Greek *the cutting away of the body of the flesh.* 2:15 Or *he stripped off.* 2:18 Or *or worshiping with angels.* 3:4 Some manuscripts read *our.*

FRIENDSHIP EXPERIENCE *continued from page 388...*

Reflect
★ What barriers stop you from going deeper in friendship with your neighbors? with God?
★ How would having fun together deepen the friendship with your neighbor? with God?

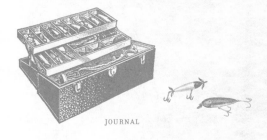

JOURNAL

> *"Telling lies about others is as harmful as hitting them with an ax,*
>
> *wounding them with a sword,*
>
> *or shooting them with a sharp arrow."*
>
> ~ Proverbs 25:18

JOURNAL

⁵So put to death the sinful, earthly things lurking within you. Have nothing to do with sexual immorality, impurity, lust, and evil desires. Don't be greedy, for a greedy person is an idolater, worshiping the things of this world. ⁶Because of these sins, the anger of God is coming.* ⁷You used to do these things when your life was still part of this world. ⁸But now is the time to get rid of anger, rage, malicious behavior, slander, and dirty language. ⁹Don't lie to each other, for you have stripped off your old sinful nature and all its wicked deeds. ¹⁰Put on your new nature, and be renewed as you learn to know your Creator and become like him. ¹¹In this new life, it doesn't matter if you are a Jew or a Gentile,* circumcised or uncircumcised, barbaric, uncivilized,* slave, or free. Christ is all that matters, and he lives in all of us.

¹²Since God chose you to be the holy people he loves, you must clothe yourselves with tenderhearted mercy, kindness, humility, gentleness, and patience. ¹³Make allowance for each other's faults, and forgive anyone who offends you. Remember, the Lord forgave you, so you must forgive others. ¹⁴Above all, clothe yourselves with love, which binds us all together in perfect harmony. ¹⁵And let the peace that comes from Christ rule in your hearts. For as members of one body you are called to live in peace. And always be thankful.

¹⁶Let the message about Christ, in all its richness, fill your lives. Teach and counsel each other with all the wisdom he gives. Sing psalms and hymns and spiritual songs to God with thankful hearts. ¹⁷And whatever you do or say, do it as a representative of the Lord Jesus, giving thanks through him to God the Father.

Instructions for Christian Households

¹⁸Wives, submit to your husbands, as is fitting for those who belong to the Lord.

¹⁹Husbands, love your wives and never treat them harshly.

²⁰Children, always obey your parents, for this pleases the Lord. ²¹Fathers, do not aggravate your children, or they will become discouraged.

²²Slaves, obey your earthly masters in everything you do. Try to please them all the time, not just when they are watching you. Serve them sincerely because of your reverent fear of the Lord. ²³Work willingly at whatever you do, as though you were working for the Lord rather than for people. ²⁴Remember that the Lord will give you an inheritance as your reward, and that

3:6 Some manuscripts read *is coming on all who disobey him.* 3:11a Greek *a Greek.* 3:11b Greek *Barbarian, Scythian.*

the Master you are serving is Christ.* [25]But if you do what is wrong, you will be paid back for the wrong you have done. For God has no favorites.

CHAPTER **4**

Masters, be just and fair to your slaves. Remember that you also have a Master—in heaven.

An Encouragement for Prayer

[2]Devote yourselves to prayer with an alert mind and a thankful heart. [3]Pray for us, too, that God will give us many opportunities to speak about his mysterious plan concerning Christ. That is why I am here in chains. [4]Pray that I will proclaim this message as clearly as I should.

[5]Live wisely among those who are not believers, and make the most of every opportunity. [6]Let your conversation be gracious and attractive* so that you will have the right response for everyone.

Paul's Final Instructions and Greetings

[7]Tychicus will give you a full report about how I am getting along. He is a beloved brother and faithful helper who serves with me in the Lord's work. [8]I have sent him to you for this very purpose—to let you know how we are doing and to encourage you. [9]I am also sending Onesimus, a faithful and beloved brother, one of your own people. He and Tychicus will tell you everything that's happening here.

[10]Aristarchus, who is in prison with me, sends you his greetings, and so does Mark, Barnabas's cousin. As you were instructed before, make Mark welcome if he comes your way. [11]Jesus (the one we call Justus) also sends his greetings. These are the only Jewish believers among my co-workers; they are working with me here for the Kingdom of God. And what a comfort they have been!

[12]Epaphras, a member of your own fellowship and a servant of Christ Jesus, sends you his greetings. He always prays earnestly for you, asking God to make you strong and perfect, fully confident that you are following the whole will of God. [13]I can assure you that he prays hard for you and also for the believers in Laodicea and Hierapolis.

[14]Luke, the beloved doctor, sends his greetings, and so does Demas. [15]Please give my greetings to our brothers and sisters* at Laodicea, and to Nympha and the church that meets in her house.

3:24 Or *and serve Christ as your Master.* **4:6** Greek *and seasoned with salt.* **4:15** Greek *brothers.*

WHAT TO SAY
AND
WHAT NOT TO SAY

FRIENDSHIP TYPE:	FRIENDSHIP LAYER:
Neighbors	*Deepening*

Top 7

The Top 7 Things Not to Do or Say

...if you're trying to deepen your friendship with neighbors (according to **Colossians 3:5-11**).

WHAT NOT TO DO:

7. **Be sexually immoral.** (It's best not to desire your neighbor's spouse.)
6. **Be greedy.** (Jealousy is always ugly. Be happy for your neighbor's good fortunes, not jealous of them.)
5. **Be angry and/or show rage.** (Whether you show it or not, anger toward your neighbor only promotes bitterness—something that does *not* lead to a happy neighborhood.)
4. **Engage in malicious behavior.** (Coercing your dog to do its business on your neighbor's lawn? Not nice. If you wouldn't want your neighbors to do it to you, don't do it to them.)
3. **Slander others.** (Gossiping about your neighbors—to them, with them, or about them—is never a good thing.)
2. **Use dirty language.** (Seriously, using foul language—especially in front of their children—just isn't a good idea.)
1. **Tell lies.** (Your neighbors aren't going to appreciate it if you lie to them.)

WHAT TO SAY AND **WHAT NOT TO SAY** *continues on page 392...*

Friendship First NEW TESTAMENT

WHAT TO SAY AND WHAT NOT TO SAY *continued from page 391…*

The Top 7 Things to Do and Say
…if you're trying to deepen your friendship with neighbors (according to **Colossians 3:12-17**).

WHAT TO DO:

7. **Be kind.** (Take 'em cookies. Invite them over for dinner. Shovel their sidewalk on a snowy morning.)

6. **Be humble.** (You don't need to one-up your neighbors at every turn. Rejoice in their successes without needing to tout yours.)

5. **Be patient.** (Your neighbors aren't perfect, and neither are you. Don't get mad every time their lawn is an inch too long or they have friends over past midnight. Remember, your friendship is worth more than that.)

4. **Forgive others.** (No matter what they do. Christ did it for you; you should do it for them.)

3. **Live in peace.** (Your neighbors aren't out to get you, and you shouldn't be out to get your neighbors. Smile. Wave. Give compliments. Be generous. A peaceful neighborhood is worth your time and energy.)

2. **Be thankful.** (God gave you those neighbors for a reason! Find the good in them—and be grateful for it!)

And above all else, the number one thing to do to deepen your friendship with your neighbors is to…

1. ***Love them!*** (It covers over a multitude of sins according to **1 Peter 4:8**.)

[16]After you have read this letter, pass it on to the church at Laodicea so they can read it, too. And you should read the letter I wrote to them.

[17]And say to Archippus, "Be sure to carry out the ministry the Lord gave you."

[18]HERE IS MY GREETING IN MY OWN HANDWRITING—PAUL. Remember my chains.

May God's grace be with you.

1 Thessalonians

AUTHOR:	DATE WRITTEN:
Paul	Approximately A.D. 51

CHAPTER 1

Greetings from Paul

This letter is from Paul, Silas,* and Timothy.

We are writing to the church in Thessalonica, to you who belong to God the Father and the Lord Jesus Christ.

May God give you grace and peace.

The Faith of the Thessalonian Believers

2 We always thank God for all of you and pray for you constantly. 3 As we pray to our God and Father about you, we think of your faithful work, your loving deeds, and the enduring hope you have because of our Lord Jesus Christ.

4 We know, dear brothers and sisters,* that God loves you and has chosen you to be his own people. 5 For when we brought you the Good News, it was not only with words but also with power, for the Holy Spirit gave you full assurance* that what we said was true. And you know of our concern for you from the way we lived when we were with you. 6 So you received the message with joy from the Holy Spirit in spite of the severe suffering it brought you. In this way, you imitated both us and the Lord. 7 As a result, you have become an example to all the believers in Greece—throughout both Macedonia and Achaia.*

8 And now the word of the Lord is ringing out from you to people everywhere, even beyond Macedonia and Achaia, for wherever we go we find people telling us about your faith in God. We don't need to tell them about it, 9 for they keep talking about the wonderful welcome you gave us and how you turned away from idols to serve the living and true God. 10 And they speak of how you are looking forward to the coming of God's

1:1 Greek *Silvanus,* the Greek form of the name.   1:4 Greek *brothers.*   1:5 Or *with the power of the Holy Spirit, so you can have full assurance.*   1:7 *Macedonia* and *Achaia* were the northern and southern regions of Greece.

No. 20-FS-394

FRIENDSHIP
STORY

FRIENDSHIP TYPE:
Friends

FRIENDSHIP LAYER:
Trust

FOUND IN SCRIPTURE

Trust Under Fire

Shadrach, Meshach, and Abednego: three inseparable friends…so inseparable, in fact, that their names are *always* mentioned together.

Theirs is a story of loyal friendship, enduring trust, and unshakeable faith.

They were three young prisoners of war—captives taken to serve in King Nebuchadnezzar's court. They were good-looking, talented, hard-working, smart guys, and they quickly rose in the ranks.

Though they were far from their families, their homes, and their land, Shadrach, Meshach, and Abednego trusted in God—and each other—and they were doing all right.

Until…the inevitable happened. It was a culture clash of mighty proportions. King Nebuchadnezzar ordered that a giant golden statue be made and that *everyone* in his kingdom be forced to bow and worship this statue. And when King Nebuchadnezzar said "everyone," he meant his prisoners of war, too, no matter what they believed. The king declared that anyone who disobeyed would be executed—burned to death in a furnace.

It was, in essence, a death sentence for the three young friends. Though they had worked hard for the king, they would not worship something he had created—because Shadrach, Meshach, and Abednego believed in only one God, a God that could not be created from gold or formed by men, and they would worship nothing but that God.

The musical instruments sounded, the kingdom bowed before the golden statue…and left three men standing alone, proud and defiant.

FRIENDSHIP STORY *continues on page 395…*

Son from heaven—Jesus, whom God raised from the dead. He is the one who has rescued us from the terrors of the coming judgment.

CHAPTER **2**
Paul Remembers His Visit

You yourselves know, dear brothers and sisters,* that our visit to you was not a failure. ²You know how badly we had been treated at Philippi just before we came to you and how much we suffered there. Yet our God gave us the courage to declare his Good News to you boldly, in spite of great opposition. ³So you can see we were not preaching with any deceit or impure motives or trickery.

⁴For we speak as messengers approved by God to be entrusted with the Good News. Our purpose is to please God, not people. He alone examines the motives of our hearts. ⁵Never once did we try to win you with flattery, as you well know. And God is our witness that we were not pretending to be your friends just to get your money! ⁶As for human praise, we have never sought it from you or anyone else.

⁷As apostles of Christ we certainly had a right to make some demands of you, but instead we were like children* among you. Or we were like a mother feeding and caring for her own children. ⁸We loved you so much that we shared with you not only God's Good News but our own lives, too.

⁹Don't you remember, dear brothers and sisters, how hard we worked among you? Night and day we toiled to earn a living so that we would not be a burden to any of you as we preached God's Good News to you. ¹⁰You yourselves are our witnesses—and so is God—that we were devout and honest and faultless toward all of you believers. ¹¹And you know that we treated each of you as a father treats his own children. ¹²We pleaded with you, encouraged you, and urged you to live your lives in a way that God would consider worthy. For he called you to share in his Kingdom and glory.

¹³Therefore, we never stop thanking God that when you received his message from us, you didn't think of our words as mere human ideas. You accepted what we said as the very word of God—which, of course, it is. And this word continues to work in you who believe.

¹⁴And then, dear brothers and sisters, you suffered persecution from your own countrymen. In this way, you imitated the

2:1 Greek *brothers;* also in 2:9, 14, 17.   2:7 Some manuscripts read *we were gentle.*

believers in God's churches in Judea who, because of their belief in Christ Jesus, suffered from their own people, the Jews. [15]For some of the Jews killed the prophets, and some even killed the Lord Jesus. Now they have persecuted us, too. They fail to please God and work against all humanity [16]as they try to keep us from preaching the Good News of salvation to the Gentiles. By doing this, they continue to pile up their sins. But the anger of God has caught up with them at last.

Timothy's Good Report about the Church

[17]Dear brothers and sisters, after we were separated from you for a little while (though our hearts never left you), we tried very hard to come back because of our intense longing to see you again. [18]We wanted very much to come to you, and I, Paul, tried again and again, but Satan prevented us. [19]After all, what gives us hope and joy, and what will be our proud reward and crown as we stand before our Lord Jesus when he returns? It is you! [20]Yes, you are our pride and joy.

CHAPTER **3**

Finally, when we could stand it no longer, we decided to stay alone in Athens, [2]and we sent Timothy to visit you. He is our brother and God's co-worker* in proclaiming the Good News of Christ. We sent him to strengthen you, to encourage you in your faith, [3]and to keep you from being shaken by the troubles you were going through. But you know that we are destined for such troubles. [4]Even while we were with you, we warned you that troubles would soon come—and they did, as you well know. [5]That is why, when I could bear it no longer, I sent Timothy to find out whether your faith was still strong. I was afraid that the tempter had gotten the best of you and that our work had been useless.

[6]But now Timothy has just returned, bringing us good news about your faith and love. He reports that you always remember our visit with joy and that you want to see us as much as we want to see you. [7]So we have been greatly encouraged in the midst of our troubles and suffering, dear brothers and sisters,* because you have remained strong in your faith. [8]It gives us new life to know that you are standing firm in the Lord.

[9]How we thank God for you! Because of you we have great joy as we enter God's presence. [10]Night and day we pray

3:2 Other manuscripts read *and God's servant;* still others read *and a co-worker,* or *and a servant and co-worker for God,* or *and God's servant and our co-worker.*   3:7 Greek *brothers.*

FRIENDSHIP STORY *continued from page 394...*

Nebuchadnezzar's anger resounded through the kingdom. He had the men seized and declared that the furnace be heated seven times hotter in preparation for their execution.

The three friends were led—unflinching—to the furnace…to their deaths. But they remained loyal to one another and to God. They believed that God would save them.

And when Nebuchadnezzar looked into the furnace, prepared to gloat over their deaths, he saw instead *four* men walking around in the furnace…unbound, unharmed, comfortable. And the fourth looked very much like an angel.

Amazed, Nebuchadnezzar called Shadrach, Meshach, and Abednego to come out of the furnace, and they came to him, without a single hair or thread burned. The king dropped to his knees in worship of this One True God—the God of Shadrach, Meshach, and Abednego.

Read the entire story in Daniel 1–3 in the Old Testament.

Experience

THE ONE THING **1** YOU CAN DO THIS WEEK

Surviving a fire isn't easy— and life certainly brings plenty of "fires"—but if you have true friends (friends you can trust), those fires can be a little less devastating. Shadrach, Meshach, and Abednego trusted God, and they also relied on each other to get through a tough time—to survive a fire. Read **Mark 2:1-12** for a glimpse at the power of trusting Jesus…and the power of being a trustworthy friend, especially during hard times.

FRIENDSHIP STORY *continues on page 396...*

FRIENDSHIP STORY *continued from page 395...*

Do you have a friend who is going through a "fire" right now? Perhaps you know a friend who is depressed, a friend who is out of work, or a friend who has just lost a loved one. That friend needs you right now; that friend needs to know he or she can trust you and rely on you. Commit to being there for that friend. Call your friend daily, take your friend on a fun outing, organize daily meals for your friend…pray for your friend.

Reflect

★ How did being tossed into the fire deepen the three Hebrews' friendship with each other? with God?

★ Why do you think Jesus wants us to trust? to be trustworthy?

★ How will your commitment during the tough times build trust in your friendships?

JOURNAL

_____

_____

_____

_____

_____

_____

_____

_____

_____

_____

earnestly for you, asking God to let us see you again to fill the gaps in your faith.

[11] May God our Father and our Lord Jesus bring us to you very soon. [12] And may the Lord make your love for one another and for all people grow and overflow, just as our love for you overflows. [13] May he, as a result, make your hearts strong, blameless, and holy as you stand before God our Father when our Lord Jesus comes again with all his holy people. Amen.

CHAPTER **4**

Live to Please God

Finally, dear brothers and sisters,* we urge you in the name of the Lord Jesus to live in a way that pleases God, as we have taught you. You live this way already, and we encourage you to do so even more. [2] For you remember what we taught you by the authority of the Lord Jesus.

[3] God's will is for you to be holy, so stay away from all sexual sin. [4] Then each of you will control his own body* and live in holiness and honor—[5] not in lustful passion like the pagans who do not know God and his ways. [6] Never harm or cheat a Christian brother in this matter by violating his wife,* for the Lord avenges all such sins, as we have solemnly warned you before. [7] God has called us to live holy lives, not impure lives. [8] Therefore, anyone who refuses to live by these rules is not disobeying human teaching but is rejecting God, who gives his Holy Spirit to you.

[9] But we don't need to write to you about the importance of loving each other,* for God himself has taught you to love one another. [10] Indeed, you already show your love for all the believers* throughout Macedonia. Even so, dear brothers and sisters, we urge you to love them even more.

[11] Make it your goal to live a quiet life, minding your own business and working with your hands, just as we instructed you before. [12] Then people who are not Christians will respect the way you live, and you will not need to depend on others.

The Hope of the Resurrection

[13] And now, dear brothers and sisters, we want you to know what will happen to the believers who have died* so you will not grieve like people who have no hope. [14] For since we believe that Jesus died and was raised to life again, we also believe that

4:1 Greek *brothers;* also in 4:10, 13.   4:4 Or *will know how to take a wife for himself;* or *will learn to live with his own wife;* Greek reads *will know how to possess his own vessel.*   4:6 Greek *Never harm or cheat a brother in this matter.*   4:9 Greek *about brotherly love.*   4:10 Greek *the brothers.*   4:13 Greek *those who have fallen asleep;* also in 4:14.

when Jesus returns, God will bring back with him the believers who have died.

15 We tell you this directly from the Lord: We who are still living when the Lord returns will not meet him ahead of those who have died.* 16 For the Lord himself will come down from heaven with a commanding shout, with the voice of the archangel, and with the trumpet call of God. First, the Christians who have died* will rise from their graves. 17 Then, together with them, we who are still alive and remain on the earth will be caught up in the clouds to meet the Lord in the air. Then we will be with the Lord forever. 18 So encourage each other with these words.

CHAPTER **5**

Now concerning how and when all this will happen, dear brothers and sisters,* we don't really need to write you. 2 For you know quite well that the day of the Lord's return will come unexpectedly, like a thief in the night. 3 When people are saying, "Everything is peaceful and secure," then disaster will fall on them as suddenly as a pregnant woman's labor pains begin. And there will be no escape.

4 But you aren't in the dark about these things, dear brothers and sisters, and you won't be surprised when the day of the Lord comes like a thief.* 5 For you are all children of the light and of the day; we don't belong to darkness and night. 6 So be on your guard, not asleep like the others. Stay alert and be clearheaded. 7 Night is the time when people sleep and drinkers get drunk. 8 But let us who live in the light be clearheaded, protected by the armor of faith and love, and wearing as our helmet the confidence of our salvation.

9 For God chose to save us through our Lord Jesus Christ, not to pour out his anger on us. 10 Christ died for us so that, whether we are dead or alive when he returns, we can live with him forever. 11 So encourage each other and build each other up, just as you are already doing.

Paul's Final Advice

12 Dear brothers and sisters, honor those who are your leaders in the Lord's work. They work hard among you and give you spiritual guidance. 13 Show them great respect and wholehearted love because of their work. And live peacefully with each other.

14 Brothers and sisters, we urge you to warn those who are

4:15 Greek *those who have fallen asleep.*   **4:16** Greek *the dead in Christ.*   **5:1** Greek *brothers;* also in 5:4, 12, 14, 25, 26, 27.   **5:4** Some manuscripts read *comes upon you as if you were thieves.*

FRIENDSHIP TYPE: *Friends*   FRIENDSHIP LAYER: *Trust*

Be Safe

So you're sitting down to dinner with your friend, and suddenly he lowers his voice and confesses a deep, dark secret…a secret he has been terrified to tell anyone.

In this particular situation, it's *really* not a good idea to let any of these pass through your lips:

  WHAT NOT TO SAY:

★ "Are you serious?! That's the most terrible thing I've ever heard!"
★ "Ha ha ha! That's a good one. You're totally kidding me…right?"
★ "I'm so disappointed in you. Wow, I'm not sure we can even be friends anymore."
★ "Oh, right, cool…hey, so do you think I should go for that promotion or not?"
★ "Well, if you think that's bad, wait'll you hear this…"

  WHAT TO SAY:

First Thessalonians 5:11 says, "So encourage each other and build each other up, just as you are already doing." Be someone your friend will trust and feel safe with. Use encouraging, helpful, loving words such as…

★ "I'm really honored that you trust me enough to share this, and I really want to live up to that trust. How can I do that?"
★ "Would you like to pray together now about this?"
★ "What specific thing can I do to help or encourage you?"
★ "This must have been very difficult for you. Would you like to tell me more about it over coffee?"
★ "Your courage and openness really inspire me in my own life. Thank you."

lazy. Encourage those who are timid. Take tender care of those who are weak. Be patient with everyone.

¹⁵See that no one pays back evil for evil, but always try to do good to each other and to all people.

¹⁶Always be joyful. ¹⁷Never stop praying. ¹⁸Be thankful in all circumstances, for this is God's will for you who belong to Christ Jesus.

¹⁹Do not stifle the Holy Spirit. ²⁰Do not scoff at prophecies, ²¹but test everything that is said. Hold on to what is good. ²²Stay away from every kind of evil.

Paul's Final Greetings

²³Now may the God of peace make you holy in every way, and may your whole spirit and soul and body be kept blameless until our Lord Jesus Christ comes again. ²⁴God will make this happen, for he who calls you is faithful.

²⁵Dear brothers and sisters, pray for us.

²⁶Greet all the brothers and sisters with Christian love.*

²⁷I command you in the name of the Lord to read this letter to all the brothers and sisters.

²⁸May the grace of our Lord Jesus Christ be with you.

5:26 Greek *with a holy kiss.*

"The family that prays together stays together."

~ Al Scalpone, copywriter for Family Theater Productions, and later the vice president of CBS-TV

2 Thessalonians

AUTHOR:	DATE WRITTEN:
Paul	Approximately A.D. 51 or 52

CHAPTER 1

Greetings from Paul

This letter is from Paul, Silas,* and Timothy.

We are writing to the church in Thessalonica, to you who belong to God our Father and the Lord Jesus Christ.

²May God our Father* and the Lord Jesus Christ give you grace and peace.

Encouragement during Persecution

³Dear brothers and sisters,* we can't help but thank God for you, because your faith is flourishing and your love for one another is growing. ⁴We proudly tell God's other churches about your endurance and faithfulness in all the persecutions and hardships you are suffering. ⁵And God will use this persecution to show his justice and to make you worthy of his Kingdom, for which you are suffering. ⁶In his justice he will pay back those who persecute you.

⁷And God will provide rest for you who are being persecuted and also for us when the Lord Jesus appears from heaven. He will come with his mighty angels, ⁸in flaming fire, bringing judgment on those who don't know God and on those who refuse to obey the Good News of our Lord Jesus. ⁹They will be punished with eternal destruction, forever separated from the Lord and from his glorious power. ¹⁰When he comes on that day, he will receive glory from his holy people—praise from all who believe. And this includes you, for you believed what we told you about him.

¹¹So we keep on praying for you, asking our God to enable you to live a life worthy of his call. May he give you the power to accomplish all the good things your faith prompts you to do. ¹²Then the name of our Lord Jesus will be honored because

1:1 Greek *Silvanus,* the Greek form of the name. 1:2 Some manuscripts read *God the Father.* 1:3 Greek *Brothers.*

WHAT TO SAY
AND
WHAT NOT TO SAY

FRIENDSHIP TYPE: *Friends*   FRIENDSHIP LAYER: *Deepening*

Work It Out

Relationships grow deeper when we're willing to work things out, forgive past hurts, and let go of grudges.

If you've had a conflict with a good friend, you know fixing it isn't easy; it takes time, sacrifice, humility…and emotional pain.

If you're in the middle of a relational battle right now, here are a few things you may *not* want to say…

WHAT NOT TO SAY:

★ **"I'm sorry you felt hurt by what I said."** That's not a true apology. When you say it like that, you're implying the person is at fault for feeling hurt, not that you're at fault for hurting the person.

★ **"I forgive you. Let's just forget it ever happened."** It's a great thought, but it's not going to happen. You can't just ignore the problem or pretend it never happened because one day it'll come up again. Before you can put it behind you, you both have to work it out and make sure you're OK about the whole thing and that there are no lingering hard feelings.

★ *(Speaking to another friend)* **"Did you hear what happened? I'm so angry!"** Keep it between you and your friend, don't gossip about your friend or complain about your friend to others. It'll only increase the bitterness in your own heart and lead to divisiveness among your group of friends.

WHAT TO SAY AND **WHAT NOT TO SAY** *continues on page 401…*

---

of the way you live, and you will be honored along with him. This is all made possible because of the grace of our God and Lord, Jesus Christ.*

CHAPTER **2**

Events prior to the Lord's Second Coming

Now, dear brothers and sisters,* let us clarify some things about the coming of our Lord Jesus Christ and how we will be gathered to meet him. [2]Don't be so easily shaken or alarmed by those who say that the day of the Lord has already begun. Don't believe them, even if they claim to have had a spiritual vision, a revelation, or a letter supposedly from us. [3]Don't be fooled by what they say. For that day will not come until there is a great rebellion against God and the man of lawlessness* is revealed—the one who brings destruction.* [4]He will exalt himself and defy everything that people call god and every object of worship. He will even sit in the temple of God, claiming that he himself is God.

[5]Don't you remember that I told you about all this when I was with you? [6]And you know what is holding him back, for he can be revealed only when his time comes. [7]For this lawlessness is already at work secretly, and it will remain secret until the one who is holding it back steps out of the way. [8]Then the man of lawlessness will be revealed, but the Lord Jesus will kill him with the breath of his mouth and destroy him by the splendor of his coming.

[9]This man will come to do the work of Satan with counterfeit power and signs and miracles. [10]He will use every kind of evil deception to fool those on their way to destruction, because they refuse to love and accept the truth that would save them. [11]So God will cause them to be greatly deceived, and they will believe these lies. [12]Then they will be condemned for enjoying evil rather than believing the truth.

Believers Should Stand Firm

[13]As for us, we can't help but thank God for you, dear brothers and sisters loved by the Lord. We are always thankful that God chose you to be among the first* to experience salvation—a salvation that came through the Spirit who makes you holy and through your belief in the truth. [14]He called you to salvation when we told you the Good News; now you can share in the glory of our Lord Jesus Christ.

1:12 Or *of our God and our Lord Jesus Christ.* **2:1** Greek *brothers;* also in 2:13, 15. **2:3a** Some manuscripts read *the man of sin.* **2:3b** Greek *the son of destruction.* **2:13** Some manuscripts read *chose you from the very beginning.*

15 With all these things in mind, dear brothers and sisters, stand firm and keep a strong grip on the teaching we passed on to you both in person and by letter.

16 Now may our Lord Jesus Christ himself and God our Father, who loved us and by his grace gave us eternal comfort and a wonderful hope, 17 comfort you and strengthen you in every good thing you do and say.

CHAPTER 3

Paul's Request for Prayer

Finally, dear brothers and sisters,* we ask you to pray for us. Pray that the Lord's message will spread rapidly and be honored wherever it goes, just as when it came to you. 2 Pray, too, that we will be rescued from wicked and evil people, for not everyone is a believer. 3 But the Lord is faithful; he will strengthen you and guard you from the evil one.* 4 And we are confident in the Lord that you are doing and will continue to do the things we commanded you. 5 May the Lord lead your hearts into a full understanding and expression of the love of God and the patient endurance that comes from Christ.

An Exhortation to Proper Living

6 And now, dear brothers and sisters, we give you this command in the name of our Lord Jesus Christ: Stay away from all believers* who live idle lives and don't follow the tradition they received* from us. 7 For you know that you ought to imitate us. We were not idle when we were with you. 8 We never accepted food from anyone without paying for it. We worked hard day and night so we would not be a burden to any of you. 9 We certainly had the right to ask you to feed us, but we wanted to give you an example to follow. 10 Even while we were with you, we gave you this command: "Those unwilling to work will not get to eat."

11 Yet we hear that some of you are living idle lives, refusing to work and meddling in other people's business. 12 We command such people and urge them in the name of the Lord Jesus Christ to settle down and work to earn their own living. 13 As for the rest of you, dear brothers and sisters, never get tired of doing good.

14 Take note of those who refuse to obey what we say in this letter. Stay away from them so they will be ashamed. 15 Don't think of them as enemies, but warn them as you would a brother or sister.*

3:1 Greek brothers; also in 3:6, 13.   3:3 Or from evil.   3:6a Greek from every brother.   3:6b Some manuscripts read you received.   3:15 Greek as a brother.

WHAT TO SAY AND WHAT NOT TO SAY continued from page 400…

WHAT TO SAY:

★ "Can we talk? I have some things I want to tell you, and I'd like to hear how you're feeling as well." Keep the lines of communication open. Be honest and vulnerable. Don't hold back anything that's going to fester bitterness in your heart—get it all out there, and tell your friend how you're really feeling. Then listen when your friend tells you how he or she is feeling. And don't just immediately try to justify your actions. Apologize. Ask for forgiveness. Offer forgiveness. Pray together.

Read Philippians 4:2-3. Don't let disagreements, bitterness, and anger destroy the friendships God has given you.

JOURNAL

Paul's Final Greetings

[16] Now may the Lord of peace himself give you his peace at all times and in every situation. The Lord be with you all.

[17] HERE IS MY GREETING IN MY OWN HANDWRITING—PAUL. I DO THIS IN ALL MY LETTERS TO PROVE THEY ARE FROM ME.

[18] May the grace of our Lord Jesus Christ be with you all.

"An enemy is a friend waiting to be made; that is the only hope for this conflict-ridden world."

~ Archbishop Desmond Tutu

1 Timothy

AUTHOR:	DATE WRITTEN:
Paul	Approximately A.D. 64

CHAPTER 1

Greetings from Paul

This letter is from Paul, an apostle of Christ Jesus, appointed by the command of God our Savior and Christ Jesus, who gives us hope.

²I am writing to Timothy, my true son in the faith.

May God the Father and Christ Jesus our Lord give you grace, mercy, and peace.

Warnings against False Teachings

³When I left for Macedonia, I urged you to stay there in Ephesus and stop those whose teaching is contrary to the truth. ⁴Don't let them waste their time in endless discussion of myths and spiritual pedigrees. These things only lead to meaningless speculations,* which don't help people live a life of faith in God.*

⁵The purpose of my instruction is that all believers would be filled with love that comes from a pure heart, a clear conscience, and genuine faith. ⁶But some people have missed this whole point. They have turned away from these things and spend their time in meaningless discussions. ⁷They want to be known as teachers of the law of Moses, but they don't know what they are talking about, even though they speak so confidently.

⁸We know that the law is good when used correctly. ⁹For the law was not intended for people who do what is right. It is for people who are lawless and rebellious, who are ungodly and sinful, who consider nothing sacred and defile what is holy, who kill their father or mother or commit other murders. ¹⁰The law is for people who are sexually immoral, or who practice homosexuality, or are slave traders,* liars, promise breakers, or who do anything else that contradicts the wholesome teaching ¹¹that comes from the glorious Good News entrusted to me by our blessed God.

1:4a Greek *in myths and endless genealogies, which cause speculation.*   **1:4b** Greek *a stewardship of God in faith.*   **1:10** Or *kidnappers.*

WHAT TO SAY 👍
AND
WHAT NOT TO SAY 👎

FRIENDSHIP TYPE:	FRIENDSHIP LAYER:
Family	*Commitment*

Selective Memory Words

Family members occupy the ringside seats when you mess up. They remember the time you paid too much for a used car, signed up for bagpipe lessons, or your prom-date haircut looked like something from *Zombies Unleashed*. Whatever the disaster, your family was there, front and center.

And you've seen their belly-flops, too.

Be a committed friend to your family by having a selective memory—a **Philippians 4:8** memory ("…what is true, and honorable, and right, and pure, and lovely, and admirable. Think about things that are excellent and worthy of praise")—when reviewing their mistakes. Words your family members will value your never saying aloud include…

WHAT NOT TO SAY:

★ Let me tell you all about the time this guy *totally* messed up…

★ Hey—I have a photo of you in that bridesmaid dress around here somewhere.

★ That happened *years* ago. You should be over it by now.

★ Quit being so sensitive. This is *funny.*

★ Has anyone else ever been trapped in a laundry chute and had to be pulled out by the fire department—*twice*? No? Well, Jack, looks like you still have the record.

WHAT TO SAY AND **WHAT NOT TO SAY** *continues on page 405…*

Friendship First NEW TESTAMENT

Paul's Gratitude for God's Mercy

¹²I thank Christ Jesus our Lord, who has given me strength to do his work. He considered me trustworthy and appointed me to serve him, ¹³even though I used to blaspheme the name of Christ. In my insolence, I persecuted his people. But God had mercy on me because I did it in ignorance and unbelief. ¹⁴Oh, how generous and gracious our Lord was! He filled me with the faith and love that come from Christ Jesus.

¹⁵This is a trustworthy saying, and everyone should accept it: "Christ Jesus came into the world to save sinners"—and I am the worst of them all. ¹⁶But God had mercy on me so that Christ Jesus could use me as a prime example of his great patience with even the worst sinners. Then others will realize that they, too, can believe in him and receive eternal life. ¹⁷All honor and glory to God forever and ever! He is the eternal King, the unseen one who never dies; he alone is God. Amen.

Timothy's Responsibility

¹⁸Timothy, my son, here are my instructions for you, based on the prophetic words spoken about you earlier. May they help you fight well in the Lord's battles. ¹⁹Cling to your faith in Christ, and keep your conscience clear. For some people have deliberately violated their consciences; as a result, their faith has been shipwrecked. ²⁰Hymenaeus and Alexander are two examples. I threw them out and handed them over to Satan so they might learn not to blaspheme God.

CHAPTER **2**
Instructions about Worship

I urge you, first of all, to pray for all people. Ask God to help them; intercede on their behalf, and give thanks for them. ²Pray this way for kings and all who are in authority so that we can live peaceful and quiet lives marked by godliness and dignity. ³This is good and pleases God our Savior, ⁴who wants everyone to be saved and to understand the truth. ⁵For there is only one God and one Mediator who can reconcile God and humanity—the man Christ Jesus. ⁶He gave his life to purchase freedom for everyone. This is the message God gave to the world at just the right time. ⁷And I have been chosen as a preacher and apostle to teach the Gentiles this message about faith and truth. I'm not exaggerating—just telling the truth.

⁸In every place of worship, I want men to pray with holy hands lifted up to God, free from anger and controversy.

9And I want women to be modest in their appearance.* They should wear decent and appropriate clothing and not draw attention to themselves by the way they fix their hair or by wearing gold or pearls or expensive clothes. 10For women who claim to be devoted to God should make themselves attractive by the good things they do.

11Women should learn quietly and submissively. 12I do not let women teach men or have authority over them.* Let them listen quietly. 13For God made Adam first, and afterward he made Eve. 14And it was not Adam who was deceived by Satan. The woman was deceived, and sin was the result. 15But women will be saved through childbearing,* assuming they continue to live in faith, love, holiness, and modesty.

CHAPTER **3**

Leaders in the Church

This is a trustworthy saying: "If someone aspires to be an elder,* he desires an honorable position." 2So an elder must be a man whose life is above reproach. He must be faithful to his wife.* He must exercise self-control, live wisely, and have a good reputation. He must enjoy having guests in his home, and he must be able to teach. 3He must not be a heavy drinker* or be violent. He must be gentle, not quarrelsome, and not love money. 4He must manage his own family well, having children who respect and obey him. 5For if a man cannot manage his own household, how can he take care of God's church?

6An elder must not be a new believer, because he might become proud, and the devil would cause him to fall.* 7Also, people outside the church must speak well of him so that he will not be disgraced and fall into the devil's trap.

8In the same way, deacons must be well respected and have integrity. They must not be heavy drinkers or dishonest with money. 9They must be committed to the mystery of the faith now revealed and must live with a clear conscience. 10Before they are appointed as deacons, let them be closely examined. If they pass the test, then let them serve as deacons.

11In the same way, their wives* must be respected and must not slander others. They must exercise self-control and be faithful in everything they do.

2:9 Or *to pray in modest apparel.*   **2:12** Or *teach men or usurp their authority.*   **2:15** Or *will be saved by accepting their role as mothers,* or *will be saved by the birth of the Child.*   **3:1** Or *an overseer,* or *a bishop;* also in 3:2, 6.   **3:2** Or *must have only one wife,* or *must be married only once;* Greek reads *must be the husband of one wife;* also in 3:12.   **3:3** Greek *must not drink too much wine;* similarly in 3:8.   **3:6** Or *he might fall into the same judgment as the devil.*   **3:11** Or *the women deacons.* The Greek word can be translated *women* or *wives.*

WHAT TO SAY AND WHAT NOT TO SAY *continued from page 404…*

WHAT TO SAY:

Consider saying these instead…

★ Hey, remember that time you scored the last-second, game-winning shot at our basketball game?

★ Yeah, we all wore some pretty crazy clothes back in those days…but you always looked good.

★ This guy is the master of house projects. If you ever need some work done, he's the man to call.

★ Has anyone else ever won the geography bee two years in a row? No? I told you, she's the *queen* of that stuff!

JOURNAL

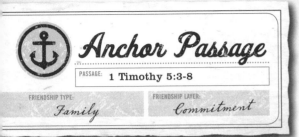

Anchor Passage

PASSAGE: **1 Timothy 5:3-8**

FRIENDSHIP TYPE: *Family*

FRIENDSHIP LAYER: *Commitment*

A Widow's Needs

Read **1 Timothy 5:3-8**.

It's never easy being widowed, but in first-century Palestine, widows were in an especially tough spot.

Women had few rights and even fewer employment opportunities. A widow without a family member to provide for her was often left destitute, with no governmental social-service net to catch her as she sank into bitter poverty.

Paul insisted that, in the church, children and grandchildren of needy widows step up and provide for their elderly relatives.

Family commitment had to stretch further than prayer requests; it needed to cover a place to live, too.

The people of Paul's time might seem hardhearted for leaving widows in distress, but consider these present-day figures: At age 65, 36 percent of American women are already widowed. And the odds that women will live at or below the poverty line? They go up with age. Many widows do no better now than when Paul wrote to Timothy.

And you know what? Those widows are in *your* church, *your* family, *your* neighborhood. What are *you* doing for them?

Anchor Passage continues on page 407...

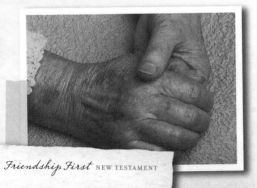

Friendship First NEW TESTAMENT

[12]A deacon must be faithful to his wife, and he must manage his children and household well. [13]Those who do well as deacons will be rewarded with respect from others and will have increased confidence in their faith in Christ Jesus.

The Truths of Our Faith

[14]I am writing these things to you now, even though I hope to be with you soon, [15]so that if I am delayed, you will know how people must conduct themselves in the household of God. This is the church of the living God, which is the pillar and foundation of the truth.

[16]Without question, this is the great mystery of our faith*:

Christ* was revealed in a human body
    and vindicated by the Spirit.*
He was seen by angels
    and announced to the nations.
He was believed in throughout the world
    and taken to heaven in glory.

CHAPTER **4**

Warnings against False Teachers

Now the Holy Spirit tells us clearly that in the last times some will turn away from the true faith; they will follow deceptive spirits and teachings that come from demons. [2]These people are hypocrites and liars, and their consciences are dead.*

[3]They will say it is wrong to be married and wrong to eat certain foods. But God created those foods to be eaten with thanks by faithful people who know the truth. [4]Since everything God created is good, we should not reject any of it but receive it with thanks. [5]For we know it is made acceptable* by the word of God and prayer.

A Good Servant of Christ Jesus

[6]If you explain these things to the brothers and sisters,* Timothy, you will be a worthy servant of Christ Jesus, one who is nourished by the message of faith and the good teaching you have followed. [7]Do not waste time arguing over godless ideas and old wives' tales. Instead, train yourself to be godly. [8]"Physical training is good, but training for godliness is much better, promising benefits in this life and in the life to come." [9]This is a trustworthy saying, and everyone should accept it. [10]This is

3:16a Or *of godliness.*   **3:16b** Greek *He who;* other manuscripts read *God.*   **3:16c** Or *in his spirit.*
4:2 Greek *are seared.*   **4:5** Or *made holy.*   **4:6** Greek *brothers.*

why we work hard and continue to struggle,* for our hope is in the living God, who is the Savior of all people and particularly of all believers.

[11] Teach these things and insist that everyone learn them. [12] Don't let anyone think less of you because you are young. Be an example to all believers in what you say, in the way you live, in your love, your faith, and your purity. [13] Until I get there, focus on reading the Scriptures to the church, encouraging the believers, and teaching them.

[14] Do not neglect the spiritual gift you received through the prophecy spoken over you when the elders of the church laid their hands on you. [15] Give your complete attention to these matters. Throw yourself into your tasks so that everyone will see your progress. [16] Keep a close watch on how you live and on your teaching. Stay true to what is right for the sake of your own salvation and the salvation of those who hear you.

CHAPTER 5

Advice about Widows, Elders, and Slaves

Never speak harshly to an older man,* but appeal to him respectfully as you would to your own father. Talk to younger men as you would to your own brothers. [2] Treat older women as you would your mother, and treat younger women with all purity as you would your own sisters.

[3] Take care of* any widow who has no one else to care for her. [4] But if she has children or grandchildren, their first responsibility is to show godliness at home and repay their parents by taking care of them. This is something that pleases God.

[5] Now a true widow, a woman who is truly alone in this world, has placed her hope in God. She prays night and day, asking God for his help. [6] But the widow who lives only for pleasure is spiritually dead even while she lives. [7] Give these instructions to the church so that no one will be open to criticism.

[8] But those who won't care for their relatives, especially those in their own household, have denied the true faith. Such people are worse than unbelievers. ⚓

4:10 Some manuscripts read *continue to suffer.*   5:1 Or *an elder.*   5:3 Or *Honor.*

Anchor Passage continued from page 406...

Experience

Ask the widows in your family some hard questions. How are they *really* doing? Many want to appear independent, so they don't reveal how tough life truly is for them.

Ask: Do you have enough money? How can I help you financially—with prescriptions, with the house payment, with anything? When is it the toughest for you? How can I be a companion for you when you're lonely?

Then select a need those widows feel, and meet it. Expensive? Maybe. Demanding? Perhaps. But the right thing to do? Absolutely. (And in the end, you'll have an invaluable friend.)

If you don't have any widows in your family, think of other people in your family who are in need. Paul called us to commit to our families, for better or for worse. How can you help those in your family who need it?

Reflect

★ Why are we so willing to let people quietly suffer?

★ What are the limits on your commitment to your family? Who qualifies for practical help, and what's the outside edge of your giving?

★ If you were elderly and alone, who would you call on for help?

DIGGING DEEPER

FRIENDSHIP TYPE:
Family

FRIENDSHIP LAYER:
Commitment

For committing to your friendship with family, check out...

➡ The Friendship Experience .... on page 409
➡ The Friendship Story .... on page 441
➡ What to Say and What Not to Say .... on page 404

Among members who say they **feel valued and respected** for what they contribute to the church community, **69% attend church weekly** and another **21%** attend almost every week.

—from "Friendship and Faith," a Gallup Research Study Commissioned by Group Publishing, Inc.

JOURNAL

9A widow who is put on the list for support must be a woman who is at least sixty years old and was faithful to her husband.* 10She must be well respected by everyone because of the good she has done. Has she brought up her children well? Has she been kind to strangers and served other believers humbly?* Has she helped those who are in trouble? Has she always been ready to do good?

11The younger widows should not be on the list, because their physical desires will overpower their devotion to Christ and they will want to remarry. 12Then they would be guilty of breaking their previous pledge. 13And if they are on the list, they will learn to be lazy and will spend their time gossiping from house to house, meddling in other people's business and talking about things they shouldn't. 14So I advise these younger widows to marry again, have children, and take care of their own homes. Then the enemy will not be able to say anything against them. 15For I am afraid that some of them have already gone astray and now follow Satan.

16If a woman who is a believer has relatives who are widows, she must take care of them and not put the responsibility on the church. Then the church can care for the widows who are truly alone.

17Elders who do their work well should be respected and paid well,* especially those who work hard at both preaching and teaching. 18For the Scripture says, "You must not muzzle an ox to keep it from eating as it treads out the grain." And in another place, "Those who work deserve their pay!"*

19Do not listen to an accusation against an elder unless it is confirmed by two or three witnesses. 20Those who sin should be reprimanded in front of the whole church; this will serve as a strong warning to others.

21I solemnly command you in the presence of God and Christ Jesus and the holy angels to obey these instructions without taking sides or showing favoritism to anyone.

22Never be in a hurry about appointing a church leader.* Do not share in the sins of others. Keep yourself pure.

23Don't drink only water. You ought to drink a little wine for the sake of your stomach because you are sick so often.

24Remember, the sins of some people are obvious, leading them to certain judgment. But there are others whose sins will not be revealed until later. 25In the same way, the good deeds

5:9 Greek *was the wife of one husband.*   5:10 Greek *and washed the feet of God's holy people?* 5:17 Greek *should be worthy of double honor.*   5:18 Deut 25:4; Luke 10:7.   5:22 Greek *about the laying on of hands.*

of some people are obvious. And the good deeds done in secret will someday come to light.

CHAPTER 6

All slaves should show full respect for their masters so they will not bring shame on the name of God and his teaching. [2]If the masters are believers, that is no excuse for being disrespectful. Those slaves should work all the harder because their efforts are helping other believers* who are well loved.

False Teaching and True Riches

Teach these things, Timothy, and encourage everyone to obey them. [3]Some people may contradict our teaching, but these are the wholesome teachings of the Lord Jesus Christ. These teachings promote a godly life. [4]Anyone who teaches something different is arrogant and lacks understanding. Such a person has an unhealthy desire to quibble over the meaning of words. This stirs up arguments ending in jealousy, division, slander, and evil suspicions. [5]These people always cause trouble. Their minds are corrupt, and they have turned their backs on the truth. To them, a show of godliness is just a way to become wealthy.

[6]Yet true godliness with contentment is itself great wealth. [7]After all, we brought nothing with us when we came into the world, and we can't take anything with us when we leave it. [8]So if we have enough food and clothing, let us be content.

[9]But people who long to be rich fall into temptation and are trapped by many foolish and harmful desires that plunge them into ruin and destruction. [10]For the love of money is the root of all kinds of evil. And some people, craving money, have wandered from the true faith and pierced themselves with many sorrows.

Paul's Final Instructions

[11]But you, Timothy, are a man of God; so run from all these evil things. Pursue righteousness and a godly life, along with faith, love, perseverance, and gentleness. [12]Fight the good fight for the true faith. Hold tightly to the eternal life to which God has called you, which you have confessed so well before many witnesses. [13]And I charge you before God, who gives life to all, and before Christ Jesus, who gave a good testimony before Pontius Pilate, [14]that you obey this command without wavering. Then no one can find fault with you from now until our

6:2 Greek *brothers.*

FRIENDSHIP
EXPERIENCE

FRIENDSHIP TYPE: *Family*   FRIENDSHIP LAYER: *Commitment*

If <u>Only</u> You Could Pick Your Family...

You've picked your friends, and you've done well. They're people you like. People who like you. People who are doing well.

But then there's your family.

Uncles who need loans. Step-brothers who think *headlock* and *hug* are interchangeable. A grandmother who has morphed into a needy widow, and you're looking down the barrel of having to help her pay rent.

Like this is *fair*? Like you *chose* these people?

Maybe you didn't choose your family members before, but you *can* choose them now.

This week decide to commit yourself to loving your family members, even if they're needy, even if it's going to cost you something to be in relationship with them.

Because no matter how uncomfortable or expensive it is to be there for your family, it's costing less than the price tag God paid to be there for you. Read **John 3:16**, and then ask yourself: Is helping Grandma so bad?

FRIENDSHIP EXPERIENCE *continues on page 410...*

Friendship First NEW TESTAMENT

FRIENDSHIP EXPERIENCE *continued from page 409...*

Experience

Look at a family member through fresh eyes.

We tend to see our family members at their worst and not notice when they're at their best, their most giving, their most caring.

Pick up the phone, and interview a few friends of a family member. Ask what those friends like about your relative. Let those opinions soften your sometimes harsh evaluations and give you new insight and appreciation. (And do it while the family member is alive. Sometimes, sadly, people only bother to find out these things at funerals.)

Now use that fresh insight as inspiration for serving that person. How can you serve your family member? With money? With time? With acts of service?

Reflect

★ Jot down your family members' names. Beside each, write what unique gifts God has given that person.

★ How can you praise and encourage those gifts in your family members? (And when will you do that?)

Lord Jesus Christ comes again. [15] For at just the right time Christ will be revealed from heaven by the blessed and only almighty God, the King of all kings and Lord of all lords. [16] He alone can never die, and he lives in light so brilliant that no human can approach him. No human eye has ever seen him, nor ever will. All honor and power to him forever! Amen.

[17] Teach those who are rich in this world not to be proud and not to trust in their money, which is so unreliable. Their trust should be in God, who richly gives us all we need for our enjoyment. [18] Tell them to use their money to do good. They should be rich in good works and generous to those in need, always being ready to share with others. [19] By doing this they will be storing up their treasure as a good foundation for the future so that they may experience true life.

[20] Timothy, guard what God has entrusted to you. Avoid godless, foolish discussions with those who oppose you with their so-called knowledge. [21] Some people have wandered from the faith by following such foolishness.

May God's grace be with you all.

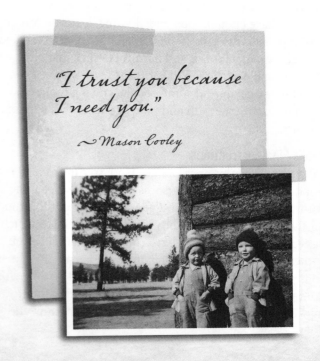

"I trust you because I need you."

~ Mason Cooley

2 Timothy

AUTHOR:	DATE WRITTEN:
Paul	Approximately A.D. 66 or 67

CHAPTER 1

Greetings from Paul

This letter is from Paul, chosen by the will of God to be an apostle of Christ Jesus. I have been sent out to tell others about the life he has promised through faith in Christ Jesus.

²I am writing to Timothy, my dear son.

May God the Father and Christ Jesus our Lord give you grace, mercy, and peace.

Encouragement to Be Faithful

³Timothy, I thank God for you—the God I serve with a clear conscience, just as my ancestors did. Night and day I constantly remember you in my prayers. ⁴I long to see you again, for I remember your tears as we parted. And I will be filled with joy when we are together again.

⁵I remember your genuine faith, for you share the faith that first filled your grandmother Lois and your mother, Eunice. And I know that same faith continues strong in you. ⁶This is why I remind you to fan into flames the spiritual gift God gave you when I laid my hands on you. ⁷For God has not given us a spirit of fear and timidity, but of power, love, and self-discipline. ⚓

⁸So never be ashamed to tell others about our Lord. And don't be ashamed of me, either, even though I'm in prison for him. With the strength God gives you, be ready to suffer with me for the sake of the Good News. ⁹For God saved us

Anchor Passage

PASSAGE: 2 Timothy 1:5-7

FRIENDSHIP TYPE: Family

FRIENDSHIP LAYER: Getting Acquainted

A Legacy of Faith

Whether you realize it or not, your family has a heritage of faith. For good or bad, your parents, grandparents, and the generations before them passed on spiritual traditions and beliefs that affect you even today. What's the legacy of faith in your family? How has each person in your family shaped what you believe?

Read **2 Timothy 1:5-7**.

Timothy came from a family of strong Christian faith. Paul knew there was something special about Timothy's mother and grandmother. Their dedication to God laid a great foundation for Timothy to build on.

But even with strong spiritual heroes such as Lois and Eunice, Timothy was encouraged to use his own spiritual gifts—to "fan the flames" of what God had given him. Regardless of our family's spiritual past, God wants each of us to create a legacy of faith for our future generations.

Anchor Passage continues on page 412...

Anchor Passage continued from page 411...

Perhaps the best place for you to start is to get acquainted with your own family. Where did they come from? What did they do for a living? What events or circumstances impacted them? How did faith influence their lives? The more you can learn about how God worked in the lives of your parents and ancestors, the more you'll understand the plans and purposes God has for the fruit that grows from your family tree.

Experience

THE ONE THING YOU CAN DO THIS WEEK — 1

Make a quick list of your family's traditions. Maybe there's something special in the way you celebrate birthdays or holidays. Perhaps certain members of your family always talk about "that summer at the lake," or maybe your dad's side of the family always makes cornbread dressing instead of bread dressing. Take a few minutes to write down all the things that come to mind.

Call the oldest living person in your family, and ask how those traditions got started. Talk about how faith had an influence in those traditions. If the person doesn't believe faith played a part in your family traditions, ask how things might have been different if faith had played a role. (And, if possible, record your conversation!)

Anchor Passage continues on page 413...

and called us to live a holy life. He did this, not because we deserved it, but because that was his plan from before the beginning of time—to show us his grace through Christ Jesus. ¹⁰And now he has made all of this plain to us by the appearing of Christ Jesus, our Savior. He broke the power of death and illuminated the way to life and immortality through the Good News. ¹¹And God chose me to be a preacher, an apostle, and a teacher of this Good News.

¹²That is why I am suffering here in prison. But I am not ashamed of it, for I know the one in whom I trust, and I am sure that he is able to guard what I have entrusted to him* until the day of his return.

¹³Hold on to the pattern of wholesome teaching you learned from me—a pattern shaped by the faith and love that you have in Christ Jesus. ¹⁴Through the power of the Holy Spirit who lives within us, carefully guard the precious truth that has been entrusted to you.

¹⁵As you know, everyone from the province of Asia has deserted me—even Phygelus and Hermogenes.

¹⁶May the Lord show special kindness to Onesiphorus and all his family because he often visited and encouraged me. He was never ashamed of me because I was in chains. ¹⁷When he came to Rome, he searched everywhere until he found me. ¹⁸May the Lord show him special kindness on the day of Christ's return. And you know very well how helpful he was in Ephesus.

CHAPTER 2

A Good Soldier of Christ Jesus

Timothy, my dear son, be strong through the grace that God gives you in Christ Jesus. ²You have heard me teach things that have been confirmed by many reliable witnesses. Now teach these truths to other trustworthy people who will be able to pass them on to others.

³Endure suffering along with me, as a good soldier of Christ Jesus. ⁴Soldiers don't get tied up in the affairs of civilian life, for then they cannot please the officer who enlisted them. ⁵And athletes cannot win the prize unless they follow the rules. ⁶And hardworking farmers should be the first to enjoy the fruit of their labor. ⁷Think about what I am saying. The Lord will help you understand all these things.

⁸Always remember that Jesus Christ, a descendant of King David, was raised from the dead. This is the Good News I

1:12 Or *what has been entrusted to me.*

preach. [9]And because I preach this Good News, I am suffering and have been chained like a criminal. But the word of God cannot be chained. [10]So I am willing to endure anything if it will bring salvation and eternal glory in Christ Jesus to those God has chosen.

[11]This is a trustworthy saying:

If we die with him,
    we will also live with him.
[12] If we endure hardship,
    we will reign with him.
If we deny him,
    he will deny us.
[13] If we are unfaithful,
    he remains faithful,
        for he cannot deny who he is.

[14]Remind everyone about these things, and command them in God's presence to stop fighting over words. Such arguments are useless, and they can ruin those who hear them.

An Approved Worker

[15]Work hard so you can present yourself to God and receive his approval. Be a good worker, one who does not need to be ashamed and who correctly explains the word of truth. [16]Avoid worthless, foolish talk that only leads to more godless behavior. [17]This kind of talk spreads like cancer, as in the case of Hymenaeus and Philetus. [18]They have left the path of truth, claiming that the resurrection of the dead has already occurred; in this way, they have turned some people away from the faith.

[19]But God's truth stands firm like a foundation stone with this inscription: "The LORD knows those who are his,"* and "All who belong to the LORD must turn away from evil."*

[20]In a wealthy home some utensils are made of gold and silver, and some are made of wood and clay. The expensive utensils are used for special occasions, and the cheap ones are for everyday use. [21]If you keep yourself pure, you will be a special utensil for honorable use. Your life will be clean, and you will be ready for the Master to use you for every good work.

[22]Run from anything that stimulates youthful lusts. Instead, pursue righteous living, faithfulness, love, and peace. Enjoy the companionship of those who call on the Lord with pure hearts.

2:19a Num 16:5.   2:19b See Isa 52:11.

Anchor Passage continued from page 412...

Reflect

★ Why do you think Paul made a point of reminding Timothy of his family's legacy of faith?

★ What legacy of faith do you hope to pass along to your children and grandchildren?

★ What's one thing you can do now that will empower you to pass a strong faith to your grandchildren?

DIGGING DEEPER

FRIENDSHIP TYPE:
Family

FRIENDSHIP LAYER:
Getting Acquainted

For being a companion of your neighbors, find...

➡ The Friendship Experience .... on page 415
➡ The Friendship Story .... on page 471
➡ What to Say and What Not to Say .... on page 467

JOURNAL

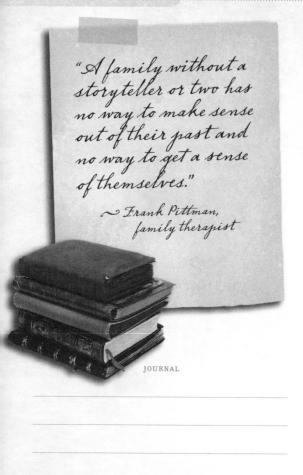

"A family without a storyteller or two has no way to make sense out of their past and no way to get a sense of themselves."

~ *Frank Pittman, family therapist*

JOURNAL

23 Again I say, don't get involved in foolish, ignorant arguments that only start fights. 24 A servant of the Lord must not quarrel but must be kind to everyone, be able to teach, and be patient with difficult people. 25 Gently instruct those who oppose the truth. Perhaps God will change those people's hearts, and they will learn the truth. 26 Then they will come to their senses and escape from the devil's trap. For they have been held captive by him to do whatever he wants.

CHAPTER 3

The Dangers of the Last Days

You should know this, Timothy, that in the last days there will be very difficult times. 2 For people will love only themselves and their money. They will be boastful and proud, scoffing at God, disobedient to their parents, and ungrateful. They will consider nothing sacred. 3 They will be unloving and unforgiving; they will slander others and have no self-control. They will be cruel and hate what is good. 4 They will betray their friends, be reckless, be puffed up with pride, and love pleasure rather than God. 5 They will act religious, but they will reject the power that could make them godly. Stay away from people like that!

6 They are the kind who work their way into people's homes and win the confidence of* vulnerable women who are burdened with the guilt of sin and controlled by various desires. 7 (Such women are forever following new teachings, but they are never able to understand the truth.) 8 These teachers oppose the truth just as Jannes and Jambres opposed Moses. They have depraved minds and a counterfeit faith. 9 But they won't get away with this for long. Someday everyone will recognize what fools they are, just as with Jannes and Jambres.

Paul's Charge to Timothy

10 But you, Timothy, certainly know what I teach, and how I live, and what my purpose in life is. You know my faith, my patience, my love, and my endurance. 11 You know how much persecution and suffering I have endured. You know all about how I was persecuted in Antioch, Iconium, and Lystra—but the Lord rescued me from all of it. 12 Yes, and everyone who wants to live a godly life in Christ Jesus will suffer persecution. 13 But evil people and impostors will flourish. They will deceive others and will themselves be deceived.

14 But you must remain faithful to the things you have been

3:6 Greek *and take captive.*

taught. You know they are true, for you know you can trust those who taught you. ¹⁵You have been taught the holy Scriptures from childhood, and they have given you the wisdom to receive the salvation that comes by trusting in Christ Jesus. ¹⁶All Scripture is inspired by God and is useful to teach us what is true and to make us realize what is wrong in our lives. It corrects us when we are wrong and teaches us to do what is right. ¹⁷God uses it to prepare and equip his people to do every good work.

CHAPTER **4**

I solemnly urge you in the presence of God and Christ Jesus, who will someday judge the living and the dead when he appears to set up his Kingdom: ²Preach the word of God. Be prepared, whether the time is favorable or not. Patiently correct, rebuke, and encourage your people with good teaching.

³For a time is coming when people will no longer listen to sound and wholesome teaching. They will follow their own desires and will look for teachers who will tell them whatever their itching ears want to hear. ⁴They will reject the truth and chase after myths.

⁵But you should keep a clear mind in every situation. Don't be afraid of suffering for the Lord. Work at telling others the Good News, and fully carry out the ministry God has given you.

⁶As for me, my life has already been poured out as an offering to God. The time of my death is near. ⁷I have fought the good fight, I have finished the race, and I have remained faithful. ⁸And now the prize awaits me—the crown of righteousness, which the Lord, the righteous Judge, will give me on the day of his return. And the prize is not just for me but for all who eagerly look forward to his appearing.

Paul's Final Words

⁹Timothy, please come as soon as you can. ¹⁰Demas has deserted me because he loves the things of this life and has gone to Thessalonica. Crescens has gone to Galatia, and Titus has gone to Dalmatia. ¹¹Only Luke is with me. Bring Mark with you when you come, for he will be helpful to me in my ministry. ¹²I sent Tychicus to Ephesus. ¹³When you come, be sure to bring the coat I left with Carpus at Troas. Also bring my books, and especially my papers.*

4:13 Greek *especially the parchments.*

FRIENDSHIP EXPERIENCE

FRIENDSHIP TYPE: *Family*   FRIENDSHIP LAYER: *Getting Acquainted*

A Visual Legacy

No family is perfect. No family has it all figured out. But every family has its strengths, and every family has a set of values and a legacy to draw from. And yet few families actually take the time to "get acquainted" with those values and to understand where the family has come from.

Second Timothy 1:5-7 shows us that Timothy was well-acquainted with the legacy of his mother and grandmother's faith, and we can learn something from that. Understanding our family's heritage of faith is an important part of strengthening our own spiritual lives and passing that faith on to future generations.

So don't let your family's faith—or it's heritage—go unnoticed in your family. Take time to understand it and to celebrate it.

Experience

THE ONE THING **1** YOU CAN DO THIS WEEK

Create a "coat of arms" that represents your family's faith. With markers, draw on poster board the outline of a coat of arms. Gather your family, and talk about the things you value most. What makes your family special? What makes you strong? What spiritual gifts do the members of your family have?

FRIENDSHIP EXPERIENCE *continues on page 416…*

FRIENDSHIP EXPERIENCE *continued from page 415...*

On the bottom two-thirds of the coat of arms, draw an image that represents your family's faith in God. Maybe an apple symbolizes your desire to bear fruit for God. Or perhaps a dog represents your family's loyalty. Along the top of the coat of arms, have each family member draw one thing that represents his or her own special contribution to the family. Be creative. Use colors. Find visual ways to represent your family's legacy of faith.

Put your coat of arms in a visible place (such as your mantle or refrigerator), and pray together that God will guide your family as you continue to grow together. Thank God for the rich symbols of faith he has brought into your lives.

Reflect

★ How does understanding your family's strengths build your faith?

★ How is getting acquainted with your family's faith heritage like getting to know God?

★ How can you ensure faith in your family's future?

14Alexander the coppersmith did me much harm, but the Lord will judge him for what he has done. 15Be careful of him, for he fought against everything we said.

16The first time I was brought before the judge, no one came with me. Everyone abandoned me. May it not be counted against them. 17But the Lord stood with me and gave me strength so that I might preach the Good News in its entirety for all the Gentiles to hear. And he rescued me from certain death.* 18Yes, and the Lord will deliver me from every evil attack and will bring me safely into his heavenly Kingdom. All glory to God forever and ever! Amen.

Paul's Final Greetings

19Give my greetings to Priscilla and Aquila and those living in the household of Onesiphorus. 20Erastus stayed at Corinth, and I left Trophimus sick at Miletus.

21Do your best to get here before winter. Eubulus sends you greetings, and so do Pudens, Linus, Claudia, and all the brothers and sisters.*

22May the Lord be with your spirit. And may his grace be with all of you.

4:17 Greek *from the mouth of a lion.*   **4:21** Greek *brothers.*

Titus

AUTHOR:	DATE WRITTEN:
Paul	Approximately A.D. 64

JOURNAL

CHAPTER **1**

Greetings from Paul

This letter is from Paul, a slave of God and an apostle of Jesus Christ. I have been sent to proclaim faith to* those God has chosen and to teach them to know the truth that shows them how to live godly lives. ²This truth gives them confidence that they have eternal life, which God—who does not lie—promised them before the world began. ³And now at just the right time he has revealed this message, which we announce to everyone. It is by the command of God our Savior that I have been entrusted with this work for him.

⁴I am writing to Titus, my true son in the faith that we share.

May God the Father and Christ Jesus our Savior give you grace and peace.

Titus's Work in Crete

⁵I left you on the island of Crete so you could complete our work there and appoint elders in each town as I instructed you. ⁶An elder must live a blameless life. He must be faithful to his wife,* and his children must be believers who don't have a reputation for being wild or rebellious. ⁷For an elder* must live a blameless life. He must not be arrogant or quick-tempered; he must not be a heavy drinker,* violent, or dishonest with money.

⁸Rather, he must enjoy having guests in his home, and he must love what is good. He must live wisely and be just. He must live a devout and disciplined life. ⁹He must have a strong belief in the trustworthy message he was taught; then he will be able to encourage others with wholesome teaching and show those who oppose it where they are wrong.

¹⁰For there are many rebellious people who engage in useless

1:1 Or *to strengthen the faith of.*   1:6 Or *must have only one wife,* or *must be married only once;* Greek reads *must be the husband of one wife.*   1:7a Or *an overseer,* or *a bishop.*   1:7b Greek *must not drink too much wine.*

WHAT TO SAY
AND
WHAT NOT TO SAY

FRIENDSHIP TYPE:
Hard-to-Love People

FRIENDSHIP LAYER:
Acceptance

"Gut Check in Aisle 9…"

The Scene: You're shopping alone at the grocery store. You're paying so much attention to the cereal choices that you don't notice that weird person from work walking up to you. It's the person everyone avoids—the one who can't tell the difference between an appropriate joke and a pencil. The person from your office seems a bit confused and asks you, with rather colorful language, how to make a dessert for a special dinner.

WHAT NOT TO SAY:

★ "I'd really prefer that you didn't use foul language around me…"

★ "I'm a Christian, and the Bible says cursing is a sin…"

★ "What would your mother say if she heard you talking like that?"

★ "Before you start thinking about treating your mouth to a dessert, maybe you should wash it out with soap first…"

WHAT TO SAY AND **WHAT NOT TO SAY** *continues on page 419…*

talk and deceive others. This is especially true of those who insist on circumcision for salvation. [11] They must be silenced, because they are turning whole families away from the truth by their false teaching. And they do it only for money. [12] Even one of their own men, a prophet from Crete, has said about them, "The people of Crete are all liars, cruel animals, and lazy gluttons."* [13] This is true. So reprimand them sternly to make them strong in the faith. [14] They must stop listening to Jewish myths and the commands of people who have turned away from the truth.

[15] Everything is pure to those whose hearts are pure. But nothing is pure to those who are corrupt and unbelieving, because their minds and consciences are corrupted. [16] Such people claim they know God, but they deny him by the way they live. They are detestable and disobedient, worthless for doing anything good.

CHAPTER **2**
Promote Right Teaching

As for you, Titus, promote the kind of living that reflects wholesome teaching. [2] Teach the older men to exercise self-control, to be worthy of respect, and to live wisely. They must have sound faith and be filled with love and patience.

[3] Similarly, teach the older women to live in a way that honors God. They must not slander others or be heavy drinkers.* Instead, they should teach others what is good. [4] These older women must train the younger women to love their husbands and their children, [5] to live wisely and be pure, to work in their homes,* to do good, and to be submissive to their husbands. Then they will not bring shame on the word of God.

[6] In the same way, encourage the young men to live wisely. [7] And you yourself must be an example to them by doing good works of every kind. Let everything you do reflect the integrity and seriousness of your teaching. [8] Teach the truth so that your teaching can't be criticized. Then those who oppose us will be ashamed and have nothing bad to say about us.

[9] Slaves must always obey their masters and do their best to please them. They must not talk back [10] or steal, but must show themselves to be entirely trustworthy and good. Then they will make the teaching about God our Savior attractive in every way. [11] For the grace of God has been revealed, bringing salvation to

1:12 This quotation is from Epimenides of Knossos.   2:3 Greek *be enslaved to much wine.*
2:5 Some manuscripts read *to care for their homes.*

all people. [12]And we are instructed to turn from godless living and sinful pleasures. We should live in this evil world with wisdom, righteousness, and devotion to God, [13]while we look forward with hope to that wonderful day when the glory of our great God and Savior, Jesus Christ, will be revealed. [14]He gave his life to free us from every kind of sin, to cleanse us, and to make us his very own people, totally committed to doing good deeds.

[15]You must teach these things and encourage the believers to do them. You have the authority to correct them when necessary, so don't let anyone disregard what you say.

CHAPTER **3**

Do What Is Good

Remind the believers to submit to the government and its officers. They should be obedient, always ready to do what is good. [2]They must not slander anyone and must avoid quarreling. Instead, they should be gentle and show true humility to everyone.

[3]Once we, too, were foolish and disobedient. We were misled and became slaves to many lusts and pleasures. Our lives were full of evil and envy, and we hated each other.

[4]But—"When God our Savior revealed his kindness and love, [5]he saved us, not because of the righteous things we had done, but because of his mercy. He washed away our sins, giving us a new birth and new life through the Holy Spirit.* [6]He generously poured out the Spirit upon us through Jesus Christ our Savior. [7]Because of his grace he declared us righteous and gave us confidence that we will inherit eternal life." [8]This is a trustworthy saying, and I want you to insist on these teachings so that all who trust in God will devote themselves to doing good. These teachings are good and beneficial for everyone.

[9]Do not get involved in foolish discussions about spiritual pedigrees* or in quarrels and fights about obedience to Jewish laws. These things are useless and a waste of time. [10]If people are causing divisions among you, give a first and second warning. After that, have nothing more to do with them. [11]For people like that have turned away from the truth, and their own sins condemn them.

Paul's Final Remarks and Greetings

[12]I am planning to send either Artemas or Tychicus to you. As soon as one of them arrives, do your best to meet me at

3:5 Greek *He saved us through the washing of regeneration and renewing of the Holy Spirit.*
3:9 Or *spiritual genealogies.*

WHAT TO SAY AND **WHAT NOT TO SAY** *continued from page 418...*

WHAT TO SAY:

★ "Well, I know a dessert that always works for my family. Do you like chocolate?"
★ "You should join us in the lunchroom next week. We like to swap recipes…"
★ "I'm not very good at making desserts, but you can never go wrong with cheesecake…"

Remember the importance of accepting people who are hard to love. Perhaps that person has sensed something about you to trust. Maybe the person knows you are a Christian. No matter the circumstances, you have a perfect opportunity to show Jesus' love through a very simple gesture such as taking a couple of minutes to walk down another aisle and point out a box of cake mix.

Even if you're in a hurry or it makes you cringe to hear people use foul language, a little grace and a smile can go a long way in showing acceptance to a person who may not otherwise get much.

The example of Saul in **Acts 9:19b-28** is a perfect one. No one could have been harder for a Christian to love than Saul. If anyone would have met Saul in the grocery store, he or she probably would have dropped the cereal and run screaming. But not Barnabas. He knew Saul had a bad reputation. But he also knew that if Jesus could love and accept Saul, then he could do the same.

JOURNAL

Nicopolis, for I have decided to stay there for the winter. [13]Do everything you can to help Zenas the lawyer and Apollos with their trip. See that they are given everything they need. [14]Our people must learn to do good by meeting the urgent needs of others; then they will not be unproductive.

[15]Everybody here sends greetings. Please give my greetings to the believers—all who love us.

May God's grace be with you all.

"An honest answer is like a kiss of friendship."

~ *Proverbs 24:26*

Philemon

AUTHOR:	DATE WRITTEN:
Paul	Approximately A.D. 60

Greetings from Paul

This letter is from Paul, a prisoner for preaching the Good News about Christ Jesus, and from our brother Timothy.

I am writing to Philemon, our beloved co-worker, ²and to our sister Apphia, and to our fellow soldier Archippus, and to the church that meets in your* house.

³May God our Father and the Lord Jesus Christ give you grace and peace.

Paul's Thanksgiving and Prayer

⁴I always thank my God when I pray for you, Philemon, ⁵because I keep hearing about your faith in the Lord Jesus and your love for all of God's people. ⁶And I am praying that you will put into action the generosity that comes from your faith as you understand and experience all the good things we have in Christ. ⁷Your love has given me much joy and comfort, my brother, for your kindness has often refreshed the hearts of God's people.

Paul's Appeal for Onesimus

⁸That is why I am boldly asking a favor of you. I could demand it in the name of Christ because it is the right thing for you to do. ⁹But because of our love, I prefer simply to ask you. Consider this as a request from me—Paul, an old man and now also a prisoner for the sake of Christ Jesus.*

¹⁰I appeal to you to show kindness to my child, Onesimus. I became his father in the faith while here in prison. ¹¹Onesimus* hasn't been of much use to you in the past, but now he is very useful to both of us. ¹²I am sending him back to you, and with him comes my own heart.

¹³I wanted to keep him here with me while I am in these

2 Throughout this letter, *you* and *your* are singular except in verses 3, 22, and 25.   **9** Or *a prisoner of Christ Jesus.*   **11** *Onesimus* means "useful."

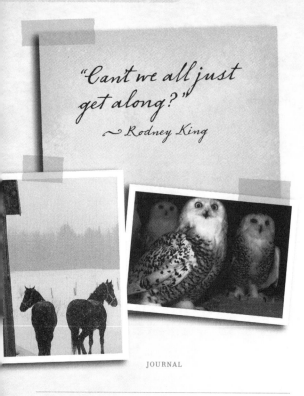

"Can't we all just get along?"
~ Rodney King

JOURNAL

chains for preaching the Good News, and he would have helped me on your behalf. ¹⁴But I didn't want to do anything without your consent. I wanted you to help because you were willing, not because you were forced. ¹⁵It seems you lost Onesimus for a little while so that you could have him back forever. ¹⁶He is no longer like a slave to you. He is more than a slave, for he is a beloved brother, especially to me. Now he will mean much more to you, both as a man and as a brother in the Lord.

¹⁷So if you consider me your partner, welcome him as you would welcome me. ¹⁸If he has wronged you in any way or owes you anything, charge it to me. ¹⁹I, PAUL, WRITE THIS WITH MY OWN HAND: I WILL REPAY IT. AND I WON'T MENTION THAT YOU OWE ME YOUR VERY SOUL!

²⁰Yes, my brother, please do me this favor* for the Lord's sake. Give me this encouragement in Christ.

²¹I am confident as I write this letter that you will do what I ask and even more! ²²One more thing—please prepare a guest room for me, for I am hoping that God will answer your prayers and let me return to you soon.

Paul's Final Greetings

²³Epaphras, my fellow prisoner in Christ Jesus, sends you his greetings. ²⁴So do Mark, Aristarchus, Demas, and Luke, my co-workers.

²⁵May the grace of the Lord Jesus Christ be with your spirit.

20 Greek *onaimen,* a play on the name Onesimus.

Hebrews

AUTHOR:	DATE WRITTEN:
Undetermined	Probably before A.D. 70

CHAPTER 1

Jesus Christ Is God's Son

Long ago God spoke many times and in many ways to our ancestors through the prophets. ²And now in these final days, he has spoken to us through his Son. God promised everything to the Son as an inheritance, and through the Son he created the universe. ³The Son radiates God's own glory and expresses the very character of God, and he sustains everything by the mighty power of his command. When he had cleansed us from our sins, he sat down in the place of honor at the right hand of the majestic God in heaven. ⁴This shows that the Son is far greater than the angels, just as the name God gave him is greater than their names.

The Son Is Greater Than the Angels

⁵For God never said to any angel what he said to Jesus:

"You are my Son.
    Today I have become your Father.*"

God also said,

"I will be his Father,
    and he will be my Son."*

⁶And when he brought his firstborn Son into the world, God said,*

"Let all of God's angels worship him."*

⁷Regarding the angels, he says,

"He sends his angels like the winds,
    his servants like flames of fire."*

1:5a Or *Today I reveal you as my Son.* Ps 2:7.   1:5b 2 Sam 7:14.   1:6a Or *when he again brings his firstborn son into the world, God will say.*   1:6b Deut 32:43.   1:7 Ps 104:4 (Greek version).

8 But to the Son he says,

> "Your throne, O God, endures forever and ever.
>   You rule with a scepter of justice.
> 9 You love justice and hate evil.
>   Therefore, O God, your God has anointed you,
>   pouring out the oil of joy on you more than on
>   anyone else."*

10 He also says to the Son,

> "In the beginning, Lord, you laid the foundation of the earth
>   and made the heavens with your hands.
> 11 They will perish, but you remain forever.
>   They will wear out like old clothing.
> 12 You will fold them up like a cloak
>   and discard them like old clothing.
> But you are always the same;
>   you will live forever."*

13 And God never said to any of the angels,

> "Sit in the place of honor at my right hand
>   until I humble your enemies,
>   making them a footstool under your feet."*

14 Therefore, angels are only servants—spirits sent to care for people who will inherit salvation.

CHAPTER 2

A Warning against Drifting Away

So we must listen very carefully to the truth we have heard, or we may drift away from it. 2 For the message God delivered through angels has always stood firm, and every violation of the law and every act of disobedience was punished. 3 So what makes us think we can escape if we ignore this great salvation that was first announced by the Lord Jesus himself and then delivered to us by those who heard him speak? 4 And God confirmed the message by giving signs and wonders and various miracles and gifts of the Holy Spirit whenever he chose.

Jesus, the Man

5 And furthermore, it is not angels who will control the future world we are talking about. 6 For in one place the Scriptures say,

1:8-9 Ps 45:6-7.   1:10-12 Ps 102:25-27.   1:13 Ps 110:1.

"What are mere mortals that you should think
about them,
or a son of man* that you should care for him?
⁷ Yet you made them only a little lower than the angels
and crowned them with glory and honor.*
⁸ You gave them authority over all things."*

Now when it says "all things," it means nothing is left out.
But we have not yet seen all things put under their authority.
⁹What we do see is Jesus, who was given a position "a little
lower than the angels"; and because he suffered death for us,
he is now "crowned with glory and honor." Yes, by God's
grace, Jesus tasted death for everyone. ¹⁰God, for whom and
through whom everything was made, chose to bring many
children into glory. And it was only right that he should make
Jesus, through his suffering, a perfect leader, fit to bring them
into their salvation.

¹¹So now Jesus and the ones he makes holy have the same
Father. That is why Jesus is not ashamed to call them his
brothers and sisters.* ¹²For he said to God,

"I will proclaim your name to my brothers and sisters.
I will praise you among your assembled people."*

¹³He also said,

"I will put my trust in him,"
that is, "I and the children God has given me."*

¹⁴Because God's children are human beings—made of flesh
and blood—the Son also became flesh and blood. For only as
a human being could he die, and only by dying could he break
the power of the devil, who had* the power of death. ¹⁵Only
in this way could he set free all who have lived their lives as
slaves to the fear of dying.

¹⁶We also know that the Son did not come to help angels;
he came to help the descendants of Abraham. ¹⁷Therefore,
it was necessary for him to be made in every respect like us,
his brothers and sisters,* so that he could be our merciful
and faithful High Priest before God. Then he could offer a
sacrifice that would take away the sins of the people. ¹⁸Since
he himself has gone through suffering and testing, he is able
to help us when we are being tested.

2:6 Or *the Son of Man.*   2:7 Some manuscripts add *You gave them charge of everything you made.*
2:6-8 Ps 8:4-6 (Greek version).   2:11 Greek *brothers;* also in 2:12.   2:12 Ps 22:22.   2:13 Isa 8:17-18.
2:14 Or *has.*   2:17 Greek *like the brothers.*

No. 21-FA-425

FRIENDSHIP STORY

FRIENDSHIP TYPE: *Jesus*   FRIENDSHIP LAYER: *Getting Acquainted*

FROM THE ARCHIVES

A Passionate Mother

Imagine bearing 19 children in 21 years, burying
nine of those children in childhood, having neighbors
who thought so much of you that they set your house
on fire, and having to make ends meet while your
husband is in debtor's prison.

Such was the not-so-easy life of Susanna Wesley.

She was a church mouse—poor preacher's wife
during a time of great turmoil within the church.
Some of the "great thinkers" at the turn of the
18th century asserted that God was distant and
unknowable—he'd set the world in motion and then
left it to run by natural law.

But Susanna, the daughter of church reformers,
believed differently, and she had the passion and
the strength to want a deeper spiritual life for her
kids. She desperately wanted her children to *know*
God—to have a friendship with God—and she would
do anything to make sure it happened.

She introduced her children to Jesus when she
taught them each to read. They would open the Bible,
and she would teach them to spell and then to read
each word, then each line, and then each verse.
Those 10 children were home-schooled by her six
hours each day year-round.

FRIENDSHIP STORY *continues on page 426…*

Friendship First NEW TESTAMENT

FRIENDSHIP STORY *continued from page 425...*

When her husband was away attending church meetings, Susanna worried that her children weren't getting enough religious instruction at church, so she held meetings at home and read aloud the best sermons she could find in her husband's library. Then they'd pray together. Neighbors soon began attending, and before long almost 200 people were meeting in Susanna's home on Sunday evenings.

Susanna even went so for as to write theological works to help her children better understand who God is.

And she did all this during a time in which women received no formal education.

Susanna's work paid rich dividends. Two of her sons, John and Charles Wesley, founded Methodism and led a great spiritual awakening across England. Thousands grew in their friendship with Christ because of one woman's passionate love for her God and her children.

"Unless the heart perceive and know Him to be its supreme good, its only happiness; unless the soul feel and acknowledge that she can find no repose, no peace, no joy, but in loving and being beloved by Him; and does accordingly rest in Him as the center of her being, the fountain of her pleasure, the origin of all virtue and goodness, her light, her life, her strength, her all; everything she wants or wishes in this world, and forever!

"In a word, HER LORD, HER GOD! Thus, let me ever know Thee, O God!"

～ Susanna Wesley

FRIENDSHIP STORY *continues on page 427...*

Friendship First NEW TESTAMENT

CHAPTER **3**

Jesus Is Greater Than Moses

And so, dear brothers and sisters who belong to God and* are partners with those called to heaven, think carefully about this Jesus whom we declare to be God's messenger* and High Priest. [2] For he was faithful to God, who appointed him, just as Moses served faithfully when he was entrusted with God's entire* house.

[3] But Jesus deserves far more glory than Moses, just as a person who builds a house deserves more praise than the house itself. [4] For every house has a builder, but the one who built everything is God.

[5] Moses was certainly faithful in God's house as a servant. His work was an illustration of the truths God would reveal later. [6] But Christ, as the Son, is in charge of God's entire house. And we are God's house, if we keep our courage and remain confident in our hope in Christ.*

[7] That is why the Holy Spirit says,

"Today when you hear his voice,
[8]   don't harden your hearts
as Israel did when they rebelled,
    when they tested me in the wilderness.
[9] There your ancestors tested and tried my patience,
    even though they saw my miracles for forty years.
[10] So I was angry with them, and I said,
'Their hearts always turn away from me.
    They refuse to do what I tell them.'
[11] So in my anger I took an oath:
    'They will never enter my place of rest.'"*

[12] Be careful then, dear brothers and sisters.* Make sure that your own hearts are not evil and unbelieving, turning you away from the living God. [13] You must warn each other every day, while it is still "today," so that none of you will be deceived by sin and hardened against God. [14] For if we are faithful to the end, trusting God just as firmly as when we first believed, we will share in all that belongs to Christ. [15] Remember what it says:

"Today when you hear his voice,
    don't harden your hearts
    as Israel did when they rebelled."*

3:1a Greek *And so, holy brothers who.* **3:1b** Greek *God's apostle.* **3:2** Some manuscripts omit *entire.* **3:6** Some manuscripts add *faithful to the end.* **3:7-11** Ps 95:7-11. **3:12** Greek *brothers.* **3:15** Ps 95:7-8.

¹⁶And who was it who rebelled against God, even though they heard his voice? Wasn't it the people Moses led out of Egypt? ¹⁷And who made God angry for forty years? Wasn't it the people who sinned, whose corpses lay in the wilderness? ¹⁸And to whom was God speaking when he took an oath that they would never enter his rest? Wasn't it the people who disobeyed him? ¹⁹So we see that because of their unbelief they were not able to enter his rest.

CHAPTER **4**
Promised Rest for God's People

God's promise of entering his rest still stands, so we ought to tremble with fear that some of you might fail to experience it. ²For this good news—that God has prepared this rest—has been announced to us just as it was to them. But it did them no good because they didn't share the faith of those who listened to God.* ³For only we who believe can enter his rest. As for the others, God said,

"In my anger I took an oath:
  'They will never enter my place of rest,'"*

even though this rest has been ready since he made the world. ⁴We know it is ready because of the place in the Scriptures where it mentions the seventh day: "On the seventh day God rested from all his work."* ⁵But in the other passage God said, "They will never enter my place of rest."*

⁶So God's rest is there for people to enter, but those who first heard this good news failed to enter because they disobeyed God. ⁷So God set another time for entering his rest, and that time is today. God announced this through David much later in the words already quoted:

"Today when you hear his voice,
  don't harden your hearts."*

⁸Now if Joshua had succeeded in giving them this rest, God would not have spoken about another day of rest still to come. ⁹So there is a special rest* still waiting for the people of God. ¹⁰For all who have entered into God's rest have rested from their labors, just as God did after creating the world. ¹¹So let us do our best to enter that rest. But if we disobey God, as the people of Israel did, we will fall.

4:2 Some manuscripts read *they didn't combine what they heard with faith.*   4:3 Ps 95:11.
4:4 Gen 2:2.   4:5 Ps 95:11.   4:7 Ps 95:7-8.   4:9 Or *a Sabbath rest.*

FRIENDSHIP STORY *continued from page 426...*

THE ONE THING YOU CAN DO THIS WEEK

Experience

Help someone get acquainted with Jesus. Tell a story about Jesus to a child you know. Find a Bible storybook, and read about Jesus together. Ask the child what his or her favorite story about Jesus is. Tell the child your favorite thing about being friends with Jesus. If you don't have any children in your life, you can invite a friend to visit your church with you. Afterward, talk together about your impressions of Jesus Christ.

Reflect
★ Read **Philippians 3:8-9**. What makes some people so passionate about introducing others to Jesus?
★ What does it take to truly become acquainted with Jesus Christ?
★ Do you feel as if you're acquainted with the real Jesus? If so, how did you come to meet him? If not, what could you do differently to get to know him?

12 For the word of God is alive and powerful. It is sharper than the sharpest two-edged sword, cutting between soul and spirit, between joint and marrow. It exposes our innermost thoughts and desires. 13 Nothing in all creation is hidden from God. Everything is naked and exposed before his eyes, and he is the one to whom we are accountable.

Christ Is Our High Priest

14 So then, since we have a great High Priest who has entered heaven, Jesus the Son of God, let us hold firmly to what we believe. 15 This High Priest of ours understands our weaknesses, for he faced all of the same testings we do, yet he did not sin. 16 So let us come boldly to the throne of our gracious God. There we will receive his mercy, and we will find grace to help us when we need it most.

CHAPTER **5**

Every high priest is a man chosen to represent other people in their dealings with God. He presents their gifts to God and offers sacrifices for their sins. 2 And he is able to deal gently with ignorant and wayward people because he himself is subject to the same weaknesses. 3 That is why he must offer sacrifices for his own sins as well as theirs.

4 And no one can become a high priest simply because he wants such an honor. He must be called by God for this work, just as Aaron was. 5 That is why Christ did not honor himself by assuming he could become High Priest. No, he was chosen by God, who said to him,

"You are my Son.
 Today I have become your Father.*"

6 And in another passage God said to him,

"You are a priest forever in the order of Melchizedek."*

7 While Jesus was here on earth, he offered prayers and pleadings, with a loud cry and tears, to the one who could rescue him from death. And God heard his prayers because of his deep reverence for God. 8 Even though Jesus was God's Son, he learned obedience from the things he suffered. 9 In this way, God qualified him as a perfect High Priest, and he became the source of eternal salvation for all those who obey him. 10 And God designated him to be a High Priest in the order of Melchizedek.

5:5 Or *Today I reveal you as my Son.* Ps 2:7.   5:6 Ps 110:4.

A Call to Spiritual Growth

[11] There is much more we would like to say about this, but it is difficult to explain, especially since you are spiritually dull and don't seem to listen. [12] You have been believers so long now that you ought to be teaching others. Instead, you need someone to teach you again the basic things about God's word.* You are like babies who need milk and cannot eat solid food. [13] For someone who lives on milk is still an infant and doesn't know how to do what is right. [14] Solid food is for those who are mature, who through training have the skill to recognize the difference between right and wrong.

CHAPTER **6**

So let us stop going over the basic teachings about Christ again and again. Let us go on instead and become mature in our understanding. Surely we don't need to start again with the fundamental importance of repenting from evil deeds and placing our faith in God. [2] You don't need further instruction about baptisms, the laying on of hands, the resurrection of the dead, and eternal judgment. [3] And so, God willing, we will move forward to further understanding.

[4] For it is impossible to bring back to repentance those who were once enlightened—those who have experienced the good things of heaven and shared in the Holy Spirit, [5] who have tasted the goodness of the word of God and the power of the age to come—[6] and who then turn away from God. It is impossible to bring such people back to repentance; by rejecting the Son of God, they themselves are nailing him to the cross once again and holding him up to public shame.

[7] When the ground soaks up the falling rain and bears a good crop for the farmer, it has God's blessing. [8] But if a field bears thorns and thistles, it is useless. The farmer will soon condemn that field and burn it.

[9] Dear friends, even though we are talking this way, we really don't believe it applies to you. We are confident that you are meant for better things, things that come with salvation. [10] For God is not unjust. He will not forget how hard you have worked for him and how you have shown your love to him by caring for other believers,* as you still do. [11] Our great desire is that you will keep on loving others as long as life lasts, in order to make certain that what you hope for will come true. [12] Then you will not become spiritually dull and indifferent. Instead, you will

5:12 Or *about the oracles of God.*   **6:10** Greek *for God's holy people.*

★

"Pass the cheesecake, please..."
Of those surveyed, 71% said they have developed friendships with others in church over a shared meal or meals.

—from "Friendship and Faith," a Gallup Research Study Commissioned by Group Publishing, Inc.

★

JOURNAL

WHAT TO SAY AND WHAT NOT TO SAY

FRIENDSHIP TYPE:	FRIENDSHIP LAYER:
Jesus	*Getting Acquainted*

Knowing vs. Knowledge

Do you have a friend who's interested in getting acquainted with Jesus? Here are a couple of enthusiasm-squashers to avoid:

WHAT NOT TO SAY:

★ The best way to know Jesus is through Scripture memory. Here are my favorite 156 verses to get you started.

★ Well, before you get to know Jesus, you have to have some background. Let's meet every night for the next six months and study Leviticus and Numbers.

★ You can't get to know Jesus if you have sin in your life. In order to be a Christian, you have to stop lying, cheating, cussing, being mean, watching bad movies…

Think about it…While memorizing, studying Scripture, and striving to be a good person are valuable activities, they don't necessarily lead you to a friendship with Jesus. After all, you wouldn't memorize a list of facts about a person you wanted to be friends with; you'd spend time with the person. You wouldn't want to be friends with a person who demanded perfection from you *before* becoming friends; you'd find a friend who really cared about you, just as you are.

Philippians 1:9 says: "I pray that your love will overflow more and more, and that you will keep on growing in knowledge and understanding."

WHAT TO SAY AND WHAT NOT TO SAY *continues on page 431…*

follow the example of those who are going to inherit God's promises because of their faith and endurance.

God's Promises Bring Hope

¹³For example, there was God's promise to Abraham. Since there was no one greater to swear by, God took an oath in his own name, saying:

¹⁴ "I will certainly bless you,
    and I will multiply your descendants beyond number."*

¹⁵Then Abraham waited patiently, and he received what God had promised.

¹⁶Now when people take an oath, they call on someone greater than themselves to hold them to it. And without any question that oath is binding. ¹⁷God also bound himself with an oath, so that those who received the promise could be perfectly sure that he would never change his mind. ¹⁸So God has given both his promise and his oath. These two things are unchangeable because it is impossible for God to lie. Therefore, we who have fled to him for refuge can have great confidence as we hold to the hope that lies before us. ¹⁹This hope is a strong and trustworthy anchor for our souls. It leads us through the curtain into God's inner sanctuary. ²⁰Jesus has already gone in there for us. He has become our eternal High Priest in the order of Melchizedek.

CHAPTER 7

Melchizedek Is Greater Than Abraham

This Melchizedek was king of the city of Salem and also a priest of God Most High. When Abraham was returning home after winning a great battle against the kings, Melchizedek met him and blessed him. ²Then Abraham took a tenth of all he had captured in battle and gave it to Melchizedek. The name Melchizedek means "king of justice," and king of Salem means "king of peace." ³There is no record of his father or mother or any of his ancestors—no beginning or end to his life. He remains a priest forever, resembling the Son of God.

⁴Consider then how great this Melchizedek was. Even Abraham, the great patriarch of Israel, recognized this by giving him a tenth of what he had taken in battle. ⁵Now the law of Moses required that the priests, who are descendants of Levi, must collect a tithe from the rest of the people of Israel,* who are also descendants of Abraham. ⁶But Melchizedek, who was

6:14 Gen 22:17.   **7:5** Greek *from their brothers.*

not a descendant of Levi, collected a tenth from Abraham. And Melchizedek placed a blessing upon Abraham, the one who had already received the promises of God. 7And without question, the person who has the power to give a blessing is greater than the one who is blessed.

8The priests who collect tithes are men who die, so Melchizedek is greater than they are, because we are told that he lives on. 9In addition, we might even say that these Levites—the ones who collect the tithe—paid a tithe to Melchizedek when their ancestor Abraham paid a tithe to him. 10For although Levi wasn't born yet, the seed from which he came was in Abraham's body when Melchizedek collected the tithe from him.

11So if the priesthood of Levi, on which the law was based, could have achieved the perfection God intended, why did God need to establish a different priesthood, with a priest in the order of Melchizedek instead of the order of Levi and Aaron?*

12And if the priesthood is changed, the law must also be changed to permit it. 13For the priest we are talking about belongs to a different tribe, whose members have never served at the altar as priests. 14What I mean is, our Lord came from the tribe of Judah, and Moses never mentioned priests coming from that tribe.

Jesus Is like Melchizedek

15This change has been made very clear since a different priest, who is like Melchizedek, has appeared. 16Jesus became a priest, not by meeting the physical requirement of belonging to the tribe of Levi, but by the power of a life that cannot be destroyed. 17And the psalmist pointed this out when he prophesied,

"You are a priest forever in the order of Melchizedek."*

18Yes, the old requirement about the priesthood was set aside because it was weak and useless. 19For the law never made anything perfect. But now we have confidence in a better hope, through which we draw near to God.

20This new system was established with a solemn oath. Aaron's descendants became priests without such an oath, 21but there was an oath regarding Jesus. For God said to him,

"The LORD has taken an oath and will not break his vow:
  'You are a priest forever.'"*

7:11 Greek *the order of Aaron?* 7:17 Ps 110:4. 7:21 Ps 110:4.

WHAT TO SAY and WHAT NOT TO SAY *continued from page 430...*

Really getting acquainted with Jesus means growing in love and understanding...along with knowledge. And that comes from knowing Jesus, not just knowing about him.

Here's what you might say instead:

WHAT TO SAY:

★ Why don't we meet regularly just to talk about life?
★ Let me tell you how Jesus has been a good friend to me.
★ Let's read about Jesus' life together; we can start with the book of Matthew.

JOURNAL

JOURNAL

²²Because of this oath, Jesus is the one who guarantees this better covenant with God.

²³There were many priests under the old system, for death prevented them from remaining in office. ²⁴But because Jesus lives forever, his priesthood lasts forever. ²⁵Therefore he is able, once and forever, to save* those who come to God through him. He lives forever to intercede with God on their behalf.

²⁶He is the kind of high priest we need because he is holy and blameless, unstained by sin. He has been set apart from sinners and has been given the highest place of honor in heaven.* ²⁷Unlike those other high priests, he does not need to offer sacrifices every day. They did this for their own sins first and then for the sins of the people. But Jesus did this once for all when he offered himself as the sacrifice for the people's sins. ²⁸The law appointed high priests who were limited by human weakness. But after the law was given, God appointed his Son with an oath, and his Son has been made the perfect High Priest forever.

CHAPTER **8**

Christ Is Our High Priest

Here is the main point: We have a High Priest who sat down in the place of honor beside the throne of the majestic God in heaven. ²There he ministers in the heavenly Tabernacle,* the true place of worship that was built by the Lord and not by human hands.

³And since every high priest is required to offer gifts and sacrifices, our High Priest must make an offering, too. ⁴If he were here on earth, he would not even be a priest, since there already are priests who offer the gifts required by the law. ⁵They serve in a system of worship that is only a copy, a shadow of the real one in heaven. For when Moses was getting ready to build the Tabernacle, God gave him this warning: "Be sure that you make everything according to the pattern I have shown you here on the mountain."*

⁶But now Jesus, our High Priest, has been given a ministry that is far superior to the old priesthood, for he is the one who mediates for us a far better covenant with God, based on better promises.

⁷If the first covenant had been faultless, there would have been no need for a second covenant to replace it. ⁸But when God found fault with the people, he said:

7:25 Or *is able to save completely.*   7:26 Or *has been exalted higher than the heavens.*   8:2 Or *tent;* also in 8:5.   8:5 Exod 25:40; 26:30.

"The day is coming, says the LORD,
  when I will make a new covenant
  with the people of Israel and Judah.
⁹ This covenant will not be like the one
  I made with their ancestors
when I took them by the hand
  and led them out of the land of Egypt.
They did not remain faithful to my covenant,
  so I turned my back on them, says the LORD.
¹⁰ But this is the new covenant I will make
  with the people of Israel on that day,* says the LORD:
I will put my laws in their minds,
  and I will write them on their hearts.
I will be their God,
  and they will be my people.
¹¹ And they will not need to teach their neighbors,
  nor will they need to teach their relatives,*
  saying, 'You should know the LORD.'
For everyone, from the least to the greatest,
  will know me already.
¹² And I will forgive their wickedness,
  and I will never again remember their sins."*

¹³ When God speaks of a "new" covenant, it means he has made the first one obsolete. It is now out of date and will soon disappear.

CHAPTER 9

Old Rules about Worship

That first covenant between God and Israel had regulations for worship and a place of worship here on earth. ²There were two rooms in that Tabernacle.* In the first room were a lampstand, a table, and sacred loaves of bread on the table. This room was called the Holy Place. ³Then there was a curtain, and behind the curtain was the second room* called the Most Holy Place. ⁴In that room were a gold incense altar and a wooden chest called the Ark of the Covenant, which was covered with gold on all sides. Inside the Ark were a gold jar containing manna, Aaron's staff that sprouted leaves, and the stone tablets of the covenant. ⁵Above the Ark were the cherubim of divine glory, whose wings stretched out over the Ark's cover, the place of atonement. But we cannot explain these things in detail now.

8:10 Greek *after those days.*   8:11 Greek *their brother.*   8:8-12 Jer 31:31-34.   9:2 Or *tent;* also in 9:11, 21.   9:3 Greek *second tent.*

No. 21-FA-433

FRIENDSHIP STORY

FRIENDSHIP TYPE: *Friends*   FRIENDSHIP LAYER: *Companionship*

FROM THE ARCHIVES

The Lion and the Hobbit

When John Ronald Reuel Tolkien and Clive Staples Lewis met at Oxford University in 1926, they didn't have a whole lot in common.

Tolkien was born in South Africa; Lewis, in Ireland. Tolkien was a devoted Roman Catholic; Lewis, a skeptic. Tolkien had a wife and children; Lewis was single and would be for most of his life. When writing, Tolkien took a long time creating complex characters and plots; Lewis wrote entire books with surprising speed.

But despite those differences, J.R.R. Tolkien and C.S. Lewis had a rich, authentic friendship that lasted for decades. And at the heart of this friendship was companionship, centered on what they did share in common: a love for writing and a passion for mythical literature. Each found in the other someone who cared just as deeply about exploring life, emotion, and truth through imagination.

Tolkien and Lewis invited a few other Oxford friends to join them as they started a writing group—a group they called "The Inklings." For years the group met together in a local pub, eating, drinking, talking, laughing, reading. They critiqued each other's work, suggested improvements, and brainstormed new ideas.

Companionship. Shared passion. Good times.

The result? A successful friendship...and two successful writers. During this time, Tolkien created much of his famous trilogy, *The Lord of the Rings*, and Lewis wrote his mythical children's books, *The Chronicles of Narnia*.

FRIENDSHIP STORY *continues on page 434...*

FRIENDSHIP STORY *continued from page 433...*

But beyond producing great books, Lewis and Tolkien's companionship had an even more significant impact. On a night in 1931, the two friends took a walk together through a favorite park. The conversation turned to faith and storytelling and the connections between them. Tolkien talked of Jesus' life, death, and resurrection and the power of that true story for all people, for all time. Tolkien spoke of Jesus as a friend and made it clear that his life was nothing without Jesus in it. Through that conversation, Lewis began to understand…He saw that Jesus' life was more than a mere moment in history; it was the fulfillment. He perceived it through a storyteller's eyes and came to realize that Jesus is the ultimate hero.

Because of his steadfast companionship—and willingness to share his life—Tolkien was able to reveal Jesus to Lewis in a way that no one else had ever been able to…in a way that finally moved Lewis to see Jesus as a friend and Savior.

Experience

THE ONE THING **1** YOU CAN DO THIS WEEK

J.R.R. Tolkien and C.S. Lewis experienced companionship through what they both cared most about. Well, get together with a close friend and do the same! What hobbies or passions do you share? If it's literature, get together and read Tolkien's and Lewis' books. If it's sports, plan a full day of playing or watching together. If it's your children, plan a day-trip to the zoo. If it's carpentry, work together on a project for your church or community. Spend time in true companionship.

FRIENDSHIP STORY *continues on page 435...*

⁶When these things were all in place, the priests regularly entered the first room* as they performed their religious duties. ⁷But only the high priest ever entered the Most Holy Place, and only once a year. And he always offered blood for his own sins and for the sins the people had committed in ignorance. ⁸By these regulations the Holy Spirit revealed that the entrance to the Most Holy Place was not freely open as long as the Tabernacle* and the system it represented were still in use.

⁹This is an illustration pointing to the present time. For the gifts and sacrifices that the priests offer are not able to cleanse the consciences of the people who bring them. ¹⁰For that old system deals only with food and drink and various cleansing ceremonies—physical regulations that were in effect only until a better system could be established.

Christ Is the Perfect Sacrifice

¹¹So Christ has now become the High Priest over all the good things that have come.* He has entered that greater, more perfect Tabernacle in heaven, which was not made by human hands and is not part of this created world. ¹²With his own blood—not the blood of goats and calves—he entered the Most Holy Place once for all time and secured our redemption forever.

¹³Under the old system, the blood of goats and bulls and the ashes of a young cow could cleanse people's bodies from ceremonial impurity. ¹⁴Just think how much more the blood of Christ will purify our consciences from sinful deeds* so that we can worship the living God. For by the power of the eternal Spirit, Christ offered himself to God as a perfect sacrifice for our sins. ¹⁵That is why he is the one who mediates a new covenant between God and people, so that all who are called can receive the eternal inheritance God has promised them. For Christ died to set them free from the penalty of the sins they had committed under that first covenant.

¹⁶Now when someone leaves a will,* it is necessary to prove that the person who made it is dead.* ¹⁷The will goes into effect only after the person's death. While the person who made it is still alive, the will cannot be put into effect.

¹⁸That is why even the first covenant was put into effect with the blood of an animal. ¹⁹For after Moses had read each of God's commandments to all the people, he took the blood of calves and goats,* along with water, and sprinkled both the

9:6 Greek *first tent.*   **9:8** Or *the first room;* Greek reads *the first tent.*   **9:11** Some manuscripts read *that are about to come.*   **9:14** Greek *from dead works.*   **9:16a** Or *covenant; also in 9:17.*   **9:16b** Or *Now when someone makes a covenant, it is necessary to ratify it with the death of a sacrifice.*   **9:19** Some manuscripts omit *and goats.*

book of God's law and all the people, using hyssop branches and scarlet wool. ²⁰Then he said, "This blood confirms the covenant God has made with you."* ²¹And in the same way, he sprinkled blood on the Tabernacle and on everything used for worship. ²²In fact, according to the law of Moses, nearly everything was purified with blood. For without the shedding of blood, there is no forgiveness.

²³That is why the Tabernacle and everything in it, which were copies of things in heaven, had to be purified by the blood of animals. But the real things in heaven had to be purified with far better sacrifices than the blood of animals.

²⁴For Christ did not enter into a holy place made with human hands, which was only a copy of the true one in heaven. He entered into heaven itself to appear now before God on our behalf. ²⁵And he did not enter heaven to offer himself again and again, like the high priest here on earth who enters the Most Holy Place year after year with the blood of an animal. ²⁶If that had been necessary, Christ would have had to die again and again, ever since the world began. But now, once for all time, he has appeared at the end of the age* to remove sin by his own death as a sacrifice.

²⁷And just as each person is destined to die once and after that comes judgment, ²⁸so also Christ died once for all time as a sacrifice to take away the sins of many people. He will come again, not to deal with our sins, but to bring salvation to all who are eagerly waiting for him.

CHAPTER 10

Christ's Sacrifice Once for All

The old system under the law of Moses was only a shadow, a dim preview of the good things to come, not the good things themselves. The sacrifices under that system were repeated again and again, year after year, but they were never able to provide perfect cleansing for those who came to worship. ²If they could have provided perfect cleansing, the sacrifices would have stopped, for the worshipers would have been puri-fied once for all time, and their feelings of guilt would have disappeared.

³But instead, those sacrifices actually reminded them of their sins year after year. ⁴For it is not possible for the blood of bulls and goats to take away sins. ⁵That is why, when Christ* came into the world, he said to God,

9:20 Exod 24:8.   9:26 Greek *the ages*.   10:5 Greek *he;* also in 10:8.

FRIENDSHIP STORY *continued from page 434...*

Companionship doesn't only mean having fun together. Just as walking together in the park and discussing stories led Tolkien and Lewis to conversations of faith, so, too, will your times of companionship lead to significant and personal conversations. Before you hang out with your friend, read **John 13:1-17**. Pray that your friendship—and companionship—will have life-changing impact.

Reflect
★ How does the companionship between Tolkien and Lewis inspire you in your friendships?
★ When have times of companionship impacted your friendships in the past?
★ How can you create more times of companionship with your friends?

JOURNAL

"You did not want animal sacrifices or sin offerings.
But you have given me a body to offer.
⁶ You were not pleased with burnt offerings
or other offerings for sin.
⁷ Then I said, 'Look, I have come to do your will, O God—
as is written about me in the Scriptures.'"*

⁸First, Christ said, "You did not want animal sacrifices or sin offerings or burnt offerings or other offerings for sin, nor were you pleased with them" (though they are required by the law of Moses). ⁹Then he said, "Look, I have come to do your will." He cancels the first covenant in order to put the second into effect. ¹⁰For God's will was for us to be made holy by the sacrifice of the body of Jesus Christ, once for all time.

¹¹Under the old covenant, the priest stands and ministers before the altar day after day, offering the same sacrifices again and again, which can never take away sins. ¹²But our High Priest offered himself to God as a single sacrifice for sins, good for all time. Then he sat down in the place of honor at God's right hand. ¹³There he waits until his enemies are humbled and made a footstool under his feet. ¹⁴For by that one offering he forever made perfect those who are being made holy.

¹⁵And the Holy Spirit also testifies that this is so. For he says,

¹⁶ "This is the new covenant I will make
with my people on that day,* says the LORD:
I will put my laws in their hearts,
and I will write them on their minds."*

¹⁷Then he says,

"I will never again remember
their sins and lawless deeds."*

¹⁸And when sins have been forgiven, there is no need to offer any more sacrifices.

A Call to Persevere

¹⁹And so, dear brothers and sisters,* we can boldly enter heaven's Most Holy Place because of the blood of Jesus. ²⁰By his death,* Jesus opened a new and life-giving way through the curtain into the Most Holy Place. ²¹And since we have a great High Priest who rules over God's house, ²²let us go right into the presence of God with sincere hearts fully trusting him. For our guilty con-

10:5-7 Ps 40:6-8 (Greek version).   10:16a Greek *after those days.*   10:16b Jer 31:33a.   10:17 Jer 31:34b.   10:19 Greek *brothers.*   10:20 Greek *Through his flesh.*

sciences have been sprinkled with Christ's blood to make us clean, and our bodies have been washed with pure water.

²³Let us hold tightly without wavering to the hope we affirm, for God can be trusted to keep his promise. ²⁴Let us think of ways to motivate one another to acts of love and good works. ²⁵And let us not neglect our meeting together, as some people do, but encourage one another, especially now that the day of his return is drawing near.

²⁶Dear friends, if we deliberately continue sinning after we have received knowledge of the truth, there is no longer any sacrifice that will cover these sins. ²⁷There is only the terrible expectation of God's judgment and the raging fire that will consume his enemies. ²⁸For anyone who refused to obey the law of Moses was put to death without mercy on the testimony of two or three witnesses. ²⁹Just think how much worse the punishment will be for those who have trampled on the Son of God, and have treated the blood of the covenant, which made us holy, as if it were common and unholy, and have insulted and disdained the Holy Spirit who brings God's mercy to us. ³⁰For we know the one who said,

> "I will take revenge.
>   I will pay them back."*

He also said,

> "The LORD will judge his own people."*

³¹It is a terrible thing to fall into the hands of the living God.

³²Think back on those early days when you first learned about Christ.* Remember how you remained faithful even though it meant terrible suffering. ³³Sometimes you were exposed to public ridicule and were beaten, and sometimes you helped others who were suffering the same things. ³⁴You suffered along with those who were thrown into jail, and when all you owned was taken from you, you accepted it with joy. You knew there were better things waiting for you that will last forever.

³⁵So do not throw away this confident trust in the Lord. Remember the great reward it brings you! ³⁶Patient endurance is what you need now, so that you will continue to do God's will. Then you will receive all that he has promised.

³⁷ "For in just a little while,
    the Coming One will come and not delay.

10:30a Deut 32:35.   10:30b Deut 32:36.   10:32 Greek *when you were first enlightened.*

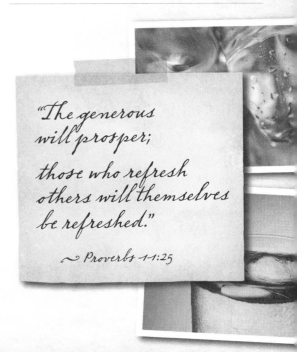

"The generous will prosper; those who refresh others will themselves be refreshed."

~ Proverbs 11:25

WHAT TO SAY 👍
AND
WHAT NOT TO SAY 👎

FRIENDSHIP TYPE: *Friends*   FRIENDSHIP LAYER: *Companionship*

Top 10

THE TOP 10 THINGS *NOT* TO DO OR SAY

...if you want to experience companionship with a friend (according to **Galatians 5:13-26**).

10. Be hostile.
9. Intentionally hurt each other.
8. Encourage each other to sin.
7. Argue.
6. Be jealous.
5. Have angry outbursts.
4. Act selfishly.
3. Be exclusive.
2. Think or act impurely.
1. Pull each other away from a friendship with Jesus.

THE TOP 10 THINGS TO DO AND SAY

...if you want to experience companionship with a friend (according to **Acts 2:43-47**).

10. Hang out a lot.
9. Be generous.
8. Worship together.
7. Serve together.
6. Do new, cool, exciting things together.
5. Show hospitality.
4. Eat together.
3. Have fun together.
2. Connect over shared interests and passions.

And above all else, the number one thing to do to experience companionship with your friends is...

1. Pull each other toward a friendship with Jesus!

Friendship First NEW TESTAMENT

---

38 And my righteous ones will live by faith.*
  But I will take no pleasure in anyone who turns away."*

39 But we are not like those who turn away from God to their own destruction. We are the faithful ones, whose souls will be saved.

CHAPTER **11**
Great Examples of Faith

Faith is the confidence that what we hope for will actually happen; it gives us assurance about things we cannot see. 2Through their faith, the people in days of old earned a good reputation.

3By faith we understand that the entire universe was formed at God's command, that what we now see did not come from anything that can be seen.

4It was by faith that Abel brought a more acceptable offering to God than Cain did. Abel's offering gave evidence that he was a righteous man, and God showed his approval of his gifts. Although Abel is long dead, he still speaks to us by his example of faith.

5It was by faith that Enoch was taken up to heaven without dying—"he disappeared, because God took him."* For before he was taken up, he was known as a person who pleased God. 6And it is impossible to please God without faith. Anyone who wants to come to him must believe that God exists and that he rewards those who sincerely seek him.

7It was by faith that Noah built a large boat to save his family from the flood. He obeyed God, who warned him about things that had never happened before. By his faith Noah condemned the rest of the world, and he received the righteousness that comes by faith.

8It was by faith that Abraham obeyed when God called him to leave home and go to another land that God would give him as his inheritance. He went without knowing where he was going. 9And even when he reached the land God promised him, he lived there by faith—for he was like a foreigner, living in tents. And so did Isaac and Jacob, who inherited the same promise. 10Abraham was confidently looking forward to a city with eternal foundations, a city designed and built by God.

11It was by faith that even Sarah was able to have a child, though she was barren and was too old. She believed* that God

10:38 Or *my righteous ones will live by their faithfulness;* Greek reads *my righteous one will live by faith.*   **10:37-38** Hab 2:3-4.   **11:5** Gen 5:24.   **11:11** Or *It was by faith that he [Abraham] was able to have a child, even though Sarah was barren and he was too old. He believed.*

would keep his promise. [12]And so a whole nation came from this one man who was as good as dead—a nation with so many people that, like the stars in the sky and the sand on the seashore, there is no way to count them.

[13]All these people died still believing what God had promised them. They did not receive what was promised, but they saw it all from a distance and welcomed it. They agreed that they were foreigners and nomads here on earth. [14]Obviously people who say such things are looking forward to a country they can call their own. [15]If they had longed for the country they came from, they could have gone back. [16]But they were looking for a better place, a heavenly homeland. That is why God is not ashamed to be called their God, for he has prepared a city for them.

[17]It was by faith that Abraham offered Isaac as a sacrifice when God was testing him. Abraham, who had received God's promises, was ready to sacrifice his only son, Isaac, [18]even though God had told him, "Isaac is the son through whom your descendants will be counted."* [19]Abraham reasoned that if Isaac died, God was able to bring him back to life again. And in a sense, Abraham did receive his son back from the dead.

[20]It was by faith that Isaac promised blessings for the future to his sons, Jacob and Esau.

[21]It was by faith that Jacob, when he was old and dying, blessed each of Joseph's sons and bowed in worship as he leaned on his staff.

[22]It was by faith that Joseph, when he was about to die, said confidently that the people of Israel would leave Egypt. He even commanded them to take his bones with them when they left.

[23]It was by faith that Moses' parents hid him for three months when he was born. They saw that God had given them an unusual child, and they were not afraid to disobey the king's command.

[24]It was by faith that Moses, when he grew up, refused to be called the son of Pharaoh's daughter. [25]He chose to share the oppression of God's people instead of enjoying the fleeting pleasures of sin. [26]He thought it was better to suffer for the sake of Christ than to own the treasures of Egypt, for he was looking ahead to his great reward. [27]It was by faith that Moses left the land of Egypt, not fearing the king's anger. He kept right on going because he kept his eyes on the one who is invisible. [28]It was by faith that Moses commanded the people of Israel

11:18 Gen 21:12.

> "An offended friend is harder to win back than a fortified city.
>
> Arguments separate friends like a gate locked with bars."
>
> ~ Proverbs 18:19

JOURNAL

to keep the Passover and to sprinkle blood on the doorposts so that the angel of death would not kill their firstborn sons.

²⁹It was by faith that the people of Israel went right through the Red Sea as though they were on dry ground. But when the Egyptians tried to follow, they were all drowned.

³⁰It was by faith that the people of Israel marched around Jericho for seven days, and the walls came crashing down.

³¹It was by faith that Rahab the prostitute was not destroyed with the people in her city who refused to obey God. For she had given a friendly welcome to the spies.

³²How much more do I need to say? It would take too long to recount the stories of the faith of Gideon, Barak, Samson, Jephthah, David, Samuel, and all the prophets. ³³By faith these people overthrew kingdoms, ruled with justice, and received what God had promised them. They shut the mouths of lions, ³⁴quenched the flames of fire, and escaped death by the edge of the sword. Their weakness was turned to strength. They became strong in battle and put whole armies to flight. ³⁵Women received their loved ones back again from death.

But others were tortured, refusing to turn from God in order to be set free. They placed their hope in a better life after the resurrection. ³⁶Some were jeered at, and their backs were cut open with whips. Others were chained in prisons. ³⁷Some died by stoning, some were sawed in half,* and others were killed with the sword. Some went about wearing skins of sheep and goats, destitute and oppressed and mistreated. ³⁸They were too good for this world, wandering over deserts and mountains, hiding in caves and holes in the ground.

³⁹All these people earned a good reputation because of their faith, yet none of them received all that God had promised. ⁴⁰For God had something better in mind for us, so that they would not reach perfection without us.

CHAPTER **12**

God's Discipline Proves His Love

Therefore, since we are surrounded by such a huge crowd of witnesses to the life of faith, let us strip off every weight that slows us down, especially the sin that so easily trips us up. And let us run with endurance the race God has set before us. ²We do this by keeping our eyes on Jesus, the champion who initiates and perfects our faith.* Because of the joy* awaiting him, he endured

11:37 Some manuscripts add *some were tested.*   **12:2a** Or *Jesus, the originator and perfecter of our faith.*   **12:2b** Or *Instead of the joy.*

the cross, disregarding its shame. Now he is seated in the place of honor beside God's throne. ³Think of all the hostility he endured from sinful people;* then you won't become weary and give up. ⁴After all, you have not yet given your lives in your struggle against sin.

⁵And have you forgotten the encouraging words God spoke to you as his children?* He said,

"My child,* don't make light of the LORD's discipline,
and don't give up when he corrects you.
⁶ For the LORD disciplines those he loves,
and he punishes each one he accepts as his child."*

⁷As you endure this divine discipline, remember that God is treating you as his own children. Who ever heard of a child who is never disciplined by its father? ⁸If God doesn't discipline you as he does all of his children, it means that you are illegitimate and are not really his children at all. ⁹Since we respected our earthly fathers who disciplined us, shouldn't we submit even more to the discipline of the Father of our spirits, and live forever?*

¹⁰For our earthly fathers disciplined us for a few years, doing the best they knew how. But God's discipline is always good for us, so that we might share in his holiness. ¹¹No discipline is enjoyable while it is happening—it's painful! But afterward there will be a peaceful harvest of right living for those who are trained in this way.

¹²So take a new grip with your tired hands and strengthen your weak knees. ¹³Mark out a straight path for your feet so that those who are weak and lame will not fall but become strong.

A Call to Listen to God

¹⁴Work at living in peace with everyone, and work at living a holy life, for those who are not holy will not see the Lord. ¹⁵Look after each other so that none of you fails to receive the grace of God. Watch out that no poisonous root of bitterness grows up to trouble you, corrupting many. ¹⁶Make sure that no one is immoral or godless like Esau, who traded his birthright as the firstborn son for a single meal. ¹⁷You know that afterward, when he wanted his father's blessing, he was rejected. It was too late for repentance, even though he begged with bitter tears.

¹⁸You have not come to a physical mountain,* to a place of

12:3 Some manuscripts read *Think of how people hurt themselves by opposing him.* 12:5a Greek *sons;* also in 12:7, 8. 12:5b Greek *son;* also in 12:6, 7. 12:5-6 Prov 3:11-12 (Greek version). 12:9 Or *and really live?* 12:18 Greek *to something that can be touched.*

No. 23-FS-441

FRIENDSHIP STORY

FRIENDSHIP TYPE:	FRIENDSHIP LAYER:
Family	*Commitment*

FOUND IN SCRIPTURE

Payback

For Joseph, it was payback time, a once-in-a-lifetime opportunity to even up the score. Men who'd betrayed Joseph and then sold him into slavery now stood right in front of him. They'd gotten away with the crime years before, but this time things were different.

This time, *Joseph* was in charge.

If revenge is sweet, Joseph was in for a tasty afternoon of dishing out justice…*if* that's what he wanted.

You see, the men who had abused Joseph weren't career criminals. They were his brothers, his own flesh and blood. They had let jealousy of their little brother simmer into bitterness and then harden into rage. They had wanted Joseph dead and gone—banished. That's why they had thrown Joseph at a slave trader who had carried the young man into Egypt. Construction projects launched by the Pharaoh consumed a steady stream of slave labor, so one more able-bodied slave was always welcome.

The last most of his brothers had seen of Joseph, he was being dragged behind a caravan deep into the desert, stumbling toward a slow death.

Now, years later, those same brothers stood before a powerful Egyptian official who literally held their lives in his hands. They had come begging for food, but there was much more at stake.

They didn't know it, but they were begging for their lives.

FRIENDSHIP STORY *continues on page 442…*

Friendship First NEW TESTAMENT

FRIENDSHIP STORY *continued from page 441...*

Joseph was second in command in Egypt, reporting only to Pharaoh. And while Joseph recognized his brothers, they didn't recognize him—giving Joseph every advantage.

Joseph could easily have his revenge. No one would have questioned Joseph's right to have his brothers killed or enslaved.

But when the moment came, Joseph wept and drew his amazed brothers to him. He tearfully explained that while his brothers' motives may have been terrible, God had used Joseph's harsh circumstances for good. What happened to Joseph was a prime example of what Paul described in **Romans 8:28** (look it up to find an encouraging promise!).

In Genesis 45:15, the writer notes that once they understood who the Egyptian official was, "they began talking freely with him."

Here's hoping the first words out of their mouths were "We're sorry."

Read the whole story of Joseph and his brothers in Genesis chapters 37 and 39–47 (in the Old Testament).

Experience

Families often fracture, and without commitment those fractures don't heal. If you have a strained or broken relationship somewhere in your family tree, use this week to try to mend it— even if you've suffered pain along the way. Send a card. Make a phone call. Open up a dialogue in any way you can. Be like Joseph and reveal who you really are and how you really feel.

And if the opportunity for revenge presents itself, don't demand payback.

Offer forgiveness.

FRIENDSHIP STORY *continues on page 443...*

flaming fire, darkness, gloom, and whirlwind, as the Israelites did at Mount Sinai. [19]For they heard an awesome trumpet blast and a voice so terrible that they begged God to stop speaking. [20]They staggered back under God's command: "If even an animal touches the mountain, it must be stoned to death."* [21]Moses himself was so frightened at the sight that he said, "I am terrified and trembling."*

[22]No, you have come to Mount Zion, to the city of the living God, the heavenly Jerusalem, and to countless thousands of angels in a joyful gathering. [23]You have come to the assembly of God's firstborn children, whose names are written in heaven. You have come to God himself, who is the judge over all things. You have come to the spirits of the righteous ones in heaven who have now been made perfect. [24]You have come to Jesus, the one who mediates the new covenant between God and people, and to the sprinkled blood, which speaks of forgiveness instead of crying out for vengeance like the blood of Abel.

[25]Be careful that you do not refuse to listen to the One who is speaking. For if the people of Israel did not escape when they refused to listen to Moses, the earthly messenger, we will certainly not escape if we reject the One who speaks to us from heaven! [26]When God spoke from Mount Sinai his voice shook the earth, but now he makes another promise: "Once again I will shake not only the earth but the heavens also."* [27]This means that all of creation will be shaken and removed, so that only unshakable things will remain.

[28]Since we are receiving a Kingdom that is unshakable, let us be thankful and please God by worshiping him with holy fear and awe. [29]For our God is a devouring fire.

CHAPTER **13**
Concluding Words

Keep on loving each other as brothers and sisters.* [2]Don't forget to show hospitality to strangers, for some who have done this have entertained angels without realizing it! [3]Remember those in prison, as if you were there yourself. Remember also those being mistreated, as if you felt their pain in your own bodies.

[4]Give honor to marriage, and remain faithful to one another in marriage. God will surely judge people who are immoral and those who commit adultery.

12:20 Exod 19:13.   **12:21** Deut 9:19.   **12:26** Hag 2:6.   **13:1** Greek *Continue in brotherly love.*

⁵Don't love money; be satisfied with what you have. For God has said,

"I will never fail you.
I will never abandon you."*

⁶So we can say with confidence,

"The LORD is my helper,
so I will have no fear.
What can mere people do to me?"*

⁷Remember your leaders who taught you the word of God. Think of all the good that has come from their lives, and follow the example of their faith.

⁸Jesus Christ is the same yesterday, today, and forever. ⁹So do not be attracted by strange, new ideas. Your strength comes from God's grace, not from rules about food, which don't help those who follow them.

¹⁰We have an altar from which the priests in the Tabernacle* have no right to eat. ¹¹Under the old system, the high priest brought the blood of animals into the Holy Place as a sacrifice for sin, and the bodies of the animals were burned outside the camp. ¹²So also Jesus suffered and died outside the city gates to make his people holy by means of his own blood. ¹³So let us go out to him, outside the camp, and bear the disgrace he bore. ¹⁴For this world is not our permanent home; we are looking forward to a home yet to come.

¹⁵Therefore, let us offer through Jesus a continual sacrifice of praise to God, proclaiming our allegiance to his name. ¹⁶And don't forget to do good and to share with those in need. These are the sacrifices that please God.

¹⁷Obey your spiritual leaders, and do what they say. Their work is to watch over your souls, and they are accountable to God. Give them reason to do this with joy and not with sorrow. That would certainly not be for your benefit.

¹⁸Pray for us, for our conscience is clear and we want to live honorably in everything we do. ¹⁹And especially pray that I will be able to come back to you soon.

²⁰ Now may the God of peace—
who brought up from the dead our Lord Jesus,
the great Shepherd of the sheep,
and ratified an eternal covenant with his blood—

13:5 Deut 31:6, 8.   13:6 Ps 118:6.   13:10 Or *tent*.

FRIENDSHIP STORY *continued from page 442…*

Reflect

★ What does commitment look like in your family? How should it look?

★ If you were committed to caring for your family in every way, how might your family interactions look different? the same?

★ What's the cost of being committed to your family?

JOURNAL

21 may he equip you with all you need
    for doing his will.
May he produce in you,*
    through the power of Jesus Christ,
every good thing that is pleasing to him.
    All glory to him forever and ever! Amen.

22 I urge you, dear brothers and sisters,* to pay attention to what I have written in this brief exhortation. 23 I want you to know that our brother Timothy has been released from jail. If he comes here soon, I will bring him with me to see you.

24 Greet all your leaders and all the believers there.* The believers from Italy send you their greetings.

25 May God's grace be with you all.

13:21 Some manuscripts read *in us.*   13:22 Greek *brothers.*   13:24 Greek *all of God's holy people.*

"Of all possessions a friend is the most precious."

~ Herodotus

James

AUTHOR:	DATE WRITTEN:
James	Probably A.D. 49

JOURNAL

CHAPTER 1

Greetings from James

This letter is from James, a slave of God and of the Lord Jesus Christ.

I am writing to the "twelve tribes"—Jewish believers scattered abroad.

Greetings!

Faith and Endurance

²Dear brothers and sisters,* when troubles come your way, consider it an opportunity for great joy. ³For you know that when your faith is tested, your endurance has a chance to grow. ⁴So let it grow, for when your endurance is fully developed, you will be perfect and complete, needing nothing.

⁵If you need wisdom, ask our generous God, and he will give it to you. He will not rebuke you for asking. ⁶But when you ask him, be sure that your faith is in God alone. Do not waver, for a person with divided loyalty is as unsettled as a wave of the sea that is blown and tossed by the wind. ⁷Such people should not expect to receive anything from the Lord. ⁸Their loyalty is divided between God and the world, and they are unstable in everything they do.

⁹Believers who are* poor have something to boast about, for God has honored them. ¹⁰And those who are rich should boast that God has humbled them. They will fade away like a little flower in the field. ¹¹The hot sun rises and the grass withers; the little flower droops and falls, and its beauty fades away. In the same way, the rich will fade away with all of their achievements.

¹²God blesses those who patiently endure testing and temptation. Afterward they will receive the crown of life that God has promised to those who love him. ¹³And remember, when you

1:2 Greek *brothers*; also in 1:16, 19.   1:9 Greek *The brother who is.*

Anchor Passage

PASSAGE: **James 2:1-13**

FRIENDSHIP TYPE: *Neighbors*

FRIENDSHIP LAYER: *Acceptance*

Members Only

Read James **2:1-13**.

You probably don't feel like you have a big problem with racial prejudice.

But if you're like most people, you do harbor some form of prejudice…even if that's not exactly what you'd call it.

Maybe it's a more subtle form of prejudice, one based on irritations, stereotypes, or personal preferences.

Maybe it's people with a lot of money who bother you. Or perhaps you try your best to avoid disabled people. Or maybe it's people of another religion who make you uncomfortable.

Most of us make judgments all the time that dictate the types of people we get to know. Maybe you're friendly toward the bikers down the street, but would you ever have them over for dinner? That business executive is nice enough, but what's the point of sharing lunch when she'll spend most of it on her cell phone?

It's easier to be with people who are more like us. But that mentality is really a form of prejudice, even if it's not an overt one.

Anchor Passage continues on page 447…

are being tempted, do not say, "God is tempting me." God is never tempted to do wrong,* and he never tempts anyone else. [14]Temptation comes from our own desires, which entice us and drag us away. [15]These desires give birth to sinful actions. And when sin is allowed to grow, it gives birth to death.

[16]So don't be misled, my dear brothers and sisters. [17]Whatever is good and perfect comes down to us from God our Father, who created all the lights in the heavens.* He never changes or casts a shifting shadow.* [18]He chose to give birth to us by giving us his true word. And we, out of all creation, became his prized possession.*

Listening and Doing

[19]Understand this, my dear brothers and sisters: You must all be quick to listen, slow to speak, and slow to get angry. [20]Human anger* does not produce the righteousness* God desires. [21]So get rid of all the filth and evil in your lives, and humbly accept the word God has planted in your hearts, for it has the power to save your souls.

[22]But don't just listen to God's word. You must do what it says. Otherwise, you are only fooling yourselves. [23]For if you listen to the word and don't obey, it is like glancing at your face in a mirror. [24]You see yourself, walk away, and forget what you look like. [25]But if you look carefully into the perfect law that sets you free, and if you do what it says and don't forget what you heard, then God will bless you for doing it.

[26]If you claim to be religious but don't control your tongue, you are fooling yourself, and your religion is worthless. [27]Pure and genuine religion in the sight of God the Father means caring for orphans and widows in their distress and refusing to let the world corrupt you.

CHAPTER 2

A Warning against Prejudice

My dear brothers and sisters,* how can you claim to have faith in our glorious Lord Jesus Christ if you favor some people over others?

[2]For example, suppose someone comes into your meeting* dressed in fancy clothes and expensive

1:13 Or *God should not be put to a test by evil people.* **1:17a** Greek *from above, from the Father of lights.* **1:17b** Some manuscripts read *He never changes, as a shifting shadow does.* **1:18** Greek *we became a kind of firstfruit of his creatures.* **1:20a** Greek *A man's anger.* **1:20b** Or *the justice.* **2:1** Greek *brothers; also in 2:5, 14.* **2:2** Greek *your synagogue.*

jewelry, and another comes in who is poor and dressed in dirty clothes. ³If you give special attention and a good seat to the rich person, but you say to the poor one, "You can stand over there, or else sit on the floor"—well, ⁴doesn't this discrimination show that your judgments are guided by evil motives?

⁵Listen to me, dear brothers and sisters. Hasn't God chosen the poor in this world to be rich in faith? Aren't they the ones who will inherit the Kingdom he promised to those who love him? ⁶But you dishonor the poor! Isn't it the rich who oppress you and drag you into court? ⁷Aren't they the ones who slander Jesus Christ, whose noble name* you bear?

⁸Yes indeed, it is good when you obey the royal law as found in the Scriptures: "Love your neighbor as yourself."* ⁹But if you favor some people over others, you are committing a sin. You are guilty of breaking the law.

¹⁰For the person who keeps all of the laws except one is as guilty as a person who has broken all of God's laws. ¹¹For the same God who said, "You must not commit adultery," also said, "You must not murder."* So if you murder someone but do not commit adultery, you have still broken the law.

¹²So whatever you say or whatever you do, remember that you will be judged by the law that sets you free. ¹³There will be no mercy for those who have not shown mercy to others. But if you have been merciful, God will be merciful when he judges you. ⚓

Faith without Good Deeds Is Dead

¹⁴What good is it, dear brothers and sisters, if you say you have faith but don't show it by your actions? Can that kind of faith save anyone? ¹⁵Suppose you see a brother or sister who has no food or clothing, ¹⁶and you say, "Good-bye and have a good day; stay warm and eat well"—but then you don't give that person any food or clothing. What good does that do?

¹⁷So you see, faith by itself isn't enough. Unless it produces good deeds, it is dead and useless.

¹⁸Now someone may argue, "Some people have faith; others have good deeds." But I say, "How can you show me your faith

2:7 Greek *slander the noble name.*　2:8 Lev 19:18.　2:11 Exod 20:13-14; Deut 5:17-18.

Anchor Passage continued from page 446...

Race. Status. Interests. Family background. None of that should matter to a Christian. Jesus is the great equalizer. Before God, we are all in need. *Anyone* who comes to God through Jesus is completely forgiven. The distinctions we make between people are ridiculous in comparison.

God offers acceptance to all people equally—and asks the same of you.

THE ONE THING YOU CAN DO THIS WEEK

Experience

Meet an acquaintance on his or her turf. For example, if you know someone who is really into scrapbooking and you're not, ask if you can see the person's pictures. Or if you know someone who is into cars, go to a stock-car race with the person. Hey, you might even have fun!

Reflect

★ What overt prejudices do you have? How can God help you get free of those prejudices?

★ What kinds of things annoy you so much that you avoid being around people who do those things?

★ What kinds of people make you fearful?

★ These are very likely hidden prejudices. What could you do to free yourself of them?

DIGGING DEEPER

FRIENDSHIP TYPE: *Neighbors*　　FRIENDSHIP LAYER: *Acceptance*

For accepting your neighbors, check out...

➡ The Friendship Experience .... on page 450

➡ The Friendship Story .... on page 457

➡ What to Say and What Not to Say .... on page 453

JOURNAL

if you don't have good deeds? I will show you my faith by my good deeds."

[19] You say you have faith, for you believe that there is one God.* Good for you! Even the demons believe this, and they tremble in terror. [20] How foolish! Can't you see that faith without good deeds is useless?

[21] Don't you remember that our ancestor Abraham was shown to be right with God by his actions when he offered his son Isaac on the altar? [22] You see, his faith and his actions worked together. His actions made his faith complete. [23] And so it happened just as the Scriptures say: "Abraham believed God, and God counted him as righteous because of his faith."* He was even called the friend of God.* [24] So you see, we are shown to be right with God by what we do, not by faith alone.

[25] Rahab the prostitute is another example. She was shown to be right with God by her actions when she hid those messengers and sent them safely away by a different road. [26] Just as the body is dead without breath,* so also faith is dead without good works.

CHAPTER 3

Controlling the Tongue

Dear brothers and sisters,* not many of you should become teachers in the church, for we who teach will be judged more strictly. [2] Indeed, we all make many mistakes. For if we could control our tongues, we would be perfect and could also control ourselves in every other way.

[3] We can make a large horse go wherever we want by means of a small bit in its mouth. [4] And a small rudder makes a huge ship turn wherever the pilot chooses to go, even though the winds are strong. [5] In the same way, the tongue is a small thing that makes grand speeches.

But a tiny spark can set a great forest on fire. [6] And the tongue is a flame of fire. It is a whole world of wickedness, corrupting your entire body. It can set your whole life on fire, for it is set on fire by hell itself.*

[7] People can tame all kinds of animals, birds, reptiles, and fish, [8] but no one can tame the tongue. It is restless and evil, full of deadly poison. [9] Sometimes it praises our Lord and Father, and sometimes it curses those who have been made in the image of

2:19 Some manuscripts read *that God is one;* see Deut 6:4. **2:23a** Gen 15:6. **2:23b** See Isa 41:8. **2:26** Or *without spirit.* **3:1** Greek *brothers;* also in 3:10. **3:6** Or *for it will burn in hell* (Greek *Gehenna*).

God. ¹⁰And so blessing and cursing come pouring out of the same mouth. Surely, my brothers and sisters, this is not right! ¹¹Does a spring of water bubble out with both fresh water and bitter water? ¹²Does a fig tree produce olives, or a grapevine produce figs? No, and you can't draw fresh water from a salty spring.*

True Wisdom Comes from God

¹³If you are wise and understand God's ways, prove it by living an honorable life, doing good works with the humility that comes from wisdom. ¹⁴But if you are bitterly jealous and there is selfish ambition in your heart, don't cover up the truth with boasting and lying. ¹⁵For jealousy and selfishness are not God's kind of wisdom. Such things are earthly, unspiritual, and demonic. ¹⁶For wherever there is jealousy and selfish ambition, there you will find disorder and evil of every kind.

¹⁷But the wisdom from above is first of all pure. It is also peace loving, gentle at all times, and willing to yield to others. It is full of mercy and good deeds. It shows no favoritism and is always sincere. ¹⁸And those who are peacemakers will plant seeds of peace and reap a harvest of righteousness.*

CHAPTER **4**

Drawing Close to God

What is causing the quarrels and fights among you? Don't they come from the evil desires at war within you? ²You want what you don't have, so you scheme and kill to get it. You are jealous of what others have, but you can't get it, so you fight and wage war to take it away from them. Yet you don't have what you want because you don't ask God for it. ³And even when you ask, you don't get it because your motives are all wrong—you want only what will give you pleasure.

⁴You adulterers!* Don't you realize that friendship with the world makes you an enemy of God? I say it again: If you want to be a friend of the world, you make yourself an enemy of God. ⁵What do you think the Scriptures mean when they say that the spirit God has placed within us is filled with envy?* ⁶But he gives us even more grace to stand against such evil desires. As the Scriptures say,

> "God opposes the proud
>   but favors the humble."*

3:12 Greek *from salt.*   3:18 Or *of good things,* or *of justice.*   4:4 Greek *You adulteresses!*   4:5 Or *that God longs jealously for the human spirit he has placed within us?* or *that the Holy Spirit, whom God has placed within us, opposes our envy?*   4:6 Prov 3:34 (Greek version).

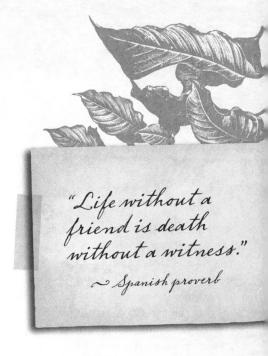

"*Life without a friend is death without a witness.*"

~ *Spanish proverb*

JOURNAL

FRIENDSHIP EXPERIENCE

FRIENDSHIP TYPE: *Neighbors*   FRIENDSHIP LAYER: *Acceptance*

Smash Through

We often blame prejudice on ignorance. And that's certainly part of the problem but not all of it—there are plenty of educated people who are also highly prejudiced. And nearly *everyone* has some level of prejudice.

Many who are free from racial prejudice harbor religious prejudice. Others make judgments about people based on what they've heard from family, from the media, or even (sadly) at church.

Prejudice is usually the result of an indulgence in stereotypes and a refusal to get to know a person or group of people.

Sure, education is great, and it may help a little, but the best cure for judgment and prejudice is exposure. It's tough to hate someone you truly know and understand.

Getting to know someone is the first step toward acceptance. If there's a person or a group you struggle with, try getting to know them. Your efforts might turn people you dislike or fear into friends. And remember, God loves those people…deeply.

FRIENDSHIP EXPERIENCE *continues on page 451…*

Friendship First NEW TESTAMENT

7 So humble yourselves before God. Resist the devil, and he will flee from you. 8 Come close to God, and God will come close to you. Wash your hands, you sinners; purify your hearts, for your loyalty is divided between God and the world. 9 Let there be tears for what you have done. Let there be sorrow and deep grief. Let there be sadness instead of laughter, and gloom instead of joy. 10 Humble yourselves before the Lord, and he will lift you up in honor.

Warning against Judging Others

11 Don't speak evil against each other, dear brothers and sisters.* If you criticize and judge each other, then you are criticizing and judging God's law. But your job is to obey the law, not to judge whether it applies to you. 12 God alone, who gave the law, is the Judge. He alone has the power to save or to destroy. So what right do you have to judge your neighbor?

Warning about Self-Confidence

13 Look here, you who say, "Today or tomorrow we are going to a certain town and will stay there a year. We will do business there and make a profit." 14 How do you know what your life will be like tomorrow? Your life is like the morning fog—it's here a little while, then it's gone. 15 What you ought to say is, "If the Lord wants us to, we will live and do this or that." 16 Otherwise you are boasting about your own plans, and all such boasting is evil.

17 Remember, it is sin to know what you ought to do and then not do it.

CHAPTER **5**

Warning to the Rich

Look here, you rich people: Weep and groan with anguish because of all the terrible troubles ahead of you. 2 Your wealth is rotting away, and your fine clothes are moth-eaten rags. 3 Your gold and silver have become worthless. The very wealth you were counting on will eat away your flesh like fire. This treasure you have accumulated will stand as evidence against you on the day of judgment. 4 For listen! Hear the cries of the field workers whom you have cheated of their pay. The wages you held back cry out against you. The cries of those who harvest your fields have reached the ears of the LORD of Heaven's Armies.

5 You have spent your years on earth in luxury, satisfying your every desire. You have fattened yourselves for the day of slaugh-

4:11 Greek *brothers.*

ter. ⁶You have condemned and killed innocent people,* who do not resist you.*

Patience and Endurance

⁷Dear brothers and sisters,* be patient as you wait for the Lord's return. Consider the farmers who patiently wait for the rains in the fall and in the spring. They eagerly look for the valuable harvest to ripen. ⁸You, too, must be patient. Take courage, for the coming of the Lord is near.

⁹Don't grumble about each other, brothers and sisters, or you will be judged. For look—the Judge is standing at the door!

¹⁰For examples of patience in suffering, dear brothers and sisters, look at the prophets who spoke in the name of the Lord. ¹¹We give great honor to those who endure under suffering. For instance, you know about Job, a man of great endurance. You can see how the Lord was kind to him at the end, for the Lord is full of tenderness and mercy.

¹²But most of all, my brothers and sisters, never take an oath, by heaven or earth or anything else. Just say a simple yes or no, so that you will not sin and be condemned.

The Power of Prayer

¹³Are any of you suffering hardships? You should pray. Are any of you happy? You should sing praises. ¹⁴Are any of you sick? You should call for the elders of the church to come and pray over you, anointing you with oil in the name of the Lord. ¹⁵Such a prayer offered in faith will heal the sick, and the Lord will make you well. And if you have committed any sins, you will be forgiven.

¹⁶Confess your sins to each other and pray for each other so that you may be healed. The earnest prayer of a righteous person has great power and produces wonderful results. ¹⁷Elijah was as human as we are, and yet when he prayed earnestly that no rain would fall, none fell for three and a half years! ¹⁸Then, when he prayed again, the sky sent down rain and the earth began to yield its crops.

Restore Wandering Believers

¹⁹My dear brothers and sisters, if someone among you wanders away from the truth and is brought back, ²⁰you can be sure that whoever brings the sinner back will save that person from death and bring about the forgiveness of many sins.

5:6a Or *killed the Righteous One.* 5:6b Or *Don't they resist you?* or *Doesn't God oppose you?* or *Aren't they now accusing you before God?* 5:7 Greek *brothers;* also in 5:9, 10, 12, 19.

FRIENDSHIP EXPERIENCE *continued from page 450...*

THE ONE THING 1 YOU CAN DO THIS WEEK

Experience

Begin by being really honest with yourself. There is likely a certain type of person you avoid, are afraid of, don't like, or feel uncomfortable around. Do you hold hidden prejudice against a race? a social or economic group? people without education? people with certain interests or behaviors?

Make an effort to get to know that race, group, or type of person. Perhaps you can start up a conversation with someone during lunch or a break at work. If you don't have direct contact with that type of person, gain exposure by learning about them. Read about their history. Search for stories about respected men and women who share the same race, economic background, or level of education.

Virtually every people group and demographic has been reached by the message of Jesus at some level. Check with a mission agency or missions program to find out what God is doing with different groups of people around the world. For the ultimate exposure, go on a mission trip and learn more (remember, a mission trip doesn't have to be to a foreign country; it could be to the inner city, a rural area, or another state).

Reflect

★ What prejudices do you struggle with? Why do you feel that way?

★ In what ways are your prejudices or judgments off-base?

★ Read **James 2:1-13**. How can you move from judgment toward acceptance?

1 Peter

AUTHOR:	DATE WRITTEN:
Peter	Approximately A.D. 62 - 64

CHAPTER **1**

Greetings from Peter

This letter is from Peter, an apostle of Jesus Christ.

I am writing to God's chosen people who are living as foreigners in the provinces of Pontus, Galatia, Cappadocia, Asia, and Bithynia.* ²God the Father knew you and chose you long ago, and his Spirit has made you holy. As a result, you have obeyed him and have been cleansed by the blood of Jesus Christ.

May God give you more and more grace and peace.

The Hope of Eternal Life

³All praise to God, the Father of our Lord Jesus Christ. It is by his great mercy that we have been born again, because God raised Jesus Christ from the dead. Now we live with great expectation, ⁴and we have a priceless inheritance—an inheritance that is kept in heaven for you, pure and undefiled, beyond the reach of change and decay. ⁵And through your faith, God is protecting you by his power until you receive this salvation, which is ready to be revealed on the last day for all to see.

⁶So be truly glad.* There is wonderful joy ahead, even though you have to endure many trials for a little while. ⁷These trials will show that your faith is genuine. It is being tested as fire tests and purifies gold—though your faith is far more precious than mere gold. So when your faith remains strong through many trials, it will bring you much praise and glory and honor on the day when Jesus Christ is revealed to the whole world.

⁸You love him even though you have never seen him. Though you do not see him now, you trust him; and you rejoice with a glorious, inexpressible joy. ⁹The reward for trusting him will be the salvation of your souls.

1:1 Pontus, Galatia, Cappadocia, Asia, and Bithynia were Roman provinces in what is now Turkey.
1:6 Or So you are truly glad.

¹⁰This salvation was something even the prophets wanted to know more about when they prophesied about this gracious salvation prepared for you. ¹¹They wondered what time or situation the Spirit of Christ within them was talking about when he told them in advance about Christ's suffering and his great glory afterward.

¹²They were told that their messages were not for themselves, but for you. And now this Good News has been announced to you by those who preached in the power of the Holy Spirit sent from heaven. It is all so wonderful that even the angels are eagerly watching these things happen.

A Call to Holy Living

¹³So think clearly and exercise self-control. Look forward to the gracious salvation that will come to you when Jesus Christ is revealed to the world. ¹⁴So you must live as God's obedient children. Don't slip back into your old ways of living to satisfy your own desires. You didn't know any better then. ¹⁵But now you must be holy in everything you do, just as God who chose you is holy. ¹⁶For the Scriptures say, "You must be holy because I am holy."*

¹⁷And remember that the heavenly Father to whom you pray has no favorites. He will judge or reward you according to what you do. So you must live in reverent fear of him during your time as "foreigners in the land." ¹⁸For you know that God paid a ransom to save you from the empty life you inherited from your ancestors. And the ransom he paid was not mere gold or silver. ¹⁹It was the precious blood of Christ, the sinless, spotless Lamb of God. ²⁰God chose him as your ransom long before the world began, but he has now revealed him to you in these last days.

²¹Through Christ you have come to trust in God. And you have placed your faith and hope in God because he raised Christ from the dead and gave him great glory.

²²You were cleansed from your sins when you obeyed the truth, so now you must show sincere love to each other as brothers and sisters.* Love each other deeply with all your heart.*

²³For you have been born again, but not to a life that will quickly end. Your new life will last forever because it comes from the eternal, living word of God. ²⁴As the Scriptures say,

1:16 Lev 11:44-45; 19:2; 20:7. **1:22a** Greek *must have brotherly love.* **1:22b** Some manuscripts read *with a pure heart.*

WHAT TO SAY AND **WHAT NOT TO SAY**

FRIENDSHIP TYPE: *Neighbors*   FRIENDSHIP LAYER: *Acceptance*

Lessons From History

   WHAT NOT TO DO:

The people of Israel were no strangers to prejudice, judgment, and discrimination. Consider the following:

★ The Egyptians refused to eat with Joseph and his family—they considered it detestable to eat with Hebrews (Genesis 43:32).

★ Naaman, a military leader suffering with leprosy, refused to follow Elisha's direction for healing because it involved washing in an Israelite river—something he was loath to do. Fortunately, Naaman's servant helped Naaman change his mind, and he was healed (2 Kings 5:1-15).

★ Haman, the most powerful official in Persia, attempted to exterminate the entire Jewish race (Esther 3).

★ When Nehemiah came to rebuild the wall around Jerusalem, men from Moab "were very displeased that someone had come to help…Israel." They did everything they could to stop the Israelites (Nehemiah 2:10).

★ The people of Edom celebrated when Jerusalem was invaded and destroyed (Obadiah 1:8-12).

WHAT TO SAY AND **WHAT NOT TO SAY** *continues on page 454…*

WHAT TO SAY AND WHAT NOT TO SAY *continued from page 453...*

WHAT TO DO:

Even though the Jews had suffered so much discrimination, the early Jewish Christians still needed a bunch of reminders not to show prejudice toward others. The following passages serve as powerful reminders for us today:

★ Don't think of anyone as impure or unclean (**Acts 10:28**).

★ Let God be the judge of others (**Romans 14:4**).

★ You don't have the right to condemn others (**Romans 2:1**).

★ Be hospitable—don't refuse to eat with anyone... no matter how different they are from you (**Galatians 2:11-21**).

★ Don't discriminate against people based on dress or status (**James 2:1-13**).

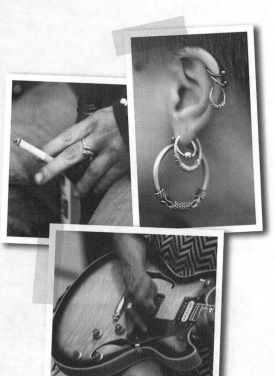

"People are like grass;
    their beauty is like a flower in the field.
The grass withers and the flower fades.
25   But the word of the Lord remains forever."*

And that word is the Good News that was preached to you.

CHAPTER **2**

So get rid of all evil behavior. Be done with all deceit, hypocrisy, jealousy, and all unkind speech. ²Like newborn babies, you must crave pure spiritual milk so that you will grow into a full experience of salvation. Cry out for this nourishment, ³now that you have had a taste of the Lord's kindness.

Living Stones for God's House

⁴You are coming to Christ, who is the living cornerstone of God's temple. He was rejected by people, but he was chosen by God for great honor.

⁵And you are living stones that God is building into his spiritual temple. What's more, you are his holy priests.* Through the mediation of Jesus Christ, you offer spiritual sacrifices that please God. ⁶As the Scriptures say,

"I am placing a cornerstone in Jerusalem,*
    chosen for great honor,
and anyone who trusts in him
    will never be disgraced."*

⁷Yes, you who trust him recognize the honor God has given him. But for those who reject him,

"The stone that the builders rejected
    has now become the cornerstone."*

⁸And,

"He is the stone that makes people stumble,
    the rock that makes them fall."*

They stumble because they do not obey God's word, and so they meet the fate that was planned for them.

⁹But you are not like that, for you are a chosen people. You are royal priests,* a holy nation, God's very own possession. As a result, you can show others the goodness of God, for he called you out of the darkness into his wonderful light.

1:24-25 Isa 40:6-8. **2:5** Greek *holy priesthood*. **2:6a** Greek *in Zion*. **2:6b** Isa 28:16 (Greek version). **2:7** Ps 118:22. **2:8** Isa 8:14. **2:9** Greek *a royal priesthood*.

10 "Once you had no identity as a people;
   now you are God's people.
Once you received no mercy;
   now you have received God's mercy."*

11 Dear friends, I warn you as "temporary residents and foreigners" to keep away from worldly desires that wage war against your very souls. 12 Be careful to live properly among your unbelieving neighbors. Then even if they accuse you of doing wrong, they will see your honorable behavior, and they will give honor to God when he judges the world.*

Respecting People in Authority

13 For the Lord's sake, respect all human authority—whether the king as head of state, 14 or the officials he has appointed. For the king has sent them to punish those who do wrong and to honor those who do right.

15 It is God's will that your honorable lives should silence those ignorant people who make foolish accusations against you. 16 For you are free, yet you are God's slaves, so don't use your freedom as an excuse to do evil. 17 Respect everyone, and love your Christian brothers and sisters.* Fear God, and respect the king.

Slaves

18 You who are slaves must accept the authority of your masters with all respect.* Do what they tell you—not only if they are kind and reasonable, but even if they are cruel. 19 For God is pleased with you when you do what you know is right and patiently endure unfair treatment. 20 Of course, you get no credit for being patient if you are beaten for doing wrong. But if you suffer for doing good and endure it patiently, God is pleased with you.

21 For God called you to do good, even if it means suffering, just as Christ suffered* for you. He is your example, and you must follow in his steps.

22 He never sinned,
   nor ever deceived anyone.*
23 He did not retaliate when he was insulted,
   nor threaten revenge when he suffered.
He left his case in the hands of God,
   who always judges fairly.

2:10 Hos 1:6, 9; 2:23.   2:12 Or *on the day of visitation.*   2:17 Greek *love the brotherhood.*   2:18 Or *because you fear God.*   2:21 Some manuscripts read *died.*   2:22 Isa 53:9.

24 He personally carried our sins
    in his body on the cross
so that we can be dead to sin
    and live for what is right.
By his wounds
    you are healed.
25 Once you were like sheep
    who wandered away.
But now you have turned to your Shepherd,
    the Guardian of your souls.

CHAPTER 3

Wives

In the same way, you wives must accept the authority of your husbands. Then, even if some refuse to obey the Good News, your godly lives will speak to them without any words. They will be won over 2 by observing your pure and reverent lives.

3 Don't be concerned about the outward beauty of fancy hairstyles, expensive jewelry, or beautiful clothes. 4 You should clothe yourselves instead with the beauty that comes from within, the unfading beauty of a gentle and quiet spirit, which is so precious to God. 5 This is how the holy women of old made themselves beautiful. They trusted God and accepted the authority of their husbands. 6 For instance, Sarah obeyed her husband, Abraham, and called him her master. You are her daughters when you do what is right without fear of what your husbands might do.

Husbands

7 In the same way, you husbands must give honor to your wives. Treat your wife with understanding as you live together. She may be weaker than you are, but she is your equal partner in God's gift of new life. Treat her as you should so your prayers will not be hindered.

All Christians

8 Finally, all of you should be of one mind. Sympathize with each other. Love each other as brothers and sisters.* Be tenderhearted, and keep a humble attitude. 9 Don't repay evil for evil. Don't retaliate with insults when people insult you. Instead, pay them back with a blessing. That is what God has called you to do, and he will bless you for it. 10 For the Scriptures say,

3:8 Greek Show brotherly love.

"If you want to enjoy life
and see many happy days,
keep your tongue from speaking evil
and your lips from telling lies.
11 Turn away from evil and do good.
Search for peace, and work to maintain it.
12 The eyes of the Lord watch over those who do right,
and his ears are open to their prayers.
But the Lord turns his face
against those who do evil."*

Suffering for Doing Good

13 Now, who will want to harm you if you are eager to do good? 14 But even if you suffer for doing what is right, God will reward you for it. So don't worry or be afraid of their threats. 15 Instead, you must worship Christ as Lord of your life. And if someone asks about your Christian hope, always be ready to explain it. 16 But do this in a gentle and respectful way.* Keep your conscience clear. Then if people speak against you, they will be ashamed when they see what a good life you live because you belong to Christ. 17 Remember, it is better to suffer for doing good, if that is what God wants, than to suffer for doing wrong!

18 Christ suffered* for our sins once for all time. He never sinned, but he died for sinners to bring you safely home to God. He suffered physical death, but he was raised to life in the Spirit.*

19 So he went and preached to the spirits in prison—20 those who disobeyed God long ago when God waited patiently while Noah was building his boat. Only eight people were saved from drowning in that terrible flood.* 21 And that water is a picture of baptism, which now saves you, not by removing dirt from your body, but as a response to God from* a clean conscience. It is effective because of the resurrection of Jesus Christ.

22 Now Christ has gone to heaven. He is seated in the place of honor next to God, and all the angels and authorities and powers accept his authority.

CHAPTER 4
Living for God

So then, since Christ suffered physical pain, you must arm yourselves with the same attitude he had, and be ready to suffer, too.

3:10-12 Ps 34:12-16.   3:16 Some English translations put this sentence in verse 15.   3:18a Some manuscripts read *died*.   3:18b Or *in spirit*.   3:20 Greek *saved through water*.   3:21 Or *as an appeal to God for*.

No. 24-FA-457
FRIENDSHIP
STORY

FRIENDSHIP TYPE: *Neighbors*   FRIENDSHIP LAYER: *Acceptance*

FROM THE ARCHIVES

End the Feud

Legend has it that the most famous feud in American history started over a hog. In 1878 Randolph McCoy reportedly accused Floyd Hatfield of stealing his pig. The Hatfields and McCoys most certainly had bad blood between them before the alleged theft. Both families competed against each other in the timber business, and differences during the Civil War likely lingered after the war had been decided.

A few years after the pig incident, Randolph's sons killed Ellison Hatfield after he shouted an insult to one of the men. "Devil Anse" Hatfield exacted justice on the McCoys by killing all three of the men who were involved. The violence grew as the McCoys raided the Hatfield territory to get their revenge. Before long, portions of Kentucky and West Virginia joined in the fighting, forcing the governors of both states to call on the National Guard to restore peace.

The battling lasted a decade, and at least a dozen people were killed.

More than 100 years later, the Hatfields and McCoys still battle one another in Pikeville, Kentucky…during an annual softball game and Tug of War. A Georgian minister by the name of Bo McCoy, Randolph McCoy's great-great-great-grandson, helped organize the first reunion; he felt the bad blood had gone on long enough. The event continues to grow and draws approximately 1,000 Hatfield and McCoy descendants every year to the delight of the county tourism agency in Pikeville.

FRIENDSHIP STORY *continues on page 458…*

Friendship First NEW TESTAMENT

FRIENDSHIP STORY *continued from page 457...*

A famous feud resolved. Hated neighbors accepted as friends. The Hatfields and McCoys are a modern-day reminder that no relationship is beyond saving. No matter how different or offensive a person is, you can show love and acceptance to that person.

Colossians 1:21-23 states that we were once enemies of God. But that didn't stop God from loving us and accepting us. God loved us *while* we were still sinners. God didn't try to get revenge on us for hurting him, nor did God wait until we got our act together before he began reaching out to us in acceptance and love. Make God's love your inspiration as you interact with your neighbors.

Experience

THE ONE THING
1
YOU CAN DO THIS WEEK

You may not have a literal feud going on with any of your neighbors, but do you have a neighborly relationship that seems strained or fractured? What about a neighbor whom you tend to avoid?

Ask God to help you take steps toward accepting that person. This week when you see the person, say "hello." Begin a conversation, ask how the person is doing, ask about his or her plans for the weekend...You'll be surprised at just how much good a simple conversation can do.

FRIENDSHIP STORY *continues on page 459...*

For if you have suffered physically for Christ, you have finished with sin.* 2You won't spend the rest of your lives chasing your own desires, but you will be anxious to do the will of God. 3You have had enough in the past of the evil things that godless people enjoy—their immorality and lust, their feasting and drunkenness and wild parties, and their terrible worship of idols.

4Of course, your former friends are surprised when you no longer plunge into the flood of wild and destructive things they do. So they slander you. 5But remember that they will have to face God, who will judge everyone, both the living and the dead. 6That is why the Good News was preached to those who are now dead*—so although they were destined to die like all people,* they now live forever with God in the Spirit.*

7The end of the world is coming soon. Therefore, be earnest and disciplined in your prayers. 8Most important of all, continue to show deep love for each other, for love covers a multitude of sins. 9Cheerfully share your home with those who need a meal or a place to stay.

10God has given each of you a gift from his great variety of spiritual gifts. Use them well to serve one another. 11Do you have the gift of speaking? Then speak as though God himself were speaking through you. Do you have the gift of helping others? Do it with all the strength and energy that God supplies. Then everything you do will bring glory to God through Jesus Christ. All glory and power to him forever and ever! Amen.

Suffering for Being a Christian

12Dear friends, don't be surprised at the fiery trials you are going through, as if something strange were happening to you. 13Instead, be very glad—for these trials make you partners with Christ in his suffering, so that you will have the wonderful joy of seeing his glory when it is revealed to all the world.

14So be happy when you are insulted for being a Christian,* for then the glorious Spirit of God* rests upon you.* 15If you suffer, however, it must not be for murder, stealing, making trouble, or prying into other people's affairs. 16But it is no shame to suffer for being a Christian. Praise God for the privilege of being called by his name! 17For the time has come for judgment, and it must begin with God's household. And if judgment begins with us, what terrible fate awaits those who have never obeyed God's Good News? 18And also,

4:1 Or *For the one* [or *One*] *who has suffered physically has finished with sin.* **4:6a** Greek *preached even to the dead.* **4:6b** Or *so although people had judged them worthy of death.* **4:6c** Or *in spirit.* **4:14a** Greek *for the name of Christ.* **4:14b** Or *for the glory of God, which is his Spirit.* **4:14c** Some manuscripts add *On their part he is blasphemed, but on your part he is glorified.*

"If the righteous are barely saved,
   what will happen to godless sinners?"*

19 So if you are suffering in a manner that pleases God, keep on doing what is right, and trust your lives to the God who created you, for he will never fail you.

CHAPTER 5
Advice for Elders and Young Men

And now, a word to you who are elders in the churches. I, too, am an elder and a witness to the sufferings of Christ. And I, too, will share in his glory when he is revealed to the whole world. As a fellow elder, I appeal to you: 2 Care for the flock that God has entrusted to you. Watch over it willingly, not grudgingly—not for what you will get out of it, but because you are eager to serve God. 3 Don't lord it over the people assigned to your care, but lead them by your own good example. 4 And when the Great Shepherd appears, you will receive a crown of never-ending glory and honor.

5 In the same way, you younger men must accept the authority of the elders. And all of you, serve each other in humility, for

"God opposes the proud
   but favors the humble."*

6 So humble yourselves under the mighty power of God, and at the right time he will lift you up in honor. 7 Give all your worries and cares to God, for he cares about you.

8 Stay alert! Watch out for your great enemy, the devil. He prowls around like a roaring lion, looking for someone to devour. 9 Stand firm against him, and be strong in your faith. Remember that your Christian brothers and sisters* all over the world are going through the same kind of suffering you are.

10 In his kindness God called you to share in his eternal glory by means of Christ Jesus. So after you have suffered a little while, he will restore, support, and strengthen you, and he will place you on a firm foundation. 11 All power to him forever! Amen.

Peter's Final Greetings

12 I have written and sent this short letter to you with the help of Silas,* whom I commend to you as a faithful brother. My

4:18 Prov 11:31 (Greek version).   5:5 Prov 3:34 (Greek version).   5:9 Greek your brothers.
5:12 Greek Silvanus.

FRIENDSHIP STORY *continued from page 458…*

Reflect
★ What does it take for people to move from being enemies to friends? What would it take for *you* to move from being someone's enemy to a friend?
★ How do you feel knowing that God has made you his friend?
★ What actions will help you show God's acceptance to people who are difficult for you to accept?

JOURNAL

JOURNAL

purpose in writing is to encourage you and assure you that what you are experiencing is truly part of God's grace for you. Stand firm in this grace.

¹³ Your sister church here in Babylon* sends you greetings, and so does my son Mark. ¹⁴ Greet each other with Christian love.*

Peace be with all of you who are in Christ.

5:13 Greek *The elect one in Babylon.* Babylon was probably symbolic for Rome.   5:14 Greek *with a kiss of love.*

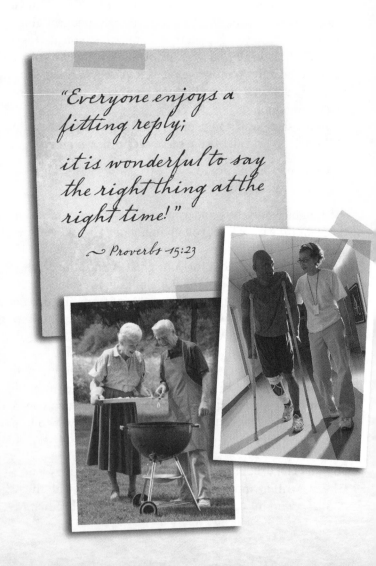

"*Everyone enjoys a fitting reply;*

it is wonderful to say the right thing at the right time!"

~ *Proverbs 15:23*

2 Peter

AUTHOR:	DATE WRITTEN:
Peter	Approximately A.D. 67

CHAPTER **1**

Greetings from Peter

This letter is from Simon* Peter, a slave and apostle of Jesus Christ.

I am writing to you who share the same precious faith we have. This faith was given to you because of the justice and fairness* of Jesus Christ, our God and Savior.

²May God give you more and more grace and peace as you grow in your knowledge of God and Jesus our Lord.

Growing in Faith

³By his divine power, God has given us everything we need for living a godly life. We have received all of this by coming to know him, the one who called us to himself by means of his marvelous glory and excellence. ⁴And because of his glory and excellence, he has given us great and precious promises. These are the promises that enable you to share his divine nature and escape the world's corruption caused by human desires.

⁵In view of all this, make every effort to respond to God's promises. Supplement your faith with a generous provision of moral excellence, and moral excellence with knowledge, ⁶and knowledge with self-control, and self-control with patient endurance, and patient endurance with godliness, ⁷and godliness with brotherly affection, and brotherly affection with love for everyone.

⁸The more you grow like this, the more productive and useful you will be in your knowledge of our Lord Jesus Christ. ⁹But those who fail to develop in this way are shortsighted or blind, forgetting that they have been cleansed from their old sins.

¹⁰So, dear brothers and sisters,* work hard to prove that you really are among those God has called and chosen. Do these

1:1a Greek *Symeon.*   **1:1b** Or *to you in the righteousness.*   **1:10** Greek *brothers.*

JOURNAL

things, and you will never fall away. [11] Then God will give you a grand entrance into the eternal Kingdom of our Lord and Savior Jesus Christ.

Paying Attention to Scripture

[12] Therefore, I will always remind you about these things—even though you already know them and are standing firm in the truth you have been taught. [13] And it is only right that I should keep on reminding you as long as I live.* [14] For our Lord Jesus Christ has shown me that I must soon leave this earthly life,* [15] so I will work hard to make sure you always remember these things after I am gone.

[16] For we were not making up clever stories when we told you about the powerful coming of our Lord Jesus Christ. We saw his majestic splendor with our own eyes [17] when he received honor and glory from God the Father. The voice from the majestic glory of God said to him, "This is my dearly loved Son, who brings me great joy."* [18] We ourselves heard that voice from heaven when we were with him on the holy mountain.

[19] Because of that experience, we have even greater confidence in the message proclaimed by the prophets. You must pay close attention to what they wrote, for their words are like a lamp shining in a dark place—until the Day dawns, and Christ the Morning Star shines* in your hearts. [20] Above all, you must realize that no prophecy in Scripture ever came from the prophet's own understanding,* [21] or from human initiative. No, those prophets were moved by the Holy Spirit, and they spoke from God.

CHAPTER 2

The Danger of False Teachers

But there were also false prophets in Israel, just as there will be false teachers among you. They will cleverly teach destructive heresies and even deny the Master who bought them. In this way, they will bring sudden destruction on themselves. [2] Many will follow their evil teaching and shameful immorality. And because of these teachers, the way of truth will be slandered. [3] In their greed they will make up clever lies to get hold of your money. But God condemned them long ago, and their destruction will not be delayed.

[4] For God did not spare even the angels who sinned. He threw them into hell,* in gloomy pits of darkness,* where they are

1:13 Greek *as long as I am in this tent* [or *tabernacle*].   1:14 Greek *I must soon put off my tent* [or *tabernacle*].   1:17 Matt 17:5; Mark 9:7; Luke 9:35.   1:19 Or *rises.*   1:20 Or *is a matter of one's own interpretation.*   2:4a Greek *Tartarus.*   2:4b Some manuscripts read *in chains of gloom.*

being held until the day of judgment. ⁵And God did not spare the ancient world—except for Noah and the seven others in his family. Noah warned the world of God's righteous judgment. So God protected Noah when he destroyed the world of ungodly people with a vast flood. ⁶Later, God condemned the cities of Sodom and Gomorrah and turned them into heaps of ashes. He made them an example of what will happen to ungodly people. ⁷But God also rescued Lot out of Sodom because he was a righteous man who was sick of the shameful immorality of the wicked people around him. ⁸Yes, Lot was a righteous man who was tormented in his soul by the wickedness he saw and heard day after day. ⁹So you see, the Lord knows how to rescue godly people from their trials, even while keeping the wicked under punishment until the day of final judgment. ¹⁰He is especially hard on those who follow their own twisted sexual desire, and who despise authority.

These people are proud and arrogant, daring even to scoff at supernatural beings* without so much as trembling. ¹¹But the angels, who are far greater in power and strength, do not dare to bring from the Lord* a charge of blasphemy against those supernatural beings.

¹²These false teachers are like unthinking animals, creatures of instinct, born to be caught and destroyed. They scoff at things they do not understand, and like animals, they will be destroyed. ¹³Their destruction is their reward for the harm they have done. They love to indulge in evil pleasures in broad daylight. They are a disgrace and a stain among you. They delight in deception* even as they eat with you in your fellowship meals. ¹⁴They commit adultery with their eyes, and their desire for sin is never satisfied. They lure unstable people into sin, and they are well trained in greed. They live under God's curse. ¹⁵They have wandered off the right road and followed the footsteps of Balaam son of Beor,* who loved to earn money by doing wrong. ¹⁶But Balaam was stopped from his mad course when his donkey rebuked him with a human voice.

¹⁷These people are as useless as dried-up springs or as mist blown away by the wind. They are doomed to blackest darkness. ¹⁸They brag about themselves with empty, foolish boasting. With an appeal to twisted sexual desires, they lure back into sin those who have barely escaped from a lifestyle of deception. ¹⁹They promise freedom, but they themselves are slaves of sin

★

Among American church members, 29% say they joined their church because of friendships within that church.

—from "Friendship and Faith," a Gallup Research Study Commissioned by Group Publishing, Inc.

★

JOURNAL

2:10 Greek *at glorious ones,* which are probably evil angels. 2:11 Other manuscripts read *to the Lord;* still others omit this phrase. 2:13 Some manuscripts read *in fellowship meals.* 2:15 Some manuscripts read *Bosor.*

WHAT TO SAY 👍
AND
WHAT NOT TO SAY 👎

FRIENDSHIP TYPE:	FRIENDSHIP LAYER:
Jesus	*Trust*

Trust Talk

Choosing to trust Jesus is a really big step for anyone. If your friend is struggling to trust Jesus, here's the kind of "encouragement" your friend *doesn't* need:

WHAT NOT TO SAY:

★ I trust Jesus for every decision. It was just yesterday that he told me what kind of toothpaste to buy.

★ What kind of idiot doesn't trust *the Creator of the universe*?

★ Your life is a *mess*. Bet things would work out better for you if you trusted Jesus more.

★ You don't trust in Jesus? Better pack *summer* clothes for your trip to hell!

Instead, aim for more *encouraging*, more *strengthening* thoughts on trust. Check out what Jesus himself said:

"Don't let your hearts be troubled. Trust in God, and trust also in me" (**John 14:1**).

Here are some more helpful truths to share with your friend:

WHAT TO SAY AND **WHAT NOT TO SAY** *continues on page 465...*

and corruption. For you are a slave to whatever controls you. [20]And when people escape from the wickedness of the world by knowing our Lord and Savior Jesus Christ and then get tangled up and enslaved by sin again, they are worse off than before. [21]It would be better if they had never known the way to righteousness than to know it and then reject the command they were given to live a holy life. [22]They prove the truth of this proverb: "A dog returns to its vomit."* And another says, "A washed pig returns to the mud."

CHAPTER **3**
The Day of the Lord Is Coming

This is my second letter to you, dear friends, and in both of them I have tried to stimulate your wholesome thinking and refresh your memory. [2]I want you to remember what the holy prophets said long ago and what our Lord and Savior commanded through your apostles.

[3]Most importantly, I want to remind you that in the last days scoffers will come, mocking the truth and following their own desires. [4]They will say, "What happened to the promise that Jesus is coming again? From before the times of our ancestors, everything has remained the same since the world was first created."

[5]They deliberately forget that God made the heavens by the word of his command, and he brought the earth out from the water and surrounded it with water. [6]Then he used the water to destroy the ancient world with a mighty flood. [7]And by the same word, the present heavens and earth have been stored up for fire. They are being kept for the day of judgment, when ungodly people will be destroyed.

[8]But you must not forget this one thing, dear friends: A day is like a thousand years to the Lord, and a thousand years is like a day. [9]The Lord isn't really being slow about his promise, as some people think. No, he is being patient for your sake. He does not want anyone to be destroyed, but wants everyone to repent. [10]But the day of the Lord will come as unexpectedly as a thief. Then the heavens will pass away with a terrible noise, and the very elements themselves will disappear in fire, and the earth and everything on it will be found to deserve judgment.*

[11]Since everything around us is going to be destroyed like this, what holy and godly lives you should live, [12]looking forward to

2:22 Prov 26:11.   **3:10** Other manuscripts read *will be burned up;* still others read *will be found destroyed.*

the day of God and hurrying it along. On that day, he will set the heavens on fire, and the elements will melt away in the flames. [13] But we are looking forward to the new heavens and new earth he has promised, a world filled with God's righteousness.

[14] And so, dear friends, while you are waiting for these things to happen, make every effort to be found living peaceful lives that are pure and blameless in his sight.

[15] And remember, the Lord's patience gives people time to be saved. This is what our beloved brother Paul also wrote to you with the wisdom God gave him—[16] speaking of these things in all of his letters. Some of his comments are hard to understand, and those who are ignorant and unstable have twisted his letters to mean something quite different, just as they do with other parts of Scripture. And this will result in their destruction.

Peter's Final Words

[17] I am warning you ahead of time, dear friends. Be on guard so that you will not be carried away by the errors of these wicked people and lose your own secure footing. [18] Rather, you must grow in the grace and knowledge of our Lord and Savior Jesus Christ.

All glory to him, both now and forever! Amen.

WHAT TO SAY AND **WHAT NOT TO SAY** *continued from page 464...*

WHAT TO SAY:

★ You can let things go and trust Jesus with them. He really does love you, and he's not going to cheat you out of the fun things in life. Jesus *wants* the best for you.

★ Trusting Jesus isn't always easy to do—it takes courage and sometimes sacrifice—but when you trust him, Jesus will give you peace.

★ Trusting Jesus doesn't make life simple or perfect; all your problems aren't going to instantly go away. But Jesus is *there* with you, and he'll give you joy in your circumstances…and hope for the future.

JOURNAL

1 John

AUTHOR:	DATE WRITTEN:
John (The Apostle)	Probably between A.D. 85 & 90

CHAPTER **1**

Introduction

We proclaim to you the one who existed from the beginning,* whom we have heard and seen. We saw him with our own eyes and touched him with our own hands. He is the Word of life. ²This one who is life itself was revealed to us, and we have seen him. And now we testify and proclaim to you that he is the one who is eternal life. He was with the Father, and then he was revealed to us. ³We proclaim to you what we ourselves have actually seen and heard so that you may have fellowship with us. And our fellowship is with the Father and with his Son, Jesus Christ. ⁴We are writing these things so that you may fully share our joy.*

Living in the Light

⁵This is the message we heard from Jesus* and now declare to you: God is light, and there is no darkness in him at all. ⁶So we are lying if we say we have fellowship with God but go on living in spiritual darkness; we are not practicing the truth. ⁷But if we are living in the light, as God is in the light, then we have fellowship with each other, and the blood of Jesus, his Son, cleanses us from all sin.

⁸If we claim we have no sin, we are only fooling ourselves and not living in the truth. ⁹But if we confess our sins to him, he is faithful and just to forgive us our sins and to cleanse us from all wickedness. ¹⁰If we claim we have not sinned, we are calling God a liar and showing that his word has no place in our hearts.

CHAPTER **2**

My dear children, I am writing this to you so that you will not sin. But if anyone does sin, we have an advocate who pleads our

1:1 Greek *What was from the beginning.* **1:4** Or *so that our joy may be complete;* some manuscripts read *your joy.* **1:5** Greek *from him.*

case before the Father. He is Jesus Christ, the one who is truly righteous. ²He himself is the sacrifice that atones for our sins—and not only our sins but the sins of all the world.

³And we can be sure that we know him if we obey his commandments. ⁴If someone claims, "I know God," but doesn't obey God's commandments, that person is a liar and is not living in the truth. ⁵But those who obey God's word truly show how completely they love him. That is how we know we are living in him. ⁶Those who say they live in God should live their lives as Jesus did.

A New Commandment

⁷Dear friends, I am not writing a new commandment for you; rather it is an old one you have had from the very beginning. This old commandment—to love one another—is the same message you heard before. ⁸Yet it is also new. Jesus lived the truth of this commandment, and you also are living it. For the darkness is disappearing, and the true light is already shining.

⁹If anyone claims, "I am living in the light," but hates a Christian brother or sister,* that person is still living in darkness. ¹⁰Anyone who loves another brother or sister* is living in the light and does not cause others to stumble. ¹¹But anyone who hates another brother or sister is still living and walking in darkness. Such a person does not know the way to go, having been blinded by the darkness.

¹² I am writing to you who are God's children
    because your sins have been forgiven through Jesus.*
¹³ I am writing to you who are mature in the faith*
    because you know Christ, who existed from the
        beginning.
  I am writing to you who are young in the faith
    because you have won your battle with the evil one.
¹⁴ I have written to you who are God's children
    because you know the Father.
  I have written to you who are mature in the faith
    because you know Christ, who existed from the
        beginning.
  I have written to you who are young in the faith
    because you are strong.
  God's word lives in your hearts,
    and you have won your battle with the evil one.

2:9 Greek *hates his brother;* similarly in 2:11. 2:10 Greek *loves his brother.* 2:12 Greek *through his name.* 2:13 Or *to you fathers;* also in 2:14.

FRIENDSHIP TYPE: *Family* FRIENDSHIP LAYER: *Getting Acquainted*

Top 10

THE TOP 10 THINGS NOT TO SAY

...if you're trying to get acquainted with your family's faith.

10. "Let's talk later..."
9. "What part of 'I'm not interested' don't you understand?"
8. "I can't pray with you right now. I need to wash my hair."
7. "Family faith? I've seen more faith in a box of thumbtacks."
6. "You mean you were actually serious about all that Christian stuff?"
5. "If this is our family tree, I think I'm in the wrong orchard."
4. "Is there going to be a quiz?"
3. "You want spirit? I'll give you some spirit."
2. "I'd rather get acquainted with the neighbors."
1. "I must've been adopted."

WHAT TO SAY AND WHAT NOT TO SAY *continues on page 468...*

Friendship First NEW TESTAMENT

WHAT TO SAY AND WHAT NOT TO SAY *continued from page 467…*

THE TOP 10 THINGS TO SAY

…if you're trying to get acquainted with your family's faith.

10. "We may not all be perfect, but we're perfect for each other."
9. "I'll never forget the way you stood strong during that tough time."
8. "Let's pray about how we can do better next time."
7. "I'd love to hear more about how God changed your life."
6. "It's good to know I always have your support."
5. "I encourage you to keep doing what's right."
4. "I'm so thankful we're growing closer!"
3. "Your story really made a difference in my life."
2. "Thank you for being a good example to me."
1. "I love you!"

JOURNAL

_____
_____
_____
_____
_____
_____
_____
_____
_____
_____
_____
_____
_____
_____
_____

Do Not Love This World

15 Do not love this world nor the things it offers you, for when you love the world, you do not have the love of the Father in you. 16 For the world offers only a craving for physical pleasure, a craving for everything we see, and pride in our achievements and possessions. These are not from the Father, but are from this world. 17 And this world is fading away, along with everything that people crave. But anyone who does what pleases God will live forever.

Warning about Antichrists

18 Dear children, the last hour is here. You have heard that the Antichrist is coming, and already many such antichrists have appeared. From this we know that the last hour has come. 19 These people left our churches, but they never really belonged with us; otherwise they would have stayed with us. When they left, it proved that they did not belong with us.

20 But you are not like that, for the Holy One has given you his Spirit,* and all of you know the truth. 21 So I am writing to you not because you don't know the truth but because you know the difference between truth and lies. 22 And who is a liar? Anyone who says that Jesus is not the Christ.* Anyone who denies the Father and the Son is an antichrist.* 23 Anyone who denies the Son doesn't have the Father, either. But anyone who acknowledges the Son has the Father also.

24 So you must remain faithful to what you have been taught from the beginning. If you do, you will remain in fellowship with the Son and with the Father. 25 And in this fellowship we enjoy the eternal life he promised us.

26 I am writing these things to warn you about those who want to lead you astray. 27 But you have received the Holy Spirit,* and he lives within you, so you don't need anyone to teach you what is true. For the Spirit* teaches you everything you need to know, and what he teaches is true—it is not a lie. So just as he has taught you, remain in fellowship with Christ.

Living as Children of God

28 And now, dear children, remain in fellowship with Christ so that when he returns, you will be full of courage and not shrink back from him in shame.

29 Since we know that Christ is righteous, we also know that all who do what is right are God's children.

2:20 Greek *But you have an anointing from the Holy One.*   **2:22a** Or *not the Messiah.*   **2:22b** Or *the antichrist.*   **2:27a** Greek *the anointing from him.*   **2:27b** Greek *the anointing.*

CHAPTER **3**

See how very much our Father loves us, for he calls us his children, and that is what we are! But the people who belong to this world don't recognize that we are God's children because they don't know him. ²Dear friends, we are already God's children, but he has not yet shown us what we will be like when Christ appears. But we do know that we will be like him, for we will see him as he really is. ³And all who have this eager expectation will keep themselves pure, just as he is pure.

⁴Everyone who sins is breaking God's law, for all sin is contrary to the law of God. ⁵And you know that Jesus came to take away our sins, and there is no sin in him. ⁶Anyone who continues to live in him will not sin. But anyone who keeps on sinning does not know him or understand who he is.

⁷Dear children, don't let anyone deceive you about this: When people do what is right, it shows that they are righteous, even as Christ is righteous. ⁸But when people keep on sinning, it shows that they belong to the devil, who has been sinning since the beginning. But the Son of God came to destroy the works of the devil. ⁹Those who have been born into God's family do not make a practice of sinning, because God's life* is in them. So they can't keep on sinning, because they are children of God. ¹⁰So now we can tell who are children of God and who are children of the devil. Anyone who does not live righteously and does not love other believers* does not belong to God.

Love One Another

¹¹This is the message you have heard from the beginning: We should love one another. ¹²We must not be like Cain, who belonged to the evil one and killed his brother. And why did he kill him? Because Cain had been doing what was evil, and his brother had been doing what was righteous. ¹³So don't be surprised, dear brothers and sisters,* if the world hates you.

¹⁴If we love our Christian brothers and sisters,* it proves that we have passed from death to life. But a person who has no love is still dead. ¹⁵Anyone who hates another brother or sister* is really a murderer at heart. And you know that murderers don't have eternal life within them.

¹⁶We know what real love is because Jesus gave up his life for us. So we also ought to give up our lives for our brothers and sisters. ¹⁷If someone has enough money to live well and sees a

"A friend may well be reckoned the masterpiece of Nature."

~ Ralph Waldo Emerson

3:9 Greek *because his seed.*   3:10 Greek *does not love his brother.*   3:13 Greek *brothers.*   3:14 Greek *the brothers; similarly in 3:16.*   3:15 Greek *hates his brother.*

JOURNAL

brother or sister* in need but shows no compassion—how can God's love be in that person?

18 Dear children, let's not merely say that we love each other; let us show the truth by our actions. 19 Our actions will show that we belong to the truth, so we will be confident when we stand before God. 20 Even if we feel guilty, God is greater than our feelings, and he knows everything.

21 Dear friends, if we don't feel guilty, we can come to God with bold confidence. 22 And we will receive from him whatever we ask because we obey him and do the things that please him.

23 And this is his commandment: We must believe in the name of his Son, Jesus Christ, and love one another, just as he commanded us. 24 Those who obey God's commandments remain in fellowship with him, and he with them. And we know he lives in us because the Spirit he gave us lives in us.

CHAPTER **4**

Discerning False Prophets

Dear friends, do not believe everyone who claims to speak by the Spirit. You must test them to see if the spirit they have comes from God. For there are many false prophets in the world. 2 This is how we know if they have the Spirit of God: If a person claiming to be a prophet* acknowledges that Jesus Christ came in a real body, that person has the Spirit of God. 3 But if someone claims to be a prophet and does not acknowledge the truth about Jesus, that person is not from God. Such a person has the spirit of the Antichrist, which you heard is coming into the world and indeed is already here.

4 But you belong to God, my dear children. You have already won a victory over those people, because the Spirit who lives in you is greater than the spirit who lives in the world. 5 Those people belong to this world, so they speak from the world's viewpoint, and the world listens to them. 6 But we belong to God, and those who know God listen to us. If they do not belong to God, they do not listen to us. That is how we know if someone has the Spirit of truth or the spirit of deception.

Loving One Another

7 Dear friends, let us continue to love one another, for love comes from God. Anyone who loves is a child of God and knows God. 8 But anyone who does not love does not know God, for God is love.

3:17 Greek *sees his brother.* **4:2** Greek *If a spirit;* similarly in 4:3.

9God showed how much he loved us by sending his one and only Son into the world so that we might have eternal life through him. 10This is real love—not that we loved God, but that he loved us and sent his Son as a sacrifice to take away our sins.

11Dear friends, since God loved us that much, we surely ought to love each other. 12No one has ever seen God. But if we love each other, God lives in us, and his love is brought to full expression in us.

13And God has given us his Spirit as proof that we live in him and he in us. 14Furthermore, we have seen with our own eyes and now testify that the Father sent his Son to be the Savior of the world. 15All who confess that Jesus is the Son of God have God living in them, and they live in God. 16We know how much God loves us, and we have put our trust in his love.

God is love, and all who live in love live in God, and God lives in them. 17And as we live in God, our love grows more perfect. So we will not be afraid on the day of judgment, but we can face him with confidence because we live like Jesus here in this world.

18Such love has no fear, because perfect love expels all fear. If we are afraid, it is for fear of punishment, and this shows that we have not fully experienced his perfect love. 19We love each other* because he loved us first.

20If someone says, "I love God," but hates a Christian brother or sister,* that person is a liar; for if we don't love people we can see, how can we love God, whom we cannot see? 21And he has given us this command: Those who love God must also love their Christian brothers and sisters.*

CHAPTER 5

Faith in the Son of God

Everyone who believes that Jesus is the Christ* has become a child of God. And everyone who loves the Father loves his children, too. 2We know we love God's children if we love God and obey his commandments. 3Loving God means keeping his commandments, and his commandments are not burdensome. 4For every child of God defeats this evil world, and we achieve this victory through our faith. 5And who can win this battle against the world? Only those who believe that Jesus is the Son of God.

6And Jesus Christ was revealed as God's Son by his baptism in

---

No. 25-FA-471

FRIENDSHIP
═══ STORY ═══

FRIENDSHIP TYPE: *Family*   FRIENDSHIP LAYER: *Getting Acquainted*

FROM THE ARCHIVES

The King of Kings

He was first and foremost a minister.

He preached Sunday after Sunday with compassion for his people and passion for his Savior.

But he was also a nationwide leader for social justice. When he read his Bible, he saw a God who looked beyond the color of a person's skin and offered the gift of grace to *everyone*. He believed in equality among all people in America and spent decades of his life speaking a gospel message that centered on God's love *in action*.

As a direct result of his Christian beliefs, he played a key role in helping American blacks achieve the same rights as whites.

His name was Martin Luther King…*Sr.*—the father of one of America's most famous and influential leaders in the 20th century.

"Daddy King" provided a living legacy for his son, Martin Luther King Jr. Because of his faith and commitment to biblical ideals, he and his wife, Alberta, created a lasting heritage for their son to follow.

MLK Jr. gave his parents the credit for influencing his faith and laying the foundation for his success. He was well-acquainted with his family's faith and referred to it often in his countless speeches around the country.

FRIENDSHIP STORY
continues on page 472…

4:19 Greek *We love.* Other manuscripts read *We love God;* still others read *We love him.* 4:20 Greek *hates his brother.* 4:21 Greek *The one who loves God must also love his brother.* 5:1 Or *the Messiah.*

FRIENDSHIP STORY *continued from page 471...*

Not only have generations of Kings lived out the love of Jesus, but their family's faithful influence has spread to millions.

Like King David, Martin Luther King Jr. wasn't a perfect leader. (Who of us is?) But the evidence of God's power in his life made a dramatic difference for generations to come. Despite his early death, despite his family's tragedies, he had a legacy of faith to follow—one given to him by his father and mother—and it was stronger than anything his enemies could throw his way.

Experience

THE ONE THING
1
YOU CAN DO THIS WEEK

Perhaps Martin Luther King Jr.'s most famous speech is his "I Have a Dream" address. What dreams do you have for your family? Gather your family, and talk about your individual dreams and goals, as well as your dreams for your family's future. Have every family member write your family's dreams on a small piece of paper. Then place those notes by each of your beds as a reminder to pray every night that God would lead you toward those dreams.

Reflect

★ Whom do you know who has a strong family heritage of faith? What do you think made that family strong?

★ What dreams do you think God has for your family's spiritual heritage?

water and by shedding his blood on the cross*—not by water only, but by water and blood. And the Spirit, who is truth, confirms it with his testimony. [7]So we have these three witnesses*—[8]the Spirit, the water, and the blood—and all three agree. [9]Since we believe human testimony, surely we can believe the greater testimony that comes from God. And God has testified about his Son. [10]All who believe in the Son of God know in their hearts that this testimony is true. Those who don't believe this are actually calling God a liar because they don't believe what God has testified about his Son.

[11]And this is what God has testified: He has given us eternal life, and this life is in his Son. [12]Whoever has the Son has life; whoever does not have God's Son does not have life.

Conclusion

[13]I have written this to you who believe in the name of the Son of God, so that you may know you have eternal life. [14]And we are confident that he hears us whenever we ask for anything that pleases him. [15]And since we know he hears us when we make our requests, we also know that he will give us what we ask for.

[16]If you see a Christian brother or sister* sinning in a way that does not lead to death, you should pray, and God will give that person life. But there is a sin that leads to death, and I am not saying you should pray for those who commit it. [17]All wicked actions are sin, but not every sin leads to death.

[18]We know that God's children do not make a practice of sinning, for God's Son holds them securely, and the evil one cannot touch them. [19]We know that we are children of God and that the world around us is under the control of the evil one.

[20]And we know that the Son of God has come, and he has given us understanding so that we can know the true God.* And now we live in fellowship with the true God because we live in fellowship with his Son, Jesus Christ. He is the only true God, and he is eternal life.

[21]Dear children, keep away from anything that might take God's place in your hearts.*

5:6 Greek *This is he who came by water and blood.* **5:7** A few very late manuscripts add *in heaven— the Father, the Word, and the Holy Spirit, and these three are one. And we have three witnesses on earth.* **5:16** Greek *a brother.* **5:20** Greek *the one who is true.* **5:21** Greek *keep yourselves from idols.*

(LETTER)

2 John

ENTRY

AUTHOR:	DATE WRITTEN:
John (the Apostle)	Approximately A.D. 90

JOURNAL

Greetings

This letter is from John, the elder.*

I am writing to the chosen lady and to her children,* whom I love in the truth—as does everyone else who knows the truth—²because the truth lives in us and will be with us forever.

³Grace, mercy, and peace, which come from God the Father and from Jesus Christ—the Son of the Father—will continue to be with us who live in truth and love.

Live in the Truth

⁴How happy I was to meet some of your children and find them living according to the truth, just as the Father commanded.

⁵I am writing to remind you, dear friends,* that we should love one another. This is not a new commandment, but one we have had from the beginning. ⁶Love means doing what God has commanded us, and he has commanded us to love one another, just as you heard from the beginning.

⁷I say this because many deceivers have gone out into the world. They deny that Jesus Christ came* in a real body. Such a person is a deceiver and an antichrist. ⁸Watch out that you do not lose what we* have worked so hard to achieve. Be diligent so that you receive your full reward. ⁹Anyone who wanders away from this teaching has no relationship with God. But anyone who remains in the teaching of Christ has a relationship with both the Father and the Son.

¹⁰If anyone comes to your meeting and does not teach the truth about Christ, don't invite that person into your home or give any kind of encouragement. ¹¹Anyone who encourages such people becomes a partner in their evil work.

1a Greek *From the elder.*   **1b** Or *the church God has chosen and its members.*   **5** Greek *I urge you, lady.*   **7** Or *will come.*   **8** Some manuscripts read *you.*

Friendship First NEW TESTAMENT

JOURNAL

Conclusion

12 I have much more to say to you, but I don't want to do it with paper and ink. For I hope to visit you soon and talk with you face to face. Then our joy will be complete.

13 Greetings from the children of your sister,* chosen by God.

13 Or *from the members of your sister church.*

"If a man does not make new acquaintances as he advances through life, he will soon find himself left alone."

~ Samuel Johnson

3 John

AUTHOR:	DATE WRITTEN:
John (the Apostle)	Approximately A.D. 90

Greetings

This letter is from John, the elder.*

I am writing to Gaius, my dear friend, whom I love in the truth.

²Dear friend, I hope all is well with you and that you are as healthy in body as you are strong in spirit. ³Some of the traveling teachers* recently returned and made me very happy by telling me about your faithfulness and that you are living according to the truth. ⁴I could have no greater joy than to hear that my children are following the truth.

Caring for the Lord's Workers

⁵Dear friend, you are being faithful to God when you care for the traveling teachers who pass through, even though they are strangers to you. ⁶They have told the church here of your loving friendship. Please continue providing for such teachers in a manner that pleases God. ⁷For they are traveling for the Lord,* and they accept nothing from people who are not believers.* ⁸So we ourselves should support them so that we can be their partners as they teach the truth.

⁹I wrote to the church about this, but Diotrephes, who loves to be the leader, refuses to have anything to do with us. ¹⁰When I come, I will report some of the things he is doing and the evil accusations he is making against us. Not only does he refuse to welcome the traveling teachers, he also tells others not to help them. And when they do help, he puts them out of the church.

¹¹Dear friend, don't let this bad example influence you. Follow only what is good. Remember that those who do good prove that they are God's children, and those who do evil prove that they do not know God.*

1 Greek *From the elder.*   **3** Greek *the brothers;* also in verses 5 and 10.   **7a** Greek *They went out on behalf of the Name.*   **7b** Greek *from Gentiles.*   **11** Greek *they have not seen God.*

★

A full 74% of church members say they have developed a friendship with people in church during worship services.

—from "Friendship and Faith," a Gallup Research Study Commissioned by Group Publishing, Inc.

★

JOURNAL

12 Everyone speaks highly of Demetrius, as does the truth itself. We ourselves can say the same for him, and you know we speak the truth.

Conclusion

13 I have much more to say to you, but I don't want to write it with pen and ink. 14 For I hope to see you soon, and then we will talk face to face.

15 *Peace be with you.

Your friends here send you their greetings. Please give my personal greetings to each of our friends there.

15 Some English translations combine verses 14 and 15 into verse 14.

Jude

AUTHOR:	DATE WRITTEN:
Jude	Approximately A.D. 65

Greetings from Jude

This letter is from Jude, a slave of Jesus Christ and a brother of James.

I am writing to all who have been called by God the Father, who loves you and keeps you safe in the care of Jesus Christ.*

2May God give you more and more mercy, peace, and love.

The Danger of False Teachers

3Dear friends, I had been eagerly planning to write to you about the salvation we all share. But now I find that I must write about something else, urging you to defend the faith that God has entrusted once for all time to his holy people. 4I say this because some ungodly people have wormed their way into your churches, saying that God's marvelous grace allows us to live immoral lives. The condemnation of such people was recorded long ago, for they have denied our only Master and Lord, Jesus Christ.

5So I want to remind you, though you already know these things, that Jesus* first rescued the nation of Israel from Egypt, but later he destroyed those who did not remain faithful. 6And I remind you of the angels who did not stay within the limits of authority God gave them but left the place where they belonged. God has kept them securely chained in prisons of darkness, waiting for the great day of judgment. 7And don't forget Sodom and Gomorrah and their neighboring towns, which were filled with immorality and every kind of sexual perversion. Those cities were destroyed by fire and serve as a warning of the eternal fire of God's judgment.

8In the same way, these people—who claim authority from their dreams—live immoral lives, defy authority, and scoff at supernatural beings.* 9But even Michael, one of the mightiest

1 Or *keeps you for Jesus Christ.*   **5** As in the best manuscripts; various other manuscripts read *[the] Lord,* or *God,* or *Christ;* one reads *God Christ.*   **8** Greek *at glorious ones,* which are probably evil angels.

of the angels,* did not dare accuse the devil of blasphemy, but simply said, "The Lord rebuke you!" (This took place when Michael was arguing with the devil about Moses' body.) [10]But these people scoff at things they do not understand. Like unthinking animals, they do whatever their instincts tell them, and so they bring about their own destruction. [11]What sorrow awaits them! For they follow in the footsteps of Cain, who killed his brother. Like Balaam, they deceive people for money. And like Korah, they perish in their rebellion.

[12]When these people eat with you in your fellowship meals commemorating the Lord's love, they are like dangerous reefs that can shipwreck you.* They are like shameless shepherds who care only for themselves. They are like clouds blowing over the land without giving any rain. They are like trees in autumn that are doubly dead, for they bear no fruit and have been pulled up by the roots. [13]They are like wild waves of the sea, churning up the foam of their shameful deeds. They are like wandering stars, doomed forever to blackest darkness.

[14]Enoch, who lived in the seventh generation after Adam, prophesied about these people. He said, "Listen! The Lord is coming with countless thousands of his holy ones [15]to execute judgment on the people of the world. He will convict every person of all the ungodly things they have done and for all the insults that ungodly sinners have spoken against him."*

[16]These people are grumblers and complainers, living only to satisfy their desires. They brag loudly about themselves, and they flatter others to get what they want.

A Call to Remain Faithful

[17]But you, my dear friends, must remember what the apostles of our Lord Jesus Christ said. [18]They told you that in the last times there would be scoffers whose purpose in life is to satisfy their ungodly desires. [19]These people are the ones who are creating divisions among you. They follow their natural instincts because they do not have God's Spirit in them.

[20]But you, dear friends, must build each other up in your most holy faith, pray in the power of the Holy Spirit,* [21]and await the mercy of our Lord Jesus Christ, who will bring you eternal life. In this way, you will keep yourselves safe in God's love.

[22]And you must show mercy to* those whose faith is waver-

9 Greek *Michael, the archangel.*   12 Or *they are contaminants among you;* or *they are stains.* 14-15 The quotation comes from intertestamental literature: Enoch 1:9.   20 Greek *pray in the Holy Spirit.*   22 Some manuscripts read *must reprove.*

ing. ²³Rescue others by snatching them from the flames of judgment. Show mercy to still others,* but do so with great caution, hating the sins that contaminate their lives.*

A Prayer of Praise

²⁴Now all glory to God, who is able to keep you from falling away and will bring you with great joy into his glorious presence without a single fault. ²⁵All glory to him who alone is God, our Savior through Jesus Christ our Lord. All glory, majesty, power, and authority are his before all time, and in the present, and beyond all time! Amen.

22-23a Some manuscripts have only two categories of people: (1) those whose faith is wavering and therefore need to be snatched from the flames of judgment, and (2) those who need to be shown mercy.   **23b** Greek *with fear, hating even the clothing stained by the flesh.*

"The heartfelt counsel of a friend is as sweet as perfume and incense."

~ Proverbs 27:9

Revelation

AUTHOR:	DATE WRITTEN:
John (The Apostle)	Approximately A.D. 95

CHAPTER **1**

Prologue

This is a revelation from* Jesus Christ, which God gave him to show his servants the events that must soon* take place. He sent an angel to present this revelation to his servant John, ²who faithfully reported everything he saw. This is his report of the word of God and the testimony of Jesus Christ.

³God blesses the one who reads the words of this prophecy to the church, and he blesses all who listen to its message and obey what it says, for the time is near.

John's Greeting to the Seven Churches

⁴This letter is from John to the seven churches in the province of Asia.*

Grace and peace to you from the one who is, who always was, and who is still to come; from the sevenfold Spirit* before his throne; ⁵and from Jesus Christ. He is the faithful witness to these things, the first to rise from the dead, and the ruler of all the kings of the world.

All glory to him who loves us and has freed us from our sins by shedding his blood for us. ⁶He has made us a Kingdom of priests for God his Father. All glory and power to him forever and ever! Amen.

⁷ Look! He comes with the clouds of heaven.
And everyone will see him—
even those who pierced him.
And all the nations of the world
will mourn for him.
Yes! Amen!

1:1a Or *of.* **1:1b** Or *suddenly,* or *quickly.* **1:4a** *Asia* was a Roman province in what is now western Turkey. **1:4b** Greek *the seven spirits.*

8 "I am the Alpha and the Omega—the beginning and the end,"* says the Lord God. "I am the one who is, who always was, and who is still to come—the Almighty One."

Vision of the Son of Man

9 I, John, am your brother and your partner in suffering and in God's Kingdom and in the patient endurance to which Jesus calls us. I was exiled to the island of Patmos for preaching the word of God and for my testimony about Jesus. 10 It was the Lord's Day, and I was worshiping in the Spirit.* Suddenly, I heard behind me a loud voice like a trumpet blast. 11 It said, "Write in a book* everything you see, and send it to the seven churches in the cities of Ephesus, Smyrna, Pergamum, Thyatira, Sardis, Philadelphia, and Laodicea."

12 When I turned to see who was speaking to me, I saw seven gold lampstands. 13 And standing in the middle of the lampstands was someone like the Son of Man.* He was wearing a long robe with a gold sash across his chest. 14 His head and his hair were white like wool, as white as snow. And his eyes were like flames of fire. 15 His feet were like polished bronze refined in a furnace, and his voice thundered like mighty ocean waves. 16 He held seven stars in his right hand, and a sharp two-edged sword came from his mouth. And his face was like the sun in all its brilliance.

17 When I saw him, I fell at his feet as if I were dead. But he laid his right hand on me and said, "Don't be afraid! I am the First and the Last. 18 I am the living one. I died, but look—I am alive forever and ever! And I hold the keys of death and the grave.*

19 "Write down what you have seen—both the things that are now happening and the things that will happen.* 20 This is the meaning of the mystery of the seven stars you saw in my right hand and the seven gold lampstands: The seven stars are the angels* of the seven churches, and the seven lampstands are the seven churches.

CHAPTER 2

The Message to the Church in Ephesus

"Write this letter to the angel* of the church in Ephesus. This is the message from the one who holds the seven stars in his right hand, the one who walks among the seven gold lampstands:

1:8 Greek *I am the Alpha and the Omega,* referring to the first and last letters of the Greek alphabet. 1:10 Or *in spirit.* 1:11 Or *on a scroll.* 1:13 Or *like a son of man.* See Dan 7:13. "Son of Man" is a title Jesus used for himself. 1:18 Greek *and Hades.* 1:19 Or *what you have seen and what they mean—the things that have already begun to happen.* 1:20 Or *the messengers.* 2:1 Or *the messenger;* also in 2:8, 12, 18.

WHAT TO SAY AND WHAT NOT TO SAY

FRIENDSHIP TYPE:	FRIENDSHIP LAYER:
Jesus	*Acceptance*

SOME THINGS YOU *DON'T* WANT TO SAY

...if someone asks you about your friendship with Jesus.

★ "I'm not exactly sure what Revelation is talking about either, but you probably want to be on our side."

★ "Yeah, you're gonna have to stop doing all that bad stuff. You're not allowed to do that anymore once you're a Christian."

★ "Everyone else is going to hell...and so will you, if you don't convert."

★ "You have to memorize a lot of verses and go to church and stuff..."

★ "Here's a Bible. Read Genesis through Revelation. Then we'll talk."

★ "Compared to income tax, tithing is chump change."

★ "The only place you can find death insurance."

SOME THINGS YOU *WANT* TO SAY

...if someone asks you about your friendship with Jesus.

Start with the Bible. Check out the book of Romans for some great passages to discuss (or read yourself if you're curious about becoming friends with Jesus):

★ **Romans 3:23**—life without Jesus.

★ **Romans 5:8**—why Jesus came to earth.

★ **Romans 6:23**—why a friendship with Jesus is important.

★ **Romans 10:9-10**—how to accept Jesus as a friend and Savior.

★ **Romans 10:13**—who gets to be friends with Jesus.

WHAT TO SAY AND **WHAT NOT TO SAY** *continues on page 482...*

WHAT TO SAY AND WHAT NOT TO SAY *continued from page 481...*

There are a bunch of other passages you can use, such as **John 3:16-18** and **Ephesians 2:8-9**, but Romans gives you a great place to start.

Hey...don't worry about saying everything just right! You don't have to get it perfect, and you don't have to be perfect. God will use your words and work in your friend's life. Just be a friend through it all, and trust God with the rest.

JOURNAL

2 "I know all the things you do. I have seen your hard work and your patient endurance. I know you don't tolerate evil people. You have examined the claims of those who say they are apostles but are not. You have discovered they are liars. 3 You have patiently suffered for me without quitting.

4 "But I have this complaint against you. You don't love me or each other as you did at first!* 5 Look how far you have fallen! Turn back to me and do the works you did at first. If you don't repent, I will come and remove your lampstand from its place among the churches. 6 But this is in your favor: You hate the evil deeds of the Nicolaitans, just as I do.

7 "Anyone with ears to hear must listen to the Spirit and understand what he is saying to the churches. To everyone who is victorious I will give fruit from the tree of life in the paradise of God.

The Message to the Church in Smyrna

8 "Write this letter to the angel of the church in Smyrna. This is the message from the one who is the First and the Last, who was dead but is now alive:

9 "I know about your suffering and your poverty—but you are rich! I know the blasphemy of those opposing you. They say they are Jews, but they are not, because their synagogue belongs to Satan. 10 Don't be afraid of what you are about to suffer. The devil will throw some of you into prison to test you. You will suffer for ten days. But if you remain faithful even when facing death, I will give you the crown of life.

11 "Anyone with ears to hear must listen to the Spirit and understand what he is saying to the churches. Whoever is victorious will not be harmed by the second death.

The Message to the Church in Pergamum

12 "Write this letter to the angel of the church in Pergamum. This is the message from the one with the sharp two-edged sword:

13 "I know that you live in the city where Satan has his throne, yet you have remained loyal to me. You refused to deny me even when Antipas, my faithful witness, was martyred among you there in Satan's city. 14 "But I have a few complaints against you. You tolerate some among you whose teaching is like that of Balaam, who showed Balak how to trip up the people of Israel. He taught

2:4 Greek *You have lost your first love.*

them to sin by eating food offered to idols and by committing sexual sin. ¹⁵In a similar way, you have some Nicolaitans among you who follow the same teaching. ¹⁶Repent of your sin, or I will come to you suddenly and fight against them with the sword of my mouth.

¹⁷"Anyone with ears to hear must listen to the Spirit and understand what he is saying to the churches. To everyone who is victorious I will give some of the manna that has been hidden away in heaven. And I will give to each one a white stone, and on the stone will be engraved a new name that no one understands except the one who receives it.

The Message to the Church in Thyatira

¹⁸"Write this letter to the angel of the church in Thyatira. This is the message from the Son of God, whose eyes are like flames of fire, whose feet are like polished bronze:

¹⁹"I know all the things you do. I have seen your love, your faith, your service, and your patient endurance. And I can see your constant improvement in all these things.

²⁰"But I have this complaint against you. You are permitting that woman—that Jezebel who calls herself a prophet—to lead my servants astray. She teaches them to commit sexual sin and to eat food offered to idols. ²¹I gave her time to repent, but she does not want to turn away from her immorality.

²²"Therefore, I will throw her on a bed of suffering,* and those who commit adultery with her will suffer greatly unless they repent and turn away from her evil deeds. ²³I will strike her children dead. Then all the churches will know that I am the one who searches out the thoughts and intentions of every person. And I will give to each of you whatever you deserve.

²⁴"But I also have a message for the rest of you in Thyatira who have not followed this false teaching ('deeper truths,' as they call them—depths of Satan, actually). I will ask nothing more of you ²⁵except that you hold tightly to what you have until I come. ²⁶To all who are victorious, who obey me to the very end,

To them I will give authority over all the nations.
²⁷ They will rule the nations with an iron rod
   and smash them like clay pots.*

2:22 Greek *a bed.*   **2:26-27** Ps 2:8-9 (Greek Version).

No. 26-FS-483

FRIENDSHIP STORY

FRIENDSHIP TYPE: *Hard-to-Love People*   **FRIENDSHIP LAYER:** *Trust*

FOUND IN SCRIPTURE

If **This** Is Friendship, Who Needs Enemies?

And to think the friendship started out so well...

David first came to the attention of King Saul when the young man dropped Goliath, a giant Philistine warrior, with a single rock to the forehead. Saul's Israelite army then rushed the field and routed the demoralized Philistines—a huge military victory.

King Saul invited David into the royal court, and before long David was a best friend of Jonathan, the king's son. Quickly David became King Saul's go-to military guy, racking up some impressive wins.

And that's when the trouble started.

The moment King Saul heard women singing David's praises, the king's jealousy kicked into high gear. Was David, the young man he'd practically adopted, planning to seize Saul's throne? Was some sort of plot underway?

Threatened, King Saul did what any royal mentor would do under the circumstances (um, not!): He decided to murder his young friend.

Nothing makes a person harder to love than when that person is actively trying to *kill* you. David headed for the hills, with Saul's troops in hot pursuit.

Here's what's amazing about this story: Saul was clearly hard to love. Hot-tempered, jealous, prone to fits of rage, the king was sometimes out of control... and he hated David.

Yet David determined that as difficult as Saul was to love, David wouldn't harm the king—*no matter what*.

FRIENDSHIP STORY

continues on page 484...

FRIENDSHIP STORY *continued from page 483...*

Twice David and his troops had the opportunity to kill Saul and avoid life as fugitives. And twice David spared Saul, saving the king's life.

Saul knew he owed his life to David. And Saul promised David safety. But did David trust Saul's reassuring words? No, and for good cause. King Saul died still at war with David, still desiring to kill the young man he had brought into the court and mentored in leadership.

The friendship between David and King Saul was never restored, and that's a tragedy. But it's also instructive.

Saul died despising a former friend, seeking to kill David. Saul's jealousy made David hard to love—and a target.

David found Saul equally hard to love, but David decided to *not* harm Saul and, if possible, to reconcile.

In the end, neither Saul nor David got what he desired.

Read more about Saul and David in 1 Samuel chapters 17–31 (in the Old Testament).

Experience

THE ONE THING
1
YOU CAN DO THIS WEEK

Consider someone you find hard to love. Would an impartial observer say you're more like Saul, actively ignoring or hurting the person? Or are you more like David, actively helping the person? Even though David never was able to reconcile his relationship with Saul, God still praised David's desire for peace.

This week be a David. Intentionally contribute something positive to that unlikable person's life. Maybe it's a smile; maybe it's a gift. Whatever it is, seek to build trust where there hasn't been any.

FRIENDSHIP STORY *continues on page 485...*

---

²⁸They will have the same authority I received from my Father, and I will also give them the morning star!

²⁹"Anyone with ears to hear must listen to the Spirit and understand what he is saying to the churches.

CHAPTER **3**

The Message to the Church in Sardis

"Write this letter to the angel* of the church in Sardis. This is the message from the one who has the sevenfold Spirit* of God and the seven stars:

"I know all the things you do, and that you have a reputation for being alive—but you are dead. ²Wake up! Strengthen what little remains, for even what is left is almost dead. I find that your actions do not meet the requirements of my God. ³Go back to what you heard and believed at first; hold to it firmly. Repent and turn to me again. If you don't wake up, I will come to you suddenly, as unexpected as a thief.

⁴"Yet there are some in the church in Sardis who have not soiled their clothes with evil. They will walk with me in white, for they are worthy. ⁵All who are victorious will be clothed in white. I will never erase their names from the Book of Life, but I will announce before my Father and his angels that they are mine.

⁶"Anyone with ears to hear must listen to the Spirit and understand what he is saying to the churches.

The Message to the Church in Philadelphia

⁷"Write this letter to the angel of the church in Philadelphia.

This is the message from the one who is holy and true,
    the one who has the key of David.
What he opens, no one can close;
    and what he closes, no one can open:*

⁸"I know all the things you do, and I have opened a door for you that no one can close. You have little strength, yet you obeyed my word and did not deny me. ⁹Look, I will force those who belong to Satan's synagogue—those liars who say they are Jews but are not—to come and bow down at your feet. They will acknowledge that you are the ones I love.

¹⁰"Because you have obeyed my command to persevere, I will protect you from the great time of testing that will come upon the whole world to test those who belong to this world.

3:1a Or *the messenger;* also in 3:7, 14.   **3:1b** Greek *the seven spirits.*   **3:7** Isa 22:22.

[11] I am coming soon.* Hold on to what you have, so that no one will take away your crown. [12] All who are victorious will become pillars in the Temple of my God, and they will never have to leave it. And I will write on them the name of my God, and they will be citizens in the city of my God—the new Jerusalem that comes down from heaven from my God. And I will also write on them my new name.

[13] "Anyone with ears to hear must listen to the Spirit and understand what he is saying to the churches.

The Message to the Church in Laodicea

[14] "Write this letter to the angel of the church in Laodicea. This is the message from the one who is the Amen—the faithful and true witness, the beginning* of God's new creation:

[15] "I know all the things you do, that you are neither hot nor cold. I wish that you were one or the other! [16] But since you are like lukewarm water, neither hot nor cold, I will spit you out of my mouth! [17] You say, 'I am rich. I have everything I want. I don't need a thing!' And you don't realize that you are wretched and miserable and poor and blind and naked. [18] So I advise you to buy gold from me—gold that has been purified by fire. Then you will be rich. Also buy white garments from me so you will not be shamed by your nakedness, and ointment for your eyes so you will be able to see. [19] I correct and discipline everyone I love. So be diligent and turn from your indifference.

[20] "Look! I stand at the door and knock. If you hear my voice and open the door, I will come in, and we will share a meal together as friends. [21] Those who are victorious will sit with me on my throne, just as I was victorious and sat with my Father on his throne.

[22] "Anyone with ears to hear must listen to the Spirit and understand what he is saying to the churches."

CHAPTER **4**

Worship in Heaven

Then as I looked, I saw a door standing open in heaven, and the same voice I had heard before spoke to me like a trumpet blast. The voice said, "Come up here, and I will show you what must happen after this." [2] And instantly I was in the Spirit,* and I saw a throne in heaven and someone sitting on it. [3] The one sitting on the throne was as brilliant as gemstones—like jasper and

3:11 Or *suddenly,* or *quickly.*   **3:14** Or *the ruler,* or *the source.*   **4:2** Or *in spirit.*

FRIENDSHIP STORY *continued from page 484...*

Reflect

★ In what ways have you experienced trust in your own life? How often was it given to you because you earned it, and how often was it a gift you hadn't yet earned?

★ When someone has betrayed your trust, what does it take to set things right and re-establish trust with you?

★ How can you work to re-establish trust with someone you betrayed...or who betrayed you?

"Now, can anything be more foolish than that men who have all the opportunities which prosperity, wealth, and great means can bestow, should secure all else which money can buy—horses, servants, splendid upholstering, and costly plate—but do not secure friends, who are, if I may use the expression, the most valuable and beautiful furniture of life?"

~ *Cicero*

Lost in Translation

WHAT NOT TO DO:

When we don't trust someone, that lack of trust usually applies to what the person says, too. Use this handy translation guide to "decode" what that hard-to-love person is *really* saying to you.

★ **"Hello."**
Translation: "So it's you again…and you're still alive. Pity."

★ **"How are you?"**
Translation: "I'm trolling for information I can use against you."

★ **"Nice haircut."**
Translation: "Spending all your money trying to compensate for that huge schnozola, eh?"

★ **"I was wondering if we could talk about something."**
Translation: "Here's where I entrap you in my wily snares of deceit."

★ **"Care for a stick of gum?"**
Translation: "I want you to feel indebted to me so I can manipulate and use you against your will. You will do my bidding, my pretty. You and your little dog, too!"

Of course, the person might actually be saying, "Hello. How are you? Nice haircut. I was wondering if we could talk about something. Care for a stick of gum?"

But why take chances?

WHAT TO SAY AND WHAT NOT TO SAY *continues on page 487…*

carnelian. And the glow of an emerald circled his throne like a rainbow. 4Twenty-four thrones surrounded him, and twenty-four elders sat on them. They were all clothed in white and had gold crowns on their heads. 5From the throne came flashes of lightning and the rumble of thunder. And in front of the throne were seven torches with burning flames. This is the sevenfold Spirit* of God. 6In front of the throne was a shiny sea of glass, sparkling like crystal.

In the center and around the throne were four living beings, each covered with eyes, front and back. 7The first of these living beings was like a lion; the second was like an ox; the third had a human face; and the fourth was like an eagle in flight. 8Each of these living beings had six wings, and their wings were covered all over with eyes, inside and out. Day after day and night after night they keep on saying,

"Holy, holy, holy is the Lord God, the Almighty—
the one who always was, who is, and who is still to come."

9Whenever the living beings give glory and honor and thanks to the one sitting on the throne (the one who lives forever and ever), 10the twenty-four elders fall down and worship the one sitting on the throne (the one who lives forever and ever). And they lay their crowns before the throne and say,

11 "You are worthy, O Lord our God,
to receive glory and honor and power.
For you created all things,
and they exist because you created what you pleased."

CHAPTER **5**
The Lamb Opens the Scroll

Then I saw a scroll* in the right hand of the one who was sitting on the throne. There was writing on the inside and the outside of the scroll, and it was sealed with seven seals. 2And I saw a strong angel, who shouted with a loud voice: "Who is worthy to break the seals on this scroll and open it?" 3But no one in heaven or on earth or under the earth was able to open the scroll and read it.

4Then I began to weep bitterly because no one was found worthy to open the scroll and read it. 5But one of the twenty-four elders said to me, "Stop weeping! Look, the Lion of the tribe of Judah, the heir to David's throne,* has won the victory. He is worthy to open the scroll and its seven seals."

4:5 Greek *They are the seven spirits.*   5:1 Or *book;* also in 5:2, 3, 4, 5, 7, 8, 9.   5:5 Greek *the root of David.* See Isa 11:10.

⁶Then I saw a Lamb that looked as if it had been slaughtered, but it was now standing between the throne and the four living beings and among the twenty-four elders. He had seven horns and seven eyes, which represent the sevenfold Spirit* of God that is sent out into every part of the earth. ⁷He stepped forward and took the scroll from the right hand of the one sitting on the throne. ⁸And when he took the scroll, the four living beings and the twenty-four elders fell down before the Lamb. Each one had a harp, and they held gold bowls filled with incense, which are the prayers of God's people. ⁹And they sang a new song with these words:

"You are worthy to take the scroll
and break its seals and open it.
For you were slaughtered, and your blood has ransomed people for God
from every tribe and language and people and nation.
¹⁰ And you have caused them to become
a Kingdom of priests for our God.
And they will reign* on the earth."

¹¹Then I looked again, and I heard the voices of thousands and millions of angels around the throne and of the living beings and the elders. ¹²And they sang in a mighty chorus:

"Worthy is the Lamb who was slaughtered—
to receive power and riches
and wisdom and strength
and honor and glory and blessing."

¹³And then I heard every creature in heaven and on earth and under the earth and in the sea. They sang:

"Blessing and honor and glory and power
belong to the one sitting on the throne
and to the Lamb forever and ever."

¹⁴And the four living beings said, "Amen!" And the twenty-four elders fell down and worshiped the Lamb.

CHAPTER **6**

The Lamb Breaks the First Six Seals

As I watched, the Lamb broke the first of the seven seals on the scroll.* Then I heard one of the four living beings say with a voice like thunder, "Come!" ²I looked up and saw a white

5:6 Greek *which are the seven spirits.*   5:10 Some manuscripts read *they are reigning.*   6:1 Or *book.*

WHAT TO SAY ᴀɴᴅ WHAT NOT TO SAY *continued from page 486...*

WHAT TO DO:

★ Throw away the translation guide.
★ Assume people mean what they say.
★ Don't try to read a subtle subtext that probably isn't there.

JOURNAL

Among respondents who report that
their church is "very friendly,"
84% of them attend churches with
fewer than 100 people.

—from "Friendship and Faith," a Gallup Research Study
Commissioned by Group Publishing, Inc.

JOURNAL

horse standing there. Its rider carried a bow, and a crown was placed on his head. He rode out to win many battles and gain the victory.

³When the Lamb broke the second seal, I heard the second living being say, "Come!" ⁴Then another horse appeared, a red one. Its rider was given a mighty sword and the authority to take peace from the earth. And there was war and slaughter everywhere.

⁵When the Lamb broke the third seal, I heard the third living being say, "Come!" I looked up and saw a black horse, and its rider was holding a pair of scales in his hand. ⁶And I heard a voice from among the four living beings say, "A loaf of wheat bread or three loaves of barley will cost a day's pay.* And don't waste* the olive oil and wine."

⁷When the Lamb broke the fourth seal, I heard the fourth living being say, "Come!" ⁸I looked up and saw a horse whose color was pale green. Its rider was named Death, and his companion was the Grave.* These two were given authority over one-fourth of the earth, to kill with the sword and famine and disease* and wild animals.

⁹When the Lamb broke the fifth seal, I saw under the altar the souls of all who had been martyred for the word of God and for being faithful in their testimony. ¹⁰They shouted to the Lord and said, "O Sovereign Lord, holy and true, how long before you judge the people who belong to this world and avenge our blood for what they have done to us?" ¹¹Then a white robe was given to each of them. And they were told to rest a little longer until the full number of their brothers and sisters*—their fellow servants of Jesus who were to be martyred—had joined them.

¹²I watched as the Lamb broke the sixth seal, and there was a great earthquake. The sun became as dark as black cloth, and the moon became as red as blood. ¹³Then the stars of the sky fell to the earth like green figs falling from a tree shaken by a strong wind. ¹⁴The sky was rolled up like a scroll, and all of the mountains and islands were moved from their places.

¹⁵Then everyone—the kings of the earth, the rulers, the generals, the wealthy, the powerful, and every slave and free person—all hid themselves in the caves and among the rocks of the mountains. ¹⁶And they cried to the mountains and the rocks,

6:6a Greek *A choinix* [1 quart or 1 liter] *of wheat for a denarius, and 3 choinix of barley for a denarius. A denarius was equivalent to a laborer's full day's wage.*   **6:6b** Or *harm.*   **6:8a** Greek *was Hades.* **6:8b** Greek *death.*   **6:11** Greek *their brothers.*

"Fall on us and hide us from the face of the one who sits on the throne and from the wrath of the Lamb. ¹⁷For the great day of their wrath has come, and who is able to survive?"

CHAPTER 7
God's People Will Be Preserved

Then I saw four angels standing at the four corners of the earth, holding back the four winds so they did not blow on the earth or the sea, or even on any tree. ²And I saw another angel coming up from the east, carrying the seal of the living God. And he shouted to those four angels, who had been given power to harm land and sea, ³"Wait! Don't harm the land or the sea or the trees until we have placed the seal of God on the foreheads of his servants."

⁴And I heard how many were marked with the seal of God— 144,000 were sealed from all the tribes of Israel:

⁵ from Judah	12,000
from Reuben	12,000
from Gad	12,000
⁶ from Asher	12,000
from Naphtali	12,000
from Manasseh	12,000
⁷ from Simeon	12,000
from Levi	12,000
from Issachar	12,000
⁸ from Zebulun	12,000
from Joseph	12,000
from Benjamin	12,000

Praise from the Great Crowd

⁹After this I saw a vast crowd, too great to count, from every nation and tribe and people and language, standing in front of the throne and before the Lamb. They were clothed in white robes and held palm branches in their hands. ¹⁰And they were shouting with a mighty shout,

"Salvation comes from our God who sits on the throne and from the Lamb!"

¹¹And all the angels were standing around the throne and around the elders and the four living beings. And they fell before the throne with their faces to the ground and worshiped God. ¹²They sang,

No. 27-TE-489

FRIENDSHIP STORY

FRIENDSHIP TYPE:	FRIENDSHIP LAYER:
Jesus	*Acceptance*

BASED ON TRUE EVENTS

The End of Pretending

He never worked at memorizing them, and he was never given an assignment. Kurt just sort of absorbed the first two chapters of Luke into his memory through all the Christmas pageants he had been in, all the Sunday school lessons he had sat through, and all the Bible classes he had taken at his Christian school. By the time Kurt was 18, he had spent more time in Bible class than a seminary student.

But his faith? Well, it was a lot like his knowledge of the first chapters of Luke—more absorbed than accepted. It was woven into almost all of his childhood experiences and memories, but it didn't really affect his life or his choices; it was just…there.

Despite years of studying the truth and learning to identify counterfeits, Kurt still hadn't really accepted that truth as a personal one for his life. And that became clear when he left home for the university.

Questions turned to confusion. Confusion turned to disillusion. Jesus, church, and those first two chapters of Luke all seemed irrelevant in the face of academic knowledge…and weekend parties.

FRIENDSHIP STORY *continues on page 490…*

Friendship First NEW TESTAMENT

FRIENDSHIP STORY *continued from page 489...*

The only thing he couldn't seem to shake was a feeling of guilt. It plagued him. He felt as if he'd betrayed something...someone. And after a series of drunken weekends, in the midst of a horrible hangover, Kurt grew tired of dealing with it. So he recklessly prayed, "God, I don't care if you're real or not, but I'm tired of pretending. If you're not real, today is the last day I pretend that you are. If you are real, I'm tired of pretending that you're not. Either way, I'm not pretending anymore."

Two days later, Kurt stopped his car on a lonely mountain road. He never saw a blinding light, and he never heard a voice from heaven. He didn't have a convincing or moving encounter with an eager Christian. He simply settled the matter in his heart. Kurt knew God was real. At that moment, Kurt accepted Jesus as his friend...and his Savior. Kurt's faith was finally his own, and he has never pretended since.

Experience

THE ONE THING 1 YOU CAN DO THIS WEEK

Kurt came to a crossroads in his faith. He went from ignoring God and his faith to deciding that he needed to know the truth, one way or the other.

Why do you believe that God is real? Use the space below to honestly answer that question for yourself. Then, sometime this week, tell someone your answer. It could be a family member, a friend, a co-worker. It could be someone who believes in Jesus or someone who doesn't. It doesn't matter, just tell someone.

_____

_____

_____

_____

FRIENDSHIP STORY *continues on page 491...*

"Amen! Blessing and glory and wisdom
    and thanksgiving and honor
and power and strength belong to our God
    forever and ever! Amen."

13 Then one of the twenty-four elders asked me, "Who are these who are clothed in white? Where did they come from?"

14 And I said to him, "Sir, you are the one who knows."

Then he said to me, "These are the ones who died in* the great tribulation.* They have washed their robes in the blood of the Lamb and made them white.

15 "That is why they stand in front of God's throne
    and serve him day and night in his Temple.
And he who sits on the throne
    will give them shelter.
16 They will never again be hungry or thirsty;
    they will never be scorched by the heat of the sun.
17 For the Lamb on the throne*
    will be their Shepherd.
He will lead them to springs of life-giving water.
    And God will wipe every tear from their eyes."

CHAPTER **8**

The Lamb Breaks the Seventh Seal

When the Lamb broke the seventh seal on the scroll,* there was silence throughout heaven for about half an hour. 2 I saw the seven angels who stand before God, and they were given seven trumpets.

3 Then another angel with a gold incense burner came and stood at the altar. And a great amount of incense was given to him to mix with the prayers of God's people as an offering on the gold altar before the throne. 4 The smoke of the incense, mixed with the prayers of God's holy people, ascended up to God from the altar where the angel had poured them out. 5 Then the angel filled the incense burner with fire from the altar and threw it down upon the earth; and thunder crashed, lightning flashed, and there was a terrible earthquake.

The First Four Trumpets

6 Then the seven angels with the seven trumpets prepared to blow their mighty blasts.

7 The first angel blew his trumpet, and hail and fire mixed

7:14a Greek *who came out of.* **7:14b** Or *the great suffering.* **7:17** Greek *on the center of the throne.* **8:1** Or *book.*

with blood were thrown down on the earth. One-third of the earth was set on fire, one-third of the trees were burned, and all the green grass was burned.

⁸Then the second angel blew his trumpet, and a great mountain of fire was thrown into the sea. One-third of the water in the sea became blood, ⁹one-third of all things living in the sea died, and one-third of all the ships on the sea were destroyed.

¹⁰Then the third angel blew his trumpet, and a great star fell from the sky, burning like a torch. It fell on one-third of the rivers and on the springs of water. ¹¹The name of the star was Bitterness.* It made one-third of the water bitter, and many people died from drinking the bitter water.

¹²Then the fourth angel blew his trumpet, and one-third of the sun was struck, and one-third of the moon, and one-third of the stars, and they became dark. And one-third of the day was dark, and also one-third of the night.

¹³Then I looked, and I heard a single eagle crying loudly as it flew through the air, "Terror, terror, terror to all who belong to this world because of what will happen when the last three angels blow their trumpets."

CHAPTER **9**

The Fifth Trumpet Brings the First Terror

Then the fifth angel blew his trumpet, and I saw a star that had fallen to earth from the sky, and he was given the key to the shaft of the bottomless pit.* ²When he opened it, smoke poured out as though from a huge furnace, and the sunlight and air turned dark from the smoke.

³Then locusts came from the smoke and descended on the earth, and they were given power to sting like scorpions. ⁴They were told not to harm the grass or plants or trees, but only the people who did not have the seal of God on their foreheads. ⁵They were told not to kill them but to torture them for five months with pain like the pain of a scorpion sting. ⁶In those days people will seek death but will not find it. They will long to die, but death will flee from them!

⁷The locusts looked like horses prepared for battle. They had what looked like gold crowns on their heads, and their faces looked like human faces. ⁸They had hair like women's hair and teeth like the teeth of a lion. ⁹They wore armor made of iron, and their wings roared like an army of chariots rushing into battle. ¹⁰They had tails that stung like scorpions, and for five

8:11 Greek *Wormwood.*   9:1 Or *the abyss,* or *the underworld;* also in 9:11.

FRIENDSHIP STORY *continued from page 490…*

Reflect

★ Read **John 3:16-19**. Why do you think people refuse Jesus' offer of friendship?

★ When have you been at a crossroads in your faith? What happened?

★ What would you say to someone who wanted to know what you believe about Jesus?

JOURNAL

"In the end, people appreciate honest criticism far more than flattery."

~ Proverbs 28:23

JOURNAL

months they had the power to torment people. ¹¹Their king is the angel from the bottomless pit; his name in Hebrew is *Abaddon,* and in Greek, *Apollyon*—the Destroyer.

¹²The first terror is past, but look, two more terrors are coming!

The Sixth Trumpet Brings the Second Terror

¹³Then the sixth angel blew his trumpet, and I heard a voice speaking from the four horns of the gold altar that stands in the presence of God. ¹⁴And the voice said to the sixth angel who held the trumpet, "Release the four angels who are bound at the great Euphrates River." ¹⁵Then the four angels who had been prepared for this hour and day and month and year were turned loose to kill one-third of all the people on earth. ¹⁶I heard the size of their army, which was 200 million mounted troops.

¹⁷And in my vision, I saw the horses and the riders sitting on them. The riders wore armor that was fiery red and dark blue and yellow. The horses had heads like lions, and fire and smoke and burning sulfur billowed from their mouths. ¹⁸One-third of all the people on earth were killed by these three plagues— by the fire and smoke and burning sulfur that came from the mouths of the horses. ¹⁹Their power was in their mouths and in their tails. For their tails had heads like snakes, with the power to injure people.

²⁰But the people who did not die in these plagues still refused to repent of their evil deeds and turn to God. They continued to worship demons and idols made of gold, silver, bronze, stone, and wood—idols that can neither see nor hear nor walk! ²¹And they did not repent of their murders or their witchcraft or their sexual immorality or their thefts.

CHAPTER **10**

The Angel and the Small Scroll

Then I saw another mighty angel coming down from heaven, surrounded by a cloud, with a rainbow over his head. His face shone like the sun, and his feet were like pillars of fire. ²And in his hand was a small scroll* that had been opened. He stood with his right foot on the sea and his left foot on the land. ³And he gave a great shout like the roar of a lion. And when he shouted, the seven thunders answered.

⁴When the seven thunders spoke, I was about to write. But I heard a voice from heaven saying, "Keep secret* what the seven thunders said, and do not write it down."

10:2 Or *book;* also in 10:8, 9, 10.   **10:4** Greek *Seal up.*

5 Then the angel I saw standing on the sea and on the land raised his right hand toward heaven. 6 He swore an oath in the name of the one who lives forever and ever, who created the heavens and everything in them, the earth and everything in it, and the sea and everything in it. He said, "There will be no more delay. 7 When the seventh angel blows his trumpet, God's mysterious plan will be fulfilled. It will happen just as he announced it to his servants the prophets."

8 Then the voice from heaven spoke to me again: "Go and take the open scroll from the hand of the angel who is standing on the sea and on the land."

9 So I went to the angel and told him to give me the small scroll. "Yes, take it and eat it," he said. "It will be sweet as honey in your mouth, but it will turn sour in your stomach!" 10 So I took the small scroll from the hand of the angel, and I ate it! It was sweet in my mouth, but when I swallowed it, it turned sour in my stomach.

11 Then I was told, "You must prophesy again about many peoples, nations, languages, and kings."

CHAPTER 11

The Two Witnesses

Then I was given a measuring stick, and I was told, "Go and measure the Temple of God and the altar, and count the number of worshipers. 2 But do not measure the outer courtyard, for it has been turned over to the nations. They will trample the holy city for 42 months. 3 And I will give power to my two witnesses, and they will be clothed in burlap and will prophesy during those 1,260 days."

4 These two prophets are the two olive trees and the two lampstands that stand before the Lord of all the earth. 5 If anyone tries to harm them, fire flashes from their mouths and consumes their enemies. This is how anyone who tries to harm them must die. 6 They have power to shut the sky so that no rain will fall for as long as they prophesy. And they have the power to turn the rivers and oceans into blood, and to strike the earth with every kind of plague as often as they wish.

7 When they complete their testimony, the beast that comes up out of the bottomless pit* will declare war against them, and he will conquer them and kill them. 8 And their bodies will lie in the main street of Jerusalem,* the city that is figuratively called "Sodom" and "Egypt," the city where their Lord was crucified.

11:7 Or *the abyss,* or *the underworld.*   11:8 Greek *the great city.*

FRIENDSHIP EXPERIENCE

FRIENDSHIP TYPE: *Family*   FRIENDSHIP LAYER: *Companionship*

The Art of Family Friendships

Love. Respect. Honor. Don't provoke anger.

The three do's and one don't of family relationships (Ephesians 5:31–6:4).

This is how you make it work. This is how you have good companionship with family members. You show love. You show respect. You show honor. You don't provoke anger.

Easier said than done? Of course.

Worth the effort? Definitely!

Try them out for yourself...

THE ONE THING 1 YOU CAN DO THIS WEEK

Experience

Practice being a good family member. On four different days this week, choose one of the four relational principles from this passage and live it out!

Love: One day really focus on showing love to your family members. Give them lots of hugs. Say, "I love you." Give gifts. Make them dinner, or take them out. Serve them.

Respect: On this day work to respect your family members. Listen when they speak. Be aware of not interrupting them. Ask their opinions on important decisions you have to make. Don't make jokes about them or mock them.

Honor: On this day spend time showing honor to your family members. Write them affirming notes. Praise them throughout the day. Recognize the things they do for the family.

FRIENDSHIP EXPERIENCE *continues on page 494...*

FRIENDSHIP EXPERIENCE *continued from page 493...*

Don't Provoke Anger: One day really concentrate on not provoking anger in your family members. Be aware of the things you say and do. Steer clear of the things you know will annoy or anger your family members. Consciously avoid pet peeves. Don't push buttons. Be nice.

At the end of each day, consider also how you can live out that same principle in your friendship with God. How can you show love to God? honor? respect? How can you avoid provoking anger in God?

Reflect

★ How do you regularly live out these principles in *your* family relationships? Why are they important to those relationships?

★ How did your family members respond to you each day? What kind of a difference did living out those principles make in your family dynamic?

★ In what ways would your friendship with God change if you daily lived out these principles?

⁹And for three and a half days, all peoples, tribes, languages, and nations will stare at their bodies. No one will be allowed to bury them. ¹⁰All the people who belong to this world will gloat over them and give presents to each other to celebrate the death of the two prophets who had tormented them.

¹¹But after three and a half days, God breathed life into them, and they stood up! Terror struck all who were staring at them. ¹²Then a loud voice from heaven called to the two prophets, "Come up here!" And they rose to heaven in a cloud as their enemies watched.

¹³At the same time there was a terrible earthquake that destroyed a tenth of the city. Seven thousand people died in that earthquake, and everyone else was terrified and gave glory to the God of heaven.

¹⁴The second terror is past, but look, the third terror is coming quickly.

The Seventh Trumpet Brings the Third Terror

¹⁵Then the seventh angel blew his trumpet, and there were loud voices shouting in heaven:

"The world has now become the Kingdom of our Lord and
of his Christ,*
and he will reign forever and ever."

¹⁶The twenty-four elders sitting on their thrones before God fell with their faces to the ground and worshiped him. ¹⁷And they said,

"We give thanks to you, Lord God, the Almighty,
the one who is and who always was,
for now you have assumed your great power
and have begun to reign.
¹⁸ The nations were filled with wrath,
but now the time of your wrath has come.
It is time to judge the dead
and reward your servants the prophets,
as well as your holy people,
and all who fear your name,
from the least to the greatest.
It is time to destroy
all who have caused destruction on the earth."

¹⁹Then, in heaven, the Temple of God was opened and the Ark of his covenant could be seen inside the Temple. Lightning

11:15 Or *his Messiah.*

flashed, thunder crashed and roared, and there was an earthquake and a terrible hailstorm.

CHAPTER 12

The Woman and the Dragon

Then I witnessed in heaven an event of great significance. I saw a woman clothed with the sun, with the moon beneath her feet, and a crown of twelve stars on her head. ²She was pregnant, and she cried out because of her labor pains and the agony of giving birth.

³Then I witnessed in heaven another significant event. I saw a large red dragon with seven heads and ten horns, with seven crowns on his heads. ⁴His tail swept away one-third of the stars in the sky, and he threw them to the earth. He stood in front of the woman as she was about to give birth, ready to devour her baby as soon as it was born.

⁵She gave birth to a son who was to rule all nations with an iron rod. And her child was snatched away from the dragon and was caught up to God and to his throne. ⁶And the woman fled into the wilderness, where God had prepared a place to care for her for 1,260 days.

⁷Then there was war in heaven. Michael and his angels fought against the dragon and his angels. ⁸And the dragon lost the battle, and he and his angels were forced out of heaven. ⁹This great dragon—the ancient serpent called the devil, or Satan, the one deceiving the whole world—was thrown down to the earth with all his angels.

¹⁰Then I heard a loud voice shouting across the heavens,

"It has come at last—
    salvation and power
and the Kingdom of our God,
    and the authority of his Christ.*
For the accuser of our brothers and sisters*
    has been thrown down to earth—
the one who accuses them
    before our God day and night.
¹¹ And they have defeated him by the blood of the Lamb
    and by their testimony.
And they did not love their lives so much
    that they were afraid to die.
¹² Therefore, rejoice, O heavens!
    And you who live in the heavens, rejoice!

12:10a Or *his Messiah.* **12:10b** Greek *brothers.*

A full 74% of church members who say they feel valued and respected at church are very likely to describe their faith as a friendship with God.

—from "Friendship and Faith," a Gallup Research Study Commissioned by Group Publishing, Inc.

JOURNAL

> "Trust in the LORD
> with all your heart;
>
> do not depend on your
> own understanding.
>
> Seek his will
> in all you do,
>
> and he will show you
> which path to take."
>
> ~ Proverbs 3:5-6

JOURNAL

_____

_____

_____

_____

_____

_____

_____

_____

_____

_____

_____

_____

_____

But terror will come on the earth and the sea,
  for the devil has come down to you in great anger,
  knowing that he has little time."

¹³When the dragon realized that he had been thrown down to the earth, he pursued the woman who had given birth to the male child. ¹⁴But she was given two wings like those of a great eagle so she could fly to the place prepared for her in the wilderness. There she would be cared for and protected from the dragon* for a time, times, and half a time.

¹⁵Then the dragon tried to drown the woman with a flood of water that flowed from his mouth. ¹⁶But the earth helped her by opening its mouth and swallowing the river that gushed out from the mouth of the dragon. ¹⁷And the dragon was angry at the woman and declared war against the rest of her children—all who keep God's commandments and maintain their testimony for Jesus.

¹⁸Then the dragon took his stand* on the shore beside the sea.

CHAPTER **13**

The Beast out of the Sea

Then I saw a beast rising up out of the sea. It had seven heads and ten horns, with ten crowns on its horns. And written on each head were names that blasphemed God. ²This beast looked like a leopard, but it had the feet of a bear and the mouth of a lion! And the dragon gave the beast his own power and throne and great authority.

³I saw that one of the heads of the beast seemed wounded beyond recovery—but the fatal wound was healed! The whole world marveled at this miracle and gave allegiance to the beast. ⁴They worshiped the dragon for giving the beast such power, and they also worshiped the beast. "Who is as great as the beast?" they exclaimed. "Who is able to fight against him?"

⁵Then the beast was allowed to speak great blasphemies against God. And he was given authority to do whatever he wanted for forty-two months. ⁶And he spoke terrible words of blasphemy against God, slandering his name and his dwelling—that is, those who dwell in heaven.* ⁷And the beast was allowed to wage war against God's holy people and to conquer them. And he was given authority to rule over every tribe and people and language and nation. ⁸And all the people who belong to this world worshiped the beast. They are the ones whose names were not writ-

12:14 Greek *the serpent;* also in 12:15. See 12:9.　**12:18** Greek *Then he took his stand;* some manuscripts read *Then I took my stand.* Some translations put this entire sentence into 13:1. **13:6** Some manuscripts read *and his dwelling and all who dwell in heaven.*

ten in the Book of Life before the world was made—the Book that belongs to the Lamb who was slaughtered.*

⁹ Anyone with ears to hear
  should listen and understand.
¹⁰ Anyone who is destined for prison
  will be taken to prison.
 Anyone destined to die by the sword
  will die by the sword.

This means that God's holy people must endure persecution patiently and remain faithful.

The Beast out of the Earth

¹¹ Then I saw another beast come up out of the earth. He had two horns like those of a lamb, but he spoke with the voice of a dragon. ¹²He exercised all the authority of the first beast. And he required all the earth and its people to worship the first beast, whose fatal wound had been healed. ¹³He did astounding miracles, even making fire flash down to earth from the sky while everyone was watching. ¹⁴And with all the miracles he was allowed to perform on behalf of the first beast, he deceived all the people who belong to this world. He ordered the people to make a great statue of the first beast, who was fatally wounded and then came back to life. ¹⁵He was then permitted to give life to this statue so that it could speak. Then the statue of the beast commanded that anyone refusing to worship it must die.

¹⁶He required everyone—small and great, rich and poor, free and slave—to be given a mark on the right hand or on the forehead. ¹⁷And no one could buy or sell anything without that mark, which was either the name of the beast or the number representing his name. ¹⁸Wisdom is needed here. Let the one with understanding solve the meaning of the number of the beast, for it is the number of a man.* His number is 666.*

CHAPTER **14**

The Lamb and the 144,000

Then I saw the Lamb standing on Mount Zion, and with him were 144,000 who had his name and his Father's name written on their foreheads. ²And I heard a sound from heaven like the roar of mighty ocean waves or the rolling of loud thunder. It was like the sound of many harpists playing together.

13:8 Or *not written in the Book of Life that belongs to the Lamb who was slaughtered before the world was made.* 13:18a Or *of humanity.* 13:18b Some manuscripts read *616.*

No. 28-FS-497

FRIENDSHIP STORY

FRIENDSHIP TYPE:	FRIENDSHIP LAYER:
Family	*Companionship*

FOUND IN SCRIPTURE

The Only Child

She was his wife...but she was barren.

He loved her...but Hannah couldn't understand why.

Especially not today. Not after another row with Peninnah, his *other* wife, his *fertile* wife. Peninnah knew just how to hurt her; she always sent her arrows straight to the heart. They had been at the Tabernacle worshiping the Lord. Elkanah had, as usual, given a larger portion of the meat to Peninnah and her children and given Hannah only one portion because she had no children. And Peninnah, as usual, had taken notice and mocked Hannah's smaller portion...her absence of children.

Even now, hours later, Peninnah's words still stung. Hannah shook her head to rid herself of the hurtful mockery. Instead she focused on Elkanah's comforting words: "Why are you crying, Hannah?" he'd asked her tenderly, "Why be downhearted just because you have no children? You have me—isn't that better than having ten sons?"

And she did love him. And she wanted to be happy with just him. But why wouldn't the Lord give her children? Why did he refuse her this happiness...this honor?

Hannah got up and went to pray in the Tabernacle. She wiped her tears as she walked. She would make another plea to the Lord. Surely the Lord would see her pain; surely he would give her comfort.

FRIENDSHIP STORY

continues on page 498...

FRIENDSHIP STORY *continued from page 497...*

She dropped to her knees and cried out, "O Lord of Heaven's Armies, if you will look upon my sorrow and answer my prayer and give me a son, then I will give him back to you. He will be yours for his entire lifetime, and as a sign that he has been dedicated to the Lord, his hair will never be cut."

There. She was finished. She would wait. She would return to Elkanah, and she would no longer be sad.

And the Lord gave her and Elkanah a son... Samuel, who grew up to be a judge, a prophet, and a great spiritual leader of Israel.

Read the whole story of Hannah, Elkanah, and Samuel in the Old Testament book of 1 Samuel.

Experience

THE ONE THING
1
YOU CAN DO THIS WEEK

Elkanah loved Hannah even during the toughest of times. He remained her companion even when societies' laws would have allowed him to leave her.

Is there someone in your family who is going through a tough time? Someone who is depressed, going through a divorce, or suffering financially? How can you be a companion during this tough time? How can you reach out in love and encouragement? Perhaps you could regularly send kind letters, maybe take the person out on regular "fun" outings, or even help out financially. And you can definitely pray for the person. Read **2 Corinthians 1:3-7** to see how God can help you comfort those in need.

Reflect

★ How has someone been a companion to you when you were struggling?

★ How can you make it a habit to encourage family members who are in need?

³This great choir sang a wonderful new song in front of the throne of God and before the four living beings and the twenty-four elders. No one could learn this song except the 144,000 who had been redeemed from the earth. ⁴They have kept themselves as pure as virgins,* following the Lamb wherever he goes. They have been purchased from among the people on the earth as a special offering* to God and to the Lamb. ⁵They have told no lies; they are without blame.

The Three Angels

⁶And I saw another angel flying through the sky, carrying the eternal Good News to proclaim to the people who belong to this world—to every nation, tribe, language, and people. ⁷"Fear God," he shouted. "Give glory to him. For the time has come when he will sit as judge. Worship him who made the heavens, the earth, the sea, and all the springs of water."

⁸Then another angel followed him through the sky, shouting, "Babylon is fallen—that great city is fallen—because she made all the nations of the world drink the wine of her passionate immorality."

⁹Then a third angel followed them, shouting, "Anyone who worships the beast and his statue or who accepts his mark on the forehead or on the hand ¹⁰must drink the wine of God's anger. It has been poured full strength into God's cup of wrath. And they will be tormented with fire and burning sulfur in the presence of the holy angels and the Lamb. ¹¹The smoke of their torment will rise forever and ever, and they will have no relief day or night, for they have worshiped the beast and his statue and have accepted the mark of his name."

¹²This means that God's holy people must endure persecution patiently, obeying his commands and maintaining their faith in Jesus.

¹³And I heard a voice from heaven saying, "Write this down: Blessed are those who die in the Lord from now on. Yes, says the Spirit, they are blessed indeed, for they will rest from their hard work; for their good deeds follow them!"

The Harvest of the Earth

¹⁴Then I saw a white cloud, and seated on the cloud was someone like the Son of Man.* He had a gold crown on his head and a sharp sickle in his hand.

14:4a Greek *They are virgins who have not defiled themselves with women.*   **14:4b** Greek *as firstfruits.*
14:14 Or *like a son of man.* See Dan 7:13. "Son of Man" is a title Jesus used for himself.

15 Then another angel came from the Temple and shouted to the one sitting on the cloud, "Swing the sickle, for the time of harvest has come; the crop on earth is ripe." 16 So the one sitting on the cloud swung his sickle over the earth, and the whole earth was harvested.

17 After that, another angel came from the Temple in heaven, and he also had a sharp sickle. 18 Then another angel, who had power to destroy with fire, came from the altar. He shouted to the angel with the sharp sickle, "Swing your sickle now to gather the clusters of grapes from the vines of the earth, for they are ripe for judgment." 19 So the angel swung his sickle over the earth and loaded the grapes into the great winepress of God's wrath. 20 The grapes were trampled in the winepress outside the city, and blood flowed from the winepress in a stream about 180 miles* long and as high as a horse's bridle.

CHAPTER 15

The Song of Moses and of the Lamb

Then I saw in heaven another marvelous event of great significance. Seven angels were holding the seven last plagues, which would bring God's wrath to completion. 2 I saw before me what seemed to be a glass sea mixed with fire. And on it stood all the people who had been victorious over the beast and his statue and the number representing his name. They were all holding harps that God had given them. 3 And they were singing the song of Moses, the servant of God, and the song of the Lamb:

"Great and marvelous are your works,
    O Lord God, the Almighty.
Just and true are your ways,
    O King of the nations.*
4 Who will not fear you, Lord,
    and glorify your name?
    For you alone are holy.
All nations will come and worship before you,
    for your righteous deeds have been revealed."

The Seven Bowls of the Seven Plagues

5 Then I looked and saw that the Temple in heaven, God's Tabernacle, was thrown wide open. 6 The seven angels who were holding the seven plagues came out of the Temple. They were clothed in spotless white linen* with gold sashes across their

14:20 Greek *1,600 stadia* [296 kilometers].   15:3 Some manuscripts read *King of the ages.*
15:6 Other manuscripts read *white stone*; still others read *white [garments] made of linen.*

"Never fear having too many friends, but beware having even one enemy."
~ Chinese proverb

JOURNAL

WHAT TO SAY 👍
AND
WHAT NOT TO SAY 👎

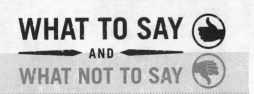

FRIENDSHIP TYPE: *Family* **FRIENDSHIP LAYER:** *Companionship*

An Explosive Situation

"I'm so stupid."

"I'm fat."

"I can never do anything right!"

"I'm such a failure."

Ever heard that from someone in your family? Most people feel like they can let down their guard with family, like they can be themselves, be vulnerable… which can sometimes lead to self-deprecation. And when that happens? It's a cry for encouragement. Answer that cry with love and encouragement, not annoyance or flippancy.

WHAT NOT TO SAY:

★ "Oh, whatever. You just had a bad day."

★ "You think *you're* stupid, guess what I did today."

★ "I wish you'd quit saying stuff like that—I get so sick of hearing it!"

★ "Well, maybe if you'd just do a better job…"

WHAT TO SAY AND **WHAT NOT TO SAY** *continues on page 501…*

chests. ⁷Then one of the four living beings handed each of the seven angels a gold bowl filled with the wrath of God, who lives forever and ever. ⁸The Temple was filled with smoke from God's glory and power. No one could enter the Temple until the seven angels had completed pouring out the seven plagues.

CHAPTER **16**

Then I heard a mighty voice from the Temple say to the seven angels, "Go your ways and pour out on the earth the seven bowls containing God's wrath."

²So the first angel left the Temple and poured out his bowl on the earth, and horrible, malignant sores broke out on everyone who had the mark of the beast and who worshiped his statue.

³Then the second angel poured out his bowl on the sea, and it became like the blood of a corpse. And everything in the sea died.

⁴Then the third angel poured out his bowl on the rivers and springs, and they became blood. ⁵And I heard the angel who had authority over all water saying,

"You are just, O Holy One, who is and who always was,
 because you have sent these judgments.
⁶ Since they shed the blood
 of your holy people and your prophets,
you have given them blood to drink.
 It is their just reward."

⁷And I heard a voice from the altar,* saying,

"Yes, O Lord God, the Almighty,
 your judgments are true and just."

⁸Then the fourth angel poured out his bowl on the sun, causing it to scorch everyone with its fire. ⁹Everyone was burned by this blast of heat, and they cursed the name of God, who had control over all these plagues. They did not repent of their sins and turn to God and give him glory.

¹⁰Then the fifth angel poured out his bowl on the throne of the beast, and his kingdom was plunged into darkness. His subjects ground their teeth in anguish, ¹¹and they cursed the God of heaven for their pains and sores. But they did not repent of their evil deeds and turn to God.

¹²Then the sixth angel poured out his bowl on the great Euphrates River, and it dried up so that the kings from the east could march their armies toward the west without hindrance.

16:7 Greek *I heard the altar.*

¹³And I saw three evil* spirits that looked like frogs leap from the mouths of the dragon, the beast, and the false prophet. ¹⁴They are demonic spirits who work miracles and go out to all the rulers of the world to gather them for battle against the Lord on that great judgment day of God the Almighty.

¹⁵"Look, I will come as unexpectedly as a thief! Blessed are all who are watching for me, who keep their clothing ready so they will not have to walk around naked and ashamed."

¹⁶And the demonic spirits gathered all the rulers and their armies to a place with the Hebrew name *Armageddon*.*

¹⁷Then the seventh angel poured out his bowl into the air. And a mighty shout came from the throne in the Temple, saying, "It is finished!" ¹⁸Then the thunder crashed and rolled, and lightning flashed. And a great earthquake struck—the worst since people were placed on the earth. ¹⁹The great city of Babylon split into three sections, and the cities of many nations fell into heaps of rubble. So God remembered all of Babylon's sins, and he made her drink the cup that was filled with the wine of his fierce wrath. ²⁰And every island disappeared, and all the mountains were leveled. ²¹There was a terrible hailstorm, and hailstones weighing seventy-five pounds* fell from the sky onto the people below. They cursed God because of the terrible plague of the hailstorm.

CHAPTER **17**

The Great Prostitute

One of the seven angels who had poured out the seven bowls came over and spoke to me. "Come with me," he said, "and I will show you the judgment that is going to come on the great prostitute, who rules over many waters. ²The kings of the world have committed adultery with her, and the people who belong to this world have been made drunk by the wine of her immorality."

³So the angel took me in the Spirit* into the wilderness. There I saw a woman sitting on a scarlet beast that had seven heads and ten horns, and blasphemies against God were written all over it. ⁴The woman wore purple and scarlet clothing and beautiful jewelry made of gold and precious gems and pearls. In her hand she held a gold goblet full of obscenities and the impurities of her immorality. ⁵A mysterious name was written on her forehead: "Babylon the Great, Mother of All Prostitutes and

16:13 Greek *unclean*.   16:16 Or *Harmagedon*.   16:21 Greek *1 talent* [34 kilograms].   17:3 Or *in spirit*.

WHAT TO SAY AND WHAT NOT TO SAY *continued from page 500...*

WHAT TO SAY:

★ **Love:** "I don't want you to feel that way about yourself. I think you're awesome. I love you. God loves you. And there's nothing that would change that."

★ **Respect:** "I know you had a hard day and it may not seem like things are ever going to get better, but they will. Do you want to talk about what happened? Maybe we can come up with some solutions together."

★ **Honor:** "You're one of the most amazing people I know. Just look at all the wonderful things you've done…[go ahead and list some things!]"

★ **Don't Provoke Anger:** [hugs] [kisses] [a listening ear] [and so on]

JOURNAL

_____

_____

_____

_____

_____

_____

_____

_____

_____

_____

_____

_____

_____

_____

_____

No. 29-TE-502

FRIENDSHIP
STORY

FRIENDSHIP TYPE: *Neighbors*

FRIENDSHIP LAYER: *Deepening*

BASED ON TRUE EVENTS

The Call of Friendship

Eight-year-old Beth wanted desperately to take violin lessons, but the teacher lived almost an hour away. Driving that far wasn't going to fit into her schedule…or her mother's.

So Beth's mother, Jean, called around the neighborhood and found enough interested children that she was able to arrange for the teacher to come to them.

Every Tuesday afternoon, Jean gathered the children at the bus stop and took them to her house. She fed them snacks, played games, and organized crafts to keep them busy while they waited for their lessons. It wasn't long before the kids were friends and the laughter upstairs was drowning out the squeaky violins downstairs!

Ten weeks went by, and the kids decided they wanted to hold a recital to show off their new

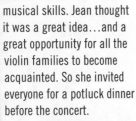

musical skills. Jean thought it was a great idea…and a great opportunity for all the violin families to become acquainted. So she invited everyone for a potluck dinner before the concert.

That was the first of many potluck violin recitals.

Over the next year, the "violin families" did a lot more together than have potlucks and listen to violin music. They went bowling, they went to movies, and they had game nights. In short, they spent a lot of time together. And they found out they had a lot in common, including a friendship with Jesus.

FRIENDSHIP STORY *continues on page 503…*

Obscenities in the World." [6]I could see that she was drunk—drunk with the blood of God's holy people who were witnesses for Jesus. I stared at her in complete amazement.

[7]"Why are you so amazed?" the angel asked. "I will tell you the mystery of this woman and of the beast with seven heads and ten horns on which she sits. [8]The beast you saw was once alive but isn't now. And yet he will soon come up out of the bottomless pit* and go to eternal destruction. And the people who belong to this world, whose names were not written in the Book of Life before the world was made, will be amazed at the reappearance of this beast who had died.

[9]"This calls for a mind with understanding: The seven heads of the beast represent the seven hills where the woman rules. They also represent seven kings. [10]Five kings have already fallen, the sixth now reigns, and the seventh is yet to come, but his reign will be brief.

[11]"The scarlet beast that was, but is no longer, is the eighth king. He is like the other seven, and he, too, is headed for destruction. [12]The ten horns of the beast are ten kings who have not yet risen to power. They will be appointed to their kingdoms for one brief moment to reign with the beast. [13]They will all agree to give him their power and authority. [14]Together they will go to war against the Lamb, but the Lamb will defeat them because he is Lord of all lords and King of all kings. And his called and chosen and faithful ones will be with him."

[15]Then the angel said to me, "The waters where the prostitute is ruling represent masses of people of every nation and language. [16]The scarlet beast and his ten horns all hate the prostitute. They will strip her naked, eat her flesh, and burn her remains with fire. [17]For God has put a plan into their minds, a plan that will carry out his purposes. They will agree to give their authority to the scarlet beast, and so the words of God will be fulfilled. [18]And this woman you saw in your vision represents the great city that rules over the kings of the world."

CHAPTER **18**
The Fall of Babylon

After all this I saw another angel come down from heaven with great authority, and the earth grew bright with his splendor. [2]He gave a mighty shout:

"Babylon is fallen—that great city is fallen!
    She has become a home for demons.

17:8 Or *the abyss,* or *the underworld.*

She is a hideout for every foul* spirit,
    a hideout for every foul vulture
    and every foul and dreadful animal.*
³ For all the nations have fallen*
    because of the wine of her passionate immorality.
The kings of the world
    have committed adultery with her.
Because of her desires for extravagant luxury,
    the merchants of the world have grown rich."

⁴Then I heard another voice calling from heaven,

"Come away from her, my people.
    Do not take part in her sins,
    or you will be punished with her.
⁵ For her sins are piled as high as heaven,
    and God remembers her evil deeds.
⁶ Do to her as she has done to others.
    Double her penalty* for all her evil deeds.
She brewed a cup of terror for others,
    so brew twice as much* for her.
⁷ She glorified herself and lived in luxury,
    so match it now with torment and sorrow.
She boasted in her heart,
    'I am queen on my throne.
I am no helpless widow,
    and I have no reason to mourn.'
⁸ Therefore, these plagues will overtake her in a single day—
    death and mourning and famine.
She will be completely consumed by fire,
    for the Lord God who judges her is mighty."

⁹And the kings of the world who committed adultery with her and enjoyed her great luxury will mourn for her as they see the smoke rising from her charred remains. ¹⁰They will stand at a distance, terrified by her great torment. They will cry out,

"How terrible, how terrible for you,
    O Babylon, you great city!
In a single moment
    God's judgment came on you."

¹¹The merchants of the world will weep and mourn for her, for there is no one left to buy their goods. ¹²She bought great

18:2a Greek *unclean;* also in each of the two following phrases. 18:2b Some manuscripts condense the last two lines to read *a hideout for every foul [unclean] and dreadful vulture.* 18:3 Some manuscripts read *have drunk.* 18:6a Or *Give her an equal penalty.* 18:6b Or *brew just as much.*

FRIENDSHIP STORY *continued from page 502…*

And it was that common bond that drew them even closer when one family experienced an unexpected, life-threatening trial…

A tearful telephone plea for prayer motivated Jean to rally the violin group in support of the family. Their 10-year-old daughter, Mary, had been diagnosed with a serious and rare cancer. They had to move away for her treatment, and their lives were in total upheaval. "Would you please pray?" the clearly distraught mother asked Jean.

The next day the families met and prayed, and instead of sharing laughter, for the first time they shared tears.

The following week, Jean started a daily e-mail prayer chain for Mary. She started each e-mail with a Scripture verse, followed by a prayer for the family based on that verse. Through this prayer chain, the families stayed connected even after Mary and her family moved away.

Brought together initially by squeaky violins, drawn closer by fun and fellowship, the families really bonded as friends while they prayed together for Mary and her family.

Over the next year, the families shared laughter and tears… and celebration. After months of praying, Mary was diagnosed cancer-free! And at a joyous potluck reunion, the families sat and listened once again to violins that, while still a little squeaky, sounded an awful lot like songbirds.

FRIENDSHIP STORY *continues on page 504…*

Friendship First NEW TESTAMENT

FRIENDSHIP STORY *continued from page 503...*

Experience

THE ONE THING
1
YOU CAN DO THIS WEEK

Think of a person or family who needs some love and encouragement. Maybe you've just been "fun" neighbors or have only seen each other at school, work, recitals, or other functions. Think of some practical ways you can deepen your friendship and encourage your neighbor. Have a "cheer-up" potluck, and invite people to bring funny stories, uplifting quotes, and encouraging Scriptures. Organize a group for a prayer chain, to send cards, to call them daily, or to bring a meal.

Reach out…and deepen your friendship.

Reflect

★ How have neighbors come to your rescue when you've been in need? How can you do the same for your neighbors?

★ How can you move your friendships with neighbors past "casual" or "fun" to meaningful?

JOURNAL

_____

_____

_____

_____

_____

_____

_____

_____

quantities of gold, silver, jewels, and pearls; fine linen, purple, silk, and scarlet cloth; things made of fragrant thyine wood, ivory goods, and objects made of expensive wood; and bronze, iron, and marble. [13] She also bought cinnamon, spice, incense, myrrh, frankincense, wine, olive oil, fine flour, wheat, cattle, sheep, horses, chariots, and bodies—that is, human slaves.

[14] "The fancy things you loved so much
    are gone," they cry.
"All your luxuries and splendor
    are gone forever,
    never to be yours again."

[15] The merchants who became wealthy by selling her these things will stand at a distance, terrified by her great torment. They will weep and cry out,

[16] "How terrible, how terrible for that great city!
    She was clothed in finest purple and scarlet linens,
    decked out with gold and precious stones and pearls!
[17] In a single moment
    all the wealth of the city is gone!"

And all the captains of the merchant ships and their passengers and sailors and crews will stand at a distance. [18] They will cry out as they watch the smoke ascend, and they will say, "Where is there another city as great as this?" [19] And they will weep and throw dust on their heads to show their grief. And they will cry out,

"How terrible, how terrible for that great city!
    The shipowners became wealthy
    by transporting her great wealth on the seas.
In a single moment it is all gone."

[20] Rejoice over her fate, O heaven
    and people of God and apostles and prophets!
For at last God has judged her
    for your sakes.

[21] Then a mighty angel picked up a boulder the size of a huge millstone. He threw it into the ocean and shouted,

"Just like this, the great city Babylon
    will be thrown down with violence
    and will never be found again.

²² The sound of harps, singers, flutes, and trumpets
  will never be heard in you again.
No craftsmen and no trades
  will ever be found in you again.
The sound of the mill
  will never be heard in you again.
²³ The light of a lamp
  will never shine in you again.
The happy voices of brides and grooms
  will never be heard in you again.
For your merchants were the greatest in the world,
  and you deceived the nations with your sorceries.
²⁴ In your* streets flowed the blood of the prophets and
    of God's holy people
  and the blood of people slaughtered all over
    the world."

CHAPTER 19

Songs of Victory in Heaven

After this, I heard what sounded like a vast crowd in heaven
shouting,

"Praise the LORD!*
  Salvation and glory and power belong to our God.
² His judgments are true and just.
  He has punished the great prostitute
who corrupted the earth with her immorality.
  He has avenged the murder of his servants."

³ And again their voices rang out:

"Praise the LORD!
  The smoke from that city ascends forever and ever!"

⁴ Then the twenty-four elders and the four living beings fell
down and worshiped God, who was sitting on the throne. They
cried out, "Amen! Praise the LORD!"
⁵ And from the throne came a voice that said,

"Praise our God,
  all his servants,
all who fear him,
  from the least to the greatest."

18:24 Greek *her.*   **19:1** Greek *Hallelujah;* also in 19:3, 4, 6. *Hallelujah* is the transliteration
of a Hebrew term that means "Praise the LORD."

"The seeds of
good deeds become
a tree of life;

a wise person
wins friends."
~ Proverbs 11:30

> "*Science will never be able to reduce the value of a sunset to arithmetic. Nor can it reduce friendship or statesmanship to a formula.*"
>
> ~ *Dr. Louis Orr, President, American Medical Association*

JOURNAL

_____

_____

_____

_____

_____

_____

_____

_____

_____

_____

_____

⁶Then I heard again what sounded like the shout of a vast crowd or the roar of mighty ocean waves or the crash of loud thunder:

"Praise the LORD!
　For the Lord our God,* the Almighty, reigns.
⁷ Let us be glad and rejoice,
　and let us give honor to him.
For the time has come for the wedding feast of the Lamb,
　and his bride has prepared herself.
⁸ She has been given the finest of pure white linen to wear."
　For the fine linen represents the good deeds of God's holy
　　people.

⁹And the angel said to me, "Write this: Blessed are those who are invited to the wedding feast of the Lamb." And he added, "These are true words that come from God."

¹⁰Then I fell down at his feet to worship him, but he said, "No, don't worship me. I am a servant of God, just like you and your brothers and sisters* who testify about their faith in Jesus. Worship only God. For the essence of prophecy is to give a clear witness for Jesus.*"

The Rider on the White Horse

¹¹Then I saw heaven opened, and a white horse was standing there. Its rider was named Faithful and True, for he judges fairly and wages a righteous war. ¹²His eyes were like flames of fire, and on his head were many crowns. A name was written on him that no one understood except himself. ¹³He wore a robe dipped in blood, and his title was the Word of God. ¹⁴The armies of heaven, dressed in the finest of pure white linen, followed him on white horses. ¹⁵From his mouth came a sharp sword to strike down the nations. He will rule them with an iron rod. He will release the fierce wrath of God, the Almighty, like juice flowing from a winepress. ¹⁶On his robe at his thigh* was written this title: King of all kings and Lord of all lords.

¹⁷Then I saw an angel standing in the sun, shouting to the vultures flying high in the sky: "Come! Gather together for the great banquet God has prepared. ¹⁸Come and eat the flesh of kings, generals, and strong warriors; of horses and their riders; and of all humanity, both free and slave, small and great."

¹⁹Then I saw the beast and the kings of the world and their armies gathered together to fight against the one sitting on the

19:6 Some manuscripts read *the Lord God.*　**19:10a** Greek *brothers.*　**19:10b** Or *is the message confirmed by Jesus.*　**19:16** Or *On his robe and thigh.*

horse and his army. ²⁰And the beast was captured, and with him the false prophet who did mighty miracles on behalf of the beast—miracles that deceived all who had accepted the mark of the beast and who worshiped his statue. Both the beast and his false prophet were thrown alive into the fiery lake of burning sulfur. ²¹Their entire army was killed by the sharp sword that came from the mouth of the one riding the white horse. And the vultures all gorged themselves on the dead bodies.

CHAPTER **20**

The Thousand Years

Then I saw an angel coming down from heaven with the key to the bottomless pit* and a heavy chain in his hand. ²He seized the dragon—that old serpent, who is the devil, Satan—and bound him in chains for a thousand years. ³The angel threw him into the bottomless pit, which he then shut and locked so Satan could not deceive the nations anymore until the thousand years were finished. Afterward he must be released for a little while.

⁴Then I saw thrones, and the people sitting on them had been given the authority to judge. And I saw the souls of those who had been beheaded for their testimony about Jesus and for proclaiming the word of God. They had not worshiped the beast or his statue, nor accepted his mark on their forehead or their hands. They all came to life again, and they reigned with Christ for a thousand years.

⁵This is the first resurrection. (The rest of the dead did not come back to life until the thousand years had ended.) ⁶Blessed and holy are those who share in the first resurrection. For them the second death holds no power, but they will be priests of God and of Christ and will reign with him a thousand years.

The Defeat of Satan

⁷When the thousand years come to an end, Satan will be let out of his prison. ⁸He will go out to deceive the nations—called Gog and Magog—in every corner of the earth. He will gather them together for battle—a mighty army, as numberless as sand along the seashore. ⁹And I saw them as they went up on the broad plain of the earth and surrounded God's people and the beloved city. But fire from heaven came down on the attacking armies and consumed them.

¹⁰Then the devil, who had deceived them, was thrown into

20:1 Or *the abyss,* or *the underworld;* also in 20:3.

FRIENDSHIP EXPERIENCE

FRIENDSHIP TYPE: *Hard-to-Love People*

FRIENDSHIP LAYER: *Trust*

Keeping Score

How hard would it be to love someone who disappoints you? who forgets to thank you for what you've done but instead asks for more? who calls you a friend but betrays your trust? How long would you even *try* to love someone like that?

Ask Jesus. He loves you no matter what you do. And if you're like the rest of us, you've proven hard-to-love and untrustworthy more than once.

Read **Romans 5:6-8**; **Luke 6:31**; and then **Ephesians 2:11-22**.

Paul asks you to love and trust hard-to-love people. Is that anything Jesus hasn't already done for you?

So how about extending a little of the grace you've already received?

Experience

THE ONE THING — **1** — **YOU CAN DO THIS WEEK**

Fully accept God's love in your life this week. It will inspire you to let that love flow through you into the lives of others (even hard-to-love others).

Tuck an index card in your purse or pocket. Make a note each time you experience joy or love this week. Each time you're forgiven. Each time you sense grace. Those are the fingerprints of God touching your world.

FRIENDSHIP EXPERIENCE *continues on page 508...*

FRIENDSHIP EXPERIENCE *continued from page 507...*

Reflect

★ What words would you use to describe Jesus' love for you?

★ What words would you use to describe your love for the hard-to-love people in your life?

★ How do you think Jesus would treat those hard-to-love people in your life? How might he want you to cooperate and participate with him?

JOURNAL

the fiery lake of burning sulfur, joining the beast and the false prophet. There they will be tormented day and night forever and ever.

The Final Judgment

[11]And I saw a great white throne and the one sitting on it. The earth and sky fled from his presence, but they found no place to hide. [12]I saw the dead, both great and small, standing before God's throne. And the books were opened, including the Book of Life. And the dead were judged according to what they had done, as recorded in the books. [13]The sea gave up its dead, and death and the grave* gave up their dead. And all were judged according to their deeds. [14]Then death and the grave were thrown into the lake of fire. This lake of fire is the second death. [15]And anyone whose name was not found recorded in the Book of Life was thrown into the lake of fire.

CHAPTER **21**

The New Jerusalem

Then I saw a new heaven and a new earth, for the old heaven and the old earth had disappeared. And the sea was also gone. [2]And I saw the holy city, the new Jerusalem, coming down from God out of heaven like a bride beautifully dressed for her husband.

[3]I heard a loud shout from the throne, saying, "Look, God's home is now among his people! He will live with them, and they will be his people. God himself will be with them.* [4]He will wipe every tear from their eyes, and there will be no more death or sorrow or crying or pain. All these things are gone forever."

[5]And the one sitting on the throne said, "Look, I am making everything new!" And then he said to me, "Write this down, for what I tell you is trustworthy and true." [6]And he also said, "It is finished! I am the Alpha and the Omega—the Beginning and the End. To all who are thirsty I will give freely from the springs of the water of life. [7]All who are victorious will inherit all these blessings, and I will be their God, and they will be my children.

[8]"But cowards, unbelievers, the corrupt, murderers, the immoral, those who practice witchcraft, idol worshipers, and all liars—their fate is in the fiery lake of burning sulfur. This is the second death."

[9]Then one of the seven angels who held the seven bowls containing the seven last plagues came and said to me, "Come with me! I will show you the bride, the wife of the Lamb."

20:13 Greek *and Hades; also in 20:14.*   **21:3** Some manuscripts read *God himself will be with them, their God.*

¹⁰So he took me in the Spirit* to a great, high mountain, and he showed me the holy city, Jerusalem, descending out of heaven from God. ¹¹It shone with the glory of God and sparkled like a precious stone—like jasper as clear as crystal. ¹²The city wall was broad and high, with twelve gates guarded by twelve angels. And the names of the twelve tribes of Israel were written on the gates. ¹³There were three gates on each side—east, north, south, and west. ¹⁴The wall of the city had twelve foundation stones, and on them were written the names of the twelve apostles of the Lamb.

¹⁵The angel who talked to me held in his hand a gold measuring stick to measure the city, its gates, and its wall. ¹⁶When he measured it, he found it was a square, as wide as it was long. In fact, its length and width and height were each 1,400 miles.* ¹⁷Then he measured the walls and found them to be 216 feet thick* (according to the human standard used by the angel).

¹⁸The wall was made of jasper, and the city was pure gold, as clear as glass. ¹⁹The wall of the city was built on foundation stones inlaid with twelve precious stones:* the first was jasper, the second sapphire, the third agate, the fourth emerald, ²⁰the fifth onyx, the sixth carnelian, the seventh chrysolite, the eighth beryl, the ninth topaz, the tenth chrysoprase, the eleventh jacinth, the twelfth amethyst.

²¹The twelve gates were made of pearls—each gate from a single pearl! And the main street was pure gold, as clear as glass.

²²I saw no temple in the city, for the Lord God Almighty and the Lamb are its temple. ²³And the city has no need of sun or moon, for the glory of God illuminates the city, and the Lamb is its light. ²⁴The nations will walk in its light, and the kings of the world will enter the city in all their glory. ²⁵Its gates will never be closed at the end of day because there is no night there. ²⁶And all the nations will bring their glory and honor into the city. ²⁷Nothing evil* will be allowed to enter, nor anyone who practices shameful idolatry and dishonesty—but only those whose names are written in the Lamb's Book of Life.

CHAPTER **22**

Then the angel showed me a river with the water of life, clear as crystal, flowing from the throne of God and of the Lamb. ²It flowed down the center of the main street. On each side of the river grew a tree of life, bearing twelve crops of fruit,* with

21:10 Or *in spirit.*   **21:16** Greek *12,000 stadia* [2,220 kilometers].   **21:17** Greek *144 cubits* [65 meters].   **21:19** The identification of some of these gemstones is uncertain.   **21:27** Or *ceremonially unclean.*   **22:2** Or *twelve kinds of fruit.*

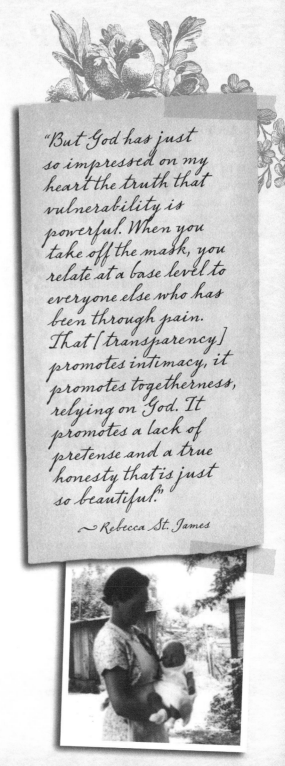

"But God has just so impressed on my heart the truth that vulnerability is powerful. When you take off the mask, you relate at a base level to everyone else who has been through pain. That [transparency] promotes intimacy, it promotes togetherness, relying on God. It promotes a lack of pretense and a true honesty that is just so beautiful."

~Rebecca St. James

FRIENDSHIP STORY

No. 30-TE-510

FRIENDSHIP TYPE: *Family*

FRIENDSHIP LAYER: *Deepening*

BASED ON TRUE EVENTS

An Accident

"Dad, I've been in an accident!"

Oh, the agony and pain those words bring, especially when they're spoken over the phone at 5 a.m.

All those reasons Cameron shouldn't have gotten his license yet came screaming into Keith's mind. What had he been thinking to give in?

Not even a week, and the kid had already sneaked the family car out of the garage to drive home a friend who had missed his curfew. And now there was an accident. Keith could feel his anger boiling…and his worry.

"Uh, are you hurt?"

"No, but the car is hanging off the road, and it's freezing out here."

"Do you have a coat?" Keith asked as he looked at the thermometer outside—it registered 10 below zero.

"No, hurry, it's freezing," Cameron insisted.

Why didn't he have a coat? Doesn't he know better? Why did he take that corner so fast? I showed him how to drive on ice…

His worry alleviated, Keith could feel his anger growing. He grabbed two coats and his keys and headed out the door, still mumbling darkly under his breath.

He arrived on the scene several minutes later and quickly herded the two cold teenagers into his warm car.

Keith turned around, mouth open, ready to begin his lecture. Before he could begin, though, Cameron began to apologize. Keith noticed how the boy was shaking. He could see the fear and the shock of the accident all over Cameron's face. Suddenly, memories of his own first accident came to Keith's mind. He remembered how scared he'd been…and how lucky.

FRIENDSHIP STORY *continues on page 511…*

a fresh crop each month. The leaves were used for medicine to heal the nations.

[3] No longer will there be a curse upon anything. For the throne of God and of the Lamb will be there, and his servants will worship him. [4] And they will see his face, and his name will be written on their foreheads. [5] And there will be no night there—no need for lamps or sun—for the Lord God will shine on them. And they will reign forever and ever.

[6] Then the angel said to me, "Everything you have heard and seen is trustworthy and true. The Lord God, who inspires his prophets,* has sent his angel to tell his servants what will happen soon.*"

Jesus Is Coming

[7] "Look, I am coming soon! Blessed are those who obey the words of prophecy written in this book.*"

[8] I, John, am the one who heard and saw all these things. And when I heard and saw them, I fell down to worship at the feet of the angel who showed them to me. [9] But he said, "No, don't worship me. I am a servant of God, just like you and your brothers the prophets, as well as all who obey what is written in this book. Worship only God!"

[10] Then he instructed me, "Do not seal up the prophetic words in this book, for the time is near. [11] Let the one who is doing harm continue to do harm; let the one who is vile continue to be vile; let the one who is righteous continue to live righteously; let the one who is holy continue to be holy."

[12] "Look, I am coming soon, bringing my reward with me to repay all people according to their deeds. [13] I am the Alpha and the Omega, the First and the Last, the Beginning and the End."

[14] Blessed are those who wash their robes. They will be permitted to enter through the gates of the city and eat the fruit from the tree of life. [15] Outside the city are the dogs—the sorcerers, the sexually immoral, the murderers, the idol worshipers, and all who love to live a lie.

[16] "I, Jesus, have sent my angel to give you this message for the churches. I am both the source of David and the heir to his throne.* I am the bright morning star."

22:6a Or *The Lord, the God of the spirits of the prophets.*   **22:6b** Or *suddenly,* or *quickly;* also in 22:7, 12, 20.   **22:7** Or *scroll;* also in 22:9, 10, 18, 19.   **22:16** Greek *I am the root and offspring of David.*